British Blast Furnace Statistics

1790–1980

British Blast Furnace Statistics 1790–1980

Philip Riden
and John G. Owen

MERTON PRIORY PRESS

Published by Merton Priory Press Ltd
7 Nant Fawr Road, Cardiff CF2 6JQ

First published 1995

ISBN 1 898937 05 2

©   P.J. Riden and J.G. Owen 1995

The authors and publisher of this volume are greatly indebted to the United Kingdom Iron and Steel Statistics Bureau for kindly allowing the inclusion here of material first published in *Iron and Steel Industry. Annual Statistics for the United Kingdom* **and its predecessors. All entries in the tables relating to individual works dated 1921 or later are from this source and copyright in entries dated 1945 or later is reserved to the Bureau.**

Typeset at Oxford University Computing Service
Printed by Hillman Printers (Frome) Ltd
Handlemaker Road
Marston Trading Estate
Frome BA11 2RW

Contents

List of Tables vi

Preface vii

Introduction

The Private Surveys, 1717–1855

    The 1717–50 Lists ix
    The 1750–88 Lists ix
    The 1790–94 List x
    The 1796 List xi
    The 1806 List xii
    The 1810 List xiii
    The 1823–30 List xiii
    The 1825–28 List xiii
    The 1827 List xiv
    Le Play's Survey of 1835–36 xiv
    The 1839 List xv
    Jessops's List of 1840 xv
    The 1841–42 List xv
    The 1842 List xvi
    The 1843 List xvi
    The 1847–48 Lists xvii
    The 1849 Lists xviii
    The 1852 List xix
    Truran's List of 1855 xix
    The Private Surveys in Retrospect xix

The Mineral Statistics, 1854–1913

    Origins and Evolution xxi
    Format and Reliability xxiii

The Trade Associations in the Later Nineteenth Century

    The British Iron Trade Association xxv
    Local Associations xxvii

Iron and Steel Statistics since 1920 xxviii

Format of this Edition

    Regional Divisions xxxi
    Name and Location of Works xxxii
    Owner's Name xxxii
    Number of Furnaces Built and In Blast xxxiv
    Note to the Tables xxxv

National and Regional Statistics xxxv

Conclusion xxxv

Select Bibliography xxxvii

National and Regional Statistics xlv

Local Statistics

    South Wales 1
    Gloucestershire 32
    Somerset and Wiltshire 35
    Sussex and Hampshire 37
    Essex 37
    Shropshire 38
    North Wales 49
    South Staffordshire and Worcestershire 55
    North Staffordshire 93
    Northamptonshire 101
    Lincolnshire 107
    Derbyshire 112
    Yorkshire, West Riding 125
    North West England 136
    North East England 152
    Scotland 179

Index of Ironworks 200

Index of Owners 203

List of Tables

National Statistics

1.1	Output of Pig Iron, 1791–1920	xlv
1.2	Output of Pig Iron, 1791–1920: Regional Percentage Shares	l
1.3	Output of Pig Iron, 1881–1905 (BITA Reports)	liv
1.4	Output of Pig Iron, 1881–1905: Regional Percentage Shares (BITA Reports)	lvi

Regional Statistics

2.1	South Wales	lviii
2.2	Gloucestershire, Somerset and Wiltshire	lx
2.3	Shropshire	lxiii
2.4	North Wales	lxv
2.5	South Staffordshire and Worcestershire	lviii
2.6	North Staffordshire	lxx
2.7	Northamptonshire	lxxiii
2.8	Lincolnshire	lxxv
2.9	Derbyshire	lxxvii
2.10	Yorkshire, West Riding	lxxx
2.11	North West England	lxxxii
2.12	North East England	lxxxv
2.13	Scotland	lxxxvii

Preface

As the reader may suspect from its bulk, this book has been some years in the making. My interest in the statistical history of the British iron industry (or counting blast furnaces, as the less charitable have called it) was first aroused by the discovery, as an undergraduate, of a letter among the records of the Butterley Co. which I recognised as the firm's reply to the enquiries conducted by the iron trade in 1797–98 which led to the compilation of a list of ironworks and their output in 1796, one of the earliest and best known of the surveys incorporated in this volume. This glimpse of the process by which one particular list was assembled made me wonder about how and why other surveys of the same period were compiled, how accurate they were, and how they related to the officially published statistics of the iron trade produced annually from 1854.

My interest in *Mineral Statistics* as a source for the history of the iron industry at local, as well as national, level was sustained during my brief appointment at Exeter University in 1976–77, where Dr Roger Burt was already engaged in his long-term project to publish the data relating to non-ferrous metal-mining contained in the series. It occurred to me that it might be possible to do something similar for the blast-furnace sector of the iron industry, combining the post-1854 material with the earlier lists of furnaces, a source for which there is no parallel in the case of the other metal industries. Thus was conceived a volume which would bring together all statistical data at national, regional and plant level over the longest possible period. I later extended the scope of the work to include the information contained in the yearbooks published by a succession of trade associations from the 1870s onwards, which from 1921 become the principal source for the statistical history of the iron and steel industry.

The work of collecting, checking and arranging the data has occupied a far longer period than I would have wished and has been interrupted on numerous occasions by other projects. As the discussion of the source material seeks to explain, the task is considerably less straightforward than might at first appear, and has involved the use of a large secondary literature, including business histories and local studies as well as maps and gazetteers, in an effort to eliminate errors and inconsistencies in the original data. The work has become easier over the years thanks to the progressive advance of computing facilities and, although the resulting publication is inevitably bulky and thus expensive, it is true to say that, without modern word-processing software, it would have been impossible even to have contemplated the publication of the data in a single volume such as this.

The other development which enabled this project to progress much faster than would otherwise have been the case was the willingness of one of my M.A. students, John Owen, to take over the central portion of the work (covering the period 1854–1913) as his dissertation project, which was completed in 1990. This in turn encouraged me to complete the outstanding loose ends concerning both the earlier private surveys and the work of the trade associations between the 1870s and the First World War, with the result that the entire project can now be published as a joint effort.

Apart from my indebtedness to Mr Owen, I have incurred numerous obligations over a long period to archivists and librarians who have supplied copies of the original source material from which the data presented here has been assembled, answered questions about the history or location of particular works or checked drafts of the various regional sections of the book. Individuals who have helped similarly include Brian Davies, David G. Edwards, the late Ifor Edwards, Dudley Fowkes, Robert Protheroe Jones, Peter King, John Powell, Lesley Richmond, Ian Standing, Barrie Trinder and Christopher Williams. British Steel, through its Secretariat and East Midlands Regional Records Centre (Mr Andy Burns), have also kindly provided information on specific points, as has the Customer Care Section of Companies House (Mr Derek Holder).

In the hope of making this book as useful as possible for readers interested in a particular company, the tables relating to individual works have been extended down to 1980. This has been made possible by the generous agreement of the United Kingdom Iron and Steel Statistics Bureau to permit the inclusion of data first published in their own annual volumes, which from 1945 to the present remain their copyright.

Why spend so much time compiling a book like this? Why include two substantially similar sets of national and regional figures for the late nineteenth century? Why publish so much detail about individual works? My answer to criticisms such as these is that the iron industry is better provided with reliable contemporary output data than any of the other leading sectors of the Industrial Revolution in Britain and that it is worth devoting some effort to making this information available in as reliable a form as possible, including regional figures as well as national aggregates. It is also worth looking at how the data was compiled and comparing the activities of the trade itself and official agencies at different dates. As for the local data, it is so rich and so useful as a basis for studies of individual enterprises that it seemed worth including in full. Few local historians interested in a particular ironworks are likely to be in a position to quarry out information relating to that works from all the sources used in this volume, whereas it will now be possible to turn at once to a table setting out what is available for virtually every site at which iron has been smelted in Britain since 1790. Similarly, anyone interested in the career of a particular ironmaster, partnership or limited company can use the index to locate all the works operated by that individual or firm. The book will, I hope, thus be useful in two ways: to provide fuller national and regional data for the output of pig iron than has hitherto been available in published statistical digests, and to provide a corpus of information which can be quarried by those interested in particular works or ironmasters. A subsidiary aim is to add to what is known about the organisation of the iron trade in Britain from the end of the eighteenth century onwards, and how the industry was affected by the general growth of interest in statistics which is a characteristic of the middle decades of the nineteenth century.

University of Wales, Cardiff
March 1995 PHILIP RIDEN

Introduction

Between 1854 and 1913 the government published detailed statistics of the output of the British iron industry each year, including data down to the level of individual works. Initially, only pig iron production was surveyed but from 1855 figures were compiled for the output of iron ore and, in later years, wrought iron and steel. The annual volumes of *Mineral Statistics*, supplemented after 1878 by the publications of a succession of trade associations, provide a mass of material for both the general history of the industry in the second half of the nineteenth century and the history of particular works and districts.

Before 1854 the historian of the iron industry is dependent for estimates of output on periodic surveys undertaken by the trade, from which it is possible to compile more detailed statistics than for most other industries of the period. Regional and national output estimates based on these surveys have been available in print for more than a century, as have some (but not all) the original lists from which the figures are drawn. Much less use has been made of the information contained in the more detailed of the pre-1854 surveys concerning individual works, nor, for that matter, have historians interested in a particular ironworks or ironmaster in the second half of the nineteenth century exploited the wealth of local detail in *Mineral Statistics*. The object of this study is to make available all the information contained in the various lists of ironworks compiled between 1794 and 1852 in a standard format which matches that adopted by *Mineral Statistics* from 1854, and to link this data with the official returns down to 1913. It then becomes possible not only to refine somewhat the regional and national output estimates for the first half of the nineteenth century but also to summarise what is known from a series of widely scattered surveys about each ironworks in Great Britain over the whole of the century and beyond.

After the First World War the initiative for the collection and publication of iron and steel statistics reverted from the government to the industry itself, whose interests were represented from 1918 by a more effective central organisation. From 1921 the lists of individual works with blast furnaces restarted, albeit in a less detailed form, and continue to be published to the present day, alongside a much wider range of statistical data than was ever collected in the nineteenth century. Details of blast furnaces in use each year since 1921 have been included here down to 1980, so as to provide the widest possible picture of one sector of the industry over nearly two centuries.

The aim of this introduction is to describe the origins, arrangement, strengths and weaknesses of the various unofficial and official lists of blast furnaces used for this study, and to set out the principles on which this edition of the material has been prepared.

The Private Surveys, 1717–1855

The 1717–50 Lists

The earliest attempts to compile lists of ironworks throughout the country date from the various occasions in the first half of the eighteenth century when the government proposed to vary the regulations controlling the import of colonial iron and the trade responded by seeking to show what damage increased imports would do to the domestic industry. Lists of furnaces and forges were made in 1717–18 and of forges only in 1736–37 and again in 1749–50.[1] These surveys have been widely used by both historians and geographers and it has become clear that none is fully comprehensive.[2] In particular, the compilation of a gazetteer of charcoal-fired furnaces, drawing on a large number of local studies, has shown that the number in use in the early eighteenth century was greater than the list of 1717 indicates.[3] Since this early eighteenth-century material, at least as far as it relates to blast furnaces, has all been incorporated in this gazetteer, it has not been included here.

The 1750–88 Lists

After 1750 there appears to have been no attempt to calculate the output of the industry until the 1780s. In 1788 a fairly detailed survey was made, which includes the number and output of furnaces in each district, with separate totals for charcoal pig (26 furnaces producing 14,500 tons) and coke pig (60 furnaces and 55,500

---

[1] For a fuller discussion of these lists see P. Riden, 'The output of the British iron industry before 1870', *Economic History Review*, 2nd series, 30 (1977), 443–59. The lists themselves were printed in E.W. Hulme, 'Statistical history of the iron trade of England and Wales, 1717–50', *Trans. Newcomen Soc.*, 9 (1928–9), 12–35.

[2] See especially the work of B.L.C. Johnson: 'The charcoal iron industry in the early eighteenth century', *Geographical Journal*, 117 (1951), 167–77, and 'The Foley partnerships: the iron industry at the end of the charcoal era', *Economic History Review*, 2nd series, 4 (1951–2), 322–40.

[3] P. Riden, *A gazetteer of charcoal-fired blast furnaces in Great Britain in use since 1660* (Cardiff, 2nd ed., 1993).

tons), although no lists of furnaces survive.[1] For bar iron, however, there is a 'List of the Forges where the method of making Bars upon the Old Plan still exists; with the number of Fineries and the Quantity of Iron which they annually make, taken on average — 1788', with a total output of 16,400 tons. By this date some 15,600 tons of bar were being produced annually by the coke-fired potting process, making a total for the entire industry of 32,000 tons.[2] A separate list of 'Charcoal Blast Furnaces which have declined blowing since the Year 1750 owing either to the want of Wood or the introduction of making Coak Iron', dated 1 January 1788, without any output estimates, appears to be part of the same survey, as does an appendix to this list naming fourteen coke-fired furnaces also abandoned by 1788.[3]

The enquiries which resulted in the lists of 1788 probably owed their origin to the iron trade's opposition to the freeing of trade first with Ireland and then with France in 1785–86; the output figures may, therefore, relate to a slightly earlier date than that of the surviving texts.[4] On the other hand, since it is impossible to establish this for certain, the regional and national totals printed here have been assigned to 1788.

The 1790–94 List

The first surviving survey of the smelting sector of the iron industry after 1717 to enumerate each blast furnace by name dates from 1794 and it is this list which forms the starting-point of the detailed local statistics presented here. Among the papers of William Wilkinson now in the Boulton & Watt Collection at Birmingham Central Library is a 'List of the different Iron Works in England, Wales, Scotland & Ireland to the Year 1794', which can fairly claim to be one of the most detailed surveys of the industry ever compiled. A much abridged, and inaccurately transcribed, version was published by Harry Scrivenor in the first (1841) edition of his *History of the Iron Trade*,[5] where it was dated May 1790, but far more information is to be found in Wilkinson's original manuscript. Under county headings arranged topographically from North East England to Gloucestershire, followed by Wales, Scotland and Ireland, the survey lists each works and names its 'Proprietor' (i.e. the ground landlord), 'Occupier' (i.e. the ironmaster) and 'Situation' (in relation to the nearest town), plus columns in which the furnace, forge and mill plant at each site are enumerated. For the furnaces, the fuel (coke or charcoal) and method of blowing (steam engine or waterwheel) are noted, together, in most cases, with the date of construction. For the forges there are columns for fineries, chaferies, melting furnaces and balling furnaces; in the next section rolling and slitting mills are distinguished; and in both cases there is a column left for the date of building. Finally, the right-hand margin has been used for comments concerning the re-use of abandoned sites, noting, for example, conversion to a tin-mill or a lead works.

There is no attempt in this list to estimate the output of either individual furnaces, districts or the country as a whole, but elsewhere in Wilkinson's papers there are figures of this sort dated December 1791.[1] These include estimates for pig iron production in each county, with the output of charcoal- and coke-fired furnaces given separately. The arrangement of the table shows that the county totals (from which, of course, the figures for the production of charcoal- and coke-smelted pig in Great Britain as a whole are obtained) have been calculated by multiplying the number of furnaces in each county by an estimate of the average weekly output of each works. A comparison of the number of works in each district used as the multiplier with the list of 1794 shows that the numbers in question have been obtained from an earlier version of this list, to which, in some counties, furnaces built in the early 1790s have been added at the end of each section. This can best be illustrated for those counties in which several coke furnaces were built in the late 1780s (e.g. Shropshire or Staffordshire), where the list begins with the charcoal furnaces and forges copied from the 1717–50 lists, then includes the early coke furnaces and accompanying forges, and finally returns to the second generation of coke furnaces built just as the list was being prepared. The 1791 list uses a figure for the number of furnaces in each county based on the first two of these three categories.

Taken together, the material of 1790–94, which has never been published in full, marks the beginning of the regular collection of statistics for the smelting branch of the iron industry. All the information in the 1794 list, as far as it relates to blast furnaces, has been included here (except for the directions as to the location of the works). The occupier's name and the number of furnaces have been entered in appropriate columns of the table printed for each works; the other details, including those relating to associated forges and mills, have been added as notes. The occupier's name has been listed under 'owner', following the terminology of *Mineral Statistics*, and the 'proprietor' has been called 'ground landlord'. The 1794 list is the only one included here

---

[1] Science Museum Library, Weale MS, I, f. 89; a variant of this list, printed by David Mushet in A. Rees, *New Cyclopaedia or Universal Dictionary of Arts and Science*, IV (1819), art. 'Blast Furnace' (no pagination) and most subsequent writers, includes only 59 coke furnaces producing 53,800 tons, which is hardly a significant discrepancy. For Mushet's authorship of this article see his *Papers on iron and steel, practical and experimental* (1840), p. 43. The figures also appear in H. Scrivenor, *History of the iron trade, from the earliest records to the present period* (1854 ed.), pp. 87–8.

[2] Birmingham Central Library, Boulton & Watt Collection, Muirhead II/5/10; cf. Riden, 'Output', pp. 446–7.

[3] For this list see P. Riden, 'Some unsuccessful blast furnaces of the early coke era', *Historical Metallurgy*, 26 (1992), 36–44.

[4] Riden, 'Output', pp. 446–7.

[5] Scrivenor, *History* (1841 ed.), pp. 359–61. The list was omitted from the second edition (1854), which is better known, partly because it was reprinted in 1967.

[1] Like the 1794 survey, the 1791 lists are in the Muirhead II section of the Boulton & Watt Collection. Cf. Riden, 'Output', p. 447, which was written before it was realised that the 1791 lists are a summary of an earlier version of the survey which survives in the manuscript of 1794.

which makes this distinction, important in the seventeenth- and eighteenth-century iron industry but less so after 1800, between landlord and tenant; later lists simply use the term 'ironmaster' or (as in 1854 and afterwards) 'owner'.

The figures drawn up in December 1791 do not name individual works; they have, however, been included in the regional statistics printed in the next section of this volume, where the total output of pig iron is given (obtained, where necessary, by combining the separate totals in the original tables for charcoal- and coke-smelted pig), together with the number of furnaces.

It should be noted that, although the list of charcoal-fired furnaces still in use in 1791 has a column headed 'No of Furnaces', the list of coke furnaces refers to the 'No of Works'. Close comparison of this list with the survey of 1794, however, shows that the figures in this column in fact refer to the number of separate furnaces, not works. In the tables here, the number of furnaces has been placed in the 'Furnaces in Blast' column, so that it is possible to obtain an estimate of average furnace output for each district. In fact, the compiler of the original tables appears to have counted the total number of furnaces in existence in 1791 and assumed all were in blast in calculating output figures. The latter, grossed up from estimates of average weekly output, are therefore rather greater than would have been the case had some allowance been made for furnaces out of blast. It would have been possible, in this volume, to have inserted the number of furnaces given in the 1791 tables in both the 'Furnaces Built' and 'Furnaces in Blast' columns, since the compiler of the original lists obviously viewed the two figures as identical. This, however, would have generated a spurious 100 per cent in the next column ('% in Blast') of the tables here, which we have preferred to avoid. Nor have we tried to count the number of works (as opposed to separate furnaces) in existence in 1791, although this could probably be done by comparison with the 1794 survey and in several districts would produce the same figure. The 1791 and 1794 rows of each regional table are therefore complementary in the information they provide, as indeed are the original lists from which the data has been taken.

The 1796 List

The estimates of 1796, occasioned by the government's proposed excise of 20s. a ton on pig iron, are well known.[1] In attempting to calculate the yield of such a tax, the Excise produced a figure of 167,312 tons from 107 furnaces in England and Wales, plus 17 furnaces and 18,300 tons in Scotland. The trade at first retaliated by reducing the England and Wales total to 133,907 tons from 103 furnaces by taking lower estimates for a number of works and eliminating four sites in North Wales, since two were no longer in use and the other two were in fact lead smelters. They made no alteration to estimates for furnaces of which they had no direct knowledge, which included the 17 in Scotland, so that the total for Great Britain was reduced to 152,207 tons. Early in 1798 the trade produced a new set of figures, this time based on returns from individual ironmasters, which, again from 120 furnaces, came to a total of 125,079 tons.[1] Manuscript copies of these surveys can be found in at least three collections; a printed version later appeared in Abraham Rees's *Cyclopaedia*.[2] Extracts for individual counties were also supplied to the Board of Agriculture's reporters and were generally published in the second ('octavo') series of county volumes, usually combined with data from the 1806 list.[3]

In its earliest form, the survey of 1796 is arranged in four columns, headed 'Name' (of the works), 'Where' (situated), 'Return' (i.e. output as estimated by the Excise), and 'May Make' (i.e. output as initially estimated by the trade). The whole of England and Wales is included under these headings and the last two columns totalled. This was followed by a list of 'Scotch Furnaces', where the trade made no alteration to the list previously compiled by the Excise. The return is dated 'Excise Office, 3 Nov. 1797', although no copy appears to survive amongst the Excise Office records themselves.[4] After the trade conducted their more detailed enquiries early in 1798, a revised version of the two tables was prepared, with a third output column, headed 'Exact Return', and the initials of the correspondent who supplied the information.[5]

Neither in England and Wales nor in Scotland is the spelling of furnace names especially good, while the second column ('Where') has led to some confusion when extracts from the list have been used in local publications, from those of the Board of Agriculture onwards. The name used in this column is that of the Excise collection within which the ironworks was situated, not the county: thus the first two names on the

---

[1] Riden, 'Output', p. 449. For both the 1796 and 1806 tax proposals see W.A. Smith, 'Combinations of West Midlands ironmasters during the industrial revolution', *West Midland Studies*, 11 (1978), 1–10; W. le Guillou, 'William Gibbons and the proposed taxes on the iron trade', *Journal of West Midlands Regional Studies*, 2 (1968), 1–5; and (most recently and in more detail), C. Evans, 'The statistical surveys of the British iron industry in 1797–98 and 1806', *Historical Metallurgy*, 27 (1993), 84–101, which draws attention to previously unnoticed manuscript versions of both surveys in the Hailstone Collection at York Minster Library.

[1] Evans, 'Statistical surveys', pp. 84–8 discusses in detail how the trade went about this exercise.

[2] Those in Birmingham Central Library, Boulton & Watt Collection, Matthew Boulton Papers, Iron Trade Box, and Science Museum Library, Weale MS, I, ff. 91–2, have long been well known; Evans, 'Statistical surveys', pp. 92–5 prints the MS in York Minster Library. The earliest published text appears to be that in Rees, *Cyclopaedia*, IV (1819), art. Blast Furnace; another was published by Scrivenor, *History* (1854 ed.), pp. 95–7.

[3] Full details of the series are given in R.E. Prothero, *English farming past and present* (6th ed., 1961), pp. xcvii–ci; for the iron industry see, e.g., John Farey's *Derbyshire* (1811–17), William Pitt's *Staffordshire* (1813) or Walter Davies's *South Wales* (1813).

[4] Now in the Public Record Office, CUST group, in which in general early Excise material makes a poor showing. Cf. Evans, 'Statistical surveys', p. 85.

[5] This is the version published in *Cyclopaedia* and by Scrivenor, loc.cit.

list, Apedale and Silverdale, were in north Staffordshire but in Chester collection; they were not in Cheshire, nor did the compiler of the list believe them to be. A similar problem arises with some of the north-east Derbyshire works, which were in Sheffield collection but not Yorkshire.

Problems of poor orthography and confusion as to location can be resolved by comparison with other sources; the question of what weight to place on the output figures for 1796 is harder to settle. It is not surprising that where the trade's estimate of the output of a particular works differed from that made by the Excise it was lower than the official figure, since it was in the ironmasters' interest to minimise the potential yield of the proposed duty. What is less clear is how the Excise arrived at their original figure, which for some works the ironmasters did not alter, or how far the trade's initial revisions were based on detailed local enquiries. From simply scanning the two output columns of the original table one can infer that, while a few of the figures appear to be returns of actual production, many are simply round-figure estimates or are multiplied from weekly totals. Indeed, the vast majority of the totals in both columns, if divided by 50 or 52, yield a dividend which is a whole number.

The figures collected by the trade in 1798 undoubtedly represent actual output much more closely, although in one instance, where an original return survives, this can be shown not to be the case. Thus in Derbyshire, the Butterley Co. made $682^1/_2$ tons of pig in a campaign from 1 January to 23 October 1796; at nearby Morley Park production totalled 692 tons between 1 January and 5 December.[1] The outputs for these works in the completed survey have been inflated to the amount that would have been produced in a 52-week campaign at the same weekly average. Since a check on the published figures of this sort appears to be available for only two out of 120 works it is clearly not possible to revise the details for every furnace; on the other hand, it is perhaps helpful to point out that a weekly average appears to underlie the annual output figure calculated for 1796, as it does in several later surveys.

Taking the material collected in these years as a whole, we have three estimates of the total output of the British iron industry in 1796, ranging from 185,612 tons (the figure first produced by the Excise) down to 125,079 tons, the trade's revised figure, itself reduced from their opening bid of 152,207 tons. The lowest of these has been adopted by all later writers as the most accurate available for 1796 and we too have accepted this figure, since it appears to rest more firmly than either of the other two on a furnace-by-furnace survey, albeit with some adjustments likely to increase rather than reduce the total. We have therefore calculated regional output estimates for 1796 using the figures for individual works given in the 'Exact Return' column of the text published in *Cyclopaedia* but in the entries for the works in question we have included the two other output estimates (i.e the 'Excise Return' and the 'Supposed Quantity', 'May Make' or 'Actual' figure) found in both the manuscript and printed versions of the survey.[1]

The earliest version of the 1796 survey has columns distinguishing the number of blast furnaces 'At Work' and 'Silent', although there are remarkably few figures in the second of these columns and the percentage of the total number of furnaces in blast, which has been calculated for each region, seems improbably high when compared with later lists. Admittedly, this was a period of rapidly rising output when the industry might be expected to have most of its plant in use, but even on later occasions when a list of furnaces was compiled close to the peak of a boom (e.g. 1810 or 1825) at least a fifth of furnaces were out of blast. In some cases, comparison with the 1794 list strongly suggests that either only a single furnace has been returned at a works where there almost certainly two or more, or that only the furnace in blast has been included. For example, Joseph Butler's works at Wingerworth, near Chesterfield, is shown as having two furnaces in 1794, as it definitely had ten years before when the lease changed hands, but only one is listed in 1796, almost certainly in error.[2] Despite problems of this sort, which are difficult to detect without detailed local investigation, a figure for the percentage of furnaces in blast has been inserted in each of the regional tables, although it should be treated with some caution.

The 1806 List

In March 1806 the government announced the introduction of a duty of 40s. a ton on pig iron and unleashed a new storm of opposition.[3] Early in May the measure was abandoned but not before the trade had produced figures showing that total production was now running at about 250,000 tons a year. This was based on a careful furnace-by-furnace survey, which lists the name of each works and its owner, the number of furnaces built and the number in and out of blast, plus the output of the works for the last available year (i.e. 1805, not 1806). The whole exercise appears to have been done very carefully and the output figures in particular look as though they are in most cases genuine estimates of annual production. The trade had clearly become more experienced in compiling surveys since 1796 and, in early manuscript versions of the list, it is

---

[1] Derbyshire Record Office, D503, Butterley Co. Letterbook, 5 March 1798 (no addressee shown).

[1] There are no serious discrepancies between those texts of the 1796 list which include all three sets of output estimates, except in the case of the Hailstone MS in York Minster Library, which has substantially different figures for the Shropshire works (for which see Evans, 'Statistical surveys', pp. 92–5).

[2] P. Riden, 'Joseph Butler, coal and iron master, 1763–1837', *Derbys. Arch. Journal*, 104 (1984), pp. 88–9. Readers with detailed knowledge of other sites listed in both 1794 and 1796 may be able to spot other instances of this kind.

[3] Riden, 'Output', p. 450; Smith, 'Combinations'; le Guillou, 'William Gibbons'; Evans, 'Statistical surveys'.

possible to see something of their method of working.[1] For each county, two or three ironmasters collected figures from their neighbours and then sent in lists to some central organiser, probably one of the partners at Soho Foundry. Thus Edward Frere of Clydach was responsible for many of the South Wales works, Joseph Butler covered much of Derbyshire, and a member of the Dalrymple family was responsible for returns from every Scottish furnace except Carron. It is noticeable that the spelling of both place- and personal names is much better than ten years before.

The details for 1806 given in the entries for individual furnaces here are taken from a copy of the list in the Boulton & Watt Collection; the text among the papers of James Weale is slightly discrepant. The output figures for the works from which returns were obtained total 242,707 tons in the Boulton & Watt version, to which 7,800 tons was added for the estimated output of eleven works from which no figures had been forthcoming, making a final total of 250,507 tons, which in later references is normally rounded off to 250,000 tons. In all 236 furnaces were listed, of which 177 (i.e. 75 per cent) were in blast. The proportion of furnaces in use conforms much more closely to that of later surveys than the figure obtained for 1796, which suggests that the number of furnaces out of use was counted properly in 1806.

Since the output figures collected on this occasion obviously relate to 1805, they have been assigned throughout this volume (for the sake of consistency with some later lists) to this latter date, even though they have traditionally been referred to, ever since they were first assembled, as belonging to 1806.

The 1810 List

By contrast with those of 1796 and 1806, the list compiled in 1810, in connection with Richard Cort's campaign in parliament and elsewhere for some reward for his father's inventions, is little known, partly because it has never been published but also because it appears to survive in only one copy, bound up with James Weale's drafts for his 'History of the Iron Trade'.[2] The return lists 223 furnaces, broken down by district, and notes that a further 45 were out of blast, but gives no furnace or district output figures. There is, however, a total output estimate of 530,000 tons, of which 130,000 tons were bar iron, leaving a pig iron total of 400,000 tons. The lack of individual output figures for each works is more than compensated for by the thoroughness of the survey and its date, coming as it does at the peak of the boom during the war with France.

Although clearly based on the survey of 1806, that of 1810 was undoubtedly derived from new enquiries: a number of works established since 1806 (some of which had gone out of use before the surveys of 1820s) are included and the number of furnaces at each site (whether in blast or not) has obviously been revised.

The 1823–30 List

After the list of 1810, there are no comprehensive national surveys until the early 1820s, merely a few local lists showing the state of the industry in certain areas during the slump following the end of the war in 1815.[1] For the 1820s, by contrast, there is a good deal of information. The widest ranging survey was that compiled by Francis Finch, later MP for Walsall and himself a South Staffordshire ironmaster, which took the form of output estimates for the principal districts (South Wales, Staffordshire, Scotland, Yorkshire, Derbyshire and the North East) for 1823 and 1830, together with the number of furnaces in each district (without distinguishing the number in blast) and the number built in each of the intervening years.[2] Furnaces and outputs are listed individually for each works but without the names of owners; comparison with the 1825 list indicates that the number of furnaces refers to the total number built at each site, not the number in blast. The output figures look as though they are genuine annual production totals, not weekly averages grossed up. The survey was made in 1825 and 1831 and may have been intended to provide 'before and after' figures to illustrate the effect of a substantial reduction in the duty on imported bar iron in 1826. Although said to have been compiled at the request of the government and referred to by Charles Poulett Thompson, the vice-president of the Board of Trade, in a Commons debate in 1832, the survey was not included in Sessional Papers. A lithographed version published in Birmingham, probably in 1832, may represent its first appearance in any form.

The 1825–28 List

For two of the years within the period covered by Finch's survey there is a separate, apparently independently compiled, output estimate by the statistician John Marshall (1783–1841), which lists works individually under district sub-headings, distinguishing the total number of furnaces from the number in blast and giving

---

[1] There are manuscripts and printed pamphlets in Birmingham Central Library, Boulton & Watt Collection, Matthew Boulton Papers, Iron Trade Box; Science Museum Library, Weale MSS, I, ff. 103–4 etc; and York Minster Library, Hailstone Collection. For the latter text and a discussion of the trade's method of working in 1806 see Evans, 'Statistical surveys', pp. 88–9, 96–8.

[2] Science Museum Library, Weale MS, III, ff. 182v–86; Riden, 'Output', p. 450.

[1] Riden, 'Output', p. 450; Evans, 'Statistical surveys', p. 101 (n. 52).

[2] Riden, 'Output', pp. 450–1 for the origins and authorship of the survey, with reference to original authorities. Finch (whose Christian name was given wrongly as Frederick in Riden, loc.cit.) sat for Walsall from 1837 until he accepted the Chiltern Hundreds in January 1841; he had previously unsuccessfully contested Lichfield (*Who's who of British Members of Parliament*, I (1976), p. 139).

output figures for 1825 and 1828. No furnace-by-furnace survey has been located for 1828 (although Marshall's figures are sufficiently detailed to make it fairly clear that one was compiled) but for 1825 information is available for each site. Manuscript versions of the list include the note that 'nearly all the works in South Wales, Shropshire, and Staffordshire, also in Yorkshire and Derbyshire', were visited to obtain this return and, in giving evidence to the 1833 Select Committee on Manufactures, the Yorkshire ironmaster Samuel Walker regarded Marshall's survey as equal in authority to Finch's.[1] In fact, for present purposes, it is superior, since it includes the minor ironmaking districts, such as North Wales and the Forest of Dean, omitted by Finch, as well as a number of works throughout the country not in the list of 1823–30. Marshall appears to have started from a copy of the 1806 survey, since works included there which had long since ceased to function reappear in 1825, generally with some comment as to their abandonment. Some of the last few charcoal-fired furnaces, for example, are listed. Like the survey of 1810, that of 1825 portrays the industry at the peak of a boom, with a large proportion of furnaces in blast.

The original version of the 1825 list evidently dates from early the following year, since a 'Remarks' column is headed 20 March 1826. In most cases, the date is not crucial, since the information concerns the use to which the output of a particular works was put (e.g. 'melting and forge' or 'in the casting trade'); where the comment is 'Building' or on the lines of 'Out of blast last week', the date is significant and has been noted in the tables printed here. Two output figures are given for each works in 1825, one weekly and the other annual; in some cases (but by no means all) the second is the first multiplied by 50 or 52. Outputs are also given for a number of works where no furnaces were in blast in 1825, presumably to indicate potential rather than actual production. All these figures are included here.

Two versions of the 1825 list are known, one in the Boulton & Watt Collection and the other among a large accumulation of solicitor's papers in the Staffordshire Record Office.[2] They are basically identical, apart from variations in the spelling of some place- and personal names, and in the phrasing of some of the comments added in March 1826. Minor discrepancies of this sort have not been noted here, although where the two texts vary materially, for example in the number of furnaces at a particular works or the number in blast, these differences have been set out in the note to each entry.

The 1827 List

Besides the better known surveys of the 1820s, there is one other output estimate of this period, of 690,000 tons in 1827, which seems to be based on detailed enquiries.[1] Output figures are given for each district, together with the number of furnaces; by comparison with adjacent lists it is clear that the latter figure is for the number of furnaces in blast, rather than the total number, and the information has been incorporated into the regional tables here on this basis. Perhaps most interesting, an attempt is made here, but not elsewhere in this period, to estimate the consumption of pig iron as between castings and bar iron and to value the resulting output of each branch of the industry, making an allowance for wastage in further working-up.[2]

Le Play's Survey of 1836

In a paper read to the British Association in 1847, G.R. Porter referred to a visit to Britain made by Frédéric Le Play (1806–82), a senior official of the French Corps des Mines, in 1836, in which he collected output figures for every ironworks in the country, presumably for the previous year, from which he produced an estimate for the total output of the industry of 1,000,000 tons p.a.[3] This is probably the origin of Sir John Guest's statement to the Select Committee on Import Duties in 1840 that Britain made about a million tons of pig in 1835 and 1.2 million the following year,[4] but where (if anywhere) the detailed figures collected by Le Play were published has not been established. His earliest biographer confirms that he visited Britain in 1835–36 but, in contrast with some of his other overseas travels during his time with the Corps des Mines, no correspondence survives from this visit, nor was a report published in *Annales des Mines*, of which Le Play was then

---

[1] Riden, 'Output', p. 451.

[2] Birmingham Central Library, Boulton & Watt Collection, Matthew Boulton Papers, Box 1, No 29; Staffs. RO, D695/1/9/81/1, Harward MSS.

[1] Riden, 'Output', p. 452. The figures appear to have been first published in the *Edinburgh Philosophical Magazine*, from where they were reprinted in the *British Almanac. The companion to the almanac* (1829), p. 196; *Mechanics' Magazine*, XIII, 352 (24 July 1830); J. Holland, *Manufactures in metal: iron and steel* (1831), p. 75; W. Needham, *The manufacture of iron* (1831), p. 30; and quite possibly elsewhere. They are also given in the statistical volume of the 1871 Coal Commission's Report (Parl. Papers, 1871 (C. 435), XVIII), III, 58.

[2] The compiler of the statistics believed that 30 per cent of pig iron went into castings and the rest into wrought iron; no further estimates of this sort seem to have been published until 1852, when Braithwaite Poole (*Statistics of British commerce*, p. 206) gave exactly the same proportions.

[3] G.R. Porter, 'On the progress, present amount, and probable future condition of the iron manufacture in Great Britain', *Report of the sixteenth meeting of the British Association* (1847), p. 102. Le Play was a long-standing correspondent of Porter's: M.Z. Brooke, *Le Play: engineer and social scientist* (1970), pp. 3, 13.

[4] *Select Committee on Import Duties* (Parl. Papers, 1840 (601), V), q. 391, which is in turn probably the source for the inclusion of the same two aggregate figures in the table printed in R.C. Taylor, *Statistics of coal* (1848), p. 330, where there is also a figure (360) for the number of furnaces in blast in 1835. This is not from the Parliamentary Paper and may indicate that Taylor had access to Le Play's original data.

joint editor and to which he contributed a regular statistical report on the French metal industries.[1]

The 1839 List

Among the essays published by David Mushet, the ironmaster and metallurgist, in his well known volume of *Papers on Iron and Steel* (1840) is one 'On the progress of the manufacture of pig iron with pit-coal, and a comparison of the value and effects of pit-coal, wood and peat-char'. Appended to this chapter is a list, arranged by region, of the ironworks in use in Great Britain in 1839, including the name of the owner, the number of furnaces in blast, out of blast and 'built or building'.[2] How the information was gathered is not explained and, indeed, the details vary slightly between different districts. Thus in North Wales we have only the names of the works, plus the furnace details, but no owners' names, whereas in South Staffordshire we have the names of the works and owners, the furnace-numbers and, in many cases, the actual output of each works, whether made by hot or cold blast, and the use to which the pig was put. For most regions Mushet also gives an 'Average Make' per furnace and the total output for the district, but how these figures were calculated is not explained. Mushet was certainly aware of the problems involved in calculating 'average' outputs over a whole county: in Derbyshire he separated the two works of the Butterley Company, 'constructed on the most powerful and comprehensive scale', from the other furnaces, giving those at Butterley and Codnor Park an average weekly make of 60 tons and the rest 40 tons.

From statements elsewhere in the same essay, it is apparent that Mushet collected similar data for 1820 and 1830, but no details are given beyond a total output of pig iron of 400,000 tons in 1820 and 650,000 tons in 1830.[3]

Mushet calculated that in 1839 there were 396 furnaces in blast, 142 out and 57 in course of construction, making in all 1,248,781 tons of pig. In 1841, in the first edition of his *History of the Iron Trade*, Harry Scrivenor printed a table listing 378 furnaces producing 1,347,790 tons, which 'we believe to be as correct an account of the quantity produced in 1839 as can be arrived at, considering that part of it is necessarily estimated', and included Mushet's figures for the same year in a footnote.[1] In his second edition of 1854, Scrivenor printed Mushet's table in the text, omitting his own altogether,[2] and mainly for this reason Mushet's figures have been used here.

Jessop's List of 1840

In October 1840, William Jessop (1783–1852), one of the owners of the Butterley Company, undertook what Porter described as 'a very elaborate inquiry' into the output of pig iron, the result of which he printed for private circulation. Jessop counted 492 furnaces in all, of which 402 were in blast, making 1,396,400 tons of pig a year. Although summary data from this survey, arranged by county, is readily accessible, Jessop's original publication has not been located.[3] The main purpose of the work appears to have been to calculate the consumption of coal by the iron industry and in particular to measure the effect of the introduction of hot blast smelting.

The 1841–42 List

At the end of 1841 the entire iron trade decided to reduce the production of pig by 25 per cent for six months from 1 January 1842, the reduction being calculated on the make for the six months ending 30 June 1841. Thomas Evans of Dowlais was made 'superintending inspector' of this exercise, no doubt assisted by local correspondents in each district.[4] An estimate of total weekly output of pig in 1841 of 25,531 tons, or 1,327,612 tons a year at a time of full working, published in March the following year, must be derived from a survey made as part of this attempted reduction in output, but it does not seem to have been noticed until now that detailed furnace-by-furnace returns were also made available at the time.[5]

---

[1] F. Le Play, *Voyages en Europe, 1829–1854* (ed. A. Le Play) (Paris, 1899), p. 12 (an obituary reprinted from *Annales des Mines*, July–Aug. 1882); the whole of the 3rd series of *Annales des Mines* (1832–41) was searched without success for a report on the British iron industry in 1835 or 1836. Le Play's modern biographer (Brooke, *Le Play*, p. 10) also mentions the visit but (despite extensive searches for similar material from his other travels in this period) failed to locate either a published or MS account, nor have we found a text.

[2] D. Mushet, *Papers on iron and steel, practical and experimental* (1840), pp. 399–428; the list of 1839 is on pp. 414–22.

[3] Ibid., pp. 413–14. Taylor, *Statistics*, p. 330 includes the figure of 400,000 tons for 1820 (but not that for 1830) and gives a figure of 170 for the number of furnaces in blast that year.

[1] Scrivenor, *History* (1841 ed.), p. 292, which is presumably the source for Taylor's figures (*Statistics*, p. 330) of 379 furnaces in blast, 50 out, 429 in all, producing 1,343,000 tons in 1839.

[2] Scrivenor, *History* (1854 ed.), p. 256, whence R. Meade, *The coal and iron industries of the United Kingdom* (1882), p. 835.

[3] There is no copy of the work, either printed or manuscript, in the Butterley Co. archive at the Derbyshire Record Office (D503), in the British Library or apparently anywhere else. A summary table was printed by Porter, 'On the progress', p. 103, and in his *Progress of the nation* (1912 ed.), pp. 238–9, as well as Meade, *Coal and iron industries*, pp. 835–6. A version also appears in Taylor, *Statistics*, p. 330, with 384 furnaces in blast, 88 out, total 492, making 1,396,400 tons.

[4] R.H. Campbell, 'The growth and fluctuations of the Scottish pig iron trade, 1828 to 1873' (Aberdeen University Ph.D. thesis, 1956), pp. 190–91. For Evans at work see M. Elsas (ed.), *Iron in the making. Dowlais Iron Company letters, 1782–1860* (Cardiff, 1960), p. 14.

[5] The summary figures were published in the *Mechanics' Magazine*, XXXVI, 231 (19 March 1842), whence Meade, *Coal and iron industries*, pp. 835–6. For the detailed local lists we are indebted to Mr Brian Davies, Curator of the Pontypridd Historical and Cultural Centre, and to Mr Robert Protheroe Jones of the National Museum of Wales for drawing our attention to an item headed 'The Iron Trade', published in the *Cardiff and Merthyr Guardian*, 12 March 1842, said there (as in the *Mechanics' Magazine*) to have been reprinted from the *Mining Journal*.

The full list of furnaces also published in March 1842 is headed by a general comment concerning the 25 per cent reduction in make, which is likewise referred to in the introductory paragraphs which preface the table for each district. The works are then listed in the usual way, with the owners' names, the total number of furnaces at each and the number in blast. The South Staffs. district is, unusually, divided into two ('North of Dudley' and 'South of Dudley'), a distinction also made in the figures published in the *Mechanics' Magazine*, which helps to confirm that the detailed list belongs with this summary. For all the major areas except South Wales a figure is given for the average weekly output of each works, presumably over the six months up to the end of June 1841. For South Wales there are no individual figures, merely an estimate of 80–85 tons a week for average furnace output. Some of the smaller districts also lack output figures, although all the furnaces are listed, including the two at Arigna in Co. Roscommon, which had not featured in surveys of this sort since 1825 (and had in any case been out of use for some time).

For each of the main districts, although not the smaller ones, the introductory paragraph includes a figure for total weekly output (based on the returns from individual furnaces), from which an annual figure has been obtained by multiplying by 52. In the form in which the survey was published in the *Cardiff and Merthyr Guardian* the weekly totals for each district are not summed to produce a national aggregate, although if one multiplies these figures by 52 the totals are identical with those published in the *Mechanics' Magazine*, which also supplies annual output figures for the smaller areas.

Although the results of this survey were not published until March 1842, the figures clearly refer to the previous year and have been treated as relating to 1841 throughout this volume. As for other years in this period, Taylor in 1848 published some slightly discrepant figures for 1841 without identifying the source.[1]

The 1842 List

In 1842 the trade tried once more to organise a reduction in make, this time of 20 per cent, and Andrew Faulds, the secretary of the Yorkshire and Derbyshire ironmasters, drew up a statement of output in the main districts in the first half of 1842 of 523,214 tons, or 1,046,428 tons in a full year, which, in his paper of 1847, G.R. Porter inflated to 1,099,142 tons, assuming that the smaller districts had the same share of output as in 1840.[1] The *Mechanics' Magazine*, in its discussion of the output estimate of 1841, thought that output had fallen to 75 per cent of the latter, suggesting that in March 1842 output was running at no more than 1,062,090 tons p.a.[2] The furnace-by-furnace survey which presumably underlay the figures collected for 1842 appears not to have been found, although the district totals, plus Porter's estimate for the smaller areas, have been inserted in the national summary table here. Once again, Taylor has slightly different figures for this year.[3]

The 1843 List

In May 1843 the *Cardiff and Merthyr Guardian* printed a list headed 'The Iron Trade. Blast Furnaces in Great Britain, January, 1843', including all the mainland districts but not Arigna in Ireland. Unlike the survey published in March 1842 there are no introductory paragraphs to the tables for each district, which have the usual columns for the names of the works and the owners, although for Shropshire only the latter are listed. For each works the number of furnaces in and out of blast is given (so that the total number at each site has to be obtained by adding these two figures, whereas in other years it is given in the original table) and a third column lists the average weekly make for every works at which at least one furnace was in blast. These figures are then grossed up into annual totals for each district by multiplying by fifty and the district totals are summed to produce a national aggregate of 1,210,550 tons.[4]

In his paper of 1847 Porter refers to the publication of what is clearly the same list in the *Glamorgan Gazette*, another South Wales weekly newspaper, and it is quite possible that it appeared there also; alternatively, he may have confused the *Gazette* with the *Cardiff and Merthyr Guardian*. Porter also mentions another version of the list, given him by Edmund Buckley, a Manchester iron merchant who was MP for Newcastle-under-Lyme between 1841 and 1847, in which the district totals produce an aggregate figure of 1,215,350 tons, a discrepancy resulting from minor differences in the figures for South Wales and Scotland and the addition of 5,000 tons in Buckley's list to the output for Northumberland and Durham.[5]

---

[1] Taylor, *Statistics*, p. 330, where he has 350 furnaces in blast, 177 out, total 527, making 1,387,551 tons of pig. In another table (p. 331), however, Taylor uses the figure of 1,327,612 tons for total output in 1841.

[1] *Report of the Midland Mining Commission* (Parl. Papers, 1843 (508), XIII), 285–7; Porter, 'On the progress', p. 103; idem, *Progress of the nation*, p. 239; *Coal Commission* (1871), III, 60–1.

[2] Loc.cit., 19 March 1842.

[3] Taylor, *Statistics*, p. 330: 339 furnaces in blast, 190 out, total 529, making 1,347,790 tons.

[4] *Cardiff and Merthyr Guardian*, 6 May 1843; once again we are indebted to Mr Davies and Mr Protheroe Jones for drawing this item to our attention.

[5] Porter, 'On the progress', pp. 105, 118. For Buckley see *Who's who of British Members of Parliament* (1976), I, p. 54. The newspaper article gives the output in South Wales as 457,350 tons (Porter has 457,355 tons) and in Scotland as 238,750 tons (238,550 tons in Porter). The major discrepancy occurs for the area described as Northumberland (which also includes Durham), where the newspaper has an output figure of 20,750, as compared with Porter's 25,750. The

Neither Porter nor the article in the *Cardiff and Merthyr Guardian* gives any clue as to why this new survey of the industry was made, although Thomas Evans of Dowlais can again be found at work, in the first three months of 1843, collecting figures from around the country.[1] His correspondents make no reference to an attempted reduction in make and so the trade may have wished merely to see how output was recovering after the slump of the previous couple of years.

Although the lists of 1842 and 1843 are so close in date, the differences between them make it clear that the second was based on fresh enquiries in each district, not merely minor revisions to the earlier survey. This is especially noticeable in South Wales, where companies which had returned a single set of furnace-numbers covering all their works in 1842 provided separate figures for each site the following year, and where a number of small works, especially in the anthracite district west of the main coalfield, appear only in 1842 or 1843 but not both.

The output estimates published in May 1843 have been assigned here to that year, rather than 1842, for which there are figures available elsewhere. This decision is open to question, given the date 'January 1843' used in the heading to the list of furnaces, although the fact that it was not published for another four months, during which time Thomas Evans was clearly collecting output information, suggests that the figures printed in May 1843 may reflect production in the earlier part of that year (rather than the previous year), even if the starting-point for the enquiry was a list of furnaces drawn up at the very beginning of the year.

The 1847–48 Lists

In his monumental compilation of 1848 on the world's coal industries, Richard Taylor supplies three aggregate output figures for British pig iron production (1,575,000 tons in 1844, 2,200,000 tons in 1845, and 2,214,000 tons in 1846) alongside those for earlier years which have already been mentioned.[2] None is accompanied by any figures for the number of furnaces built or in blast, nor have sources been identified for the data.

The next output estimate for which a furnace-by-furnace survey can be located is that contained in a list headed 'Number of Furnaces and Make of Iron in Great Britain in the Year, January 1848', printed by H.S. Tremenheere, the official charged with enforcing the provisions of the Coal Mines Act of 1842, as an appendix to his report on the mining districts in 1849, accompanied by a copy of the 1806 list.[1] The list was also published by Braithwaite Poole in his *Statistics of British Commerce* (1852) and by Henry English in his *Mining Almanack* (1850), where it was placed alongside the 1806 list and other earlier figures.[2] The phrasing of the title given to the list by Tremenheere is slightly odd, although contemporaries evidently regarded the output figures as relating to 1847 and this date has been adopted here.[3] The authorship of the list cannot be identified but in layout it resembles more closely than any of its predecessors that followed by Robert Hunt of the Mining Records Office in *Mineral Statistics* from 1854, apart from the inclusion of furnaces out of blast at each works as well as the total number and the number in blast.

What is perhaps most interesting about the list, given its similarity in style and closeness in date to those of 1854 and later, is its treatment of output estimates. For some districts a figure is given alongside each works under the heading 'Make per Year', although this is clearly notional, since in every case the figure divides by 52 into a round number and has obviously been obtained from a figure for weekly output. For the three most important areas, however (South Staffs., South Wales and Scotland), there is no pretence at giving totals for individual works, merely an average for a typical furnace, from which a district total has been derived. Again, the figure for average furnace output for the whole year has been obtained by multiplying the weekly estimate by 52. Presumably the trade was opposed to supplying the true output figures from individual works (even if these could be obtained in the case of smaller or less well managed concerns) and so those who wished to compile national figures had to proceed in this rather unsatisfactory manner.

Once the publication of annual returns under official auspices began in 1854, Robert Hunt stressed that although he never published output figures for an individual works (or for small districts, where the output of a particular firm would be apparent) his district and national totals were based on returns from individual ironmasters; indeed, as the years went by, Hunt increasingly laboured the position of trust he believed himself to enjoy, among both ironmasters and those engaged in the other mining industries. It may well be, however, that his summary output figures are based, at least in part, on the same technique of grossing up from weekly

---

first two variations may be no more than copying errors; the third possibly implies varying opinions as to the output of the six works in the North East. The lower figure has been used here. Taylor's output figure for 1843 (*Statistics*, p. 330) is 1,215,000 (with no furnace-numbers), which is obviously derived from Porter's total.

[1] Elsas, *Iron in the making*, pp. 15–16.
[2] Taylor, *Statistics*, pp. 330, 331.

---

[1] *Report of the Commissioner appointed under 5 & 6 Vict. c. 99 to inquire into the operation of that Act, and into the state of the population in the mining districts* (Parl. Papers, 1849 [1109], XXII, 395), pp. 26–7. For Tremenheere himself see O.O.G.M. MacDonagh, 'Coal mine regulation: the first decade, 1842–52', in R. Robson (ed.), *Ideas and institutions of Victorian Britain. Essays in honour of George Kitson Clark* (1967), pp. 58–86, and R.K. Webb, 'A Whig inspector', *Journal of Modern History*, 27 (1955), 352–64.

[2] B. Poole, *Statistics of British commerce* (1852), pp. 203–6 (where the output for Yorkshire is given as 66,560 tons p.a., whereas Porter's figure is 67,600); H. English (comp.), *The Mining Almanack for 1850*, pp. 349–57.

[3] Scrivenor, *History* (1854 ed.), p. 295n., Porter, *Progress of the nation*, p. 240, the 1871 Coal Commission, III, p. 61, and Meade, *Coal and iron industries*, p. 836, all treat the output figures as relating to 1847.

estimates. They should not, therefore, be treated as more authoritative than earlier, privately produced, estimates, either because they were published by a government department or because Hunt kept his method of calculation secret.

Alongside the figures for 1847 (433 furnaces in blast, 190 out, making 1,999,608 tons of iron p.a.), Porter also published a summary table for 1848, listing the number of furnaces in and out of blast in each of the principal districts (amounting to 452 furnaces in blast and 174 out for the country as a whole), together with output estimates totalling 2,093,736 tons for the whole of Great Britain.[1] No furnace-by-furnace survey underlying this table has been found but the district figures have been included in the regional statistics here.

The 1849 Lists

There are two, apparently independent, lists of blast furnaces dating from 1849. One was prepared by Hunt to accompany the report of the Royal Commission on the Application of Iron to Railway Structures and published as a plan of the British Isles on which coal and iron measures were marked, together with blast furnaces.[2] The furnaces were numbered and keyed to a list headed 'Names of Iron Furnaces in Blast, July 1849'. The number of furnaces said to be in blast in the country as a whole (573) is substantially higher than the figure published for 1847 (433), or (for those districts included there) in the other list of 1849. This suggests that, in some cases at least, the total number of furnaces built was returned, rather than the number in use. Indeed, in a somewhat uncharacteristic admission, Hunt noted that 'It is possible that some Works have been omitted in this list, as the information has been obtained with great difficulty'. In fact, comparison with the 1847 list suggests that it is substantially complete, although the rendering of place-names is poor in places.[3] Perhaps more interestingly, it is clear that Hunt's first list of blast furnaces in *Mineral Statistics* (1854) is based on the survey of 1849, which includes two works identified only by their owner's name ('Jarvis & Co.' in South Wales and 'Leather & Co.' in the West Riding), both of which reappear in this form in 1854 (but not thereafter), and also uses the name 'Typwca' for Cwmbran Ironworks in Monmouthshire, which in 1854 has its own entry, although there is a duplicate, with no furnace-numbers, for Typwca.

No output figures were included on the map prepared by Hunt for the Royal Commission, but what is clearly the same list of works was published in summary form by Braithwaite Poole three years later, together with an estimate for the output of pig iron over the twelve months ending July 1849 amounting to 2,697,240 tons from 573 furnaces at 178 works. The furnace-numbers are divided by district but the output is not.[1]

A second list dating from 1849 was published by Henry English, the editor of the *Mining Journal*, in the 1850 edition of his *Mining Almanack*.[2] Headed 'Pig-Iron Works and Furnaces, 1849', it includes tables covering Scotland, South Wales, South Staffordshire and Worcestershire, and 'Newcastle' (i.e. Durham and Northumberland), listing the works and their owners, plus the number of furnaces in and out of blast. Only for Scotland is there any attempt at an estimate of output, where it is suggested that 'Each furnace [is] producing, on an average, 6,000 tons per annum; the greater number, however, *actually* putting out *upwards* of 7,000 tons'; there is also an extra column in the Scottish table for furnaces under construction.

The order in which the works appears indicates that English was starting from Tremenheere's list of 1848, although there are enough differences in the furnace-numbers to show that it is based on fresh enquiries. English's list also differs substantially from Hunt's map and table of 1849 and in any case includes only four districts, which makes it clear that it was not copied from the Parliamentary Paper. The only clue as to how it was compiled comes from a note at the end expressing the hope that 'some of our correspondents will favour us with returns from other places'. The appeal does not seem to have met with any response, since the following year's edition of the *Mining Almanack* (the last to be published) omitted any iron trade statistics and (like the first edition of 1849) was concerned almost entirely with non-ferrous metal mining, which was where the main interests of its compiler lay. Very few copies of this short-lived series appear to survive, which may explain why the list of furnaces of 1849 has hitherto been overlooked.[3]

For the districts included in both Hunt's survey and that compiled by English, the latter has been used as the basis for entries here dated 1849, since more detail is given, although any significant discrepancy with the other list has been noted. For the smaller areas not covered by English, an entry has been inserted based on Hunt's list, which, although only brief, at least helps to establish the approximate date of opening of works built after 1847 but before 1854.

---

[1] Porter, *Progress of the nation*, p. 240; the 1871 Coal Commission (III, p. 61) also cites the figures.

[2] *Report of the Commissioners appointed to inquire into the application of iron to railway structures* (Parl. Papers, 1849 [1123], XXIX.1), p. 459. The list of works and an abridged version of the map were published by Alan Birch in his *Economic history of the British iron and steel industry, 1784–1879* (1967), pp. 389–90.

[3] Perhaps the most extreme case is the appearance of the British Iron Co.'s Abersychan (Mon.) works as the 'Bristol Iron Works'!

---

[1] Poole, *Statistics*, p. 206.

[2] English, *Mining Almanack for 1850*, pp. 358–61.

[3] The only location listed in the *British union catalogue of periodicals* is the British Library (press-mark P.P. 2061). In passing it should be pointed out that Braithwaite Poole's reference (*Statistics*, p. 207) to the *Mining Almanack* of 1850 (p. 363) as the authority for figures for 'The production of wrought iron during the last 4 years, officially made up' simply leads back to an inadequately headed table listing production and stock figures for Scottish *pig*, obviously taken from the series compiled by the Scotch Pig Iron Assocation (for which see below, p. xxvii). There are no puddled iron output figures until 1881 (B.R. Mitchell, *Abstract of British historical statistics* (Cambridge, 1971), p. 135; this series was dropped from Mitchell's replacement volume, *British historical statistics* (Cambridge, 1988) as being of insufficient general interest: see p. 275).

The 1852 List

In 1852 Robert Hunt, who had been appointed Keeper of Mining Records at the Geological Survey in 1845, prepared a 'Note on the coal raised and iron made in South Staffordshire' for the annual *Records of the School of Mines*.[1] The information was supplied by Kenyon and Samuel Blackwell of Russell's Hall Ironworks, Dudley, and included the total tonnage of coal raised and its value, plus the quantities of pig and bar iron made in the district. In addition, lists were printed of the blast furnaces in South Staffordshire (including the adjacent part of Worcestershire) and of forges and mills in the district. Although not a national survey, this list is of interest partly because it helps to elucidate the particularly complex history of the South Staffordshire district, with its multiplicity of small ironworks with similar names in close proximity to one another, but also because it may have been a trial run for the lists covering the whole country which by this date were planned for inclusion in *Mineral Statistics*. The format was very similar to that adopted two years later, with columns for the name of ironworks, the owner's name, and the number of furnaces built and in blast. The acknowledgment to the Blackwells is also of interest, since it may indicate that some use of regional correspondents (as opposed to direct application to every single works) continued into the era of *Mineral Statistics*. No details of individual furnace output were provided for South Staffs. in 1852, merely an overall figure for the district, and this again reflects the procedure later adopted by *Mineral Statistics*.

Only for South Staffordshire has a published list of furnaces in 1852 been located but similar details appear to have been collected for other areas, since a summary table showing furnace-numbers and output in each district, the latter totalling 2,701,000 tons for the whole of Great Britain, was published in 1854, if not before.[2] An interesting feature of the summary table is that it divides South Wales into two, separating the much smaller blast furnaces on the anthracite coalfield in the west from those of the main bituminous coalfield in the east. This distinction is not made in any previous list but was a feature of early volumes of *Mineral Statistics*, which further suggests that the 1852 survey was compiled by Hunt on much the same lines as the series which began two years later.

Truran's List of 1855

In general, privately published surveys which attempted to cover the whole country after 1854 may be disregarded, since they are clearly derived from *Mineral Statistics*;[1] there is on the other hand a good deal of material for two districts, Scotland and the North East, which was compiled independently and is in some cases superior to the data in *Mineral Statistics*.[2] The one general survey which does appear to be based on detailed enquiries by its author is that published by William Truran, a native of Cornwall who became works manager at Dowlais, in his treatise on *The Iron Manufacture of Great Britain* (1855). Included as an appendix to this book is a list of 'Pig Iron Works in Great Britain in 1855',[3] which provides a useful check on the earliest editions of *Mineral Statistics*, although the format adopted by Truran differs from Hunt's. Only the works are named, not the owners, and a figure is given for the total number of furnaces at each site but not for the number in blast. It is impossible to identify for certain which earlier survey Truran was working from, although for South Wales and South Staffordshire there are features in Truran's list otherwise found only in that of 1849 published by Henry English.

Unusually, Truran gives output figures, both weekly and annual, for each works, but the latter are merely the former multiplied by 52 and the number of furnaces. This in itself diminishes the value of his work, since his figures are improbably high for many works, but worse still is his practice of assuming that all the furnaces at every works were in blast, which produces an inflated total for the output of each district. He also includes some works which were undoubtedly abandoned by 1855 (for example, Duckmanton, Derbyshire) and at least one that was never brought into use, Shakemantle, in the Forest of Dean, which was described as 'Building' in 1839 but does not appear in any other list. This strongly suggests that Truran also made use of Mushet's work but without attempting to revise it properly using either the surveys of the 1840s or the first issue of *Mineral Statistics*, which may not have been available when his own book went to press. In general, Truran's output figures should be treated with caution.

The Private Surveys in Retrospect

By the early 1850s, when the compilation and publication of output statistics was taken over by a government agency, the iron trade could look back over half a century of privately produced surveys, all, it seems,

---

[1] R. Hunt, 'Note on the coal raised and iron made at present (December 1852) in South Staffordshire', *Records of the School of Mines*, I, Part 2 (1853), 342–8.

[2] Scrivenor, *History* (1854 ed.), p. 302; Meade, *Coal and iron industries*, p. 837. Both authors cite Braithwaite Poole's *Statistics of British commerce* (1852) as the source for the table (Meade presumably simply following Scrivenor). In fact it does not appear in this compilation (which does print the detailed list of 1848 in full) but was included in Poole's later work, *The commerce of Liverpool* (1854), p. 48, with no indication of the source. The latter presumably appeared before Scrivenor's revised edition went to press and, in including the extra information, Scrivenor confused which of Poole's books he had taken it from.

[1] For example, except for the North East, the material on the iron industry in W. Fordyce, *A history of coal, coke, coal fields, ... iron, its ores, and processes of manufacture* (1860; new ed. Newcastle, 1973), is simply taken from *Mineral Statistics* for 1858, which would have been the most up-to-date figures available when Fordyce was writing, presumably sometime in 1859.

[2] Below, pp. xxvii–xviii.

[3] W. Truran, *The iron manufacture of Great Britain theoretically and practically considered* (1855), pp. 172–6.

assembled in much the same way, although for a variety of purposes. Indeed, the ironmasters probably had more experience of working together to compile statistics than any other comparable group and certainly more than the coalowners, whose output also began to be measured officially in 1854.[1] All would have been used to receiving requests for basic information concerning their works and its operations over the previous six or twelve months and most seem to have been willing to allow at least some details of output to be published in the trade press and elsewhere. A smaller number in each district had obviously built up considerable experience in assembling information from their neighbours and returning it to either a central co-ordinator within the trade, such as Thomas Evans, or a writer such as David Mushet or William Truran. Underlying much of this work were the regional associations of ironmasters whose activities in the middle decades of the nineteenth century, between the demise of the meetings which were a feature of the Napoleonic War period and just after, and before the establishment of modern trade organisations in the 1870s, remain largely unexplored.[2]

The establishment of officially published annual output statistics in the mid-1850s should thus be seen as a culmination of a long tradition of voluntary activity on similar lines, not the sudden imposition of government interference into the affairs of an industry which had hitherto operated without any sort of collective action, such as the compilation of output figures, as seems mostly to have been the case in the coal trade.[3] The smoothness of the transition is illustrated by Hunt's work in compiling lists of 1848 and 1849, followed by that of 1852 for South Staffordshire, which lead on directly to the national series two years later. Both these lists, like those going back to the 1790s, had been assembled on the basis of information supplied voluntarily, and it is striking that throughout the period from 1854 until after the First World War, when the task of compiling and publishing statistics was handed back to the trade, the iron and steel figures in *Mineral Statistics* continued to be collected without any statutory intervention (except in part in the case of the output of ore). This is in marked contrast to the basis on which most of the other series in *Mineral Statistics* were compiled.

It is impossible to say whether the quality of the data relating to the iron industry was adversely affected by the absence of compulsory powers to require returns. Certainly Robert Hunt appears not to have believed this, and he made a point, in the introduction to several of the volumes of *Mineral Statistics* for which he was responsible, of praising the way in which a voluntary system worked and stressing the completeness of the returns.

One of the other features of the data in *Mineral Statistics* to which Hunt repeatedly referred was the fact that he never published output data referring to individual works, or groups of works so small that the output of a particular company might be recognisable. Indeed, he gave no clue at all as to how he arrived at the district output totals which were then summed to produce a figure for the entire country. On the other hand, given the continuity between the surveys undertaken by the trade in the first half of the nineteenth century and those published in *Mineral Statistics* from 1854 it seems likely that the same methods were used. It is therefore instructive to consider what these were and how reliable were the results they produced.

As the description of the privately compiled lists has demonstrated, most appear to have arrived at a figure for the total output of pig iron in each district by taking the average weekly output of either each works in that district or each furnace. The more carefully compiled lists allowed for the number of furnaces out of blast (whereas, for example, Truran's survey of 1855 did not) and the most thorough clearly tried to work from separate figures for each works, not merely a figure for the 'typical' blast furnace in the district as a whole. On the other hand, even the more elaborate surveys of the 1840s, which are the immediate precursors of those in *Mineral Statistics*, seem to have arrived at annual totals for each district by multiplying weekly figures by 50 or 52. Such a calculation obviously assumes that the number of furnaces in blast remained constant over twelve months and that the weekly output figure did not change significantly during the same period.

For a district as a whole, it may have been true that these assumptions were sufficiently valid to form the basis of aggregate output estimates for the whole year. It is possible that for every furnace in use when a survey was taken that was later decommissioned for repairs another was put back into use, and that for every furnace that closed down for good a new one was blown-in for the first time. It seems unlikely, however, that such symmetry was achieved very often and therefore the district totals calculated from weekly data can only be approximations to the true annual output. On the other hand, they are all we have for the period before 1854 and are certainly better than the data available for many other industries in this period. From 1854 onwards, we cannot establish how the output figures for each district were calculated, although it seems likely that similar principles were followed.

We should perhaps be more cautious in using the output figures returned for individual works in the pre-1854 surveys. Some of the annual totals may reflect the actual output of the works over twelve months but most

---

[1] Cf. M.W. Flinn, *The history of the British coal industry. Volume 2. 1700–1830: The Industrial Revolution* (Oxford, 1984), pp. 25–35; S. Pollard, 'A new estimate of British coal production, 1750–1850', *Economic History Review*, 2nd series 33 (1980), 212–35.

[2] For the early part of the century see T.S. Ashton, *Iron and steel in the industrial revolution* (Manchester, 1963), pp. 162–85, augmented by Birch, *British iron and steel industry*, pp. 104–18, to which little has since been added, apart from one local study: M.J. Daunton, 'The Dowlais Iron Company in the iron industry', *Welsh History Review*, 6 (1972), 16–48. See also below, pp. xxvii–xxviii.

[3] Cf. the output estimates of Flinn, *History of the British coal industry*, pp. 25–35, and Pollard, 'A new estimate', which both rely mainly on indirect evidence. The Erewash Valley Coal Owners' Association, however, did collect some data from its establishment in 1803 (P. Riden, *The Butterley Company, 1790–1830* (2nd ed., Chesterfield, 1990), pp. 160–66; A.R. Griffin and C.P. Griffin, 'The role of the coalowners' associations in the East Midlands in the nineteenth century', *Renaissance and Modern Studies*, 17 (1973), 95–121).

seem to have been obtained by multiplying a weekly figure by either 50 or 52; indeed, as we have seen, in at least one case the actual output during 1796 at two Derbyshire furnaces was inflated in the final list on the assumption that both had worked throughout the year, even when this was apparently not true. In several later surveys it is obvious that the annual figure is no more than the product of multiplying the weekly output but we have no means of establishing for how much of the year that weekly figure was maintained. The problem is most serious at works which either had only one furnace or those at which every furnace was said to be in blast, where simple multiplication is likely to exaggerate the actual annual output. At works with several furnaces, not all of which were in blast when the count was taken, it is at least possible to assume (perhaps rather dubiously) that the number in use remained the same throughout the year, even if several different furnaces were employed during the year to maintain that figure. On balance, however, multiplying weekly averages to obtain annual totals at plant level is likely to overestimate, rather than underestimate, output.

The Mineral Statistics, 1854–1920

Origins and Evolution

Three years after the establishment of the Geological Survey in 1835, the council of the British Association passed a resolution pressing for the establishment of a Mining Records Office, to serve as a 'Depository for the preservation of documents recording the mining operations of the United Kingdom.'[1] The Treasury accepted the proposal and in September 1840 the Mining Records Office was established under the direction of the Geological Survey, with Thomas Jordan as the first Keeper of Mining Records. Jordan held this appointment for nearly five years; on his resignation in 1845 he was succeeded by Robert Hunt, who was to be the driving force behind the collection and publication of mining statistics for almost thirty years.[2]

Hunt was born at Devonport in 1807, the posthumous son of a naval officer.[3] He received some training as a chemist and was also a pioneer of photography. Before his appointment as Keeper of Mining Records, Hunt had been a lecturer at the Royal School of Mines at Camborne; even after he moved to London he retained links with Cornwall and especially with technical education in the county. He wrote extensively on mining and scientific subjects and was elected a fellow of the Royal Society in 1854. Besides editing the long series of *Mineral Statistics*, Hunt also compiled handbooks for the Great Exhibition of 1851 and that of 1862, and undertook all the statistical work for the Coal Commission of 1869–71, which was published as Volume III of the commission's report.[1] He died in 1887, four years after his retirement from the Mining Records Office.

The Museum of Practical Geology had already been in existence for several years when, in 1853, Northcote and Trevelyan reported that 'The Mining Record Office is an interesting and valuable department of the institution ... But the produce of the iron, coal and some other important mineral substances has not been ascertained, nor can the department be expected to obtain it with any accuracy, unless it is enabled to make systematic inquiries, by sending officers of its own to collect and organise information.'[2] Their report led to the preparation two years later of the first volume of *Mineral Statistics*, compiled by Robert Hunt, with data on the coal and iron industries combined with series for other mining industries previously published elsewhere. Annual volumes, publishing data for the preceding year, continued to appear under the Geological Survey's imprint until 1882.[3] Interestingly, in the same year as *Mineral Statistics* was first published, Harry Scrivenor proposed that the iron trade should establish its own statistical bureau, under his direction.[4]

After Hunt's retirement in 1883, an inter-departmental committee was appointed, which recommended that the Mining Records Office should be transferred to the Home Office and its staff come under the direction of the Inspectors of Mines. The inspectors had for many years been collecting information somewhat similar to that published in *Mineral Statistics* and, especially since the passing of the Coal Mines Regulation Act and the Metalliferous Mines Act in 1872 had made the return of output and other figures from both branches of the mining industry a statutory requirement, there had been increasing antagonism between Hunt and the inspectorate, which was ended only by his retirement.[5] This controversy, which centred on the undesirability of two departments collecting the same information from mine-owners and subsequently publishing figures which often varied considerably, did not, for the most part, affect the iron industry's contribution to *Mineral Statistics*, since only Hunt collected details of pig iron output and other

---

[1] For the Geological Survey's origins and development see J.S. Flett, *The first hundred years of the Geological Survey of Great Britain* (1937); for the origins of the Mining Records Office see Hunt's introduction to *Mineral Statistics* for 1871.

[2] Hunt, loc.cit. previous note; cf. Flett, *First hundred years*, p. 251 for Jordan's service record.

[3] *DNB*; Flett, *First hundred years*, p. 250 for his civil service career.

[1] Parl. Papers, 1871 (C. 435), XVIII.

[2] Quoted, ibid., p. 65.

[3] It is important to emphasise that, until 1882, *Mineral Statistics* was not included in Sessional Papers, nor did the series receive the same relatively wide circulation as the Geological Survey *Memoirs*. There is a complete set for the period 1853–81 in the British Library, which were published on microfilm in 1985 by Microform Academic Publishers of Wakefield. This edition is accompanied by a very useful printed 'Introduction' by Roger Burt and Peter Waite (itself reprinted from the Northern Mine Research Society's *British Mining No 23. Memoirs*, 1983), which has been drawn on here for the complicated bibliographical history of *Mineral Statistics*, both before and after the Mining Records Office was transferred to the Home Office.

[4] *Journal of the Society of Arts*, 3 (1855), 163, 229, 375.

[5] See the work of Burt and Waite (which is unfortunately unpaginated) cited in n. 3 for a fuller account of this problem.

series, the inspectorate concerning themselves purely with iron-ore mining. When the Mining Records Office was transferred to the Home Office, however, the collection of blast furnace and other data was continued, on the same voluntary basis as before, by Hunt's former assistants, Richard Meade and James B. Jordan, who became 'Clerks of the Mineral Statistics'. Meade, best remembered today for his monumental *Coal and Iron Industries of the United Kingdom* (1882), had been appointed Hunt's assistant as long ago as 1841 and had joined the Mining Records Office in 1858.[1] He retired in 1889 but Jordan, who had also been appointed in 1858, continued at the Home Office until 1897, so that for half a century just three men had been involved in the compilation of *Mineral Statistics*.[2]

It is worth stressing that, even after 1882, the figures relating to the smelting and manufacture (as opposed to the mining) of iron were still collected on a voluntary basis by the Mining Records Office and not under the Inspectors of Mines' considerable statutory powers. The method of compilation used in Hunt's day (i.e. personal appeals to individual owners, presumably supplemented by estimates and interpolation where no actual figures were forthcoming) appears not to have changed. There is, therefore, no reason to believe that the blast furnace data became any more (or any less) reliable after it began to be issued in a Command Paper, rather than a departmental publication.

Jordan's retirement coincided with a further reorganisation of the publication of *Mineral Statistics*, although this was only partly occasioned by his departure. In 1893 the Royal Commission on Mining Royalties had raised doubts about the accuracy of some of the data in *Mineral Statistics* relating to the coal industry. A departmental committee was set up the same year to consider the matter, which in April 1894 took evidence from Bennet Brough, the secretary of the Iron and Steel Institute. Brough suggested that *Mineral Statistics* might usefully be enlarged to include figures for the production of coke (and presumably its consumption by the iron and steel industry); he also made the slightly odd comment that 'official returns of the quantity of iron and steel produced in Great Britain would be very valuable', pointing out that similar data was published for France and the United States.[3] This remark only becomes intelligible if one remembers that, even after 1882, all the iron and steel figures in *Mineral Statistics*, apart from those relating to iron-ore mining, continued to be supplied voluntarily and so might not be regarded as 'official returns'; indeed, they were in this period subject to some criticism in the annual statistical reports of the British Iron Trade Association, established in 1875.[4]

The departmental committee reported in September 1894, making a number of recommendations, some of which were adopted, although others, which required legislation, were never implemented. The committee said nothing about the iron and steel section of *Mineral Statistics*.[1] It is possible that the reorganisation of 1897 also owed something to the committee's work, as well as apparently following James Jordan's retirement. From 1897 until the First World War, *Mineral Statistics* appeared under the overall title *Mines and Quarries: General Report and Statistics* and was divided into four parts, of which Part III contained the data previously issued as *Mineral Statistics*.[2]

The last detailed list of blast furnaces to be included in the Chief Inspector of Mines' annual report was that for 1913, published, as usual, in Part III of the report dated the following year.[3] The same volume of Sessional Papers also contained the Chief Inspector's report for 1914 in which, as a comment in Part II confirmed, all the statistical tables had been shortened as far as possible, because of the outbreak of war.[4] Part III of the 1914 report included the usual summary of pig iron output by county but no list of individual furnaces, nor any specific explanation for the omission.[5]

The publication of mining statistics continued on similar lines for the remainder of the First World War and on to 1920, with summary figures for pig iron output but no details at plant level. In the latter year, however, Part III of the Chief Inspector's Report failed to appear as a Sessional Paper but was issued later in 1921 as a non-Parliamentary Paper by the Mines Department, a sub-department of the Board of Trade, headed by a parliamentary secretary designated the Secretary for Mines, who took over the Home Secretary's responsibilities for the Mines Inspectorate and other aspects of the government's dealings with the coal industry previously the concern of the Board of Trade.[6] The report included the familiar summary table of pig iron output by county and various other statistics relating to the iron and steel industry, but the pre-war publication of a complete list of furnaces and their owners was not revived. In 1922 the Chief Inspector's Report was subsumed within the *First Annual Report of the Secretary for Mines* for the year to 31 December 1921 and contained the same iron and steel statistics as in the previous year. This arrangement continued throughout the inter-war period, with the eighteenth

---

[1] Burt and Waite, 'Introduction'; Flett, *First hundred years*, p. 254.

[2] Burt and Waite, 'Introduction'; Flett, *First hundred years*, p. 251.

[3] Burt and Waite, 'Introduction'; *Report of the Departmental Committee on Mining and Mineral Statistics* (Parl. Papers, 1895 [C. 7609], XLII.1), p. 19.

[4] Below, p. xxvi.

[1] *Rep. Dept Cttee Mining and Mineral Statistics*, pp. 20ff.

[2] The bibliographical details are given in Burt and Waite, 'Introduction'.

[3] Parl. Papers, 1914–16 [Cd 7741], LXXX.537, Table 23.

[4] Parl. Papers, 1914–16 [Cd 8135], LXXX.819, p. 5.

[5] Parl. Papers, 1914–16 [Cd 8141], LXXX.819, Table 99.

[6] Mines Department, *Mines and Quarries: General Report, with Statistics. For 1920. By H.M. Chief Inspector of Mines. Part III. Output* (1921). A copy of this rather elusive volume, which fills the gap evident in the entry for 1920 under 'Mines III.10 (Statistics)' in the *Index of House of Commons Papers 1900–1949*, p. 481, can be found in the BL at the press-mark BS 21/17(1). For the Mines Department see B. Supple, *The history of the British coal industry. Vol. 4. 1913–1946: The political economy of decline* (Oxford, 1987), p. 144n.

(and, as it proved, last) report, that for 1938, appearing in 1939. The iron and steel figures, however, were only included in the first eight reports, up to that for 1928, before their publication (as well as collection) was handed entirely to the industry's main trade association.[1]

Format and Reliability

The layout adopted by Hunt in 1854, the origins of which can be traced back to the surveys of the 1840s and indeed earlier, involved listing each furnace under district subheadings on lines long familiar in the industry. Besides the name of the works, Hunt also printed the owner's name, the number of furnaces built and the number in blast. Other tables summarised the statistical data for each district, including estimated pig iron output, but no output figures for individual works were published. In addition, the number of works, the number of furnaces built and the number in blast were calculated from the lists for each district, from which in turn data for Great Britain as a whole was worked out.

It should be added that on one occasion (1857) Hunt listed the furnace at Creevelea, Co. Leitrim, so that the grand totals could be said to relate to the entire United Kingdom. In fact, both the works at Creevelea and that at Arigna, Co. Roscommon, which was listed in 1825 and 1842, were in use over a longer period than their brief appearance in British statistical sources would suggest.[2] *Mineral Statistics* cannot, therefore, claim to provide a reliable account of attempts to establish an iron-smelting industry in Ireland in the nineteenth century, although Irish iron-ore mining appears to have been treated rather better.

The method of presenting the list of blast furnaces established by Hunt did not change fundamentally between 1854 and 1913, although the original district subheadings were later refined to show more clearly the county in which each furnace lay. Thus the Worcestershire works around Dudley were properly distinguished from those elsewhere in the Black Country, whereas to begin with (as in the pre-1854 private surveys), the entire district was labelled 'South Staffordshire'. The Scottish furnaces were also assigned to counties, although separate output figures were only published for those with a number of works. In South Wales, as the industry contracted, the practice of dividing the region into an 'anthracite' district to the west and a 'bituminous' district to the east was abandoned in favour of county headings, but again the number of works in Breconshire and West Wales was too small for individual outputs to be published. Elsewhere also, for example in Somerset and Wiltshire, a single figure was published to represent the output of two counties where the number of works was so small that an individual concern might have been recognisable had a total been published for only one county.

Under each district or county heading the furnaces were normally listed in alphabetical order, as one might expect. Ironworks sometimes changed their name, although often the entry was not moved to its new place in an alphabetical sequence for several years. In South Staffordshire, which in the middle decades of the nineteenth century still had several dozen works within a very small area, a simple alphabetical listing was for a time abandoned in favour of grouping the furnaces by district and arranging these district names (Bilston, Dudley, Walsall, Wolverhampton etc) alphabetically. This chopping and changing with the Black Country section of the list, coupled with the problem of like-sounding names for different works, makes it more difficult than in any other area to be sure that entries for the same works each year have been placed under the same heading. Every effort has been made to avoid duplicates and ghosts but it is here that these are most likely to be found.

Besides the special difficulties with the Black Country, there are a number of general problems to be overcome in reworking the blast furnace lists from *Mineral Statistics*, especially in the earlier years. Place-names, particularly in Wales, are often misspelt; works with similar names are confused; owners' names vary from year to year in ways which suggest that typographical errors passed into print unnoticed; and furnace-numbers sometimes also vary inexplicably. Later in the nineteenth century, mainly in districts where output was declining and there were mergers between once separate concerns (notably in Shropshire and South Wales), figures for individual sites are not always given separately or have become confused.

Difficulties over the entries for particular works in any one year can often be resolved by comparison with entries for adjacent years, or by checking secondary sources. What concerned contemporary critics rather more, and remains a problem in using the data today, were shortcomings in the calculation of district totals, from which the national figures were derived, since these were of course quoted far more widely than the sub-totals, much less the details of individual works.

At first sight, the calculation of the number of works, the number of furnaces built and the number in blast seems simple enough, since the figures for each district were merely the sum of the individual entries printed under each subheading. The reality, however, was less straightforward. For most works in most years, the figure returned for furnaces in blast was a whole number, which may often have been something of a generalisation on the part of the owner of the works, whose furnaces may not all have been in use for the whole of the previous year but who was disinclined to recall the exact dates of blowing-in or blowing-out.

---

[1] Mines Department, *First Annual Report of the Secretary for Mines for the year ending 31st December 1921 and the Annual Report of H.M. Chief Inspector of Mines for the same period, with a statistical appendix to both reports* (1922). This volume (and its successors to 1938) can be found in the BL at BS 27(5); they form a sequel to the report cited in the previous note. See below, p. xxviii, for iron and steel statistics after 1920.

[2] We are indebted to the county librarians of Leitrim and Roscommon for kindly supplying copies of local publications relating to these two works, which both operated intermittently during the nineteenth century.

Other ironmasters did supply more detail, some of which was printed in *Mineral Statistics*. A comment on the lines of 'For six months only' is easy enough to interpret at a works with only one furnace in blast, but where there were two or more are we to infer that the entire plant was shut down for half the year or did some furnaces remain in use for the whole twelve months? Some explanatory notes are even less helpful ('For a few weeks only' or 'In blast part of the year'); a few are downright confusing. Thus a return might list five furnaces at a particular works, with all of them in blast, but with a note reading 'Two furnaces for three months, three furnaces for five months and five furnaces for four months'. This might mean that (say) two furnaces were in use between January and March, a third was lit in April and the other two were blown-in in September, a total of 41 'furnace-months' out of a possible 60, or an average number in blast for the year of just under $3^1/_2$, rather than the 5 printed in the main table. From 1889 *Mineral Statistics* tried to be more precise, printing the number of furnaces in blast as a whole number plus a fraction expressed in twelfths. In general, however, it is often difficult to decide exactly what is meant and so in this edition all fractions of furnaces in blast have been rounded up or down to the nearest whole number. The effect of this has been to reduce the number of furnaces in blast at some sites, because of the tendency of *Mineral Statistics* to print figures in the tables which did not accommodate qualifications expressed in footnotes.

The difficulty with the figures given in the original returns for the number of works and the total number of furnaces in each district has a somewhat different origin. All the tables in *Mineral Statistics* were presumably left standing in type from year to year, even if the linking passages of narrative were set from scratch for each edition, and one imagines that the data for each table was supplied to the printer as a marked-up copy of the same table as published the previous year. In this situation there was a strong tendency, with the list of blast furnaces, to leave unamended an entry for a particular works for which no return had been received, for example because the company in question had gone out of business. In modern practice, such an entry would be marked to show that it had not been revised; in any case, a telephone call would be sufficient to establish whether a firm had forgotten to send in a return or had disappeared. Hunt and his colleagues no doubt did their best, with the less sophisticated means of communication at their disposal, to chase up backsliders but seem to have been prepared to let an entry continue to be published for several years without having heard from the firm in question, a procedure made simpler by the practice of working from standing type. In a few cases, companies continued to be listed after they had been wound-up and liquidated. This can be detected, where an owner was a registered company, by an examination of the Companies Registration Office file for the firm in question, and several instances of this have been identified. There may even be cases where furnaces continued to appear after they had been demolished or at least become derelict, although this could only be confirmed by a more detailed investigation of individual works than we have attempted.

Even if, as was usually the case, such entries included a nil return for the number of furnaces in blast, this practice could still distort the derived data at district and national level, by producing higher figures for the number of works and the number of furnaces than was really the position on the ground. This would not only affect the aggregate figures for the industry as a whole, but also distort two ratios which can be calculated from the data in *Mineral Statistics* at both district and national level — that between the number of works and the total number of furnaces in existence, and between the total number of furnaces and the number in blast (the latter also being affected by the problems already discussed concerning the calculation of the number in blast at each works). It would also affect estimates for the output of pig iron per works and per furnace, although not the more important figure for output per furnace in blast.

It might be argued, in support of the Mining Records Office's policy, that contemporaries were not to know that a particular works might not be restarted, possibly by a new company, and so it was reasonable to continue to list the site. Indeed, there are instances of this happening, where in some cases the works continued to have an entry throughout the period in which it was out of use, while in others a site disappeared and reappeared. This is a fair point, since Hunt and his colleagues could not predict the future. On the other hand, the fact remains that, with the benefit of hindsight, one can see that a certain amount of dead matter remained in type after it should have been struck out and that this may affect the statistics derived from the lists of ironworks.

It would in theory have been possible, for this edition, to have reworked all the district (and thus national) figures for the number of works and number of furnaces from the entries for individual sites, eliminating cases where works which had in practice closed down were still counted. On the other hand, not only would this have been exceedingly laborious, especially for the larger districts, but the results would probably not have been commensurate with the effort involved. There would still have been a number of doubtful cases, not all of which could have been sorted out from secondary sources, for many of which there would be no archival material to fall back on, so that the figures would still have remained only an approximation of the true position. By contrast with the figures compiled by the trade associations, both before and after 1920, *Mineral Statistics* never assigned a precise date to its lists of works and furnaces (e.g. 31 December) and only from 1892 were the figures explicitly said to be an average for the year as a whole, although this may have been true of earlier years. Anyone who wishes to compile more precise information for a particular area or year may start by going through all the entries for individual works printed here, but must then be prepared to follow up a much larger number of loose ends than the compilers of a volume such as this might reasonably be expected to do.

The most serious problem with the pig iron data in *Mineral Statistics*, the one which attracted most criticism from the trade at the time and about which the detailed tables for each district offer no help, concerns the figures for output. How did Hunt (and his successors) produce their total tonnages for each county (or group of counties), which were then summed to produce the statistic which was by far the most widely quoted by the iron trade from the entire volume, the total output of pig iron in Great Britain in a particular year? Did he really obtain an annual output figure from every single works, or even one for average weekly output which could then be multiplied, with more or less sophistication, by the proportion of the year for which the furnaces in question were in blast? Or did he, as he seems to have done in 1848, settle for a reasonable sample of actual output figures in each district, secured from those works which were able and willing to supply the information, and interpolate data for the other works in the area by comparison with those for which he had returns or with the help of correspondents in the trade locally? How far was the annual output figure for each district based on aggregate output returns from individual works and how far was it estimated by multiplying weekly figures by 50 or 52?

None of these questions can apparently be answered, partly because none of Hunt's working papers seem to have survived.[1] Hunt always stressed the care with which he compiled all the figures in *Mineral Statistics*; he was at pains to emphasise that he never revealed details of the output of individual works; he also repeated, year after year, that he enjoyed a unique position of trust in all branches of the mining industry, which enabled him to collect so much information on a voluntary basis. Some of these protestations were clearly directed at the Inspectors of Mines, rather than his critics in the trade, since after the regulation of both collieries and metalliferous mines became far more comprehensive in 1872 (including the statutory requirement to return output and other statistics to the inspectors), a good deal of Hunt's work at the Geological Survey was duplicated by the Home Office, as the Treasury were not slow to notice.[2] Equally, there is no doubt that Hunt did enjoy a special standing in the coal trade, the iron industry and in the various branches of non-ferrous metal mining and smelting, a position reflected in his appointment to the staff of the Coal Commission of 1869–71, to whose report he contributed, almost single-handed, a comprehensive statistical survey which is still of value today.[1] Only in the years immediately after Hunt's retirement were a handful of entries for individual furnaces printed with the comment 'Production estimated', although of course the estimate itself was not published. This may reflect a decision by Hunt's successors to bring more openness to the collection of the pig iron data for *Mineral Statistics*; if so, the attempt was abandoned after a few years and never repeated. The proportion of total output based on estimates in 1883 and later must have been well under 5 per cent, judging by the small number of companies whose entries are flagged in this way.

The Trade Associations in the Later Nineteenth Century

The British Iron Trade Association

Whatever their shortcomings, the historian has little choice but to use Hunt's *Mineral Statistics*, at least up to 1871, since they are, for the most part, all that is available. After this date, the Inspectors of Mines' reports provide an alternative source for the mining industries but not for iron and steel (except for iron-ore mining), where the Mining Records Office continued unchallenged for a little longer. In 1875, however, the first modern trade association was formed for the industry, the British Iron Trade Association, one of whose main objects was the compilation and publication of statistics.[2] The association's secretary from 1877 until 1908 was John Stephen Jeans (1846–1913), who was originally a journalist and later became chief proprietor of the *Iron and Coal Trades Review*, the *Foundry Trade Journal* and other trade papers. He also, from 1877 until 1893, combined the secretaryship of BITA with the same office at the Iron and Steel Institute, established in 1869 as a scientific society for the industry, as had his predecessor, John Jones.[3] The association, set up chiefly as a result of initiatives by the ironmasters of the North of England, initially had its headquarters at Mid-

---

[1] Home Office out-letters and registered files relating to Mines and Quarries up to 1920 now form POWE 4 and POWE 6 respectively at the Public Record Office, but contain nothing that sheds light on the compilation of the iron and steel figures in *Mineral Statistics*. Nor are there papers still in the custody of the Geological Survey or at the Mining Records Office at Bootle, where it is now part of the Health & Safety Executive. No private papers of Hunt's relating to this subject have been located. We are indebted to the PRO, the Geological Survey, the Health & Safety Executive and the Historical Manuscripts Commission for help in trying to trace any material relating to the compilation of *Mineral Statistics*.

[2] See the prefaces to *Mineral Statistics*, especially from 1871 until Hunt's retirement; cf. also Burt and Waite, 'Introduction'.

[1] i.e. Vol. III of the Royal Commission's Report (Parl. Papers, 1871 (C. 435), XVIII).

[2] See the preface to *The iron, steel and allied trades in 1877. Annual report to the members of the British Iron Trade Association* (BITA, 1878). Similar accounts, not always completely accurate, of the origins of statistical work by the trade appear in the prefaces to the first volumes issued by all the later organisations mentioned in this section. See also *The British Iron and Steel Federation. An account of the principal trade association in the steel industry* (BISF, 1963), pp. 27–30, and R.M. Shone, 'Statistics relating to the U.K. iron and steel industry', *Journal of the Royal Statistical Society Series A*, 118 (1950), 464–86. For BITA generally see J.C. Carr and W. Taplin, *History of the British steel industry* (Oxford, 1962), pp. 94–5, 254, and D.L Burn, *The economic history of steeelmaking, 1867–1939. A study in competition* (Cambridge, 1940), pp. 31–2.

[3] Carr and Taplin, *History*, pp. 45–7; see also P. Carden, 'The Institute and the technical press', *Journal of the Iron & Steel Institute*, 211 (1973), 859, and B.H. Tripp, 'The Iron and Steel Institute, 1869–1969: an historical sketch', Ibid., 207 (1969), 243.

dlesbrough and was dominated by Cleveland interests for much of its thirty years of active life.

BITA issued its first annual report early in 1878, containing a largely narrative survey of the industry during the previous year, accompanied by some rather haphazardly arranged statistics. In his preface, Jeans did not disguise the fact that the series had been established because of misgivings over *Mineral Statistics*, arguing that the volume was published nearly twelve months after the end of the year to which it related and that the iron and steel figures formed only a small part of a report mainly concerned with the mining industries. Both points had some validity and the second in particular was to acquire more weight after the transfer of the Mining Records Office to the Home Office in 1883. In addition, however, Jeans cast doubt on the accuracy of the data for the iron industry, although without attempting a detailed critique of Hunt's methods. He did, on the other hand, explain how he assembled the pig iron figures for successive BITA reports which he continued to compile until 1906. For Cleveland and the West of Scotland, local associations existed which collected statistics for their areas (by this date the two most important centres of the industry) and these Jeans had been allowed to use. For the rest of the industry (amounting in 1878 to 199 works out of a total of 265) Jeans had approached each company individually for an output figure for the previous year.[1] As always with such compilations, Jeans lavished thanks on those who had responded to his request and stressed that no figures relating to particular works would ever be published. He did not, however, reveal precisely how successful he had been in obtaining true annual output figures, whether at plant or district level, although in 1887, after BITA had engaged a firm of accountants to audit Jeans's work, a note was appended to the table of pig iron output indicating that about 5 per cent of the returns from individual works had been estimated, and in 1900–02 similar notes indicated that between 6 and 7 per cent of the output was based on estimates.[2] Nor did he present the data as fully as Hunt did in *Mineral Statistics*. There were no lists of furnaces, merely tables giving the number of furnaces in use and the total output of pig in each district, from which a national total was obtained.

The BITA reports cannot, therefore, be used as an alternative to *Mineral Statistics* for a detailed study of the late nineteenth-century iron industry at local level, although they do yield an alternative series of output figures, arranged under slightly different regional headings. On the other hand, even here the degree of novelty is limited. In later years, Jeans stressed that the great majority of companies approached had co-operated in supplying figures for his report, even though they had already made a similar return to the Mining Records Office. It does not seem to have occurred to him that most, if not all, firms would simply have sent the same figure in reply to both enquiries, a pretty obvious course of action which would go far towards explaining why the eventual output figure for the country as a whole published by BITA was remarkably close to that produced by the Mining Records Office. Jeans appears to have regarded his achievement in obtaining a figure so similar to that published by the Inspectors of Mines as a vindication of his efforts;[1] to a later generation, detached from contemporary arguments between the trade and the government as to the accuracy of each other's figures, it tends to make one ask how much BITA's work added to what was being done by the Mining Records Office.[2]

In fact, the association's reports do have considerable value, both as an annual review of all branches of the iron and steel industry, and as a source of much wider (rather than necessarily better) statistics, which supply more detail concerning, for example, the output of different types of pig iron, and prices. To begin with, it is true, the arrangement of the tables fluctuates somewhat but within a few years a settled format was established which continues down to 1905.[3] The two series of reports should really be used alongside each other in a full study of the iron and steel industry from the late 1870s up to the First World War, although in general historians have preferred to rely on the data in *Mineral Statistics*.[4] This may be partly because of a general tendency to favour figures published in Parliamentary Papers over those collected by trade assocations (which in this case may reflect misplaced confidence in 'official' statistics); it may also owe something to the elusive character of the BITA reports.[5]

---

[1] BITA Annual Report (1877), pp. 16–17.

[2] BITA Annual Report (1887), p. 7; 1900, p. 14; 1901, p. 11; 1902, p. 6. This suggests a slightly higher reliance on estimates than the Mining Records Office admitted to the mid-1880s (cf. above, p. xxv).

[1] See, e.g., the 1890 Report, pp. iv–v, where Jeans observes than his estimate of pig iron output in Great Britain was within 0.3 per cent of that published in *Mineral Statistics*.

[2] It night be possible to answer this question more fully had BITA's own internal records survived, but this appears not to be the case. Carr and Taplin, whose book was published in 1962, made use of papers then at the British Iron & Steel Federation inherited from its immediate predecessor, the National Federation of Iron & Steel Manufacturers (*History*, p. v; these are presumably now with British Steel), but make no mention of any BITA archive. Nor have we found any reference elsewhere to the association's records.

[3] Carr and Taplin's description of the reports as 'the chief extant source of information regarding the fortunes of the industry during the last quarter of the nineteenth century' (*History*, p. 47) is perhaps overgenerous, but while Burn's criticism of the association generally as 'Narrow and ill-defined in its objects, timid in its concessions to the claims of organisation, imperfect in operation within its limited sphere' may be justified, his reporting on 'good authority' that its methods of collecting and handling statistics were 'rather chaotic' sounds like hearsay and his comment that their presentation in the annual reports supports this view is an overstatement (*Economic history*, p. 32 and note).

[4] Thus B.R. Mitchell, *British historical statistics* (Cambridge, 1988), pp. 279–83, relies on *Mineral Statistics* for iron ore and pig iron output figures from 1854, although he makes use of BITA and later trade association figures for other series (Ibid., pp. 286–90).

[5] The BITA reports cover the years 1877–1905 and were published between 1878 and 1906. Both the British Library set (at 8275 f.1) and that in the Bodleian (at Soc. 17981 e.12) are incomplete and there are none in the other copyright libraries. The best set, which is still imperfect, appears to be that in the Mitchell Library, Glasgow. The reports of 1893 and 1894 refer to a *Bulletin* issued by the association, which appeared monthly and published statistics in

BITA's last separately published report appeared in 1906, when the association was at the height of its prestige. The following year, however, Jeans, who had given the best years of his life to the organisation, had a breakdown and, after prolonged leave of absence, left in 1908; he died in 1913. His successor, C.J.F. Scott, lacked the same drive and experience and the association went into a decline, aggravated by divisions over tariff reform.[1] The collection of statistics continued but the results were published in the *Iron and Coal Trades Review*, rather than as separate reports; some material was also included in a series of Board of Trade publications containing comparative statistics for the iron and steel industry in different countries issued between 1903 and 1913.[2]

1906 also saw the establishment of a new Iron, Steel & Allied Trades Federation at the initiative of North Eastern producers unhappy with the defeat of tariff reform in the general election of that year. Although BITA welcomed the new organisation, to which it affiliated, it seems thereafter to have taken little action itself on major issues. The association was formally wound up in 1915, three years before ISATF was itself remodelled as the National Federation of Iron & Steel Manufacturers. ISATF briefly took over the statistical work of BITA, which later passed to the Statistical Bureau set up by the National Federation in 1919.[3] From this date, as the next section of this introduction explains, responsibility for the collection and publication of iron and steel statistics reverted entirely to the industry itself, so that there were no longer two sets of figures to compare.

Local Associations

Before considering the period since the First World War, something should be said about the locally compiled statistics for Cleveland and Scotland referred to by Jeans in his initial BITA report and used by him in every subsequent volume. The longer and more important series relates to Scotland and begins in 1845, the year which saw the establishment in Liverpool of the Scotch Pig Iron Association, set up to collect statistical information for the merchants and ironmasters who made up its membership and to establish a store in Glasgow where iron might be warehoused on reasonable terms.[1] The old established firm of William Connal & Co. were appointed storekeepers and their circulars appear to be the ultimate source for the various more detailed statistics of the Scottish pig iron trade which become available from 1845. Confusingly, however, several slightly discrepant series exist, at least down to 1866, when the market was reorganised and the Glasgow Association of Iron Brokers took over the publication of the figures, which thereafter seem to have been used by both *Mineral Statistics* and, from 1878, the British Iron Trade Association. Although the Glasgow iron ring failed to secure statutory recognition of its activities in 1890, the market survived until 1916.[2]

In the 1950s, Professor R.H. Campbell, in what remains the only historical discussion of the reliability of the pig iron figures in *Mineral Statistics*, located four other series for the output of pig iron in Scotland between 1845 and 1865,[3] in addition to Connal's own lists and the figures compiled by Hunt, who in 1856 published yet another set for 1845–56 in *Mineral Statistics*, alongside his own.[4] The same figures were also published in the *Journal of the Iron and Steel Institute*'s regular 'Notes on the Iron and Steel Industries of the United Kingdom'.[5] Some of the series are slightly discrepant in earlier years, although the fact that they all begin in 1845, when Connal became storekeepers, makes it clear that all owe their origin to the activities of the Scotch Pig Iron Association. Not unreasonably, therefore, Campbell suggested that the output figures given in Connal's own price lists were probably the most trustworthy. These do not differ greatly from those in *Mineral Statistics*, which from 1866 appears to have used the figures without attempting to compile a separate series independently. Campbell, on the other hand, stressed the differences between Connal's figures and those in *Mineral Statistics*, and pointed out that in general the other series he located tended to be closer to the former than the latter. This, however, is no more than one would expect, since

---

advance of their appearance in the annual report. It began in 1891 and continued for 25 issues before the title was absorbed by the *Iron and Coal Trades Review* (see *British union catalogue of periodicals*, sn. British Iron Trade Association).

[1] Carr and Taplin, *History*, pp. 254–5.

[2] These reports are referred to by Burn, *Economic history*, p. 336, although he failed to note that those issued between 1910 and 1913 were preceded by a series of less detailed papers with a slightly different title which begins in 1903 and contains figures back to 1890 (cf. *Index to House of Commons Papers, 1900–1949*, p. 378, Iron and Steel, IV, Production and Consumption). Some of the material in both series is said to be from the BITA reports and some is from *Mineral Statistics*; neither contains any additional information which cannot be found in one or other of these sources.

[3] Carr and Taplin, *History*, p. 343.

---

[1] The following account is based on Birch, *Iron and steel industry*, pp. 238–40; R.H. Campbell, 'Developments in the Scottish pig iron trade, 1844–8', *Journal of Economic History*, 15 (1955), 209–26; idem, 'Fluctuations in stocks: a nineteenth-century case-study', *Oxford Economic Papers*, New Series, 9 (1957), 41–55; and C.C. Bewsher, *The Glasgow Royal Exchange. Centenary. 1827–1927* (Glasgow, 1927), pp. 31–8.

[2] R.H. Campbell, 'Statistics of the Scottish pig iron trade 1830 to 1865', *Journal of the West of Scotland Iron & Steel Institute*, 64 (1956–7), 282–9; Birch, *British iron and steel industry*, pp. 239–40.

[3] Campbell, 'Statistics', p. 284, which identifies series similar to those published by Connal's in J. Barclay, *Statistics of the Scotch iron trade* (Glasgow, 1850), p. 19 (for 1846–9); F.J. Rowan, 'On the iron trade of Scotland', *Journal of the Iron & Steel Institute* (1885) Part 2, 376–93 (1845–85, together with other series, some from Connal, some from *Mineral Statistics*, and some from other sources); H. Bumby et al., 'The iron and steel industries of the west of Scotland', Ibid., 60 (1901), p. 18 (1875–1900); and the *Supplement to the Mining Journal*, 17 Oct. 1863 (1946–62). Campbell's source E is in fact a duplicate reference to one of the sources given under D in his list.

[4] *Mineral Statistics* (1856), p. 79.

[5] See, e.g., *JISI* (1872) Part 2, p. 368 or (1876) Part 2, p. 497; we have not made a systematic search but it is obvious that the figures were included regularly in the section of the journal which evolved into the modern abstracts service.

all the series which begin in 1845 clearly derive from information collected by Connal, whereas *Mineral Statistics* did not spawn variants in the same way. Connal's figures may indeed be more accurate than those in *Mineral Statistics*, since they were compiled locally by the trade itself, but should not be preferred simply because they exist in several versions, as if this established their superiority by sheer weight of numbers. In addition, Campbell's criticism of one particular figure said to be from *Mineral Statistics* (the output of pig in 1865), is based on a mistranscription; the figure actually printed in *Mineral Statistics* differs from that in Connal's list by only a few hundred tons in a year in which Scottish pig iron production was some 1.16m. tons.

Campbell was quite justified in pointing out that Connal's figures, and those derived from them, are superior to those in *Mineral Statistics* in that they include details of coastal and foreign shipments and stocks in makers' hands or warrant stores, although in some years Hunt inserted information of this sort from Connal's lists, as did the BITA reports. Both also regularly reprinted Connal's table of monthly pig iron prices on the Glasgow market.

Rather less has been written about the Cleveland Ironmasters' Association, although it is clear that the collection of statistics formed part of their activities from their establishment in 1866.[1] Monthly returns collected by the association were published in the local press and also from 1877 in the monthly reports of the Middlesbrough Chamber of Commerce, which from time to time printed retrospective data back to 1870, including details of individual companies.[2] The figures in fact begin in 1868 and were regularly used by Jeans from 1878 for the BITA reports.[3] Like the Scottish series, they were also published in the *Journal of the Iron and Steel Institute*.[4]

In most years, the BITA reports give pride of place, and most space, to Scotland and Cleveland, partly because these were, during the period in which the association was active, the most important ironmaking districts, but partly perhaps because more information was readily available. There is far less, for example, about the West Cumberland industry, even though the district had a local ironmasters' association and a system of marketing based on warrants similar to that which existed in Glasgow and Middlesbrough, which might have led to the collection of statistics.[1] In fact, no evidence has been found in *Mineral Statistics*, the BITA reports or local sources to suggest that ironmasters' associations in other districts compiled systematic statistics or even coordinated the return of figures to the Mining Records Office and BITA, both of whom appear to have dealt individually with works outside Scotland and Cleveland. Whilst the degree of organisation among producers at district level varied considerably, even at the end of the nineteenth century, all the local associations seem to have been concerned purely with wages, prices and other commercial questions, rather than the collection or publication of statistics.[2] Similarly, local bodies modelled on the Iron & Steel Institute or the engineering institutions devoted themselves to technical matters.[3]

Iron and Steel Statistics since 1920

Throughout the period 1920–28, the information relating to the iron and steel industry included in the Mines Department's reports was not collected by the department itself but was supplied by the National Federation of Iron & Steel Manufacturers, founded in 1918, which was the successor of two earlier attempts to set up a national organisation for the industry.

As we have seen, although BITA ceased to issue annual reports as separate publications after 1906, the association continued to collect statistics until its dissolution in 1915.[4] Meanwhile, a new body, the Iron, Steel & Allied Trades Federation, had been founded at Middlesbrough in 1906, with its headquarters at the Royal Exchange. Following the demise of BITA, ISATF added the collection of statistics to its work and opened a Statistical Bureau at 28 Victoria St, SW1, supervised by George Christopher Lloyd, who had been secretary of the Iron and Steel Institute since 1908.[5] ISATF issued three reports, for 1915, 1916 and 1917, which included summary data for pig iron production but no detailed lists of furnaces. The reports, by contrast with

---

[1] Cf. U. Wengenroth, *Enterprise and technology. The German and British steel industries, 1865–1895* (Cambridge, 1994), pp. 136n., 167n. The minute books cited there are now at British Steel's Irthlingborough Records Centre. One of the early secretaries of the CIA was John Jones, who was also the first secretary of BITA between its establishment in 1875 and his death in 1877 (Carr and Taplin, *History*, pp. 45–6).

[2] Information kindly supplied by Middlesbrough Public Library.

[3] BITA Report (1878), p. 18 gives figures for Cleveland which differ from those printed in *Mineral Statistics*; both in 1878 and later Jeans acknowledged the Cleveland Ironmasters' Association as the source of all his data for this district.

[4] See, e.g., *JISI* (1872) Part 2, p. 367, where monthly pig iron figures are given for 1871 and 1872, and *JISI* (1876) Part 2, p. 493, where annual figures for 1868–76 are printed; in both cases the Cleveland Ironmasters' Association is identified as the source.

[1] Carr and Taplin, *History*, p. 150; Birch, *Iron and steel industry*, p. 204.

[2] Carr and Taplin, *History*, pp. 64–8, 145–50.

[3] For bodies such as the South Wales Institute of Engineers, the West of Scotland Iron & Steel Institute, the Staffordshire Iron & Steel Institute or the Chesterfield & Derbyshire Institute of Mining, Civil & Mechanical Engineers see R.A. Buchanan, *The Engineers: a history of the engineering profession in Britain, 1750–1914* (1989), ch. 7. We have not searched their proceedings systematically but any signs of interest in the collection of statistics would undoubtedly emerge from the pages of the *Journal of the Iron & Steel Institute*, whose literature reviews were extremely comprehensive from its inception in 1869.

[4] Above, p. xxvii.

[5] Iron, Steel & Allied Trades Federation, *Statistical Report for 1915. Statistics of the iron and steel industries, including statistics of coal, coke and iron ore, of the British Empire and foreign countries* (ISATF, 1916), Preface. Cf. also Carr and Taplin, *History*, p. 343; Tripp, 'Historical sketch', pp. 427–8.

those of BITA, consisted entirely of tables, with no narrative discussion.[1]

ISATF was itself wound up in 1918 and succeeded (on 11 November, Armistice Day) by the National Federation of Iron & Steel Manufacturers, which proved a rather more durable body and was the immediate predecessor of the modern British Iron & Steel Federation.[2] NFISM took over ISATF's statistical work, retaining Lloyd as supervisor of the bureau at Victoria Street, from where a report on the industry for 1918 was issued in July the following year,[3] its format virtually identical to those for 1915–17.

In January 1920 the new federation began the publication of a *Monthly Statistical Bulletin*, which has continued to appear, with one change of title, ever since, except during the Second World War.[4] The annual reports, however, were not resumed until 1923, when the first volume of *Statistics of the Iron and Steel Industries* was issued from the Federation's new offices at Caxton House, Tothill St, SW1. This included pig iron statistics arranged by district and also, in an unnumbered table following the summary figures, a list of 'Blast Furnaces in the United Kingdom at 31st December 1921'; there was no attempt to produce a similar list for 1920, even though the report in general covered both 1920 and 1921. Nor does the Federation appear ever to have issued any statistics for 1919.[5]

Once established, the format of the annual volume did not change greatly during the rest of the Federation's existence. The collection of statistics bulked large in the routine work of the organisation, which was regarded as one of the most effective of the major trade associations in this respect.[6] Figures for 1922 were contained in a book published in December 1923, which included a similar unnumbered table of blast furnaces in existence at the end of the year, and a third edition appeared in February 1925 with data for 1923. Some mystery attaches to the issue for 1924, which is missing from the British Library set, although there is a copy in the hands of the Federation's present-day successor.[1] On the other hand, none of the pig iron figures reprinted in other years up to 1928 in the Mines Department's annual report were included in 1924,[2] which possibly suggests that the Federation published their book unusually late and neglected to deposit a copy at the British Museum.

In April 1934 the National Federation was succeeded by the British Iron and Steel Federation, which had a rather different structure and closer links with government, partly as a consequence of the granting of tariff protection to the industry two years before.[3] The change from NFISM to BISF did not greatly affect the work of the Statistical Bureau, although in 1936 the annual volume was rearranged and the list of blast furnaces was henceforth for some years printed as Table 1. The districts within which the works were grouped in the table were also changed to conform with the boundaries adopted by the Federation for electoral purposes. The books for 1935 and 1936 were described as the 14th and 15th editions respectively (i.e. counting from that published in 1923) but this numbering was then abandoned. The 1937 issue named the Federation's headquarters, still at Tothill St, as Steel House for the first time.

The Federation was able to publish statistics for 1938 in a volume issued the following year but the series was then suspended until September 1945, when a book appeared summarising production during the years 1939–44, the data coming from Iron and Steel Control, which was thanked for agreeing to its publication so soon after the war ended. A complete list of blast furnaces in existence in each of the years covered was included, a relatively straightforward compilation, since there was virtually no new construction or dismantling of plant during the war. Publication of annual volumes was resumed the following year (1946), as was the *Monthly Statistical Bulletin*.[4]

The short-lived nationalisation and subsequent denationalisation of the steel industry in 1951–53 did not directly affect the statistical work of the Federation, although with effect from the issue for 1955 the annual volume was published under the joint auspices of BISF

---

[1] The other contrast with the BITA series is that all three ISATF reports can be found in the British Library (at 08244 h.29), the Bodleian (at Per. 1799 d.87) and no doubt elsewhere.

[2] See the preface to National Federation of Iron & Steel Manufacturers, *Statistical Report – 1918. Statistics of the iron and steel industries of the British Empire and other countries, including statistics of coal, iron ore, and other minerals used in the industries* (NFISM, 1919). The BL's copy of this is at Ac. 4461/2, whereas the rest of the NFISM reports (and their BISF successors) are at 08225 dd. See also *The British Iron and Steel Federation*, pp. 27–30; Carr and Taplin, *History*, pp. 343–5; Burn, *Economic history*, pp. 375–6.

[3] i.e. the report cited in the previous note. For other statistics covering the period of the First World War, and a general account of the industry in these years, see F.H. Hatch, *The iron and steel industry of the United Kingdom under war conditions. A record of the work of the Iron and Steel Production Department of the Ministry of Munitions* (1919), and *Report of the Departmental Committee appointed to consider the position of the Iron and Steel Trades after the War* (Parl. Papers, 1918 [Cd 9071], XIII.423).

[4] The BL's set of these bulletins (up to the change of title in 1955) is at Ac. 4461 and is catalogued under BISF, rather than NFISM.

[5] There are no parts earlier than that for 1921 in the BL (except for the 1918 report referred to earlier) or at the present-day Iron & Steel Statistics Bureau in Croydon, to whom we are indebted for help on this point. When, in a couple of later years, the BISF reports were numbered, the edition numbers fit if one counts the report for 1920–21 as the first.

[6] Carr and Taplin, *History*, pp. 390–1; Burn, *Economic history*, p. 376 takes another sideswipe at BITA's statistics, which he describes as 'erratic and of uncertain value', by contrast with those of the Federation, which were 'always admirable and uniform within their rather limited scope'.

---

[1] i.e. the Iron & Steel Statistics Bureau, to whom we are indebted for a copy of the blast furnace table.

[2] *Fourth Annual Report of the Secretary for Mines for the year ending 31st December 1924* (1925). The report offers no explanation for the non-availability of the iron and steel figures.

[3] *The British Iron and Steel Federation*, pp. 27–30; Burn, *Economic history*, pp. 452–3; Carr and Taplin, *History*, pp. 495–508.

[4] The Federation did not, however, deposit copies of the annual volume at the British Museum after that for 1947. A complete set is in the hands of the Iron & Steel Statistics Bureau, to whom we are indebted for copies of the blast furnace tables for 1948–50. The *Monthly Statistical Bulletin* continued to be sent to the Museum.

and the Iron and Steel Board.¹ A complete list of blast furnaces and their owners (plus, from 1953, the location of the works) continued to be published on much the same lines as it had since 1921. The monthly publication was also issued jointly from 1955 as *Iron and Steel Monthly Statistics*.² The Iron and Steel Board, established in its second incarnation to supervise the denationalised industry, rather than make steel itself, reported initially to the Ministry of Supply, from 1955 to the Board of Trade and from 1957 to the Ministry of Power.³

When the steel industry was returned to public ownership in 1967, with the take-over by the British Steel Corporation of thirteen privately owned companies plus Richard Thomas & Baldwins, which had never been denationalised, the British Iron and Steel Federation was wound up.⁴ Its statistical work, however, was continued, more or less unchanged, by the United Kingdom Iron and Steel Statistics Bureau, an independent organisation funded by BSC, which took over responsibility for the publication of the annual report. This arrangement survived the privatisation of British Steel, although the ISSB now draws its income from several sources and is incorporated as a limited company.⁵ In this form, the reports, including a list of blast furnaces in existence at 31 December each year, continue to appear, seventy years after the series began in roughly its present form and almost two centuries after the first comprehensive survey of the modern iron industry was compiled.⁶ The only significant change since 1967, apart from the disappearance of all but one owner's name, came in 1970, when the arrangement of the works according to the old BISF electoral districts was abandoned in favour of using the government's standard regions.

The lists of blast furnaces published by NFISM and BISF from 1921, although not directly comparable to those included in *Mineral Statistics* between 1854 and 1913, have been used here as the basis of entries for those works at which pig iron continued to be produced after the First World War. At the end of 1921 there were 486 furnaces in the United Kingdom, a number which had fallen to 189 by December 1938. The data is thus useful in charting the decline and fall of a large number of works during this period, as it is for following the fortunes of the industry between the end of the Second World War and the establishment of the British Steel Corporation in 1967. The lack of any figures for the number of furnaces in blast (as opposed to the number in existence) is a weakness, both in seeking to compare data for individual works before and after the First World War and in any attempt to measure the performance of the industry at district or national level during the (mostly depressed) years between the wars, when a large proportion of furnaces were out of blast, but for the sake of completeness, if nothing more, information from the post-1921 tables has been included here. Both NFISM and BISF gradually increased the range of statistics collected for both smelting and other branches of the industry and thus more could have been extracted at district and national level for this period than has been.¹ At plant level, details of blast furnace hearth size were given from 1946. On the other hand, to have included more material from the original returns would have further lengthened an already substantial volume, whose main aim is to make available data for the nineteenth century, when there were far more ironworks and less information is readily accessible about many of them. In any case, the more recent BISF handbooks, if not all those issued since 1921, are fairly widely available and the data in them easier to extract than is the case with earlier sources.²

The post-1921 lists of furnaces initially only printed the names of owners, rather than works, and in general companies with several plants in a particular district returned a single figure for all their furnaces. Only from 1953 were works named and separate details given for the number of furnaces at each. Whilst it is generally easy enough to match up post-1921 entries with those for 1913 by relying on continuity in ownership and secondary sources, it has not always been possible to distribute the total number of furnaces owned by a company in any one district between different sites before 1953.

The later figures may seem rather monotonous, compared with those from before the First World War, with few changes in ownership apparent and little movement either up or down in the number of furnaces at any particular works. In both cases, the stability may be deceptive. In an age in which all the surviving furnaces were in the hands of limited liability concerns, actual ownership might well (and indeed did) change without the name of the company changing, and fluctuations in production would generally be accommodated by varying the number of furnaces in blast rather than the number in existence. It might also be argued that since so much information is readily available about modern steel companies, it was pointless to include

---

¹ *Iron and Steel Annual Statistics for the United Kingdom* (Iron & Steel Board and British Iron & Steel Federation, 1956–67). The BL has only the reports for 1955–59 inclusive (at BS 135/8); there is a complete set at the Iron & Steel Statistics Bureau.

² The BL set is kept at a different press-mark (BS 135/7) from that for the earlier monthly bulletins, which reflects the arrival of the Ministry of Supply as joint publisher with BISF.

³ See the introductory note to the list of its surviving records at the PRO, where they form the one-class group BE. There is nothing in the archive which adds to what can be discovered about the statistical work of the Board and BISF from their publications.

⁴ J. Vaisey, *The history of British steel* (1974), p. 180.

⁵ We are indebted to the Iron & Steel Statistics Bureau for confirming details of its history since 1967.

⁶ The current title of the series is *Iron and Steel Industry. Annual Statistics for the United Kingdom*, published by ISSB Ltd (incorporating the Iron & Steel Statistics Bureau), Canterbury House, 2 Sydenham Road, Croydon CR9 2LZ.

¹ Shone, 'Statistics relating to the U.K. iron and steel industry', provides a thorough guide to the contents of both the monthly and annual publications in the post-war period. Sir Robert Shone was head of the statistics department at BISF between 1936 and 1939, before moving to a succession of more senior positions in Iron & Steel Control and the Iron & Steel Board: see obituaries in *The Times*, 16 and 30 Dec. 1992.

² See also Mitchell, *British historical statistics*, pp. 283–5.

details of furnaces and ownership beyond 1913. Despite their shortcomings, however, the lists of furnaces in the NFISM/BISF publications at least enable the story to be completed for each site and provide a quick means of reference to ownership, size of works and closure date, details which are not always easily available for some of the smaller companies in the inter-war period. The long timespan adopted here may also be of interest in enabling the reader to see which of the hundreds of sites at which blast furnaces were erected from the late eighteenth century onwards proved most durable as centres of production.

In theory, it would have been possible to have continued the entries for the works taken over by BSC down to the most recent year for which the Statistical Bureau's annual report was available when this book went to press. On the other hand, the individual interest of the entries inevitably wanes once virtually all blast furnaces passed into the hands of a single owner, although the name British Steel Corporation was only used from 1970. We have therefore decided to print details down to 1980, the year after the last independently owned furnace (Brymbo, which first appears in the list of 1794, and where important remains of an eighteenth-century furnace are still standing) was shut down, and a year which saw the closure of several BSC plants.[1] For those works which remained in use in 1981 or later, the date of their last appearance in the ISSB reports is noted here, as is the continued operation of four sites today, with a total of eleven blast furnaces, at Redcar in the North East, Scunthorpe on Humberside and Port Talbot and Llanwern in South Wales.

Format of this Edition

Since no two surveys from the period prior to 1854 are arranged in exactly the same way, whereas the format of *Mineral Statistics* changed hardly at all between then and 1913, nor did that adopted from 1921 differ from it fundamentally, it seemed sensible to present the data here according to that devised by Robert Hunt and to re-arrange material from before 1854 under the same headings as those used after that date. Each ironworks therefore has a table in which the columns are headed in the same way as in *Mineral Statistics*.

For ironworks which operated both before and after that year these tables contain annual entries from 1854 onwards, preceded by entries for the years for which there are private surveys in which the works in question appears. No entry has been made if the works was not included (whether or not it appears to have been in use), since the book would have been rather pointlessly lengthened had numerous rows been added to some of the tables with blanks in all the columns. In this context it is worth remembering that some of the pre-1854 surveys omitted the smaller ironmaking districts altogether and therefore the absence of a particular works may not necessarily mean that it was not in use. In addition, as already discussed, some surveys were more thorough than others even for districts which were included.

The establishment of the most appropriate dates for the various pre-1854 lists has already been discussed, including the decision to treat information from the well-known survey of 1806 as referring to the previous year.[1] There are, of course, no problems of this sort from 1854 onwards.

The data for 1921 onwards has also been cast into the same form as that for 1854–1913, including (for the sake of consistency of layout) a column for the number of furnaces in blast, even though this was no longer printed in the original source. For this period the number of furnaces in existence refers specifically to the position at 31 December each year; mid-year closures were sometimes noted in notes to the table but in other years works simply disappeared. Between 1892 and 1913 the number is an average for the year as a whole; up to 1891 the position is unclear.[2]

A gap has been inserted into a table to indicate a break in the continuity of the figures, either because the works was out of use for a time or (more commonly) because the furnace-numbers switch from relating to one site to including several. The reason for the break is explained in the note to the table, except for the gap between 1913 and 1921, which simply indicates the change from *Mineral Statistics* to the NFISM reports. No gap has been left between the last of the private surveys and 1854, since the discontinuity is less marked.[3]

Regional Divisions

The ironworks have been divided into districts consisting in some cases of individual counties, in others of two or more, or alternatively of only part of a county. Most of these districts are units which have long been familiar to historians of the industry and seemed to us preferable to either the counties used in the later volumes of *Mineral Statistics*, the BISF electoral districts or the standard regions. A regional arrangement is easier for iron and steel than for some industries, since throughout the period covered here production was concentrated in a limited number of reasonably well defined districts, even though the relative importance of those areas changed drastically.

In general, regions have been defined broadly, rather than narrowly, so that 'South Wales' extends from Monmouthshire through the main coalfield and its anthracite extension to Pembrokeshire, although the charcoal-fired furnace at Tintern (Mon.) has been placed with neighbouring Forest of Dean sites under Glouces-

---

[1] 1980 is also the terminal date chosen for series from all sectors of the economy included in Mitchell, *British historical statistics*.

[1] Above, p. xiii.
[2] Above, p. xxiv.
[3] Above, pp. xix–xx.

tershire. 'North East England' includes Northumberland and Durham as well as the Cleveland district, and (perhaps most dubiously) 'North West England' extends from Cheshire to West Cumberland, although the works at Lawton, near Crewe, has been put in North Staffordshire. The short-lived furnace at Moira (Leics.) has been added to Derbyshire, as have two later Nottinghamshire works; the other Leicestershire site, Holwell, has been included with Lincolnshire, since this was the county with which it was grouped in *Mineral Statistics*, although arguably it might have been better placed with Northamptonshire. Scotland has been treated as a single unit, as it has always been in work on the iron and steel industry; indeed this is the one region whose boundaries remain consistent in all the original sources from 1790 to 1980. Staffordshire has been divided into 'North' and 'South' as is traditional in the industry; so too is the separation of the West Riding from Cleveland. Geographers (or others) unhappy with an attempt by historians to define 'regions' can always construct their own regional data from the details of individual furnaces.

The districts under which the works have been listed have themselves been arranged geographically, starting with South Wales in the south-west and proceeding to North East England before finishing with Scotland. This seemed to us to have more logic than a simple alphabetical order, once we had decided not to organise the furnaces purely by county.

Name and Location of the Works

Under each regional heading the ironworks have been listed alphabetically, using the name by which they were most commonly known in contemporary lists, with cross-references where this differs from that by which the site is known today or where a works was also known by another name when it was in use. The suffixes 'Old' and 'New' have been added in brackets to distinguish two works at the same place where these terms were used in the original lists; where those words come at the beginning of a name they are part of the place-name. Where there were two or more works in the same town not otherwise distinguished, roman numerals have been used to separate them.

In general, place-names have been spelt as they are published by the Ordnance Survey today, with a handful of exceptions. In Wales, where the orthography of Welsh place-names on Ordnance Survey maps has been vastly improved since most of the ironworks listed here were active, a number of works have been given names whose spelling differs from that used in some of the owners' registered titles, although 'Cwmafan' (Glam.) seemed to us a little too odd for a works always known locally as Cwmavon. Where a name cannot be located on the current 1:50,000 Ordnance Survey map what appears to be the best contemporary form has been adopted. This is a particular problem with several of the older South Staffs. furnaces, although here some of the names survive as street names.

Considerable effort has been made to identify correctly the name of the county in which each works stood, using that term to mean the geographical county as it existed prior to the establishment of administrative counties and county boroughs in England and Wales in 1889 and the parallel changes in Scotland. It is nonetheless possible that occasionally we have identified the county in which a town with the same name as an ironworks is situated and failed to notice that the works, although nearby, was actually in another county. For example, local knowledge has saved us from the error of placing Hirwaun Ironworks in Glamorgan (since it stood on the opposite bank of the River Cynon from the village named after the works it was in fact in Brecknock) or Amman Ironworks in Carmarthenshire (although close to Ammanford, it was actually in the Glamorgan parish of Llangiwg), but it is unlikely that we have escaped entirely from slips of this sort. The district which presents most difficulty in this exercise is, once again, the Black Country, where not only were there a number of small works which are difficult to find even on contemporary maps but where administrative geography before 1889 (and indeed since) is extraordinarily complex. We are reasonably confident that works labelled 'Staffs.' were in that county rather than Worcestershire, although some errors may yet be revealed by readers with an encyclopaedic knowledge of the district.[1]

After a good deal of consideration, we have decided further to tempt the palate of the hypercritical reviewer by including a four-figure National Grid reference for as many works as possible. This has been done in the belief that geographers using the volume (and perhaps also archaeologists, if not necessarily historians) will welcome locational data that can immediately be fed into modern information systems, which obsolete county suffixes cannot. Welsh readers may also appreciate this extra clue as to which 'Pentwyn' or 'Clydach' is being referred to. Where a works has been securely located on a map the grid reference for the appropriate 1km. square has been printed opposite the name of the works at the head of each entry. Where we have not been able to locate the works precisely we have given the Ordnance Survey four-figure reference for the place-name in question in square brackets, in some cases with a question mark where we are not certain that we have identified the place correctly. There remains, mostly in the Black Country, a residue of sites which we have failed to locate sufficiently precisely to feel able to give a map reference at all.

Owner's Name

In general, owners' names have been printed as they appear in the original lists, both before and after 1854. It should be noted that some of the earlier surveys did not include the owners' names, or recorded them

---

[1] We are considerably indebted in this respect to Mr Peter King of Stourbridge for making available his detailed knowledge of the Black Country iron industry, which has reduced the likely number of mis-identifications in this area.

incompletely, and that occasionally *Mineral Statistics* also failed to give an name, typically when a new works was listed for the first time. Inevitably, where owners are named, some mistakes are either apparent or may be suspected. Obvious typographical errors in *Mineral Statistics* and the other printed lists have been corrected, generally by comparison with entries for adjacent years, and dubious spellings compared with secondary sources. We have not, however, changed the owner's name in this edition from that which appears in the original source simply because there is a conflict with the modern literature, although we have commented on what appear to be glaring inconsistencies. Nor have we always adopted a single spelling for an owner's name from the earlier surveys, unless we are quite certain which one is right. Comparison with contemporary directories is of little help in this respect, since their spelling of personal names is unlikely to be any better than that found in the lists of ironworks.

During the first sixty years covered by this volume, most ironworks were operated by individuals or partnerships, plus a handful of early, unregistered joint-stock concerns. Some partnerships used a locative name more or less consistently, in which case that has been used here. Occasionally, a literal minded respondent might supply the names of those forming the partnership, otherwise the actual owners of the business cannot be identified from the sources used here. For example, the owner of Butterley Works in Derbyshire was usually returned as the Butterley Co., but in 1866 the owners were entered in *Mineral Statistics* as 'F. Wright and W. Jessop', the partners who owned the company.

The Joint Stock Companies Act of 1844 was the first statute to establish a clear distinction between private partnerships and joint-stock companies, by providing that all companies formed after 1 November 1844 which had more than 25 members, or with shares which were freely transferable, were to be registered and thus become incorporated as joint-stock companies.[1] The Act introduced the Registrar of Joint Stock Companies (later known simply as the Registrar of Companies) as the responsible authority for registration in England (including Wales) and Ireland but not Scotland. It did not, however, remove the personal liability of all the company's members for its debts, which was done only with the Limited Liability Act of 1855. A year later, the Joint Stock Companies Act of 1856 repealed previous legislation and laid down the basic framework within which limited liability companies operated until after the First World War.

From the mid-1850s an increasing number of iron companies listed in *Mineral Statistics* have the abbreviation 'Ltd' after their name. It therefore seemed useful, for several reasons, to check both these names and others against the printed *Index of Registered Companies July 1856 to June 1920*,[1] which conveniently ends at much the same date as the detailed blast furnace lists in *Mineral Statistics*. This exercise not only enabled us to correct a number of owners' names given wrongly in *Mineral Statistics* and to remove others which proved to be mangled versions of those given correctly elsewhere in the entry for a particular works; it also demonstrated that *Mineral Statistics* would, on its own, be a most unsatisfactory source from which to measure the adoption of limited liability in the iron industry.[2] Numerous companies against whose name 'Ltd' did not appear in Hunt's returns proved, on comparison with the printed index, to have been registered under the 1856 Act. In addition, a few were registered with unlimited liability under that of 1844.[3] There were also a handful of concerns described as 'Ltd' in *Mineral Statistics* which could not be found in the index and appear to have been given the title in error.

Most of the inconsistencies between *Mineral Statistics* and the Companies House index could be reconciled without difficulty and changes made to the form in which the owner's name has been printed here. In a couple of dozen cases, however, generally where there were several registered companies with names similar to that used in *Mineral Statistics*, the Companies House files themselves were examined and a note to this effect, giving the piece numbers, added to the entry here.[4] Ideally, one would have examined every surviving file relating to a iron company whose name appears in this volume; a moment's reflection will presumably persuade the reader that with at least 600 registered companies involved, this was hardly a practical proposition, nor was it necessary for the task undertaken here. As far as we have discovered, the printed index for the period 1856–1920 can be relied upon and, in particular, its rendering of company names is clearly to be preferred

---

[1] PRO Records Information Leaflet No 54, *Registration of Companies and Businesses*, is an excellent brief guide to this subject; for more detail see J. Armstrong and S. Jones, *Business documents. Their origins, sources and uses in historical research* (1987) and L. Richmond and B. Stockford, *Company archives. The survey of the records of 1000 of the first registered companies in England and Wales* (Aldershot, 1986), pp. xviii–xx. C.T. Watts and M.J. Watts, 'Company records as a source for the family historian', *Genealogist's Magazine*, 21 (2) (1983), 44–54 remains useful, although some of the details concerning Companies House are out of date: see E.D. Probert, *Company and business records for family historians* (Birmingham, 1994). For Scotland see R.H. Campbell, 'The law and the joint-stock company in Scotland', in P.L. Payne (ed.), *Studies in Scottish business history* (1967), 136–51, and P.L. Payne, *The early Scottish limited companies, 1856–1895. An historical and analytical survey* (Edinburgh, 1980).

[1] A copy of this two-volume work can be found in the Reference Room at the PRO; inexplicably, considering that it is printed, no copy has survived to reach Companies House at Cardiff.

[2] As H.A. Shannon did so many years ago in 'The coming of general limited liability', *Economic History*, 2 (1930–33), 267–91.

[3] For these companies (and those registered under the 1856 Act before 1860) class BT 41 should be checked, as well as the better known BT 31. For example, Armstrong and Jones, *Business documents*, pp. 39–45, use BT 31/435/1677, relating to the Oakerthorpe Iron & Coal Co. Ltd, to illustrate the value of these files, without drawing attention to BT 41/522/2864, the file opened for the same company when it was first registered.

[4] i.e. Public Record Office, classes BT 41 and BT 31 in the case of companies registered in England and Wales. Some checking was also done at the Scottish Record Office, where the equivalent files transferred from Companies House, Edinburgh, form class BT 2. The Scottish material is easier to use, partly because there is less of it, but also because the SRO has the actual register from Companies House (BT 1), which is quicker to consult than the individual files.

to either *Mineral Statistics* or any other list of iron-works.

Unfortunately, it is not possible to be absolutely certain that every registered company (for which there may or may not be a Companies House file in existence today)[1] which owned blast furnaces listed here has been identified. The printed index is arranged in strict alphabetical order, so that Smith & Co. Ltd appears under S but J. Smith & Co. Ltd will be under J. Checking an alphabetical list of blast furnace owners against this index presents no problems with companies like Dowlais or Butterley whose names begin with a place-name, nor with partnerships such as Bolckow, Vaughan or Harrison Ainslie, which retained much the same name when they were converted into limited liability concerns. Similarly, Alfred Hickman Ltd or C. & T. Bagnall Ltd can be found, as long as one remembers to look under A and C, rather than H and B. The problem arises with names such as these last two in cases where *Mineral Statistics* does not use the term 'Ltd' and therefore, in compiling a list of owners to check against the Companies House index, one uses the usual inverted form of name (Hickman, Alfred; Bagnall, C. & T.). With over 2,500 owners listed in this volume prior to the First World War, it is once again impractical to check every possible name which appears to be that of an individual or an unregistered partnership to see whether the name, or some version of it (which might then only be confirmed by an examination of an actual Companies House file) corresponds with that of a registered company in existence at about the right period.

For the period after 1921, the position becomes somewhat simpler. The number of owners drops rapidly during the inter-war period; virtually all were registered companies; and the NFISM/BISF returns generally printed owners' names more accurately than was the case up to 1913. We have nonetheless checked the names against Companies House records and, as with those listed in *Mineral Statistics*, added the registered number and date of incorporation to the entry for each company in the Index of Owners in this volume.[2]

Clearly any process of checking data collected for this book against other sources and possibly adding information in footnotes or otherwise has to stop somewhere, or else this project would never have been brought to a conclusion and the results would have been too long to publish in book form. We have, therefore, decided not to cite bibliographical references at the end of each entry, except in a few special cases, but to list regional and local works, and business histories, in a Select Bibliography at the end of this Introduction. The ironworks to which any particular book or article refers is normally self-evident. Nor have we attempted to locate business records relating to the companies listed here, a task recently completed by the Historical Manuscripts Commission.[1] The only archival material cited here are the Companies House files (i.e. PRO classes BT 31 and BT 41) we have consulted to elucidate the details of ownership at some sites.

Number of Furnaces Built and In Blast

The problems surrounding the figures printed in *Mineral Statistics* for both the number of furnaces at each works and the number in blast have already been discussed.[2] Another problem which affects the data after 1854, rather than before, is the inclusion of two or more works owned by the same company in a single entry, with furnace-numbers given for the company, rather than each site. In many cases it would be possible to split the number of furnaces in existence between the different sites by comparison with other years but this would generally be much more difficult to do accurately for the number in blast, a figure which obviously fluctuated far more. We have therefore followed the principle of not splitting either figure but of giving the combined total under one heading (usually that for the works after which the company was named, or the site which remained in use longest out of several, or simply the one which comes first alphabetically), with a note below the table explaining (where this can be deduced) which other works are included in the furnace-numbers for a particular year or years. There are cross-references in the notes attached to the entries for sites thus subsumed under other headings but blanks have been inserted in the furnace-number columns in such entries.

Perhaps not surprisingly, the compilers of *Mineral Statistics* themselves sometimes became confused when companies made single returns for several works, printing the combined figures under one head and at the same time printing separate figures for other works under those headings. We hope, by careful comparison with other years, to have eliminated this double-counting, which again has been discussed in the notes to each table.

---

[1] See Richmond and Stockford, *Company archives*, pp. xix–xx and PRO Leaflet 54 for the increasingly complicated and selective rules governing the retention of this material, which have been changed several times over the last forty years, and for the rather elaborate procedure one has to follow at the PRO to establish that the file for a particular company has definitely been destroyed. The compilation of a single database, combining the typed lists at Kew and the card index at West Register House with the on-line information available at the Companies House search-rooms and other finding-aids kept at Cardiff would make the use of this important source much easier.

[2] There are printed lists of companies on the register at 30 June 1930 and 30 June 1937 available at Kew but for a company not included in these volumes which was dissolved more than 20 years ago (and therefore does not appear on the Companies House database) it is necessary to apply at Companies House for information from a card index not directly accessible to the public. We are indebted to the Customer Care Section of Companies House for help in this respect and also to British Steel's Secretariat and East Midlands Regional Records Centre.

[1] Royal Commission on Historical Manuscripts, *Records of British business and industry 1760–1914. Metal processing and engineering* (1994). The compilers of this invaluable guide appear not to have checked the names of registered companies against Companies House records and therefore there are occasional discrepancies between the forms used there and here.

[2] Above, pp. xxiii–xxiv.

After 1921 the returns generally printed a single figure for the total number of furnaces owned by each company in each district, at any rate until 1953, when disaggregated data reappeared. A few of these combined totals can safely be split, either by comparison with pre-1913 data or other information (chiefly histories of the companies concerned), but in general the totals have been left alone and the number of works embraced within them listed in the note. The biggest problem of this sort concerns the Bolckow, Vaughan group in the North East, especially after the merger with Dorman Long in 1929, for which until 1953 only a single total was printed for all their blast furnace sites.

Some of the pre-1854 lists included not only the number of furnaces built and in blast at each works but also a rather redundant figure for the number out of blast, which has not been included here. On the other hand, in some of the early lists, only the total number of furnaces was given and not the number in blast. Here a dash has been inserted, as it has in some entries for 1854 or later where *Mineral Statistics* failed to include a figure in either or both of the right-hand columns of the table. Users of the tables should note the distinction between a dash (meaning no data is given in the original source) and figure nought, meaning that no furnaces were built or in blast.

Notes to the Tables

Most entries are followed by a footnote, which varies considerably in length, partly as a function of the longevity or otherwise of the works in question but also depending on the complexity of the original information. Some of the points discussed in these notes have already been mentioned; otherwise they contain additional information taken from the original lists which cannot be fitted into the body of the table.

By far the most important (and difficult) type of information given is that relating to output found in some of the pre-1854 surveys. All available output data (however reliable or otherwise) is given in the note, together with the extra comments in the 1825 survey and the additional information concerning plant in that of 1794. It should be emphasised once again that many of these output figures are clearly no more than estimates, that figures for average weekly output are likely to be more reliable than annual figures grossed up from them, and that, after 1854, only district averages are given. In general, information in the footnotes for the 1854–1913 period, and from 1921 onwards, is confined to discussing inconsistencies in the data, especially where furnace-numbers for two or more works have been combined under a single heading, and noting the occasional comments given in the original returns which go beyond the basic details of ownership and furnace-numbers.

National and Regional Statistics

Immediately following this Introduction we have printed tables summarising the figures from the pre-1854 surveys and from *Mineral Statistics* by region, which are themselves then summarised for the whole country. For each district the tables include the number of works in use, the number of furnaces built and in blast and the estimated annual output, as recorded in the original source. We have not continued the tables beyond 1920 since, as we have already noted, the data for this period is far more accessible and easier to use in the form in which it was first published than is the case with the earlier material.[1] We have, however, printed the annual output figures, again broken down by region, published by the British Iron Trade Association and its successors for the period 1878–1918, to facilitate comparison with those compiled officially.

Users of this volume may wish to calculate further series from those we have collected from the original sources; we have contented ourselves by including only three here: the percentage of furnaces in blast, and the average output per works and per furnace. These have been calculated for each district for every year for which there is sufficient original data. Average furnace output obviously cannot be given if no output figures were printed for a particular district at the time, nor for the smaller areas whose output was combined in later nineteenth-century issues of *Mineral Statistics*. Nor can figures showing the proportion of furnaces in blast be worked out for 1794, 1823 or 1830, since only the total number of furnaces at each works is given for these years. In addition, although the 1796 list does describe a handful of furnaces as out of blast, the percentage in blast derived from that survey seems improbably high. It is also possible that Mushet's list of 1839 is suspect in the same way.[2]

Conclusion

The reader who has followed this explanation of how this book has been compiled will, we hope, appreciate that the tables which fill most of its pages represent considerably more than a mere rearrangement of data by works instead of year. Not only have we brought together information from three separate types of source, including some material which has never before been published, but we have gone to some trouble to verify and improve the raw data, as well as reducing it to a form that can be published within the covers of a single volume.

At the very least, fuller regional statistics for one sector of the iron industry in the long run are now available. We hope, however, that this book will have a wider purpose in providing an outline of the rise and fall of virtually every site at which iron has been

---

[1] Above, p. xxx.
[2] Above, pp. xii, xv.

smelted since the end of the eighteenth century.[1] This may encourage more work at local level on particular ironworks and owners, especially in the period after 1830, when less of this sort has been done. The book may also be of value to geographers seeking to map the details of iron-smelting since the 1790s.

The more the local history of the industry in this period is studied, the more likely errors of omission and commission are likely to be detected. We have done our utmost to check and re-check the data here back to the sources from which it has been taken and we have used a range of secondary literature to try to identify errors in the original lists. We obviously hope that no fundamental errors will come to light which seriously damage the overall value of the work and that those who notice minor slips, either in our work or that of the compilers of the statistics on which ours are based, will appreciate just how difficult it is to collect information consistently and accurately for an industry as large as that surveyed here, even for one year, much less for nearly two hundred. The tables which form the bulk of this book contain some 25,000 rows; if errors are found in a couple of dozen that will mean the work is 99.9 per cent accurate, which we feel will be an adequate tribute to the thousands of ironmasters who originally supplied information about individual works, and to the much smaller number of statisticians and others who produced the regional and national surveys summarised here. Even if the incidence of errors is somewhat greater than 0.1 per cent, this will not, we feel, jeopardise the iron industry's claim to be one of the branches of private enterprise best served by contemporary statistics both during the Industrial Revolution and since.

---

[1] It would be nice to claim that absolutely every blast furnace built in this period is included here, but this is not the case. For example, Whitecliff (Glos.), which operated briefly and unsuccessfully for a few years around 1800–10, was omitted from the lists of 1805 and 1810, and there are probably later instances of very short-lived enterprises which failed to be recorded in contemporary lists. Although this slightly weakens the value of this work as a catalogue of sites, the omissions are too trivial to affect the summary statistics for each region.

Select Bibliography

The following is in no sense a comprehensive bibliography of nineteenth- and twentieth-century ironmaking in Britain, or even the blast furnace sector of the industry, but merely a list of works referred to in the Introduction and a guide to secondary sources relating to the works included in the chapters of local statistics. It concentrates chiefly on regional histories of the industry, accounts of individual works and business histories. Particular efforts have been made to locate material containing either maps or statistics. The many histories of towns and villages which describe local ironworks have generally been omitted, unless they contain especially important material. So too have most contemporary descriptions of works in the trade press and local newspapers, sale catalogues, directors' reports to shareholders and similar printed primary sources, as well as unpublished manuscript or typescript histories, including undergraduate dissertations. Only the main references have been included for the small number of charcoal-fired furnaces which appear here, since Riden's *Gazetteer* (1993) has a much fuller bibliography. Similarly, works relating solely to iron ore mining have been omitted, since these are listed by Burt and Waite (1988).

Mineral Statistics and its successors, and also the annual statistical reports of the various trade associations, have been listed in simple form: fuller details are given in the Introduction.

In all cases, the place of publication is London except where indicated.

Bibliographies and Archive Guides

Armstrong, J., and Jones, S., *Business documents. Their origins, sources and uses in historical research* (1987).
Burt, R., and Waite, P., *Bibliography of the history of British metal mining* (Exeter University, 1988).
Greenwood, J., *The industrial archaeology and industrial history of northern England: a bibliography* (The Author, 1985).
Greenwood, J., *The industrial archaeology and industrial history of the English Midlands: a bibliography* (Cranfield, 1987).
Probert, E.D., *Company and business records for family historians* (Fed. Family Hist. Socs., 1994).
Richmond, L., and Stockford, B., *Company archives. The survey of the records of 1000 of the first registered companies in England and Wales* (Aldershot, 1986).
Royal Commission on Historical Manuscripts, *Records of British business and industry. 1760–1914. Metal processing and engineering* (1994).
Watts, C.T., and Watts, M.J., 'Company records as a source for the family historian', *Genealogist's Magazine*, 21 (2) (1983), 44–54.

Parliamentary Papers

Select Committee on Import Duties (1840 (601), V).
Report of the Midland Mining Commission (1843 (508), XIII).
Report of the Commissioner appointed under 5 & 6 Vict. c. 99 to inquire into the operation of that Act, and into the state of the population in the mining districts (1849 [1109], XXII).
Report of the Commissioners appointed to inquire into the application of iron to railway structures (1849 [1123], XXIX).
Report of the Royal Commission on the Coal Trade (1871 [C. 435], XVIII).
Mineral Statistics (Annual, for 1882–1919).
Report of the Departmental Committee on Mining and Mineral Statistics (1895 [C. 7609], XLII).
Report of the Departmental Committee appointed to consider the position of the Iron and Steel Trades after the War (1918 [Cd 9071], XIII).

Statistics

British Iron & Steel Federation, *Statistics of the Iron and Steel Industries* (Annual, for 1934–55).
British Iron Trade Association, *Annual Report* (Annual, for 1877–1905).
English, H. (comp.), *The Mining Almanack for 1850* (1850).
Evans, C., 'The statistical surveys of the British iron industry in 1797–98 and 1806', *Historical Metallurgy*, 27 (1993), 84–101.
Geological Survey, *Mineral Statistics* (Annual, for 1854–81).
Hulme, E.W., 'Statistical history of iron trade of England and Wales, 1717–50', *Trans. Newcomen Soc.*, 9 (1928–29), 12–35.
Hunt, R., 'Note on the coal raised and iron made at present (December, 1852) in South Staffordshire', *Records of the School of Mines*, 1 (Part 2) (1853), 342–8.
Iron & Steel Board and British Iron & Steel Federation, *Iron and steel annual statistics for the United Kingdom* (Annual, 1956–67).
Iron, Steel & Allied Trades Federation, *Statistical Report* (Annual, for 1915–17).
Marshall, J., *An account of the rise, progress and present extent of the production, exportation and consumption of iron in Great Britain* (1829).
Marshall, J., *Digest of all the accounts relating to the population, productions, revenues, financial operations ... of the United Kingdom* (1833).
Mines Department, *Mines and Quarries: General Report with Statistics. For 1920* (1921).
Mines Department, *Annual Report of the Secretary for Mines* (Annual, for 1921–38).
Mitchell, B.R., *Abstract of British historical statistics* (Cambridge, 1971).

Mitchell, B.R., *British historical statistics* (Cambridge, 1988).
National Federation of Iron & Steel Manufacturers, *Statistical Report* (Annual, for 1918–33).
Poole, B., *Statistics of British commerce* (1852).
Poole, B., *The commerce of Liverpool* (1854).
Porter, G.R., 'On the progress, present amount, and probable future condition of the iron manufacture in Great Britain', *Reports of the sixteenth meeting of the British Association* (1847), 99–119.
Porter, G.R., *The progress of the nation* (ed. F.W. Hirst, 1912).
Riden, P., 'The output of the British iron industry before 1870', *Economic History Review*, 2nd series, 30 (1977), 443–59.
Shone, R.M., 'Statistics relating to the U.K. iron and steel industry', *Journal of the Royal Statistical Society, Series A*, 118 (1950), 464–86.
Taylor, R.C., *Statistics of coal* (1848).

General Histories

Ashton, T.S., *Iron and steel in the industrial revolution* (Manchester, new imp. 1963).
Bell, I.L., *The iron trade of the United Kingdom* (1886).
Birch, A., *The economic history of the British iron and steel industry 1784–1879* (1967).
The British Iron and Steel Federation. An account of the principal trade association in the steel industry (BISF, 1963).
Burn, D.L., *The economic history of steelmaking, 1867–1939. A study in competition* (Cambridge, 1940).
Carden, P., 'The Institute and the technical press', *Journal of the Iron and Steel Institute*, 211 (1973), 859.
Carr, J.C., and Taplin, W., *History of the British steel industry* (Oxford, 1962).
Fordyce, W., *A history of coal, coke, coal fields, ... iron, its ores, and processes of manufacture* (1860; new ed. Newcastle, 1973).
Guillou, W. le, 'William Gibbons and the proposed taxes on the iron trade', *Journal of West Midlands Regional Studies*, 2 (1968), 1–5.
Hatch, F.H., *The iron and steel industry of the United Kingdom under war conditions. A record of the work of the Iron and Steel Production Department of the Ministry of Munitions* (1919).
Holland, J., *Manufactures in metal: iron and steel* (1831).
Johnson, B.L.C., 'The charcoal iron industry in the early eighteenth century', *Geographical Journal*, 117 (1951), 167–77.
Johnson, B.L.C., 'The Foley partnerships: the iron industry at the end of the charcoal era', *Economic History Review*, 2nd series 4 (1951–52), 322–40.
Meade, R., *The coal and iron industries of the United Kingdom* (1882).
[Mushet, D.], 'Blast Furnace', in *Cyclopaedia or universal dictionary of arts and sciences* (1819), IV.
Mushet, D., *Papers on iron and steel, practical and experimental* (1840).
Needham, W., *The manufacture of iron* (1831).
Riden, P., 'Some unsuccessful blast furnaces of the early coke era', *Historical Metallurgy*, 26 (1992), 36–44.

Riden, P., *A gazetteer of charcoal-fired blast furnaces in Great Britain in use since 1660* (Cardiff, 2nd ed. 1993).
Scrivenor, H., *History of the iron trade, from the earliest records to the present period* (1841; 2nd ed. 1854; new imp. of 2nd ed. 1967).
Smith, W.A., 'Combinations of West Midlands ironmasters during the industrial revolution', *West Midland Studies*, 11 (1978), 1–10.
Tripp, B.H., 'The Iron and Steel Institute, 1869–1969: an historical sketch', *Journal of the Iron and Steel Institute*, 207 (1969), 243.
Truran, W., *The iron manufacture of Great Britain theoretically and practically considered* (1855).
Vaisey, J., *The history of British steel* (1974).
Wengenroth, U., *Enterprise and technology. The German and British steel industries, 1865–1895* (Cambridge, 1994).

Regional Studies

South Wales

Addis, J.P., *The Crawshay dynasty. A study in industrial organisation and development, 1765–1867* (Cardiff, 1957).
Atkinson, M., and Baber, C., *The growth and decline of the South Wales iron industry, 1760–1880* (Cardiff, 1987).
Chappell, E.L., *Historic Melingriffith: an account of Pentyrch Iron Works* (Cardiff, 1940).
Daunton, M.J., 'The Dowlais Iron Company in the iron industry, 1800–1850', *Welsh History Review*, 6 (1972), 16–48.
Elsas, M. (ed.), *Iron in the making. Dowlais Iron Company letters, 1782–1860* (Glamorgan Record Office, 1960).
England, J., 'The Dowlais iron works, 1759–93', *Morgannwg*, 3 (1959), 41–60.
Evans, C., *'Labyrinth of flames'. Work and social conflict in early industrial Merthyr Tydfil* (Cardiff, 1993).
Evans, C., and Hayes, G.G.L. (ed.), *The letterbook of Richard Crawshay, 1788–1797* (S. Wales Record Soc., 6, 1990).
Havill, E.A., 'William Tait and the Dowlais Ironworks', *Trans. Cymmrodorion Soc.* (1983), 97–114.
Higgins, L.S., 'John Brogden & Sons: industrial pioneers in mid-Glamorgan', *Glamorgan Historian*, 10 (1974), 148–56.
Ince, L., *The Neath Abbey Iron Company* (Eindhoven, 1984).
John, A.H., and Williams, G. (ed.), *Glamorgan County History. V. Industrial Glamorgan from 1700 to 1970* (Cardiff, 1980).
John, H., 'The iron industry of Maesteg in the nineteenth century: an outline', *Journal of the S.E. Wales Ind. Arch. Soc.*, 2 (2) (1976), 5–16.
Jones, E., *A history of GKN* (1987–90).
Knight, J., 'The Blaenavon Iron and Coal Company, 1836–1864. A Victorian joint-stock venture', *Bull. Board of Celtic Studies*, 28 (178–80), 631–44.
Lloyd, J., *The early history of the old South Wales ironworks, 1760–1840* (1906).
Minchinton, W.E., 'The place of Brecknock in the industrialization of South Wales', *Brycheiniog*, 7 (1961), 1–46.
Moxham, M., 'Description of plant for iron smelting by water-gas, recently erected at Trimsaran', *Proc. S. Wales Inst. Engineers*, 14 (1884–5), 295–302.

Owen, J.A., *The history of the Dowlais Iron Works, 1759–1970* (Risca, 1977).

Phillips, M., 'The early development of the iron and tinplate industries of the Port Talbot district', *Trans. Aberafan & Margam District Historical Soc.*, 5 (1932–3), 11–30.

Rees, D.M., *Mines, mills and furnaces. An introduction to industrial archaeology in Wales* (National Museum of Wales, 1969).

Riden, P., *John Bedford and the ironworks at Cefn Cribwr* (Cardiff, 1992).

Roberts, C.W., *A legacy from Victorian enterprise. The Briton Ferry Ironworks and the daughter companies* (Gloucester, 1983).

Wilson, A., 'The excavation of Clydach Ironworks', *Industrial Archaeology Review*, 10 (1988), 16–36.

Gloucestershire

Anstis, R., *The industrial Teagues and the Forest of Dean* (Gloucester, 1990).

Bridgewater, N.P., and Morton, G.R., 'Bromley Hill Furnace, Forest of Dean', *Bull. Historical Metallurgy Group*, 2 (1968), 43–46.

Hart, C., *The industrial history of Dean with an introduction to its industrial archaeology* (Newton Abbot, 1971).

Newman, R., 'The origins of the Cinderford coke iron furnace', *Gloucs. Ind. Arch. Soc. Journal* (1982), 12–16.

Osborn, F.M., *The story of the Mushets* (1952).

Standing, I.J., 'The Whitecliff Ironworks in the Forest of Dean. Part 1. 1798–1808', *Gloucs. Ind. Arch. Soc. Journal* (1980), 18–28.

Standing, I.J., '"Dear Mushet": a history of the Whitecliff Ironworks. Part 2. 1808–1810', *Gloucs. Ind. Arch. Soc. Journal* (1981), 32–71.

Standing, I.J., 'The Whitecliff Ironworks in the Forest of Dean', *Gloucs. Ind. Arch. Soc. Journal* (1986), 2–19.

Somerset and Wiltshire

Cogswell, R.J., 'Westbury Ironworks' (Unpublished typescript, 1988, in Wiltshire County Library, Trowbridge).

Hooper, T.J., 'The Wiltshire iron industry' (Unpublished typescript, 1980, in Wiltshire County Library, Trowbridge).

Parkhouse, N., 'Seend Ironworks', *Archive*, 4 (n.d.), 58–64.

Sussex and Hampshire

Beswick, W.R., Broomhall, P.J., and Bickersteth, J.D., 'Ashburnham blast furnace: a definitive date for its closure', *Sussex Arch. Collections*, 122 (1984), 226–7.

Cleere, H., and Crossley, D., *The iron industry of the Weald* (Cardiff, 2nd ed. 1995).

Crossley, D.W., and Saville, R.V. (ed.), *The Fuller letters 1728–1755. Guns, slaves and finance* (Sussex Record Soc., 76, 1991).

Shropshire

Gale, W.K.V., and Nicholls, C.R., *The Lilleshall Company Limited: a history 1764–1964* (Buxton, 1979).

Raistrick, A., *Dynasty of ironfounders. The Darbys and Coalbrookdale* (Newton Abbot, 2nd ed. 1970).

Smith, S.B., 'The construction of the Blists Hill Ironworks', *Industrial Archaeology Review*, 3 (2), 170–78.

Smith, S.B., 'New light on the Bedlam furnaces, Ironbridge, Telford', *Historical Metallurgy*, 13 (1979), 21–30.

Trinder, B., *The industrial revolution in Shropshire* (Chichester, 2nd ed. 1981).

North Wales

The story of Brymbo (Brymbo, 1959).

British Steel Corporation, *Full circle: the story of steelmaking on Deeside* (1980).

Davies, A.S., 'The early iron industry in North Wales', *Trans. Newcomen Soc.*, 25 (1945–7), 83–90.

Edwards, I., 'Iron production in North Wales: the canal era, 1795–1850', *Trans. Denbighs. Hist. Soc.*, 14 (1965), 141–84.

Edwards, I., 'The British Iron Company', *Trans. Denbighs. Hist. Soc.*, 31 (1982), 109–48.

Edwards, I., 'The New British Iron Company', *Trans. Denbighs. Hist. Soc.*, 32 (1983), 98–134.

Mostyn History Preservation Society, 'Mostyn Ironworks 1800–1964', *Archive*, 2 (n.d.), 2–14.

Redhead, B., and Gooddie, S., *The Summers of Shotton* (1987).

Reid, A., *Continuous venture. The story of a steel works* (Shotton, 1948).

Richards, P.S., 'The Darwen & Mostyn Iron Company', *Flints. Hist. Soc. Journal*, 24 (1969–70), 84–94.

Richards, P.S., 'The Hawarden Bridge, Shotton, Chester, iron and steel works of Messrs John Summers & Co.', *Flints. Hist. Soc. Journal*, 25 (1971–2), 103–23.

Williams, C.J., *Industry in Clwyd. An illustrated history* (Clwyd Record Office, 1986).

South Staffordshire

Gale, W.K.V., *The Coneygre story* (Coneygre Foundry, 1954).

Gale, W.K.V., *The Black Country iron industry. A technical history* (Metals Society, 2nd ed. 1979).

Gale, W.K.V., *A history of Bromford, 1780–1980* (Bromford Iron & Steel Co., 1981).

Gale, W.K.V., 'Patent Shaft steel works', *Blackcountryman*, 14 (3) (1981), 18–22.

Guillou, M. le, 'Developments in the south Staffordshire iron and steel industry 1850–1913, in the light of home and foreign competition' (Keele University Ph.D. thesis, 1972–3).

Holden, L., 'Bradley and Foster', *Blackcountryman*, 5 (2) (1972), 11–15.

Hoskison, T.M., 'The Earl of Dudley's Level New Furnaces', *Trans. Newcomen Soc.*, 28 (1951–53), 153–61.

Hunt, L.B., 'The Parker brothers. Black Country ironmasters', *Historical Metallurgy*, 13 (1979), 31.

Knox, C., *Steel at Brierley Hill: the story of Round Oak Steel Works 1857–1957* (Round Oak Steel Works, 1957).

Morton, G.R., and Guillou, M. le, 'Alfred Hickman Ltd 1866–1932', *West Midland Studies*, 3 (1969), 1–30.

Morton, G.R., and Guillou, M. le, 'The rise and fall of the South Staffordshire pig iron industry', *British Foundryman*, 60 (7), (1967), 269–86.

Morton, G.R., and Smith, W.A., 'The Bradley Ironworks of John Wilkinson', *Journal of the Iron & Steel Institute*, 204 (1966), 661–78.

Mutton, N., 'The Foster family, 1786–1899. A study of a Midlands industrial dynasty' (London University External Ph.D. thesis, 1974).

Raybould, T.J., 'The development and organisation of Lord Dudley's mineral estates, 1774–1845', *Economic History Review*, 2nd series, 21 (1968), 529–44.

Raybould, T.J., *The economic emergence of the Black Country. A study of the Dudley estate* (Newton Abbot, 1972).

Rostron, P., 'M. & W. Grazebrook's Netherton ironworks', *Blackcountryman*, 12 (2), (1979), 47–50.

Smith, W.A., 'The contribution of the Gibbons family to technical developments in the iron and coal industries', *West Midland Studies*, 4 (1970–71), 46–55.

Smith, W.A., 'John Wilkinson and the industrial revolution in South Staffordshire', *West Midland Studies*, 5 (1972), 24–27.

Worpell, J.G., 'The iron and coal trades of the South Staffordshire area covering the period 1843–1853', *West Midland Studies*, 9 (1976), 34–48.

North Staffordshire

Hardman, B.M., 'The early history of the Silverdale Ironworks', *J. Staffs. Ind. Arch. Soc.*, 3 (1972), 1–20.

Hardman, B.M., 'The iron and steel industry of north Staffordshire and south Cheshire in the pre-coke smelting era', *N. Staffs. Journal of Field Studies*, 15 (1975), 83–92.

Sherlock, R., *The industrial archaeology of Staffordshire* (Newton Abbot, 1976).

Simons, P.E., 'Silverdale iron, 1792–1902: a study of the effects of management and technological changes on the fluctuating economic fortunes of a north Staffordshire iron company' (Keele University M.A. thesis, 1978).

Northamptonshire

Beaver, S.H., 'The iron industry of Northamptonshire, Rutland and south Lincolnshire', *Geography*, 18 (1933), 102–17.

Beaver, S.H., 'The development of the Northamptonshire iron industry, 1851–1930', in Stamp, L.D., and Wooldridge, S.W. (ed.), *London essays in geography* (1951), 33–58.

Pocock, D.C.D., 'Iron and steel at Corby', *East Midland Geographer*, 2 (15) (1961), 3–10.

Scopes, F., *The development of Corby Works* (Corby, 1968).

Starmer, G.H., 'Ironworks in Northamptonshire', *CBA Group 9 Bulletin*, 11 (1979), 17–35.

Starmer, G.H., 'Islip iron furnaces and tramways', *Bull. Northants. Federation of Archaeological Societies*, 3 (April 1969), 30–32; 4 (April 1970), 25–28.

Stewarts and Lloyds, 1903–1953 (Stewarts & Lloyds, n.d.).

Lincolnshire

Appleby-Frodingham Steel Company, Scunthorpe, Lincolnshire (Bradford, 1961).

Ayres, H.S., 'A hundred years of ironmaking at Appleby-Frodingham', *Journal of the Iron and Steel Institute*, 203 (1965), 1081–93.

'Century of iron making at Scunthorpe'. *Metallurgia*, 72 (1965), 220–24.

Daff, T., 'The establishment of ironmaking at Scunthorpe, 1858–77', *Bulletin of Economic Research*, 25 (2) (1973), 104–21.

Daff, T., 'Scunthorpe's first furnace', *Journal of the Iron and Steel Institute*, 206 (1968), 693–99.

Dove, G., 'The Frodingham iron field, north Lincolnshire', *Journal of the Iron and Steel Institute* (1876), 318–41.

Dove, G., 'On the iron industry of Frodingham', *Proc. Inst. Mech. Engineers* (1885), 413–21.

Henderson, J., 'Notes on the early history of the iron making industry of north Lincolnshire', *Proc. Lincs. Iron & Steel Institute*, 1 (1918–20), 121–6.

Iron & Coal Trades Review, *Appleby-Frodingham Steel Company. Branch of the United Steel Companies Ltd. A technical survey* (n.d.).

Isaac, S.R., 'Steelmaking at Redbourn', *Journal of the Iron and Steel Institute*, 193 (1955), 44–8.

Kendall, O.D., 'Iron and steel industry of Scunthorpe', *Economic Geography*, 14 (1938), 271–81.

John Lysaght Ltd, *The Lysaght century, 1857–1957* (Bristol, 1957).

Lysaght's Scunthorpe works: Normanby Park Steelworks, Scunthorpe, Lincolnshire (Manchester, n.d.).

Peddie, P., *The United Steel Companies Ltd, 1918–1968* (Manchester, 1969).

Pocock, D.C.D., 'Iron and steel at Scunthorpe', *East Midland Geographer*, 3 (1962–65), 124–38.

Walshaw, G.R., and Behrendt, C.A.J., *The history of Appleby-Frodingham* (Appleby-Frodingham Steel Co., 1950).

Derbyshire

A hundred years of enterprise: centenary of the Clay Cross Company, 1837–1937 (Clay Cross Co., 1937).

Chapman, S.D., *Stanton and Staveley: a business history* (Cambridge, 1981).

Chapman, S.D., *The Clay Cross Company 1837–1987* (Clay Cross, 1987).

Cranstone, D., 'The iron industry of the Ashby coalfield', *Leics. Industrial History Soc. Bulletin*, 8 (1985), 23–31.

Cranstone, D., *Moria Furnace: a Napoleonic blast furnace in Leicestershire* (N.W. Leics. District Council, 1985).

Jenkins, D.E., 'John Brocksopp: yeoman ironmaster of Hasland', *Derbys. Arch. Journal*, 112 (1992), 69–78.

Lewis, V., *The iron dale* (Stanton Ironworks Co., 1959).

Lindsay, J., 'The Butterley coal and iron works, 1792–1816', *Derbys. Arch. Journal*, 85 (1975), 25–43.

Mottram, R.H., and Coote, C., *Through five generations. The history of the Butterley Company* (1950).

Palmer, M., and Palmer, D., 'Moira Furnace', *Industrial Archaeology Review*, 1 (1976), 63–69.

Riden, P., 'Joseph Butler, coal and iron master, 1763–1837', *Derbys. Arch. Journal*, 104 (1984), 87–95.

Riden, P., 'The ironworks at Alderwasley and Morley Park' *Derbys. Arch. Journal*, 108 (1988), 77–107.

Riden, P., 'The ironworks at Alderwasley and Morley Park: a postscript', *Derbys. Arch. Journal*, 109 (1989), 175–9.

Riden, P., *The Butterley Company, 1790–1830* (Derbyshire Record Soc., 16, 1990).

Robinson, P., *The Smiths of Chesterfield: a history of the Griffin Foundry, Brampton, 1775–1833* (Chesterfield, 1957).

Warren, K., 'The Derbyshire iron industry since 1780', *East Midland Geographer*, 16 (1961), 17–33.

Yorkshire, West Riding

Andrews, C.R., *The story of Wortley Ironworks* (3rd ed., Nottingham, 1975).

Baker, H.G., *Samuel Walker and his partners: the Kimberworth ironfounders of 1745–1782* (Rotherham, 1946).

Clayton, A.K., *The story of the Elsecar and Milton iron works from their opening until the year 1848* (Cusworth Hall Museum, 1973).

Dodsworth, C., 'Further observations on the Bowling Ironworks', *Industrial Archaeology*, 6 (1969), 114–23.

Dodsworth, C., 'The Low Moor Ironworks, Bradford', *Industrial Archaeology*, 8 (1971), 122–64.

Ferns, J.L., 'The Walker Company of Rotherham: practical proof of its greatness', *Industrial Archaeology*, 12 (1977), 206–20.

Firth, G., 'The origins of Low Moor Ironworks, Bradford, 1788–1800', *Yorks. Arch. Journal*, 49 (1977), 127–39.

Hey, D.G., 'The ironworks at Chapeltown', *Trans. Hunter Arch. Soc.*, 10 (1971–77), 252–9.

Hey, D.G., 'The nailmaking background of the Walkers and the Booths', *Trans. Hunter Arch. Soc.*, 10 (1971–77), 31–36.

Hopkinson, G.G., 'The development of lead mining and of the coal and iron industries in north Derbyshire and south Yorkshire (Sheffield University Ph.D. thesis, 1958).

John, A.H. (ed.), *Minutes relating to Messrs Samuel Walker & Co., Rotherham, iron founders and steeel refiners, 1741–1829, and Messrs Walkers, Parker & Co., lead manufacturers, 1788–1898* (Council for the Preservation of Business Archives, 1951).

Long, H., 'Bowling Ironworks', *Industrial Archaeology*, 5 (1968), 171–77.

Norman, W.L., 'Fall Ings, Wakefield. Some notes on an eighteenth-century foundry', *Industrial Archaeology*, 6 (1969), 74–79.

Royston, G.P., *A history of the Park Gate Iron and Steel Company 1823–1923* (Park Gate Iron & Steel Co., 1923).

Ward, H.D., '"Best Yorkshire" from west Yorkshire', *Journal of the Iron and Steel Institute*, 210 (1972), 396–405.

North West England

Andrews, P.W.S., and Brunner, E., *Capital development in steel. A study of the United Steel Companies* (Oxford, 1951).

Ashmore, O., *The industrial archaeology of north-west England* (Manchester, 1982).

Birch, A., 'The Haigh Ironworks, 1789–1856: a nobleman's enterprise during the Industrial Revolution', *Bull. John Rylands Library*, 25 (1953), 316–33.

Boswell, J.S., 'Hope, inefficiency or public duty? The United Steel Companies and West Cumberland, 1918–1939', *Business History*, 22 (1980), 35–50.

Harris, A., 'Askam iron: the development of Askam-in-Furness, 1850–1920', *Trans. Cumberland & Westmorland Antiquarian & Archaeological Society*, 65 (1965), 381–407.

Fell, A., *The early iron industry of Furness and district* (Ulverston, 1908).

Lancaster, J.Y., and Wattleworth, D.R., *The iron and steel industry of West Cumberland. An historical survey* (Workington, 1977).

Lord, W.M., 'The development of the Bessemer process in Lancashire, 1856–1900', *Trans. Newcomen Soc.*, 25 (1945–7), 163–80.

Marshall, J.D., *Furness and the industrial revolution. An economic history of Furness, 1771–1900, and the town of Barrow, 1757–1897* (Barrow-in-Furness, 1958).

Peddie, R., *The United Steel Companies Ltd. 1918–1968. A history* (United Steel Co. Ltd, 1969).

Price, J.W.A., 'Iron making at Halton', *Contrebis*, 9 (1982), 23–29.

Workington Iron & Steel Co.: branch of the United Steel Companies Ltd (Workington Iron & Steel Co., n.d.).

North East England

Almond, J.K., 'Production of iron and steel at Tudhoe Works, County Durham', *Metallurgist*, 9 (1977), 127–8.

Atkinson, F., *The industrial archaeology of north-east England* (Newton Abbot, 1974).

Bolckow, Vaughan & Co., *Thomas and Gilchrist, 1879–1929. Bolckow & Vaughan* (Middlesbrough, 1929).

Bradley, W.G.B., 'The struggle for existence of a small works in the iron and steel industry', *Cleveland Industrial Archaeology*, 8 (1978), 15–24.

Edwards, K.H.R., *Chronology of the development of the iron and steel industries of Tees-side* (Wigan, 1955).

Hempstead, C.A. (ed.), *Cleveland iron and steel. Background and nineteenth-century history* (British Steel, 1979).

Herbert, J., 'Portrack Lane Iron Works', *Industrial Archaeology Review*, 4 (1980), 272–5.

Hornsby, R.M., *History of the Consett Iron Company* (Consett Iron Co., 1958).

Hoskison, T.M., 'Northumberland blast furnace plants in the 19th century', *Trans. Newcomen Soc.*, 25 (1945–7), 73–82.

Irving, R.J., 'New industries for old? Some investment decisions of Sir W.G. Armstong, Whitworth & Co. Ltd, 1900–1914', *Business History*, 17 (1975), 150–75.

Jeans, J.S., *Pioneers of the Cleveland iron trade* (Middlesbrough, 1875).

Jones, G., 'A description of Messrs Bell Brothers' blast-furnaces from 1844–1908', *Journal of the Iron and Steel Institute*, 78 (1908), 59–72.

Kirby, M.W., *Men of politics and business. A history of the Quaker Pease dynasty of north east England, 1750–1939* (1981).

Linsley, S.M., 'Hareshaw and Ridsdale ironworks', *Northumbria*, No 12 (Spring 1978), 15–17; No 13 (Summer 1978), 11–14.

Lillie, W., *The history of Middlesbrough. An illustration of the evolution of English industry* (Middlesbrough, 1968).

Richardson, H.W., and Bass, J.M., 'The profitability of the Consett Iron Company before 1914', *Business History*, 7 (1965), 71–93.

Ridley, Viscount, *The development of the iron and steel industry in north west Durham* (Tyneside Geographical Society, 1961).

Tylecote, R.F., 'Recent research on nineteenth-century Northumberland blast furnace sites', *Industrial Archaeology*, 8 (1971), 341–59.

Tylecote, R.F., 'Weardale iron and steel making 1876–95', *Metallurgist*, 8 (1976), 269–71.

Warren, K., *Consett Iron. 1840 to 1980. A study in industrial location* (Oxford, 1990).

Willis, W.G., *Skinningrove Iron Company Ltd. A history* (Skinningrove Iron Co., n.d.).

Willis, A.G., *South Durham Steel & Iron Co. Ltd* (S. Durham Steel & Iron Co., 1969).

Wilson, A.S., 'The Consett Iron Company Limited. A case study in Victorian business history' (Durham University M.Phil. thesis, 1973).

Wilson, A.S., 'The origin of the Consett Iron Company, 1840–1864', *Durham University Journal*, New Series, 34 (1972–3), 90–102.

Scotland

Bumby, H., Wylie, W., and Archibald, H., 'The iron and steel industries of the west of Scotland', *Journal of the Iron and Steel Institute*, 60 (1901), 9–28.

Butt, J., 'The Scottish iron and steel industry before the hot-blast', *Journal of the West of Scotland Iron and Steel Institute*, 73 (1965–6), 193–220.

Butt, J., *The industrial archaeology of Scotland* (Newton Abbot, 1967).

Butt, J., 'Glenbuck Iron Works', *Ayrshire Collections*, 2nd series, 8 (1967–9), 68–75.

Butt, J., 'Capital and enterprise in the Scottish iron industry, 1780–1840', in Butt, J., and Ward, J.T. (ed.), *Scottish themes. Essays in honour of Professor S.G.E. Lythe* (Edinburgh, 1976), 67–79.

Byres, T.J., 'Entrepreneurship in the Scottish heavy industries, 1870–1900', in Payne, P.L. (ed.), *Studies in Scottish business history* (1967), 250–96.

Cadell, P., *The iron mills at Cramond* (Edinburgh, 1973).

Campbell, R.H., 'Investment in the Scottish pig iron trade, 1830–1843', *Scottish Journal of Political Economy*, 1 (1954), 233–49.

Campbell, R.H., 'Developments in the Scottish pig iron trade, 1844–8', *Journal of Economic History*, 17 (1955), 209–26.

Campbell, R.H., 'The growth and fluctuations of the Scottish pig iron trade, 1828 to 1873' (Aberdeen University Ph.D. thesis, 1956).

Campbell, R.H., 'Statistics of the Scottish pig iron trade 1830 to 1865', *Journal of the West of Scotland Iron and Steel Institute*, 64 (1956–7), 282–89.

Campbell, R.H., 'Fluctuations in stocks: a nineteenth-century case-study', *Oxford Economic Papers*, New Series, 9 (1957), 41–55.

Campbell, R.H., *Carron Company* (Edinburgh, 1961).

Campbell, R.H., 'The law and the joint-stock company in Scotland'. in P.L. Payne (ed.), *Studies in Scottish business history* (1967), 136–51.

Carvel, J.L., *The Coltness Iron Company. A study in private enterprise* (1948).

Corrins, R.D., 'William Baird & Company, coal and iron masters, 1830–1914' (Strathclyde University Ph.D. thesis, 1974).

Donnachie, I.L., and Butt, J., 'The Wilsons of Wilsontown Ironworks (1779–1813): a study in entrepreneurial failure', *Explorations in Entrepreneurial History*, 2nd series, 4 (1967), 150–68.

Hume, J.R., *The industrial archaeology of Scotland. 1. The Lowlands and Borders* (1976).

Hume, J.R., *The industrial archaeology of Scotland. 2. The Highland and Islands* (1977).

Hume, J.R., and Butt, J., 'Muirkirk 1786–1802: the creation of a Scottish industrial community', *Scottish Historical Review*, 45 (1966), 160–83.

Hume, J.R.. and Moss, M.S., *Beardmore: the history of a Scottish industrial giant* (1979).

McEwan, A.M.C., 'Shotts Iron company, 1800–1850' (Strathclyde University M.Litt. thesis, 1972).

Marwick, W.H., 'A bibliography of Scottish business history', in Payne, P.L. (ed.), *Studies in Scottish business history* (1967), 77–99.

Mayer, J., 'On the rise and progress of the iron manufacture in Scotland', *Journal of the Iron and Steel Institute* (1872) Part II, 28–43.

Muir, A., *The story of Shotts. A short history of the Shotts Iron Company Limited* (Edinburgh, 1952).

Payne, P.L., 'Rationality and personality: a study of mergers in the Scottish iron and steel industry, 1916–1936', *Business History*, 19 (1977), 162–91.

Payne, P.L., *Colvilles and the Scottish steel industry* (Oxford, 1979).

Payne, P.L., *The early Scottish limited companies, 1856–1895. An historical and analytical survey* (Edinburgh, 1980).

Quinn, E., 'The Ravenscraig decision' (Strathclyde University Ph.D. thesis, 1981).

Rowan, F.J., 'On the iron trade of Scotland', *Journal of the Iron and Steel Institute* (1885), 376–93.

Smith, D.L., *The Dalmellington Iron Company. Its engines and men* (Newton Abbot, 1967).

National and Regional Statistics

Table 1.1: Output of Pig Iron, 1788–1920

Year	Great Britain	South Wales	Gloucs etc	Shrop-shire	North Wales	South Staffs	North Staffs	North-ants	Lin-coln	Derby-shire	York-shire	North West	North East	Scot-land	Others
1788	66	12.5	2.6	24.9	0.4	3.8	0.8	-	-	4.5	5.1	4.1	-	7.0	0.3
1791	89	17.5	2.0	31.9	0.8	7.3	0.5	-	-	4.7	7.0	3.9	-	13.5	0.3
1796	149	39.6	1.0	42.8	1.8	14.9	2.2	-	-	7.6	16.5	3.8	-	18.6	-
1805	250	72.9	4.1	55.0	2.1	45.9	2.6	-	-	10.0	25.6	1.3	-	22.8	7.8
1823	454	182.3	-	57.9	-	133.6	-	-	-	14.0	27.3	-	2.4	24.5	12.0
1825	578	223.5	-	81.8	13.1	172.2	4.0	-	-	19.2	35.3	-	-	29.2	-
1827	690	272.0	-	78.0	24.0	211.3	4.8	-	-	20.5	43.0	-	-	36.5	-
1828	703	279.5	-	81.2	25.2	214.7	4.8	-	-	22.4	33.0	-	-	37.7	4.2
1830	678	277.6	-	73.4	-	212.6	-	-	-	18.0	28.9	-	5.3	37.5	25.0
1839	1,249	453.9	18.2	80.9	33.8	346.2	18.2	-	-	34.4	52.4	0.8	13.0	197.0	-
1840	1,397	505.0	15.5	82.8	26.5	407.2	20.5	-	-	31.0	56.0	-	11.0	241.0	-
1841	1,328	468.0	6.2	70.5	18.7	347.1	32.2	-	-	30.0	55.1	-	12.5	287.3	-
1842	1,098	317.4	-	81.3	-	279.3	23.0	-	-	27.6	46.9	-	-	270.1	52.7
1843	1,211	457.4	8.0	76.2	19.8	300.3	21.8	-	-	25.8	42.0	-	20.8	238.8	-
1847	2,000	706.7	-	88.4	16.1	320.3	65.5	-	-	95.2	67.6	-	99.8	540.0	-
1848	2,094	631.3	-	111.0	22.3	465.9	67.1	-	-	78.0	59.8	-	94.4	564.0	-
1852	2,701	666.0	-	120.0	30.0	725.0	90.0	-	-	-	-	-	145.0	775.0	150.0
1854	3,070	750.0	22.0	124.8	32.9	743.6	104.0	-	-	127.5	73.4	20.0	275.0	796.6	-
1855	3,218	840.0	19.5	121.7	31.4	754.0	101.5	-	-	116.6	90.8	16.6	298.5	827.5	-
1856	3,586	777.2	24.1	109.7	47.7	777.2	130.6	-	-	107.0	96.2	25.5	510.8	880.5	-
1857	3,659	970.8	24.2	117.1	37.0	657.3	134.1	11.5	-	112.2	117.0	31.7	527.6	918.0	-

Year	Great Britain	South Wales	Gloucs etc	Shrop-shire	North Wales	South Staffs	North Staffs	North-ants	Lin-coln	Derby-shire	York-shire	North West	North East	Scot-land	Others
1858	3,456	886.5	25.6	101.0	28.2	597.8	135.3	9.7	-	131.6	85.9	29.1	499.8	925.5	-
1859	3,713	985.3	42.3	149.5	27.0	473.3	143.5	12.8	-	139.3	85.0	76.6	618.0	960.6	-
1860	3,827	969.0	50.3	145.2	49.4	469.5	147.0	7.6	-	125.9	98.1	169.2	658.7	937.0	-
1861	3,712	886.3	40.5	140.8	46.7	395.7	187.7	7.7	-	129.7	142.9	164.5	619.9	950.0	-
1862	3,944	893.3	52.0	126.0	31.7	410.2	184.5	13.5	-	131.0	112.1	242.0	667.2	1,080.0	-
1863	4,510	847.8	64.0	135.6	51.1	691.2	176.5	14.6	-	170.0	104.7	270.2	824.4	1,160.0	-
1864	4,768	937.6	65.3	130.7	51.1	628.8	218.0	-	-	174.7	112.1	336.5	931.6	1,158.8	22.8
1865	4,805	845.0	65.5	117.3	51.9	692.6	206.3	-	-	189.4	123.2	312.4	1,012.5	1,163.5	25.7
1866	4,524	927.5	59.8	121.2	25.5	532.6	210.3	19.2	13.8	200.0	119.7	405.0	895.4	994.0	-
1867	4,761	886.2	71.2	123.6	32.8	515.6	202.3	25.2	25.6	160.0	109.0	428.6	1,149.8	1,031.0	-
1868	4,970	894.3	75.8	145.2	37.0	532.2	229.9	35.6	34.0	159.3	100.1	442.2	1,216.6	1,068.0	-
1869	5,446	801.0	81.3	197.4	38.5	569.6	231.9	41.5	33.8	188.4	105.8	565.8	1,440.9	1,150.0	-
1870	5,964	979.2	93.6	112.3	42.7	588.5	303.4	43.2	31.7	180.0	77.7	677.9	1,627.6	1,206.0	-
1871	6,628	1,045.9	100.0	129.5	41.9	725.7	268.3	60.5	31.1	270.5	114.5	856.9	1,823.3	1,160.0	-
1872	6,742	1,002.6	98.1	133.0	54.7	673.5	275.9	59.4	37.0	283.4	148.6	964.6	1,921.1	1,090.0	-
1873	6,566	817.8	93.0	135.1	67.5	673.4	241.2	58.5	52.1	296.4	151.5	986.1	2,000.8	993.0	-
1874	5,992	714.7	78.3	126.1	51.9	452.4	273.5	53.8	67.3	301.7	163.9	879.5	2,020.8	807.7	-
1875	6,366	541.8	59.8	121.0	55.1	470.5	241.4	80.7	111.7	272.1	267.2	1,044.9	2,049.3	1,050.0	-
1876	6,556	756.1	57.6	106.7	32.7	465.9	213.6	84.9	125.2	300.7	235.5	989.9	2,084.2	1,103.0	-
1877	6,609	711.0	50.8	102.2	26.7	428.3	255.4	106.9	116.9	328.2	229.0	1,162.3	2,109.0	982.0	-
1878	6,381	741.1	42.4	81.0	23.1	392.9	231.5	138.4	125.0	306.1	219.5	1,159.2	2,018.8	902.0	-
1879	5,996	669.9	40.0	60.8	19.0	325.8	210.4	165.3	131.7	291.5	218.8	1,163.0	1,767.3	932.0	-
1880	7,749	889.7	37.5	88.3	57.8	384.6	225.0	178.7	207.7	366.8	306.6	1,541.2	2,416.4	1,049.0	-
1881	8,144	911.0	30.9	79.4	46.8	374.3	273.5	189.8	187.9	367.6	256.3	1,616.7	2,634.1	1,176.0	-

Year	Great Britain	South Wales	Gloucs etc	Shrop-shire	North Wales	South Staffs	North Staffs	North-ants	Lin-coln	Derby-shire	York-shire	North West	North East	Scot-land	Others
1882	8,588	934.4	53.0	80.5	53.1	398.4	275.6	192.1	201.6	445.7	321.4	1,792.2	2,712.6	1,126.9	-
1883	8,529	906.3	46.3	77.7	39.4	429.7	267.9	216.6	237.1	422.2	304.4	1,673.2	2,779.5	1,129.0	-
1884	7,812	851.4	24.0	53.2	34.5	356.9	296.3	196.2	259.4	437.5	248.3	1,561.1	2,505.0	988.0	-
1885	7,416	792.8	24.3	44.7	40.3	344.1	268.9	190.3	235.4	444.0	165.9	1,383.7	2,477.6	1,003.6	-
1886	7,010	666.6	32.3	40.9	35.3	294.5	233.5	197.9	242.3	346.3	137.3	1,410.3	2,436.7	935.8	-
1887	7,559	767.4	28.5	52.0	37.9	293.4	260.2	236.4	251.9	296.1	178.5	1,700.7	2,524.2	932.2	-
1888	7,999	870.9	40.1	61.0	33.3	366.4	279.2	236.8	298.7	362.7	190.8	1,600.0	2,631.3	1,027.8	-
1889	8,323	826.4	38.1	52.4	68.0	372.7	276.2	230.8	336.2	470.1	229.0	1,662.2	2,782.5	978.2	-
1890	7,904	824.7	39.1	43.1	64.5	327.0	255.8	225.0	268.4	463.7	248.6	1,569.6	2,837.6	737.1	-
1891	7,406	760.6	37.9	47.8	53.7	350.1	232.3	194.4	284.8	471.0	228.4	1,440.1	2,631.2	674.1	-
1892	6,709	684.0	34.6	50.0	45.6	337.5	241.4	177.8	279.6	481.4	261.5	1,198.7	1,944.5	972.5	-
1893	6,977	680.4	34.4	39.5	30.5	330.2	199.0	143.8	216.6	343.1	155.0	1,297.5	2,713.9	793.1	-
1894	7,427	708.9	25.5	39.8	29.8	332.7	210.1	223.3	343.6	376.7	225.2	1,295.6	2,973.9	642.2	-
1895	7,703	704.7	-	49.0	41.3	338.3	193.6	254.7	349.2	413.5	195.1	1,189.0	2,926.2	1,048.8	-
1896	8,660	780.4	-	46.7	49.2	389.3	236.2	274.5	361.0	455.5	289.5	1,451.4	3,211.9	1,114.0	-
1897	8,797	804.8	-	38.5	53.3	400.0	242.7	249.8	363.5	488.8	294.8	1,526.4	3,197.6	1,136.5	-
1898	8,610	495.3	-	42.1	58.8	405.5	268.4	250.8	381.8	529.2	297.5	1,619.1	3,198.6	1,062.5	-
1899	9,421	929.4	-	40.6	66.6	414.8	283.2	279.3	409.0	572.0	305.6	1,698.7	3,251.4	1,170.8	-
1900	8,960	908.1	-	39.2	-	398.5	272.6	247.9	388.7	561.6	290.6	1,585.9	3,109.6	1,156.9	-
1901	7,929	700.1	-	40.7	-	340.9	225.4	206.1	322.0	457.5	247.0	1,432.6	2,820.1	1,136.4	-
1902	8,680	800.3	-	40.9	-	380.2	249.0	247.2	386.2	519.0	284.1	1,540.1	2,960.9	1,271.7	-
1903	8,935	875.6	-	46.8	-	397.4	245.6	253.6	386.2	546.9	298.4	1,485.8	3,108.1	1,290.8	-
1904	8,694	804.9	-	-	55.5	393.7	286.7	267.2	376.7	551.0	263.4	1,219.5	3,123.9	1,351.1	-
1905	9,608	912.2	-	-	66.3	430.4	304.1	273.4	443.4	568.3	293.2	1,455.8	3,485.8	1,375.1	-

Year	Great Britain	South Wales	Gloucs etc	Shrop-shire	North Wales	South Staffs	North Staffs	North-ants	Lin-coln	Derby-shire	York-shire	North West	North East	Scot-land	Others
1906	10,180	900.3	-	-	73.7	452.0	348.6	289.5	497.0	640.1	335.9	1,566.8	3,698.7	1,376.9	-
1907	10,114	928.7	-	-	62.8	469.8	355.9	288.5	481.6	675.6	332.6	1,447.6	3,681.8	1,389.5	-
1908	9,057	802.7	-	-	63.6	449.1	322.8	295.7	491.8	637.7	281.6	1,097.9	3,389.1	1,224.8	-
1909	9,532	742.9	-	-	77.5	482.4	334.7	315.1	475.1	645.7	292.3	1,239.0	3,550.1	1,377.2	-
1910	10,012	787.8	-	-	75.0	495.4	354.2	365.6	512.3	687.3	313.4	1,313.7	3,679.5	1,427.8	-
1911	9,526	718.0	-	-	75.0	473.5	355.7	386.3	496.4	665.8	283.9	1,121.1	3,542.0	1,408.6	-
1912	8,752	755.9	-	-	44.2	442.2	350.1	350.7	450.2	585.9	265.0	1,063.0	3,258.8	1,185.5	-
1913	10,260	889.2	-	-	50.9	467.5	383.1	386.1	531.1	698.7	302.7	1,312.6	3,869.2	1,369.3	-
1914	8,924	753.4	-	-	46.1	419.9	333.9	339.4	471.6	640.6	263.5	1,222.9	3,306.6	1,126.0	-
1915	8,724	829.0	-	-	33.5	425.6	345.0	294.9	533.1	558.1	284.7	1,304.1	3,006.5	1,109.2	-
1916	8,919	855.5	-	-	45.3	410.3	339.4	284.5	533.2	498.5	293.3	1,437.1	3,097.3	1,124.9	-
1917	9,338	778.6	-	-	49.0	433.5	368.1	300.4	649.2	543.5	307.3	1,521.6	3,230.1	1,156.9	-
1918	9,107	880.7	-	-	44.2	413.3	371.6	314.5	638.8	566.9	281.8	1,512.3	2,991.9	1,091.4	-
1919	7,418	598.8	-	-	41.7	318.7	335.1	244.0	535.4	482.5	239.2	1,211.9	2,506.8	903.4	-
1920	8,035	692.0	-	-	-	-	-	283.0	657.3	563.3	260.0	1,341.2	2,638.6	902.6	697.2

Note: All figures are in thousands of tons.

Source: 1788–1852: Private surveys as discussed in the Introduction; aggregate estimates mentioned there are only included here if the original source also contains regional figures.

1854–1920: *Mineral Statistics*. Since this is also the source for the table in B.R. Mitchell, *British Historical Statistics* (Cambridge, 1988), pp. 281–3, it should be noted that the sole discrepancy between that table and the one printed here occurs in 1906, when a mistranscription of the output from Scotland (1,451,000 tons in Mitchell; the total in *Mineral Statistics* is as above) has generated an error in the total for Great Britain (10,184,000 tons in Mitchell; 10,109,453 tons in *Mineral Statistics*). It should also be noted that here the figures in the second column have been obtained by summing the figures in the columns to the right (instead of transcribing the total for Great Britain printed in *Mineral Statistics*); in some years this produces a total which varies from the latter by ± 1,000 tons.

Figures entered in the final column ('Others') include the following:

1788: Output from the Weald.
1791: As 1788.
1806: Contemporary estimate of output from furnaces not making returns.
1823: Marshall's estimate of output from furnaces not included in Finch's original survey.
1828: Combined output of minor districts not separately enumerated.
1830: As 1823.
1842: Porter's estimate of the output of the minor districts, based on the proportions of the 1840 list.
1852: Combined output of Derbyshire and Yorkshire.
1864: Combined output of Northamptonshire and Lincolnshire.
1865: As 1864.
1920: Combined output of Shropshire, South Staffs. and North Staffs.

See the appropriate sections of the Introduction and Tables 2.1–2.13 for further discussion.

Table 1.2: Output of Pig Iron, 1788–1920: Regional Percentage Shares

Year	Great Britain 000 tons	South Wales %	Gloucs etc %	Shropshire %	North Wales %	South Staffs %	North Staffs %	Northants %	Lincoln %	Derbyshire %	Yorkshire %	North West %	North East %	Scotland %	Others %
1788	66	19	4	38	1	6	1	-	-	7	8	6	-	11	..
1791	89	20	2	36	1	8	1	-	-	5	8	4	-	15	..
1796	149	27	1	29	1	10	1	-	-	5	11	3	-	12	-
1805	250	29	2	22	1	18	1	-	-	4	10	1	-	9	3
1823	454	40	-	13	-	29	-	-	-	3	6	-	1	5	3
1825	578	39	-	14	2	30	1	-	-	3	6	-	-	5	-
1827	690	39	-	11	3	31	1	-	-	3	6	-	-	5	-
1828	703	40	-	12	4	31	1	-	-	3	5	-	-	5	1
1830	678	41	-	11	-	31	-	-	-	3	4	-	1	6	4
1839	1,249	36	1	6	3	28	1	-	-	3	4	0	1	16	-
1840	1,397	36	1	6	2	29	1	-	-	2	4	-	1	17	-
1841	1,328	35	..	5	1	26	2	-	-	2	4	-	1	22	-
1842	1,098	29	-	7	-	25	2	-	-	3	4	-	-	25	5
1843	1,211	38	1	6	2	25	2	-	-	2	3	-	2	20	-
1847	2,000	35	-	4	1	16	3	-	-	5	3	-	5	27	-
1848	2,094	30	-	5	1	22	3	-	-	4	3	-	5	27	-
1852	2,701	25	-	4	1	27	3	-	-	-	-	-	5	29	6
1854	3,070	24	1	4	1	24	3	-	-	4	2	1	9	26	-
1855	3,218	26	1	4	1	23	3	-	-	4	3	1	9	26	-
1856	3,587	24	1	3	1	22	4	-	-	3	3	1	14	25	-
1857	3,659	27	1	3	1	18	4	..	-	3	3	1	14	25	-

Year	Great Britain 000 tons	South Wales %	Gloucs etc %	Shropshire %	North Wales %	South Staffs %	North Staffs %	Northants %	Lincoln %	Derbyshire %	Yorkshire %	North West %	North East %	Scotland %	Others %
1858	3,456	26	1	3	1	17	4	..	-	4	2	1	14	27	-
1859	3,713	27	1	4	1	13	4	..	-	4	2	2	17	26	-
1860	3,827	25	1	4	1	12	4	..	-	3	3	4	17	24	-
1861	3,712	24	1	4	1	11	5	..	-	3	4	4	17	26	-
1862	3,944	23	1	3	1	10	5	..	-	3	3	6	17	27	-
1863	4,510	19	1	3	1	15	4	..	-	4	2	6	18	26	-
1864	4,768	20	1	3	1	13	5	-	-	4	2	7	20	24	0
1865	4,805	18	1	2	1	14	4	-	-	4	3	7	21	24	1
1866	4,524	21	1	3	1	12	5	..	..	4	3	9	20	22	-
1867	4,761	19	1	3	1	11	4	1	1	3	2	9	24	22	-
1868	4,970	18	2	3	1	11	5	1	1	3	2	9	24	21	-
1869	5,446	15	1	4	1	10	4	1	1	3	2	10	26	21	-
1870	5,964	16	2	2	1	10	5	1	1	3	1	11	27	20	-
1871	6,628	16	2	2	1	11	4	1	0	4	2	13	28	17	-
1872	6,742	15	1	2	1	10	4	1	1	4	2	14	28	16	-
1873	6,566	12	1	2	1	10	4	1	1	5	2	15	30	15	-
1874	5,992	12	1	2	1	8	5	1	1	5	3	15	34	13	-
1875	6,366	9	1	2	1	7	4	1	2	4	4	16	32	16	-
1876	6,556	12	1	2	..	7	3	1	2	5	4	15	32	17	-
1877	6,609	11	1	2	..	6	4	2	2	5	3	18	32	15	-
1878	6,381	12	1	1	..	6	4	2	2	5	3	18	32	14	-
1879	5,996	11	1	1	..	5	4	3	2	5	4	19	29	16	-
1880	7,749	11	..	1	1	5	3	2	3	5	4	20	31	14	-

Year	Great Britain 000 tons	South Wales %	Gloucs etc %	Shrop-shire %	North Wales %	South Staffs %	North Staffs %	North-ants %	Lin-coln %	Derby-shire %	York-shire %	North West %	North East %	Scot-land %	Others %
1881	8,144	11	..	1	1	5	3	2	2	5	3	20	32	14	-
1882	8,588	11	1	1	1	5	3	2	2	5	4	21	32	13	-
1883	8,529	11	1	1	..	5	3	3	3	5	4	20	33	13	-
1884	7,812	11	..	1	..	5	4	3	3	6	3	20	32	13	-
1885	7,416	11	..	1	1	5	4	3	3	6	2	19	33	14	-
1886	7,010	10	..	1	1	4	3	3	3	5	2	20	35	13	-
1887	7,559	10	..	1	1	4	3	3	3	4	2	22	33	12	-
1888	7,999	11	1	1	..	5	3	3	4	5	2	20	33	13	-
1889	8,323	10	..	1	1	4	3	3	4	6	3	20	33	12	-
1890	7,904	10	..	1	1	4	3	3	3	6	3	20	36	9	-
1891	7,406	10	1	1	1	5	3	3	4	6	3	19	36	9	-
1892	6,709	10	1	1	1	5	4	3	4	7	4	18	29	14	-
1893	6,977	10	..	1	..	5	3	2	3	5	2	19	39	11	-
1894	7,427	10	..	1	..	4	3	3	5	5	3	17	40	9	-
1895	7,703	9	-	1	1	4	3	3	5	5	3	15	38	14	-
1896	8,660	9	-	1	1	4	3	3	4	5	3	17	37	13	-
1897	8,797	9	-	..	1	5	3	3	4	6	3	17	36	13	-
1898	8,610	6	-	..	1	5	3	3	4	6	3	19	37	12	-
1899	9,421	10	-	..	1	4	3	3	4	6	3	18	35	12	-
1900	8,960	10	-	..	-	4	3	3	4	6	3	18	35	13	-
1901	7,929	9	-	1	-	4	3	3	4	6	3	18	36	14	-
1902	8,680	9	-	..	-	4	3	3	4	6	3	18	34	15	-
1903	8,935	10	-	1	-	4	3	3	4	6	3	17	35	14	-

Year	Great Britain 000 tons	South Wales %	Gloucs etc %	Shrop- shire %	North Wales %	South Staffs %	North Staffs %	North- ants %	Lin- coln %	Derby- shire %	York- shire %	North West %	North East %	Scot- land %	Others %
1904	8,694	9	-	-	1	5	3	3	4	6	3	14	36	16	-
1905	9,608	9	-	-	1	4	3	3	5	6	3	15	36	14	-
1906	10,180	9	-	-	1	4	3	3	5	6	3	15	36	14	-
1907	10,114	9	-	-	1	5	4	3	5	7	3	14	36	14	-
1908	9,057	9	-	-	1	5	4	3	5	7	3	12	37	14	-
1909	9,532	8	-	-	1	5	4	3	5	7	3	13	37	14	-
1910	10,012	8	-	-	1	5	4	4	5	7	3	13	37	14	-
1911	9,526	8	-	-	1	5	4	4	5	7	3	12	37	15	-
1912	8,752	9	-	-	1	5	4	4	5	7	3	12	37	14	-
1913	10,260	9	-	-	..	5	4	4	5	7	3	13	38	13	-
1914	8,924	8	-	-	1	5	4	4	5	7	3	14	37	13	-
1915	8,724	10	-	-	..	5	4	3	6	6	3	15	34	13	-
1916	8,919	10	-	-	1	5	4	3	6	6	3	16	35	13	-
1917	9,338	8	-	-	1	5	4	3	7	6	3	16	35	12	-
1918	9,107	10	-	-	..	5	4	3	7	6	3	17	33	12	-
1919	7,418	8	-	-	1	4	5	3	7	7	3	16	34	12	-
1920	8,035	9	-	-	-	-	-	4	8	7	3	17	33	11	9

See Table 1.1. for sources. The symbol .. indicates that the share is less than 0.5%.

Table 1.3: Output of Pig Iron, 1877–1918 (BITA, ISATF and NFISM Reports)

Year	Great Britain	South Wales	Gloucs etc	Shrop-shire	North Wales	South Staffs	North Staffs	North-ants	Lin-coln	Derby-shire	York-shire	North West	North East	Scot-land	Others
1877	6,609	-	-	-	-	-	-	-	-	-	-	-	2,138.4	982.0	3,488.6
1878	6,381	741.1	-	81.0	23.1	392.9	231.5	-	-	306.1	215.1	-	2,023.2	902.0	1,465.0
1879	6,010	669.9	40.0	60.8	19.0	325.8	210.4	165.3	131.7	291.5	218.8	1,162.9	1,781.4	932.0	-
1880	7,722	877.4	45.0	90.3	53.0	334.4	239.8	167.5	214.5	357.0	285.8	1,497.3	2,510.9	1,049.0	-
1881	8,377	857.6	50.0	80.3	46.1	395.6	293.7	206.3	187.9	377.3	330.1	1,706.1	2,670.3	1,176.0	-
1882	8,493	883.3	48.0	80.5	48.7	398.4	317.1	192.1	201.6	445.7	279.3	1,783.9	2,688.7	1,126.0	-
1883	8,490	887.3	47.0	71.0	39.4	394.0	285.4	201.0	236.6	457.1	284.8	1,697.0	2,760.7	1,129.0	-
1884	7,529	817.9	20.1	54.2	27.8	317.7	256.1	196.2	224.8	374.7	245.6	1,521.6	2,484.3	988.0	-
1885	7,297	777.6	11.6	46.3	36.8	293.2	253.6	166.7	232.8	489.2	160.4	1,366.6	2,458.9	1,003.6	-
1886	6,871	645.9	5.2	32.5	15.6	278.9	206.6	204.8	226.7	383.7	126.4	1,402.4	2,406.3	935.8	-
1887	7,442	755.8	26.0	51.9	37.8	296.1	249.2	208.6	230.2	320.9	170.4	1,654.5	2,508.2	932.2	-
1888	7,899	883.5	32.5	61.0	27.3	339.6	274.1	235.4	250.0	400.7	167.4	1,584.4	2,615.0	1,027.8	-
1889	8,245	835.0	35.3	52.4	60.2	377.1	283.6	228.1	293.4	495.6	215.5	1,598.9	2,771.2	998.9	-
1890	7,875	822.0	33.5	43.1	64.5	352.8	248.3	174.4	226.3	510.9	248.6	1,506.4	2,846.1	798.3	-
1891	-	-	-	-	-	-	-	-	-	-	-	-	-	-	-
1892	6,617	683.3	34.6	50.1	45.6	346.7	238.8	162.0	212.1	518.0	244.7	1,166.2	1,937.5	977.2	-
1893	6,830	679.6	27.5	38.4	30.5	329.4	190.4	142.3	194.3	359.4	155.6	1,174.4	2,724.2	783.9	-
1894	7,365	708.9	68.6	19.0	29.8	315.9	195.8	212.4	287.4	437.9	202.3	1,267.8	2,963.4	655.6	-
1895	7,896	704.1	40.7	50.0	41.3	353.3	196.4	265.3	299.1	495.2	216.1	1,220.9	2,916.4	1,096.9	-
1896	8,563	806.9	23.8	46.7	49.2	326.7	215.8	232.4	299.2	503.7	282.7	1,426.2	3,170.0	1,180.0	-
1897	8,789	763.3	21.5	38.6	53.3	360.2	239.3	250.0	306.6	531.9	299.2	1,437.9	3,300.0	1,187.6	-

Year	Great Britain	South Wales	Gloucs etc	Shrop-shire	North Wales	South Staffs	North Staffs	North-ants	Lin-coln	Derby-shire	York-shire	North West	North East	Scot-land	Others
1898	8,681	507.3	22.3	42.1	58.9	375.7	241.3	280.6	319.0	594.4	297.5	1,573.6	3,178.1	1,190.3	-
1899	9,305	943.0	-	43.7	88.6	394.4	304.5	274.6	332.5	651.8	305.5	1,648.5	3,151.5	1,166.8	-
1900	8,909	858.5	-	45.3	77.7	255.9	279.2	270.6	350.6	653.0	276.4	1,617.0	3,070.5	1,153.9	-
1901	7,852	673.4	-	40.7	36.9	338.6	190.6	225.7	249.9	535.8	246.8	1,385.9	2,813.6	1,114.0	-
1902	8,518	756.3	-	40.9	61.9	364.7	229.0	246.1	309.7	622.5	258.8	1,470.5	2,862.1	1,295.1	-
1903	8,811	785.7	-	46.8	71.7	400.6	230.7	240.4	318.8	598.8	277.2	1,474.5	3,078.1	1,288.1	-
1904	8,562	779.6	-	47.6	74.5	373.2	246.0	223.9	321.5	603.3	263.4	1,074.2	3,215.5	1,339.7	-
1905	9,593	886.7	-	47.8	84.8	415.8	258.7	231.2	366.7	641.3	289.7	1,453.4	3,538.4	1,378.4	-
1915	8,435	829.5	-	-	-	434.3	345.0	-	554.0	-	284.7	1,197.4	2,892.6	1,104.4	792.7
1916	9,048	855.5	-	-	-	414.8	339.4	-	551.8	-	293.3	1,485.4	3,097.3	1,144.8	865.6
1917	9,420	793.4	-	-	-	444.3	368.1	-	565.6	-	308.2	1,570.6	3,250.5	1,211.4	908.2
1918	9,072	852.5	-	-	-	414.4	371.6	-	563.3	-	284.1	1,551.2	3,056.9	1,053.0	925.4

Note: All figures are in thousands of tons.

Sources: 1877–1905: British Iron Trade Association Annual Reports. In 1877 precise output figures were given only for Great Britain, Scotland and Cleveland (including Durham), with round-figure estimates for most, but not all, the other districts. Only the Cleveland and Scotland district totals are printed here, with the remainder of the total given for Great Britain placed under 'Others'. In 1878 figures apparently based on detailed enquiries were given for most, but not all, the other districts, which together sum to less than the total for Great Britain, so that once again a residual has been printed in the final column. We have failed to locate a copy of a BITA Report containing figures for 1891.

For some years, slightly revised figures were printed in the report for the year following that in which they first appeared and these later totals have been used here.

From 1899 the output from Gloucestershire, Wiltshire and Somerset was combined with that from North Wales and a single total is printed here under the latter heading.

'Derbyshire' here includes Nottinghamshire and Leicestershire.

1915–1918: Iron, Steel & Allied Trades Federation and National Federation of Iron & Steel Manufacturers Annual Reports. For these years a single figure (printed here under 'Others') was published for the Midland districts (Derbyshire, Leicestershire, Northamptonshire and Nottinghamshire); any output from Wiltshire was included with South Staffs. and Worcestershire; and output from Shropshire was included with North Staffs.

Table 1.4: Output of Pig Iron, 1877–1905: Regional Percentage Shares (BITA etc Reports)

Year	Great Britain (tons)	South Wales %	Gloucs etc %	Shrop-shire %	North Wales %	South Staffs %	North Staffs %	North-ants %	Lin-coln %	Derby-shire %	York-shire %	North West %	North East %	Scot-land %	Others %
1877	6,609	-	-	-	-	-	-	-	-	-	-	-	32.4	14.9	52.8
1878	6,381	11.6	-	1.3	0.4	6.2	3.6	-	-	4.8	3.4	-	31.7	14.1	23.0
1879	6,010	11.2	0.7	1.0	0.3	5.4	3.5	2.8	2.2	4.9	3.6	19.4	29.6	15.5	-
1880	7,722	11.4	0.6	1.2	0.7	4.3	3.1	2.2	2.8	4.6	3.7	19.4	32.5	13.6	-
1881	8,377	9.9	1.0	1.0	1.0	5.0	4.0	2.0	2.0	5.0	4.0	19.8	31.7	13.9	-
1882	18,493	10.0	1.0	1.0	1.0	5.0	4.0	2.0	2.0	5.0	3.0	21.0	32.0	13.0	-
1883	8,490	10.1	1.0	1.0	..	5.1	3.0	2.0	3.0	5.1	3.0	20.2	33.3	13.1	-
1884	7,529	11.1	..	1.0	..	4.0	3.0	3.0	3.0	5.1	3.0	20.2	33.3	13.1	-
1885	7,297	10.9	..	1.0	1.0	4.0	3.0	2.0	3.0	6.9	2.0	18.8	33.7	13.9	-
1886	6,871	9.1	..	..	..	4.0	3.0	3.0	3.0	6.1	2.0	20.2	35.4	14.1	-
1887	7,442	10.0	..	1.0	1.0	4.0	3.0	3.0	3.0	4.0	2.0	22.0	34.0	13.0	-
1888	7,899	11.2	..	1.0	..	4.1	3.1	3.1	3.1	5.1	2.0	20.4	33.7	13.3	-
1889	8,245	9.9	..	1.0	1.0	5.0	3.0	3.0	4.0	5.9	3.0	18.8	33.7	11.9	-
1890	7,875	10.2	..	1.0	1.0	4.1	3.1	2.0	3.1	6.1	3.1	19.4	36.7	10.2	-
1891	-	-	-	-	-	-	-	-	-	-	-	-	-	-	-
1892	6,617	9.9	1.0	1.0	1.0	5.0	4.0	2.0	3.0	7.9	4.0	17.8	28.7	14.9	-
1893	6,830	10.1	..	1.0	..	5.1	3.0	2.0	3.0	5.1	2.0	17.2	40.4	11.1	-
1894	7,365	10.0	1.0	..	..	4.0	3.0	3.0	4.0	6.0	3.0	17.0	40.0	9.0	-
1895	7,896	9.0	1.0	1.0	1.0	4.0	2.0	3.0	4.0	6.0	3.0	15.0	37.0	14.0	-
1896	8,563	8.9	..	1.0	1.0	4.0	3.0	3.0	3.0	5.9	3.0	16.8	36.6	13.9	-
1897	8,789	9.0	..	..	1.0	4.0	3.0	3.0	3.0	6.0	3.0	16.0	38.0	14.0	-

Year	Great Britain (tons)	South Wales %	Gloucs etc %	Shrop-shire %	North Wales %	South Staffs %	North Staffs %	North-ants %	Lin-coln %	Derby-shire %	York-shire %	North West %	North East %	Scot-land %	Others %
1898	8,681	6.0	..	..	1.0	4.0	3.0	3.0	4.0	7.0	3.0	18.0	37.0	14.0	-
1899	9,305	10.0	-	..	1.0	4.0	3.0	3.0	4.0	7.0	3.0	18.0	34.0	13.0	-
1900	8,909	10.0	-	1.0	1.0	3.0	3.0	3.0	4.0	7.0	3.0	18.0	34.0	13.0	-
1901	7,852	9.0	-	1.0	..	4.0	2.0	3.0	3.0	7.0	3.0	18.0	36.0	14.0	-
1902	8,518	9.0	-	..	1.0	4.0	3.0	3.0	4.0	7.0	3.0	17.0	34.0	15.0	-
1903	8,811	8.7	-	1.0	1.0	4.9	2.9	2.9	3.9	6.8	2.9	16.5	34.0	14.6	-
1904	8,562	8.8	-	1.0	1.0	3.9	2.9	2.9	3.9	6.9	2.9	12.8	37.3	15.7	-
1905	9,593	9.0	-	1.0	1.0	4.0	3.0	2.0	4.0	7.0	3.0	15.0	37.0	14.0	-
1915	8,435	9.8	-	-	-	5.1	4.1	-	6.6	-	3.4	14.2	34.3	13.1	9.4
1916	9,048	9.5	-	-	-	4.6	3.8	-	6.1	-	3.2	16.4	34.2	12.7	9.6
1917	9,420	8.4	-	-	-	4.7	3.9	-	6.0	-	3.3	16.7	34.5	12.9	9.6
1918	9,072	9.4	-	-	-	4.6	4.1	-	6.2	-	3.1	17.1	33.7	11.6	10.2

See Table 1.3 for sources and methods. The symbol .. indicates that the share is less than 0.05%.

Table 2.1: South Wales

Year	No of Works	Furnaces Built	Furnaces in Blast	% in Blast	Total Annual Output (Tons)	Annual Output per Works (Tons)	Annual Output per Furnace (Tons)
1788	-	-	15	-	12,500	-	833
1791	-	-	19	-	17,534	-	923
1794	20	22	-	-	-	-	-
1796	19	26	25	96	34,391	1,810	1,376
1805	26	46	35	76	72,911	2,804	2,083
1810	22	52	42	81	-	-	-
1823	23	72	-	-	182,325	7,927	-
1825	36	108	80	74	223,520	6,209	2,794
1827		-	90	-	272,000	-	3,022
1828		100	89	89	279,512	-	3,141
1830	34	113	-	-	277,643	8,166	-
1839	41	127	122	96	453,880	11,070	3,720
1840	-	163	132	81	505,000	-	3,826
1841	42	162	116	72	468,000	11,143	4,034
1843	42	168	121	72	457,350	10,889	3,780
1847	46	193	150	78	706,680	15,363	4,711
1848	-	196	139	71	631,280	-	4,542
1849	48	203	148	73	-	-	-
1852	-	197	147	75	666,000	-	4,531
1854	48	169	121	72	750,000	15,625	6,198
1855	44	187	148	79	840,000	19,091	5,676
1856	48	199	162	81	877,150	18,274	5,415
1857	49	207	164	79	970,727	19,811	5,919
1858	49	199	148	74	886,478	18,091	5,990
1859	49	203	147	72	985,290	20,108	6,703
1860	49	214	139	65	969,025	19,776	6,971
1861	45	200	137	69	886,300	19,696	6,469
1862	45	197	125	63	893,309	19,851	7,146
1863	45	197	123	62	847,753	18,839	6,892
1864	44	197	133	68	937,621	21,310	7,050
1865	40	195	128	66	845,035	21,126	6,602
1866	39	193	132	68	927,454	23,781	7,026
1867	32	187	115	62	886,234	27,695	7,706
1868	24	184	108	59	894,255	37,261	8,280
1869	29	178	112	63	800,972	27,620	7,152

Year	No of Works	Furnaces Built	Furnaces in Blast	% in Blast	Total Annual Output (Tons)	Annual Output per Works (Tons)	Annual Output per Furnace (Tons)
1870	24	174	114	66	979,193	40,800	8,589
1871	29	167	112	67	1,045,916	36,066	9,339
1872	31	154	115	75	1,002,623	32,343	8,718
1873	29	148	101	68	817,789	28,200	8,097
1874	30	139	88	63	714,724	23,824	8,122
1875	29	153	79	52	541,809	18,683	6,858
1876	21	134	69	51	756,121	36,006	10,958
1877	19	150	60	40	710,958	37,419	11,849
1878	18	145	57	39	741,136	41,174	13,002
1879	18	143	54	38	669,858	37,214	12,405
1880	18	141	69	49	889,738	49,430	12,895
1881	21	141	67	48	910,965	43,379	13,596
1882	18	139	62	45	934,434	51,913	15,072
1883	19	127	60	47	906,263	47,698	15,104
1884	19	134	49	37	851,391	44,810	17,375
1885	20	132	41	31	792,784	39,639	19,336
1886	16	126	31	25	666,596	41,662	21,503
1887	13	119	33	28	767,448	59,034	23,256
1888	15	120	39	33	870,940	58,063	22,332
1889	15	84	36	43	826,392	55,093	22,955
1890	15	84	35	42	824,722	54,981	23,563
1891	14	88	31	35	760,566	54,326	24,534
1892	11	87	25	29	684,007	62,182	27,360
1893	10	79	23	29	680,445	68,045	29,585
1894	9	73	22	30	708,914	78,768	32,223
1895	10	75	21	28	704,676	70,468	33,556
1896	10	73	25	34	780,421	78,042	31,217
1897	10	74	24	32	804,816	80,482	33,534
1898	17	72	17	24	495,315	29,136	29,136
1899	16	69	28	41	929,415	58,088	33,193
1900	16	70	29	41	[a]908,114	56,757	31,314
1901	16	66	18	27	700,052	43,753	38,892
1902	9	59	19	32	800,262	88,918	42,119
1903	9	55	19	35	875,584	97,287	46,083

[a] Between 1900 and 1903 the output of pig in Flintshire was included in the total for Monmouthshire and that for Denbighshire in Glamorgan. The South Wales total printed above is therefore inflated by about 60,000 tons p.a., the probable output of North Wales in these years.

Year	No of Works	Furnaces Built	Furnaces in Blast	% in Blast	Total Annual Output (Tons)	Annual Output per Works (Tons)	Annual Output per Furnace (Tons)
1904	10	56	19	34	804,850	80,485	42,361
1905	9	56	19	34	912,217	101,357	48,011
1906	9	43	21	49	900,302	100,034	42,872
1907	10	35	20	57	928,653	92,865	46,433
1908	9	34	14	41	802,746	89,194	57,339
1909	8	33	12	36	742,911	92,864	61,909
1910	9	33	15	45	787,812	87,535	52,521
1911	9	33	12	36	718,004	79,778	59,834
1912	9	31	13	42	755,869	83,985	58,144
1913	11	31	12	39	889,210	80,837	74,101
1914	8	31	10	32	753,367	94,171	75,337
1915	8	29	13	45	829,002	103,625	63,769
1916	8	29	14	48	855,525	106,941	61,109
1917	8	26	15	58	778,572	97,322	51,905
1918	9	26	16	62	880,651	97,850	55,041
1919	9	27	10	37	598,782	66,531	59,878
1920	8	29	11	38	692,019	86,502	62,911

Table 2.2: Gloucestershire, Somerset and Wiltshire[a]

Year	No of Works	Furnaces Built	Furnaces in Blast	% in Blast	Total Annual Output (Tons)	Annual Output per Works (Tons)	Annual Output per Furnace (Tons)
1788	-	-	4	-	2,600	-	650
1791	-	-	4	-	2,000	-	500
1794	5	5	-	-	-	-	-
1796	6	6	4	67	1,397	233	349
1805	5	6	6	100	4,073	815	679
1810	5	7	5	71	-	-	-
1825	5	5	-	-	-	-	-

[a] The pre-1854 returns for Gloucestershire (the only one of the three counties included in this table for this period) are defective in several respects and therefore difficult to summarise. There are no figures for 1823–30, 1828 or 1847–48, and for 1843 and 1849 only Cinderford is listed. In 1805 and 1810 the furnaces at Cinderford are said to comprise two separate businesses, although the works has been counted as one here. In 1825 there was no explicit statement as to whether any of the furnaces were in blast or not. Soudley was not included in *Mineral Statistics* until 1854 and has therefore been omitted from this table in earlier years, although it appears in the 1841 list.

Year	No of Works	Furnaces Built	Furnaces in Blast	% in Blast	Total Annual Output (Tons)	Annual Output per Works (Tons)	Annual Output per Furnace (Tons)
1839	4	8	5	63	18,200	4,550	3,640
1840	-	4	4	100	15,500	-	3,875
1841	4	8	3	38	6,240	1,560	2,080
1843	1	3	2	67	8,000	8,000	4,000
1849	1	-	3	-	-	-	-
1854	4	7	5	71	21,990	5,498	4,398
1855	4	7	4	57	19,500	4,875	4,875
1856	5	10	5	50	24,132	4,826	4,826
1857	7	13	6	46	24,182	3,455	4,030
1858	8	15	6	40	25,620	3,203	4,270
1859	8	15	9	60	42,250	5,281	4,694
1860	8	15	9	60	50,293	6,287	5,588
1861	8	15	6	40	40,493	5,062	6,749
1862	8	16	7	44	51,968	6,496	7,424
1863	8	16	10	63	64,001	8,000	6,400
1864	7	14	10	71	65,312	9,330	6,531
1865	7	14	10	71	65,471	9,353	6,547
1866	5	15	10	67	59,817	11,963	5,982
1867	5	16	6	38	71,186	14,237	11,864
1868	5	16	9	56	75,847	15,169	8,427
1869	6	17	11	65	81,306	13,551	7,391
1870	6	17	12	71	93,601	15,600	7,800
1871	6	18	13	72	99,997	16,666	7,692
1872	6	18	12	67	98,081	16,347	8,173
1873	6	18	12	67	92,993	15,499	7,749
1874	6	19	9	47	78,254	13,042	8,695
1875	6	16	9	56	59,819	9,970	6,647
1876	5	19	8	42	57,587	11,517	7,198
1877	6	18	7	39	50,752	8,459	7,250
1878	2	18	4	22	42,351	21,176	10,588
1879	2	15	4	27	40,000	20,000	10,000
1880	2	15	4	27	37,351	18,676	9,338
1881	2	14	3	21	30,906	15,453	10,302
1882	3	13	4	31	52,991	17,664	13,248
1883	4	13	4	31	46,268	11,567	11,567
1884	2	16	2	13	23,987	11,994	11,994
1885	2	16	2	13	24,335	12,168	12,168

Year	No of Works	Furnaces Built	Furnaces in Blast	% in Blast	Total Annual Output (Tons)	Annual Output per Works (Tons)	Annual Output per Furnace (Tons)
1886	3	15	3	20	32,302	10,767	10,767
1887	3	15	2	13	28,500	9,500	14,250
1888	2	15	2	13	40,094	20,047	20,047
1889	2	9	2	22	38,109	19,055	19,055
1890	2	4	2	50	39,104	19,552	19,552
1891	2	6	2	33	37,944	18,972	18,972
1892	2	6	2	33	34,643	17,322	17,322
1893	2	6	2	33	34,373	17,187	17,187
1894	2	5	1	20	25,459	12,730	25,459
1895	1	2	1	50	[a]-	-	-
1896	1	2	1	50	-	-	-
1897	1	1	1	100	-	-	-
1898	1	1	1	100	-	-	-
1899	1	2	1	50	-	-	-
1900	1	2	1	50	-	-	-
1901	1	2	0	-	-	-	-
1902	0	2	0	-	-	-	-
1903	1	2	0	-	-	-	-
1904	1	2	1	50	-	-	-
1905	1	2	1	50	-	-	-
1906	1	2	1	50	-	-	-
1907	1	2	1	50	-	-	-
1908	1	2	1	50	-	-	-
1909	0	2	0	-	-	-	-
1910	0	2	0	-	-	-	-
1911	0	2	0	-	-	-	-
1912	0	2	0	-	-	-	-
1913	0	2	0	-	-	-	-
1914	0	2	0	-	-	-	-
1915	0	2	0	-	-	-	-
1916	0	2	0	-	-	-	-
1917	0	2	0	-	-	-	-
1918	0	2	0	-	-	-	-
1919	0	2	0	-	-	-	-
1920	0	2	0	-	-	-	-

[a] From 1895 any output from Westbury (the only West of England ironworks still in use) was included in the total published for Worcestershire, which has here been combined with the output for South Staffordshire.

Table 2.3: Shropshire

Year	No of Works	Furnaces Built	Furnaces in Blast	% in Blast	Total Annual Output (Tons)	Annual Output per Works (Tons)	Annual Output per Furnace (Tons)
1788	-	-	24	-	24,900	-	1,038
1791	-	-	25	-	31,896	-	1,276
1794	16	25	-	-	-	-	-
1796	16	30	25	83	33,701	2,106	1,348
1805	19	42	30	71	54,967	2,893	1,832
1810	19	45	35	78	-	-	-
1823	16	38	-	-	57,923	3,620	-
1825	21	47	33	70	81,820	3,896	2,479
1827	-	-	31	-	78,000	-	2,516
1828	-	48	31	65	81,224	-	2,620
1830	20	48	-	-	73,418	3,671	-
1839	14	34	29	85	80,940	5,781	2,791
1840	-	31	24	77	82,750	-	3,448
1841	15	36	24	67	70,460	4,697	2,936
1843	15	36	27	75	76,200	5,080	2,822
1847	15	34	28	82	88,400	5,893	3,157
1848	-	35	31	89	111,000	-	3,581
1849	14	-	31	-	-	-	-
1852	-	40	27	68	120,000	-	4,444
1854	13	34	28	82	124,800	9,600	4,457
1855	13	34	26	76	121,680	9,360	4,680
1856	14	35	27	77	109,722	7,837	4,064
1857	13	31	26	84	117,141	9,011	4,505
1858	13	32	25	78	101,016	7,770	4,041
1859	14	37	30	81	149,480	10,677	4,983
1860	13	32	26	81	145,200	11,169	5,585
1861	13	31	23	74	140,791	10,830	6,121
1862	13	31	23	74	125,981	9,691	5,477
1863	12	31	22	71	135,557	11,296	6,162
1864	12	30	23	77	130,666	10,889	5,681
1865	11	29	23	79	117,343	10,668	5,102
1866	11	29	23	79	121,161	11,015	5,268
1867	11	29	22	76	123,604	11,237	5,618
1868	8	29	24	83	145,154	18,144	6,048
1869	10	29	23	79	197,443	19,744	8,584

Year	No of Works	Furnaces Built	Furnaces in Blast	% in Blast	Total Annual Output (Tons)	Annual Output per Works (Tons)	Annual Output per Furnace (Tons)
1870	8	29	22	76	112,300	14,038	5,105
1871	10	25	19	76	129,467	12,947	6,814
1872	11	29	22	76	133,046	12,095	6,048
1873	11	29	21	72	135,149	12,286	6,436
1874	11	28	20	71	126,055	11,460	6,303
1875	11	26	20	77	120,996	11,000	6,050
1876	10	24	16	67	106,711	10,671	6,669
1877	8	23	14	61	102,180	12,773	7,299
1878	6	28	11	39	80,965	13,494	7,360
1879	4	23	7	30	60,790	15,198	8,684
1880	5	24	12	50	88,338	17,668	7,362
1881	5	24	10	42	79,412	15,882	7,941
1882	5	24	10	42	80,475	16,095	8,048
1883	5	22	9	41	77,716	15,543	8,635
1884	4	22	7	32	53,224	13,306	7,603
1885	4	21	6	29	44,732	11,183	7,455
1886	4	17	6	35	40,938	10,235	6,823
1887	4	15	6	40	52,047	13,012	8,675
1888	4	16	7	44	61,005	15,251	8,715
1889	3	16	6	38	52,438	17,479	8,740
1890	3	11	6	55	43,084	14,361	7,181
1891	3	10	6	60	47,781	15,927	7,964
1892	3	10	6	60	49,955	16,652	8,326
1893	3	10	5	50	39,504	13,168	7,901
1894	3	10	4	40	39,832	13,277	9,958
1895	3	10	6	60	49,010	16,337	8,168
1896	3	8	6	75	46,724	15,575	7,787
1897	3	9	7	78	38,507	12,836	5,501
1898	3	7	5	71	42,102	14,034	8,420
1899	3	9	4	44	40,597	13,532	10,149
1900	3	9	4	44	39,177	13,059	9,794
1901	3	9	5	56	40,660	13,553	8,132
1902	3	9	4	44	40,870	13,623	10,218
1903	3	9	4	44	46,778	15,593	11,695
1904	2	6	3	50	[a]-	-	-

[a] From 1904 a single figure was published in *Mineral Statistics* for the output of pig in Shropshire and North Staffordshire, which has been printed here under the latter heading.

Year	No of Works	Furnaces Built	Furnaces in Blast	% in Blast	Total Annual Output (Tons)	Annual Output per Works (Tons)	Annual Output per Furnace (Tons)
1905	2	6	3	50	-	-	-
1906	2	6	3	50	-	-	-
1907	2	6	3	50	-	-	-
1908	2	6	3	50	-	-	-
1909	2	6	3	50	-	-	-
1910	2	6	3	50	-	-	-
1911	2	6	3	50	-	-	-
1912	2	6	2	33	-	-	-
1913	2	6	2	33	-	-	-
1914	1	3	1	33	-	-	-
1915	1	3	2	67	-	-	-
1916	1	3	2	67	-	-	-
1917	1	3	2	67	-	-	-
1918	1	3	2	67	-	-	-
1919	1	3	2	67	-	-	-
1920	1	3	2	67	-	-	-

Table 2.4: North Wales

Year	No of Works	Furnaces Built	Furnaces in Blast	% in Blast	Total Annual Output (Tons)	Annual Output per Works (Tons)	Annual Output per Furnace (Tons)
1788	-	-	1	-	400	-	400
1791	-	-	1	-	780	-	780
1794	3	3	-	-	-	-	-
1796	3	3	2	67	1,294	431	647
1805	3	4	3	75	2,075	692	692
1810	3	4	3	75	-	-	-
1825	9	14	8	57	13,100	1,456	1,638
1827	-	-	12	-	24,000	-	2,000
1828	-	-	-	-	25,168	-	-
1839	11	20	13	65	33,800	3,073	2,600
1840	-	15	12	80	26,500	-	2,208
1841	12	22	6	27	18,720	1,560	3,120
1843	10	20	8	40	19,750	1,975	2,469
1847	7	11	4	36	16,120	2,303	4,030

Year	No of Works	Furnaces Built	Furnaces in Blast	% in Blast	Total Annual Output (Tons)	Annual Output per Works (Tons)	Annual Output per Furnace (Tons)
1848	-	14	5	36	22,256	-	4,451
1849	7	-	8	-	-	-	-
1852	-	13	6	46	30,000	-	5,000
1854	7	11	9	82	32,900	4,700	3,656
1855	6	11	8	73	31,420	5,237	3,928
1856	6	10	9	90	47,682	7,947	5,298
1857	8	14	6	43	37,049	4,631	6,175
1858	8	13	6	46	28,150	3,519	4,692
1859	8	13	6	46	26,980	3,373	4,497
1860	8	14	8	57	49,360	6,170	6,170
1861	8	12	5	42	46,658	5,832	9,332
1862	8	13	5	38	31,719	3,965	6,344
1863	8	13	7	54	51,076	6,385	7,297
1864	9	14	8	57	51,108	5,679	6,389
1865	9	14	7	50	51,874	5,764	7,411
1866	4	10	5	50	25,515	6,379	5,103
1867	3	9	5	56	32,843	10,948	6,569
1868	3	9	4	44	37,046	12,349	9,262
1869	3	8	6	75	38,530	12,843	6,422
1870	3	8	6	75	42,695	14,232	7,116
1871	3	8	5	63	41,893	13,964	8,379
1872	5	11	8	73	54,692	10,938	6,837
1873	5	13	8	62	67,463	13,493	8,433
1874	4	11	8	73	51,868	12,967	6,484
1875	4	11	7	64	55,099	13,775	7,871
1876	3	11	4	36	32,723	10,908	8,181
1877	3	11	4	36	26,715	8,905	6,679
1878	2	11	3	27	23,091	11,546	7,697
1879	2	11	3	27	18,953	9,477	6,318
1880	3	10	7	70	57,812	19,271	8,259
1881	4	11	7	64	46,833	11,708	6,690
1882	4	10	6	60	53,138	13,285	8,856
1883	3	10	5	50	39,377	13,126	7,875
1884	2	10	4	40	34,486	17,243	8,622
1885	3	10	4	40	40,261	13,420	10,065
1886	3	10	5	50	35,318	11,773	7,064
1887	3	10	5	50	37,910	12,637	7,582

Year	No of Works	Furnaces Built	Furnaces in Blast	% in Blast	Total Annual Output (Tons)	Annual Output per Works (Tons)	Annual Output per Furnace (Tons)
1888	3	10	4	40	33,296	11,099	8,324
1889	3	10	6	60	68,001	22,667	11,334
1890	3	10	5	50	64,539	21,513	12,908
1891	3	8	4	50	53,677	17,892	13,419
1892	2	8	4	50	45,573	22,787	11,393
1893	2	7	3	43	30,527	15,264	10,176
1894	2	7	2	29	29,775	14,888	14,888
1895	2	7	3	43	41,269	20,635	13,756
1896	2	7	2	29	49,206	24,603	24,603
1897	2	6	3	50	53,290	26,645	17,763
1898	3	6	3	50	58,811	19,604	19,604
1899	3	6	3	50	66,586	22,195	22,195
1900	3	5	4	80	[a]-	-	-
1901	3	6	3	50		-	-	-
1902	3	5	3	60		-	-	-
1903	2	5	3	60		-	-	-
1904	2	3	2	67	55,477	27,739	27,739
1905	2	3	3	100	66,270	33,135	22,090
1906	2	3	3	100	73,703	36,852	24,568
1907	2	3	3	100	62,825	31,413	20,942
1908	2	4	2	50	63,621	31,811	31,811
1909	2	4	3	75	77,478	38,739	25,826
1910	2	4	3	75	75,047	37,524	25,016
1911	2	4	3	75	74,957	37,479	24,986
1912	2	3	3	100	[b]44,214	22,107	14,738
1913	2	3	3	100	50,880	25,440	16,960
1914	2	5	3	60	46,133	23,067	15,378
1915	2	5	3	60	33,523	16,762	11,174
1916	2	4	3	75	45,346	22,673	15,115
1917	2	4	3	75	48,992	24,496	16,331
1918	2	4	2	50	44,177	22,089	22,089
1919	2	4	2	50	41,661	20,831	20,831
1920	2	4	2	50	[c]-	-	-

[a] Between 1900 and 1903 the output of pig from Flintshire was combined with that for Monmouthshire and that from Denbighshire with Glamorgan. The output of North Wales in these years is therefore subsumed here within the total printed for South Wales.

[b] Between 1912 and 1919 the output printed here relates to Denbighshire only; output from Flintshire was combined in *Mineral Statistics* with that for Lancashire and is therefore included here in the figure printed for North West England.

[c] Output included with that for Lancashire in the original returns; included here under North West England.

Table 2.5: South Staffordshire and Worcestershire

Year	No of Works	Furnaces Built	Furnaces in Blast	% in Blast	Total Annual Output (Tons)	Annual Output per Works (Tons)	Annual Output per Furnace (Tons)
1788[a]	-	-	5	-	3,750	-	750
1791	-	-	14	-	7,280	-	520
1794	9	15	-	-	-	-	-
1796	10	16	14	88	13,211	1,321	944
1805	22	39	29	74	45,896	2,086	1,583
1810	26	50	47	94	-	-	-
1823	43	84	-	-	133,590	3,107	-
1825	52	103	78	76	172,204	3,312	2,208
1827	-	-	-	-	[b]211,250	-	-
1828	-	-	-	-	214,664	-	-
1830	56	123	-	-	212,604	3,797	-
1839	53	126	106	84	346,213	6,532	3,266
1840	-	135	116	86	407,150	-	3,510
1841	55	133	85	64	347,100	6,311	4,084
1843	52	129	76	59	300,250	5,774	3,951
1847	57	139	79	57	320,320	5,620	4,055
1848	-	137	112	82	465,920	-	4,160
1849	64	148	88	59	-	-	-
1852	64	159	127	80	[c]725,000	11,328	5,709
1854	65	175	145	83	743,600	11,440	5,128
1855	65	178	146	82	754,000	11,600	5,164
1856	64	171	147	86	777,171	12,143	5,287
1857	66	180	153	85	657,295	9,959	4,296
1858	64	186	147	79	597,809	9,341	4,067
1859	71	184	124	67	[d]473,300	6,666	3,817
1860	72	181	109	60	469,500	6,521	4,307
1861	68	182	114	63	395,650	5,818	3,471
1862	71	192	107	56	410,220	5,778	3,834

[a] In 1788 and 1791 figures were returned for Staffordshire as a whole; they have been split here on the assumption that the only North Staffs. furnace included in either year was Apedale.

[b] In 1827 and 1828 figures were given for Staffordshire as a whole; the output figures have been split here between North and South Staffordshire using the proportions of the 1825 list (i.e. 2.2 : 97.8); no attempt has been made to divide the furnace-numbers.

[c] The detailed list of South Staffs. furnaces is 1852 is accompanied by an output estimate of 650,000 tons, but in the summary table covering the whole country published elsewhere a figure of 725,000 tons is given for South Staffs, and this has been used here.

[d] In 1859 the output of South Staffs. is given as 475,300 tons in the detailed table of furnaces, but 473,300 tons in the summary list from which the national total has been calculated. The discrepancy is probably no more than a typographical error and an arbitrary decision has been made to use the lower total, since otherwise the accepted national figure for 1859 would be affected.

Year	No of Works	Furnaces Built	Furnaces in Blast	% in Blast	Total Annual Output (Tons)	Annual Output per Works (Tons)	Annual Output per Furnace (Tons)
1863	73	200	110	55	691,157	9,468	6,283
1864	68	172	105	61	628,793	9,247	5,989
1865	64	172	114	66	692,627	10,822	6,076
1866	54	167	112	67	532,635	9,864	4,756
1867	49	177	92	52	515,638	10,523	5,605
1868	41	172	89	52	532,234	12,981	5,980
1869	48	164	95	58	569,562	11,866	5,995
1870	56	171	114	67	588,540	10,510	5,163
1871	53	163	108	66	725,716	13,693	6,720
1872	58	145	108	74	673,470	11,612	6,236
1873	55	142	99	70	673,397	12,244	6,802
1874	50	154	81	53	452,400	9,048	5,585
1875	53	155	76	49	470,540	8,878	6,191
1876	41	147	65	44	465,946	11,365	7,168
1877	34	146	57	39	428,276	12,596	7,514
1878	33	147	55	37	392,949	11,908	7,145
1879	29	140	44	31	325,780	11,234	7,404
1880	30	137	46	34	384,556	12,819	8,360
1881	31	135	46	34	374,321	12,075	8,137
1882	29	133	48	36	398,443	13,739	8,301
1883	29	123	46	37	429,723	14,818	9,342
1884	25	119	37	31	356,873	14,275	9,645
1885	24	116	34	29	344,079	14,337	10,120
1886	21	107	29	27	294,468	14,022	10,154
1887	20	104	31	30	293,400	14,670	9,465
1888	19	95	35	37	366,351	19,282	10,467
1889	18	87	35	40	372,677	20,704	10,648
1890	18	85	31	36	326,991	18,166	10,548
1891	17	83	30	36	350,062	20,592	11,669
1892	17	65	31	48	337,538	19,855	10,888
1893	17	66	26	39	330,177	19,422	12,699
1894	17	65	23	35	332,665	19,569	14,464
1895	15	60	21	35	a338,335	22,556	16,111
1896	15	57	22	39	389,294	25,953	17,695
1897	16	56	25	45	400,019	25,001	16,001

a From 1895 the output for Worcestershire published in *Mineral Statistics* includes any pig produced at Westbury (Wilts.), the only surviving West of England ironworks, and this figure is thus also included in those printed here for the Black Country.

Year	No of Works	Furnaces Built	Furnaces in Blast	% in Blast	Total Annual Output (Tons)	Annual Output per Works (Tons)	Annual Output per Furnace (Tons)
1898	22	57	24	42	405,541	18,434	16,898
1899	20	50	22	44	414,830	20,742	18,856
1900	19	47	22	47	398,499	20,974	18,114
1901	18	43	17	40	340,859	18,937	20,051
1902	13	40	18	45	380,193	29,246	21,122
1903	13	39	19	49	397,379	30,568	20,915
1904	13	39	17	44	393,742	30,288	23,161
1905	13	39	18	46	430,441	33,111	23,913
1906	13	38	20	53	452,000	34,769	22,600
1907	13	38	20	53	469,778	36,137	23,489
1908	14	38	19	50	449,076	32,077	23,636
1909	14	38	21	55	482,405	34,458	22,972
1910	14	40	20	50	495,407	35,386	24,770
1911	13	35	20	57	473,488	36,422	23,674
1912	12	35	20	57	442,153	36,846	22,108
1913	13	31	20	65	467,462	35,959	23,373
1914	12	31	17	55	419,896	34,991	24,700
1915	13	31	18	58	425,580	32,737	23,643
1916	13	30	18	60	410,302	31,562	22,795
1917	12	32	17	53	433,475	36,123	25,499
1918	12	32	18	56	413,336	34,445	22,963
1919	12	32	14	44	318,685	26,557	22,763
1920	12	32	16	50	[a] -	-	-

Table 2.6: North Staffordshire

Year	No of Works	Furnaces Built	Furnaces in Blast	% in Blast	Total Annual Output (Tons)	Annual Output per Works (Tons)	Annual Output per Furnace (Tons)
1788[b]	-	-	1	-	750	-	750
1791	-	-	1	-	520	-	520
1794	2	2	-	-	-	-	-
1796	2	2	2	100	1,959	980	980

[a] An output of 697,221 tons printed in the original returns includes South Staffs. and Worcs., North Staffs. and Shropshire.
[b] See note to South Staffs. table concerning the Staffordshire figures for 1788 and 1791.

Year	No of Works	Furnaces Built	Furnaces in Blast	% in Blast	Total Annual Output (Tons)	Annual Output per Works (Tons)	Annual Output per Furnace (Tons)
1805	3	3	3	100	2,594	865	865
1810	3	4	4	100	-	-	-
1825	4	6	3	50	4,031	1,008	1,344
1827	-	-	-	-	ᵃ4,750	-	-
1828	-	-	-	-	4,828	-	-
1839	6	10	7	70	18,200	3,033	2,600
1840	-	16	7	44	20,500	-	2,929
1841	7	18	12	67	32,240	4,606	2,687
1843	7	18	8	44	21,750	3,107	2,719
1847	7	19	16	84	65,520	9,360	4,095
1848	-	21	14	67	67,080	-	4,791
1849	8	-	19	-	-	-	-
1852	-	21	17	81	90,000	-	5,294
1854	7	28	21	75	104,000	14,857	4,952
1855	7	28	20	71	101,500	14,500	5,075
1856	7	28	20	71	130,560	18,651	6,528
1857	7	27	23	85	134,057	19,151	5,829
1858	7	27	22	81	135,308	19,330	6,150
1859	7	29	24	83	143,500	20,500	5,979
1860	8	31	25	81	146,950	18,369	5,878
1861	8	32	24	75	187,700	23,463	7,821
1862	8	33	23	70	184,455	23,057	8,020
1863	8	33	25	76	176,504	22,063	7,060
1864	9	35	25	71	217,996	24,222	8,720
1865	8	35	27	77	206,268	25,784	7,640
1866	8	35	28	80	210,335	26,292	7,512
1867	6	35	23	66	202,332	33,722	8,797
1868	7	36	25	69	229,913	32,845	9,197
1869	7	37	27	73	231,913	33,130	8,589
1870	9	43	37	86	303,378	33,709	8,199
1871	7	35	30	86	268,300	38,329	8,943
1872	8	36	31	86	275,925	34,491	8,901
1873	9	36	29	81	241,166	26,796	8,316
1874	8	39	28	72	273,501	34,188	9,768
1875	8	39	26	67	241,398	30,175	9,285

ᵃ For 1827–28 see the note to the South Staffs. table.

Year	No of Works	Furnaces Built	Furnaces in Blast	% in Blast	Total Annual Output (Tons)	Annual Output per Works (Tons)	Annual Output per Furnace (Tons)
1876	8	37	25	68	213,569	26,696	8,543
1877	8	35	25	71	255,383	31,923	10,215
1878	9	35	24	69	231,534	25,726	9,647
1879	8	35	24	69	210,374	26,297	8,766
1880	9	36	24	67	225,023	25,003	9,376
1881	9	37	25	68	273,532	30,392	10,941
1882	9	37	25	68	275,577	30,620	11,023
1883	9	38	25	66	267,911	29,768	10,716
1884	10	39	24	62	296,256	29,626	12,344
1885	10	40	23	58	268,925	26,893	11,692
1886	9	40	21	53	233,500	25,944	11,119
1887	8	40	19	48	260,201	32,525	13,695
1888	8	39	19	49	279,169	34,896	14,693
1889	8	38	20	53	276,219	34,527	13,811
1890	9	37	22	59	255,777	28,420	11,626
1891	8	37	19	51	232,254	29,032	12,224
1892	8	38	17	45	241,416	30,177	14,201
1893	7	38	14	37	199,010	28,430	14,215
1894	5	38	14	37	210,069	42,014	15,005
1895	5	34	13	38	193,647	38,729	14,896
1896	5	34	14	41	236,176	47,235	16,870
1897	6	34	16	47	242,688	40,448	15,168
1898	8	34	17	50	268,357	33,545	15,786
1899	8	34	21	62	283,212	35,402	13,486
1900	8	34	20	59	272,617	34,077	13,631
1901	8	34	14	41	225,388	28,174	16,099
1902	5	34	15	44	249,002	49,800	16,600
1903	5	32	15	47	245,594	49,119	16,373
1904	5	29	14	48	[a]286,720	57,344	20,480
1905	5	29	13	45	304,148	60,830	23,396
1906	5	29	15	52	348,605	69,721	23,240
1907	5	29	16	55	355,872	71,174	22,242
1908	5	29	15	52	322,829	64,566	21,522
1909	5	27	14	52	334,723	66,945	23,909
1910	5	27	15	56	354,231	70,846	23,615

[a] From 1904 the output published in *Mineral Statistics* and here for North Staffs. also includes Shropshire.

Year	No of Works	Furnaces Built	Furnaces in Blast	% in Blast	Total Annual Output (Tons)	Annual Output per Works (Tons)	Annual Output per Furnace (Tons)
1911	5	27	14	52	355,749	71,150	25,411
1912	5	27	14	52	350,058	70,012	25,004
1913	6	27	13	48	383,118	63,853	29,471
1914	5	27	12	44	333,864	66,773	27,822
1915	5	24	14	58	345,020	69,004	24,644
1916	5	23	12	52	339,431	67,886	28,286
1917	5	21	13	62	368,068	73,614	28,313
1918	5	21	13	62	371,637	74,327	28,587
1919	5	20	12	60	335,128	67,026	27,927
1920	5	21	12	57	[a]-	-	-

Table 2.7: Northamptonshire

Year	No of Works	Furnaces Built	Furnaces in Blast	% in Blast	Total Annual Output (Tons)	Annual Output per Works (Tons)	Annual Output per Furnace (Tons)
1857	2	3	3	100	11,500	5,750	3,833
1858	2	3	3	100	9,750	4,875	3,250
1859	2	4	3	75	12,800	6,400	4,267
1860	2	4	3	75	7,595	3,798	2,532
1861	2	4	3	75	7,730	3,865	2,577
1862	2	4	3	75	13,471	6,736	4,490
1863	2	5	3	60	14,590	7,295	4,863
1864	2	4	3	75	[b]-	-	-
1865	2	5	4	80	-	-	-
1866	4	9	6	67	19,174	4,794	3,196
1867	4	9	5	56	25,184	6,296	5,037
1868	3	8	6	75	35,584	11,861	5,931
1869	4	8	7	88	41,500	10,375	5,929
1870	3	10	10	100	43,166	14,389	4,317
1871	5	12	9	75	60,512	12,102	6,724

[a] See note to South Staffs. table.
[b] In 1864 and 1865 a single output was returned for Northamptonshire and Lincolnshire, although separate furnace-numbers were given for each county. The figure was 22,823 tons in 1864 and 25,728 tons in 1865.

Year	No of Works	Furnaces Built	Furnaces in Blast	% in Blast	Total Annual Output (Tons)	Annual Output per Works (Tons)	Annual Output per Furnace (Tons)
1872	4	10	9	90	59,424	14,856	6,603
1873	5	16	10	63	58,480	11,696	5,848
1874	7	18	14	78	53,760	7,680	3,840
1875	7	18	12	67	80,689	11,527	6,724
1876	7	20	11	55	84,916	12,131	7,720
1877	6	20	13	65	106,948	17,825	8,227
1878	6	20	15	75	138,370	23,062	9,225
1879	7	23	17	74	165,317	23,617	9,725
1880	7	23	17	74	178,714	25,531	10,513
1881	7	23	17	74	189,841	27,120	11,167
1882	7	26	15	58	192,115	27,445	12,808
1883	7	26	18	69	216,641	30,949	12,036
1884	7	28	15	54	196,212	28,030	13,081
1885	8	30	16	53	190,261	23,783	11,891
1886	7	31	13	42	197,853	28,265	15,219
1887	7	28	15	54	236,390	33,770	15,759
1888	6	30	14	47	236,841	39,474	16,917
1889	6	24	17	71	230,820	38,470	13,578
1890	9	24	15	63	225,046	25,005	15,003
1891	8	23	12	52	194,395	24,299	16,200
1892	6	26	10	38	177,817	29,636	17,782
1893	6	26	9	35	143,815	23,969	15,979
1894	6	27	13	48	223,348	37,225	17,181
1895	6	26	14	54	254,744	42,457	18,196
1896	6	26	14	54	274,462	45,744	19,604
1897	6	26	13	50	249,824	41,637	19,217
1898	8	27	13	48	250,835	31,354	19,295
1899	7	24	14	58	279,301	39,900	19,950
1900	7	21	13	62	247,908	35,415	19,070
1901	7	21	10	48	206,101	29,443	20,610
1902	6	20	11	55	247,245	41,208	22,477
1903	6	20	12	60	253,571	42,262	21,131
1904	6	20	12	60	267,235	44,539	22,270
1905	6	20	12	60	273,366	45,561	22,781
1906	6	20	13	65	289,541	48,257	22,272
1907	6	20	12	60	288,507	48,085	24,042
1908	6	20	12	60	295,675	49,279	24,640

Year	No of Works	Furnaces Built	Furnaces in Blast	% in Blast	Total Annual Output (Tons)	Annual Output per Works (Tons)	Annual Output per Furnace (Tons)
1909	6	18	12	67	315,066	52,511	26,256
1910	7	20	13	65	365,564	52,223	28,120
1911	7	20	14	70	386,332	55,190	27,595
1912	7	20	14	70	350,746	50,107	25,053
1913	7	20	13	65	386,056	55,151	29,697
1914	7	20	12	60	339,407	48,487	28,284
1915	7	20	11	55	294,854	42,122	26,805
1916	6	20	11	55	284,520	47,420	25,865
1917	7	20	11	55	300,350	42,907	27,305
1918	7	20	13	65	314,467	44,924	24,190
1919	7	20	10	50	244,006	34,858	24,401
1920	7	20	11	55	282,950	40,421	25,723

Table 2.8: Lincolnshire

Year	No of Works	Furnaces Built	Furnaces in Blast	% in Blast	Total Annual Output (Tons)	Annual Output per Works (Tons)	Annual Output per Furnace (Tons)
1864	3	11	6	55	[a]-	-	-
1865	3	5	3	60	-	-	-
1866	3	6	3	50	13,765	4,588	4,588
1867	3	6	5	83	25,579	8,526	5,116
1868	3	6	5	83	33,999	11,333	6,800
1869	3	6	5	83	33,786	11,262	6,757
1870	3	6	4	67	31,690	10,563	7,923
1871	3	7	4	57	30,122	10,041	7,531
1872	3	9	7	78	36,989	12,330	5,284
1873	3	13	9	69	52,076	17,359	5,786
1874	3	15	8	53	67,266	22,422	8,408
1875	5	21	14	67	111,683	22,337	7,977
1876	6	21	16	76	125,198	20,866	7,825
1877	5	21	10	48	116,857	23,371	11,686

[a] See note to the Northamptonshire table concerning the returns for 1864–65.

Year	No of Works	Furnaces Built	Furnaces in Blast	% in Blast	Total Annual Output (Tons)	Annual Output per Works (Tons)	Annual Output per Furnace (Tons)
1878	5	21	11	52	125,043	25,009	11,368
1879	6	21	14	67	131,678	21,946	9,406
1880	6	21	15	71	207,704	34,617	13,847
1881	5	21	14	67	187,937	37,587	13,424
1882	5	21	17	81	201,561	40,312	11,857
1883[a]	7	22	20	91	237,068	33,867	11,853
1884	7	23	18	78	259,398	37,057	14,411
1885	7	23	16	70	235,381	33,626	14,711
1886	6	24	15	63	242,342	40,390	16,156
1887	6	24	16	67	251,869	41,978	15,742
1888	6	24	17	71	298,673	49,779	17,569
1889	7	24	20	83	336,175	48,025	16,809
1890	7	24	16	67	268,405	38,344	16,775
1891	6	24	15	63	284,766	47,461	18,984
1892	6	25	16	64	279,556	46,593	17,472
1893	7	25	13	52	216,575	30,939	16,660
1894	7	25	17	68	343,616	49,088	20,213
1894	7	25	17	68	349,232	49,890	20,543
1896	7	25	17	68	361,029	51,576	21,237
1897	6	25	18	72	363,487	60,581	20,194
1898	6	26	17	65	381,824	63,637	22,460
1899	6	26	20	77	408,989	68,165	20,449
1900	6	26	19	73	388,745	64,791	20,460
1901	6	25	14	56	321,969	53,662	22,998
1902	6	25	17	68	386,207	64,368	22,718
1903	6	25	16	64	386,179	64,363	24,136
1904	6	25	15	60	376,674	62,779	25,112
1905	6	23	14	61	443,408	73,901	31,672
1906	6	23	18	78	497,006	82,834	27,611
1907	6	19	16	84	481,600	80,267	30,100
1908	6	18	16	89	491,845	81,974	30,740
1909	6	18	15	83	475,091	79,182	31,673
1910	6	20	16	80	512,335	85,389	32,021
1911	6	20	16	80	496,383	82,731	31,024
1912	6	21	14	67	450,156	75,026	32,154

[a] From 1883 the Lincolnshire furnace-numbers and output figures include Holwell Ironworks, Leics.

Year	No of Works	Furnaces Built	Furnaces in Blast	% in Blast	Total Annual Output (Tons)	Annual Output per Works (Tons)	Annual Output per Furnace (Tons)
1913	6	21	16	76	531,117	88,520	33,195
1914	6	21	14	67	471,647	78,608	33,689
1915	6	21	16	76	533,067	88,845	33,317
1916	6	21	16	76	533,195	88,866	33,325
1917	7	26	20	77	649,191	92,742	32,460
1918	7	26	20	77	638,794	91,256	31,940
1919	7	26	19	73	535,445	76,492	28,181
1920	7	26	20	77	657,347	93,907	32,867

Table 2.9: Derbyshire

Year	No of Works	Furnaces Built	Furnaces in Blast	% in Blast	Total Annual Output (Tons)	Annual Output per Works (Tons)	Annual Output per Furnace (Tons)
1788	-	-	8	-	4,500	-	563
1791	-	-	9	-	4,680	-	520
1794	7	10	-	-	-	-	-
1796	8	8	8	100	7,347	918	918
1805[a]	12	19	12	63	9,969	831	831
1810	12	22	17	77	-	-	-
1823	10	15	-	-	14,038	1,404	-
1825	11	21	14	67	19,184	1,744	1,370
1827	-	-	14	-	20,500	-	1,464
1828	-	18	14	78	22,360	-	1,597
1830	10	18	-	-	17,999	1,800	-
1839	7	16	14	88	34,372	4,910	2,455
1840	-	18	13	72	31,000	-	2,385
1841	7	15	14	93	29,952	4,279	2,139
1843	7	18	10	56	25,750	3,679	2,575
1847	12	30	19	63	95,160	7,930	5,008
1848	-	30	20	67	78,000	-	3,900
1849	13	-	21	-	-	-	-
1854[b]	13	33	25	76	127,500	9,808	5,100

[a] The figures for 1805 and 1810 include the furnace at Moira (Leics.) but those for 1810 exclude the two furnaces said then to have existed at Alderwasley, since this appears to be a duplicate of the entry for Morley Park.

Year	No of Works	Furnaces Built	Furnaces in Blast	% in Blast	Total Annual Output (Tons)	Annual Output per Works (Tons)	Annual Output per Furnace (Tons)
1855	14	33	24	73	116,550	8,325	4,856
1856	13	32	26	81	106,960	8,228	4,114
1857	15	34	25	74	112,160	7,477	4,486
1858	15	34	28	82	131,577	8,772	4,699
1859	16	36	27	75	139,250	8,703	5,157
1860	16	37	23	62	125,850	7,866	5,472
1861	16	37	24	65	129,715	8,107	5,405
1862	17	44	32	73	131,005	7,706	4,094
1863	17	42	31	74	170,026	10,002	5,485
1864	17	43	31	72	174,743	10,279	5,637
1865	15	41	34	83	189,364	12,624	5,570
1866	15	42	33	79	199,867	13,324	6,057
1867	14	43	30	70	160,028	11,431	5,334
1868	11	42	28	67	159,312	14,483	5,690
1869	13	43	31	72	188,353	14,489	6,076
1870	12	43	30	70	179,772	14,981	5,992
1871	12	46	38	83	270,485	22,540	7,118
1872	14	46	38	83	283,375	20,241	7,457
1873	13	47	39	83	296,468	22,805	7,602
1874	13	50	38	76	301,687	23,207	7,939
1875	13	51	38	75	272,065	20,928	7,160
1876	12	54	35	65	300,719	25,060	8,592
1877	12	53	37	70	328,203	27,350	8,870
1878	12	55	38	69	306,141	25,512	8,056
1879	13	53	35	66	291,455	22,420	8,327
1880[a]	12	54	40	74	366,792	30,566	9,170
1881	12	57	42	74	367,614	30,635	8,753
1882	14	58	45	78	445,735	31,838	9,905
1883	13	58	39	67	422,214	32,478	10,826
1884	12	59	38	64	437,513	36,459	11,514
1885	11	56	35	63	443,953	40,359	12,684
1886	11	53	27	51	346,332	31,485	12,827
1887	8	52	24	46	296,118	37,015	12,338
1888	10	52	30	58	362,744	36,274	12,091

[b] There is no separate data for 1852 for Derbyshire, which is combined with Yorkshire, with a total of 42 furnaces, 35 in blast, and an output for the two counties of 150,000 tons p.a.

[a] From this date the two Nottinghamshire works at Bennerley and Bestwood are included in the Derbyshire returns.

Year	No of Works	Furnaces Built	Furnaces in Blast	% in Blast	Total Annual Output (Tons)	Annual Output per Works (Tons)	Annual Output per Furnace (Tons)
1889	11	54	38	70	470,114	42,738	12,371
1890	13	56	37	66	463,660	35,666	12,531
1891	13	55	38	69	470,951	36,227	12,393
1892	11	56	36	64	481,449	43,768	13,374
1893	11	56	28	50	343,115	31,192	12,254
1894	10	56	29	52	376,726	37,673	12,991
1894	10	56	32	57	413,454	41,345	12,920
1896	10	55	35	64	455,487	45,549	13,014
1897	11	56	39	70	488,472	44,407	12,525
1898	13	53	41	77	529,208	40,708	12,908
1899	13	52	44	85	571,994	44,000	13,000
1900	13	54	43	80	561,626	43,202	13,061
1901	13	54	36	67	457,519	35,194	12,709
1902	11	54	37	69	519,010	47,183	14,027
1903	11	51	38	75	546,947	49,722	14,393
1904	11	51	37	73	550,984	50,089	14,891
1905	11	51	37	73	568,310	51,665	15,360
1906	12	48	42	88	640,091	53,341	15,240
1907	13	50	43	86	675,589	51,968	15,711
1908	12	48	35	73	637,661	53,138	18,219
1909	12	48	34	71	645,660	53,805	18,990
1910	12	48	37	77	687,305	57,275	18,576
1911	12	48	36	75	665,751	55,479	18,493
1912	12	48	39	81	585,937	48,828	15,024
1913	12	48	41	85	698,703	58,225	17,042
1914	12	48	35	73	640,566	53,381	18,302
1915	12	48	30	63	558,148	46,512	18,605
1916	12	48	26	54	498,542	41,545	19,175
1917	12	48	31	65	543,534	45,295	17,533
1918	12	49	34	69	566,934	47,245	16,675
1919	12	49	32	65	482,455	40,205	15,077
1920	12	49	32	65	563,267	46,939	17,602

Table 2.10: Yorkshire, West Riding

Year	No of Works	Furnaces Built	Furnaces in Blast	% in Blast	Total Annual Output (Tons)	Annual Output per Works (Tons)	Annual Output per Furnace (Tons)
1788	-	-	7	-	5,100	-	729
1791	-	-	10	-	7,040	-	704
1794	9	14	-	-	-	-	-
1796	10	13	13	100	12,707	1,271	977
1805	14	27	23	85	25,621	1,830	1,114
1810	18	36	34	94	-	-	-
1823	14	26	-	-	27,311	1,951	-
1825	14	33	22	67	35,308	2,522	1,605
1827	-	-	24	-	43,000	-	1,792
1828	-	34	17	50	32,968	-	1,939
1830	14	27	-	-	28,926	2,066	-
1839	13	29	24	83	52,416	4,032	2,184
1840	-	32	25	78	56,000	-	2,240
1841	13	30	24	80	55,068	4,236	2,295
1843	13	30	18	60	42,000	3,231	2,333
1847	13	28	23	82	[a]67,600	5,200	2,939
1848	-	31	20	65	59,800	-	2,990
1849	13	-	29	-	-	-	-
1854[b]	14	28	21	75	73,444	5,246	3,497
1855	13	32	23	72	90,840	6,988	3,950
1856	13	34	23	68	96,200	7,400	4,183
1857	13	36	25	69	117,000	9,000	4,680
1858	13	33	24	73	85,936	6,610	3,581
1859	13	34	24	71	84,950	6,535	3,540
1860	13	34	25	74	98,100	7,546	3,924
1861	12	34	27	79	142,865	11,905	5,291
1862	12	35	26	74	112,121	9,343	4,312
1863	12	35	24	69	104,745	8,729	4,364
1864	12	35	25	71	112,093	9,341	4,484
1865	14	38	29	76	123,233	8,802	4,249
1866	10	36	29	81	119,747	11,975	4,129

[a] Braithwaite Poole's version of the 1847 list (*Statistics of British commerce*, p. 206) gives the output for Yorkshire as 66,560 tons p.a., whereas the sum of the individual furnace outputs as printed by him on p. 204 is 66,550 tons. Every other version of the list gives the Yorkshire total as 67,600 tons, which has been used here.

[b] For the absence of Yorkshire data for 1852 see note to the Derbyshire table.

Year	No of Works	Furnaces Built	Furnaces in Blast	% in Blast	Total Annual Output (Tons)	Annual Output per Works (Tons)	Annual Output per Furnace (Tons)
1867	12	36	25	69	109,002	9,084	4,360
1868	9	38	22	58	100,050	11,117	4,548
1869	12	38	23	61	105,765	8,814	4,598
1870	8	38	22	58	77,717	9,715	3,533
1871	9	39	25	64	114,549	12,728	4,582
1872	11	40	30	75	148,636	13,512	4,955
1873	12	40	30	75	151,511	12,626	5,050
1874	13	44	31	70	163,856	12,604	5,286
1875	13	50	38	76	267,153	20,550	7,030
1876	16	49	34	69	235,451	14,716	6,925
1877	14	48	30	63	229,027	16,359	7,634
1878	12	48	29	60	219,547	18,296	7,571
1879	11	49	31	63	218,805	19,891	7,058
1880	11	47	33	70	306,560	27,869	9,290
1881	12	46	25	54	256,300	21,358	10,252
1882	19	47	28	60	321,430	16,917	11,480
1883	13	46	28	61	304,381	23,414	10,871
1884	10	48	22	46	248,313	24,831	11,287
1885	9	42	17	40	165,857	18,429	9,756
1886	9	38	16	42	137,307	15,256	8,582
1887	10	38	16	42	178,455	17,846	11,153
1888	10	35	19	54	190,846	19,085	10,045
1889	10	38	22	58	229,029	22,903	10,410
1890	10	38	19	50	248,581	24,858	13,083
1891	10	38	18	47	228,354	22,835	12,686
1892	9	37	21	57	261,537	29,060	12,454
1893	9	39	13	33	155,027	17,225	11,925
1894	9	39	14	36	225,185	25,021	16,085
1895	8	39	11	28	195,123	24,390	17,738
1896	8	39	17	44	289,497	36,187	17,029
1897	9	34	19	56	294,846	32,761	15,518
1898	9	27	18	67	297,490	33,054	16,527
1899	9	27	19	70	305,583	33,954	16,083
1900	9	28	18	64	290,601	32,289	16,145
1901	8	24	15	63	247,005	30,876	16,467
1902	8	24	16	67	284,061	35,508	17,754
1903	8	24	15	63	298,406	37,301	19,894

Year	No of Works	Furnaces Built	Furnaces in Blast	% in Blast	Total Annual Output (Tons)	Annual Output per Works (Tons)	Annual Output per Furnace (Tons)
1904	7	22	13	59	263,412	37,630	20,262
1905	8	25	15	60	293,231	36,654	19,549
1906	8	25	16	64	335,852	41,982	20,991
1907	8	23	16	70	332,590	41,574	20,787
1908	7	25	12	48	281,617	40,231	23,468
1909	7	25	12	48	292,274	41,753	24,356
1910	7	25	12	48	313,358	44,765	26,113
1911	6	24	10	42	283,888	47,315	28,389
1912	5	22	11	50	264,990	52,998	24,090
1913	6	21	12	57	302,695	50,449	25,225
1914	5	21	11	52	263,509	52,702	23,955
1915	5	21	11	52	284,658	56,932	25,878
1916	5	21	11	52	293,339	58,668	26,667
1917	5	21	13	62	307,292	61,458	23,638
1918	5	22	12	55	281,771	56,354	23,481
1919	5	22	10	45	239,202	47,840	23,920
1920	5	18	10	56	259,590	51,918	25,959

Table 2.11: North West England[a]

Year	No of Works	Furnaces Built	Furnaces in Blast	% in Blast	Total Annual Output (Tons)	Annual Output per Works (Tons)	Annual Output per Furnace (Tons)
1788	-	-	7	-	4,100	-	586
1791	-	-	7	-	3,914	-	559
1794	8	9	-	-	-	-	-
1796	5	5	5	100	2,814	563	563
1805	6	9	6	67	1,291	215	215
1810	5	8	5	-	-	-	-
1825	7	8	-	-	-	-	-
1839	-	-	-	-	800	-	-

[a] There are no returns for North West England for 1823–30, 1841, 1843 or 1847–48 and deficiencies in some of the other pre-1854 lists. The furnace at Dukinfield (Cheshire) is included in 1794 and 1825, but not 1796, 1805 or 1810; that at Haigh (Lancs.) appears in 1794, 1805 and 1810 but not 1796. In 1849 only Cleator Moor was listed and the charcoal-fired furnaces entirely omitted.

Year	No of Works	Furnaces Built	Furnaces in Blast	% in Blast	Total Annual Output (Tons)	Annual Output per Works (Tons)	Annual Output per Furnace (Tons)
1854	4	5	5	100	20,000	5,000	4,000
1855	4	6	5	83	16,574	4,144	3,315
1856	5	10	5	50	25,530	5,106	5,106
1857	6	11	8	73	31,748	5,291	3,969
1858	8	13	8	62	29,104	3,638	3,638
1859	9	22	14	64	76,588	8,510	5,471
1860	9	23	16	70	169,200	18,800	10,575
1861	9	25	18	72	164,542	18,282	9,141
1862	9	27	18	67	242,018	26,891	13,445
1863	8	32	22	69	270,200	33,775	12,282
1864	8	31	25	81	336,493	42,062	13,460
1865	10	40	26	65	312,355	31,236	12,014
1866	7	43	31	72	405,023	57,860	13,065
1867	7	43	28	65	428,640	61,234	15,309
1868	8	46	31	67	442,231	55,279	14,266
1869	9	48	36	75	565,769	62,863	15,716
1870	12	66	51	77	677,906	56,492	13,292
1871	15	75	63	84	856,928	57,129	13,602
1872	17	83	68	82	964,616	56,742	14,186
1873	16	92	70	76	986,148	61,634	14,088
1874	19	98	63	64	879,512	46,290	13,961
1875	20	101	63	62	1,044,892	52,245	16,586
1876	21	96	57	59	989,871	47,137	17,366
1877	20	100	60	60	1,162,345	58,117	19,372
1878	19	103	57	55	922,396	48,547	16,182
1879	19	100	65	65	1,162,981	61,210	17,892
1880	21	100	77	77	1,541,227	73,392	20,016
1881	23	104	79	76	1,616,737	70,293	20,465
1882	23	104	80	77	1,792,180	77,921	22,402
1883	23	105	69	66	1,673,215	72,748	24,249
1884	22	104	61	59	1,561,120	70,960	25,592
1885	20	103	52	50	1,383,733	69,187	26,610
1886	22	104	54	52	1,410,276	64,103	26,116
1887	20	104	62	60	1,700,699	85,035	27,431
1888	21	101	56	55	1,599,978	76,189	28,571
1889	21	98	59	60	1,662,181	79,151	28,173
1890	21	96	59	61	1,569,640	74,745	26,604

Year	No of Works	Furnaces Built	Furnaces in Blast	% in Blast	Total Annual Output (Tons)	Annual Output per Works (Tons)	Annual Output per Furnace (Tons)
1891	20	98	46	47	1,440,055	72,003	31,306
1892	19	97	44	45	1,198,723	63,091	27,244
1893	18	97	41	42	1,297,453	72,081	31,645
1894	17	97	41	42	1,295,643	76,214	31,601
1895	16	91	37	41	1,189,038	74,315	32,136
1896	17	92	43	47	1,451,421	85,378	33,754
1897	18	87	44	51	1,526,368	84,798	34,690
1898	19	86	48	56	1,619,063	85,214	33,730
1899	19	82	52	63	1,698,702	89,405	32,667
1900	19	81	50	62	1,585,925	83,470	31,719
1901	19	81	42	52	1,432,582	75,399	34,109
1902	17	81	42	52	1,540,102	90,594	36,669
1903	16	76	39	51	1,485,785	92,862	38,097
1904	15	75	30	40	1,219,494	81,300	40,650
1905	17	73	35	48	1,455,808	85,636	41,595
1906	17	73	39	53	1,566,814	92,166	40,175
1907	17	71	38	54	1,447,635	85,155	38,096
1908	14	70	27	39	1,097,900	78,421	40,663
1909	15	67	29	43	1,239,028	82,602	42,725
1910	16	66	32	48	1,313,728	82,108	41,054
1911	16	63	27	43	1,121,133	70,071	41,523
1912	16	64	25	39	[a]1,062,979	66,436	42,519
1913	18	69	33	48	1,312,601	72,922	39,776
1914	17	69	29	42	1,222,850	71,932	42,167
1915	16	69	30	43	1,304,073	81,505	43,469
1916	16	69	34	49	1,437,106	89,819	42,268
1917	17	69	36	52	1,521,566	89,504	42,266
1918	17	67	36	54	1,512,317	88,960	42,009
1919	18	68	33	49	1,211,865	67,326	36,723
1920	15	61	32	52	[b]1,341,209	89,414	41,913

[a] In 1912–19 the output (but not the furnace-numbers) printed in *Mineral Statistics* and here for Lancashire also includes Flintshire.
[b] This figure includes the output of Denbighs. and Flintshire.

Table 2.12: North East England

Year	No of Works	Furnaces Built	Furnaces in Blast	% in Blast	Total Annual Output (Tons)	Annual Output per Works (Tons)	Annual Output per Furnace (Tons)
1805	1	2	1	50	-	-	-
1810	1	2	2	100	-	-	-
1823	1	2	-	-	2,379	2,379	-
1825	1	2	-	-	-	-	-
1830	2	4	-	-	5,327	2,664	-
1839	3	5	5	100	13,000	4,333	2,600
1840	-	6	5	83	11,000	-	2,200
1841	5	9	4	44	12,480	2,496	3,120
1843	7	-	8	-	20,750	2,964	2,594
1847	10	33	22	67	99,840	9,984	4,538
1848	-	32	17	53	94,380	-	5,552
1849	12	36	21	58	-	-	-
1852	-	39	25	64	145,000	-	5,800
1854	23	78	59	76	275,000	11,957	4,661
1855	25	85	64	75	298,520	11,941	4,664
1856	32	95	71	75	510,770	15,962	7,194
1857	33	101	64	63	527,588	15,988	8,244
1858	32	101	70	69	499,816	15,619	7,140
1859	35	110	75	68	617,966	17,656	8,240
1860	37	112	69	62	658,679	17,802	9,546
1861	36	111	65	59	619,946	17,221	9,538
1862	36	113	67	59	667,202	18,533	9,958
1863	37	132	87	66	824,431	22,282	9,476
1864	40	126	90	71	931,553	23,289	10,351
1865	42	148	108	73	1,012,478	24,107	9,375
1866	28	155	109	70	895,414	31,979	8,215
1867	27	156	93	60	1,149,754	42,583	12,363
1868	22	159	87	55	1,216,581	55,299	13,984
1869	26	159	92	58	1,440,858	55,418	15,662
1870	29	162	120	74	1,627,557	56,123	13,563
1871	31	146	121	83	1,823,294	58,816	15,069
1872	33	141	127	90	1,921,052	58,214	15,126
1873	34	142	130	92	2,000,811	58,847	15,391
1874	40	157	136	87	2,020,848	50,521	14,859
1875	37	159	128	81	2,049,319	55,387	16,010

Year	No of Works	Furnaces Built	Furnaces in Blast	% in Blast	Total Annual Output (Tons)	Annual Output per Works (Tons)	Annual Output per Furnace (Tons)
1876	33	159	127	80	2,084,185	63,157	16,411
1877	30	163	116	71	2,109,020	70,301	18,181
1878	26	165	100	61	2,018,765	77,645	20,188
1879	27	165	103	62	1,767,346	65,457	17,159
1880	26	167	112	67	2,416,418	92,939	21,575
1881	30	169	117	69	2,634,051	87,802	22,513
1882	21	168	120	71	2,712,601	129,171	22,605
1883	31	163	123	75	2,779,523	89,662	22,598
1884	30	162	102	63	2,504,954	83,498	24,558
1885	29	159	97	61	2,477,606	85,435	25,542
1886	29	159	94	59	2,436,721	84,025	25,923
1887	27	158	94	59	2,524,241	93,490	26,854
1888	28	158	98	62	2,631,258	93,974	26,850
1889	28	153	101	66	2,782,466	99,374	27,549
1890	28	153	103	67	2,837,599	101,343	27,550
1891	28	149	92	62	2,631,183	93,971	28,600
1892	25	139	72	52	1,944,548	77,782	27,008
1893	26	144	87	60	2,713,914	104,381	31,194
1894	26	138	93	67	2,973,867	114,380	31,977
1895	26	139	92	66	2,926,157	112,545	31,806
1896	26	133	96	72	3,211,926	123,536	33,458
1897	25	127	96	76	3,197,641	127,906	33,309
1898	28	124	96	77	3,198,626	114,237	33,319
1899	28	125	97	78	3,251,396	116,121	33,520
1900	26	121	95	79	3,109,594	119,600	32,733
1901	26	121	79	65	2,820,116	108,466	35,698
1902	25	115	79	69	2,960,867	118,435	37,479
1903	25	114	81	71	3,108,050	124,322	38,371
1904	26	114	77	68	3,123,915	120,151	40,570
1905	26	116	83	72	3,485,762	134,068	41,997
1906	26	115	87	76	3,628,651	139,564	41,709
1907	26	116	90	78	3,681,758	141,606	40,908
1908	26	117	78	67	3,389,079	130,349	43,450
1909	26	116	80	69	3,550,104	136,542	44,376
1910	26	115	83	72	3,679,473	141,518	44,331
1911	26	116	79	68	3,542,032	136,232	44,836
1912	25	115	78	68	3,258,842	130,354	41,780

Year	No of Works	Furnaces Built	Furnaces in Blast	% in Blast	Total Annual Output (Tons)	Annual Output per Works (Tons)	Annual Output per Furnace (Tons)
1913	26	115	85	74	3,869,214	148,816	45,520
1914	25	112	75	67	3,306,567	132,263	44,088
1915	26	113	70	62	3,006,458	115,633	42,949
1916	24	113	71	63	3,097,298	129,054	43,624
1917	25	113	75	66	3,230,110	129,204	43,068
1918	25	113	74	65	2,991,904	119,676	40,431
1919	25	115	68	59	2,506,796	100,272	36,865
1920	25	114	69	61	2,638,564	105,543	38,240

Table 2.13: Scotland

Year	No of Works	Furnaces Built	Furnaces in Blast	% in Blast	Total Annual Output (Tons)	Annual Output per Works (Tons)	Annual Output per Furnace (Tons)
1788	-	-	8	-	7,000	-	875
1791	-	-	14	-	13,480	-	963
1794	8	17	-	-	-	-	-
1796	8	17	17	100	16,086	2,011	946
1805	12	27	18	67	22,840	1,903	1,269
1810	12	[a]29	26	90	-	-	-
1823	8	22	-	-	24,500	3,063	-
1825	9	25	17	68	29,200	3,244	1,718
1827	-	-	18	-	36,500	-	2,028
1828	-	25	18	72	37,700	-	2,094
1830	10	27	-	-	37,500	3,750	-
1839	18	55	55	100	196,960	10,942	3,581
1840	-	70	64	91	241,000	-	3,766
1841	21	92	65	71	287,300	13,681	4,420
1843	21	98	62	63	238,750	11,369	3,851
1847	24	130	90	69	539,962	22,498	6,000
1848	-	130	94	72	564,000	-	6,000
1849	27	143	114	80	-	-	-
1852	-	144	113	78	775,000	-	6,858

[a] This figure has been adjusted from 30, the sum of the original entries, on the assumption that the return showing 2 furnaces at Craleckan is an error for 1.

REGIONAL STATISTICS

Year	No of Works	Furnaces Built	Furnaces in Blast	% in Blast	Total Annual Output (Tons)	Annual Output per Works (Tons)	Annual Output per Furnace (Tons)
1854	32	156	118	76	796,640	24,895	6,751
1855	33	160	122	76	827,500	25,076	6,783
1856	33	161	127	79	880,500	26,682	6,933
1857	32	165	124	75	918,000	28,688	7,403
1858	32	177	132	75	925,500	28,922	7,011
1859	33	175	125	71	960,550	29,108	7,684
1860	33	175	131	75	937,000	28,394	7,153
1861	31	169	124	73	950,000	30,645	7,661
1862	31	171	125	73	1,080,000	34,839	8,640
1863	31	169	134	79	1,160,000	37,419	8,657
1864	31	170	131	77	1,158,750	37,379	8,845
1865	32	180	141	78	1,163,478	36,359	8,252
1866	27	165	98	59	994,000	36,815	10,143
1867	30	167	112	67	1,031,000	34,367	9,205
1868	30	167	123	74	1,068,000	35,600	8,683
1869	29	165	132	80	1,150,000	39,655	8,712
1870	28	156	123	79	1,206,000	43,071	9,805
1871	27	156	127	81	1,160,000	42,963	9,134
1872	27	154	130	84	1,090,000	40,370	8,385
1873	27	156	126	81	993,000	36,778	7,881
1874	26	163	123	75	807,677	31,065	6,556
1875	26	159	119	75	1,050,000	40,385	8,824
1876	26	156	119	76	1,103,000	42,423	9,269
1877	27	152	109	72	982,000	36,370	9,009
1878	21	152	95	63	902,000	42,952	9,495
1879	22	151	97	64	932,000	42,364	9,608
1880	24	149	113	76	1,049,000	43,708	9,283
1881	24	151	115	76	1,176,000	49,000	10,226
1882	23	149	110	74	1,126,890	48,995	10,244
1883	24	147	108	73	1,129,000	47,042	10,454
1884	24	144	98	68	988,000	41,167	10,082
1885	21	144	92	64	1,003,562	47,789	10,908
1886	21	141	86	61	935,801	44,562	10,881
1887	20	141	84	60	932,240	46,612	11,098
1888	18	141	85	60	1,027,774	57,099	12,091
1889	18	134	84	63	978,203	54,345	11,645
1890	18	126	65	52	737,066	40,948	11,339

Year	No of Works	Furnaces Built	Furnaces in Blast	% in Blast	Total Annual Output (Tons)	Annual Output per Works (Tons)	Annual Output per Furnace (Tons)
1891	17	122	64	52	674,076	39,652	10,532
1892	17	125	77	62	972,493	57,205	12,630
1893	16	123	64	52	793,055	49,566	12,391
1894	16	114	52	46	642,243	40,140	12,351
1895	16	106	76	72	1,048,774	65,548	13,800
1896	16	109	80	73	1,114,038	69,627	13,925
1897	16	106	80	75	1,136,507	71,032	14,206
1898	19	105	78	74	1,062,547	55,924	13,622
1899	19	107	85	79	1,170,830	61,623	13,774
1900	19	106	85	80	1,156,885	60,889	13,610
1901	18	101	83	82	1,136,396	63,133	13,692
1902	17	103	86	84	1,271,716	74,807	14,787
1903	17	103	88	85	1,290,790	75,929	14,668
1904	17	101	86	85	1,351,147	79,479	15,711
1905	17	101	88	87	1,375,125	80,890	15,626
1906	17	100	92	92	1,376,888	80,993	14,966
1907	17	102	91	89	1,389,474	81,734	15,269
1908	16	102	77	75	1,224,802	76,550	15,907
1909	17	102	84	82	1,377,247	81,015	16,396
1910	17	102	87	85	1,427,828	83,990	16,412
1911	17	102	85	83	1,408,555	82,856	16,571
1912	17	102	78	76	1,185,520	69,736	15,199
1913	17	102	87	85	1,369,259	80,545	15,739
1914	17	102	72	71	1,125,967	66,233	15,638
1915	17	101	72	71	1,109,177	65,246	15,405
1916	17	102	76	75	1,124,862	66,168	14,801
1917	17	102	81	79	1,156,924	68,054	14,283
1918	17	102	78	76	1,091,396	64,200	13,992
1919	17	102	68	67	903,376	53,140	13,285
1920	17	102	68	67	902,550	53,091	13,273

Local Statistics

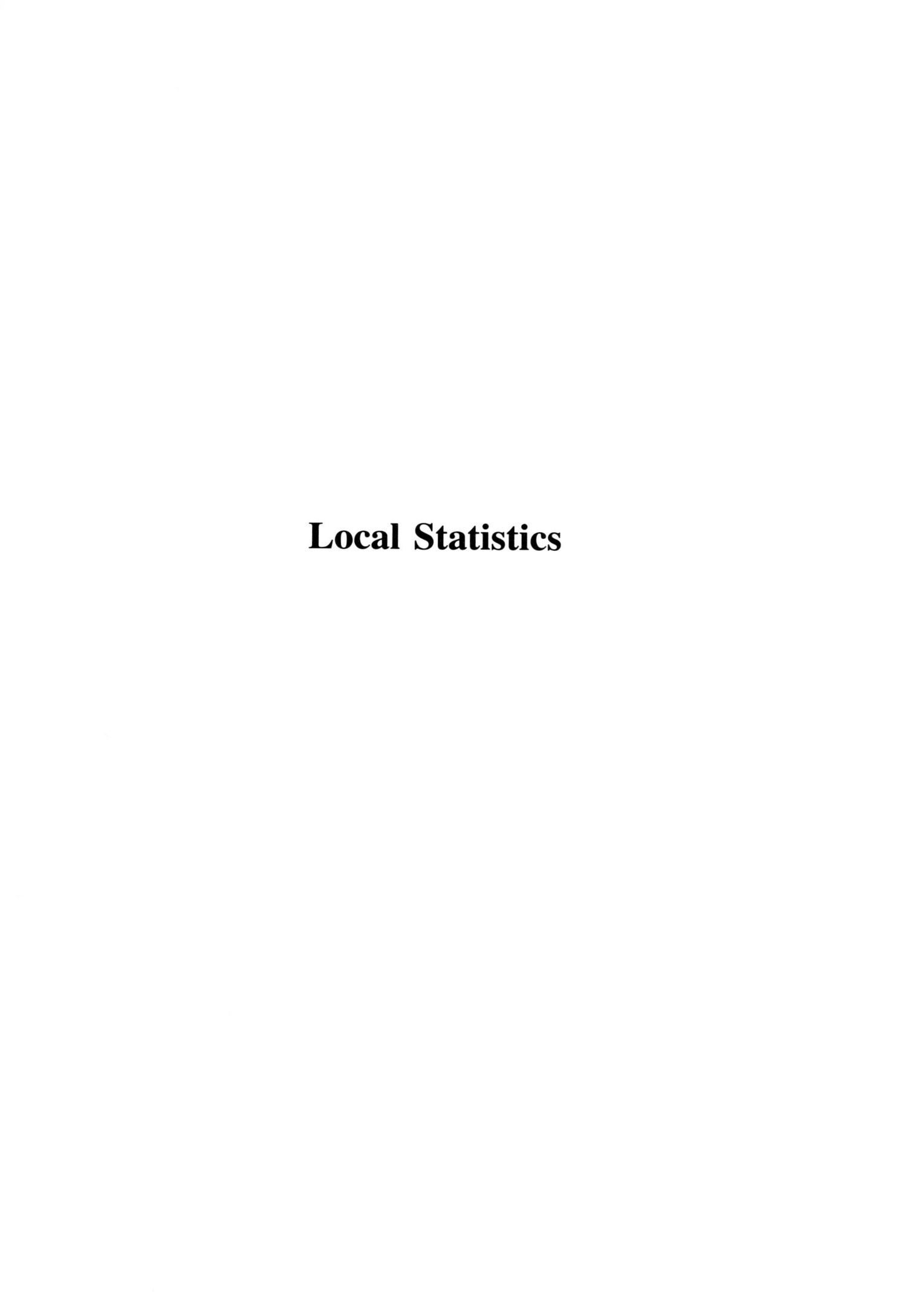

South Wales

Abbey Tintern: see Tintern, Glos.

Aberaman, Glam. [SO 0100]

Year	Owner	Built	In Blast
1849	C. Bailey	2	2
1854	Crawshay Bailey	3	0
1855	Crawshay Bailey	3	3
1856	Crawshay Bailey	3	3
1857	Crawshay Bailey	3	3
1858	Crawshay Bailey	3	3
1859	Crawshay Bailey	3	3
1860	Crawshay Bailey	3	3
1861	Crawshay Bailey	3	3
1862	Crawshay Bailey	3	3
1863	Crawshay Bailey	3	3
1864	Crawshay Bailey	3	3
1865	Crawshay Bailey	3	3
1866	Crawshay Bailey	3	3

Truran: output 120 tons a week from each of 3 furnaces. 1866: 'Now stopped, and not likely to go on again'.

'Abercarne': see Abercraf

Abercraf, Brecs. [SN 8112]

Year	Owner	Built	In Blast
1854	T. Walters	1	1
1855	T. Walters	1	1
1856	T. Walters	1	1
1857	T. Walters	1	1
1858	T. Walters	1	1
1859	T. Walters	1	1
1860	T. Walters	1	1
1861	T. Walters	1	1
1862	T. Walters	1	0
1863	T. Walters	1	0
1864	T. Walters	1	0
1865	T. Walters	1	0

Truran has an entry for 'Abercarne', with one furnace producing 50 tons a week, which can only, by a process of elimination, belong here. It cannot refer to Abercarn, Mon., since the works appears in the anthracite section of the South Wales list.

Aberdare, Glam. [SN 9904]

Year	Owner	Built	In Blast
1805	Scales & Co.	2	2
1810	Scales & Co.	3	3
1823	—	3	-
1825	Scales, Fothergill & Co.	3	3
1830	—	3	-
1839	Thompson & Co.	3	3
1841	Thompson & Co.	3	2
1843	Joint Stock	3	2
1847	Thompson & Co.	3	3
1849	Fothergill & Co.	6	5
1854	Aberdare Iron Co.	3	2
1855	Aberdare Iron Co.	3	3
1856	Aberdare Iron Co.	3	3
1857	Aberdare Iron Co.	3	3
1858	Aberdare Iron Co.	7	6
1859	Aberdare Iron Co.	6	5
1860	Aberdare Iron Co.	6	1
1861	Fothergill & Hankey	6	5
1862	Fothergill & Hankey	5	5
1863	Fothergill & Hankey	5	4
1864	Fothergill & Hankey	5	4
1865	Fothergill & Hankey	5	3
1866	Fothergill & Hankey	5	4
1867	Fothergill, Hankey & Lewis	5	4
1868	R. Fothergill & T.A. Hankey	5	3
1869	Fothergill, Hankey & Lewis	5	3
1870	Aberdare Iron Co.	5	4
1871	Aberdare Iron Co.	5	4
1872	Aberdare Iron Co.	5	3
1873	Aberdare Iron Co.	5	3
1874	Aberdare Iron Co.	5	3
1875	Aberdare Iron Co.	5	0
1876	Aberdare Iron Co.	5	0
1877	Aberdare & Plymouth Co. Ltd	5	0
1878	Aberdare & Plymouth Co. Ltd	5	0
1879	Aberdare & Plymouth Co. Ltd	5	0
1880	Aberdare & Plymouth Co. Ltd	5	0
1881	Aberdare & Plymouth Co. Ltd	5	0
1882	Aberdare & Plymouth Co. Ltd	3	0
1883	Aberdare & Plymouth Co. Ltd	3	0
1884	Aberdare & Plymouth Co. Ltd	3	0
1885	Aberdare & Plymouth Co. Ltd	3	0
1886	Aberdare & Plymouth Co. Ltd	3	0
1887	Aberdare & Plymouth Co. Ltd	3	0
1888	Aberdare Works & Collieries Co.	3	0
1889	Aberdare Works & Collieries Co.	3	0
1890	Aberdare Works & Collieries Co.	3	0
1891	Aberdare Works & Collieries Co.	3	0
1892	Aberdare Works & Collieries Co.	3	0
1893	Aberdare Works & Collieries Co.	3	0
1894	Aberdare Works & Collieries Co.	3	0
1895	Aberdare Works & Collieries Co.	3	0
1896	Aberdare Works & Collieries Co.	3	0
1897	Aberdare Works & Collieries Co.	3	0

1805: output 3,586 tons p.a. From 1823 onwards, figures for Aberdare were usually combined with those for Abernant (qv): in 1823 the 3 furnaces at Aberdare and the 3 at Abernant together produced 5,676 tons; in 1830 an output of 12,571 tons was given for the 6 furnaces together. 1825: weekly output of the two works 230 tons (11,440 p.a.), 'melting and forge'. The Staffs RO version of the list has 3 furnaces in blast at Aberdare; the B&W text has 2. 1839 and 1847: 6 furnaces, all in blast, at Aberdare and Abernant, which has been split as above and under Abernant, below. 1843: output 102 tons a week. 1849: furnace-numbers for Aberdare and Abernant combined as above in English; Hunt's list has 6 furnaces in blast. In 1854 these two works were bracketed with a third, 'Iswydcoed' (i.e. Llwydcoed, which is in fact the district of Aberdare where Aberdare Ironworks was located, not a separate works), with the number of furnaces at all three given as 3 (2 in blast). Truran: output (at Aberdare) 125 tons a week from each of three furnaces. In 1856–57 furnace-numbers were given separately for Aberdare and Abernant but for 1858–81 they were combined and have been printed here under Aberdare. From 1869 the Aberdare site was called Llwydcoed. See also next entry.

Abernant, Glam. [SO 0103]

Year	Owner	Built	In Blast
1805	Tappenden	2	1
1810	Tappenden & Co.	3	3
1823	—	3	-
1825	Scales, Fothergill & Co.	1	1
1830	—	3	-
1839	Thompson & Co.	3	3
1841	Thompson & Co.	3	3
1843	Joint Stock	3	3
1847	Thompson & Co.	3	3
1849	Fothergill & Co.	-	-
1854	Aberdare Iron Co.	-	-
1855	Aberdare Iron Co.	-	-
1856	Aberdare Iron Co.	3	2
1857	Aberdare Iron Co.	3	2
1858	Aberdare Iron Co.	-	-
1859	Aberdare Iron Co.	-	-
1860	Aberdare Iron Co.	-	-
1861	Fothergill & Hankey	-	-
1862	Fothergill & Hankey	-	-
1863	Fothergill & Hankey	-	-
1864	Fothergill & Hankey	-	-
1865	Fothergill & Hankey	-	-
1866	Fothergill & Hankey	-	-
1867	Fothergill, Hankey & Lewis	-	-
1868	R. Fothergill & T.A. Hankey	-	-
1869	Fothergill, Hankey & Lewis	-	-
1870	Aberdare Iron Co.	-	-
1871	Aberdare Iron Co.	-	-
1872	Aberdare Iron Co.	-	-
1873	Aberdare Iron Co.	-	-
1874	Aberdare Iron Co.	-	-
1875	Aberdare Iron Co.	-	-
1876	Aberdare Iron Co.	-	-
1877	Aberdare & Plymouth Co. Ltd	-	-
1878	Aberdare & Plymouth Co. Ltd	-	-
1879	Aberdare & Plymouth Co. Ltd	-	-
1880	Aberdare & Plymouth Co. Ltd	-	-
1881	Aberdare & Plymouth Co. Ltd	-	-
1882	Aberdare & Plymouth Co. Ltd	2	0
1883	Aberdare & Plymouth Co. Ltd	2	0
1884	Aberdare & Plymouth Co. Ltd	2	0
1885	Aberdare & Plymouth Co. Ltd	2	0
1886	Aberdare & Plymouth Co. Ltd	2	0
1887	Aberdare & Plymouth Co. Ltd	2	0
1888	Aberdare Works & Collieries Co.	2	0
1889	Aberdare Works & Collieries Co.	2	0
1890	Aberdare Works & Collieries Co.	2	0

1805: output 4,376 tons p.a. 1823–30: see Aberdare. 1825: combined output of Aberdare and Abernant 230 tons weekly, 11,440 tons p.a., 'melting and forge'. The Staffs RO version of the list has the single furnace in blast; the B&W text has it out of blast. In 1839 and 1847 Aberdare and Abernant were again combined (6 furnaces, all in blast), and have been split as above and under Aberdare. 1843: output (at Abernant) 136 tons a week. 1849: see Aberdare. In 1854 (only) the owner at Aberdare and Abernant was given as the Abernant Iron Co., apparently in error. Truran: output (at Abernant only) 115 tons a week from each of three furnaces. Separate furnace-numbers are given for Aberdare and Abernant in 1856–57; for 1858–81 they are combined and have been printed here under Aberdare. From 1869 the Abernant entry is called 'Abernant and Taffvale'.

Abernant (Glyn-neath), Glam. [SN 8806]

Year	Owner	Built	In Blast
1854	Neath Abbey Co.	3	1
1855	—	1	0
1856	Abernant Iron Co.	3	3
1857	Abernant Iron Co.	3	3
1858	Abernant Iron Co.	3	0
1859	Abernant Iron Co.	3	1
1860	Abernant Iron Co.	3	1
1861	Abernant Iron Co.	3	1
1862	Abernant Iron Co.	3	0
1863	Abernant Iron Co.	3	0
1864	Abernant Iron Co.	3	0
1865	Abernant Iron Co.	3	0
1866	Abernant Iron Co.	3	0
1867	Abernant Iron Co.	3	0

These figures relate to the works at Abernant in the Neath Valley, as opposed to Abernant in the Cynon Valley (see preceding entry). 1854: entry headed Neath Valley appears to belong here, given the number of furnaces (cf. also Venallt). The 1855 entry appears under Glyn-neath and is evidently defective. Truran: output 80 tons a week from each of three furnaces. 1861: furnace in blast for a portion of the year only.

Abersychan, Mon. SO 2503

Year	Owner	Built	In Blast
1825	British Iron Co. (Small, Share & Co.)	4	0
1830	—	6	-
1839	British Iron Co.	4	4
1841	British Iron Co.	6	3
1843	British Iron Co.	6	2
1847	British Iron Co.	6	4
1849	New British Iron Co.	6	3
1854	Ebbw Vale Co.	6	4
1855	Ebbw Vale Co. (Darby, Brown & Co.)	6	4

Year	Owner	Built	In Blast
1856	Ebbw Vale Co. (Darby, Brown & Co.)	6	6
1857	Ebbw Vale Co. (Darby, Brown & Co.)	6	6
1858	Ebbw Vale Co.	6	6
1859	Ebbw Vale Co.	6	6
1860	Ebbw Vale Co.	6	4
1861	Ebbw Vale Co.	6	2
1862	Ebbw Vale Iron Co.	6	0
1863	Ebbw Vale Iron Co.	6	0
1864	Ebbw Vale Iron Co.	6	4
1865	Ebbw Vale Co. Ltd	6	4
1866	Ebbw Vale Co. Ltd	6	4
1867	Ebbw Vale Co. Ltd	6	5
1868	Ebbw Vale Co. Ltd	6	4
1869	Ebbw Vale Co. Ltd	6	5
1870	Ebbw Vale Co. Ltd	-	-
1871	Ebbw Vale Co. Ltd	-	-
1872	Ebbw Vale Steel Iron & Coal Co. Ltd	-	-
1873	Ebbw Vale Steel Iron & Coal Co. Ltd	-	-
1874	Ebbw Vale Steel Iron & Coal Co. Ltd	-	-
1875	Ebbw Vale Steel Iron & Coal Co. Ltd	-	-
1876	Ebbw Vale Steel Iron & Coal Co. Ltd	6	4
1877	Ebbw Vale Steel Iron & Coal Co. Ltd	6	2
1878	Ebbw Vale Steel Iron & Coal Co. Ltd	6	2
1879	Ebbw Vale Steel Iron & Coal Co. Ltd	6	3
1880	Ebbw Vale Steel Iron & Coal Co. Ltd	6	4
1881	Ebbw Vale Steel Iron & Coal Co. Ltd	6	4
1882	Ebbw Vale Steel Iron & Coal Co. Ltd	6	4
1883	Ebbw Vale Steel Iron & Coal Co. Ltd	6	3
1884	Ebbw Vale Steel Iron & Coal Co. Ltd	6	0
1885	Ebbw Vale Steel Iron & Coal Co. Ltd	6	0
1886	Ebbw Vale Steel Iron & Coal Co. Ltd	6	0
1887	Ebbw Vale Steel Iron & Coal Co. Ltd	6	0
1888	Ebbw Vale Steel Iron & Coal Co. Ltd	6	0
1889	Ebbw Vale Steel Iron & Coal Co. Ltd	6	0

1823–30: 6 furnaces built in 1826; output 10,640 tons in 1840. 1825: 'Building' (20 March 1826). The Staffs RO version of the list has 4 furnaces; the B&W text has 2 and gives the second partner's name as 'Hare'; both lists agree that the furnaces were not in blast. 1839: 2 furnaces building. 1843: output 178 tons a week. 1849: Hunt's list has 5 furnaces in blast. Truran: output 160 tons a week from each of 6 furnaces. In 1870–75 furnace-numbers for all the Ebbw Vale Co.'s works are combined under Ebbw Vale (qv).

Amman, 'Amwain': see Brynamman; Cwmavon; Oakwood

Banwen, Glam. [SN 8509]

Year	Owner	Built	In Blast
1847	Joint stock company	2	0
1849	Banwen Co.	2	0
1854	Not occupied	2	0
1855	—	2	0
1856	—	2	0
1857	—	2	0
1858	—	2	0
1859	—	2	0
1860	—	2	0
1861	Llewelyn & Co.	2	2
1862	Llewelyn & Co.	2	0
1863	Llewelyn & Co.	2	0
1864	Llewelyn & Co.	2	0
1865	Llewelyn & Co.	2	0
1866	Llewelyn & Co.	2	0
1867	Llewelyn & Co.	2	0
1868	Llewelyn & Co.	2	0
1869	Llewelyn & Co.	2	0
1870	Llewelyn & Co.	2	0
1871	Llewelyn & Co.	2	0

1849: Hunt's list has 1 furnace in blast. Truran: output 60 tons a week from each of 2 furnaces.

Beaufort, Brecs. [SO 1611]

Year	Owner	Built	In Blast
1794	Messrs Kendall	1	-
1796	—	1	1
1805	Kendall & Co.	2	2
1810	Kendall & Co.	2	2
1823	—	3	-
1825	Kendall & Co.	4	4
1830	—	4	-
1839	Bailey Bros.	6	6
1841	Bailey Bros.	6	6
1843	Bailey Bros.	8	7
1847	J. & J. Bailey	14	12
1849	Messrs Bailey	14	14
1854	Joseph & C. Bailey	7	7
1855	Sir Jos. & C. Bailey	7	7
1856	Sir Jos. & C. Bailey	7	7
1857	Sir Jos. & C. Bailey	8	7
1858	Sir Jos. & C. Bailey	8	7
1859	Sir Jos. & C. Bailey	8	7
1860	Sir Jos. & C. Bailey	8	7
1861	Sir Jos. & C. Bailey	7	6
1862	Sir Jos. & C. Bailey	7	6
1863	Sir Jos. & C. Bailey	7	6
1864	Sir Jos. & C. Bailey	7	6
1865	Sir Jos. & C. Bailey	7	6
1866	Sir Jos. & C. Bailey	5	5
1867	J. & C. Bailey	5	5
1868	J. & C. Bailey	5	5
1869	J. & C. Bailey	7	6
1870	J. & C. Bailey	7	6
1871	Nant-y-Glo & Blaina Iron Works Co. Ltd	6	4
1872	Nant-y-Glo & Blaina Iron Works Co. Ltd	7	6

Year	Owner	Built	In Blast
1874	Nant-y-Glo & Blaina Iron Works Co. Ltd	-	-
1875	Nant-y-Glo & Blaina Iron Works Co. Ltd	-	-
1876	Nant-y-Glo & Blaina Iron Works Co. Ltd	5	0
1877	Nant-y-Glo & Blaina Iron Works Co. Ltd	3	0
1878	Nant-y-Glo & Blaina Iron Works Co. Ltd	3	0

The ground landlord in 1794 was the Duke of Beaufort; the furnace was coke-fired, blown by water, and built in 1780; there were two melting fineries, built in 1787. 1796: output 1,560 tons p.a., i.e. 30 tons a week, Excise and actual; 1,660 tons Exact Return. 1805: output 4,696 tons p.a. 1823: 5,243 tons p.a.; fourth furnace built in 1824; output in 1830 7,276 tons p.a. 1825: output 170 tons a week, 8,320 tons p.a., 'melting and forge' (B&W); 'melting iron' (Staffs RO). The B&W text has 2 furnaces in blast; the Staffs RO version has 4. 1843: output 525 tons a week. 1847: furnace-numbers include Beaufort and Nantyglo (qv), as they do in English's list of 1849; Hunt's list has 7 furnaces in blast at each works. Truran: output (at Beaufort) 120 tons a week from each of 7 furnaces. Beaufort was taken over by the Nant-y-Glo & Blaina Co. in 1871; the reappearance of J. & C. Bailey as owners in 1872 in *Mineral Statistics* is clearly in error and has been corrected above. There is no reference at all to Beaufort in 1873 and in 1874–75 furnace-numbers are given for all the Nant-y-Glo Co.'s works under Nantyglo (qv).

Blaenavon, Mon. SO 2509

Year	Owner	Built	In Blast
1794	Hill & Co.	3	-
1796	—	3	3
1805	Hill & Co.	4	3
1810	Hill & Hopkins	5	5
1823	—	5	-
1825	Hill & Co.	5	4
1830	—	5	-
1839	Blaenavon Iron Co.	5	5
1841	Blaenavon Iron Co.	5	4
1843	Joint Stock	5	4
1847	Blaenavon Iron Co.	5	4
1849	Blaenavon Iron Co.	5	4
1854	Blaenavon Iron Co.	5	5
1855	Blaenavon Iron Co.	5	4
1856	Blaenavon Iron Co.	5	4
1857	Blaenavon Iron Co.	5	4
1858	Blaenavon Iron Co.	-	-
1859	Blaenavon Iron Co.	-	-
1860	Blaenavon Iron Co.	6	6
1861	Blaenavon Iron Co.	6	5
1862	Blaenavon Iron Co.	6	6
1863	Blaenavon Iron Co.	6	5
1864	Blaenavon Co. Ltd	6	6
1865	Blaenavon Co. Ltd	6	5
1866	Blaenavon Co. Ltd	6	6
1867	Blaenavon Co. Ltd	6	6
1868	Blaenavon Co. Ltd	7	7
1869	Blaenavon Co. Ltd	9	8
1870	Blaenavon Co. Ltd	9	9
1871	Blaenavon Co. Ltd	10	8
1872	Blaenavon Iron & Steel Co. Ltd	10	8
1873	Blaenavon Iron & Steel Co. Ltd	10	7
1874	Blaenavon Iron & Steel Co. Ltd	10	7
1875	Blaenavon Iron & Steel Co. Ltd	10	7
1876	Blaenavon Iron & Steel Co. Ltd	10	6
1877	Blaenavon Iron & Steel Co. Ltd	10	6
1878	Blaenavon Iron & Steel Co. Ltd	9	5
1879	Blaenavon Iron & Steel Co. Ltd	9	4
1880	Blaenavon Iron & Steel Co. Ltd	9	5
1881	Blaenavon Iron & Steel Co. Ltd	8	5
1882	Blaenavon Co. Ltd	9	6
1883	Blaenavon Co. Ltd	8	6
1884	Blaenavon Co. Ltd	9	6
1885	Blaenavon Co. Ltd	6	4
1886	Blaenavon Co. Ltd	9	4
1887	Blaenavon Co. Ltd	6	4
1888	Blaenavon Co. Ltd	6	4
1889	Blaenavon Co. Ltd	9	4
1890	Blaenavon Co. Ltd	9	4
1891	Blaenavon Co. Ltd	9	4
1892	Blaenavon Co. Ltd	9	4
1893	Blaenavon Co. Ltd	9	3
1894	Blaenavon Co. Ltd	9	4
1895	Blaenavon Co. Ltd	9	3
1896	Blaenavon Co. Ltd	9	4
1897	Blaenavon Co. Ltd	9	4
1898	Blaenavon Co. Ltd	9	3
1899	Blaenavon Co. Ltd	9	4
1900	Blaenavon Co. Ltd	9	5
1901	Blaenavon Co. Ltd	9	0
1902	Blaenavon Co. Ltd	9	0
1903	Blaenavon Co. Ltd	9	0
1904	Blaenavon Co. Ltd	9	1
1905	Blaenavon Co. Ltd	9	2
1906	Blaenavon Co. Ltd	9	2
1907	Blaenavon Co. Ltd	3	2
1908	Blaenavon Co. Ltd	2	1
1909	Blaenavon Co. Ltd	2	1
1910	Blaenavon Co. Ltd	2	1
1911	Blaenavon Co. Ltd	2	1
1912	Blaenavon Co. Ltd	2	1
1913	Blaenavon Co. Ltd	2	1
1921	Blaenavon Co. Ltd	3	-
1922	Blaenavon Co. Ltd	3	-
1923	Blaenavon Co. Ltd	3	-
1924	Blaenavon Co. Ltd	3	-
1925	Blaenavon Co. Ltd	3	-
1926	Blaenavon Co. Ltd	3	-
1927	Blaenavon Co. Ltd	3	-
1928	Blaenavon Co. Ltd	3	-
1929	Blaenavon Co. Ltd	3	-
1930	Blaenavon Co. Ltd	3	-
1931	Blaenavon Co. Ltd	3	-
1932	Blaenavon Co. Ltd	3	-
1933	Blaenavon Co. Ltd	3	-

The ground landlord in 1794 was the Earl of Abergavenny; the furnaces were coke-fired, blown by engine and built in 1789. 1796: 3 furnaces each said to be producing 1,820 tons p.a., i.e. 35 tons a week; total output 5,460 tons p.a., Excise and actual; 4,318 tons Exact Return. 1805: output 7,846 tons p.a. 1823: output 16,882 tons p.a. 1830: 13,843 tons p.a. 1825: 290 tons a week, 14,560 tons p.a., 'melting and forge'. The Staffs RO version of the list has 4 furnaces in blast; the B&W text has 3. 1839: 2 building. 1843: output 540 tons a week. 1849: Hunt's list has 5 furnaces in blast. Truran: output 120 tons a week from each of 5 furnaces. In 1867 the output was described as cold blast and in 1881 one furnace was rebuilding. The first limited liability company (registered in 1864) is not named at all in *Mineral Statistics*; the second was registered in 1870 but only appears as owner from 1872; and the third was registered in 1880 but only appears from 1882.

Blaendare, Mon. ST 2799

Year	Owner	Built	In Blast
1794	D. Tanner	1	-
1796	—	1	1
1805	Barnaby	1	0
1810	—	2	2
1825	—	1	-

In 1794 Tanner was also listed as ground landlord; the furnace was coke-fired, built in 1790, and blown by engine. 1796: output 1,404 tons p.a., i.e. 27 tons a week, Excise and actual; 1,500 tons Exact Return. The furnace was out of blast in 1805 but apparently back in use by 1810. In 1825 Blaendare was grouped with Melincourt and several other small charcoal-fired furnaces against all of which the compiler commented: 'Am not acquainted with these furnaces and have taken them from an old list'. The furnace was almost certainly out of blast but strictly speaking the compiler had not received a return for any of these works. For the later works on or very close to the site of Blaendare see Pontypool (II).

Blaengwrach: see Venallt

Blain: see Cwmavon

Blaina, Mon. [SO 1908]

Year	Owner	Built	In Blast
1825	G. Jones	2	1
1830	—	3	-
1839	Russell & Brown	2	2
1841	Cwmcelyn & Blaina Co.	6	3
1843	Joint Stock	3	3
1847	Cruttwell, Allies & Co.	6	4
1849	Messrs Cruttwell	6	3
1854	Cruttwell & Levick	7	4
1855	Cruttwell, Levick & Co.	3	2
1856	Cruttwell, Levick & Co.	3	2
1857	Cruttwell, Levick & Co.	9	5
1858	Fred. Levick	2	2
1859	Fred. Levick	2	2
1860	Fred. Levick	2	2
1861	Fred. Levick & R. Simpson	6	6
1862	Fred. Levick & R. Simpson	6	6
1863	Levick & Simpson	6	6
1864	Levick & Simpson	6	4
1865	Levick & Simpson	6	5
1866	Levick & Simpson	6	5
1867	Levick & Simpson	6	5
1868	Levick & Simpson	6	0
1869	Levick & Simpson	2	0
1870	Levick & Simpson	2	0
1871	Nant-y-Glo & Blaina Iron Works Co. Ltd	4	3
1872	Nant-y-Glo & Blaina Iron Works Co. Ltd	-	-
1873	Nant-y-Glo & Blaina Iron Works Co. Ltd	-	-
1874	Nant-y-Glo & Blaina Iron Works Co. Ltd	-	-
1875	Nant-y-Glo & Blaina Iron Works Co. Ltd	-	-
1876	Nant-y-Glo & Blaina Iron Works Co. Ltd	3	2
1877	Nant-y-Glo & Blaina Iron Works Co. Ltd	3	0
1878	Nant-y-Glo & Blaina Iron Works Co. Ltd	3	0
1879	Nant-y-Glo & Blaina Iron Works Co. Ltd	3	0
1880	Nant-y-Glo & Blaina Iron Works Co. Ltd	3	0
1881	Blaina Furnaces Co. Ltd	3	2
1882	Blaina Furnaces Co. Ltd	3	2
1883	Blaina Furnaces Co. Ltd	3	2
1884	Blaina Furnaces Co. Ltd	3	2
1885	Blaina Furnaces Co. Ltd	3	2
1886	Pyle Works Ltd	2	1
1891	Pyle & Blaina Works Ltd	2	2
1892	Pyle & Blaina Works Ltd	2	1
1893	Pyle & Blaina Works Ltd	2	1
1894	Pyle & Blaina Works Ltd	2	1
1895	Pyle & Blaina Works Ltd	2	1
1896	Pyle & Blaina Works Ltd	2	1
1897	Pyle & Blaina Works Ltd	2	1
1898	Pyle & Blaina Works Ltd	2	1
1899	Pyle & Blaina Works Ltd	2	1
1900	Pyle & Blaina Works Ltd	2	1
1901	Pyle & Blaina Works Ltd	2	1
1902	Pyle & Blaina Works Ltd	2	1
1903	Pyle & Blaina Works Ltd	2	1
1904	Pyle & Blaina Works Ltd	2	1
1905	Pyle & Blaina Works Ltd	2	2
1906	Pyle & Blaina Works Ltd	2	2
1907	Pyle & Blaina Works Ltd	2	1
1908	Pyle & Blaina Works Ltd	2	1
1909	Pyle & Blaina Works Ltd	2	0
1910	Pyle & Blaina Works Ltd	2	1
1911	Pyle & Blaina Works Ltd	2	0
1912	Pyle & Blaina Works Ltd	2	0
1913	Pyle & Blaina Works Ltd	2	0

The 1823–30 list gives 1824 as the year of construction for all 3 furnaces; output in 1830 4,905 tons p.a. 1825: output 55 tons a week, 2,600 tons p.a., 'melting and forge'. 1843: output 197 tons a week. For 1841, 1847 and 1849 furnace-numbers for Blaina above include Cwm-celyn (qv), and in 1854, 1857 and 1861–70 those for Blaina include Cwm-celyn and Coalbookvale (qv). There is no entry for Cwm-celyn in 1871. In 1872–75 numbers for Blaina and Nantyglo are combined under the latter heading (qv). Truran: output 150 tons a week from each of 3 furnaces at Blaina alone. The entry printed above for 1886 appears in *Mineral Statistics* under Monmouthshire but may belong with the works at Cefn Cwsc (qv), near Pyle (Glam.), with which Blaina was subsequently associated.

'Brin': see Onllwyn

Briton Ferry, Glam. [SS 7394]

Year	Owner	Built	In Blast
1856	Briton Ferry Iron Co.	2	2
1857	Briton Ferry Iron Co.	2	2
1858	Briton Ferry Iron Co.	2	2
1859	Briton Ferry Iron Co.	2	1
1860	Briton Ferry Iron Co.	2	2
1861	Briton Ferry Iron Co.	2	2
1862	Briton Ferry Iron Co.	2	2
1863	Willett & Davey	2	2
1864	Willett & Davey	2	2
1865	Willett & Davey	2	2
1866	Willett & Davey	2	2
1867	Willett & Davey	2	2
1868	Willett & Davey	2	0
1869	Willett & Davey	2	1
1870	Townshend, Wood & Co.	2	2
1871	Townshend, Wood & Co.	2	2
1872	Townshend, Wood & Co.	2	2
1873	Townshend, Wood & Co.	2	2
1874	Townshend, Wood & Co.	2	2
1875	Townshend, Wood & Co.	2	1
1876	Townshend, Wood & Co.	2	2
1877	Townshend, Wood & Co.	2	2
1878	Townshend, Wood & Co.	2	2
1879	Townshend, Wood & Co.	2	1
1880	Townshend, Wood & Co.	2	2
1881	Townshend, Wood & Co.	2	0
1882	Townshend, Wood & Co.	2	2
1883	George Henry Davey	2	1
1884	George Henry Davey	2	1
1885	George Henry Davey	2	1
1886	George Henry Davey	2	0
1887	Unoccupied	2	0
1888	Martin & Co.	2	0
1889	Briton Ferry Works Reconstruction Co. Ltd	2	0
1890	Briton Ferry Works Reconstruction Co Ltd	2	1
1891	Briton Ferry Works Reconstruction Co Ltd	2	1
1892	Briton Ferry Works Reconstruction Co. Ltd	2	1
1893	Briton Ferry Works Ltd	2	1
1894	Briton Ferry Works Ltd	2	1
1895	Briton Ferry Works Ltd	2	1
1896	Briton Ferry Works Ltd	2	1
1897	Briton Ferry Works Ltd	2	2
1898	Briton Ferry Works Ltd	2	1
1899	Briton Ferry Works Ltd	2	1
1900	Briton Ferry Works Ltd	2	1
1901	Briton Ferry Works Ltd	2	1
1902	Briton Ferry Works Ltd	2	1
1903	Briton Ferry Works Ltd	2	1
1904	Briton Ferry Works Ltd	2	1
1905	Briton Ferry Works Ltd	2	1
1906	Briton Ferry Works Ltd	2	1
1907	Briton Ferry Works Ltd	2	1
1908	Briton Ferry Works Ltd	2	1
1909	Briton Ferry Works Ltd	2	1
1910	Briton Ferry Works Ltd	2	1
1911	Briton Ferry Works Ltd	2	1
1912	Briton Ferry Works Ltd	2	1
1913	Briton Ferry Works Ltd	2	1
1921	Briton Ferry Works Ltd	2	-
1922	Briton Ferry Works Ltd	2	-
1923	Briton Ferry Works Ltd	2	-
1924	Briton Ferry Works Ltd	2	-
1925	Briton Ferry Works Ltd	2	-
1926	Briton Ferry Works Ltd	2	-
1927	Briton Ferry Works Ltd	2	-
1928	Briton Ferry Works Ltd	2	-
1929	Briton Ferry Works Ltd	2	-
1930	Briton Ferry Works Ltd	2	-
1931	Briton Ferry Works Ltd	2	-
1932	Briton Ferry Works Ltd	2	-
1933	Briton Ferry Works Ltd	2	-
1934	Briton Ferry Works Ltd	2	-
1935	Guest Keen Baldwins Iron & Steel Co. Ltd	2	-
1936	Guest Keen Baldwins Iron & Steel Co. Ltd	2	-
1937	Guest Keen Baldwins Iron & Steel Ltd	2	-
1938	Guest Keen Baldwins Iron & Steel Co. Ltd	1	-
1939	Guest Keen Baldwins Iron & Steel Co. Ltd	1	-
1940	Guest Keen Baldwins Iron & Steel Co. Ltd	1	-
1941	Guest Keen Baldwins Iron & Steel Co. Ltd	1	-
1942	Guest Keen Baldwins Iron & Steel Co. Ltd	1	-
1943	Guest Keen Baldwins Iron & Steel Co. Ltd	1	-
1944	Guest Keen Baldwins Iron & Steel Co. Ltd	1	-
1945	Guest Keen Baldwins Iron & Steel Co. Ltd	1	-
1946	Guest Keen Baldwins Iron & Steel Co. Ltd	1	-
1947	Guest Keen Baldwins Iron & Steel Co. Ltd	1	-
1948	Briton Ferry Works Ltd	1	-
1949	Briton Ferry Works Ltd	1	-
1950	Briton Ferry Works Ltd	1	-
1951	Briton Ferry Works Ltd	1	-
1952	Briton Ferry Works Ltd	1	-
1953	Briton Ferry Works Ltd	1	-
1954	Briton Ferry Works Ltd	1	-
1955	Briton Ferry Works Ltd	1	-
1956	Briton Ferry Works Ltd	1	-
1957	Briton Ferry Works Ltd	1	-
1958	Briton Ferry Works Ltd	1	-

Bryn: see Onllwyn

Brynamman, Glam. [SN 7114]

Year	Owner	Built	In Blast
1847	Llewellyn & Co.	2	2
1849	—	2	2

Year	Owner	Built	In Blast
1854	L. Llewellyn	2	2
1855	L. Llewellyn	2	2
1856	L. Llewellyn	2	2
1857	L. Llewellyn	2	2
1858	L. Llewellyn	2	1
1859	Frances Strickley	2	2
1860	L. Llewellyn	2	2
1861	Henry Strick & Co.	2	1
1862	Henry Strick & Co.	2	1
1863	Henry Strick & Co.	2	1
1864	Henry Strick & Co.	2	1
1865	Henry Strick & Co.	2	1
1866	Henry Strick & Co.	2	1
1867	Henry Strick & Co.	3	2
1868	Henry Strick & Co.	3	2
1869	Amman Iron Co.	3	3
1870	Amman Iron Co.	3	3
1871	Amman Iron Co.	3	3
1872	Amman Iron Co.	3	3
1873	Amman Iron Co.	3	3
1874	Amman Iron Co.	3	3
1875	Amman Iron Co.	3	3
1876	Amman Iron Co.	3	2
1877	Amman Iron Co.	3	3
1878	Amman Iron Co.	3	2
1879	Amman Iron Co.	3	2
1880	Amman Iron Co.	3	2
1881	Amman Iron Co.	3	2
1882	Amman Iron Co.	3	3
1883	Amman Iron Co.	3	2
1884	Amman Iron Co.	3	3
1885	Amman Iron Co.	3	1
1886	Amman Iron & Tinplate Co.	3	1
1887	Amman Iron Co.	3	1
1888	Amman Iron Co.	3	1
1889	Amman Iron Co.	3	1
1890	Amman Iron Co.	3	0
1891	Amman Iron Co.	3	0
1892	Amman Iron Co.	3	0
1893	Amman Iron Co.	3	0

1847: a works owned by Llewellyn & Co., with 2 furnaces, both in blast, at 'Amwain' is probably that at Brynamman, since the place-name as it stands is meaningless and the other details all match. 1849: works called Amman by English; Hunt's list uses the name Brynamman; cf. also an entry for 'Oakwood and Amwain' (see Oakwood). 1854: the return is said to be for two works, each with one furnace, both owned by Llewellyn. Truran: output 60 tons a week from each of 2 furnaces. In 1865-70 there is an entry under 'Amman' under Glamorgan in *Mineral Statistics*, which appears to be a duplicate of that under Brynamman, Carms., since there is nowhere in Glamorgan called 'Amman', both works had 3 furnaces, and the owner at 'Amman' was the Amman Iron Co., as it was at Brynamman from 1869. From 1871 there is only one entry in *Mineral Statistics*, placed (correctly, since the furnaces were in the parish of Llangiwg) under Glamorgan.

Bryn-du, Glam. SS 8383

Year	Owner	Built	In Blast
1841	—	2	0
1843	O'Neil & Co.	2	0

An entry under Pyle in 1843 must, given the owner's name, belong with one for Bryn-du in 1841. See also Cefn Cwsc, which appears as Pyle in the 1839 list.

Bute, Mon. [SO 1009]

Year	Owner	Built	In Blast
1825	Forman & Co.	3	0
1830	—	3	-
1839	Rhymney Iron Co.	3	3
1841	Rhymney Co.	-	-
1843	Joint Stock	-	-
1847	Rhymney Iron Co.	-	-
1849	Rhymney Iron Co.	-	-
1854	Rhymney Iron Co.	-	-
1855	Rhymney Iron Co.	-	-
1856	Rhymney Iron Co.	5	5
1857	Rhymney Iron Co.	5	4
1858	Rhymney Iron Co.	5	5
1859	Rhymney Iron Co.	5	5
1860	Rhymney Iron Co.	5	4

1825 is the only year from the era of unofficial statistics for which separate figures are given for Bute and the neighbouring Rhymney works (qv). The furnaces at Bute were said to be 'Building' in 1825; no output is given. 1823-30: 3 furnaces at Rhymney in 1823, 6 in 1830; the 3 additional furnaces were built in 1826. These were presumably those at Bute, since in 1825 they were under construction. See under Rhymney for output figures. 1839: 6 furnaces built and in blast at the two works and another 2 furnaces building, although at which works is not stated. 1841: see Rhymney. 1847: 10 furnaces at the two works (9 in blast). 1849: Hunt's list has 10 furnaces in blast. 1854-55: 9 furnaces (8 in blast): these have been entered under Rhymney. Separate figures were given for 1856-60 but from 1861 a single return was published under Rhymney (qv), as it was by Truran.

Caerphilly, Glam. ST 1487

Year	Owner	Built	In Blast
1794	Harford & Partridge	1	-
1796	—	1	1
1805	Harford & Co.	1	0
1825	—	1	0

The furnace was described as 'old' and blown by water in 1794, when the ground landlord was John Morgan; there was also a rolling and slitting mill at the works. 1796: output 600 tons p.a. (i.e. 12 tons a week), Excise and actual; 695 tons Exact Return. 1805: 'Silent'. See Melincourt for the comment appended to the entry for Caerphilly and other abandoned charcoal-fired sites in the 1825 list; the Staffs RO version of the list notes 'No returns' against these works.

Cambrian: see Llynvi

Cardiff Iron & Steel, Glam. ST 2075

Year	Owner	Built	In Blast
1891	Dowlais Iron Co.	-	-
1892	Dowlais Iron Co.	-	-
1893	Dowlais Iron Co.	-	-
1894	Dowlais Iron Co.	-	-
1895	Dowlais Iron Co.	-	-
1896	Dowlais Iron Co.	-	-
1897	Dowlais Iron Co.	4	2
1898	Dowlais Iron Co.	4	1
1899	Dowlais Iron Co.	4	2
1900	Guest Keen & Co. Ltd	4	2
1901	Guest Keen & Co. Ltd	4	2
1902	Guest Keen & Nettlefolds Ltd	4	2
1903	Guest Keen & Nettlefolds Ltd	4	2
1904	Guest Keen & Nettlefolds Ltd	4	2
1905	Guest Keen & Nettlefolds Ltd	4	2
1906	Guest Keen & Nettlefolds Ltd	4	2
1907	Guest Keen & Nettlefolds Ltd	4	2
1908	Guest Keen & Nettlefolds Ltd	4	2
1909	Guest Keen & Nettlefolds Ltd	4	2
1910	Guest Keen & Nettlefolds Ltd	4	2
1911	Guest Keen & Nettlefolds Ltd	4	2
1912	Guest Keen & Nettlefolds Ltd	4	2
1913	Guest Keen & Nettlefolds Ltd	4	2
1921	Guest Keen & Nettlefolds Ltd	9	-
1922	Guest Keen & Nettlefolds Ltd	9	-
1923	Guest Keen & Nettlefolds Ltd	7	-
1924	Guest Keen & Nettlefolds Ltd	8	-
1925	Guest Keen & Nettlefolds Ltd	8	-
1926	Guest Keen & Nettlefolds Ltd	7	-
1927	Guest Keen & Nettlefolds Ltd	7	-
1928	Guest Keen & Nettlefolds Ltd	7	-
1929	Guest Keen & Nettlefolds Ltd	7	-
1930	British (Guest, Keen, Baldwins) Iron & Steel Co. Ltd	7	-
1931	British (Guest, Keen, Baldwins) Iron & Steel Co. Ltd	5	-
1932	British (Guest, Keen, Baldwins) Iron & Steel Co. Ltd	6	-
1933	British (Guest, Keen, Baldwins) Iron & Steel Co. Ltd	6	-
1934	British (Guest, Keen, Baldwins) Iron & Steel Co. Ltd	3	-
1935	Guest Keen Baldwins Iron & Steel Co. Ltd	3	-
1936	Guest Keen Baldwins Iron & Steel Co. Ltd	4	-
1937	Guest Keen Baldwins Iron & Steel Co. Ltd	3	-
1938	Guest Keen Baldwins Iron & Steel Co. Ltd	3	-
1939	Guest Keen Baldwins Iron & Steel Co. Ltd	4	-
1940	Guest Keen Baldwins Iron & Steel Co. Ltd	4	-
1941	Guest Keen Baldwins Iron & Steel Co. Ltd	4	-
1942	Guest Keen Baldwins Iron & Steel Co. Ltd	4	-
1943	Guest Keen Baldwins Iron & Steel Co. Ltd	4	-
1944	Guest Keen Baldwins Iron & Steel Co. Ltd	4	-
1945	Guest Keen Baldwins Iron & Steel Co. Ltd	4	-
1946	Guest Keen Baldwins Iron & Steel Co. Ltd	4	-
1947	Guest Keen Baldwins Iron & Steel Co. Ltd	4	-
1948	Guest Keen Baldwins Iron & Steel Co. Ltd	4	-
1949	Guest Keen Baldwins Iron & Steel Ltd	4	-
1950	Guest Keen Baldwins Iron & Steel Ltd	4	-
1951	Guest Keen Baldwins Iron & Steel Co. Ltd	4	-
1952	Guest Keen Baldwins Iron & Steel Co. Ltd	4	-
1953	Guest Keen Baldwins Iron & Steel Co. Ltd	4	-
1954	Guest Keen Iron & Steel Co. Ltd	4	-
1955	Guest Keen Iron & Steel Co. Ltd	4	-
1956	Guest Keen Iron & Steel Co. Ltd	4	-
1957	Guest Keen Iron & Steel Co. Ltd	3	-
1958	Guest Keen Iron & Steel Co. Ltd	4	-
1959	Guest Keen Iron & Steel Co. Ltd	4	-
1960	Guest Keen Iron & Steel Co. Ltd	4	-
1961	Guest Keen Iron & Steel Works	4	-
1962	Guest Keen Iron & Steel Works	4	-
1963	Guest Keen Iron & Steel Works	4	-
1964	Guest Keen Iron & Steel Works	4	-
1965	Guest Keen Iron & Steel Works	4	-
1966	Guest Keen Iron & Steel Works	4	-
1967	Guest Keen Iron & Steel Works	4	-
1968	East Moors Works	4	-
1969	East Moors Works	4	-
1970	British Steel Corporation	4	-
1971	British Steel Corporation	4	-
1972	British Steel Corporation	4	-
1973	British Steel Corporation	4	-
1974	British Steel Corporation	4	-
1975	British Steel Corporation	4	-
1976	British Steel Corporation	4	-
1977	British Steel Corporation	4	-

This is the works known in modern times as East Moors, although this name was only used as the 'owner' in 1968–69 and for the location of the plant from 1970. In 1891–96 furnace-numbers were combined with those for Dowlais (qv) and for a few years from 1921 the furnace-numbers above include Dowlais. Between 1961 and 1965 the owner was described as a branch of GKN Steel Co. Ltd. East Moors closed in 1978.

Carmarthen, Carms. SN 4220

Year	Owner	Built	In Blast
1794	Mr Morgan	1	-
1796	—	1	1
1805	Morgan	1	1
1825	Morgan	2	0

In 1794 Mr Morgan was also the ground landlord. The furnace was charcoal-fired, blown by water and described as 'old'; the forge consisted of two fineries, a chafery and a tinmill. 1796: output 1,056 tons p.a., Excise and actual; 290 tons Exact Return. 1805: no output. See Melincourt for the comment appended to the entry for Carmarthen and other charcoal-fired sites in 1825.

Cefn Cribwr, Glam. SS 8583

Year	Owner	Built	In Blast
1794	Green & Price	1	-
1830	—	1	-
1841	—	1	0
1849	—	1	0

This site is listed in 1794 as 'Cefn Crififi', described as being at Cowbridge (which is actually nearly ten miles away to the east). The ground landlord was — Bedford and the occupiers Green & Price; the furnace was coke-fired and said to have been built in 1790. 1823–30: nil return for 1823; note that one furnace was built in 1824; no output in 1830. 1849: Hunt's list claims the furnace to have been in blast, as does Truran (output 90 tons a week), but the works was abandoned by this period.

Cefn Cwsc, Glam. SS 8583

Year	Owner	Built	In Blast
1839	Millens & Co.	0	0
1841	Melin	2	2
1843	Mellins & Co.	2	1
1847	Maling [&] Co.	5	2
1849	H. Scale	3	1
1854	North British Banking Co.	3	0
1855	North British Banking Co.	2	0
1856	North British Banking Co.	2	0
1857	North British Banking Co.	2	0
1858	North British Banking Co.	2	0
1859	North British Banking Co.	2	0
1860	North British Banking Co.	2	0
1884	Pyle Works Ltd	2	1
1885	Pyle Works Ltd	2	1
1887	Pyle Works Ltd	1	1
1888	Pyle Works Ltd, in liquidation	1	1
1889	Pyle & Blaina Works Ltd	1	1
1890	Pyle & Blaina Works Ltd	1	1
1891	Pyle & Blaina Works Ltd	1	1
1892	Pyle & Blaina Works Ltd	2	1
1893	Pyle & Blaina Works Ltd	2	0
1894	Pyle & Blaina Works Ltd	2	0
1895	Pyle & Blaina Works Ltd	2	0
1896	Pyle & Blaina Works Ltd	1	1
1897	Pyle & Blaina Works Ltd	1	0
1898	Cefn Iron Works Ltd	1	0
1899	Cefn Iron Works Ltd	1	1
1900	Cefn Iron Works Ltd	1	0
1901	Cefn Iron Works Ltd	1	0

The 1839 list names the works as 'Pyle'; assuming the owner's name is a poor form of Malins & Co., an identification with Cefn Cwsc, about two miles from Pyle, seems reasonable. There were 2 furnaces building in 1839. 1841: an entry for 'Melin's Works' probably belongs here, given the number of furnaces and its position in the original list immediately after the adjacent works at Cefn Cribwr (qv). 1843: given the owner's name, an entry under 'Porthcawl' must belong here; output was said to be 60 tons a week. The 1847 return couples Cefn Cwsc with Garth (qv), the two sites having 5 furnaces in all (2 in blast). In 1854 Cefn Cwsc has a separate entry but was out of use, although the following year Truran lists 3 furnaces with a weekly output of 90 tons each at the site. From 1884 the works is called Pyle. An entry in *Mineral Statistics* for 1886 under Monmouthshire, said to refer to Blaina but with Pyle Works Ltd as the owner, may belong here, although it has been printed under Blaina (qv); it is not clear from what date the two works came under common ownership.

Clydach, Brecs. SO 2213

Year	Owner	Built	In Blast
1794	Cooke & Frere	1	-
1796	—	1	1
1805	Frere, Cooke & Co.	2	1
1810	Frere & Co.	2	2
1823	—	2	-
1825	Frere & Co.	3	2
1830	—	3	-
1839	Powell & Co.	4	4
1841	—	4	3
1843	Powell & Co.	4	3
1847	Powell & Co.	4	4
1849	Powell & Co.	4	4
1854	Powell & Co.	4	3
1855	Powell & Co.	4	3
1856	Powell & Co.	4	3
1857	Powell & Co.	4	3
1858	Powell & Co.	4	3
1859	Clydach Iron Co.	4	3
1860	Clydach Iron Co.	4	3
1861	Clydach Iron Co.	4	3
1862	Clydach Iron Co.	4	0
1863	Clydach Iron Co.	4	0
1864	Clydach Iron Co.	4	0
1865	New Clydach Sheet & Bar Iron Co. Ltd	4	0
1866	New Clydach Sheet & Bar Iron Co. Ltd	4	0
1867	New Clydach Sheet & Bar Iron Co. Ltd	4	0
1868	New Clydach Sheet & Bar Iron Co. Ltd	4	0
1869	New Clydach Sheet & Bar Iron Co.	4	0
1870	New Clydach Sheet & Bar Iron Co.	4	0
1871	John Jayne	4	0

The ground landlord in 1794 was — Hanbury Esq.; the furnace was coke-fired. 1796: weekly output 35 tons, i.e. 1,820 tons p.a., Excise and actual; 1,625 tons Exact Return. 1805: output 2,802 tons p.a. 1823: 5,200 tons p.a.; third furnace added in 1826; output 10,190 tons p.a. in 1830. 1825: weekly output 115 tons, 5,720 tons p.a., 'used by themselves'. In 1839 (and in the Staffs RO version of the 1825 list) the works is called 'Llanelly', the name usually used for the charcoal-fired furnace lower down the valley (qv). 1843: output 280 tons a week. Truran: output 90 tons a week from each of 4 furnaces. 1861: 'Out of blast since October last'.

Coalbrookvale, Mon. [SO 1909]

Year	Owner	Built	In Blast
1823	—	1	-
1825	Brewer & Co.	2	2
1830	—	2	-
1839	Brewer & Co.	2	2
1841	Brewer & Co.	4	4
1843	Brewer & Co.	4	4
1847	Brewer & Co.	2	1
1849	Brewer & Co.	5	5
1854	Cruttwell & Levick	-	-
1855	Cruttwell, Levick & Co.	2	2
1856	Cruttwell, Levick & Co.	2	2
1857	Cruttwell, Levick & Co.	-	-
1858	Fred. Levick	2	1
1859	Fred. Levick	2	2
1860	Fred. Levick	2	1
1861	Fred. Levick & R. Simpson	-	-
1862	Fred. Levick & R. Simpson	-	-
1863	Levick & Simpson	-	-
1864	Levick & Simpson	-	-
1865	Levick & Simpson	-	-
1866	Levick & Simpson	-	-
1867	Levick & Simpson	-	-
1868	Levick & Simpson	-	-
1869	Levick & Simpson	-	-
1870	Levick & Simpson	-	-
1871	Nant-y-Glo & Blaina Iron Works Co. Ltd	-	-
1872	Nant-y-Glo & Blaina Iron Works Co. Ltd	-	-
1873	Nant-y-Glo & Blaina Iron Works Co. Ltd	-	-
1874	Nant-y-Glo & Blaina Iron Works Co. Ltd	-	-
1875	Nant-y-Glo & Blaina Iron Works Co. Ltd	-	-
1876	Nant-y-Glo & Blaina Iron Works Co. Ltd	1	0
1877	Nant-y-Glo & Blaina Iron Works Co. Ltd	1	0
1878	Nant-y-Glo & Blaina Iron Works Co. Ltd	1	0
1879	Nant-y-Glo & Blaina Iron Works Co. Ltd	1	0
1880	Nant-y-Glo & Blaina Iron Works Co. Ltd	1	0
1881	Nant-y-Glo & Blaina Iron Works Co. Ltd	1	0
1882	Nant-y-Glo & Blaina Iron Works Co. Ltd	-	-

1823–30: output in 1823 2,704 tons p.a.; second furnace built 1824; output in 1830 2,780 tons p.a. 1825: output 108 tons a week, 5,200 p.a., 'melting and forge'; the Staffs RO version of the list has 2 furnaces in blast, the B&W text has 1. 1839: 1 furnace building. 1841 and 1843: furnace-numbers appear to include another works, although at this date Cwm-celyn and Blaina were still under separate ownership, as was Nantyglo. 1843: output 260 tons a week. In 1854, 1857 and 1861–70 furnace-numbers for Coalbrookvale are combined with those for Cwm-celyn and Blaina under the latter (qv). Truran: output (at Coalbrookvale alone) 100 tons week from each of 5 furnaces. In 1872–75 furnace-numbers for Coalbrookvale are included in those printed under Nantyglo (qv). In 1871 they are not combined and the blanks indicate that the works was out of use. 1882: Works dismantled.

'Coelbrook': see Gwendraeth

Cwmavon, Glam. [SS 7892]

Year	Owner	Built	In Blast
1823	Vigors & Smith	1	-
1825	Vigors & Co.	1	1
1830	Vigors & Smith	1	-
1839	Vigors & Co.	2	2
1841	Miners' Co.	2	2
1847	Copper Mining Co.	7	6
1849	Copper Miners of England	4	4
1854	Governor & Co. of Copper Mines	4	4
1855	Governor & Co. of Copper Mines	5	5
1856	Governor & Co. of Copper Mines	5	5
1857	Governor & Co. of Copper Mines	5	5
1858	Governor & Co. of Copper Mines	5	4
1859	Governor & Co. of Copper Mines	5	4
1860	Governor & Co. of Copper Mines	5	3
1861	Governor & Co. of Copper Mines	2	2
1862	Governor & Co. of Copper Mines	5	4
1863	Governor & Co. of Copper Mines	7	5
1864	Governor & Co. of Copper Mines	7	6
1865	Governor & Co. of Copper Mines	7	6
1866	Governor & Co. of Copper Mines	7	5
1867	Governor & Co. of Copper Miners in England	7	3
1868	Governor & Co. of Copper Miners in England	7	3
1869	Governor & Co. of Copper Miners in England	7	3
1870	Governor & Co. of Copper Miners in England	7	3
1871	Governor & Co. of Copper Miners in England	7	3
1872	Governor & Co. of Copper Miners in England	6	4
1873	Governor & Co. of Copper Miners in England	6	3
1874	Governor & Co. of Copper Miners in England	4	3
1875	Governor & Co. of Copper Miners in England	4	2
1876	Governor & Co. of Copper Miners in England	3	2
1877	Governor & Co. of Copper Miners in England	3	2

Year	Owner	Built	In Blast
1878	Governor & Co. of Copper Miners in England	2	2
1879	Governor & Co. of Copper Miners in England	2	2
1880	Governor & Co. of Copper Miners in England	2	2
1881	Cwm Avon Estate & Works Co. Ltd	2	1
1882	Cwm Avon Estate (Receiver of)	2	1
1883	Cwm Avon Estate (Receiver of)	2	1
1884	Cwm Avon Works Proprietors	2	1
1885	Cwm Avon Works Proprietors	2	1
1886	Cwm Avon Works Proprietors	2	1
1887	Cwm Avon Works Proprietors	2	1
1888	Cwm Avon Works Proprietors	2	1
1889	Wright Butler & Co. Ltd	2	1
1890	Wright Butler & Co. Ltd	2	1
1891	Wright Butler & Co. Ltd	2	1
1892	Wright Butler & Co. Ltd	2	0
1893	Wright Butler & Co. Ltd	2	0
1894	Wright Butler & Co. Ltd	2	0
1895	Wright Butler & Co. Ltd	2	0
1896	Wright Butler & Co. Ltd	2	0
1897	Wright Butler & Co. Ltd	2	0
1898	Wright Butler & Co. Ltd	2	0
1899	Wright Butler & Co. Ltd	2	0
1900	Wright Butler & Co. Ltd	2	0
1901	Wright Butler & Co. Ltd	2	0
1902	Baldwin's Ltd	2	0
1903	Baldwin's Ltd	2	0
1904	Baldwin's Ltd	2	0
1905	Baldwin's Ltd	2	0
1906	Baldwin's Ltd	2	0
1907	Baldwin's Ltd	2	0
1908	Baldwin's Ltd	2	0
1909	Baldwin's Ltd	2	0
1910	Baldwin's Ltd	2	0
1911	Baldwin's Ltd	2	0
1921	Baldwin's Ltd	2	-
1922	Baldwin's Ltd	2	-
1923	Baldwin's Ltd	2	-
1924	Baldwin's Ltd	2	-
1925	Baldwin's Ltd	2	-
1926	Baldwin's Ltd	2	-
1927	Baldwin's Ltd	2	-
1928	Baldwin's Ltd	2	-

Exceptionally, the 1823–30 list gives the owner's name for this works. Output 1,560 tons in 1823, 1,950 in 1830. The entry in the 1825 list names the works as 'Blain' and has been assigned to this site on the basis of the owner's name; output 30 tons a week, 1,820 tons p.a., 'used by himself'. The 1839 and 1841 lists use the name 'Cwm Bychan', which has been assigned here for the same reason, plus the proximity of Mynydd Bychan to Cwmavon. 1847: furnace-numbers must include Oakwood (qv), for which there is no separate entry that year; in 1849 an entry for 'Oakwood and Amwain' in English's list appears to couple the two again, although Cwmavon has its own entry. Hunt's list names Cwmavon only, but with 7 furnaces in blast, which must also include both sites. The two were definitely combined between 1863 and 1875. Truran lists output (at Cwmavon alone) as 100 tons a week from each of 4 furnaces but also has an entry for Oakwood, with 5 furnaces each producing 100 tons a week. This figure matches that given in the 1849 list and must include an element of double-counting, since there were never as many as 9 furnaces at the two sites.

Cwmbran, Mon. ST 2895

Year	Owner	Built	In Blast
1847	R.J. Blewitt	1	1
1849	R.J. Blewett	1	1
1854	Cwmbran Iron Co.	1	1
1855	J. Lawrence	1	1
1856	J. Lawrence	1	1
1857	J. Lawrence	1	1
1858	J. Lawrence	1	1
1859	J. Lawrence	1	1
1860	R.S. Roper & Co.	1	1
1861	R.S. Roper & Co.	1	1
1862	R.S. Roper & Co.	2	1
1863	R.S. Roper & Co.	2	2
1864	R.S. Roper & Co.	2	2
1865	R.S. Roper & Co.	2	2
1866	R.S. Roper & Co.	2	2
1867	R.S. Roper & Co.	2	2
1868	R.S. Roper & Co.	2	2
1869	R.S. Roper & Co.	2	2
1870	Cwmbran Iron Co.	2	2
1871	Cwmbran Iron Co.	2	2
1872	Patent Nut & Bolt Co. Ltd	2	2
1873	Patent Nut & Bolt Co. Ltd	2	2
1874	Patent Nut & Bolt Co. Ltd	2	1
1875	Patent Nut & Bolt Co. Ltd	2	1
1876	Patent Nut & Bolt Co. Ltd	2	1
1877	Patent Nut & Bolt Co. Ltd	2	1
1878	Patent Nut & Bolt Co. Ltd	2	1
1879	Patent Nut & Bolt Co. Ltd	2	1
1880	Patent Nut & Bolt Co. Ltd	2	2
1881	Patent Nut & Bolt Co. Ltd	2	2
1882	Patent Nut & Bolt Co. Ltd	2	1
1883	Patent Nut & Bolt Co. Ltd	2	1
1884	Patent Nut & Bolt Co. Ltd	2	1
1885	Patent Nut & Bolt Co. Ltd	2	1
1886	Patent Nut & Bolt Co. Ltd	2	1
1887	Patent Nut & Bolt Co. Ltd	1	1
1888	Patent Nut & Bolt Co. Ltd	1	1
1889	Patent Nut & Bolt Co. Ltd	1	1
1890	Patent Nut & Bolt Co. Ltd	1	0
1891	Patent Nut & Bolt Co. Ltd	1	0
1892	Patent Nut & Bolt Co. Ltd	1	0
1893	Patent Nut & Bolt Co. Ltd	1	0
1894	Patent Nut & Bolt Co. Ltd	1	0
1895	Patent Nut & Bolt Co. Ltd	1	1
1896	Patent Nut & Bolt Co. Ltd	1	1
1897	Patent Nut & Bolt Co. Ltd	1	1
1898	Patent Nut & Bolt Co. Ltd	1	0
1899	Patent Nut & Bolt Co. Ltd	1	1
1900	Patent Nut & Bolt Co. Ltd	1	1
1901	Guest Keen & Co. Ltd	1	1
1902	Guest Keen & Nettlefolds Ltd	1	1
1903	Guest Keen & Nettlefolds Ltd	1	1
1904	Guest Keen & Nettlefolds Ltd	1	1
1905	Guest Keen & Nettlefolds Ltd	1	1
1906	Guest Keen & Nettlefolds Ltd	1	1
1907	Guest Keen & Nettlefolds Ltd	1	1
1908	Guest Keen & Nettlefolds Ltd	1	1
1909	Guest Keen & Nettlefolds Ltd	1	0
1910	Guest Keen & Nettlefolds Ltd	1	1
1911	Guest Keen & Nettlefolds Ltd	1	1
1912	Guest Keen & Nettlefolds Ltd	1	1
1913	Guest Keen & Nettlefolds Ltd	1	1

1849: Hunt's list uses the name Typwca for this works; the name reappears in *Mineral Statistics* in 1854, with no other information, when Cwmbran has its own entry as above. Truran: output 170 tons a week from a single furnace. 1883: 'Production estimated'.

Cwm Bychan: see Cwmavon

Cwm-celyn, Mon. [SO 2008]

Year	Owner	Built	In Blast
1839	Cwm Celyn Co.	0	0
1841	Cwmcelyn & Blaina Co.	-	-
1843	Joint Stock	3	3
1847	Cruttwell, Allies & Co.	-	-
1849	Messrs Cruttwell	-	-
1854	Cruttwell & Levick	-	-
1855	Cruttwell, Levick & Co	2	2
1856	Cruttwell, Levick & Co.	2	2
1857	Cruttwell, Levick & Co.	-	-
1858	Fred. Levick	2	2
1859	Fred. Levick	2	2
1860	Fred. Levick	2	2
1861	Fred. Levick & R. Simpson	-	-
1862	Fred. Levick & R. Simpson	-	-
1863	Levick & Simpson	-	-
1864	Levick & Simpson	-	-
1865	Levick & Simpson	-	-
1866	Levick & Simpson	-	-
1867	Levick & Simpson	-	-
1868	Levick & Simpson	-	-
1869	Levick & Simpson	-	-
1870	Levick & Simpson	-	-

1839: 4 furnaces building. Furnace-numbers combined with Blaina (qv) in 1841, 1847, 1849, 1854 and 1861–70. 1843: output (at Cwm-celyn) 273 tons a week. Truran: output 210 tons a week from each of 3 furnaces.

Cwm Neath: see Venallt

Cyfarthfa, Glam. SO 0307

Year	Owner	Built	In Blast
1794	Messrs Crawshay	2	-
1796	—	3	3
1805	R. Crawshay	4	4
1810	Crawshay & Co.	6	4
1823	—	8	-
1825	Crawshay	7	7
1830	—	9	-
1839	William Crawshay	7	7
1841	W. Crawshay	11	9
1843	Crawshay & Co.	7	6
1847	W. Crawshay	15	13
1849	Crawshay & Co.	7	6
1854	W. Crawshay & Sons	7	6
1855	W. Crawshay & Sons	7	6
1856	W. Crawshay & Sons	7	7
1857	W. Crawshay & Sons	7	7
1858	W. Crawshay & Sons	7	7
1859	W. Crawshay & Sons	7	7
1860	W. Crawshay & Sons	7	7
1861	William Crawshay	7	7
1862	William Crawshay	7	6
1863	William Crawshay	11	11
1864	William Crawshay	11	11
1865	William Crawshay	11	10
1866	William Crawshay	11	10
1867	Robert Crawshay	11	8
1868	Robert Crawshay	11	9
1869	Robert Crawshay	11	9
1870	Robert Crawshay	11	9
1871	Robert Crawshay	11	9
1872	Robert Crawshay	11	9
1873	Robert Crawshay	11	8
1874	Robert Crawshay	11	4
1875	Robert Crawshay	10	0
1876	Robert Crawshay	6	0
1877	Robert Crawshay	6	0
1878	Robert Crawshay	6	0
1879	Crawshay Brothers	10	0
1880	Crawshay Brothers	10	6
1881	Crawshay Brothers	10	0
1882	Crawshay Brothers	6	0
1883	Crawshay Brothers	0	0
1884	Crawshay Brothers	7	1
1885	Crawshay Brothers	7	2
1886	Crawshay Brothers	7	2
1887	Crawshay Brothers	7	2
1888	Crawshay Brothers	7	3
1889	Crawshay Brothers	8	3
1890	Crawshay Brothers	8	3
1891	Crawshay Brothers	8	4
1892	Crawshay Brothers, Cyfarthfa, Ltd	8	3
1893	Crawshay Brothers, Cyfarthfa, Ltd	8	3
1894	Crawshay Brothers, Cyfarthfa, Ltd	8	3
1895	Crawshay Brothers, Cyfarthfa, Ltd	8	3
1896	Crawshay Brothers, Cyfarthfa, Ltd	8	3
1897	Crawshay Brothers, Cyfarthfa, Ltd	8	3
1898	Crawshay Brothers, Cyfarthfa, Ltd	9	3
1899	Crawshay Brothers, Cyfarthfa, Ltd	9	4
1900	Crawshay Brothers, Cyfarthfa, Ltd	9	4
1901	Crawshay Brothers, Cyfarthfa, Ltd	9	4
1902	Crawshay Brothers, Cyfarthfa, Ltd	9	3
1903	Crawshay Brothers, Cyfarthfa, Ltd	9	3
1904	Crawshay Brothers, Cyfarthfa, Ltd	9	2
1905	Crawshay Brothers, Cyfarthfa, Ltd	9	2
1906	Crawshay Brothers, Cyfarthfa, Ltd	5	3
1907	Crawshay Brothers, Cyfarthfa, Ltd	5	3
1908	Crawshay Brothers, Cyfarthfa, Ltd	5	1
1909	Crawshay Brothers, Cyfarthfa, Ltd	5	0
1910	Crawshay Brothers, Cyfarthfa, Ltd	5	0
1911	Crawshay Brothers, Cyfarthfa, Ltd	5	0
1912	Crawshay Brothers, Cyfarthfa, Ltd	5	0

Year	Owner	Built	In Blast
1913	Crawshay Brothers, Cyfarthfa, Ltd	5	0
1921	Crawshay Brothers, Cyfarthfa, Ltd	5	-
1922	Crawshay Brothers, Cyfarthfa, Ltd	5	-
1923	Crawshay Brothers, Cyfarthfa, Ltd	5	-
1924	Crawshay Brothers, Cyfarthfa, Ltd	5	-
1925	Crawshay Brothers, Cyfarthfa, Ltd	5	-
1926	Crawshay Brothers, Cyfarthfa, Ltd	5	-

The ground landlord in 1794 was Lord Talbot; the furnaces were coke-fired, blown by engine and built in 1767; at the forge there were 8 'Corts' (i.e. puddling) furnaces, 3 melting fineries, and 3 balling furnaces, against which the date 1767 is also written (but clearly cannot apply to the puddling plant); there was also a rolling mill built in 1790. In 1796 three furnaces were said to be producing 2,000 tons p.a. each (i.e. 40 tons a week), Excise and actual; 7,204 tons Exact Return. 1805: output 10,460 tons p.a. In 1823 the output was given as 24,200 tons p.a. and in 1830 as 29,000 tons p.a.; the additional furnace was built in 1824. The 1825 list returns a weekly output of 390 tons from Cyfarthfa, coupled with Ynysfach (qv) to give an aggregate annual figure for the two of 28,000 tons. The B&W text comments 'Use it themselves'; the Staffs RO version adds 'No 1 sometimes'. 1841: furnace-numbers above appear to include Ynysfach with Cyfarthfa, but not Hirwaun. 1843: output 420 tons a week. 1847: furnace-numbers include Cyfarthfa, Ynysfach and Hirwaun (qqv). 1849: English gives the furnace-numbers as 11 built, 16 in blast, 1 out: the 16 must be a misprint for 10, in which case the figures clearly include Ynysfach, which has its own entry (4 built, all in blast) and the details printed above have therefore been adjusted. Hunt's list has 7 furnaces in blast at Cyfarthfa (alone). Truran: output (at Cyfarthfa alone) 100 tons a week from each of 7 furnaces. Furnace-numbers above for 1863–75 and 1879–81 include Ynysfach. In 1879 the entry includes the comment (presumably referring to Cyfarthfa only): 'Operations resumed December 1879, the works having been standing for several years'. From 1891 the Cyfarthfa furnace-numbers are said to include Treforest works at Pontypridd (qv), although 3 furnaces (none in blast) continue to be listed under the latter heading until 1898.

Dowlais, Glam.   SO 0608

Year	Owner	Built	In Blast
1794	Dowlais Co.	2	-
1796	—	3	3
1805	Tait & Co.	3	3
1810	Tait & Co.	3	3
1823	—	8	-
1825	Guest, Lewis & Co.	11	11
1830	—	12	-
1839	Guest, Lewis & Co.	14	14
1841	Guest & Co.	18	18
1843	Guest & Co.	18	17
1847	Guest & Co.	18	18
1849	Sir J.J. Guest & Co.	18	16
1854	Dowlais Iron Co.	18	16
1855	Guest & Co.	18	16
1856	Guest & Co.	18	16
1857	Guest & Co.	18	16
1858	Guest & Co.	18	16
1859	Guest & Co.	18	15
1860	Guest & Co.	18	15
1861	Dowlais Iron Co.	17	15
1862	Trustees of Sir J.J. Guest Bt	18	14
1863	Trustees of Sir J.J. Guest Bt	18	14
1864	Dowlais Iron Co.	18	15
1865	Dowlais Iron Co.	17	16
1866	Dowlais Iron Co.	17	16
1867	Dowlais Iron Co.	17	15
1868	Dowlais Iron Co.	17	15
1869	Dowlais Iron Co.	18	16
1870	Dowlais Iron Co.	18	16
1871	Dowlais Iron Co.	17	17
1872	Dowlais Iron Co.	17	16
1873	Dowlais Iron Co.	18	16
1874	Dowlais Iron Co.	18	15
1875	Dowlais Iron Co.	18	14
1876	Dowlais Iron Co.	14	12
1877	Dowlais Iron Co.	18	13
1878	Dowlais Iron Co.	18	13
1879	Dowlais Iron Co.	18	11
1880	Dowlais Iron Co.	17	13
1881	Dowlais Iron Co.	16	13
1882	Dowlais Iron Co.	18	14
1883	Dowlais Iron Co.	16	13
1884	Dowlais Iron Co.	18	10
1885	Dowlais Iron Co.	18	9
1886	Dowlais Iron Co.	16	7
1887	Dowlais Iron Co.	16	7
1888	Dowlais Iron Co.	16	8
1889	Dowlais Iron Co.	15	8
1890	Dowlais Iron Co.	15	8
1891	Dowlais Iron Co.	18	8
1892	Dowlais Iron Co.	18	7
1893	Dowlais Iron Co.	18	7
1894	Dowlais Iron Co.	18	6
1895	Dowlais Iron Co.	18	6
1896	Dowlais Iron Co.	17	7
1897	Dowlais Iron Co.	14	5
1898	Dowlais Iron Co.	14	4
1899	Dowlais Iron Co.	14	6
1900	Guest Keen & Co. Ltd	14	6
1901	Guest Keen & Co. Ltd	14	5
1902	Guest Keen & Nettlefolds Ltd	8	5
1903	Guest Keen & Nettlefolds Ltd	8	5
1904	Guest Keen & Nettlefolds Ltd	8	5
1905	Guest Keen & Nettlefolds Ltd	8	5
1906	Guest Keen & Nettlefolds Ltd	8	5
1907	Guest Keen & Nettlefolds Ltd	6	4
1908	Guest Keen & Nettlefolds Ltd	6	3
1909	Guest Keen & Nettlefolds Ltd	5	3
1910	Guest Keen & Nettlefolds Ltd	5	3
1911	Guest Keen & Nettlefolds Ltd	5	2
1912	Guest Keen & Nettlefolds Ltd	5	2
1913	Guest Keen & Nettlefolds Ltd	5	2

The ground landlord in 1794 was Lord Cardiff. The furnaces were coke-fired, blown by engine, and said to have been built in 1758. 1796: Excise outputs for the three furnaces were 1,400, 1,350 and 1,350 tons p.a. (i.e. 28 or 27 tons a week), 4,100 tons total; the 'actual' outputs were 1,800, 1,850 and 1,800 tons p.a. (37 or 36 tons a week), 5,400 tons total; and the Exact Return was 2,800 tons p.a. total. 1805: output 6,800 tons p.a. 1823–30: output 22,287 tons in 1823 and 32,611 tons in 1830; 3 new furnaces were built in 1825 and one in 1828. 1825: output 580 tons a week (28,600 tons p.a.), 'forge and a little melting' (B&W) or 'Sometimes a little Nos 1–3' (Staffs RO). The Staffs RO version of the list has all 11 furnaces in blast, the B&W text has 8. 1839: 4 furnaces building. 1843: output 1,470 tons a week. 1849: Hunt's list has 14 furnaces in blast, probably meaning those at Dowlais only. Truran divides the number of furnaces between Dowlais and the adjacent Ifor Works (14 and 4 respectively) but assigns the same average weekly output of 116 tons per furnace to both plants; *Mineral Statistics* returned a single figure for the two works, although both names are listed in 1855–60, as they are in 1849. In 1879–80 1 furnace was said to be building and in 1883 2 furnaces. For 1891–96 furnace-numbers include both the two works at Merthyr Tydfil and Cardiff Iron & Steel (qv). After 1921 furnace-numbers for both Dowlais and Cardiff were returned as a single figure, for which see under Cardiff.

Duffryn, Glam. SO 0603

Year	Owner	Built	In Blast
1825	R. & A. Hill	2	1
1839	R. & A. Hill	3	3
1841	R. & A. Hill	-	-
1843	R. & A. Hill	4	3
1847	A. Hill	-	-
1854	Anthony Hill & Co.	-	-
1855	Anthony Hill	-	-
1856	Anthony Hill	5	4
1857	Anthony Hill	5	4
1858	Anthony Hill	5	4
1859	Anthony Hill	5	5
1860	Anthony Hill	5	5
1861	Anthony Hill	5	5
1862	Trustees of the late Anthony Hill	-	-
1863	Fothergill, Hankey & Bateman	-	-
1864	Fothergill, Hankey & Bateman	-	-
1865	Fothergill, Hankey & Bateman	-	-
1866	Fothergill, Hankey & Bateman	-	-
1867	Fothergill, Hankey & Lewis	-	-
1868	R. Fothergill & T.A. Lewis	-	-
1869	Fothergill, Hankey & Lewis	-	-
1870	Plymouth Iron Co.	-	-
1871	Fothergill & Hankey	-	-
1872	Fothergill & Hankey	-	-
1873	Fothergill & Hankey	-	-
1874	Fothergill & Hankey	-	-

There is no entry for Duffryn in the 1823–30 list, but see under Plymouth, where references to furnaces built in 1825 and 1827 may in fact relate to the first two furnaces at the adjacent Duffryn works. 1825: one furnace in blast and another building at Duffryn; output 104 tons a week, 5,460 p.a. There is also an additional note that the furnace averaged 104½ tons a week for six months and has made 111 tons in a week. 1839: 1 furnace building. In 1841, 1847 and 1854–55 Duffryn furnace-numbers are combined with those for Plymouth (qv); Truran gives a separate figure for the latter year: the 4 furnaces at Duffryn had an average weekly output of 120 tons each. 1843: output (at Duffryn) 300 tons a week. For 1862–74 furnace-numbers for Duffryn were once again coupled with those for Plymouth.

East Moors: see Cardiff Iron & Steel

Ebbw Vale, Mon. SO 1708

Year	Owner	Built	In Blast
1794	J. Homfray & Watt	1	-
1796	—	1	1
1805	Harford & Co.	2	1
1810	Harfords & Co.	1	0
1823	—	3	-
1825	Harford & Co.	3	3
1830	—	3	-
1839	Harford & Co.	3	3
1841	Harfords & Co.	4	3
1843	Harfords & Co.	4	3
1847	Darby & Co.	9	8
1849	Darby & Co.	4	4
1854	Ebbw Vale Co.	4	3
1855	Ebbw Vale Iron & Coal Co.	4	3
1856	Ebbw Vale Iron Co.	4	4
1857	Ebbw Vale Iron Co.	5	4
1858	Ebbw Vale Iron Co.	4	3
1859	Ebbw Vale Iron Co.	4	3
1860	Ebbw Vale Iron Co.	4	3
1861	Ebbw Vale Iron Co.	4	2
1862	Ebbw Vale Iron Co.	4	2
1863	Ebbw Vale Iron Co.	4	2
1864	Ebbw Vale Iron Co.	3	2
1865	Ebbw Vale Co. Ltd	3	0
1866	Ebbw Vale Co. Ltd	13	8
1867	Ebbw Vale Co. Ltd	13	8
1868	Ebbw Vale Co. Ltd	13	9
1869	Ebbw Vale Co. Ltd	3	3
1870	Ebbw Vale Co. Ltd	21	16
1871	Ebbw Vale Co. Ltd	21	17
1872	Ebbw Vale Steel Iron & Coal Co. Ltd	22	18
1873	Ebbw Vale Steel Iron & Coal Co. Ltd	21	17
1874	Ebbw Vale Steel Iron & Coal Co. Ltd	21	16
1875	Ebbw Vale Steel Iron & Coal Co. Ltd	21	13
1876	Ebbw Vale Steel Iron & Coal Co. Ltd	4	3
1877	Ebbw Vale Steel Iron & Coal Co. Ltd	4	4
1878	Ebbw Vale Steel Iron & Coal Co. Ltd	3	3
1879	Ebbw Vale Steel Iron & Coal Co. Ltd	4	3
1880	Ebbw Vale Steel Iron & Coal Co. Ltd	4	4
1881	Ebbw Vale Steel Iron & Coal Co. Ltd	4	4
1882	Ebbw Vale Steel Iron & Coal Co. Ltd	4	4
1883	Ebbw Vale Steel Iron & Coal Co. Ltd	4	4
1884	Ebbw Vale Steel Iron & Coal Co. Ltd	4	4
1885	Ebbw Vale Steel Iron & Coal Co. Ltd	4	4

Year	Company		
1886	Ebbw Vale Steel Iron & Coal Co. Ltd	4	4
1887	Ebbw Vale Steel Iron & Coal Co. Ltd	4	4
1888	Ebbw Vale Steel Iron & Coal Co. Ltd	5	5
1889	Ebbw Vale Steel Iron & Coal Co. Ltd	4	3
1890	Ebbw Vale Steel Iron & Coal Co. Ltd	4	4
1891	Ebbw Vale Steel Iron & Coal Co. Ltd	4	3
1892	Ebbw Vale Steel Iron & Coal Co. Ltd	3	2
1893	Ebbw Vale Steel Iron & Coal Co. Ltd	4	3
1894	Ebbw Vale Steel Iron & Coal Co. Ltd	4	4
1895	Ebbw Vale Steel Iron & Coal Co. Ltd	4	3
1896	Ebbw Vale Steel Iron & Coal Co. Ltd	4	3
1897	Ebbw Vale Steel Iron & Coal Co. Ltd	4	3
1898	Ebbw Vale Steel Iron & Coal Co. Ltd	6	2
1899	Ebbw Vale Steel Iron & Coal Co. Ltd	6	5
1900	Ebbw Vale Steel Iron & Coal Co. Ltd	4	3
1901	Ebbw Vale Steel Iron & Coal Co. Ltd	4	3
1902	Ebbw Vale Steel Iron & Coal Co. Ltd	4	3
1903	Ebbw Vale Steel Iron & Coal Co. Ltd	6	5
1904	Ebbw Vale Steel Iron & Coal Co. Ltd	7	5
1905	Ebbw Vale Steel Iron & Coal Co. Ltd	7	4
1906	Ebbw Vale Steel Iron & Coal Co. Ltd	7	5
1907	Ebbw Vale Steel Iron & Coal Co. Ltd	7	5
1908	Ebbw Vale Steel Iron & Coal Co. Ltd	7	4
1909	Ebbw Vale Steel Iron & Coal Co. Ltd	7	4
1910	Ebbw Vale Steel Iron & Coal Co. Ltd	7	5
1911	Ebbw Vale Steel Iron & Coal Co. Ltd	7	3
1912	Ebbw Vale Steel Iron & Coal Co. Ltd	7	5
1913	Ebbw Vale Steel Iron & Coal Co. Ltd	7	4
1921	Ebbw Vale Steel Iron & Coal Co. Ltd	8	-
1922	Ebbw Vale Steel Iron & Coal Co. Ltd	8	-
1923	Ebbw Vale Steel Iron & Coal Co. Ltd	9	-
1924	Ebbw Vale Steel Iron & Coal Co. Ltd	9	-
1925	Ebbw Vale Steel Iron & Coal Co. Ltd	9	-
1926	Ebbw Vale Steel Iron & Coal Co. Ltd	5	-
1927	Ebbw Vale Steel Iron & Coal Co. Ltd	5	-
1928	Ebbw Vale Steel Iron & Coal Co. Ltd	5	-
1929	Ebbw Vale Steel Iron & Coal Co. Ltd	5	-
1930	Ebbw Vale Steel Iron & Coal Co. Ltd	5	-
1931	Ebbw Vale Steel Iron & Coal Co. Ltd	5	-
1932	Ebbw Vale Steel Iron & Coal Co. Ltd	5	-
1933	Ebbw Vale Steel Iron & Coal Co. Ltd	5	-
1934	Ebbw Vale Steel Iron & Coal Co. Ltd	5	-
1935	Ebbw Vale Steel Iron & Coal Co. Ltd	5	-
1936	Richard Thomas & Co. Ltd	0	-
1937	Richard Thomas & Co. Ltd	1	-
1938	Richard Thomas & Co. Ltd	2	-
1939	Richard Thomas & Baldwins Ltd	2	-
1940	Richard Thomas & Baldwins Ltd	2	-
1941	Richard Thomas & Baldwins Ltd	2	-
1942	Richard Thomas & Baldwins Ltd	2	-
1943	Richard Thomas & Baldwins Ltd	2	-
1944	Richard Thomas & Baldwins Ltd	2	-
1945	Richard Thomas & Baldwins Ltd	3	-
1946	Richard Thomas & Baldwins Ltd	3	-
1947	Richard Thomas & Baldwins Ltd	3	-
1948	Richard Thomas & Baldwins Ltd	3	-
1949	Richard Thomas & Baldwins Ltd	3	-
1950	Richard Thomas & Baldwins Ltd	3	-
1951	Richard Thomas & Baldwins Ltd	2	-
1952	Richard Thomas & Baldwins Ltd	2	-
1953	Richard Thomas & Baldwins Ltd	2	-
1954	Richard Thomas & Baldwins Ltd	3	-
1955	Richard Thomas & Baldwins Ltd	3	-
1956	Richard Thomas & Baldwins Ltd	3	-
1957	Richard Thomas & Baldwins Ltd	3	-
1958	Richard Thomas & Baldwins Ltd	3	-
1959	Richard Thomas & Baldwins Ltd	3	-
1960	Richard Thomas & Baldwins Ltd	3	-
1961	Richard Thomas & Baldwins Ltd	3	-
1962	Richard Thomas & Baldwins Ltd	3	-
1963	Richard Thomas & Baldwins Ltd	3	-
1964	Richard Thomas & Baldwins Ltd	3	-
1965	Richard Thomas & Baldwins Ltd	3	-
1966	Richard Thomas & Baldwins Ltd	3	-
1967	Richard Thomas & Baldwins Ltd	3	-
1968	Richard Thomas & Baldwins Ltd	3	-
1969	Richard Thomas & Baldwins Ltd	3	-
1970	British Steel Corporation	3	-
1971	British Steel Corporation	3	-
1972	British Steel Corporation	3	-
1973	British Steel Corporation	3	-
1974	British Steel Corporation	3	-

The ground landlord in 1794 was John Miles; the furnace was coke-fired, blown by engine, and built in 1790. 1796: output 30 tons a week (1,560 p.a.), Excise and actual, at 'Penyea' (i.e. Penycae), i.e. Ebbw Vale; Exact Return 397 tons p.a. 1805: output 3,664 tons p.a. In 1823 and 1830 Ebbw Vale was coupled with Sirhowy (qv), with 6 furnaces at the two sites producing 10,425 tons p.a. in 1823 and 26,020 in 1830; the figures can safely be split by reference to the 1825 list. The output in 1825 was given as 150 tons a week, 7,020 p.a., 'use it themselves'. The B&W text lists 1 furnace in blast, the Staffs RO version has 3. 1839: 1 furnace building. 1843: output 291 tons a week. In 1847 figures were again given for Ebbw Vale and Sirhowy together. Truran: output 130 tons a week from each of 4 furnaces at Ebbw Vale alone. In 1866–68 furnace-numbers printed above include Ebbw Vale, Sirhowy and Victoria (qv); in 1870–75 the figures include those three works plus Abersychan and Pontypool (qqv). In 1869 and from 1876 onwards each Ebbw Vale Co. plant has separate furnace-numbers in *Mineral Statistics*, printed here under the appropriate headings. In 1878 one furnace was said to be 'Building' at Ebbw Vale. In 1898–99 and from 1903 the furnace-numbers above include Victoria.

Forest Iron & Steel: see Pontypridd

Furnace Isaf: see Plymouth

Gadlys, Glam. SO 0003

Year	Owner	Built	In Blast
1830	—	1	-
1839	Wayne & Co.	1	1
1841	Wayne & Co.	2	1
1843	Wayne & Co.	2	1
1847	Wayne & Co.	2	1
1849	Wayne & Co.	2	1
1854	Wayne & Co.	2	2
1855	Wayne & Co.	2	2
1856	Wayne & Co.	4	2
1857	Wayne & Co.	4	2
1858	Wayne & Co.	4	2
1859	Wayne & Co.	4	3
1860	Wayne & Co.	4	3
1861	Wayne & Co.	4	3
1862	Gadlys Iron Co.	4	4
1863	Gadlys Iron Co.	4	4
1864	Gadlys Iron Co.	4	4
1865	Gadlys Iron Co.	4	4
1866	Gadlys Iron Co.	4	4
1867	Gadlys Iron Co.	4	3
1868	Wayne & Co.	4	2
1869	Wayne & Co.	4	3
1870	Wayne & Co.	4	2
1871	Gadlys Iron Co.	4	2
1872	Gadlys Coal & Iron Co. Ltd	4	2
1873	Wayne's Merthyr Steam Coal & Iron Works Ltd	4	2
1874	Wayne's Merthyr Steam Coal & Iron Works Ltd	4	2
1875	Wayne's Merthyr Steam Coal & Iron Works Ltd	4	0
1876	Wayne's Merthyr Steam Coal & Iron Works Ltd	4	1
1877	Wayne's Merthyr Steam Coal & Iron Works Ltd	4	0
1878	Wayne's Merthyr Steam Coal & Iron Works Ltd	4	0
1879	Wayne's Merthyr Steam Coal & Iron Works Ltd	4	0
1880	Wayne's Merthyr Steam Coal & Iron Works Ltd	4	0
1881	Wayne's Merthyr Steam Coal & Iron Works Ltd	4	0
1882	Wayne's Merthyr Steam Coal & Iron Works Ltd	4	0
1883	Wayne's Merthyr Steam Coal & Iron Works Ltd	4	0
1884	Wayne's Merthyr Steam Coal & Iron Works Ltd	4	0
1885	Wayne's Merthyr Steam Coal & Iron Works Ltd	4	0

The 1823–30 list gives a nil return for the former year and notes that the first furnace was built in 1828, although no output is given for 1830. 1839: 1 furnace building. 1843: output 45 tons a week. Truran: output 90 tons a week from each of 2 furnaces.

Garth, Glam. [SS 8690]

Year	Owner	Built	In Blast
1847	Maling [&] Co.	-	-
1849	Messrs Scale	3	0
1854	—	-	-

1847: 5 furnaces in all (2 in blast) at Garth and Cefn Cwsc (qv). 1849: Hunt's list has 3 furnaces in blast. In 1854 *Mineral Statistics* lists the name Garth but with blanks in every column. The name does not occur again in the official returns but Truran gives separate figures for Cefn Cwsc and Garth, with an output for the latter of 95 tons a week from each of 3 furnaces. It seems unlikely that in fact the works was then in use, although the number of furnaces balances correctly with the 5 returned for the two sites in 1847 and the 2 listed at Cefn Cwsc in 1855–60.

Glamorgan Coal & Iron Co.: see Tondu

Glyn-neath: see Abernant (Glyn-neath)

Golynos, Mon. SO 2504

Year	Owner	Built	In Blast
1839	Golynos Co.	2	2
1841	Golynos Co.	2	2
1843	Joint Stock	2	2
1847	Williams & Co.	8	5
1849	Williams & Co.	8	7
1854	Williams & Co.	7	4
1855	Williams & Co.	7	4
1856	Williams & Co.	7	4
1857	Williams & Co.	7	4
1858	Crawshay Bailey & William Morgan	6	4
1859	Crawshay Bailey & William Morgan	6	4
1860	Crawshay Bailey & William Morgan	6	4
1861	Crawshay Bailey & William Morgan	5	0
1862	Partridge & Sons	2	0
1863	Partridge & Sons	2	1
1864	Golynos Iron Co.	5	3
1865	Golynos Iron Co.	5	0

Year	Owner	Built	In Blast
1866	Golynos Iron Co.	5	0
1867	Golynos Iron Co.	5	0
1868	Golynos Iron Co.	5	0

1843: output 184 tons a week. 1847–49: furnace-numbers include Golynos, Pentwyn and Varteg (qqv); those for 1854–61 include Golynos and Varteg; those for 1862–63 are for Golynos only; and those for 1864–68 are for Golynos and Varteg. Truran gives separate figures for the two works in 1855: output at Golynos was 120 tons a week from each of 2 furnaces.

Gwendraeth, Carms. [SN 5011?]

Year	Owner	Built	In Blast
1843	—	1	0
1847	Watney & Co.	3	2
1849	Watney & Co.	3	1
1854	T. Watney & Co.	2	2
1855	T. Watney & Co.	2	1
1856	T. Watney & Co.	3	0
1857	T. Watney & Co.	3	0
1858	T. Watney & Co.	3	0
1859	T. Watney	3	0
1860	Daniel Watney	2	1
1861	Daniel Watney	2	1
1862	Daniel Watney	3	0
1863	Daniel Watney	2	0
1864	Daniel Watney	2	0
1865	Daniel Watney	2	0
1866	Daniel Watney	2	0
1867	Daniel Watney	2	0
1868	Daniel Watney	3	0
1869	Daniel Watney	3	0
1870	Daniel Watney	3	0
1871	Daniel Watney	2	0

1847: no output; owner's name given as 'Walneg'. 1849: owner's name given by English as 'Walvey & Co.'; Hunt lists 2 furnaces in blast at a works named 'Coelbrook', which appears to belong here, given its position on his map and assuming that the name is intended to be Coal Brook, i.e. Nantyglo, a tributary of the Gwendraeth. Truran: output 80 tons a week from each of 3 furnaces.

Hirwaun, Brecs. SN 9505

Year	Owner	Built	In Blast
1794	Mr Glover	1	-
1796	—	1	1
1805	Bouzer & Co.	1	1
1810	Bouzer & Co.	2	2
1823	—	2	-
1825	Crawshay	3	3
1830	—	4	-
1839	W. Crawshay	4	4
1841	W. Crawshay	4	3
1843	Crawshay & Co.	4	4
1847	W. Crawshay	-	-
1849	Crawshay & Co.	4	4
1854	W. Crawshay	-	-
1855	Francis Crawshay	4	4
1856	Francis Crawshay	4	4
1857	Francis Crawshay	4	4
1858	Francis Crawshay	4	4
1859	Francis Crawshay	4	4
1860	Francis Crawshay	4	0
1861	Francis Crawshay	4	0
1862	Marquess of Bute	4	0
1863	Marquess of Bute	4	0
1864	Hinde & Cosham	4	2
1865	Hinde & Cosham	4	2
1866	Hirwain Coal & Iron Co. Ltd	4	0
1867	Hirwain Coal & Iron Co. Ltd	4	0
1868	Hirwain Coal & Iron Co. Ltd	4	0
1869	Hirwain Coal & Iron Co. Ltd	4	0
1870	Hirwain Coal & Iron Co. Ltd	4	0
1871	Hirwain Coal & Iron Co. Ltd	4	0
1881	Stuart Iron, Steel & Tin Plate Co. Ltd	4	0
1882	Stuart Iron, Steel & Tin Plate Co. Ltd	4	0
1883	Stuart Iron, Steel & Tin Plate Co. Ltd	4	0
1884	Stuart Iron, Steel & Tin Plate Co. Ltd	4	0
1885	Stuart Iron, Steel & Tin Plate Co. Ltd	4	0
1886	Stuart Iron, Steel & Tin Plate Co. Ltd	4	0
1887	Stuart Iron, Steel & Tin Plate Co. Ltd	4	0
1888	Unoccupied	4	0

The ground landlord in 1794 was Lord Cardiff; the furnace was coke-fired, blown by engine and said to have been built in 1758. 1796: output 28 tons a week (1,400 p.a.), Excise and actual; Exact Return 1,050 tons. 1805: 450 tons. 1823–30: 4,160 tons from 2 furnaces in 1823; 2 more furnaces built 1824; output in 1830 9,360 tons. 1825: output 140 tons a week, 7,020 p.a., 'use it themselves'. The Staffs RO version of the list also adds 'No 1 sometimes'. 1843: output 200 tons a week. 1847: furnace-numbers returned for Cyfarthfa, Ynysfach and Hirwaun together (15 furnaces built, 13 in blast). 1849: Hunt's list has 5 furnaces in blast at Hirwaun. In 1854 Hirwaun was coupled with Varteg (qv) in obvious error, since the two works were never under common ownership and Varteg was normally combined with Golynos; in any case, no furnace-numbers are given. At Hirwaun, the furnaces were said to be in blast for six months in 1859 and in 1866 two furnaces were said to be in blast for three months and the others had been repaired the previous year. From 1881 the works was entered under 'Merthyr, Hirwain'. Truran: output 130 tons a week from each of 4 furnaces.

Ifor: see Dowlais

Jarvis: see Venallt

Kilgetty, Pembs. SN 1407

Year	Owner	Built	In Blast
1854	Not occupied	1	0
1855	Pembroke Iron & Coal Co.	1	0
1856	Pembroke Iron & Coal Co.	2	0

Year	Owner	Built	In Blast
1857	Pembroke Iron & Coal Co.	2	0
1858	Pembroke Iron & Coal Co.	2	1
1859	Pembroke Iron & Coal Co.	2	1
1860	Pembrokeshire Iron & Coal Co. Ltd	2	1
1861	Pembrokeshire Iron & Coal Co. Ltd	2	0
1862	Pembrokeshire Iron & Coal Co. Ltd	2	0
1863	Vickerman & Co.	2	0
1864	Vickerman & Co.	2	1
1865	Vickerman & Co.	2	1
1866	Vickerman & Co.	2	2
1867	Vickerman & Co.	2	1
1868	Vickerman & Co.	2	1
1869	Vickerman & Co.	2	0
1870	Vickerman & Co.	2	0
1871	Vickerman & Co.	2	0

This site is called Saundersfoot until 1859, thereafter Kilgetty. Truran: output 60 tons a week from each of 2 furnaces. 1857: 1 furnace in blast for 3 months. 1859: the first word of the owner's name has been emended from 'Penhale' in the original list.

Landore, Glam. [SS 6696]

Year	Owner	Built	In Blast
1885	Swansea Blast Furnace Co. Ltd	2	1
1886	Swansea Blast Furnace Co. Ltd	2	1
1887	Swansea Hematite Iron Co. Ltd	2	1
1888	Swansea Hematite Iron Co. Ltd	2	1
1889	Swansea Hematite Iron Co. Ltd	2	1
1890	Swansea Hematite Iron Co. Ltd	2	1
1891	Swansea Hematite Iron Co. Ltd	2	1
1892	Swansea Hematite Iron Co. Ltd	2	1
1893	Swansea Hematite Iron Co. Ltd	2	1
1894	Swansea Hematite Iron Co. Ltd	2	1
1895	Swansea Hematite Iron Co. Ltd	2	1
1896	Swansea Hematite Iron Co. Ltd	2	2
1897	Swansea Hematite Iron Co. Ltd	2	1
1898	Swansea Hematite Iron Co. Ltd	2	1
1899	Swansea Hematite Iron Co. Ltd	2	2
1900	Wright Butler & Co. Ltd	2	1
1901	Wright Butler & Co. Ltd	2	1
1902	Baldwin's Ltd	2	1
1903	Baldwin's Ltd	2	2
1904	Baldwin's Ltd	2	1
1905	Baldwin's Ltd	2	1
1906	Baldwin's Ltd	2	1
1907	Baldwin's Ltd	2	1
1908	Baldwin's Ltd	2	0
1909	Baldwin's Ltd	2	1
1910	Baldwin's Ltd	2	1
1911	Baldwin's Ltd	2	1
1912	Baldwin's Ltd	2	1
1913	Baldwin's Ltd	2	1
1921	Baldwin's Ltd	2	-
1922	Baldwin's Ltd	2	-
1923	Baldwin's Ltd	2	-
1924	Baldwin's Ltd	2	-
1925	Baldwin's Ltd	2	-
1926	Baldwin's Ltd	2	-
1927	Baldwin's Ltd	2	-
1928	Baldwin's Ltd	2	-
1929	Baldwin's Ltd	2	-
1920	Baldwin's Ltd	2	-
1931	Baldwin's Ltd	2	-
1932	Baldwin's Ltd	2	-
1933	Baldwin's Ltd	2	-
1934	Baldwin's Ltd	1	-
1935	Baldwin's Ltd	1	-
1936	Baldwin's Ltd	1	-
1937	Baldwin's Ltd	1	-

See under Millbrook for an earlier works sometimes known as Millbrook and Landore. Baldwin's furnace at Landore was dismantled in 1938.

Llanelli, Carms. SN 5001

Year	Owner	Built	In Blast
1796	—	1	1
1805	A. Raby	2	2
1810	A. Raby	2	0
1825	Raby	2	0

1796: output 1,664 tons p.a., Excise and actual; Exact Return 1,560 tons. 1805: output 2,267 tons p.a. In 1825 the entry is accompanied by the same comment as that made against Melincourt (qv).

Llanelly, Brecs. SO 2313

Year	Owner	Built	In Blast
1794	D. Tanner	1	-

The ground landlord was — Hanbury Esq.; the single charcoal-fired furnace was described as 'old', and there were two melting fineries at the forge. See Clydach for the nearby coke-fired furnaces which are occasionally called Llanelly in later lists.

Llanwern, Mon. ST 3786

Year	Owner	Built	In Blast
1962	Richard Thomas & Baldwins Ltd	1	-
1963	Richard Thomas & Baldwins Ltd	2	-
1964	Richard Thomas & Baldwins Ltd	2	-
1965	Richard Thomas & Baldwins Ltd	2	-
1966	Richard Thomas & Baldwins Ltd	2	-
1967	Richard Thomas & Baldwins Ltd	2	-
1968	Richard Thomas & Baldwins Ltd	2	-
1969	Richard Thomas & Baldwins Ltd	2	-
1970	British Steel Corporation	2	-
1971	British Steel Corporation	2	-
1972	British Steel Corporation	2	-
1973	British Steel Corporation	2	-
1974	British Steel Corporation	3	-
1975	British Steel Corporation	3	-
1976	British Steel Corporation	3	-
1977	British Steel Corporation	3	-
1978	British Steel Corporation	3	-
1979	British Steel Corporation	3	-
1980	British Steel Corporation	3	-

The location of the works, which remains in use today, was given as Newport until 1969, thereafter Llanwern.

Llwydcoed: see Aberdare

Llynvi Vale, Glam. SS 8491

Year	Owner	Built	In Blast
1839	Cambrian Co.	0	0
1841	Cambrian Co.	2	2
1843	Joint Stock	4	2
1847	Cambrian Iron Co.	3	2
1849	Cambrian Iron Co.	4	2
1854	Llynvi Iron Co.	4	2
1855	Llynvi Iron Co.	4	3
1856	Llynvi Iron Co.	4	3
1857	Llynvi Iron Co.	4	3
1858	Llynvi Iron Co.	4	3
1859	Llynvi Vale Iron Co.	4	4
1860	Llynvi Vale Iron Co.	4	3
1861	Llynvi Vale Iron Co.	4	3
1862	Llynvi Vale Iron Co.	7	3
1863	Llynvi Vale Iron Co.	7	3
1864	Llynvi Vale Iron Co.	7	4
1865	Llynvi Vale Iron Co.	7	4
1866	Llynvi Vale Iron Co.	7	3
1867	Llynvi Vale Iron Co. Ltd	7	3
1868	Llynvi Vale Iron Co. Ltd	7	3
1869	Llynvi Vale Iron Co. Ltd	7	4
1870	Llynvi Vale Iron Co. Ltd	7	4
1871	Llynvi Vale Iron Co. Ltd	7	4
1872	Llynvi, Tondu & Ogmore Coal & Iron Co. Ltd	7	4
1873	Llynvi, Tondu & Ogmore Coal & Iron Co. Ltd	7	4
1874	Llynvi, Tondu & Ogmore Coal & Iron Co. Ltd	0	0
1875	Llynvi, Tondu & Ogmore Coal & Iron Co. Ltd	7	2
1876	Llynvi, Tondu & Ogmore Coal & Iron Co. Ltd	6	2
1877	Llynvi, Tondu & Ogmore Coal & Iron Co. Ltd	6	2
1878	Llynvi, Tondu & Ogmore Coal & Iron Co. Ltd	6	1
1879	Llynvi, Tondu & Ogmore Coal & Iron Co. Ltd	6	1
1880	Llynvi, Tondu & Ogmore Coal & Iron Co. Ltd	6	2
1881	Llynvi, Tondu & Ogmore Coal & Iron Co. Ltd	7	1
1882	Llynvi & Tondû Co. Ltd	7	2
1883	Llynvi & Tondû Co. Ltd	7	1
1884	Llynvi & Tondû Co. Ltd	6	1
1885	Llynvi & Tondû Co. Ltd	7	1
1886	Llynvi & Tondû Co. Ltd	7	0
1887	Llynvi & Tondû Co. Ltd	6	0
1888	North's Navigation Collieries Syndicate Ltd	6	0

The entries above for 1839–47 appear under the heading 'Cambrian'. In 1839 4 furnaces were said to be building but none was in blast. 1843: output 100 tons a week. In 1847 there was a second entry under Llynvi, with the owner given as 'Joint Stock Co.' and 1 of the 3 furnaces in blast. This and the entry under Cambrian appear to be duplicates, since there was no other works in South Wales called Cambrian. 1849: Hunt's list has 3 furnaces in blast at Llynvi. Truran: output (at Llynvi) 90 tons a week from each of 4 furnaces. From 1862 the furnace-numbers above include Maesteg (qv). A Llynvi Vale Iron Co. was registered, with unlimited liability, in 1856, although this name was not used in *Mineral Statistics* until 1859; a new company, with the same name but limited liability, was registered in 1867. The Llynvi & Tondû Co. Ltd was registered in 1880 but does not appear as owner until 1882.

Machen: see Rudry

Maesteg, Glam. SS 8591

Year	Owner	Built	In Blast
1830	—	1	-
1839	Smith & Co.	2	2
1841	Smith & Co.	2	1
1843	Smith & Co.	4	2
1847	Maesteg Iron Co.	3	2
1849	Maesteg Iron Co.	3	0
1854	Maesteg Iron Co.	-	-
1855	Llynvi Iron Co.	3	3
1856	Llynvi Iron Co.	3	3
1857	Llynvi Iron Co.	3	3
1858	Llynvi Iron Co.	4	4
1859	Llynvi Vale Iron Co.	4	4
1860	Llynvi Vale Iron Co.	4	4

The 1823–30 list has a nil return for 1823 and notes that the single furnace was built in 1828 and had an output of 2,430 tons p.a. in 1830. There is a footnote that 1 furnace was built at Maesteg in 1831. 1843: output 120 tons a week. 1849: Hunt's list has 3 furnaces in blast. No furnace-numbers are given in 1854. There is no entry in Truran for Maesteg, nor in *Mineral Statistics* in 1861. For 1862 and later see under Llynvi, where problems of owners' names are also discussed.

Margam: see Port Talbot

Melincourt, Glam. SN 8201

Year	Owner	Built	In Blast
1794	Dr Lettsom for Myers' Executors	1	-
1796	—	1	1
1805	Myers	1	1
1810	Myers & Co.	1	1
1825	Myers & Co.	1	0

The ground landlord was listed in 1794 as Lord Talbot; the furnace was by this date coke-fired but was still blown by water and described as 'old'. 1796: output 648 tons p.a., Excise and actual; Exact Return 503 tons. 1805: 950 tons p.a. No output is given for 1825 but instead the following comment, which also appears alongside other closed (but not necessarily charcoal-fired) works: 'I am not acquainted with these furnaces and have taken them from an old list of mine. They are probably worked with charcoal' (this is the wording in the Staffs RO version of the list; that in the B&W text varies slightly).

Melingriffith: see Pentyrch

Millbrook and Landore, Glam. [SS 6595]

Year	Owner	Built	In Blast
1825	Bevan	1	0
1839	Sir John Morris Bt	1	1
1841	Sir J. Morris	2	0
1843	Sir John Morris	1	0
1847	Sir John Morris Bt	1	1
1847	Millbrook Iron Co.	1	1
1849	Sir J. Morris	2	0
1854	Sir J. Morris	1	0
1855	Sir G.B. Morris	1	0
1856	Sir G.B. Morris	1	0
1857	Sir G.B. Morris	1	0
1858	Sir G.B. Morris	1	0

1825: an entry under Morriston evidently belongs here and has the comment 'Supposed now in blast' (B&W) or 'I believe now in blast' (Staffs RO), i.e. presumably in March 1826. 1841: an entry for 2 furnaces, both out of blast, under Millbrook must include Landore. 1843: entry under Landore only, output nil. 1847: 2 entries, one under Millbrook, the other under Landore, both printed above. 1849: one entry, headed 'Millbrook, or Landore'. Neither appears in Truran. In 1854 *Mineral Statistics* use both names; later entries name Millbrook only but must include both sites. See Landore for the later works there.

Morriston: see Millbrook

Nantyglo, Mon. [SO 1910]

Year	Owner	Built	In Blast
1805	Hill & Co.	2	0
1810	Jos. Bailey	2	0
1823	—	5	-
1825	Bailey Bros.	7	5
1830	—	7	-
1839	Bailey Bros.	8	8
1841	Bailey Bros.	7	6
1843	Bailey Bros.	8	7
1847	J. & J. Bailey	-	-
1849	Messrs Bailey	-	-
1854	Joseph & C. Bailey	-	-
1855	Sir Jos. H. Bailey	7	7
1856	Sir Jos. H. Bailey	7	7
1857	Sir Jos. H. Bailey	7	7
1858	Sir Jos. H. Bailey	7	0
1859	Sir Jos. H. Bailey	7	0
1860	Sir Jos. H. Bailey	7	0
1861	Sir Jos. H. Bailey	7	6
1862	Sir Jos. & C. Bailey	7	6
1863	J. & C. Bailey	7	6
1864	J. & C. Bailey	7	5
1865	J. & C. Bailey	7	5
1866	J. & C. Bailey	7	5
1867	J. & C. Bailey	7	5
1868	J. & C. Bailey	7	5
1869	J. & C. Bailey	7	5
1870	Jos. & Crawshay Bailey	7	5
1871	Nant-y-Glo & Blaina Iron Works Co. Ltd	7	4
1872	Nant-y-Glo & Blaina Iron Works Co. Ltd	11	7
1873	Nant-y-Glo & Blaina Iron Works Co. Ltd	11	3
1874	Nant-y-Glo & Blaina Iron Works Co. Ltd	11	4
1875	Nant-y-Glo & Blaina Iron Works Co. Ltd	11	5
1876	Nant-y-Glo & Blaina Iron Works Co. Ltd	2	0
1877	Nant-y-Glo & Blaina Iron Works Co. Ltd	3	0
1878	Nant-y-Glo & Blaina Iron Works Co. Ltd	3	0
1879	Nant-y-Glo & Blaina Iron Works Co. Ltd	3	0
1880	Nant-y-Glo & Blaina Iron Works Co. Ltd	3	0
1881	Nant-y-Glo & Blaina Iron Works Co. Ltd	2	0
1882	Nant-y-Glo & Blaina Iron Works Co. Ltd	-	-

1805: no output returned. 1823–30: output for 1823 17,751 tons p.a.; additional furnace built 1826 and another 1827; output for 1830 23,883 tons. 1825: output 340 tons a week, 16,900 p.a., 'use it themselves'. The Staffs RO version of the list has 7 furnacs, 5 in blast; the B&W text has 5 furnaces, 3 in blast. 1843: output 570 tons a week. 1847: furnace-numbers for Nantyglo and Beaufort given together under the latter heading (qv), as they are by English in 1849; Hunt's list has 7 furnaces in blast at Nantyglo. In 1854 blanks appear in both furnace-number columns. Truran: output (at Nantyglo alone) 120 tons a week from each of 8 furnaces. In 1861 the furnace-numbers printed for Nantyglo in *Mineral Statistics* (12 built, 6 in blast) evidently also include Beaufort, although separate figures are given under Beaufort (7 furnaces, 6 in blast). If the latter figures are subtracted from those under Nantyglo, the balance appears to be 2 furnaces short in the 'Built' column but correct in the 'In Blast' column. Figures have been inserted above on the assumption that there were in fact 7 furnaces at Nantyglo throughout this period. Furnace-numbers printed above for 1872–73 include Nantyglo, Blaina and Coalbrookvale (qqv) and those for 1874–75 include those three works plus Beaufort. 1882: Works dismantled.

Neath Abbey, Glam. SS 7397

Year	Owner	Built	In Blast
1794	Phillips & Wilson	-	-
1796	—	2	2
1805	Foxes & Co.	2	0
1810	Foxes & Co.	2	0
1823	—	2	-
1825	Price	2	2
1830	—	2	-
1839	Foxes & Co.	2	1
1841	Fox & Co.	2	0
1843	Price & Co.	2	0
1847	J. Price	2	2
1849	Neath Abbey Iron Co.	2	0

No ground landlord is named in 1794, nor any details of plant, except that the furnace(s) was (or were) blown by engine. The entry has the appearance of a late addition to the list. 1796:

output 30 tons a week from each of 2 furnaces, i.e. 3,120 tons p.a., Excise and actual; Exact Return 1,759 tons. 1805: no output. 1823: output nil. 1830: 2,374 tons p.a. 1825: weekly output 74 tons, 3,640 p.a., 'castings etc'. 1843: no output. 1849: Hunt's list has 2 furnaces in blast.

Neath Valley: see Abernant (Glyn-neath); Venallt

Newport: see Llanwern

Oakwood, Glam. [SS 7892?]

Year	Owner	Built	In Blast
1839	Oakwood Co.	2	0
1841	Oakwood Co.	2	0
1847	Copper Mining Co.	-	-
1849	W. Llewellyn	5	5
1855	Governor & Co. of Copper Mines	2	0
1856	Governor & Co. of Copper Mines	2	0
1857	Governor & Co. of Copper Mines	2	2
1858	Governor & Co. of Copper Mines	2	2
1859	Governor & Co. of Copper Mines	2	2
1860	Governor & Co. of Copper Mines	2	1
1861	Governor & Co. of Copper Mines	2	1
1862	Governor & Co. of Copper Mines	2	2
1863	Governor & Co. of Copper Mines	-	-
1864	Governor & Co. of Copper Mines	-	-
1865	Governor & Co. of Copper Mines	-	-
1866	Governor & Co. of Copper Mines	-	-
1867	Governor & Co. of Copper Miners in England	-	-
1868	Governor & Co. of Copper Miners in England	-	-
1869	Governor & Co. of Copper Miners in England	-	-
1870	Governor & Co. of Copper Miners in England	-	-
1871	Governor & Co. of Copper Miners in England	-	-
1872	Governor & Co. of Copper Miners in England	-	-
1873	Governor & Co. of Copper Miners in England	-	-
1874	Governor & Co. of Copper Miners in England	-	-
1875	Governor & Co. of Copper Miners in England	-	-

1847: furnace-numbers for Oakwood and Cwmavon combined under the latter heading (qv). Both the 1849 list and Truran have a separate entry for Cwmavon but evidently also combined the two works under Oakwood, for which Truran returns an output of 100 tons a week from each of 5 furnaces. Since there were never as many as 9 furnaces at the two sites together this must be double-counting. In 1849 the site is named as 'Oakwood and Amwain' by English and the name of the owner appears to be wrong: L. Llewellyn was the owner of Amman Ironworks, Brynamman (qv), whose name is given as 'Amwain' in 1847; there is thus a two-fold error arising from confusion over this misspelling. From 1863 furnace-numbers for Oakwood and Cwmavon are given under Cwmavon.

Onllwyn, Glam. [SN 8410]

Year	Owner	Built	In Blast
1847	John Williams	2	2
1849	J. Williams, Swansea	2	2
1854	W. Llewellyn	2	1
1855	L. Llewellyn	2	1
1856	L. Llewellyn	2	1
1857	L. Llewellyn	2	1
1858	W. Llewellyn & Son	2	1
1859	W. Parsons	2	1
1860	W. Parsons	2	1
1861	William Parsons	2	1
1862	William Parsons	2	2
1863	William Parsons	2	2
1864	Onllwyn Iron & Coal Co. Ltd	2	2
1865	Onllwyn Iron & Coal Co. Ltd	2	2
1866	Onllwyn Iron & Coal Co. Ltd	2	2
1867	Onllwyn Iron & Coal Co. Ltd	2	0
1868	Onllwyn Iron & Coal Co. Ltd	1	0
1869	Onllwyn Iron & Coal Co. Ltd	2	0
1870	Onllwyn Iron & Coal Co. Ltd	2	0
1871	Onllwyn Iron & Coal Co. Ltd	-	-

In 1855–60 *Mineral Statistics* names the works as 'Onllwyn or Brin' (i.e. Bryn). Truran: output 60 tons a week from each of 2 furnaces.

Pembrey, Carms. SN 4301

Year	Owner	Built	In Blast
1830	—	2	-

Nil return for 1823; note that two furnaces were built in 1824; no output given for 1830.

Penallt: see Venallt

Penrhiwtyn, Glam. [SS 7495]

Year	Owner	Built	In Blast
1805	A. Raby	1	0
1810	A. Raby	1	0
1825	Raby	1	0

1805: no output. 1825: no output; the works appears with others, some in the Forest of Dean, most of them charcoal-fired, said to have been taken from an old list.

Pentwyn, Mon. SO 2603

Year	Owner	Built	In Blast
1825	Hunt	3	0
1830	—	3	-
1839	Pentwyn Co.	3	2
1841	Pentwyn Co.	3	2
1843	Joint Stock	3	2
1847	Williams & Co.	-	-
1849	Williams & Co.	-	-

Year	Owner	Built	In Blast
1854	—	-	-
1857	Ebbw Vale Co.	3	0
1858	Ebbw Vale Co.	3	0
1859	Ebbw Vale Co.	3	0
1860	Ebbw Vale Iron Co.	3	0
1861	Ebbw Vale Iron Co.	3	0
1862	Ebbw Vale Iron Co.	3	0
1863	Ebbw Vale Iron Co.	3	0
1864	Ebbw Vale Iron Co.	3	0
1865	Ebbw Vale Co. Ltd	4	2
1866	Ebbw Vale Co. Ltd	4	2
1867	Ebbw Vale Co. Ltd	4	2
1868	Ebbw Vale Co. Ltd	4	0

1823–30: nil return for the former year; note that 3 furnaces were built in 1825 and that they were making 5,391 tons p.a. in 1830. 1825: 'Building'; 1 furnace said to be in blast in the Staffs RO version of list, but none in the B&W text, which (alone) has the comment that one furnace had blown up. 1843: output 150 tons a week. In 1847 and 1849 Pentwyn was coupled with Varteg and Golynos (qv); there are no entries under Pentwyn in 1855–56. Truran: output (at Pentwyn) 120 tons a week from each of 3 furnaces.

Pentyrch, Glam. ST 1283

Year	Owner	Built	In Blast
1794	Mr Lewis	0	-
1796	—	1	0
1823	—	1	-
1825	Blakemore	1	1
1830	—	1	-
1839	R. Blakemore	2	2
1841	R. Blakemore	2	1
1843	Blakemore & Co.	2	1
1847	T.W. Booker	2	1
1849	T.W. Booker	2	1
1854	T.W. Booker	2	1
1855	T.W. Booker	2	2
1856	T.W. Booker	2	0
1857	T.W. Booker	2	2
1858	T.W. Booker	2	2
1859	T.W. Booker	2	2
1860	T.W. Booker	2	2
1861	T.W. Booker & Co.	2	1
1862	T.W. Booker & Co.	2	2
1863	T.W. Booker & Co.	2	2
1864	T.W. Booker & Co.	2	2
1865	T.W. Booker & Co.	2	2
1866	T.W. Booker & Co.	2	2
1867	Thomes William Booker & Co.	2	2
1868	Thomas William Booker & Co.	2	2
1869	Thomas William Booker & Co.	2	2
1870	Thomas William Booker & Co.	2	2
1871	Thomas William Booker & Co.	2	2
1872	Thomas W. Booker & Co. Ltd	2	2
1873	Thomas W. Booker & Co. Ltd	2	2
1874	Thomas W. Booker & Co. Ltd	2	2
1875	Thomas W. Booker & Co. Ltd	3	2
1876	Thomas W. Booker & Co. Ltd	3	3
1877	Thomas W. Booker & Co. Ltd	3	1
1878	Thomas W. Booker & Co. Ltd	3	1
1879	Thomas W. Booker & Co. Ltd	3	1
1880	Thomas W. Booker & Co. Ltd	3	1
1881	Thomas W. Booker & Co. Ltd	3	1
1882	Thomas W. Booker & Co. Ltd	3	1
1883	Thomas W. Booker & Co. Ltd	3	1
1884	Cardiff Iron & Tin Plate Co. Ltd	3	1
1885	Cardiff Iron & Tin Plate Co. Ltd	3	1
1886	Cardiff Iron & Tin Plate Co. Ltd	3	0
1887	Cardiff Iron & Tin Plate Co. Ltd	3	0
1888	Cardiff Iron & Tin Plate Co. Ltd	3	0

The 1794 list names the ground landlord as Lord Talbot, but the only indication of plant is a figure 0 in the column for coke furnaces, against which are the comments 'water' (blown) and 'old'. 1796: furnace out of blast; no output. The output in 1823 is given as 1,235 tons p.a., in 1830 as 2,412 tons p.a. 1825: output 30 tons a week, 1,820 tons a year, 'used by himself'. 1843: output 35 tons a week. 1849: Hunt's list has 2 furnaces in blast. Truran: output 100 tons a week from each of 2 furnaces. From 1866 onwards the works is named as 'Pentyrch and Melingriffith' (or vice versa): the latter was the site of a tinplate works owned by the same firm.

Penycae: see Ebbw Vale

Penydarren, Glam. [SO 0505]

Year	Owner	Built	In Blast
1794	Messrs Homfray	1	-
1796	—	2	2
1805	S. Homfray & Co.	3	3
1810	Homfray	4	4
1823	—	5	-
1825	Forman & Co.	5	5
1830	—	5	-
1839	Thompson & Co.	6	6
1841	Thompson & Co.	6	5
1843	Joint Stock	7	6
1847	Thompson & Co.	7	6
1849	Thompson & Co.	7	5
1854	Thompson & Co.	-	-
1855	William Forman	6	6
1856	William Forman	7	7
1857	William Forman	7	7
1858	William Forman	7	7
1859	William Forman	7	0
1860	Penydarren Iron Co.	7	0
1861	Penydarren Iron Co.	7	0
1862	William Henry Forman	7	0
1863	Davis, Williams & Phillips	7	0
1864	Davis, Williams & Phillips	7	1
1865	Aberdare Iron Co.	6	0
1866	Aberdare Iron Co.	6	0
1867	Aberdare Iron Co.	6	0
1868	R. Fothergill & T.A. Hankey	6	0
1869	Aberdare Iron Co.	7	0
1875	Aberdare & Plymouth Co. Ltd	7	0
1876	Aberdare & Plymouth Co. Ltd	-	-
1877	Aberdare & Plymouth Co. Ltd	7	0
1878	Aberdare & Plymouth Co. Ltd	7	0
1879	Aberdare & Plymouth Co. Ltd	7	0
1880	Aberdare & Plymouth Co. Ltd	-	-
1881	Aberdare & Plymouth Co. Ltd	-	-

Year	Owner	Built	In Blast
1882	Aberdare & Plymouth Co. Ltd	7	0
1883	Aberdare & Plymouth Co. Ltd	7	0
1884	Aberdare & Plymouth Co. Ltd	7	0
1885	Aberdare & Plymouth Co. Ltd	7	0
1886	Aberdare & Plymouth Co. Ltd	7	0
1887	Aberdare & Plymouth Co. Ltd	7	0
1888	Mortgagees of Plymouth Works	7	0

The ground landlord in 1794 was Lewis Evans; the furnace was coke-fired, blown by engine and said to have been built in 1785. The forge consisted of 2 chaferies, 3 melting fineries and 3 balling furnaces, built in 1787. 1796: two furnaces each producing 2,000 tons p.a. (i.e. 40 tons a week), Excise and actual, 4,000 tons total; Exact Return 4,100 tons total. 1805: output 7,803 tons. 1823: output 15,547 tons p.a. 1830: 17,015 tons. 1825: weekly output 312 tons, 15,600 p.a., 'use it themselves'. The Staffs RO version of the list has all 5 furnace in blast, the B&W text has 4. 1843: output 480 tons a week. 1849: Hunt's list has 7 furnaces in blast. In 1854 there are blanks in the furnace-number columns. Truran: output 100 tons a week from each of 7 furnaces. 1861: 'These works are now closed'. In 1876 and 1880–81 Penydarren and Plymouth (qv) were coupled together, with 5 furnaces listed in 1876 and 17 in 1880–81, none in use. In the table above figures have been inserted on the assumption that there were 7 furnaces at Penydarren throughout these years. The figure of 5 probably arose from an attempt to separate Plymouth from the adjacent works at Duffryn (qv), since both sites had 5 furnaces; Duffryn, however, had closed in 1861 and lost its own entry in *Mineral Statistics* in 1874.

Plymouth, Glam.   SO 0604

Year	Owner	Built	In Blast
1794	Mr Hill	1	-
1796	—	1	1
1805	R. Hill & Son	3	3
1810	Hill & Struttle	4	4
1823	—	3	-
1825	R. & A. Hill	4	4
1830	—	5	-
1839	R. & A. Hill	4	4
1841	R. & A. Hill	8	5
1843	R. & A. Hill	4	4
1847	A. Hill	8	7
1849	A. Hill & Co.	8	8
1854	Anthony Hill & Co.	9	8
1855	Anthony Hill & Co.	9	8
1856	Anthony Hill	5	4
1857	Anthony Hill	5	5
1858	Anthony Hill	5	5
1859	Anthony Hill	5	5
1860	Anthony Hill	5	5
1861	Anthony Hill	5	5
1862	Trustees of the late Anthony Hill	11	10
1863	Fothergill, Hankey & Bateman	11	10
1864	Fothergill, Hankey & Bateman	11	10
1865	Fothergill, Hankey & Bateman	10	10
1866	Fothergill, Hankey & Bateman	11	10
1867	Fothergill, Hankey & Lewis	10	7
1868	R. Fothergill & T.A. Hankey	10	7
1869	Fothergill, Hankey & Lewis	10	7
1870	Plymouth Iron Co.	10	7
1871	Fothergill & Hankey	10	5
1872	Fothergill & Hankey	10	4
1873	Fothergill & Hankey	10	3
1874	Fothergill & Hankey	10	2
1875	Aberdare & Plymouth Co. Ltd	10	0
1876	Aberdare & Plymouth Co. Ltd	10	0
1877	Aberdare & Plymouth Co. Ltd	10	0
1878	Aberdare & Plymouth Co. Ltd	10	0
1879	Aberdare & Plymouth Co. Ltd	10	0
1880	Aberdare & Plymouth Co. Ltd	10	0
1881	Aberdare & Plymouth Co. Ltd	10	0
1882	Aberdare & Plymouth Co. Ltd	10	0
1883	Aberdare & Plymouth Co. Ltd	10	0
1884	Aberdare & Plymouth Co. Ltd	10	0
1885	Aberdare & Plymouth Co. Ltd	10	0
1886	Aberdare & Plymouth Co. Ltd	10	0
1887	Aberdare & Plymouth Co. Ltd	10	0
1888	Mortgagees of Plymouth Works	10	0

The ground landlord in 1794 was the Earl of Plymouth; the furnace was coke-fired, blown by engine and built in 1766. 1796: output 2,000 tons p.a. (i.e. 40 tons a week), Excise and actual; Exact Return 2,200 tons. 1805: output 5,789 tons p.a. 1810: second partner's name given as 'Stittle' in MS. 1823: output 16,387 tons p.a.; a fourth furnace is listed as built in 1825 and another in 1827 (these may have been the first two furnaces at Duffryn (qv), which has an entry in the 1825 list but not in that of 1823–30); in 1830 output was 18,582 tons p.a. 1825: 230 tons a week, 11,440 tons p.a.; 'use it themselves' (B&W), 'No 1 sometimes' (Staffs RO). In 1841, 1847 and 1849 furnace-numbers were given for Plymouth (also known as Furnace Isaf, i.e. the Lower Furnace, in the latter year) and Duffryn (qv) together. 1843: output (at Plymouth) 200 tons a week. *Mineral Statistics* combines the two sites in 1854–55 and from 1862. Truran provides separate figures: output at Plymouth was 100 tons a week in 1855 from each of 5 furnaces. For furnace-numbers at Penydarren, Plymouth and Duffryn in 1876 and 1880–81 see under Penydarren.

Pontrhydyfen, Glam.   [SS 7994]

Year	Owner	Built	In Blast
1830	—	2	-
1841	—	2	0
1843	Reynolds & Co.	2	0

1823–30: nil return for 1823; 2 furnaces built 1826; output nil in 1830. An entry for Pontrhydyryn in 1843 has been placed here, since the furnace-numbers and its position in the list compared with that of 1841 both fit, added to which there were never any blast furnaces associated with Pontrhydyryn tinplate works (near Cwmbran, Mon.), which seems the only other candidate.

Pontrhydyryn: see Pontrhydyfen

Pontypool [I], Mon.   SO 2600

Year	Owner	Built	In Blast
1794	D. Tanner	1	-
1805	Leigh	1	1

The ground landlord in 1794 was — Hanbury Esq.; the furnace was charcoal-fired and 'old'. Forge plant consisted of 3 fineries, 2 chaferies, a wire-mill and a rolling and a slitting mill; there is a marginal note 'Tin Mill'. In 1805 the furnace was said to be in blast but no output was given. This furnace was at Trosnant, about a mile west of Pontypool, in the hamlet now called Old Furnace.

Pontypool [II], Mon.   ST 2799

Year	Owner	Built	In Blast
1823	—	3	-
1825	Leigh & George	3	3
1830	—	3	-
1839	C.H. Leigh	4	3
1841	C.H. Leigh	3	2
1843	C.H. Leigh	4	1
1847	C.H. Leigh	4	1
1849	C.H. Leigh	3	2
1854	Pontypool Iron Co.	4	4
1855	Pontypool Iron Co.	4	4
1856	Pontypool Iron Co.	4	4
1857	Pontypool Iron Co.	4	4
1858	Pontypool Iron Co.	4	4
1859	Pontypool Iron Co.	4	4
1860	Pontypool Iron Co.	4	4
1861	Pontypool Iron Co.	4	4
1862	Pontypool Iron Co.	4	4
1863	Pontypool Iron Co.	4	4
1864	Pontypool Iron Co.	4	4
1865	Ebbw Vale Co. Ltd	4	4
1866	Ebbw Vale Co. Ltd	4	4
1867	Ebbw Vale Co. Ltd	4	3
1868	Ebbw Vale Co. Ltd	4	3
1869	Ebbw Vale Co. Ltd	4	1
1870	Pontypool Iron Co.	-	-
1871	Pontypool Iron Co.	-	-
1872	Ebbw Vale Steel Iron & Coal Co. Ltd	-	-
1873	Ebbw Vale Steel Iron & Coal Co. Ltd	-	-
1874	Ebbw Vale Steel Iron & Coal Co. Ltd	-	-
1875	Ebbw Vale Steel Iron & Coal Co. Ltd	-	-
1876	Ebbw Vale Steel Iron & Coal Co. Ltd	4	3
1877	Ebbw Vale Steel Iron & Coal Co. Ltd	4	3
1878	Ebbw Vale Steel Iron & Coal Co. Ltd	4	3
1879	Ebbw Vale Steel Iron & Coal Co. Ltd	4	2
1880	Ebbw Vale Steel Iron & Coal Co. Ltd	4	2
1881	Ebbw Vale Steel Iron & Coal Co. Ltd	4	2
1882	Ebbw Vale Steel Iron & Coal Co. Ltd	4	2
1883	Ebbw Vale Steel Iron & Coal Co. Ltd	2	2
1884	Ebbw Vale Steel Iron & Coal Co. Ltd	2	1
1885	Ebbw Vale Steel Iron & Coal Co. Ltd	1	1
1886	Ebbw Vale Steel Iron & Coal Co. Ltd	1	1
1887	Ebbw Vale Steel Iron & Coal Co. Ltd	1	1
1888	Ebbw Vale Steel Iron & Coal Co. Ltd	1	1
1889	Ebbw Vale Steel Iron & Coal Co. Ltd	1	1
1890	Ebbw Vale Steel Iron & Coal Co. Ltd	1	0
1891	Ebbw Vale Steel Iron & Coal Co. Ltd	1	0
1892	Ebbw Vale Steel Iron & Coal Co. Ltd	1	0
1893	Ebbw Vale Steel Iron & Coal Co. Ltd	1	0

The 1823–30 list refers to the works as 'Race'; the furnaces were in fact at Upper Race, SW of Pontypool, at or very near the site occupied at an earlier date by Blaendare Ironworks (qv). 1823: output 3,173 tons p.a. 1830: 2,421 tons. 1825: output 160 tons a week, 7,800 p.a.; 'melting and forge' (B&W), 'melting iron in part' (Staffs RO). The B&W text has all 3 furnaces out of blast; the Staffs RO version has all 3 in use. 1841: named as 'Rhas' (i.e. Race), Pontypool. 1843: output 110 tons a week. The 1847 list names the works as 'Pontypool and Blacadare', i.e. Blaendare. 1849: Hunt lists two separate works at Pontypool and 'Blainder', each with 3 furnaces in blast; these are clearly duplicate entries for a single works. Truran: output 120 tons a week from each of 3 furnaces. 1859: 3 furnaces on cold blast, 1 on hot blast. 1863: all output cold blast. In 1870–75 furnace-numbers for all the Ebbw Vale Co.'s works are combined under Ebbw Vale (qv); the reappearance of the Pontypool Iron Co. as the owner at Pontypool in 1870–71 is almost certainly an error. 1883: 'Discontinued in March 1883'.

Pontypridd, Glam.   SS 0888

Year	Owner	Built	In Blast
1859	Francis Crawshay	3	0
1860	Francis Crawshay	3	0
1861	Francis Crawshay	3	0
1862	Francis Crawshay	3	0
1863	Francis Crawshay	3	0
1864	Francis Crawshay	3	0
1865	Francis Crawshay	3	0
1866	Francis Crawshay	3	0
1867	Francis Crawshay	3	0
1868	Francis Crawshay	2	0
1869	Francis Crawshay	2	0
1870	Francis Crawshay	2	0
1871	Francis Crawshay	2	0
1872	Forest Iron & Steel Co. Ltd	2	1
1873	Forest Iron & Steel Co. Ltd	3	2
1874	Forest Iron & Steel Co. Ltd	3	1
1875	Forest Iron & Steel Co. Ltd	3	2
1876	Forest Iron & Steel Co. Ltd	2	2
1877	Forest Iron & Steel Co. Ltd	3	2
1878	Forest Iron & Steel Co. Ltd	3	2
1879	Forest Iron & Steel Co. Ltd	3	2
1880	Forest Iron & Steel Co. Ltd	3	2
1881	Forest Iron & Steel Co. Ltd	3	2
1882	Forest Iron & Steel Co. Ltd	3	2

Year	Owner	Built	In Blast
1883	Forest Iron & Steel Co. Ltd	3	2
1884	Forest Iron & Steel Co. Ltd	3	2
1885	Forest Iron & Steel Co. Ltd	3	0
1886	Forest Iron & Steel Co. Ltd	3	0
1887	Forest Iron & Steel Co. Ltd	3	0
1888	Forest Iron & Steel Co. Ltd	3	2
1889	Forest Iron & Steel Co. Ltd	3	2
1890	Forest Iron & Steel Co. Ltd	3	1
1891	Forest Iron & Steel Co. Ltd	3	0
1892	Forest Iron & Steel Co. Ltd	3	0
1893	Forest Iron & Steel Co. Ltd	3	0
1894	Forest Iron & Steel Co. Ltd	3	0
1895	Forest Iron & Steel Co. Ltd	3	0
1896	Forest Iron & Steel Co. Ltd	3	0
1897	Forest Iron & Steel Co. Ltd	3	0
1898	Forest Iron & Steel Co. Ltd	3	0

1859: 2 furnaces ready for blast; 1 two-thirds ready. 1872: Furnaces blown-in 21 Nov. 1872. From 1891 the furnace-numbers given for the Crawshays' main works at Cyfarthfa (qv) are said to include those for Pontypridd, although the 3 furnaces at the latter site (none in blast) continue to appear under that heading.

Porthcawl: see Cefn Cwsc

Port Talbot, Glam. SS 7887

Year	Owner	Built	In Blast
1921	Baldwin's Ltd	2	-
1922	Baldwin's Ltd	2	-
1923	Baldwin's Ltd	2	-
1924	Baldwin's Ltd	2	-
1925	Baldwin's Ltd	2	-
1926	Baldwin's Ltd	2	-
1927	Baldwin's Ltd	2	-
1928	Baldwin's Ltd	2	-
1929	Baldwin's Ltd	2	-
1930	British (Guest, Keen, Baldwins) Iron & Steel Co. Ltd	2	-
1931	British (Guest, Keen, Baldwins) Iron & Steel Co. Ltd	2	-
1932	British (Guest, Keen, Baldwins) Iron & Steel Co. Ltd	2	-
1933	British (Guest, Keen Baldwins) Iron & Steel Co. Ltd	2	-
1934	British (Guest, Keen Baldwins) Iron & Steel Co. Ltd	2	-
1935	Guest Keen Baldwins Iron & Steel Co. Ltd	2	-
1936	Guest Keen Baldwins Iron & Steel Co. Ltd	2	-
1937	Guest Keen Baldwins Iron & Steel Co. Ltd	2	-
1938	Guest Keen Baldwins Iron & Steel Co. Ltd	2	-
1939	Guest Keen Baldwins Iron & Steel Co. Ltd	2	-
1940	Guest Keen Baldwins Iron & Steel Co. Ltd	2	-
1941	Guest Keen Baldwins Iron & Steel Co. Ltd	3	-
1942	Guest Keen Baldwins Iron & Steel Co. Ltd	3	-
1943	Guest Keen Baldwins Iron & Steel Co. Ltd	3	-
1944	Guest Keen Baldwins Iron & Steel Co. Ltd	3	-
1945	Guest Keen Baldwins Iron & Steel Co. Ltd	2	-
1946	Guest Keen Baldwins Iron & Steel Co. Ltd	3	-
1947	Steel Company of Wales Ltd	3	-
1948	Steel Company of Wales Ltd	2	-
1949	Steel Company of Wales Ltd	2	-
1950	Steel Company of Wales Ltd	2	-
1951	Steel Company of Wales Ltd	2	-
1952	Steel Company of Wales Ltd	3	-
1953	Steel Company of Wales Ltd	3	-
1954	Steel Company of Wales Ltd	3	-
1955	Steel Company of Wales Ltd	3	-
1956	Steel Company of Wales Ltd	4	-
1957	Steel Company of Wales Ltd	4	-
1958	Steel Company of Wales Ltd	4	-
1959	Steel Company of Wales Ltd	5	-
1960	Steel Company of Wales Ltd	5	-
1961	Steel Company of Wales Ltd	5	-
1962	Steel Company of Wales Ltd	5	-
1963	Steel Company of Wales Ltd	5	-
1964	Steel Company of Wales Ltd	5	-
1965	Steel Company of Wales Ltd	5	-
1966	Steel Company of Wales Ltd	5	-
1967	Steel Company of Wales Ltd	5	-
1968	Steel Company of Wales Ltd	5	-
1969	Steel Company of Wales Ltd	5	-
1970	British Steel Corporation	5	-
1971	British Steel Corporation	5	-
1972	British Steel Corporation	5	-
1973	British Steel Corporation	5	-
1974	British Steel Corporation	5	-
1975	British Steel Corporation	5	-
1976	British Steel Corporation	5	-
1977	British Steel Corporation	5	-
1978	British Steel Corporation	4	-
1979	British Steel Corporation	4	-
1980	British Steel Corporation	4	-

The works are called Margam from 1921 to 1938; Margam and Port Talbot in 1938–46; Margam in 1947–52; and Port Talbot from 1953. They remain in use today.

Pyle: see Bryn-du; Cefn Cwsc

Race: see Pontypool

Rhymney and Bute, Mon. [SO 1107]

Year	Owner	Built	In Blast
1805	Crawshay	-	-
1810	B. Hall	2	2
1823	—	3	-
1825	Forman & Co.	3	3
1830	—	3	-
1839	Rhymney Iron Co.	3	3
1841	Rhymney Co.	9	7
1843	Joint Stock	10	9
1847	Rhymney Iron Co.	10	9
1849	Rhymney Iron Co.	10	9

Year	Owner	Built	In Blast
1854	Rhymney Iron Co.	9	8
1855	Rhymney Iron Co.	9	8
1856	Rhymney Iron Co.	4	4
1857	Rhymney Iron Co.	4	4
1858	Rhymney Iron Co.	4	4
1859	Rhymney Iron Co.	4	4
1860	Rhymney Iron Co.	4	4
1861	Rhymney Iron Co.	9	6
1862	Rhymney Iron Co.	8	8
1863	Rhymney Iron Co.	9	7
1864	Rhymney Iron Co.	9	7
1865	Rhymney Iron Co.	9	7
1866	Rhymney Iron Co.	9	7
1867	Rhymney Iron Co.	9	7
1868	Rhymney Iron Co.	9	7
1869	Rhymney Iron Co.	9	7
1870	Rhymney Iron Co.	9	6
1871	Rhymney Iron Co.	9	6
1872	Rhymney Iron Co. Ltd	9	7
1873	Rhymney Iron Co. Ltd	9	7
1874	Rhymney Iron Co. Ltd	9	7
1875	Rhymney Iron Co. Ltd	9	6
1876	Rhymney Iron Co. Ltd	9	5
1877	Rhymney Iron Co. Ltd	9	5
1878	Rhymney Iron Co. Ltd	9	6
1879	Rhymney Iron Co. Ltd	9	5
1880	Rhymney Iron Co. Ltd	9	6
1881	Rhymney Iron Co. Ltd	9	8
1882	Rhymney Iron Co. Ltd	9	7
1883	Rhymney Iron Co. Ltd	9	7
1884	Rhymney Iron Co. Ltd	9	5
1885	Rhymney Iron Co. Ltd	9	4
1886	Rhymney Iron Co. Ltd	9	3
1887	Rhymney Iron Co. Ltd	9	4
1888	Rhymney Iron Co. Ltd	9	5
1889	Rhymney Iron Co. Ltd	9	4
1890	Rhymney Iron Co. Ltd	9	4
1891	Rhymney Iron Co. Ltd	9	1
1892	Rhymney Iron Co. Ltd	9	0
1893	Rhymney Iron Co. Ltd	9	0
1894	Rhymney Iron Co. Ltd	9	0
1895	Rhymney Iron Co. Ltd	9	0
1896	Rhymney Iron Co. Ltd	9	0
1897	Rhymney Iron Co. Ltd	9	0
1898	Rhymney Iron Co. Ltd	9	0
1899	Rhymney Iron Co. Ltd	9	0
1900	Rhymney Iron Co. Ltd	9	0
1901	Rhymney Iron Co. Ltd	9	0
1902	Rhymney Iron Co. Ltd	9	0
1903	Rhymney Iron Co. Ltd	9	0
1904	Rhymney Iron Co. Ltd	9	0
1905	Rhymney Iron Co. Ltd	9	0

Although there are blanks in the furnace-number columns, the 1805 list, which uses the name Union, returns an output of 2,322 tons p.a. The 1810 list refers only to the older of the two adjacent works, Rhymney; that of 1823–30 refers to the building of three additional furnaces in 1826, presumably meaning Bute Ironworks, which has a separate entry in the 1825 list, where again the furnaces are said to be 'Building'. The B&W version of the 1825 list has 2 furnaces in blast, the Staffs RO text has 3. Output in 1825 was returned as 100 tons a week, 7,020 tons p.a., 'use it themselves'. In 1830 6 furnaces are listed, apparently 3 at each site: see also Bute. Output in 1823 5,500 tons; output in 1830 7,608 tons. 1839: 2 furnaces building; works called 'Rhymney and Bute'. The figures for 1841, 1843, 1847–55 and from 1861 onwards also refer to both works, although the works is called Rhymney only in *Mineral Statistics*. 1843: output (at Rhymney and Bute) 590 tons a week. 1849: Hunt lists 10 furnaces in blast. Truran: output 125 tons a week from each of 9 furnaces, i.e. those at both the Rhymney and Bute works; there is no separate entry for the latter. 1875: Furnaces in blast for 9 months only (3 months strike and lock-out).

Rudry, Glam. ST 1988

Year	Owner	Built	In Blast
1830	Christopher Pope	1	-
1854	—	-	-

The 1823–30 list has an entry for 'Rhydry', consisting of a nil return in 1823, a note that one furnace was built in 1828, and that output in 1830 was 220 tons. In 1854 the name 'Machen' appears in the list of works, but with no other information; this must refer to the same site as that called Rudry thirty years earlier.

Saundersfoot: see Kilgetty

Sirhowy, Mon. [SO 1410]

Year	Owner	Built	In Blast
1794	Mr Atkinson	1	-
1796	—	1	1
1805	Fothergill & Co.	2	2
1810	Fothergill	2	2
1823	—	3	-
1825	Harford & Co.	4	3
1830	—	3	-
1839	Harford & Co.	4	4
1841	Harfords & Co.	5	3
1843	Harfords & Co.	4	4
1847	Darby & Co.	-	-
1849	Darby & Co.	5	4
1854	Ebbw Vale Co.	5	3
1855	Ebbw Vale Iron & Coal Co.	5	4
1856	Ebbw Vale Iron Co.	5	4
1857	Ebbw Vale Iron Co.	4	4
1858	Ebbw Vale Iron Co.	4	4
1859	Ebbw Vale Iron Co.	5	3
1860	Ebbw Vale Iron Co.	5	3
1861	Ebbw Vale Iron Co.	5	2
1862	Ebbw Vale Iron Co.	5	3
1863	Ebbw Vale Iron Co.	5	3
1864	Ebbw Vale Iron Co.	5	3
1865	Ebbw Vale Co. Ltd	5	3
1866	Ebbw Vale Co. Ltd	-	-
1867	Ebbw Vale Co. Ltd	-	-
1868	Ebbw Vale Co. Ltd	-	-
1869	Ebbw Vale Co. Ltd	5	3
1870	Ebbw Vale Co. Ltd	-	-
1871	Ebbw Vale Co. Ltd	-	-

Year	Owner	Built	In Blast
1872	Ebbw Vale Steel Iron & Coal Co. Ltd	-	-
1873	Ebbw Vale Steel Iron & Coal Co. Ltd	-	-
1874	Ebbw Vale Steel Iron & Coal Co. Ltd	-	-
1875	Ebbw Vale Steel Iron & Coal Co. Ltd	-	-
1876	Ebbw Vale Steel Iron & Coal Co. Ltd	4	4
1877	Ebbw Vale Steel Iron & Coal Co. Ltd	4	3
1878	Ebbw Vale Steel Iron & Coal Co. Ltd	3	3
1879	Ebbw Vale Steel Iron & Coal Co. Ltd	4	3
1880	Ebbw Vale Steel Iron & Coal Co. Ltd	4	4
1881	Ebbw Vale Steel Iron & Coal Co. Ltd	4	3
1882	Ebbw Vale Steel Iron & Coal Co. Ltd	4	3
1883	Ebbw Vale Steel Iron & Coal Co. Ltd	2	2

The ground landlord in 1794 was Col. T. Johns; the furnace was coke-fired, blown by water and said to have been built in 1778. 1796: output 1,820 tons p.a. (i.e. 35 tons a week), Excise and actual; Exact Return 1,930 tons. 1805: 3,700 tons p.a. The 1823–30 list combines Sirhowy with Ebbw Vale (qv), with 6 furnaces making 10,425 tons p.a. in 1823 and 26,020 tons in 1830. A seventh furnace was erected (at Sirhowy) in 1831. The 1825 list has separate entries for the two works, from which it is possible to calculate furnace-numbers for 1823 and 1830. Output in 1825 160 tons a week, 7,800 tons p.a.; 'use it themselves'. The Staffs RO text has 4 furnaces, 3 in blast; the B&W version has 3 furnaces, 2 in blast. 1843: output 380 tons a week. 1847: furnace-numbers for Ebbw Vale and Sirhowy combined under former heading. 1849: Hunt lists 5 furnaces in blast. Truran: output (at Sirhowy alone) 130 tons a week from each of 5 furnaces. See Ebbw Vale for furnace-numbers in 1866–68 and 1870–75.

Taffvale: see Abernant

Tintern: see under Gloucestershire

Tondu, Glam. SS 8984

Year	Owner	Built	In Blast
1839	Sir Robert Price & Co.	-	-
1843	Sir Robert Price	1	0
1847	Sir R. Price	2	1
1849	Sir R. Price	2	1
1854	Messrs Brogden	2	1
1855	Brogden & Sons	2	2
1856	Brogden & Sons	2	2
1857	Brogden & Sons	2	2
1858	Brogden & Sons	2	2
1859	Brogden & Sons	2	2
1860	Brogden & Sons	2	2
1861	John Brogden & Sons	2	2
1862	John Brogden & Sons	2	2
1863	John Brogden & Sons	2	2
1864	John Brogden & Sons	2	2
1865	John Brogden & Sons	2	2
1866	John Brogden & Sons	2	2
1867	John Brogden & Sons	2	2
1868	John Brogden & Sons	2	2
1869	John Brogden & Sons	2	2
1870	John Brogden & Sons	2	2
1871	Llynvi, Tondu & Ogmore Coal & Iron Co. Ltd	2	2
1872	Llynvi, Tondu & Ogmore Coal & Iron Co. Ltd	2	2
1873	Llynvi, Tondu & Ogmore Coal & Iron Co. Ltd	2	2
1874	Llynvi, Tondu & Ogmore Coal & Iron Co. Ltd	2	2
1875	Llynvi, Tondu & Ogmore Coal & Iron Co. Ltd	2	2
1876	Llynvi, Tondu & Ogmore Coal & Iron Co. Ltd	2	2
1877	Llynvi, Tondu & Ogmore Coal & Iron Co. Ltd	2	1
1878	Llynvi, Tondu & Ogmore Coal & Iron Co. Ltd	2	1
1879	Llynvi, Tondu & Ogmore Coal & Iron Co. Ltd	2	2
1880	Llynvi, Tondu & Ogmore Coal & Iron Co. Ltd	2	1
1881	Llynvi, Tondu & Ogmore Coal & Iron Co. Ltd	2	2
1882	Llynvi & Tondû Co. Ltd	2	2
1883	Llynvi & Tondû Co. Ltd	2	2
1884	Llynvi & Tondû Co. Ltd	2	2
1885	Llynvi & Tondû Co. Ltd	2	0
1886	Llynvi & Tondû Co. Ltd	2	1
1887	Llynvi & Tondû Co. Ltd	1	1
1888	North's Navigation Collieries Syndicate Ltd	1	1
1889	North's Navigation Collieries Syndicate Ltd	1	1
1890	North's Navigation Collieries (1889) Ltd	1	1
1891	North's Navigation Collieries (1889) Ltd	2	1
1892	North's Navigation Collieries (1889) Ltd	1	1
1893	North's Navigation Collieries (1889) Ltd	1	1
1894	North's Navigation Collieries (1889) Ltd	1	1
1895	North's Navigation Collieries (1889) Ltd	1	1
1896	North's Navigation Collieries (1889) Ltd	1	0
1897	North's Navigation Collieries (1889) Ltd	1	0
1898	North's Navigation Collieries (1889) Ltd	1	0
1899	North's Navigation Collieries (1889) Ltd	1	0
1900	North's Navigation Collieries (1889) Ltd	1	0
1901	North's Navigation Collieries (1889) Ltd	1	0
1902	North's Navigation Collieries (1889) Ltd	1	0
1903	North's Navigation Collieries (1889) Ltd	1	0

Year	Owner	Built	In Blast
1904	North's Navigation Collieries (1889) Ltd	1	0
1905	North's Navigation Collieries (1889) Ltd	1	0
1906	North's Navigation Collieries (1889) Ltd	1	0
1907	North's Navigation Collieries (1889) Ltd	1	0
1908	North's Navigation Collieries (1889) Ltd	1	0
1909	North's Navigation Collieries (1889) Ltd	1	0
1910	North's Navigation Collieries (1889) Ltd	1	0
1911	North's Navigation Collieries (1889) Ltd	1	0
1912	North's Navigation Collieries (1889) Ltd	1	0
1913	North's Navigation Collieries (1889) Ltd	1	0

1839: named as 'Glamorgan Coal & Iron Co.'; the owner's name identifies the works as Tondu but no furnaces are listed. 1843: no output. 1849: Hunt lists 2 furnaces in blast. Truran: output 90 tons a week from each of 2 furnaces. In 1878 the owner was said to be in liquidation.

Tredegar, Mon. SO 1409

Year	Owner	Built	In Blast
1805	S. Homfray & Co.	2	2
1810	Fothergill	4	4
1823	—	5	-
1825	Homfray & Co.	5	5
1830	—	5	-
1839	Thompson & Co.	5	5
1841	Thompson & Co.	7	6
1843	Joint Stock	7	6
1847	Tredegar Iron Co.	7	7
1849	Tredegar Iron Co.	7	7
1854	Tredegar Iron Co.	8	8
1855	Tredegar Iron Co.	8	8
1856	Tredegar Iron Co.	8	8
1857	Tredegar Iron Co.	9	8
1858	Tredegar Iron Co.	9	7
1859	Tredegar Iron Co.	9	8
1860	Tredegar Iron Co.	9	8
1861	Tredegar Iron Co.	9	7
1862	Tredegar Iron Co.	9	8
1863	Tredegar Iron Co.	9	7
1864	Tredegar Iron Co.	9	7
1865	Tredegar Iron Co.	7	2
1866	Forman & Fothergill	9	6
1867	Forman & Fothergill	9	7
1868	Forman & Fothergill	9	7
1869	Forman & Fothergill	9	7
1870	Forman & Fothergill	9	7
1871	W.H. Forman & R. Fothergill	9	7
1872	Tredegar Iron Co.	9	7
1873	Tredegar Iron & Coal Co. Ltd	9	6
1874	Tredegar Iron & Coal Co. Ltd	9	6
1875	Tredegar Iron & Coal Co. Ltd	9	5
1876	Tredegar Iron & Coal Co. Ltd	9	4
1877	Tredegar Iron & Coal Co. Ltd	9	3
1878	Tredegar Iron & Coal Co. Ltd	9	3
1879	Tredegar Iron & Coal Co. Ltd	9	4
1880	Tredegar Iron & Coal Co. Ltd	9	6
1881	Tredegar Iron & Coal Co. Ltd	8	5
1882	Tredegar Iron & Coal Co. Ltd	6	5
1883	Tredegar Iron & Coal Co. Ltd	7	5
1884	Tredegar Iron & Coal Co. Ltd	7	4
1885	Tredegar Iron & Coal Co. Ltd	5	3
1886	Tredegar Iron & Coal Co. Ltd	5	3
1887	Tredegar Iron & Coal Co. Ltd	5	4
1888	Tredegar Iron & Coal Co. Ltd	5	3
1889	Tredegar Iron & Coal Co. Ltd	5	3
1890	Tredegar Iron & Coal Co. Ltd	5	4
1891	Tredegar Iron & Coal Co. Ltd	5	3
1892	Tredegar Iron & Coal Co. Ltd	5	2
1893	Tredegar Iron & Coal Co. Ltd	5	0
1894	Tredegar Iron & Coal Co. Ltd	5	0
1895	Tredegar Iron & Coal Co. Ltd	5	0
1896	Tredegar Iron & Coal Co. Ltd	5	0
1897	Tredegar Iron & Coal Co. Ltd	5	0
1898	Tredegar Iron & Coal Co. Ltd	5	0
1899	Tredegar Iron & Coal Co. Ltd	5	2
1900	Tredegar Iron & Coal Co. Ltd	6	2
1901	Tredegar Iron & Coal Co. Ltd	2	0
1902	Tredegar Iron & Coal Co. Ltd	2	0

1805: output 4,500 tons p.a. 1823–30: 16,385 tons p.a. in 1823, 18,514 tons in 1830. 1825: output 290 tons a week (14,300 tons p.a.), 'use it themselves'. 1843: 501 tons a week. 1849: Hunt's list has 9 furnaces in blast. Truran: output 110 tons a week from each of 8 furnaces. 1878: 2 furnaces rebuilding. 1882: 1 furnace building.

Treforest: see Pontypridd

Trimsaran, Carms. SN 4405

Year	Owner	Built	In Blast
1843	—	1	0
1847	Nartoh & Co.	2	0
1849	Martole & Co.	2	0
1854	Nortole & Co.	-	-
1855	E.H. Thomas	2	0
1856	E.H. Thomas	2	0
1857	E.H. Thomas	2	0
1858	E.H. Thomas	2	0
1859	—	2	0
1860	Frederick Harrison	2	0
1893	Anthracite Iron & Steel Co. Ltd	2	0
1894	Anthracite Iron & Steel Co. Ltd	2	0
1895	Anthracite Iron & Steel Co. Ltd	2	0
1896	Anthracite Iron & Steel Co. Ltd	2	0
1897	Anthracite Iron & Steel Co. Ltd	2	0
1898	Anthracite Iron & Steel Co. Ltd	2	0
1899	Anthracite Iron & Steel Co. Ltd	2	0
1900	Anthracite Iron & Steel Co. Ltd	2	0
1901	C.E. & H.M. Peel, Swansea	2	0
1902	C.E. & H.M. Peel, Swansea	2	0

1843: no output. The owners named in 1847–54 are presumably identical but which is correct is not clear. 1849: Hunt lists 3 furnaces in blast. Truran: output 60 tons a week from each of 2 furnaces. 1893: 1 furnace in blast for 3 months.

Trosnant: see Pontypool

Typwca: see **Cwmbran**

Union: see **Rhymney**

Varteg, Mon. SO 2605

Year	Owner	Built	In Blast
1805	Knight & Co.	1	1
1810	Varteg Co.	1	1
1823	—	2	-
1825	Kenrick & Co.	3	2
1830	—	5	-
1839	Kenrick & Co.	5	5
1841	Kenrick & Co.	5	0
1843	Kenrick & Co.	5	0
1847	Williams & Co.	-	-
1849	Williams & Co.	-	-
1854	Williams & Co.	-	-
1855	Williams & Co.	-	-
1856	Williams & Co.	-	-
1857	Williams & Co.	-	-
1858	Crawshay Bailey & William Morgan	-	-
1859	Crawshay Bailey & William Morgan	-	-
1860	Crawshay Bailey & William Morgan	-	-
1861	Crawshay Bailey & William Morgan	-	-
1862	Partridge & Sons	-	-
1863	Partridge & Sons	-	-
1864	Golynos Iron Co.	-	-
1865	Golynos Iron Co.	-	-
1866	Golynos Iron Co.	-	-
1867	Golynos Iron Co.	-	-
1868	Golynos Iron Co.	-	-

1805: output 900 tons p.a. 1823–30: notes construction of additional furnaces in 1824, 1826 and 1830; output 6,512 tons p.a. in 1823 and 13,356 tons in 1830. 1825: output 160 tons a week, 7,800 tons p.a., 'melting and forge'. The Staffs RO version of the list has 3 furnaces in blast, the B&W text has 2. 1843: no output. The 1847 list couples Varteg with Pentwyn and Golynos (qqv), with a total of 8 furnaces (5 in blast) at the three sites, as does English in 1849. Hunt lists 2 furnaces in blast at Varteg alone in 1849. In 1854-68 Varteg was combined with Golynos (qv). Truran: output (at Varteg alone) 120 tons a week from each of 5 furnaces.

Venallt, Glam. SN 8604

Year	Owner	Built	In Blast
1839	Arthur & Co.	0	0
1841	—	1	0
1843	Jevons, Wood & Co.	1	0
1847	Iwons & Co.	2	2
1849	Jevons & Co.	2	0
1854	Aberdare Iron Co.	2	0
1855	Fothergill, Brown & Co. (Aberdare Iron Co.)	2	0
1856	Fothergill, Brown & Co. (Aberdare Iron Co.)	2	0
1857	Fothergill, Brown & Co. (Aberdare Iron Co.)	2	0
1858	Fothergill & Co. (Aberdare Iron Co.)	2	0
1859	Aberdare Iron Co.	2	0
1860	N. Vaughan	2	0
1861	N. Vaughan	2	0
1862	N. Vaughan	2	0
1863	N. Vaughan	2	0
1869	Neath Abbey Co.	2	0
1870	Neath Abbey Co.	2	0

1839: an entry for Neath Valley, with 2 furnaces building, appears to belong here. 1841: an entry for Blaengwrach has been assumed to belong here. 1843: a works named 'Cwm Neath' has been identified as Venallt from the owner's name. In 1847 and English's list of 1849 the site appears as 'Penallt', the name also used by Truran; neither has an entry for Venallt, whereas 'Penallt' does not appear in *Mineral Statistics*, which suggests that the two names refer to the same works. Hunt's list of 1849 has an entry for 'Jarvis & Co.' (i.e. the name of the owner, rather than the works), with 2 furnaces in blast, which appears to belong here. In 1854 *Mineral Statistics* has an entry with the same heading but no other information, whereas there is a separate entry for Venallt as above. 1861: 'Dismantled and not likely to resume operations'; there appears to have been an abortive revival in 1869–70. The owner's name in 1847 is presumably a poor form of Jevons, rather than Izons, the South Staffs. firm. Truran: output 60 tons a week from each of 2 furnaces.

Victoria, Mon. [SO 1707]

Year	Owner	Built	In Blast
1839	Victoria Coal & Iron Co.	2	2
1841	Victoria	4	3
1843	Joint Stock	3	0
1847	Joint Stock Co.	4	2
1849	Darby & Co.	4	2
1854	Ebbw Vale Co.	4	2
1855	Ebbw Vale Iron Co.	4	2
1856	Ebbw Vale Iron Co.	4	3
1857	Ebbw Vale Iron Co.	4	3
1858	Ebbw Vale Iron Co.	4	3
1859	Ebbw Vale Iron Co.	4	3
1860	Ebbw Vale Iron Co.	4	3
1861	Ebbw Vale Iron Co.	4	2
1862	Ebbw Vale Iron Co.	4	3
1863	Ebbw Vale Iron Co.	4	3
1864	Ebbw Vale Iron Co.	4	3
1865	Ebbw Vale Co. Ltd	4	3
1866	Ebbw Vale Co. Ltd	-	-
1867	Ebbw Vale Co. Ltd	-	-
1868	Ebbw Vale Co. Ltd	-	-
1869	Ebbw Vale Co. Ltd	3	3
1870	Ebbw Vale Co. Ltd	-	-
1871	Ebbw Vale Co. Ltd	-	-
1872	Ebbw Vale Steel Iron & Coal Co. Ltd	-	-
1873	Ebbw Vale Steel Iron & Coal Co. Ltd	-	-
1874	Ebbw Vale Steel Iron & Coal Co. Ltd	-	-
1875	Ebbw Vale Steel Iron & Coal Co. Ltd	-	-

Year	Owner	Built	In Blast
1876	Ebbw Vale Steel Iron & Coal Co. Ltd	3	3
1877	Ebbw Vale Steel Iron & Coal Co. Ltd	3	2
1878	Ebbw Vale Steel Iron & Coal Co. Ltd	2	2
1879	Ebbw Vale Steel Iron & Coal Co. Ltd	3	2
1880	Ebbw Vale Steel Iron & Coal Co. Ltd	2	2
1881	Ebbw Vale Steel Iron & Coal Co. Ltd	1	1
1882	Ebbw Vale Steel Iron & Coal Co. Ltd	1	1
1883	Ebbw Vale Steel Iron & Coal Co. Ltd	3	3
1884	Ebbw Vale Steel Iron & Coal Co. Ltd	3	2
1885	Ebbw Vale Steel Iron & Coal Co. Ltd	2	2
1886	Ebbw Vale Steel Iron & Coal Co. Ltd	2	2
1887	Ebbw Vale Steel Iron & Coal Co. Ltd	2	2
1888	Ebbw Vale Steel Iron & Coal Co. Ltd	2	2
1889	Ebbw Vale Steel Iron & Coal Co. Ltd	2	2
1890	Ebbw Vale Steel Iron & Coal Co. Ltd	2	2
1891	Ebbw Vale Steel Iron & Coal Co. Ltd	2	2
1892	Ebbw Vale Steel Iron & Coal Co. Ltd	2	2
1893	Ebbw Vale Steel Iron & Coal Co. Ltd	2	2
1894	Ebbw Vale Steel Iron & Coal Co. Ltd	2	2
1895	Ebbw Vale Steel Iron & Coal Co. Ltd	2	2
1896	Ebbw Vale Steel Iron & Coal Co. Ltd	2	2
1897	Ebbw Vale Steel Iron & Coal Co. Ltd	2	2
1898	Ebbw Vale Steel Iron & Coal Co. Ltd	-	-
1899	Ebbw Vale Steel Iron & Coal Co. Ltd	-	-
1900	Ebbw Vale Steel Iron & Coal Co. Ltd	2	1
1901	Ebbw Vale Steel Iron & Coal Co. Ltd	2	1
1902	Ebbw Vale Steel Iron & Coal Co. Ltd	2	2
1903	Ebbw Vale Steel Iron & Coal Co. Ltd	-	-
1904	Ebbw Vale Steel Iron & Coal Co. Ltd	-	-
1905	Ebbw Vale Steel Iron & Coal Co. Ltd	-	-
1906	Ebbw Vale Steel Iron & Coal Co. Ltd	-	-
1907	Ebbw Vale Steel Iron & Coal Co. Ltd	-	-
1908	Ebbw Vale Steel Iron & Coal Co. Ltd	-	-
1909	Ebbw Vale Steel Iron & Coal Co. Ltd	-	-
1910	Ebbw Vale Steel Iron & Coal Co. Ltd	-	-
1911	Ebbw Vale Steel Iron & Coal Co. Ltd	-	-
1912	Ebbw Vale Steel Iron & Coal Co. Ltd	-	-
1913	Ebbw Vale Steel Iron & Coal Co. Ltd	-	-

1839: 2 furnaces building. 1843: no output. 1849: Hunt lists 4 furnaces in blast. Truran: output 200 tons a week from each of 4 furnaces. In 1866–68 and 1870–75 furnace-numbers for Victoria are combined with those for other Ebbw Vale Co. works under Ebbw Vale (qv). 1882: 2 furnaces building. 1883: 2 furnaces started July 1883. In 1898–99 and from 1903 furnace-numbers combined with Ebbw Vale.

Ynyscedwyn, Brecs. SN 7809

Year	Owner	Built	In Blast
1794	Mr Parsons	1	-
1796	—	1	1
1805	Parsons	1	1
1810	Parsons & Co.	1	1
1823	—	1	-
1825	Reynolds	2	2
1830	—	2	-
1839	George Crane	3	3
1841	George Crane	3	3
1843	Crane & Co.	3	2
1847	Crane & Co.	7	5
1849	Ynyscedwyn Iron Co.	7	5
1854	Ynyscedwyn Iron Co.	7	5
1855	Ynyscedwyn Iron Co.	7	4
1856	Ynyscedwyn Iron Co.	6	5
1857	Ynyscedwyn Iron Co.	6	4
1858	Ynyscedwyn Iron Co.	6	5
1859	Ynyscedwyn Iron Co.	6	5
1860	Ynyscedwyn Iron Co.	6	4
1861	Ynyscedwyn Iron Co.	6	2
1862	Ynyscedwyn Iron Co.	6	1
1863	Ynyscedwyn Iron Co.	6	0
1864	Ynyscedwyn Iron Co. Ltd	6	1
1865	Ynyscedwyn Iron Co. Ltd	6	1
1866	Ynyscedwyn Iron Co. Ltd	2	2
1867	Ynyscedwyn Iron Co. Ltd	2	2
1868	Ynyscedwyn Iron Co. Ltd	2	2
1869	Ynyscedwyn Iron Co. Ltd	2	0
1870	Ynyscedwyn Iron Co. Ltd	2	0
1871	Ynyscedwyn Iron Co. Ltd	2	2
1872	Ynyscedwyn Iron Co. Ltd	2	2
1873	Ynyscedwyn Iron Co. Ltd	2	2
1874	Ynyscedwyn Iron, Steel & Coal Co. Ltd	2	2
1875	Ynyscedwyn Iron, Steel & Coal Co. Ltd	2	2
1876	Ynyscedwyn Iron, Steel & Coal Co. Ltd	2	2
1877	Ynyscedwyn Iron, Steel & Coal Co. Ltd	2	0
1878	Ynyscedwyn Iron, Steel & Coal Co. Ltd	2	0

1884	Crane Iron, Steel & Coal Co. Ltd	2	0
1885	Crane Iron, Steel & Coal Co. Ltd	2	0
1886	Crane Iron, Steel & Coal Co. Ltd	2	0
1887	Crane Iron, Steel & Coal Co. Ltd	2	0
1888	Crane Iron, Steel & Coal Co. Ltd	2	0

The 1794 list names the ground landlord as Thomas Aubrey Esq.; the furnace was charcoal-fired. 1796: output 1,352 tons p.a., i.e. 26 tons a week, Excise and actual; Exact Return 800 tons. 1805: no output returned. 1823: output 1,498 tons p.a. 1830: 2,111 tons. 1825: weekly output 73 tons, 3,640 tons p.a. 1843: 140 tons a week. 1849: Hunt lists 7 furnaces in blast. Truran: output 80 tons a week from each of 7 furnaces. 1864: new furnace put in blast for a short time only. 1873: 'No Return' (although the figures above are printed in *Mineral Statistics*).

Ynysfach, Glam. SO 0406

Year	Owner	Built	In Blast
1825	Crawshay	2	2
1839	William Crawshay	2	2
1841	W. Crawshay	-	-
1843	Crawshay & Co.	4	4
1847	W. Crawshay	-	-
1849	W. Crawshay	4	4
1854	W. Crawshay & Sons	4	4
1855	W. Crawshay & Sons	4	4
1856	W. Crawshay & Sons	4	4
1857	W. Crawshay & Sons	4	4
1858	W. Crawshay & Sons	4	4
1859	William Crawshay & Sons	4	4
1860	William Crawshay & Sons	4	4
1861	William Crawshay	4	4
1862	William Crawshay	4	4
1863	William Crawshay	-	-
1864	William Crawshay	-	-
1865	William Crawshay	-	-
1866	William Crawshay	-	-
1867	Robert Crawshay	-	-
1868	Robert Crawshay	-	-
1869	Robert Crawshay	-	-
1870	Robert Crawshay	-	-
1871	Robert Crawshay	-	-
1872	Robert Crawshay	-	-
1873	Robert Crawshay	-	-
1874	Robert Crawshay	-	-
1875	Robert Crawshay	-	-
1876	Robert Crawshay	4	0
1877	Robert Crawshay	4	0
1878	Robert Crawshay	4	0
1879	Crawshay Brothers	-	-
1880	Crawshay Brothers	-	-
1881	Crawshay Brothers	-	-
1882	Crawshay Brothers	4	0
1883	Crawshay Brothers	4	0

1825: weekly output 170 tons at Ynysfach; annual figure for Ynysfach and Cyfarthfa (qv) together 28,000 tons, 'use it themselves; No 1 sometimes'. The Staffs RO version of the list has 2 furnaces in blast; the B&W text has 1. 1839: 2 furnaces building. 1841: see Cyfarthfa. 1843: output 360 tons a week. 1847: furnace-numbers returned for Cyfarthfa, Hirwaun (qqv) and Ynysfach together, with 15 furnaces (13 in blast) at the three sites. Truran: output at Ynysfach 100 tons a week from each of 4 furnaces. In 1863–75 and 1879–81 furnace-numbers combined with Cyfarthfa.

Ystalyfera, Glam. [SN 7608]

Year	Owner	Built	In Blast
1839	Brancker & Co.	1	1
1841	Brancker & Co.	2	2
1843	Sir T. Brancker & Co.	3	3
1847	Ystalyfera Iron Co.	11	6
1849	Ystalyfera Iron Co.	11	4
1854	Ystalyfera Iron Co.	10	7
1855	Ystalyfera Iron Co.	10	7
1856	Ystalyfera Iron Co.	11	9
1857	Ystalyfera Iron Co.	11	9
1858	Ystalyfera Iron Co.	11	7
1859	Ystalyfera Iron Co.	11	7
1860	Ystalyfera Iron Co.	11	5
1861	Ystalyfera Iron Co.	11	7
1862	Ystalyfera Iron Co.	11	7
1863	Ystalyfera Iron Co.	11	7
1864	Ystalyfera Iron Co.	11	6
1865	Ystalyfera Iron Co.	11	6
1866	Ystalyfera Iron Co.	11	6
1867	Ystalyfera Iron Co.	11	6
1868	Ystalyfera Iron Co.	11	6
1869	Ystalyfera Iron Co.	11	6
1870	Ystalyfera Iron Co.	11	6
1871	Ystalyfera Iron Co.	11	6
1872	Ystalyfera Iron Co.	11	6
1873	Ystalyfera Iron Co.	11	5
1874	Ystalyfera Iron Co.	11	5
1875	Ystalyfera Iron Co.	11	4
1876	Ystalyfera Iron Co.	11	4
1877	Ystalyfera Iron Co.	11	4
1878	Ystalyfera Iron Co.	11	4
1879	Ystalyfera Iron Co.	11	4
1880	Ystalyfera Iron Co.	11	4
1881	Ystalyfera Iron Co.	11	3
1882	Ystalyfera Iron Co.	11	2
1883	Ystalyfera Iron Co.	9	2
1884	Ystalyfera Iron Co.	9	2
1885	Ystalyfera Iron Co.	11	2
1886	Ystalyfera Iron Co.	11	0
1887	Ystalyfera Iron & Tin Plate Co. Ltd	11	0
1888	Ystalyfera Iron & Tin Plate Co. Ltd	11	0
1889	Ystylyfera Iron & Tin Plate Co. Ltd	11	0
1890	Ystylyfera Iron & Tin Plate Co. Ltd	11	0
1891	Ystylyfera Iron & Tin Plate Co. Ltd	11	0
1892	Ystylyfera Iron & Tin Plate Co. Ltd	11	0

1839: 1 furnace building. 1843: output 150 tons a week. 1849: Hunt lists 11 furnaces in blast. 1854: 2 works listed at Ystalyfera, both owned by the same company, with 5 furnaces at each and a total of 7 furnaces (not split between the two sites) in blast. The two remain combined in later years. Truran: output 80 tons a week from each of 11 furnaces.

Gloucestershire

Abbey Tintern: see Tintern

Bishopswood　　　　　　　　　　　　　　SO 5918

Year	Owner	Built	In Blast
1794	William Partridge	1	-
1796	—	1	1
1805	William Partridge	1	1
1810	Partridge	1	1
1825	—	1	1

In 1794 the ground landlord was Lord Foley; the only plant listed was a single charcoal furnace and a finery. 1796: output 500 tons p.a., Excise and actual, 947 tons Exact Return. 1805: output 653 tons. In 1825 Bishopswood is one of several charcoal furnaces bracketed with Melincourt, Glam. (qv), with the comment: 'Am not acquainted with these furnaces and have taken them from an old list of mine. They are probably worked with charcoal'; no output is shown for any.

Bromley Hill: see Oakwood

Cinderford　　　　　　　　　　　　　　[SO 5710]

Year	Owner	Built	In Blast
1796	—	1	1
1805a	Teague & Co.	2	2
1805b	Protheroe		
1810a	Teague	2	0
1810b	Protheroe	1	1
1825	Whitehouse & Co.	1	-
1839	—	3	3
1841	Crawshay & Co.	3	2
1843	Crawshay & Co.	3	2
1849	—	-	3
1854	Alloway & Crawshay	3	3
1855	Alloway & Crawshay	3	3
1856	Alloway & Crawshay	4	3
1857	Alloway & Crawshay	4	3
1858	Alloway & Crawshay	4	3
1859	Alloway & Crawshay	4	3
1860	Cinderford Iron Co.	4	2
1861	Cinderford Iron Co.	4	2
1862	Henry Crawshay	4	3
1863	Henry Crawshay	4	3
1864	Henry Crawshay	4	3
1865	Henry Crawshay	4	3
1866	Henry Crawshay	4	3
1867	Henry Crawshay	4	2
1868	Henry Crawshay	4	2
1869	Henry Crawshay	4	3
1870	Henry Crawshay	4	3
1871	Henry Crawshay	3	3
1872	Henry Crawshay	4	3
1873	Henry Crawshay & Co.	4	3
1874	Henry Crawshay & Co.	4	3
1875	Henry Crawshay & Co.	4	3
1876	Henry Crawshay & Co.	4	2
1877	Henry Crawshay & Co.	4	2
1878	Henry Crawshay & Co.	4	2
1879	Henry Crawshay & Co.	4	2
1880	Henry Crawshay & Co.	4	2
1881	Henry Crawshay & Co.	4	2
1882	Henry Crawshay & Co.	3	2
1883	Henry Crawshay & Co.	3	1
1884	Henry Crawshay & Co.	3	1
1885	Henry Crawshay & Co.	3	1
1886	Henry Crawshay & Co.	3	1
1887	Henry Crawshay & Co.	3	1
1888	Henry Crawshay & Co.	3	1
1889	Henry Crawshay & Co.	3	1
1890	Henry Crawshay & Co.	1	1
1891	Henry Crawshay & Co.	3	1
1892	Henry Crawshay & Co. Ltd	3	1
1893	Henry Crawshay & Co. Ltd	3	1
1894	Henry Crawshay & Co. Ltd	3	0

1796: 20 tons p.a. Excise, actual and Exact Return; works called Forest of Dean. 1805: two entries with one set of furnace-numbers as above but two output figures, 800 tons p.a. and 450 tons p.a. 1810: only one name (Dean Forest) appears in the list of works, followed by two owners (as above) and two sets of furnace-numbers. 1825: no note as to whether the furnace was in blast or not and the comment 'No Returns'. 1841: output not stated but cf. the comment made of the Forest of Dean as a whole: 'The operations here may be said to be confined to the works of Messrs Crawshay and Allaway [i.e. Cinderford], the furnace of Mushet's [i.e. Darkhill, qv] being an experimental cupelo furnace'. 1843: output at Cinderford, the only Dean works listed, 160 tons a week. Truran: output 100 tons a week from each of 3 furnaces. The works was generally called the Forest of Dean Ironworks in pre-1854 lists, although it appears as Cinderford in 1839. In *Mineral Statistics* it is called Cinderford in 1854–59 and 1882–94 and Newnham in 1860–81.

Darkhill　　　　　　　　　　　　　　SO 5908

Year	Owner	Built	In Blast
1839	—	1	0
1841	Mushet	1	1
1854	Messrs Mushet	1	0
1855	Messrs Mushet	1	0
1856	Messrs Mushet	1	0
1857	Messrs Mushet	1	0
1858	Messrs Mushet	1	0
1859	Messrs Mushet	1	0

1841: No output shown, although the furnace was said to be in blast. Cf. the general comment about the Forest of Dean printed above under Cinderford, which indicates that Darkhill was 'an experimental cupelo furnace'.

Flaxley
SO 6915

Year	Owner	Built	In Blast
1794	— Crawley Esq.	1	-
1796	—	1	1
1805	T.B. Crawley	1	1
1810	Crawley & Co.	1	1
1825	—	1	-

In 1794 Crawley was both owner and occupier; there was 1 charcoal furnace, 2 fineries and a chafery. 1796: output 360 tons, Excise, actual and Exact Return. 1805: output 379 tons. In 1825 no return was received and so there was no information as to owner, output or whether the furnace was in blast.

Forest of Dean: see Cinderford

Great Western: see Soudley

Lydney
SO 6202

Year	Owner	Built	In Blast
1794	Daniel Harford	1	-
1796	—	1	0

In 1794 the ground landlord was — Bathurst Esq.; there was 1 charcoal furnace, 2 fineries, 2 chaferies, 1 balling furnace and a rolling and slitting mill.

Newnham: see Cinderford

Oakwood
SO 6006

Year	Owner	Built	In Blast
1854	Ebbw Vale Co.	1	0
1855	Ebbw Vale Co.	1	0
1856	Ebbw Vale Co.	1	0
1857	Ebbw Vale Co.	1	0
1858	Ebbw Vale Co.	1	0
1859	Ebbw Vale Co.	1	0
1859	Ebbw Vale Co.	1	0
1860	Ebbw Vale Co.	1	0
1861	Ebbw Vale Co.	1	0
1862	Ebbw Vale Co.	1	0
1863	Ebbw Vale Co.	1	0
1864	Ebbw Vale Co.	1	0
1865	Ebbw Vale Co. Ltd	1	0
1866	Ebbw Vale Co. Ltd	1	0
1867	Ebbw Vale Co. Ltd	1	0
1868	Ebbw Vale Co. Ltd	1	0
1869	Ebbw Vale Co. Ltd	1	0
1870	Ebbw Vale Co. Ltd	1	0
1871	Ebbw Vale Co. Ltd	1	0
1872	Ebbw Vale Steel Iron & Coal Co. Ltd	1	0
1873	Ebbw Vale Steel Iron & Coal Co. Ltd	1	0
1874	Ebbw Vale Steel Iron & Coal Co. Ltd	1	0
1875	Ebbw Vale Steel Iron & Coal Co. Ltd	1	0
1876	Ebbw Vale Steel Iron & Coal Co. Ltd	1	0
1877	Ebbw Vale Steel Iron & Coal Co. Ltd	0	0

Truran uses the alternative name Bromley for this works and assigns an output of 80 tons a week to the single furnace, which in fact may never have worked at all.

Parkend
[SO 6108]

Year	Owner	Built	In Blast
1839	—	2	1
1841	James & Montague	2	0
1854	James & Greenham	2	2
1855	James & Greenham	2	1
1856	James & Greenham	2	2
1857	James & Greenham	2	2
1858	James & Greenham	2	1
1859	James & Greenham	2	1
1860	James & Greenham	2	1
1861	James & Greenham	2	1
1862	Forest of Dean Iron Co.	2	1
1863	Forest of Dean Iron Co.	2	2
1864	Forest of Dean Iron Co.	2	2
1865	Forest of Dean Iron Co.	2	2
1866	Forest of Dean Iron Co.	3	2
1867	Forest of Dean Iron Co.	3	2
1868	Forest of Dean Iron Co.	3	2
1869	Forest of Dean Iron Co.	3	2
1870	Forest of Dean Iron Co.	3	3
1871	Forest of Dean Iron Co.	3	2
1872	Forest of Dean Iron Co.	3	2
1873	Forest of Dean Iron Co.	3	2
1874	Forest of Dean Iron Co.	3	2
1875	Forest of Dean Iron Co.	3	2
1876	Forest of Dean Iron Co. Ltd	3	2
1877	Forest of Dean Iron Co. Ltd	3	1
1878	Forest of Dean Iron Co. Ltd	3	0
1879	Forest of Dean Iron Co. Ltd	3	0
1880	Forest of Dean Iron Co. Ltd	3	0
1881	Forest of Dean Iron Co. Ltd	3	0
1882	Henry Crawshay & Sons	3	0
1883	Henry Crawshay & Sons	3	0
1884	Henry Crawshay & Sons	3	0
1885	Henry Crawshay & Sons	3	0
1886	Henry Crawshay & Sons	3	0
1887	Henry Crawshay & Sons	3	0
1888	Henry Crawshay & Sons	3	0
1889	Henry Crawshay & Sons	3	0

1841: output nil; cf. comment under Cinderford. Truran: output 90 tons a week from each of 2 furnaces.

Redbrook
SO 5410

Year	Owner	Built	In Blast
1794	H. Partridge	1	-
1796	—	1	0
1805	Davies & Co.	1	1
1810	Davies & Co.	1	1
1825	—	1	-

The ground landlord in 1794 was Lord Gage; there was 1 charcoal furnace, 1 chafery, 1 balling furnace and a rolling mill. In 1796 the furnace was explicitly said to be out of blast. 1805: output 804 tons. In 1825 no owner was named and there was no return as to output or whether the furnace was in blast.

Shakemantle

The 1839 list notes 2 furnaces building at 'Shackmantle', which fail to reappear in any later list. Despite this, Truran returns an output 100 tons a week from each of 2 furnaces at Shakemantle, a site which is not listed at all in *Mineral Statistics*. It does not appear to be an alternative name for another works and was apparently a project which came to Truran's notice but never materialised. His notional output figure is therefore grossly misleading, especially in such a small district as the Forest of Dean.

Soudley SO 6510

Year	Owner	Built	In Blast
1839	—	2	1
1841	—	2	0
1856	B. Gibbons Jun.	2	0
1857	B. Gibbons Jun.	2	0
1858	B. Gibbons Jun.	2	0
1859	B. Gibbons Jun.	2	0
1860	Benjamin Gibbons	2	1
1861	Benjamin Gibbons	2	0
1862	Benjamin Gibbons	2	1
1863	Benjamin Gibbons	2	1
1864	Goold Brothers	2	1
1865	Goold Brothers	2	1
1866	Goold Brothers	2	0
1867	Goold Brothers	2	1
1868	Goold Brothers	2	1
1869	Goold Brothers	2	1
1870	Goold Brothers	2	1
1871	Goold Brothers	2	1
1872	Goold Brothers	2	1
1873	Goold Brothers	2	1
1874	Goold Brothers	2	1
1875	Great Western Iron Co. Ltd	2	1
1876	Great Western Iron Co. Ltd	2	1
1877	Great Western Iron Co. Ltd	2	1
1878	Great Western Iron Co. Ltd	2	0
1879	Great Western Iron Co. Ltd	2	0
1880	Great Western Iron Co. Ltd	2	0
1881	George Benton	2	0
1882	George Benton	2	0
1883	George Benton	2	0
1884	George Benton	2	0
1885	George Benton	2	0
1886	George Benton	2	0
1887	Executors of late George Benton	2	0
1888	Executors of late George Benton	2	0

1841: output nil; cf. comment under Cinderford. The works appears as Soudley in 1839 and 1856–74, Great Western thereafter. Truran: output 90 tons a week from each of 2 furnaces.

Tintern, Mon. SO 5100

Year	Owner	Built	In Blast
1794	D. Tanner	1	-
1796	—	1	1
1805	Thompson	1	1
1810	Thompson & Co.	1	1
1825	—	1	-

This furnace stood on the Angidy Brook, a west bank tributary of the Wye, and was therefore in Monmouthshire but is more appropriately included with the other Forest of Dean works in Gloucestershire. In 1794 it was called 'Abbey Tintern'; the ground landlord was the Duke of Beaufort; and there was one 'old' charcoal furnace, 4 fineries, 2 chaferies and a wire mill. 1796: output 70 tons, Excise, actual and Exact Return. 1805: output 987 tons. In 1825 Tintern was one of a number of charcoal furnaces bracketed with Melincourt, South Wales (qv), from which no return was received as to owner, output or whether the furnace was in blast (cf. Bishopswood).

Somerset and Wiltshire

Ashton Vale, Somerset [ST 5670]

Year	Owner	Built	In Blast
1860	Knight, Abbots & Co.	1	1
1861	Edwin Knight & Co.	1	1
1862	Edwin Knight & Co.	1	0
1863	Edwin Knight & Co.	1	1
1864	Edwin Knight & Co.	1	1
1865	Ashton Vale Iron Co. Ltd	1	1
1866	Ashton Vale Iron Co. Ltd	1	1
1867	Ashton Vale Iron Co. Ltd	2	1
1868	Ashton Vale Iron Co. Ltd	2	1
1869	Ashton Vale Iron Co. Ltd	2	1
1870	Ashton Vale Iron Co. Ltd	2	1
1871	Ashton Vale Iron Co. Ltd	1	1
1872	Ashton Vale Iron Co. Ltd	1	1
1873	Ashton Vale Iron Co. Ltd	1	1
1874	Ashton Vale Iron Co. Ltd	1	1
1875	Ashton Vale Iron Co. Ltd	1	1
1876	Ashton Vale Iron Co. Ltd	1	0
1877	Ashton Vale Iron Co. Ltd	1	0
1878	Ashton Vale Iron Co. Ltd	1	0
1879	Ashton Vale Iron Co. Ltd	1	0
1880	Ashton Vale Iron Co. Ltd	1	0
1881	Ashton Vale Iron Co. Ltd	1	0
1882	Ashton Vale Iron Co. Ltd	1	1
1883	Ashton Vale Iron Co. Ltd	1	1
1884	Ashton Vale Iron Co. Ltd	1	0
1885	Ashton Furnace Co.	1	0
1886	Ashton Furnace Co.	1	1
1887	Ashton Furnace Co.	1	0
1888	Ashton Furnace Co.	1	0
1889	Ashton Furnace Co.	1	0
1890	Ashton Furnace Co.	1	0
1891	Ashton Furnace Co.	1	0
1892	Ashton Furnace Co.	1	0
1893	Ashton Furnace Co.	1	0

Pennywell Road, Somerset [ST 6073]

Year	Owner	Built	In Blast
1857	Langford & Co.	1	1
1858	Langford & Co.	1	1
1859	George Chick	1	1
1860	George Chick	1	0
1861	George Chick	1	0
1862	George Chick	1	0
1863	Keeling & Chick	1	0
1864	Keeling & Chick	1	0
1865	—	1	0

1857: In blast for a few months only.

Seend, Wilts. [ST 9461]

Year	Owner	Built	In Blast
1858	Sarl & Sons	2	0
1859	Sarl & Sons	2	0
1860	Sarl & Sons	2	2
1861	Sarl & Sons	2	0
1862	Sarl & Sons	2	0
1863	Westbury Iron Co.	2	0
1870	W. & S.S. Malcolm & Co.	1	1
1871	W. & S.S. Malcolm & Co.	3	2
1872	Malcolm & Co.	3	2
1873	Malcolm & Co.	3	2
1874	Ducal Iron & Coal Co.	3	0
1875	Ducal Iron & Coal Co.	3	0
1876	Ducal Iron & Coal Co.	3	0
1877	Ducal Iron & Coal Co.	3	0
1878	Ducal Iron & Coal Co.	3	0
1884	Richard Berridge	3	0
1885	Richard Berridge	3	0
1886	Richard Berridge	3	0
1887	Executors of late Richard Berridge	3	0
1888	Executors of late Richard Berridge	3	0

Cf. Dolydd, North Wales.

Westbury, Wilts. [ST 8650]

Year	Owner	Built	In Blast
1857	Greenwell & Co.	2	0
1858	Westbury Iron Co. Ltd	2	1
1859	Westbury Iron Co. Ltd	2	2
1860	Westbury Iron Co. Ltd	2	2
1861	Westbury Iron Co. Ltd	2	2
1862	Westbury Iron Co. Ltd	3	2
1863	—	3	2
1864	Westbury Iron Co. Ltd	3	3
1865	Westbury Iron Co. Ltd	3	3
1866	Westbury Iron Co. Ltd	4	3
1867	Westbury Iron Co. Ltd	4	3
1868	Westbury Iron Co. Ltd	4	2
1869	Westbury Iron Co. Ltd	4	3
1870	Westbury Iron Co. Ltd	4	3
1871	Westbury Iron Co. Ltd	4	3
1872	Westbury Iron Co. Ltd	4	3
1873	Westbury Iron Co. Ltd	4	3
1874	Westbury Iron Co. Ltd	4	2
1875	Westbury Iron Co. Ltd	4	2
1876	Westbury Iron Co. Ltd	4	2
1877	Westbury Iron Co. Ltd	4	2
1878	Westbury Iron Co. Ltd	4	2
1879	Westbury Iron Co. Ltd	4	2
1880	Westbury Iron Co. Ltd	4	2
1881	Westbury Iron Co. Ltd	3	1
1882	Westbury Iron Co. Ltd	3	2

1883	Westbury Iron Co. Ltd	3	2
1884	Westbury Iron Co. Ltd	3	1
1885	Westbury Iron Co. Ltd	3	1
1886	Westbury Iron Co. Ltd	3	1
1887	Westbury Iron Co. Ltd	3	1
1888	Westbury Iron Co. Ltd	3	1
1889	Westbury Iron Co. Ltd	2	1
1890	Westbury Iron Co. Ltd	2	1
1891	Westbury Iron Co. Ltd	2	1
1892	Westbury Iron Co. Ltd	2	1
1893	Westbury Iron Co. Ltd	2	1
1894	Westbury Iron Co. Ltd	2	1
1895	Westbury Iron Co. Ltd	2	1
1896	Westbury Iron Co. Ltd	2	1
1897	Westbury Iron Co. Ltd	1	1
1898	Westbury Iron Co. Ltd	1	1
1899	Westbury Iron Co. Ltd	1	2
1900	Westbury Iron Co. Ltd	2	1
1901	Westbury Iron Co. Ltd	2	0
1902	Westbury Iron, Mining & Smelting Co.	2	0
1903	New Westbury Iron Co. Ltd	2	0
1904	New Westbury Iron Co. Ltd	2	1
1905	New Westbury Iron Co. Ltd	2	1
1906	New Westbury Iron Co. Ltd	2	1
1907	New Westbury Iron Co. Ltd	2	1
1908	New Westbury Iron Co. Ltd	2	1
1909	New Westbury Iron Co. Ltd	2	0
1910	New Westbury Iron Co. Ltd	2	0
1911	New Westbury Iron Co. Ltd	2	0
1912	New Westbury Iron Co. Ltd	2	0
1913	New Westbury Iron Co. Ltd	2	0
1921	New Westbury Iron Co. Ltd	2	-
1922	New Westbury Iron Co. Ltd	2	-
1923	New Westbury Iron Co. Ltd	2	-
1924	New Westbury Iron Co. Ltd	2	-
1925	New Westbury Iron Co. Ltd	2	-
1926	New Westbury Iron Co. Ltd	2	-
1927	New Westbury Iron Co. Ltd	2	-
1928	New Westbury Iron Co. Ltd	2	-
1929	New Westbury Iron Co. Ltd	2	-
1930	New Westbury Iron Co. Ltd	1	-
1931	New Westbury Iron Co. Ltd	1	-
1932	New Westbury Iron Co. Ltd	1	-
1933	New Westbury Iron Co. Ltd	1	-
1934	New Westbury Iron Co. Ltd	1	-
1935	New Westbury Iron Co. Ltd	1	-
1936	New Westbury Iron Co. Ltd	1	-
1937	New Westbury Iron Co. Ltd	1	-
1938	New Westbury Iron Co. Ltd	1	-

1857: 'Expected soon to be in blast'. Dismantled 1939.

Sussex and Hampshire

Ashburnham, Sussex TQ 6817

Year	Owner	Built	In Blast
1794	Lord Ashburnham	1	-
1796	—	1	1

No ground landlord was returned for the Wealden works in 1794; Ashburnham was listed as a charcoal furnace, with an illegible note in the right-hand margin. 1796: output returned as 172 tons 15 cwt (Excise), 173 tons (actual and Exact Return).

Heathfield, Sussex TQ 5918

Year	Owner	Built	In Blast
1794	J. Fuller	1	-

There is an illegible note in the right-hand margin of the original return but no other information.

Warsash, Hants. SU 4906

Year	Owner	Built	In Blast
1869	—	1	1
1870	Harrison Ainslie & Co.	1	0
1871	Harrison Ainslie & Co.	1	0
1872	Harrison Ainslie & Co.	1	0
1873	Harrison Ainslie & Co.	1	0
1874	Harrison Ainslie & Co.	1	1
1875	Harrison Ainslie & Co.	1	0
1876	Harrison Ainslie & Co.	1	0
1877	Harrison Ainslie & Co.	1	1
1878	Harrison Ainslie & Co.	1	0
1879	Harrison Ainslie & Co.	1	0
1880	Harrison Ainslie & Co.	1	0
1881	Harrison Ainslie & Co.	1	0
1882	Harrison Ainslie & Co.	1	0
1883	Harrison Ainslie & Co.	1	0
1884	Harrison Ainslie & Co.	1	0
1885	Harrison Ainslie & Co.	1	0

In 1869 the name Southampton appears in the 'Owner' column, presumably meaning where the works was situated; there is also a comment that this was a charcoal furnace. In 1870 there is the additional information that the furnace was erected in 1868, put into blast in 1869 but was not in blast in 1870.

Essex

Dagenham [TQ 4884]

Year	Owner	Built	In Blast
1934	Ford Motor Co. Ltd	1	-
1935	Ford Motor Co. Ltd	1	-
1936	Ford Motor Co. Ltd	1	-
1937	Ford Motor Co. Ltd	1	-
1938	Ford Motor Co. Ltd	1	-
1939	Ford Motor Co. Ltd	1	-
1940	Ford Motor Co. Ltd	1	-
1941	Ford Motor Co. Ltd	1	-
1942	Ford Motor Co. Ltd	1	-
1943	Ford Motor Co. Ltd	1	-
1944	Ford Motor Co. Ltd	1	-
1945	Ford Motor Co. Ltd	1	-
1946	Ford Motor Co. Ltd	1	-
1947	Ford Motor Co. Ltd	1	-
1948	Ford Motor Co. Ltd	1	-
1949	Ford Motor Co. Ltd	1	-
1950	Ford Motor Co. Ltd	1	-
1951	Ford Motor Co. Ltd	1	-
1952	Ford Motor Co. Ltd	1	-
1953	Ford Motor Co. Ltd	1	-
1954	Ford Motor Co. Ltd	1	-
1955	Ford Motor Co. Ltd	1	-
1956	Ford Motor Co. Ltd	1	-
1957	Ford Motor Co. Ltd	1	-
1958	Ford Motor Co. Ltd	1	-
1959	Ford Motor Co. Ltd	1	-
1960	Ford Motor Co. Ltd	1	-
1961	Ford Motor Co. Ltd	1	-
1962	Ford Motor Co. Ltd	2	-
1963	Ford Motor Co. Ltd	1	-
1964	Ford Motor Co. Ltd	1	-
1965	Ford Motor Co. Ltd	1	-
1966	Ford Motor Co. Ltd	1	-
1967	Ford Motor Co. Ltd	1	-
1968	Ford Motor Co. Ltd	1	-
1969	Ford Motor Co. Ltd	1	-
1970	Ford Motor Co. Ltd	1	-
1971	Ford Motor Co. Ltd	1	-
1972	Ford Motor Co. Ltd	1	-
1973	Ford Motor Co. Ltd	1	-
1974	Ford Motor Co. Ltd	1	-
1975	Ford Motor Co. Ltd	1	-
1976	Ford Motor Co. Ltd	1	-
1977	Ford Motor Co. Ltd	1	-

Shropshire

Abdon: see Bouldon

Barnetts Leasow, Broseley [SJ 6703?]

Year	Owner	Built	In Blast
1805	Jesson	2	1
1810	Jesson	2	1
1823	—	2	-
1825	J. Bradley & Co.	2	1
1830	—	2	-

1805: output 574 tons p.a. 1823: output 2,755 tons p.a. 1825: output 40 tons a week, 2,080 p.a., 'use it themselves'. 1830: 1,316 tons p.a.

Bedlam: see Madeley Wood

Benthall [SJ 6602]

Year	Owner	Built	In Blast
1794	Messrs Banhest	2	-
1796	—	1	1
1805	Harries	1	1
1810	Harries & Co.	2	1
1823	—	1	-
1825	F.B. Harries	2	0
1830	—	1	-

In 1794 the ground landlord was named as S. Harris Esq.; the furnaces were coke-fired, blown by engine and built in 1785. 1796: Excise output 2,367 tons 10 cwt p.a, may make 1,600 tons p.a. (i.e. 32 tons a week), Exact Return 1,334 tons (Hailstone MS agrees but adds: 'Has been standing'). 1805: output 1,294 tons p.a. 1823, 1825, 1830: no output listed; 'not likely to work again' (March 1826).

Billingsley [SO 7085]

Year	Owner	Built	In Blast
1805	Stokes	2	0
1810	Stokes	2	1

No output is given in 1805.

Blists Hill SJ 6903

Year	Owner	Built	In Blast
1839	Madeley Wood Co.	1	1
1841	Madeley Wood Co.	2	2
1843	Madeley Wood Iron Co.	5	3
1847	Madeley Wood Co. (William Anstice & Co.)	3	2
1849	—	-	3
1854	John Anstice	3	3
1855	John Anstice	3	3
1856	John Anstice	3	3
1857	Madeley Wood Co.	3	3
1858	Madeley Wood Co.	3	3
1859	Madeley Wood Co.	3	3
1860	Madeley Wood Co.	3	3
1861	Madeley Wood Co.	3	3
1862	Madeley Wood Co.	3	3
1863	Madeley Wood Co.	3	2
1864	Madeley Wood Co.	3	3
1865	Madeley Wood Co.	3	3
1866	Madeley Wood Co.	3	3
1867	Madeley Wood Co.	3	3
1868	Madeley Wood Co.	3	3
1869	Messrs Anstice	3	3
1870	Messrs Anstice	3	3
1871	Messrs Anstice	3	3
1872	Madeley Wood Co.	3	3
1873	Madeley Wood Co.	3	3
1874	Madeley Wood Co.	3	2
1875	Madeley Wood Co.	3	3
1876	Madeley Wood Co.	3	3
1877	Madeley Wood Co.	3	3
1878	Madeley Wood Co.	3	2
1879	Madeley Wood Co.	3	1
1880	Madeley Wood Co.	3	3
1881	Madeley Wood Co.	3	3
1882	Madeley Wood Co.	3	3
1883	Madeley Wood Co.	3	2
1884	Madeley Wood Co.	3	2
1885	Madeley Wood Co.	3	2
1886	Madeley Wood Co.	3	2
1887	Madeley Wood Co.	3	2
1888	Madeley Wood Co.	3	2
1889	Madeley Wood Co.	3	2
1890	Madeley Wood Co.	3	2
1891	Madeley Wood Co.	3	2
1892	Madeley Wood Co.	3	2
1893	Madeley Wood Co.	3	2
1894	Madeley Wood Co.	3	1
1895	Madeley Wood Co.	3	2
1896	Madeley Wood Co.	3	2
1897	Madeley Wood Co.	3	2
1898	Madeley Wood Co.	3	2
1899	Madeley Wood Co.	3	1
1900	Madeley Wood Co.	3	1
1901	Madeley Wood Co.	3	2
1902	Madeley Wood Co.	3	1
1903	Madeley Wood Co.	3	1
1904	Madeley Wood Co.	3	1
1905	Madeley Wood Co.	3	1
1906	Madeley Wood Co.	3	1
1907	Madeley Wood Co.	3	1
1908	Madeley Wood Co.	3	1
1909	Madeley Wood Co.	3	1
1910	Madeley Wood Co.	3	1

Year	Owner	Built	In Blast
1911	Madeley Wood Co.	3	1
1912	Madeley Wood Co.	3	0
1913	Madeley Wood Co.	3	0
1922	Madeley Wood Co. Ltd	3	-
1923	Madeley Wood Co. Ltd	3	-
1924	Madeley Wood Co. Ltd	3	-
1925	Madeley Wood Co. Ltd	3	-
1926	Madeley Wood Co. Ltd	3	-

1841: output 110 tons a week. 1843: furnace-numbers above include Madeley Wood (qv); output from 3 furnaces 162 tons a week. 1847: output (probably at Blists Hill only) 7,280 tons p.a. (70 tons a week from each furnace). Truran: output (at Blists Hill) 80 tons a week from each of 3 furnaces. In 1858–59 the furnaces were noted as operating on cold blast. The owner's name is misprinted as 'John Austrie' in 1854–55. *Mineral Statistics* names the works as Madeley Wood throughout, although from 1911 Blists Hill appears alongside what was properly the name of the company, rather than the site. There is no entry for the Madeley Wood Co. in 1921 but it reappears in 1922 for a few years.

Bouldon [SO 5485]

Year	Owner	Built	In Blast
1794	Sir W. Blount	1	-
1796	—	2	0

In 1794 the site is called 'Coalford and Bouldon', owned and occupied by Sir W. Blount, and consisting of a single charcoal furnace. In 1796 the same name is used, but 2 furnaces were listed, both out of blast. The furnace at 'Coalford' may have been the one at Abdon: see Riden, *Gazetteer*, pp. 55–6.

Bringewood, Herefs. SO 4575

Year	Owner	Built	In Blast
1794	Downing & Cooley	1	-
1796	—	1	1

The ground landlord in 1794 was Richard Knight Esq.; the single charcoal furnace was blown by water and there was a forge containing 3 fineries and a chafery. 1796: output 500 tons, Excise and actual, Exact Return 250 tons (Hailstone MS agrees). The site was in Shropshire during the working life of the furnace but later Herefordshire.

Broseley [SJ 6701]

Year	Owner	Built	In Blast
1794	Messrs Banhest	1	-
1796	—	1	1
1805	Banks & Co.	1	1
1810	Banks & Co.	1	1
1823	—	2	-
1825	John Onions	2	1
1830	—	2	-

The ground landlord in 1794 was — Davenport Esq.; the furnace was coke-fired, blown by engine and built in 1786. 1796: Excise 1,775 tons p.a., may make 1,400 tons p.a. (i.e. 28 tons a week), Exact Return 1,076 tons 10 cwt (Hailstone MS has 1,076 tons and adds 'Standing'). 1805: 1,451 tons p.a. 1823: output nil. 1825: two works, distinguished as Broseley New and Broseley Old, both owned by John Onions, each with one furnace. Both are listed as out of blast in the B&W text; the Staffs RO version has one furnace in blast at Broseley New, said to make 26 tons a week, 1,300 tons p.a., 'Castings and No 2'. 1830: 270 tons p.a. The distinction made in 1825 probably reflects the fact that there were two separate furnaces at Broseley, the earlier of which was called Coneybury in 1794, both of which were operated by Banks and Onions and are therefore most conveniently considered together.

Calcutts [SJ 6802]

Year	Owner	Built	In Blast
1794	Mr Brodie	1	-
1796	—	2	2
1805	Brodie & Co.	5	1
1810	Brodie & Co.	5	2
1823	—	2	-
1825	W. Hazledine	2	1
1830	—	2	-

The ground landlord in 1794 was Sir O. Paul; the furnace was coke-fired, blown by engine and built in 1775. 1796: called Jackfield; output for 2 furnaces 4,471 and 2,615 tons p.a. (Excise); 2,080 tons p.a. (i.e. 40 tons a week), actual for each, 4,160 tons total; Exact Return 1,820 tons p.a. (35 tons a week) total; Hailstone MS assigns outputs of 1,300 and 1,200 tons to the 2 furnaces. 1805: output 2,269 tons p.a. 1823: 1,833 tons p.a. 1825: 26 tons a week, 1,300 tons p.a., 'Castings & No 2'. 1830: output nil.

Castle: see Dawley Castle

Clee Hill [SN 6075]

Year	Owner	Built	In Blast
1794	Messrs Botfield & Co.	1	-
1805	George & Co.	1	1
1810	George & Co.	1	1
1825	Wilkinson's Executors	-	-

In 1794 the ground landlord was Lord Craven; the furnace was coke-fired, blown by engine and built in 1783. 1805: output 303 tons, returned by T. Botfield. 1825: no output, no furnace numbers; the Staffs RO text has no owner's name and a 'Quaere' in the Remarks column. See also Cornbrook.

Coalbrookdale SJ 6604

Year	Owner	Built	In Blast
1794	Dale Co.	2	-
1796	—	3	2
1805	Dale Co.	2	2
1810	Coalbrookdale Co.	2	2
1823	—	2	-
1825	B. Dickenson & Co.	2	0
1830	—	2	-

In 1794 the ground landlord was Mr Reynolds; the furnaces were coke-fired, blown by engine and said to have been built in 1720. 1796: Excise return output for each furnace 3,382$^1/_2$ tons, 3,275 and 517$^1/_2$; the 'may make' figures were 2,080 tons, 2,080 (i.e. 40 tons a week) and nil; the Exact Return total was 2,659 tons 11 cwt; the Hailstone MS has 1,500, 1,400 and 500 tons, with the comment 'Melts old cast iron' against the last figure. 1805: 2,962 tons. 1823, 1825, 1830: no output, but with the comment in 1825: 'Melting Iron'.

'Coalford': see Bouldon

Coneybury: see Broseley

Cornbrook [SN 6075]

Year	Owner	Built	In Blast
1796	—	1	1
1805	Botfield	1	1
1810	Botfield & Co.	1	1
1825	Wilkinson's Executors	-	-

1796: output 1,000 tons p.a. (i.e. 20 tons a week), Excise and actual, 482 tons Exact Return (Hailstone MS agrees). 1805: 292 tons. 1825: no furnace-numbers or output; the Staffs RO text does not even name an owner. See also Clee Hill.

Dark Lane [SJ 7008?]

Year	Owner	Built	In Blast
1841	Botfields & Co.	2	2
1843	J.N. & B. Botfield	9	7
1847	W. & B. Botfield	8	6
1854	B. Botfield	2	2
1855	B. Botfield	2	2
1856	B. Botfield	2	2
1857	B. Botfield	2	2
1858	B. Botfield	2	2
1859	B. Botfield	2	2
1860	Beriah Botfield	2	2
1861	Beriah Botfield	2	1
1862	Beriah Botfield	5	3
1863	Mrs Isabella Botfield	4	3
1864	Mrs Isabella Botfield	4	3
1865	Mrs Isabella Botfield	4	3
1866	Reps. of late Beriah Botfield	4	3
1867	Leighton & Grenfell	4	3
1868	Leighton & Grenfell	4	3
1869	Leighton & Grenfell	4	3
1870	Leighton & Grenfell	4	2
1871	Leighton & Grenfell	4	2
1872	Haybridge Iron Co. Ltd	4	3
1873	Haybridge Iron Co. Ltd	4	3
1874	Haybridge Iron Co. Ltd	4	3

1841: output 110 tons a week. In 1843 furnace-numbers and output were combined for the Botfields' three works (Dark Lane, Old Park and Stirchley) and are given above; the output from 7 furnaces in blast was said to be 294 tons a week. 1847: the output of 18,720 p.a. (i.e. 60 tons a week from each of 6 furnaces) includes Stirchley. In 1863 Mrs Botfield was said to be of Finchley Iron Works and in 1867 Leighton & Grenfell were described as the Representatives of the late B. Botfield. The furnace-numbers above for 1862 include Dark Lane, Hinkshay and Langley (qqv); those for 1863–74 include Dark Lane and Hinkshay.

Dawley Castle [SJ 6906]

Year	Owner	Built	In Blast
1810	Dale & Co.	1	1
1823	—	2	-
1825	B. Dickenson & Co.	2	2
1830	—	2	-
1839	Coalbrookdale Co.	2	2
1841	Coalbrookdale Co.	2	2
1843	Coalbrookdale Co.	7	6
1847	Coalbrookdale Co. (A. Darby & Co.)	8	8
1849	—	-	2
1854	Coalbrookdale Co.	2	2
1855	Coalbrookdale Co.	2	2
1856	Coalbrookdale Co.	2	2
1857	Coalbrookdale Co.	2	2
1858	Coalbrookdale Co.	2	1
1859	Coalbrookdale Co.	2	2
1860	Coalbrookdale Co.	2	2
1861	Coalbrookdale Co.	2	2
1862	Coalbrookdale Co.	6	4
1863	Coalbrookdale Co.	2	2
1864	Coalbrookdale Co.	7	4
1865	Coalbrookdale Co.	2	2
1866	Coalbrookdale Co.	2	2
1867	Coalbrookdale Co.	5	3
1868	Coalbrookdale Co.	2	2
1869	Coalbrookdale Co.	2	2
1870	Coalbrookdale Co.	2	2
1871	Coalbrookdale Co.	5	3
1872	Coalbrookdale Iron Co.	5	3
1873	Coalbrookdale Iron Co.	5	3
1874	Coalbrookdale Iron Co.	5	3
1875	Coalbrookdale Iron Co.	5	3
1876	Coalbrookdale Iron Co.	4	2
1877	Coalbrookdale Iron Co.	4	2
1878	Coalbrookdale Iron Co.	2	1
1879	Coalbrookdale Iron Co.	4	1
1880	Coalbrookdale Iron Co.	2	1
1881	Coalbrookdale Co. Ltd	2	1
1882	Coalbrookdale Co. Ltd	2	0
1883	Coalbrookdale Co. Ltd	2	1
1884	Coalbrookdale Co. Ltd	2	0
1885	Coalbrookdale Co. Ltd	2	0
1886	Coalbrookdale Co. Ltd	2	0

1823–30: output 4,925 tons p.a. in 1823, 4,312 tons p.a. in 1830. 1825: called 'Castle or Dawley' in B&W, 'Castle' in Staffs RO; output 120 tons a week, 5,900 p.a., 'use it themselves'. 1839, 1841: called 'Castle'. 1841: output 110 tons a week. In 1843 figures from all three Coalbrookdale Co. works (Dawley Castle, Horsehay and Lightmoor) were combined as above; output from 6 furnaces in blast was said to be 348 tons a week. The 1847 figures also relate to all three works, for which which an aggregate output of 24,960 tons was returned, i.e. 60 tons a week from each of 8 furnaces. Truran: The Dawley site is called 'Castle'; weekly output 90 tons from each of 2 furnaces. In *Mineral Statistics* the works is called Castle in 1854–59 and 1871, Dawley in 1861 and Dawley Castle in other years. The furnace-numbers above include those for Horsehay, Lawley and Lightmoor in 1862 and 1864; Lawley and Lightmoor only in 1867, 1871–77 and 1879. 1883: furnace in blast for seven months only.

Donnington Wood [SJ 7012]

Year	Owner	Built	In Blast
1794	William Reynolds & Co.	1	-
1796	—	3	2
1805	Bishton	3	2
1810	Bishton & Co.	5	4
1823	—	3	-
1825	Lilleshall Co.	3	3
1830	—	5	-
1839	Lilleshall Co.	3	3
1841	Lilleshall Co.	3	2
1843	Lilleshall Iron Co.	-	-
1847	Lilleshall Co.	-	-
1849	—	-	2

In 1794 the ground landlords were 'the three Lords'; the furnace was coke-fired, blown by engine and built in 1785. There were four melting furnaces built in 1786. 1796: 3 furnaces listed, 2 in blast and 1 out. Outputs given for 2 furnaces: Excise returns 2,340 and 2,380 tons p.a., 'actual' figures 2,080 tons (i.e. 40 tons a week) for each; Exact Return 3,323 tons total; Hailstone MS has 2,000 and 1,850 tons. 1805: output bracketed with Wrockwardine (qv) as 7,400 tons p.a. from 4 furnaces in blast. 1810: furnace-numbers above include Donnington and Wrockwardine; see also Snedshill. 1823–30: output 8,074 tons p.a. in 1823; two furnaces built in 1828 in lieu of the two at Wrockwardine, which are blown out; output 15,110 tons in 1830. 1825: output given for Snedshill, Wrockwardine and Lilleshall (i.e. Lodge Wood) (qqv) together in the Staffs RO text (Donnington is omitted entirely), and Donnington, Snedshill, Wrockwardine and Lilleshall in the B&W text, the three (or four) works making 365 tons a week, 18,200 tons p.a., 'forge iron'. The owner's name is given as 'Lilleshall & Co.' in 1825, apparently in error. 1841: output 110 tons a week. 1843–47: see Lodge Wood. Truran: output (at Donnington Wood) 80 tons a week from each of 3 furnaces.

Hadley [SJ 6811]

Year	Owner	Built	In Blast
1805	Wilkinson	2	2
1810	Fereday & Co.	2	2
1823	—	2	-
1825	Wilkinson's Executors	2	0
1830	—	2	-

1805: output 3,612 tons p.a. 1823: 2,080 tons p.a. 1825: no output, 'Not likely to work again'. 1830: output nil. The works is called New Hadley in 1805 and 1810.

Hinkshay SJ 6907

Year	Owner	Built	In Blast
1854	B. Botfield	2	0
1855	B. Botfield	2	0
1856	B. Botfield	2	1
1857	B. Botfield	2	2
1858	B. Botfield	2	2
1859	B. Botfield	2	2
1860	Beriah Botfield	2	1
1861	Beriah Botfield	2	1
1862	Beriah Botfield	-	-
1863	Mrs Isabella Botfield	-	-
1864	Mrs Isabella Botfield	-	-
1865	Mrs Isabella Botfield	-	-
1866	Reps. of late Beriah Botfield	-	-
1867	Leighton & Grenfell	-	-
1868	Leighton & Grenfell	-	-
1869	Leighton & Grenfell	-	-
1870	Leighton & Grenfell	-	-
1871	Leighton & Grenfell	-	-
1872	Haybridge Iron Co. Ltd	-	-
1873	Haybridge Iron Co. Ltd	-	-
1874	Haybridge Iron Co. Ltd	-	-
1875	Haybridge Iron Co. Ltd	2	2
1876	Haybridge Iron Co. Ltd	2	1
1877	Haybridge Iron Co. Ltd	2	0
1878	Haybridge Iron Co. Ltd	2	0
1879	Haybridge Iron Co. Ltd	2	0
1880	Haybridge Iron Co. Ltd	2	0
1881	Haybridge Iron Co. Ltd	2	0

In 1854–59 this works is called The Jerry. In 1862–74 furnace-numbers are given for Dark Lane and Hinkshay together under Dark Lane (qv); in 1875–77 numbers for Hinkshay and Lawley (qv) are bracketed together in *Mineral Statistics*, almost certainly in error, and the figures printed above for 1875–81 probably relate to Hinkshay only.

Hollinswood [SJ 6909]

Year	Owner	Built	In Blast
1794	J. Wilkinson	1	-

The ground landlord was Sir William Jerningham; the furnace was coke-fired, blown by engine and built in 1787.

Horsehay [SJ 6707]

Year	Owner	Built	In Blast
1794	R. Reynolds & Co.	1	-
1796	—	1	1
1805	Dale Co.	2	2
1810	Dale & Co.	3	3
1823	—	3	-
1825	B. Dickenson & Co.	3	3
1830	—	3	-
1839	Coalbrookdale Co.	3	3
1841	Coalbrookdale Co.	3	1
1843	Coalbrookdale Iron Co.	-	-
1847	Coalbrookdale Co.	-	-
1849	Coalbrookdale Co.	-	5
1854	Coalbrookdale Co.	3	2
1855	Coalbrookdale Co.	3	1
1856	Coalbrookdale Co.	3	1
1857	Coalbrookdale Co.	2	1
1858	Coalbrookdale Co.	2	1
1859	Coalbrookdale Co.	2	0
1860	Coalbrookdale Co.	2	0
1861	Coalbrookdale Co.	1	0
1862	Coalbrookdale Co.	-	-
1863	Coalbrookdale Co.	2	0
1864	Coalbrookdale Co.	-	-

In 1794 the ground landlord was Mr Slaney; the furnace was coke-fired, blown by engine and built in 1758. Unspecified forge plant was said to have been built in 1786. 1796: Excise return 4,927 tons 10 cwt p.a., 'may make' 2,080 tons (i.e. 40 tons a week), Exact Return 1,458 tons 4 cwt; Hailstone MS has 1,500 tons. 1805: 3,834 tons. 1823: 4,854 tons. 1825: 170 tons a week, 8,320 tons p.a., 'use it themselves'. 1830: 6,833 tons. 1841: output 60 tons a week. 1843, 1847: furnace-numbers and output for all Coalbrookdale Co. works combined under Dawley Caste (qv). 1849: furnace-numbers for Horsehay and Lightmoor combined as above. Truran: output (at Horsehay) 90 tons a week from each of 3 furnaces. For 1862 and 1864 furnace-numbers for Horsehay and Dawley Castle are combined under the latter site (qv).

Jackfield: see Calcutts

The Jerry: see Hinkshay

Ketley [SJ 6710]

Year	Owner	Built	In Blast
1794	R. Reynolds & Co.	4	-
1796	—	5	3
1805	Reynolds & Co.	4	3
1810	Reynolds & Co.	4	4
1823	—	3	-
1825	Williams & Co.	3	3
1830	—	3	-
1839	Ketley Co.	3	2
1841	Ketley Co.	3	2
1843	Ketley Iron Co.	3	2
1847	Ketley Co. (J. Williams & Co.)	3	2
1849	—	-	2
1854	Ketley Co.	3	1
1855	Ketley Co.	3	1
1856	Ketley Co.	2	1
1857	Ketley Co.	2	1
1858	Ketley Co.	2	1
1859	Ketley Co.	2	1
1860	Ketley Co.	2	1
1861	Ketley Co.	2	1
1862	Ketley Co.	2	1
1863	Ketley Co.	1	1
1864	Ketley Co.	1	1
1865	Ketley Co.	1	1
1866	Ketley Co.	1	1
1867	Ketley Co.	1	1
1868	Ketley Co.	1	1
1869	Ketley Co.	1	1
1870	Ketley Co.	1	1
1871	Ketley Co.	1	1
1872	Ketley Co.	1	1
1873	Ketley Co.	1	1
1874	Ketley Co.	1	1
1875	Ketley Co.	1	1
1876	Ketley Co.	1	1
1877	Ketley Co.	1	0
1878	Ketley Co.	1	0

The ground landlord in 1794 was Lord Stafford; the furnaces were coke-fired, blown by engine and built 1758. There were 2 fineries and 6 melting furnaces built in 1786, and a rolling and slitting mill built in 1787. 1796: 5 furnaces listed, 3 in blast, for which output figures were given as 2,530, 2,460 and 2,600 tons p.a. (Excise returns); 'may make' 2,080 tons p.a. (40 tons a week) in each case; Exact Return 5,068 tons 19 cwt total; Hailstone MS has 1,900 tons for each of 3 furnaces. 1805: 7,510 tons p.a. 1823: 4,984 tons. 1825: 2 furnaces in blast in B&W text, 3 in Staffs RO version. Output 155 tons a week, 7,800 p.a., 'melting and forge iron'. 1830: 5,763 tons. 1841: output 110 tons a week. 1843: output 109 tons a week. 1847: 6,240 tons (60 tons a week from each furnace). Truran: output 80 tons a week from each of 3 furnaces.

Langley [SJ 6907]

Year	Owner	Built	In Blast
1825	Bishton & Wright	1	1
1830	—	2	-
1839	Ketley Co.	2	1
1841	Mortgagees of Langley Co.	1	1
1843	Langley Iron Co.	1	0
1847	Langley Co. (Wombridge & Co.)	2	1
1849	—	-	2
1854	Thomas Hinde & Co.	1	1
1855	Thomas Hinde & Co.	1	1
1856	Thomas Hinde & Co.	1	0
1857	B. Botfield	1	0
1858	B. Botfield	1	0
1859	B. Botfield	1	0
1860	Beriah Botfield	1	0
1861	Beriah Botfield	1	0
1862	Beriah Botfield	-	-

The 1823–30 list notes the building of one furnace in 1824 and another in 1826; output in 1830 was 4,325 tons p.a. 1825: 46 tons a week, 2,340 p.a., 'melting iron'. 1839: called Langley. 1841: output 60 tons a week. 1843: output nil. Truran: output 89 (*sic*) tons a week from each of 2 furnaces. 1847: 3,120 tons p.a. (60 tons a week). 1862: see Dark Lane.

Lawley [SJ 6608]

Year	Owner	Built	In Blast
1825	Williams & Co.	1	1
1830	—	1	-
1839	Ketley Co.	1	1
1841	Lawley Co.	1	1
1843	Lawley Iron Co.	1	1
1847	Coalbrookdale Co.	-	-
1854	Coalbrookdale Co.	1	1
1855	Coalbrookdale Co.	1	1
1856	Coalbrookdale Co.	1	1
1857	Coalbrookdale Co.	1	1
1858	Coalbrookdale Co.	1	1
1859	Coalbrookdale Co.	1	1
1860	Coalbrookdale Co.	1	1
1861	Coalbrookdale Co.	1	1
1862	Coalbrookdale Co.	-	-
1863	Coalbrookdale Co.	1	1
1864	Coalbrookdale Co.	-	-
1865	Coalbrookdale Co.	1	1
1866	Coalbrookdale Co.	1	1
1867	Coalbrookdale Co.	-	-
1868	Coalbrookdale Co.	1	0
1869	Coalbrookdale Co.	1	0
1870	Coalbrookdale Co.	1	0
1871	Coalbrookdale Co.	-	-
1872	Coalbrookdale Iron Co.	-	-
1873	Coalbrookdale Iron Co.	-	-
1874	Coalbrookdale Iron Co.	-	-
1875	Coalbrookdale Iron Co.	-	-
1876	Coalbrookdale Iron Co.	-	-
1877	Coalbrookdale Iron Co.	-	-
1878	Coalbrookdale Iron Co.	1	0

The 1823–30 list notes that the furnace was built in 1824 and was making 3,073 tons p.a. in 1830. 1825: output 46 tons a week, 2,340 p.a., 'melting and forge iron'. 1841: output 60 tons a week. 1843: output 47 tons a week. 1847: furnace-numbers and output for all Coalbrookdale Co. works combined under Dawley Castle (qv). Truran: output (at Lawley) 80 tons a week from a single furnace. In 1862, 1864, 1867 and 1871–74 furnace-numbers for Lawley and Dawley Castle are combined under the latter heading. In 1875–77 Lawley is bracketed with Hinkshay (qv), almost certainly in error, since neither the furnace-numbers for Dawley nor those for Hinkshay change in a way which suggests that Lawley has been transferred from the former to the latter. For this reason, the owner's name given above for 1875–77 has been changed from Haybridge Iron Co. (which owned Hinkshay) back to the Coalbrookdale Co. (which owned Dawley).

Lightmoor [SJ 6705]

Year	Owner	Built	In Blast
1794	Messrs Homfray	2	-
1796	—	3	3
1805	Addenbrooke & Co.	3	3
1810	Addenbrooke & Co.	3	3
1823	—	3	-
1825	Addenbrooke & Pidcock	3	3
1830	—	3	-
1839	Coalbrookdale Co.	2	0
1841	Coalbrookdale Co.	2	2
1843	Coalbrookdale Iron Co.	-	-
1847	Coalbrookdale Co.	-	-
1849	Coalbrookdale Co.	-	-
1854	Coalbrookdale Co.	2	2
1855	Coalbrookdale Co.	2	2
1856	Coalbrookdale Co.	2	1
1857	Coalbrookdale Co.	2	1
1858	Coalbrookdale Co.	2	1
1859	Coalbrookdale Co.	2	1
1860	Coalbrookdale Co.	2	2
1861	Coalbrookdale Co.	2	1
1862	Coalbrookdale Co.	-	-
1863	Coalbrookdale Co.	2	1
1864	Coalbrookdale Co.	-	-
1865	Coalbrookdale Co.	2	1
1866	Coalbrookdale Co.	2	1
1867	Coalbrookdale Co.	-	-
1868	Coalbrookdale Co.	2	2
1869	Coalbrookdale Co.	2	2
1870	Coalbrookdale Co.	2	2
1871	Coalbrookdale Co.	-	-
1872	Coalbrookdale Iron Co.	-	-
1873	Coalbrookdale Iron Co.	-	-
1874	Coalbrookdale Iron Co.	-	-
1875	Coalbrookdale Iron Co.	-	-
1876	Coalbrookdale Iron Co.	-	-
1877	Coalbrookdale Iron Co.	-	-
1878	Coalbrookdale Iron Co.	2	1
1879	Coalbrookdale Iron Co.	-	-
1880	Coalbrookdale Iron Co.	2	0
1881	Coalbrookdale Co. Ltd	2	0
1882	Coalbrookdale Co. Ltd	2	1
1883	Coalbrookdale Co. Ltd	2	0
1884	Coalbrookdale Co. Ltd	2	0
1885	Coalbrookdale Co. Ltd	2	0

In 1794 the ground landlord was Lord Craven; the furnaces were coke-fired, blown by engine and built in 1758. 1796: separate outputs were returned by the Excise for three furnaces of 3,665, 3,361 and 1,920 tons p.a.; the 'may make' figure for each was given as 2,080 tons (40 tons a week); Exact Return 3,498 tons 15 cwt total; Hailstone MS has 1,750 tons, 1,750 tons and nil. 1805: 5,601 tons p.a. 1823: 6,052 tons p.a. 1825: 155 tons a week, 7,800 tons p.a., 'melting and forge iron'. 1830: 6,194 tons p.a. 1841: 120 tons a week. 1843–47: furnace-numbers and output for all Coalbrookdale Co. works combined under Dawley Castle (qv). 1849: see Horsehay. Truran: output (at Lightmoor) 90 tons a week from each of 2 furnaces. In 1862, 1864, 1867, 1871–77 and 1879 furnace-numbers for Lightmoor and Dawley Castle are combined under the latter heading (qv).

Lilleshall: see Lodge Wood

Lodge Wood [SJ 6705]

Year	Owner	Built	In Blast
1825	Lilleshall Co.	2	0
1830	—	-	-
1839	Lilleshall Co.	2	2
1841	Lilleshall Co.	2	2
1843	Lilleshall Iron Co.	7	5
1847	Lilleshall Co. (Horton, Simms & Ball)	7	6
1849	Lilleshall Co.	-	6
1854	Lilleshall Co.	4	4
1855	Lilleshall Co.	4	4
1856	Lilleshall Co.	4	4
1857	Lilleshall Co.	4	4
1858	Lilleshall Co.	4	4
1859	Lilleshall Co.	4	4
1860	Lilleshall Co.	4	4
1861	Lilleshall Co.	4	4
1862	Lilleshall Co.	8	7
1863	Lilleshall Co.	9	8
1864	Lilleshall Co.	8	8
1865	Lilleshall Iron Co.	9	7
1866	Lilleshall Iron Co.	9	7
1867	Lilleshall Iron Co.	9	7
1868	Lilleshall Iron Co.	9	8
1869	Lilleshall Iron Co.	9	8
1870	Lilleshall Iron Co.	9	8
1871	Lilleshall Iron Co.	9	8
1872	Lilleshall Iron Co.	9	8
1873	Lilleshall Iron Co.	9	7
1874	Lilleshall Iron Co.	8	7
1875	Lilleshall Iron Co.	9	7
1876	Lilleshall Iron Co.	5	3
1877	Lilleshall Iron Co.	5	3
1878	Lilleshall Iron Co.	5	2
1879	Lilleshall Iron Co.	5	2
1880	Lilleshall Co. Ltd	5	3
1881	Lilleshall Co. Ltd	5	2
1882	Lilleshall Co. Ltd	5	3
1883	Lilleshall Co. Ltd	5	3
1884	Lilleshall Co. Ltd	5	1
1885	Lilleshall Co. Ltd	5	1
1886	Lilleshall Co. Ltd	5	1
1887	Lilleshall Co. Ltd	5	1
1888	Lilleshall Co. Ltd	5	1
1889	Lilleshall Co. Ltd	5	0

1825: the B&W text gives an output for Lilleshall (the parish in which Lodge Wood is situated), Donnington Wood, Wrockwardine and Snedshill (qqv) together of 365 tons a week, 18,200 p.a., 'forge iron', but splits the furnace-numbers between the works; the Staffs RO text only lists Snedshill, Wrockwardine and Lilleshall, and does not give separate furnace-numbers. For 1823–30 see Donnington Wood. 1841: output (at Lodge Wood) 110 tons a week. 1843: figures include all three Lilleshall Co. sites (Donnington Wood, Lodge Wood and Snedshill), for which an output of 383 tons a week from 5 furnaces is given. 1847: both the output (18,720 tons p.a., i.e. 60 tons a week from 6 furnaces) and the furnace-numbers are for all the works owned by the Lilleshall Co. 1849: combined return as above under Lilleshall for Lodge Wood and Snedshill. Truran: output (at Lodge) 89 (*sic*) tons a week from each of 2 furnaces. Between 1862 and 1875 furnace-numbers above include Priorslee (qv).

Madeley Court [SJ 6905]

Year	Owner	Built	In Blast
1843	James Foster	3	3
1847	J. Foster	3	3
1849	—	-	3
1854	W.O. Foster	3	2
1855	W.O. Foster	3	2
1856	W.O. Foster	3	2
1857	W.O. Foster	3	2
1858	W.O. Foster	3	2
1859	W.O. Foster	3	2
1860	John Bradley & Co.	3	2
1861	W.O. Foster	3	2
1862	W.O. Foster	3	2
1863	William Orme Foster MP	3	2
1864	William Orme Foster MP	3	2
1865	William Orme Foster MP	3	2
1866	William Orme Foster MP	3	2
1867	William Orme Foster MP	3	2
1868	William Orme Foster	3	2
1869	William Orme Foster	3	2
1870	William Orme Foster	3	2
1871	William Orme Foster	3	2
1872	William Orme Foster	3	2
1873	William Orme Foster	3	2
1874	William Orme Foster	3	2
1875	William Orme Foster	3	2
1876	William Orme Foster	3	2
1877	William Orme Foster	2	2
1878	William Orme Foster	3	2
1879	William Orme Foster	3	1
1880	William Orme Foster	3	2
1881	William Orme Foster	3	1
1882	William Orme Foster	3	1
1883	William Orme Foster	3	1
1884	William Orme Foster	3	1
1885	William Orme Foster	3	1
1886	William Orme Foster	3	1
1887	William Orme Foster	3	1
1888	William Orme Foster	3	1
1889	William Orme Foster	3	1
1890	William Orme Foster	3	1
1891	William Orme Foster	3	1
1892	William Orme Foster	3	1

Year	Owner	Built	In Blast
1893	William Orme Foster	3	1
1894	William Orme Foster	3	1
1895	William Orme Foster	3	1
1896	William Orme Foster	1	1
1897	William Orme Foster	3	1
1898	William Orme Foster	1	1
1899	William Orme Foster	3	1
1900	William Orme Foster	3	1
1901	William H. Foster	3	1
1902	William H. Foster	3	1
1903	William H. Foster	3	1

1847: works name omitted in Parliamentary Paper text and given as Paine's Lane Works in Braithwaite Poole; it has been identified as Madeley Court from the owner's name and by elimination; output 9,360 tons p.a. (60 tons a week from each furnace). The owner's name appears as 'W.F. Foster' in 1857, which is presumably a misprint; whether there is also an error in 1860 is less clear. W.O. Foster was Liberal MP for Staffordshire, South, 1857–68.

Madeley Wood [SJ 6703]

Year	Owner	Built	In Blast
1794	Dale Co.	2	-
1796	—	1	1
1805	Reynolds & Co.	2	2
1810	Madeley Wood Co.	4	2
1823	—	3	-
1825	W. Anstice & Co.	3	2
1830	—	3	-
1839	Madeley Wood Co.	3	2
1841	Madeley Wood Co.	3	1
1843	Madeley Wood Co.	-	-

In 1794 the ground landlord was R. Reynolds; the furnaces were coke-fired, blown by engine and said to have been built in 1759. 1796: Excise return 3,777 tons 10 cwt p.a., 'may make' 2,080 tons (40 tons a week), Exact Return 1,856 tons 8 cwt; Hailstone MS has 1,750 tons. 1805: 2,951 tons p.a. 1823: 2,475 tons p.a. 1825: 80 tons a week, 4,160 p.a. 1830: 3,471 tons p.a. The 1823–30 list also says that 1 furnace was erected at Madeley Wood in 1832. 1841: output 60 tons a week. The 1839 list uses the local name 'Bedlam' for the works, as does Truran, who gives an output of 80 tons a week from a single furnace, although whether the site was still in use by 1855 seems dubious. In 1843 furnace-numbers and output were given for Madeley Wood and Blists Hill together (see Blists Hill) and from 1847 only the latter appears to be listed for the Madeley Wood Co.

Malinslee: see Old Park

New Broseley: see Broseley

New Hadley: see Hadley

Oakengates: see Priorslee

Oldbury: see under South Staffs.

Old Lodge: see Lodge Wood

Old Park [SJ 6809]

Year	Owner	Built	In Blast
1794	H. Brown & Botfield	2	-
1796	—	3	3
1805	Botfield	4	3
1810	Botfield & Co.	4	4
1823	—	4	-
1825	T.W. & B. Botfield	4	3
1830	—	4	-
1839	Botfield Esq.	3	3
1841	Botfields & Co.	3	1
1843	J.N. & B. Botfield	-	-
1847	W. & B. Botfield	-	-
1849	—	-	2
1854	B. Botfield	4	4
1855	B. Botfield	4	3
1856	B. Botfield	4	3
1857	Old Park Iron Co. Ltd	3	2
1858	Old Park Iron Co. Ltd	4	3
1859	Old Park Iron Co. Ltd	4	4
1860	Old Park Iron Co. Ltd	4	4
1861	Old Park Iron Co. Ltd	4	3
1862	Old Park Iron Co. Ltd	4	3
1863	Old Park Iron Co. Ltd	4	2
1864	Old Park Iron Co. Ltd	4	2
1865	Old Park Iron Co. Ltd	4	3
1866	Old Park Iron Co. Ltd	4	3
1867	Old Park Iron Co. Ltd	4	2
1868	Old Park Iron Co. Ltd	4	2
1869	Old Park Iron Co. Ltd	4	2
1870	Old Park Iron Co. Ltd	4	2
1871	Old Park Iron Co. Ltd	-	-
1872	Old Park Iron Co. Ltd	4	2
1873	Old Park Iron Co. Ltd	4	2
1874	Wellington Iron & Coal Co. Ltd	4	2
1875	Wellington Iron & Coal Co. Ltd	3	2
1876	Wellington Iron & Coal Co. Ltd	2	1
1877	Wellington Iron & Coal Co. Ltd	3	1
1878	Edward Cheney	3	0
1879	Edward Cheney	3	0
1880	Edward Cheney	3	0
1881	Edward Cheney	3	0
1882	Edward Cheney	3	0
1883	Edward Cheney	3	0
1884	A.C. Cure	3	0
1885	Haybridge Iron Co. Ltd	2	0

In 1794 the works is called Park; the ground landlord was Haw. Browne Esq.; the furnaces were coke-fired, blown by engine and built in 1790. 1796: separate Excise returns for 3 furnaces of 3,825, 3,792 tons 10 cwt and 3,715 tons p.a.; 'may make' totals of 2,080 tons p.a. (40 tons a week) for each; Exact Return 5,952 tons total; Hailstone MS has 2,000 tons for each of 3 furnaces. 1805: 8,359 tons p.a. 1823: 6,900. 1825: details given as above in Staffs RO text; the B&W text gives the owner's name as J.W. & B. Botfield and has only 1 furnace in blast. Output in both texts 155 tons a week, 7,800 p.a. 'melting and forge'. 1830: output 15,300 tons p.a. including Stirchley (qv), where 4 furnaces were built in 1827. 1841: output (at Old Park) 55 tons a week. 1843–47: furnace-numbers and output for Botfield's three works (Dark Lane, Old Park and Stirchley) combined under Dark Lane (qv). Truran: output (at Old Park) 90 tons a week from each of 3 furnaces. *Mineral Statistics* gives the name of this works as

Stirchley Old Park in 1854–57; Old Park, Shifnal, in 1858–65; Malinslee and Stirchley in 1866; Old Park in 1867–74; and Wellington in 1875–77. For one year only (1859) *Mineral Statistics* has a separate entry for Stirchley, with no owner's name and 5 furnaces, 4 in blast. In 1878 there are entries for both Old Park and Wellington, which appear to be duplicates since the furnace-numbers are identical. Under Old Park the owner in 1878 is given as Edward Cheney, under Wellington it appears as the Wellington Coal & Iron Co., which was presumably owned by Cheney. In 1871, there is an entry for Old Park but with no furnace-numbers; in 1876 (under Wellington) one of the two furnaces was said to be 'Building'.

Paine's Lane Works: see Madeley Court

Park: see Old Park

Priorslee [SJ 7009]

Year	Owner	Built	In Blast
1847	Lilleshall Co.	-	-
1849	—	-	2
1854	Lilleshall Co.	4	4
1855	Lilleshall Co.	4	4
1856	Lilleshall Co.	4	4
1857	Lilleshall Co.	4	4
1858	Lilleshall Co.	4	4
1859	Lilleshall Co.	4	4
1860	Lilleshall Co.	4	4
1861	Lilleshall Co.	4	4
1862	Lilleshall Co.	-	-
1863	Lilleshall Co.	-	-
1864	Lilleshall Co.	-	-
1865	Lilleshall Co.	-	-
1866	Lilleshall Co.	-	-
1867	Lilleshall Co.	-	-
1868	Lilleshall Co.	-	-
1869	Lilleshall Co.	-	-
1870	Lilleshall Co.	-	-
1871	Lilleshall Co.	-	-
1872	Lilleshall Co.	-	-
1873	Lilleshall Co.	-	-
1874	Lilleshall Co.	-	-
1875	Lilleshall Co.	-	-
1876	Lilleshall Co.	4	3
1877	Lilleshall Co.	3	3
1878	Lilleshall Co.	3	3
1879	Lilleshall Co.	3	2
1880	Lilleshall Co. Ltd	4	3
1881	Lilleshall Co. Ltd	4	3
1882	Lilleshall Co. Ltd	4	2
1883	Lilleshall Co. Ltd	4	2
1884	Lilleshall Co. Ltd	4	3
1885	Lilleshall Co. Ltd	4	2
1886	Lilleshall Co. Ltd	4	2
1887	Lilleshall Co. Ltd	4	2
1888	Lilleshall Co. Ltd	5	3
1889	Lilleshall Co. Ltd	5	3
1890	Lilleshall Co. Ltd	5	3
1891	Lilleshall Co. Ltd	4	3
1892	Lilleshall Co. Ltd	4	3
1893	Lilleshall Co. Ltd	4	2
1894	Lilleshall Co. Ltd	4	2
1895	Lilleshall Co. Ltd	4	3
1896	Lilleshall Co. Ltd	4	3
1897	Lilleshall Co. Ltd	3	2
1898	Lilleshall Co. Ltd	3	2
1899	Lilleshall Co. Ltd	3	2
1900	Lilleshall Co. Ltd	3	2
1901	Lilleshall Co. Ltd	3	2
1902	Lilleshall Co. Ltd	3	2
1903	Lilleshall Co. Ltd	3	2
1904	Lilleshall Co. Ltd	3	2
1905	Lilleshall Co. Ltd	3	2
1906	Lilleshall Co. Ltd	3	2
1907	Lilleshall Co. Ltd	3	2
1908	Lilleshall Co. Ltd	3	2
1909	Lilleshall Co. Ltd	3	2
1910	Lilleshall Co. Ltd	3	2
1911	Lilleshall Co. Ltd	3	2
1912	Lilleshall Co. Ltd	3	2
1913	Lilleshall Co. Ltd	3	2
1921	Lilleshall Co. Ltd	3	-
1922	Lilleshall Co. Ltd	3	-
1923	Lilleshall Co. Ltd	3	-
1924	Lilleshall Co. Ltd	3	-
1925	Lilleshall Co. Ltd	3	-
1926	Lilleshall Co. Ltd	3	-
1927	Lilleshall Co. Ltd	3	-
1928	Lilleshall Co. Ltd	3	-
1929	Lilleshall Co. Ltd	3	-
1930	Lilleshall Co. Ltd	3	-
1931	Lilleshall Co. Ltd	3	-
1932	Lilleshall Co. Ltd	3	-
1933	Lilleshall Co. Ltd	3	-
1934	Lilleshall Co. Ltd	3	-
1935	Lilleshall Co. Ltd	3	-
1936	Lilleshall Co. Ltd	3	-
1937	Lilleshall Co. Ltd	3	-
1938	Lilleshall Co. Ltd	3	-
1939	Lilleshall Co. Ltd	3	-
1940	Lilleshall Co. Ltd	3	-
1041	Lilleshall Co. Ltd	3	-
1942	Lilleshall Co. Ltd	3	-
1943	Lilleshall Co. Ltd	3	-
1944	Lilleshall Co. Ltd	3	-
1945	Lilleshall Co. Ltd	3	-
1946	Lilleshall Co. Ltd	2	-
1947	Lilleshall Co. Ltd	2	-
1948	Lilleshall Iron & Steel Co. Ltd	2	-
1949	Lilleshall Iron & Steel Co. Ltd	2	-
1950	Lilleshall Iron & Steel Co. Ltd	2	-
1951	Lilleshall Iron & Steel Co. Ltd	2	-
1952	Lilleshall Iron & Steel Co. Ltd	2	-
1953	Lilleshall Iron & Steel Co. Ltd	2	-
1954	Lilleshall Iron & Steel Co. Ltd	2	-
1955	Lilleshall Iron & Steel Co. Ltd	2	-
1956	Lilleshall Iron & Steel Co. Ltd	2	-
1957	Lilleshall Iron & Steel Co. Ltd	2	-
1958	Lilleshall Iron & Steel Co. Ltd	2	-

For 1847 and 1862–75 see Lodge Wood. From 1953 (as in 1849) the location of the works is given as Oakengates.

Queenswood [SJ 6910]

Year	Owner	Built	In Blast
1805	Reynolds & Co.	1	1
1810	Reynolds & Co.	1	1

The output in 1805 was given as 2,605 tons p.a.

Snedshill [SJ 6910?]

Year	Owner	Built	In Blast
1794	J. Wilkinson	2	-
1796	—	2	2
1805	Bishton & Co.	3	2
1810	Bishton & Co.	3	2
1823	—	2	-
1825	Lilleshall Co.	2	2
1830	—	2	-
1839	Lilleshall Co.	2	2
1841	Lilleshall Co.	2	1
1843	Lilleshall Iron Co.	-	-

The ground landlord in 1794 was Sir William Jerningham; the furnaces were coke-fired, blown by engine and built in 1778. 1796: Excise outputs for two furnaces of 2,460 and 2,340 tons p.a.; 'may make' 1,700 tons p.a. (35 tons a week) each; Exact Return 3,367 tons total; Hailstone MS has 1,750 tons and 1,750 tons. 1805: 3,950 tons p.a. 1810: Snedshill bracketed with Donnington Wood (qv) and Wrockwardine but also listed separately with furnace-numbers as above. 1823: 2,786 tons p.a. 1825: output included in total for all the Lilleshall Co. works (Snedshill, Donnington Wood, Wrockwardine and Lilleshall (i.e. Lodge Wood) (qqv)): 365 tons a week, 18,200 tons p.a., 'forge iron'. The Staffs RO text also combines furnace-numbers but the B&W version splits them between the different works. 1830: output 317 tons p.a. 1841: output 60 tons a week. 1843: furnace-numbers and output for all three Lilleshall Co. sites (Donnington Wood, Lodge Wood and Snedshill) give under Donnington Wood. Truran: output (at Snedshill) 89 (*sic*) tons a week from each of 2 furnaces.

Stirchley SJ 7007

Year	Owner	Built	In Blast
1825	T.W. & B. Botfield	3	3
1830	—	4	-
1839	Botfield Esq.	4	4
1841	Botfields & Co.	4	2
1843	J.N. & B. Botfield	-	-
1847	W. & B. Botfield	-	-
1859	—	5	4
1882	Haybridge Iron Co. Ltd	2	0
1883	Haybridge Iron Co. Ltd	0	0

1823–30: 4 furnaces built 1827; output in 1830 is included in the figure for Old Park (qv). 1825: Details in Staffs RO text as above; B&W text names owner as J.W. & B. Botfield and lists 4 furnaces built, 3 in blast. Output (in both versions) 94 tons a week, 4,680 tons p.a., 'melting and forge' (B&W), 'melting iron' (Staffs RO). 1841: output 110 tons a week. 1843: furnace-numbers and output (294 tons a week from 7 furnaces) for all Botfield's works combined under Dark Lane (qv). 1847: Furnace-numbers and output (18,720 tons p.a., i.e. 60 tons a week from each of 6 furnaces) were returned for Old Park and Stirchley together; see under Dark Lane. See under Old Park for confusion in *Mineral Statistics* between this works and Stirchley; only in 1859 does Stirchley have an entry of its own, which lacks an owner's name but includes the comment, 'In blast till the end of May'. Truran: output (at Stirchley) 90 tons a week from each of 4 furnaces. There was evidently an attempted revival in 1882–83, although in the latter year the comment 'Dismantled' is appended to the return.

Stirchley Old Park: see Old Park

'Urmbridge': see Wombridge

Wellington: see Old Park

Willey SJ 6700

Year	Owner	Built	In Blast
1794	J. Wilkinson	1	-
1796	—	1	1
1805	Wilkinson	1	0

The ground landlord in 1794 was Geo. Forrester; the furnace was coke-fired, blown by engine and built in 1757. 1796: Excise output figure 3,702 tons 10 cwt p.a.; 'may make' 1,600 tons (i.e. 32 tons a week); Exact Return 1,554 tons 10 cwt; Hailstone MS has 1,544 tons and the comment: 'Will soon stop'. 1805: no output.

Wombridge [SJ 6811]

Year	Owner	Built	In Blast
1823	—	2	-
1825	Jukes, Collins & Co.	3	3
1830	—	3	-
1839	James Foster	3	3
1841	James Foster	3	2
1849	—	-	2

1823: output 5,084 tons p.a.; third furnace built 1824. 1825: owner named as above in B&W text; the second name is Collin in the Staffs RO version. Output 155 tons a week, 7,800 tons p.a., 'used by J. Bradley & Co.'. 1830: output 7,134 tons p.a. 1839: called 'Urmbridge'. 1841: output 110 tons a week. 1843: 181 tons a week. Truran: output at 'Urmbridge' 80 tons a week from each of 3 furnaces.

Wrockwardine [SJ 7011]

Year	Owner	Built	In Blast
1805	Bishton	2	2
1810	Bishton & Co.	-	-

Year	Owner	Built	In Blast
1823	—	2	-
1825	Lilleshall Co.	2	1
1830	—	2	-
1847	Lilleshall Co.	-	-

1805 output for Wrockwardine and Donnington Wood (qv) 7,400 tons p.a. 1810: furnace-numbers combined with those for Donnington Wood. 1823–30: output (at Wrockwardine) 5,121 tons p.a. in 1823; note that 2 furnaces were built at Donnington Wood in 1828 in lieu of those at Wrockwardine, which are blown out. 1825: coupled with Donnington Wood, Lilleshall (Lodge Wood) and Snedshill (qqv), the four works producing in all 365 tons a week, 18,200 tons p.a., 'forge iron'. 1847: furnace-numbers and output returned together for all the Lilleshall Co. works under Lodge Wood.

Unidentified

Year	Owner	Built	In Blast
1856	T. Holroyd & Co.	2	2

This entry, which appears for one year only, cannot be matched with any other works in Shropshire (under which heading it is placed), nor can T. Holroyd be identified.

North Wales

Aberderfyn, Denbighs. [SJ 2947?]

Year	Owner	Built	In Blast
1825	Welsh Iron Co.	2	0

'Building'. The works, which was near that at Ponciau (qv), is not named in the Staffs RO version of the list.

'Aberdovey': see Dyfi

Acrefair, Denbighs. SJ 2742

Year	Owner	Built	In Blast
1825	British Iron Co.	2	1
1839	—	3	3
1841	British Iron Co.	3	2
1843	British Iron Co.	3	2
1847	British Iron Co.	3	1
1849	—	-	1
1854	New British Iron Co.	3	3
1855	New British Iron Co.	3	2
1856	New British Iron Co.	3	2
1857	New British Iron Co.	3	2
1858	New British Iron Co.	3	2
1859	New British Iron Co.	2	2
1860	New British Iron Co.	3	2
1861	New British Iron Co.	3	1
1862	New British Iron Co.	3	1
1863	New British Iron Co.	3	2
1864	New British Iron Co.	3	2
1865	New British Iron Co.	3	2
1866	New British Iron Co.	3	1
1867	New British Iron Co.	3	1
1868	New British Iron Co.	3	1
1869	New British Iron Co.	3	1
1870	New British Iron Co.	3	1
1871	New British Iron Co.	3	1
1872	New British Iron Co.	3	1
1873	New British Iron Co.	3	1
1874	New British Iron Co.	3	1
1875	New British Iron Co.	3	1
1876	New British Iron Co.	3	0
1877	New British Iron Co.	3	0
1878	New British Iron Co.	3	0
1879	New British Iron Co.	3	0
1880	New British Iron Co.	2	1
1881	New British Iron Co.	2	0
1882	New British Iron Co.	2	1
1883	New British Iron Co. Ltd	2	0
1884	New British Iron Co. Ltd	2	1
1885	New British Iron Co. Ltd	2	1
1886	New British Iron Co. Ltd	2	1
1887	New British Iron Co. Ltd	2	1
1888	New British Iron Co. Ltd	2	0
1889	New British Iron Co.	2	0
1890	—	2	0

1825: output 36 tons a week, 1,800 p.a., 'melting'. The works is called 'Old Ruabon' in the Staffs RO version of the list, which is slightly confusing, since the Rowlands' furnace at Ruabon (qv), by then out of use, is called by this name elsewhere; the furnace at Pant (qv) also appears under Ruabon in 1825. 1841: called 'Acrefair, or Ruabon Works'. 1843: output: 200 tons a week. 1847: the entry headed 'British Company' in North Wales can, by a process of elimination, only be Ruabon, where the output was 5,200 tons p.a., i.e. 100 tons a week. Truran: output 100 tons a week from each of 3 furnaces. 1856: note that 1 furnace at Ruabon made 300 tons of pig in a week. 1860: 'New British Iron Co.' used as name of works. 1890: Appears as Ruabon, with no owner's name.

British: see Acrefair

Brymbo, Denbighs. SJ 2952

Year	Owner	Built	In Blast
1794	J. Wilkinson	1	-
1796	—	1	0
1805	Wilkinson	2	1
1810	Jones	2	2
1825	John Thompson	2	1
1839	—	2	2
1841	Brymbo Iron Co.	2	0
1843	Joint Stock Co.	2	1
1847	Brymbo Iron Co.	2	1
1849	—	-	2
1854	Brymbo Co.	2	2
1855	Brymbo Co.	2	2
1856	Brymbo Co.	2	2
1857	Brymbo Co.	2	2
1858	Darby & Co.	2	2
1859	Darby & Co.	2	2
1860	Darby & Co.	2	2
1861	Darby & Co.	2	2
1862	Darby & Co.	2	2
1863	Brymbo Iron Co.	2	2
1864	Brymbo Iron Co.	2	2
1865	Brymbo Iron Co.	2	2
1866	Brymbo Iron Co.	2	2
1867	Brymbo Iron Co.	2	2
1868	Brymbo Iron Co.	2	2
1869	Brymbo Iron Co.	3	1
1870	Brymbo Iron Co.	3	2
1871	Brymbo Iron Co.	2	2
1872	Brymbo Iron Co.	2	2
1873	Brymbo Iron Co.	3	2
1874	Brymbo Iron Co.	3	2
1875	Brymbo Iron Co.	3	2
1876	Brymbo Iron Co.	3	1
1877	Brymbo Iron Co.	3	2
1878	Brymbo Iron Co.	3	1
1879	Brymbo Iron Co.	3	2
1880	Brymbo Iron Co.	3	2
1881	Brymbo Iron Co.	3	2

Year	Owner	Built	In Blast
1882	Brymbo Iron Co.	3	1
1883	Brymbo Iron Co.	3	1
1884	Brymbo Steel Co. Ltd	3	0
1885	Brymbo Steel Co. Ltd	3	0
1886	Brymbo Steel Co. Ltd	3	1
1887	Brymbo Steel Co. Ltd	3	1
1888	Brymbo Steel Co. Ltd	3	2
1889	Brymbo Steel Co. Ltd	3	2
1890	Brymbo Steel Co. Ltd	3	2
1891	Brymbo Steel Co. Ltd	3	2
1892	Brymbo Steel Co. Ltd	3	2
1893	Brymbo Steel Co. Ltd	2	1
1894	Brymbo Steel Co. Ltd	2	1
1895	Brymbo Steel Co. Ltd	2	1
1896	Brymbo Steel Co. Ltd	2	1
1897	Brymbo Steel Co. Ltd	2	1
1898	Brymbo Steel Co. Ltd	2	1
1899	Brymbo Steel Co. Ltd	2	1
1900	Brymbo Steel Co. Ltd	1	1
1901	Brymbo Steel Co. Ltd	2	1
1902	Brymbo Steel Co. Ltd	1	1
1903	Brymbo Steel Co. Ltd	1	1
1904	Brymbo Steel Co. Ltd	1	1
1905	Brymbo Steel Co. Ltd	1	1
1906	Brymbo Steel Co. Ltd	1	1
1907	Brymbo Steel Co. Ltd	1	1
1908	Brymbo Steel Co. Ltd	2	1
1909	Brymbo Steel Co. Ltd	2	1
1910	Brymbo Steel Co. Ltd	2	1
1911	Brymbo Steel Co. Ltd	2	1
1912	Brymbo Steel Co. Ltd	1	1
1913	Brymbo Steel Co. Ltd	1	1
1921	Brymbo Steel Co. Ltd	1	-
1922	Brymbo Steel Co. Ltd	1	-
1923	Brymbo Steel Co. Ltd	1	-
1924	Brymbo Steel Co. Ltd	1	-
1925	Brymbo Steel Co. Ltd	1	-
1926	Brymbo Steel Co. Ltd	1	-
1927	Brymbo Steel Co. Ltd	1	-
1928	Brymbo Steel Co. Ltd	1	-
1929	Brymbo Steel Co. Ltd	1	-
1930	Brymbo Steel Co. Ltd	1	-
1931	Brymbo Steel Co. Ltd	1	-
1932	Brymbo Steel Co. Ltd	1	-
1933	Brymbo Steel Co. Ltd	1	-
1934	Brymbo Steel (Successors) Co. Ltd	1	-
1935	Brymbo Steel (Successors) Co. Ltd	1	-
1936	Brymbo Steel Co. Ltd	1	-
1937	Brymbo Steel Co. Ltd	1	-
1938	Brymbo Steel Co. Ltd	1	-
1939	Brymbo Steel Co. Ltd	1	-
1940	Brymbo Steel Co. Ltd	1	-
1941	Brymbo Steel Co. Ltd	1	-
1942	Brymbo Steel Co. Ltd	1	-
1943	Brymbo Steel Co. Ltd	1	-
1944	Brymbo Steel Co. Ltd	1	-
1945	Brymbo Steel Co. Ltd	1	-
1946	Brymbo Steel Co. Ltd	1	-
1947	Brymbo Steel Co. Ltd	1	-
1948	Brymbo Steel Works Ltd	1	-
1949	Brymbo Steel Works Ltd	1	-
1950	Brymbo Steel Works Ltd	1	-
1951	Brymbo Steel Works Ltd	1	-
1952	Brymbo Steel Works Ltd	1	-
1953	Brymbo Steel Works Ltd	1	-
1954	Brymbo Steel Works Ltd	1	-
1955	Brymbo Steel Works Ltd	1	-
1956	Brymbo Steel Works Ltd	1	-
1957	Brymbo Steel Works Ltd	1	-
1958	Brymbo Steel Works Ltd	1	-
1959	Brymbo Steel Works Ltd	1	-
1960	Brymbo Steel Works Ltd	1	-
1961	Brymbo Steel Works	1	-
1962	Brymbo Steel Works	1	-
1963	Brymbo Steel Works	1	-
1964	Brymbo Steel Works	1	-
1965	Brymbo Steel Works	1	-
1966	Brymbo Steel Works	1	-
1967	Brymbo Steel Works	1	-
1968	Brymbo Steel Works	1	-
1969	Brymbo Steel Works	1	-
1970	British Steel Corporation	1	-
1971	British Steel Corporation	1	-
1972	British Steel Corporation	1	-
1973	Brymbo Steel Works Ltd	1	-
1974	Brymbo Steel Works Ltd	1	-
1975	Brymbo Steel Works Ltd	1	-
1976	Brymbo Steel Works Ltd	1	-
1977	Brymbo Steel Works Ltd	1	-
1978	Brymbo Steel Works Ltd	1	-

The ground landlord in 1794 was also J. Wilkinson; the furnace was coke-fired and said to have been built in 1796 (*sic*). 1796: Excise output 884 tons p.a.; nil for 'May Make' and Exact Return; described as 'Silent' (inititialled J.W.). The 1796 list also includes a furnace called Brymbo Gate, to which the Excise assigned an output of 728 tons p.a., but which was a leadworks, as were two other sites wrongly identified as blast furnaces. 1805: output 462 tons p.a., returned by Thomas Jones. 1825: output 40 tons a week, 2,000 p.a., 'melting'. 1841: no output shown (nor for any other North Wales works) but cf. the comment 'that one furnace at Brymbo is expected to be shortly in blast, being only stopped for repairs'. 1843: output 55 tons a week. 1847: output 6,240 tons p.a., i.e. 60 tons a week from each furnace. The Parliamentary Papers version of the 1847 list names 4 works in North Wales (Brymbo, Coed Talon, Plas Issa and Ruabon), at which a total of 5 furnaces were in blast and 6 out, but with no figures for individual works. Braithwaite Poole's version divides the number of furnaces in blast between different works but not the figures for the number built or the number out of blast. The total number of furnaces built at each works can be deduced from adjacent lists. Truran: output (at Brymbo only) 70 tons a week from each of 2 furnaces. Between 1961 and 1964 the owner was described as a branch of GKN Steel Co. Ltd; in 1978 the owner's name appears beneath the heading GKN Rolled & Bright Steel Ltd.

Cefn, Denbighs. [SJ 2742?]

Year	Owner	Built	In Blast
1841	Messrs Pickering	1	0

This appears to be a reference to a short-lived (if not abortive) furnace at Cefn-mawr or Cefn-bychan, near Acrefair.

Coed Talon, Flintshire [SJ 2658]

Year	Owner	Built	In Blast
1825	Welsh Iron & Coal Co.	2	1

Year	Owner	Built	In Blast
1839	—	5	4
1841	Oakley	5	3
1843	E. Oakley	5	2
1847	Edward Oakley	5	1
1849	—	-	2
1854	—	1	0
1855	Oakley & Co.	1	0
1864	—	1	0
1865	—	1	0

1825: output 36 tons a week, 1,800 p.a., 'melting'. 1839–43: furnace-numbers include the adjacent works at Leeswood (qv), although in 1841 there is the comment that 'Of the number of furnaces in blast at Coed Talon we are unacquainted'. 1843: output of the two works 80 tons a week. 1847: output at Coed Talon and Leeswood 1,560 tons p.a., i.e. 30 tons a week; see also note under Brymbo. Truran: output 50 tons a week from each of 5 furnaces (i.e. those at Coed Talon and Leeswood).

Dolydd, Denbighs. [SJ 2742]

Year	Owner	Built	In Blast
1857	Great Western Iron Co. Ltd	2	0
1858	Great Western Iron Co. Ltd	2	0
1859	Great Western Iron Co. Ltd	2	0
1860	Great Western Iron Co. Ltd	2	0
1861	Great Western Iron Co. Ltd	-	-
1862	Great Western Iron Co. Ltd	1	0
1863	Great Western Iron Co. Ltd	1	0
1864	Great Western Iron Co. Ltd	1	0
1865	—	1	0

1857: Building. The company, registered under the name given above on 19 April 1858, proposed to operate ironworks in Denbighshire and at Seend, Wilts. (qv). A winding-up order was made on 7 July 1859 but the company was not struck off until 1902 (BT 31/335/1195). *Mineral Statistics* consistently gives the name as 'Great Western Co. Ltd' under Dolydd.

Dyfi, Cards. SN 6895

Year	Owner	Built	In Blast
1794	Messrs Kendall	1	-
1796	—	1	1
1805	Kendall	1	1
1810	Kendall	1	1

In 1794 the ground landlord was Lewis Edwards Esq.; the furnace, called 'Aberdovey', was charcoal-fired but a 'Q' has been entered against method of blowing (it was, of course, by water: see Riden, *Gazetteer*, pp. 69–71). 1796: output 200 tons p.a. Excise and actual, Exact Return 150 tons. 1805: output 150 tons.

Ffrwd, Denbighs. [SJ 3055]

Year	Owner	Built	In Blast
1825	John Thompson	1	0
1839	—	2	1
1841	— Thompson	2	0
1843	Thompson	2	2
1849	—	-	1
1854	Frood Iron Co.	1	1
1855	Sparrow & Co.	1	1
1856	Sparrow & Co.	1	1
1857	W. Sparrow & Co.	2	1
1858	James Sparrow	1	1
1859	James Sparrow	2	1
1860	James Sparrow & Poole	2	1
1861	James Sparrow & Poole	2	1
1862	James Sparrow & Poole	2	1
1863	Sparrow & Poole	2	1
1864	Sparrow & Poole	2	2
1865	Sparrow & Poole	2	2
1866	Sparrow & Poole	2	1
1867	Sparrow & Poole	2	2
1868	Sparrow & Poole	2	1
1869	Sparrow & Poole	2	2
1870	Sparrow & Poole	2	2
1871	Sparrow & Poole	3	2
1872	Sparrow & Poole	3	2
1873	Sparrow & Poole	3	2
1874	Sparrow & Poole	3	2
1875	Sparrow & Poole	3	2
1876	Sparrow & Poole	3	2
1877	Sparrow & Poole	3	2
1878	James Sparrow & Son	3	1
1879	James Sparrow & Son	3	1
1880	James Sparrow & Son	3	2
1881	James Sparrow & Son	2	1
1882	James Sparrow & Son	2	1
1883	James Sparrow & Son	2	0
1884	James Sparrow & Son	2	0
1885	James Sparrow & Son	2	0
1886	James Sparrow & Son	2	0
1887	James Sparrow & Son	2	0
1888	James Sparrow & Son	2	1
1889	James Sparrow & Son	2	1
1890	James Sparrow & Son	2	1
1891	James Sparrow & Son	2	0
1892	James Sparrow & Son	2	0
1893	James Sparrow & Son	2	0
1894	James Sparrow & Son	2	0
1895	James Sparrow & Son	2	0
1896	James Sparrow & Son	2	0
1897	James Sparrow & Son	2	0
1898	James Sparrow & Son	2	0
1899	James Sparrow & Son	2	0
1900	James Sparrow & Son	2	1
1901	James Sparrow & Son	2	1
1902	James Sparrow & Son	2	0
1903	James Sparrow & Son	2	0

The 1825 list has an entry for a furnace (said to be 'Building') at Plas Main and in the Staffs RO version there is an MS addition, 'Frood'. On the strength of this, plus the continuity of ownership, the entry is assumed to be refer to the works later known as Ffrwd. The National Grid reference above is for the place-name which appears as Plas Maen on the modern map. 1843: output nil. Truran: output 60 tons a week from each of 2 furnaces. 1870: 1 furnace in course of construction.

Leeswood, Flintshire [SJ 2759]

Year	Owner	Built	In Blast
1839	—	-	-

Year	Owner		
1841	Oakley	-	-
1843	E. Oakley	-	-
1847	Edward Oakley	-	-
1849	—	-	2
1854	Oakley & Co.	2	1
1855	Messrs Dalton	2	1
1856	Messrs Dalton	2	2
1857	Messrs Dalton	2	0
1858	—	2	0
1859	—	0	
1860	Messrs Gandy	2	1
1861	Sharp & Co.	2	1
1862	Leeswood Iron Co. Ltd	2	1
1863	Leeswood Iron Co. Ltd	2	2
1864	Leeswood Iron Co. Ltd	2	2
1865	Leeswood Iron Co. Ltd	2	1
1866	Leeswood Iron Co. Ltd	2	1
1867	Leeswood Iron Co. Ltd	2	0
1868	Leeswood Iron Co. Ltd	2	0
1872	Leeswood Iron Co. Ltd	2	1
1873	Leeswood Iron Co. Ltd	2	1

1839–47: furnace-numbers (and in 1843 output) combined with Coed Talon (qv), as is Truran's output estimate of 1855. 1856: 'Blown out April 1857'.

Llwyneinion, Denbighs. [SJ 2847]

Year	Owner	Built	In Blast
1825	Welsh Iron & Coal Co.	2	2
1839	—	2	1
1841	—	2	0
1843	—	2	0

1825: output 80 tons a week, 2,000 p.a., 'melting'. The B&W text gives the owner's name as above; it is Welsh Coal & Iron Co. in the Staffs RO version. Truran: output 60 tons a week from each of 2 furnaces.

Mostyn, Flintshire [SJ 1580]

Year	Owner	Built	In Blast
1872	John Lankaster & Co.	2	2
1873	John Lankaster & Co.	2	2
1874	Mostyn Coal & Iron Co. Ltd	2	2
1875	Mostyn Coal & Iron Co. Ltd	2	1
1876	Mostyn Coal & Iron Co. Ltd	2	0
1877	Mostyn Coal & Iron Co. Ltd	2	0
1878	Mostyn Coal & Iron Co. Ltd	2	0
1879	Mostyn Coal & Iron Co. Ltd	2	0
1880	Mostyn Coal & Iron Co. Ltd	2	2
1881	Mostyn Coal & Iron Co. Ltd	3	3
1882	Mostyn Coal & Iron Co. Ltd	3	2
1883	Mostyn Coal & Iron Co. Ltd	3	3
1884	Mostyn Coal & Iron Co. Ltd	3	3
1885	Mostyn Coal & Iron Co. Ltd	3	3
1886	Mostyn Coal & Iron Co. Ltd	3	3
1887	Darwen & Mostyn Iron Co. Ltd	3	3
1888	Darwen & Mostyn Iron Co. Ltd	3	1
1889	Darwen & Mostyn Iron Co. Ltd	3	3
1890	Darwen & Mostyn Iron Co. Ltd	3	2
1891	Darwen & Mostyn Iron Co. Ltd	3	2
1892	Darwen & Mostyn Iron Co. Ltd	3	2
1893	Darwen & Mostyn Iron Co. Ltd	3	2
1894	Darwen & Mostyn Iron Co. Ltd	3	1
1895	Darwen & Mostyn Iron Co. Ltd	3	2
1896	Darwen & Mostyn Iron Co. Ltd	3	1
1897	Darwen & Mostyn Iron Co. Ltd	2	2
1898	Darwen & Mostyn Iron Co. Ltd	2	2
1899	Darwen & Mostyn Iron Co. Ltd	2	2
1900	Darwen & Mostyn Iron Co. Ltd	2	2
1901	Darwen & Mostyn Iron Co. Ltd	2	1
1902	Darwen & Mostyn Iron Co. Ltd	2	2
1903	Darwen & Mostyn Iron Co. Ltd	2	2
1904	Darwen & Mostyn Iron Co. Ltd	2	1
1905	Darwen & Mostyn Iron Co. Ltd	2	2
1906	Darwen & Mostyn Iron Co. Ltd	2	2
1907	Darwen & Mostyn Iron Co. Ltd	2	2
1908	Darwen & Mostyn Iron Co. Ltd	2	1
1909	Darwen & Mostyn Iron Co. Ltd	2	2
1910	Darwen & Mostyn Iron Co. Ltd	2	2
1911	Darwen & Mostyn Iron Co. Ltd	2	2
1912	Darwen & Mostyn Iron Co. Ltd	2	2
1913	Darwen & Mostyn Iron Co. Ltd	2	2
1921	Darwen & Mostyn Iron Co. Ltd	5	-
1922	Darwen & Mostyn Iron Co. Ltd	5	-
1923	Darwen & Mostyn Iron Co. Ltd	5	-
1924	Darwen & Mostyn Iron Co. Ltd	5	-
1925	Darwen & Mostyn Iron Co. Ltd	5	-
1926	Darwen & Mostyn Iron Co. Ltd	5	-
1927	Darwen & Mostyn Iron Co. Ltd	5	-
1928	Darwen & Mostyn Iron Co. Ltd	5	-
1929	Darwen & Mostyn Iron Co. Ltd	3	-
1930	Darwen & Mostyn Iron Co. Ltd	4	-
1931	Darwen & Mostyn Iron Co. Ltd	4	-
1932	Darwen & Mostyn Iron Co. Ltd	4	-
1933	Darwen & Mostyn Iron Co. Ltd	4	-
1934	Darwen & Mostyn Iron Co. Ltd	4	-
1935	Darwen & Mostyn Iron Co. Ltd	4	-
1936	Darwen & Mostyn Iron Co. Ltd	2	-
1937	Darwen & Mostyn Iron Co. Ltd	2	-
1938	Darwen & Mostyn Iron Co. Ltd	2	-
1939	Darwen & Mostyn Iron Co. Ltd	2	-
1940	Darwen & Mostyn Iron Co. Ltd	2	-
1941	Darwen & Mostyn Iron Co. Ltd	2	-
1942	Darwen & Mostyn Iron Co. Ltd	2	-
1943	Darwen & Mostyn Iron Co. Ltd	2	-
1944	Darwen & Mostyn Iron Co. Ltd	2	-
1945	Darwen & Mostyn Iron Co. Ltd	2	-
1946	Darwen & Mostyn Iron Co. Ltd	1	-
1947	Darwen & Mostyn Iron Co. Ltd	1	-
1948	Darwen & Mostyn Iron Co. Ltd	1	-
1949	Darwen & Mostyn Iron Co. Ltd	1	-
1950	Darwen & Mostyn Iron Co. Ltd	2	-
1951	Darwen & Mostyn Iron Co. Ltd	1	-
1952	Darwen & Mostyn Iron Co. Ltd	1	-
1953	Darwen & Mostyn Iron Co. Ltd	1	-
1954	Darwen & Mostyn Iron Co. Ltd	1	-
1955	Darwen & Mostyn Iron Co. Ltd	2	-
1956	Darwen & Mostyn Iron Co. Ltd	2	-
1957	Darwen & Mostyn Iron Co. Ltd	2	-
1958	Darwen & Mostyn Iron Co. Ltd	2	-
1959	Darwen & Mostyn Iron Co. Ltd	2	-
1960	Darwen & Mostyn Iron Co. Ltd	2	-
1961	Darwen & Mostyn Iron Co. Ltd	2	-
1962	Darwen & Mostyn Iron Co. Ltd	2	-
1963	Darwen & Mostyn Iron Co. Ltd	2	-
1964	Darwen & Mostyn Iron Co. Ltd	2	-

After 1921 the figures include the company's other works at Darwen, Lancs. (qv). From 1953 the location of the surviving works is given as Mostyn. In 1960–64 the suffix 'Ltd' is omitted from the company's title in the original returns, presumably in error.

Newbridge, Denbighs. [SJ 2841]

Year	Owner	Built	In Blast
1825	British Iron Co.	1	1
1839	—	1	0
1841	British Iron Co.	1	0

1825: Output 36 tons a week, 1,800 p.a., 'melting'.

New British Iron Co.: see Acrefair

Old Ruabon: see Acrefair; Ruabon

Pant, Denbighs. [SJ 2945]

Year	Owner	Built	In Blast
1825	R.T. & R. Greenhow	1	1
1839	—	2	0
1841	Late Greenhowe	3	0
1843	—	2	0

In 1825 this works is listed under Ruabon, but is not identical with the Rowlands' works there (nor should it be confused with Acrefair, which was sometimes also called Ruabon). The output at the Greenhows' works in 1825 was 35 tons a week, 1,700 p.a., 'melting'. Truran: output 50 tons a week from each of 2 furnaces.

Plas Issa, Denbighs. [SJ 2744?]

Year	Owner	Built	In Blast
1839	—	1	1
1841	Roberts, Rogers & Co.	1	1
1843	—	1	1
1847	British Iron Co.	1	1
1854	Samuel Giller	1	1
1855	Samuel Gillar	1	1
1856	Samuel Gillar	1	1
1857	J. Jukes & Co.	1	1
1858	Ponkey Iron Co. Ltd	1	1
1859	Ponkey Iron Co. Ltd	1	1
1860	Ponkey Iron Co. Ltd	1	1
1861	Ponkey Iron Co. Ltd	1	0
1862	Ponkey Iron Co. Ltd	1	0
1863	Ponkey Iron Co. Ltd	1	0
1864	Ponkey Iron Co. Ltd	1	0
1865	Ponkey Iron Co. Ltd	1	0

1843: output 60 tons a week. 1847: output 3,120 tons p.a.; cf. note under Brymbo concerning the total number of furnaces at each works in N. Wales at this date. Truran: output 60 tons a week from a single furnace.

Plaskynaston, Denbighs. [SJ 2742?]

Year	Owner	Built	In Blast
1839	—	1	0
1841	T.E. Ward	1	0
1843	—	2	0
1854	Moss & Jukes	1	1
1855	Joseph Jukes	1	1
1856	Joseph Jukes	1	1
1857	J. Jukes & Co.	1	0
1858	John Dickin	1	0
1859	John Dickin	1	0
1860	John Dickin	1	0
1861	John Dickin	1	0
1862	Buckley, Newton & Co.	1	0
1863	Buckley, Newton & Co.	1	0
1864	Buckley, Newton & Co.	1	0
1865	Buckley, Newton & Co.	1	0
1866	Buckley, Newton & Co.	1	0

Truran: output 50 tons a week from a single furnace.

Plas Main: see Ffrwd

Ponciau, Denbighs. [SJ 2947]

Year	Owner	Built	In Blast
1825	John Thompson	1	1
1839	—	1	1
1841	Kyrke & Burton	1	0
1843	Kirk & Co.	1	0
1857	John Dickin	1	0
1858	Ponkey Iron Co. Ltd	1	0
1859	Ponkey Iron Co. Ltd	1	0
1860	Ponkey Iron Co. Ltd	1	1
1861	Ponkey Iron Co. Ltd	1	0
1862	Ponkey Iron Co. Ltd	1	0
1863	Ruabon Coal Co. Ltd	1	0
1864	Ruabon Coal Co. Ltd	1	0
1865	Ruabon Coal Co. Ltd	1	0

1825: output 40 tons a week, 2,000 p.a., 'melting'. 1857: Building. 1860: Out of blast since July 1860. Truran: output 50 tons a week from a single furnace.

Ruabon, Denbighs. [SJ 2945]

Year	Owner	Built	In Blast
1794	Jones & Rowland	1	-
1796	—	1	1
1805	E. Rowland & Co.	1	1
1810	Rowland	1	1

1794: the ground landlord was R. Myddleton; the furnace was coke-fired and built in 1790. 1796: Excise and actual output 1,560 tons p.a. (i.e. 30 tons a week), Exact Return 1,144 tons. 1805: output 1,463 tons p.a.

Ruabon: see also Acrefair; Pant

Shotton, Flintshire SJ 3070

Year	Owner	Built	In Blast
1953	John Summers & Sons Ltd	1	-
1954	John Summers & Sons Ltd	1	-
1955	John Summers & Sons Ltd	2	-
1956	John Summers & Sons Ltd	2	-
1957	John Summers & Sons Ltd	2	-
1958	John Summers & Sons Ltd	2	-
1959	John Summers & Sons Ltd	2	-
1960	John Summers & Sons Ltd	2	-
1961	John Summers & Sons Ltd	2	-
1962	John Summers & Sons Ltd	2	-
1963	John Summers & Sons Ltd	2	-
1964	John Summers & Sons Ltd	2	-
1965	John Summers & Sons Ltd	2	-
1966	John Summers & Sons Ltd	2	-
1967	John Summers & Sons Ltd	2	-
1968	John Summers & Sons Ltd	2	-
1969	John Summers & Sons Ltd	2	-
1970	British Steel Corporation	2	-
1971	British Steel Corporation	2	-
1972	British Steel Corporation	2	-
1973	British Steel Corporation	2	-
1974	British Steel Corporation	2	-
1975	British Steel Corporation	2	-
1976	British Steel Corporation	2	-
1977	British Steel Corporation	2	-
1978	British Steel Corporation	2	-

Southsea, Denbighs. [SJ 3051]

1839: 2 furnaces contemplated.

South Staffordshire and Worcestershire

Bankfield: see Broadwaters

Barbor's Field, Bilston, Staffs. [SO 9596?]

Year	Owner	Built	In Blast
1825	Thomas Banks	1	0
1830	—	2	-
1859	T. Banks & Son	2	1
1860	T. Banks & Son	2	0
1861	Shale & Fowler	2	0
1862	Shale & Fowler	2	0
1863	Barbor's Field Co.	2	2
1864	Barbor's Field Co.	2	1
1865	Barbor's Field Co.	2	2
1866	Barbor's Field Co.	2	2
1867	Barbor's Field Co.	2	2
1868	Barbor's Field Co.	2	2
1869	Barbor's Field Co.	2	2
1870	Barbor's Field Co.	2	2
1871	Barbor's Field Co.	2	2
1872	Barbor's Field Co.	2	2
1873	Barbor's Field Co.	2	2
1874	Barbor's Field Co.	2	2
1875	Barbor's Field Co.	2	2
1876	Barbor's Field Co.	2	1
1877	Barbor's Field Co.	2	1
1878	Barbor's Field Co.	2	1
1879	Barbor's Field Co.	2	0
1880	Barbor's Field Co.	2	0
1881	Barbor's Field Co.	2	1
1882	Barbor's Field Co.	2	1
1883	Barbor's Field Co.	2	1
1884	Barbor's Field Co.	2	2
1885	Barbor's Field Co.	2	0
1886	Barbor's Field Co.	2	0
1887	Unoccupied	2	0
1888	Unoccupied	2	0
1889	Unoccupied	2	0
1890	Unoccupied	2	0
1891	Unoccupied	2	0
1892	Unoccupied	2	0
1893	Unoccupied	2	0
1894	Unoccupied	2	0
1895	Unoccupied	2	0
1896	Unoccupied	2	0
1897	Unoccupied	2	0
1898	Unoccupied	2	0
1899	Unoccupied	2	0
1900	Unoccupied	2	0
1901	W.H. Fowler, Cheltenham	2	0
1902	W.H. Fowler, Cheltenham	2	0
1903	W.H. Fowler, Cheltenham	2	0
1904	W.H. Fowler, Cheltenham	2	0
1905	W.H. Fowler, Cheltenham	2	0
1906	W.H. Fowler, Cheltenham	2	0
1907	W.H. Fowler, Cheltenham	2	0
1908	W.H. Fowler, Cheltenham	2	0
1909	W.H. Fowler, Cheltenham	2	0
1910	W.H. Fowler, Cheltenham	2	0

1823–30: nil return for 1823; one furnace built 1826 and another in 1828; output in 1830 5,720 tons p.a. 1825: no output; 'Not yet built' (20 March 1826).

Batterfield, ?Staffs.

Year	Owner	Built	In Blast
1825	Izons & Co.	1	0

No output was returned.

Bentley, Walsall, Staffs. [SO 9898]

Year	Owner	Built	In Blast
1839	Earl of Lichfield	2	2
1841	Countess of Lichfield's Trust[ee]s	4	1
1843	Earl of Lichfield	4	2
1847	Earl of Lichfield	4	0
1849	Earl of Lichfield	4	0
1852	Countess of Lichfield	4	0
1854	H. Clarke	3	1
1855	Clarke & Jerome	4	0
1856	Riley & Co.	3	0
1857	Riley & Co.	3	1
1858	Riley & Co.	3	0
1859	Chillington & Co.	2	0
1860	Chillington Iron Co.	2	1
1861	Chillington Iron Co.	2	2
1862	Chillington Iron Co.	-	-
1863	Chillington Iron Co.	-	-
1864	Chillington Iron Co.	-	-
1865	Chillington Iron Co.	-	-
1866	Chillington Iron Co.	-	-
1867	Chillington Iron Co.	-	-
1868	Chillington Iron Co.	-	-
1869	Chillington Iron Co.	-	-
1871	Chillington Iron Co.	2	2
1872	Chillington Iron Co. Ltd	2	2
1873	Chillington Iron Co. Ltd	2	2
1874	Chillington Iron Co. Ltd	2	1
1875	Chillington Iron Co. Ltd	2	1
1876	Chillington Iron Co. Ltd	2	0
1877	Chillington Iron Co. Ltd	2	0
1878	Chillington Iron Co. Ltd	2	0
1879	Chillington Iron Co. Ltd	2	0
1880	Chillington Iron Co. Ltd	2	0
1881	Chillington Iron Co. Ltd	2	0
1882	Chillington Iron Co. Ltd	2	0
1883	Chillington Iron Co. Ltd	0	0

1823–30: Note that 2 furnaces were erected at Bentley in 1832. 1839: output 50 tons a week, 5,000 p.a. (actual); 'foundry and forge'; hot blast. 1841: output 80 tons a week. 1843: output 160 tons a week. Truran: output 100 tons a week from each of 4 furnaces. 1862–69: furnace-numbers included in the figures printed under Chillington (qv). The works is called Bentley Heath up to 1860, Bentley thereafter. 1883: Dismantled.

Bilston, Staffs. [SO 9396]

Year	Owner	Built	In Blast
1794	B. Gibbons	2	-
1796	—	2	2
1805	Bickley & Gibbons	3	2
1810	Bickley	3	2
1823	—	4	-
1825	W. Sparrow & Co.	4	4
1830	—	4	-
1839	George Jones	3	2
1841	George Jones	3	2
1843	George Jones	3	2
1847	G. Jones	3	2
1849	George Jones	3	2
1852	G. Jones	3	3
1854	Geo. Jones	3	2

The ground landlord of a works described as 'Ettinsall [i.e. Ettingshall] or Bilston' in 1794 was Mrs Bickley; the furnaces were coke-fired, blown by engine and built in 1788. 1796: output 2,340 tons p.a. (i.e. 45 tons a week), Excise and actual, Exact Return 1,429 tons. 1805: 3,550 tons p.a. 1823–30: output at Bilston 7,696 tons p.a. in 1823, 4,680 tons in 1830. 1825: 150 tons a week (8,000 tons p.a.), 'forge consumed by them'. 1839: 50 tons a week at Bilston, 14,447 p.a. (actual) for Bilston and Coseley (New) (qv); 'forge, in part'; cold blast. 1847: an otherwise isolated entry for New Duffield appears to belong here. In 1854 two works are named at Bilston, as they are by Truran, one distinguished in each case as 'Bilston (New)'. Truran's entry for 'Bilston', presumably meaning the site listed above, assigns an output of 110 tons a week from each of 3 furnaces. 1841: output 170 tons a week. 1843: output 170 tons a week.

Bilston (New), Staffs. [SO 9497]

Year	Owner	Built	In Blast
1839	W. Baldwin & Co.	2	2
1841	W. Baldwin & Co.	2	1
1843	W. Baldwin	2	1
1847	Baldwin & Co.	2	1
1852	Blackwell & Co.	2	2
1854	Blackwell & Co.	5	5
1855	S.H. Blackwell & Co.	5	4
1856	S.H. Blackwell & Co.	5	5
1857	S.H. Blackwell & Co.	5	5
1858	S.H. Blackwell & Co.	5	4
1859	S.H. Blackwell & Co.	5	4
1860	S.H. Blackwell & Co.	5	3
1861	S.H. Blackwell & Co.	5	0
1862	S.H. Blackwell & Co.	5	0
1863	S.H. Blackwell & Co.	5	0

1839: output 50 tons a week, 5,180 p.a. (actual); 'forge, worked'; cold blast. 1841: output 70 tons a week. 1843: output 85 tons a week. Truran: output 125 tons a week from each of 5 furnaces. *Mineral Statistics* uses the name 'New Furnaces, Bilston' for this site.

Bilston Brook, Staffs. [SO 9497]

Year	Owner	Built	In Blast
1810	Prices & Co.	2	2
1823	—	2	-
1825	Thomas Price	2	1
1830	—	2	-
1839	Executors of T.B. Price	2	2
1841	J. Parsons	2	2
1843	Executors of T.B. Price	2	1
1847	J. Parson	2	0
1849	John Parsons	2	0
1852	G. Hickman & Son	2	2
1854	Hickman & Sons	3	2
1855	G.H. & A. Hickman	3	2
1856	G.H. & A. Hickman	3	2
1857	G.H. & A. Hickman	3	2
1858	G.H. & A. Hickman	3	2
1859	G.H. & A. Hickman	3	3
1860	Samuel Griffiths	3	3
1861	Samuel Griffiths	3	2
1862	Benjamin Gibbons	2	1
1863	Benjamin Gibbons	2	1
1864	Emily Gibbons	3	1
1865	Brook Furnace Iron Co.	3	2
1866	Brook Furnace Iron Co.	3	2
1867	Brook Furnace Co.	3	2
1868	Brook Furnace Co.	3	2
1869	Brook Furnace Co.	3	2
1870	Brook Furnace Co.	3	2
1871	Bilston Brook Furnace Co.	3	2
1872	Bilston Brook Furnace Co.	2	2
1873	Bilston Brook Furnace Co.	2	2
1874	Bilston Brook Furnace Co.	2	0
1875	Bilston Brook Furnace Co.	3	2
1876	Brook Furnace Co.	3	1
1877	Brook Furnace Co.	3	1
1878	Brook Furnaces Iron Co.	3	1
1879	Brook Furnaces Iron Co.	3	0
1880	Brook Furnaces Iron Co.	3	0

1810: Works not named; identified from name of owner. Output in 1823 was given as 4,345 tons p.a., in 1825 as 90 tons a week (4,500 p.a.; 'Forge, consumed by them') and in 1830 as 3,771 tons. 1839: output 45 tons a week, 4,665 p.a. (actual); 'forge sale, worked; cold blast'. 1841: output 140 tons a week. 1843: output 70 tons a week. Truran: output 80 tons a week from each of 2 furnaces. *Mineral Statistics* in certain years uses the name 'Brook, Bilston' for this site.

Bilston: see also Ettingshall; Millfield; Spring Vale; Stonefield

Birchfield, ?Staffs. [SP 0790?]

Year	Owner	Built	In Blast
1825	W. Sparrow & Co.	2	0

'Building' (20 March 1826).

Birchills (Old), Walsall, Staffs. [SP 0099]

Year	Owner	Built	In Blast
1823	—	2	-
1825	Mrs Walker	2	1
1830	—	2	-
1839	E. Tyler	1	1
1841	E. Tyler	1	1
1843	E. Tyler	1	0
1847	E. Tyler	1	1
1849	P. Williams & Sons	1	1
1852	P. Williams & Sons	2	1
1854	P. Williams & Sons	2	1
1855	P. Williams & Sons	2	0
1856	F.C. Perry	2	0
1857	F.C. Perry	2	2
1858	F.C. Perry	2	2
1859	F.C. Perry	2	1
1860	F.C. Perry	2	0
1861	Williams Brothers	2	0
1862	Williams Brothers	2	0
1863	Williams Brothers	2	0
1864	Williams Brothers	2	0
1865	Williams Brothers	2	0
1866	Williams Brothers	2	0
1867	Williams Brothers	2	0
1868	Williams Brothers	2	0
1871	Williams Brothers	2	0
1874	Castle Coal & Iron Co. Ltd	2	0
1875	Castle Coal & Iron Co. Ltd	2	1
1876	Castle Coal & Iron Co. Ltd	2	1
1877	Castle Coal & Iron Co. Ltd	2	1
1878	Castle Coal & Iron Co. Ltd	2	0
1879	Castle Coal & Iron Co. Ltd	2	0
1880	Castle Coal & Iron Co. Ltd	2	0
1881	Castle Coal & Iron Co. Ltd	2	1
1882	Castle Coal & Iron Co. Ltd	3	2
1883	Castle Coal & Iron Co. Ltd	2	2
1884	Castle Coal & Iron Co. Ltd	2	0
1885	Castle Coal & Iron Co. Ltd	2	0
1886	Castle Coal & Iron Co. Ltd	2	0
1887	Castle Coal & Iron Co. Ltd	2	0
1888	Castle Coal & Iron Co. Ltd	2	0
1889	Castle Coal & Iron Co. Ltd	2	0
1890	Jones Brothers, Walsall, Ltd	2	0
1891	Jones Brothers, Walsall, Ltd	2	1
1892	Jones Brothers, Walsall, Ltd	2	1
1893	Jones Brothers, Walsall, Ltd	2	1
1894	John Russell & Co. Ltd	2	0
1895	John Russell & Co. Ltd	2	1
1896	John Russell & Co. Ltd	2	1
1897	John Russell & Co. Ltd	2	1
1898	John Russell & Co. Ltd	2	1
1899	John Russell & Co. Ltd	2	0
1900	John Russell & Co. Ltd	2	0
1901	John Russell & Co. Ltd	2	0
1902	John Russell & Co. Ltd	2	0
1903	John Russell & Co. Ltd	2	0
1904	John Russell & Co. Ltd	2	0
1905	John Russell & Co. Ltd	2	0
1906	John Russell & Co. Ltd	2	0
1907	John Russell & Co. Ltd	2	0
1908	Birchills Furnaces Ltd	2	1
1909	Birchills Furnaces Ltd	2	1
1910	Birchills Furnaces Ltd	2	1
1911	Birchills Furnaces Ltd	2	1
1912	Birchills Furnaces Ltd	2	1
1913	Birchills Furnaces Ltd	2	1
1921	Birchills Furnaces Ltd	2	-
1922	Birchills Furnaces Ltd	2	-
1923	Birchills Furnaces Ltd	2	-
1924	Birchills Furnaces Ltd	2	-

1823–30: 2 furnaces listed in both years but no output shown in either. 1825: output 40 tons a week, 1,800 p.a, 'consumed by herself'. 1839: output 45 tons a week, 2,340 p.a. (estimated); 'forge, sale'; hot blast. 1841: output 60 tons a week. 1843: output nil. Truran: output 90 tons a week from each of 2 furnaces. The works is called 'Roughwood' in 1859–60 and 1871 and 'Castle' from 1878. In 1859 there are two entries, one under 'Birchills, Roughwood', with details as above, and the other under Roughwood, with the owner named as Charles F. Perry. In 1860 the only entry is under Roughwood, with details as above. In 1861–63 there are entries under Roughwood (as well as for the two Birchills sites), which appear to duplicate those for Birchills (Old): the furnace-numbers agree exactly, as do the owners in 1862–63; in 1861 the owner under Roughwood is named as 'F.C. Perry (late)'. 1883: Production estimated.

Birchills (New), Walsall, Staffs. [SP 0099]

Year	Owner	Built	In Blast
1847	G. Jones	2	0
1849	George Jones	2	2
1852	G. Jones	4	3
1854	Geo. Jones	5	4
1855	Geo. Jones	5	5
1856	Geo. Jones	5	5
1857	John Jones	5	4
1858	Henry Smith	5	3
1859	Henry Smith	5	2
1860	Henry Smith	5	2
1861	John Jones	5	2
1862	John Jones	5	3
1863	John Jones	5	2
1864	John Jones	5	3
1865	John Jones	5	2
1866	John Jones	5	2
1867	John Jones	5	0
1868	John Jones	4	0
1869	Brayford	3	1
1870	J. Brayford	3	1
1871	Late John Brayford	3	0

Truran: output 110 tons a week from each of 4 furnaces. In 1860 there is a second entry, under 'New Birchills', John Jones owner, with 5 furnaces, 2 in blast, which appears to be a duplicate of that under 'Birchills, New' printed above.

Birds Wharf: see Millfields

Blowers Green, Dudley, Worcs. [SO 9389]

Year	Owner	Built	In Blast
1805	Grazebrook	1	1
1810	Grazebrook & Co.	1	1
1823	—	2	-
1825	Grazebrook & Sons	2	2
1830	—	2	-

1805: output 2,436 tons p.a. 1823: 5,348 tons; 1830: 5,237 tons. 1825: 100 tons a week, 5,000 tons p.a., 'casting trade'.

Bloxwich: see Green Lane; Hatherton

Bovereux, Bilston, Staffs.

Year	Owner	Built	In Blast
1849	Baldwin & Co.	2	1
1852	Baldwin & Co.	2	2
1854	Baldwin & Co.	2	2
1855	William Baldwin & Co.	2	1
1856	William Baldwin & Co.	2	2
1857	William Baldwin & Co.	2	1
1858	William Baldwin & Co.	2	1
1859	William Baldwin & Co.	2	2
1860	William Baldwin & Co.	2	1
1861	William Baldwin & Co.	2	0
1862	William Baldwin & Co.	2	0
1863	William Baldwin & Co.	7	0
1865	William Baldwin & Co.	7	0
1866	William Baldwin & Co.	7	0
1867	William Baldwin & Co.	7	0
1868	William Baldwin & Co.	7	0
1869	William Baldwin & Co.	7	0
1870	William Baldwin & Co.	7	1
1871	William Baldwin & Co.	2	0
1872	Tame Iron Co.	2	1
1873	James & Thomas Holcroft	2	2
1874	Tame Iron Co.	2	1
1875	Tame Iron Co.	2	2
1876	Tame Iron Co.	2	2
1877	Tame Iron Co.	2	2
1878	Tame Iron Co.	2	2
1879	Tame Iron Co.	2	0
1880	Thomas Holcroft	2	1
1881	Thomas Holcroft	2	1
1882	Reps. of late William Baldwin	2	1
1883	Tame Iron Co.	2	1
1884	Tame Iron Co.	2	0
1885	Tame Iron Co.	2	0
1886	Unoccupied	2	0

1849: Hunt lists 2 furnaces in blast. Truran: output 110 tons a week from each of 2 furnaces. The site is called Bovereux Lower in 1862–70, Bovereux thereafter. In 1863–70 the furnace-numbers evidently include a second works, possibly Wallbut (qv). Bovereux is not listed at all in 1864.

Brades Hall, Tipton, Staffs. [SO 9790]

Year	Owner	Built	In Blast
1862	James & George Onions	4	3
1863	J.C. Cohen	2	2
1864	James & George Onions	2	2
1865	James & George Onions	2	2
1866	James & George Onions	4	4
1867	James & George Onions	4	4
1868	James & George Onions	4	2
1869	James & George Onions	4	2
1870	James & George Onions	4	2
1875	W. & G. Onions	2	0
1876	W. & E. Onions	2	0
1877	W. & E. Onions	2	0
1878	W. & E. Onions	2	0
1879	W. & E. Onions	2	0
1880	W. & E. Onions	2	0
1881	W. & E. Onions	2	1
1882	T. & S. Roberts	2	1
1883	T. & S. Roberts	2	1
1884	J. & S. Roberts	2	1
1885	J. & S. Roberts	2	1
1886	J. & S. Roberts	2	0
1887	J. & S. Roberts	2	0
1888	J. & S. Roberts	2	0
1889	J. & S. Roberts	2	0
1890	J. & S. Roberts	2	0
1891	J. & S. Roberts	2	0

In 1862 and 1866–70 the furnace-numbers include Netherton (Old) (qv). 1883: Production estimated.

Bradley, Staffs. SO 9595

Year	Owner	Built	In Blast
1794	J. Wilkinson	2	-
1796	—	3	3
1805	Wilkinson	3	2
1810	Fereday	3	3
1823	—	3	-
1825	J.T. Fereday	3	3
1830	—	3	-
1839	J. Wilkinson & Co.	1	1
1843	J. Wilkinson & Son	1	0
1847	Trustees of J. Wilkin[son]	1	1

Wilkinson is also listed as ground landlord in 1794; the furnaces were coke-fired, blown by engine and said to have been built in 1772. The forge consisted of 6 melting furnaces, 6 balling furnaces and a rolling and slitting mill; a date of building of 1787 is written against the mill. 1796:' Excise output 3,640 tons; actual 3,000 tons (i.e. 60 tons a week); Exact Return 1,920 tons. 1805: 3,566 tons p.a. The 1823-30 list (only) distinguishes Bradley works from 'Bradley Lower'. The two have been treated here as one; at the former the two furnaces made 4,195 tons in 1823 and 4,194 tons in 1830; the figures for Bradley Lower were 1,920 and 2,113 tons from one furnace. 1825: output 140 tons a week, 6,500 p.a., 'forge, consumed by themselves '. The B&W text of the 1825 list has 2 furnaces, both in blast; the Staffs RO version has 3 furnaces, all in blast. The latter has been taken as correct here, in view of the figures given in 1823–30. 1839: 65 tons a week, 3,314 p.a. (actual); 'foundry'; hot blast. 1843: output nil. The name 'Wilkin' in 1847 is presumably an error for Wilkinson.

Bradley (New), Staffs. [SO 9595]

Year	Owner	Built	In Blast
1860	G.B. Thorneycroft & Co.	2	0
1861	G.B. Thorneycroft & Co.	2	2
1862	G.B. Thorneycroft & Co.	2	1
1863	G.B. Thorneycroft & Co.	2	2
1864	G.B. Thorneycroft & Co.	2	2
1865	G.B. Thorneycroft & Co.	2	2
1867	G.B. Thorneycroft & Co.	2	0
1868	G.B. Thorneycroft & Co.	2	0
1869	G.B. Thorneycroft & Co.	2	0
1870	G.B. Thorneycroft & Co.	2	2
1871	G.B. Thorneycroft & Co.	2	2
1872	G.B. Thorneycroft & Co.	2	2
1874	G.B. Thorneycroft & Co.	2	1
1875	G.B. Thorneycroft & Co.	2	1
1876	G.B. Thorneycroft & Co.	2	0
1877	G.B. Thorneycroft & Co.	2	0
1878	G.B. Thorneycroft & Co.	2	0
1879	G.B. Thorneycroft & Co.	2	0

Brettell Lane, Staffs. [SO 9085]

Year	Owner	Built	In Blast
1825	Wheeley	2	0
1830	—	2	-
1839	W. & J. Wheeley	2	2
1841	J. Wheeley & Co.	2	2
1843	W. & J. Wheely	2	0
1847	J. & W. Wheeley	2	1
1849	John Wheeley & Co.	2	0
1852	Hall, Holcroft & Pearson	2	1
1854	Hall, Holcroft & Pearson	2	2
1855	Hall, Holcroft & Pearson	2	2
1856	Hall, Holcroft & Pearson	2	2
1857	Hall, Holcroft & Pearson	2	2
1858	Hall, Holcroft & Pearson	2	2
1859	Hall, Holcroft & Pearson	2	2
1860	Hall, Holcroft & Pearson	2	1
1861	Hall, Holcroft & Pearson	2	2
1862	Hall, Holcroft & Pearson	2	2
1863	Hall, Holcroft & Pearson	2	2
1864	Hall, Holcroft & Pearson	2	2
1865	Hall, Holcroft & Pearson	2	1
1866	Hall, Holcroft & Pearson	-	-
1867	Hall, Holcroft & Pearson	-	-
1868	Hall, Holcroft & Pearson	-	-
1869	Hall, Holcroft & Pearson	-	-
1870	Hall, Holcroft & Pearson	-	-

1823–30: nil return for 1823; notes construction of two furnaces in 1825; output in 1830 2,949 tons p.a. 1825: 'Building. 1 [furnace] in blast next week' (comment dated 20 March 1826). The B&W text has 2 furnaces in built, 1 in blast; the Staffs RO text has both furnaces in blast; in fact none appears to have operated in 1825 itself. 1839: output 57 tons a week, 5,928 p.a. (actual); 'forge'; cold blast. 1841: output 120 tons a week. 1843: output nil. Truran: output 85 tons a week from each of 2 furnaces. 1866–70: furnace-numbers combined with those for Level, Old (qv).

Bridge, Bilston, Staffs. [SO 9497]

Year	Owner	Built	In Blast
1866	David Jones	1	1
1867	David Jones	1	1
1868	David Jones	1	1
1869	David Jones	1	1

In 1869 the number of furnaces in blast is printed as 2 in *Mineral Statistics*, presumably in error.

Brierley, Staffs. [SO 9286]

Year	Owner	Built	In Blast
1794	Bank & Onions	2	-
1796	—	2	1
1805	Onions	2	0
1810	Onions & Co.	2	2
1823	—	1	-
1830	—	1	-

Bank & Onions were also ground landlords in 1794; the furnaces were coke-fired, blown by engine and built in 1790. The forge consisted of 2 chaferies, 3 melting furnaces and 2 balling furnaces, built in 1788. 1796: Excise and actual output 1,300 tons p.a. (i.e. 25 tons a week), from the 1 furnace then in blast; Exact Return 1,046 tons 19 cwt. 1805: no output. 1823–30: 1 furnace listed in both years but no output shown in either.

Brierley Hill, Staffs. [SO 9286]

Year	Owner	Built	In Blast
1805	Izons & Co.	1	1
1810	Izons & Co.	1	1
1823	—	2	-
1825	J. Bradley & Co.	2	1
1830	—	2	-

1805: output 817 tons p.a. 1823: 4,348 tons p.a. 1825: 95 tons a week, 4,500 p.a., 'used by themselves'. In 1825 the works was called Brierley and has been placed here, rather than in the previous entry, on the basis of the owner's name; Onions were not listed as owning any works in South Staffs in 1825. 1830: output nil.

Broadwaters, Wednesbury, Staffs. [SO 9795?]

Year	Owner	Built	In Blast
1823	—	2	-
1825	Matthews & Co.	2	1
1830	—	2	-
1839	Sir H. St Paul	2	0
1841	Sir H. St Paul, Thorneycroft & Co.	2	1
1843	Sir H. St Paul	2	1

Year	Owner	Built	In Blast
1847	Sir Horace St Paul	2	1
1849	Colbourn, Groucutt & Co.	2	2
1852	Colbourn, Groucutt & Co.	2	2
1854	Samuel Groucutt & Sons	2	2
1855	Samuel Groucutt & Sons	2	2
1856	Samuel Groucutt & Sons	2	2
1857	Samuel Groucutt & Sons	2	2
1858	Samuel Groucutt & Sons	3	3
1859	Samuel Groucutt & Sons	3	3
1860	Samuel Groucutt & Sons	3	3
1861	Samuel Groucutt & Sons	3	3
1862	Samuel Groucutt & Sons	3	3
1863	Samuel Groucutt & Sons	3	3
1864	Samuel Groucutt & Sons	3	2
1865	Samuel Groucutt & Sons	3	2
1866	Samuel Groucutt & Sons	3	2
1867	Samuel Groucutt & Sons	3	2
1868	Samuel Groucutt & Sons	3	2
1869	Samuel Groucutt & Sons	3	0
1870	Samuel Groucutt & Sons	3	3
1871	Samuel Groucutt & Sons	3	3
1872	Samuel Groucutt & Sons	3	3
1873	Samuel Groucutt & Sons	3	3
1874	Samuel Groucutt & Sons	3	2
1875	Samuel Groucutt & Sons	3	1
1876	Samuel Groucutt & Sons	3	1
1877	Samuel Groucutt & Sons	3	1
1878	Samuel Groucutt & Sons	3	0
1879	Samuel Groucutt & Sons	3	0
1880	Samuel Groucutt & Sons	3	1
1881	Samuel Groucutt & Sons	3	1
1882	Samuel Groucutt & Sons	3	1
1883	Samuel Groucutt & Sons	3	1
1885	Samuel Groucutt & Sons	3	0
1886	Samuel Groucutt & Sons	3	0
1887	Samuel Groucutt & Sons	3	0

1823: output nil. 1830: 6,368 tons p.a. 1825: output 50 tons a week, 3,000 tons p.a. The B&W text has 2 furnaces in blast (with no comment), the Staffs RO version has 2 and the comment: 'If the demand was good, 2 would blow'. 1841: output 70 tons a week. 1843: output 70 tons a week. The entries above for 1825, 1843 and 1847 are for a works called Waterloo which has been assumed to belong here since the owner's name and furnace-numbers match. In 1866 the site is called 'Broadwaters and Bankfield'; there are no other references to the latter name and there is no change in the furnace-numbers for Broadwaters.

Bromford: see Withymoor

Bromley Hall: see Corbyn's Hall (New) [I]

Brook: see Bilston Brook

Buffery (Old), Dudley, Worcs. [SO 9489]

Year	Owner	Built	In Blast
1823	—	1	-
1825	Salisbury & Co.	1	1
1830	—	1	-
1839	Joseph Haden	1	1
1841	Joseph Haden	1	1
1843	J. Haden	1	1
1847	J. Haden	1	0

1823: output 2,646 tons p.a. 1825: 40 tons a week, 1,800 tons p.a., 'casting trade'. 1830: 2,158 tons p.a. 1839: output 50 tons a week, 2,600 p.a. (actual); 'forge'; cold blast. 1841: output 60 tons a week. 1843: output 50 tons a week. Only one works at Buffery is listed in 1847, which has been assigned to the older site on the basis of the owner's name.

Buffery (New), Dudley, Worcs. [SO 9489]

Year	Owner	Built	In Blast
1823	—	3	-
1825	Wainwright, Jones & Co.	3	3
1830	—	3	-
1839	Blackwell, Jones & Co.	3	3
1841	Blackwell, Jones & Co.	3	2
1843	Blackwell, Jones & Co.	3	2
1849	Jones & Oakes	0	0
1870	J. Jones	1	1
1872	John Jones & Son	1	1
1873	John Jones & Son	1	1
1874	John Jones & Son	1	0
1875	John Jones & Son	1	1
1876	John Jones & Son	1	1
1877	John Jones & Son	1	1
1878	John Jones & Son	1	1
1879	John Jones & Son	1	0
1880	John Jones & Son	1	1
1881	John Jones & Son	1	1
1882	John Jones & Sons	1	1
1883	J. & G. Dunn	1	0
1884	J. & G. Dunn	1	0

1823–30: output 6,551 tons p.a. in 1823, 5,246 tons in 1830. 1825: 120 tons a week, 5,750 tons p.a., 'melting iron'. 1839: output 70 tons a week, $11,631\frac{1}{2}$ p.a. (actual); 'forge'; cold blast. 1841: output 160 tons a week. 1843: output 143 tons a week. Cf. Buffery (Old) for 1847.

Bull Field, ?Staffs.

Year	Owner	Built	In Blast
1841	J. Dunning	1	1

Output 70 tons a week.

Bumble Hole: see Netherton (New)

Cape, Smethick, Staffs. [SP 0387]

Year	Owner	Built	In Blast
1864	Cape Iron Co.	1	1
1865	Cape Iron Co.	1	1
1866	Benjamin Richard	1	1
1867	Benjamin Richard	1	1
1868	Benjamin Richard	2	0
1869	Benjamin Richard	2	0
1870	Benjamin Richard	2	0
1871	—	1	0

Capponfield, Bilston, Staffs. SO 9495

Year	Owner	Built	In Blast
1805	Smith, Read & Co.	2	2
1810	Smith, Read & Co.	2	2
1823	—	2	-
1825	W. Aston	2	2
1830	—	2	-
1839	J. Bagnall & Sons	3	2
1841	J. Bagnall & Sons	3	2
1843	J. Bagnell & Son	3	3
1847	J. Bagnall & Sons	3	2
1849	John Bagnall & Sons	3	2
1852	J. Bagnall & Sons	3	3
1854	John Bagnall & Sons	3	2
1855	John Bagnall & Sons	3	2
1856	John Bagnall & Sons	3	3
1857	John Bagnall & Sons	3	3
1858	John Bagnall & Sons	3	3
1859	John Bagnall & Sons	3	2
1860	John Bagnall & Sons	3	2
1861	John Bagnall & Sons	3	2
1862	John Bagnall & Sons	-	-
1863	John Bagnall & Sons	-	-
1864	John Bagnall & Sons	-	-
1865	John Bagnall & Sons	-	-
1866	John Bagnall & Sons	-	-
1867	John Bagnall & Sons	-	-
1868	John Bagnall & Sons	-	-
1869	John Bagnall & Sons	-	-
1870	John Bagnall & Sons	3	1
1871	John Bagnall & Sons	3	2
1872	John Bagnall & Sons	3	2
1873	John Bagnall & Sons	3	2
1874	John Bagnall & Sons	3	2
1875	John Bagnall & Sons Ltd	3	1
1876	John Bagnall & Sons Ltd	3	0
1877	John Bagnall & Sons Ltd	3	0
1878	John Bagnall & Sons Ltd	3	0
1879	John Bagnall & Sons Ltd	3	2
1880	John Bagnall & Sons Ltd	3	1
1881	John Bagnall & Sons Ltd	3	2
1882	T. & I. Bradley	2	2
1883	T. & I. Bradley	2	1
1884	T. & I. Bradley	3	1
1885	T. & I. Bradley	3	2
1886	T. & I. Bradley	3	1
1887	T. & I. Bradley	3	1
1888	T. & I. Bradley	3	2
1889	T. & I. Bradley	3	2
1890	T. & I. Bradley	3	1
1891	T. & I. Bradley	3	1
1892	T. & I. Bradley	3	2
1893	T. & I. Bradley	3	2
1894	T. & I. Bradley	2	2
1895	T. & I. Bradley	3	2
1896	T. & I. Bradley	2	2
1897	T. & I. Bradley	3	2
1898	T. & I. Bradley Ltd	3	2
1899	T. & I. Bradley Ltd	2	2
1900	T. & I. Bradley Ltd	3	2
1901	T. & I. Bradley Ltd	3	1
1902	T. & I. Bradley Ltd	3	1
1903	T. & I. Bradley Ltd	3	1
1904	T. & I. Bradley Ltd	3	1
1905	T. & I. Bradley Ltd	3	1
1906	T. & I. Bradley Ltd	2	1
1907	T. & I. Bradley Ltd	2	1
1908	T. & I. Bradley Ltd	2	1
1909	T. & I. Bradley Ltd	2	1
1910	T. & I. Bradley Ltd	2	1
1911	T. & I. Bradley Ltd	2	0
1912	T. & I. Bradley Ltd	2	0
1913	T. & I. Bradley Ltd	2	0
1921	T. & I. Bradley Ltd	2	-
1922	T. & I. Bradley Ltd	2	-
1923	T. & I. Bradley Ltd	2	-
1924	T. & I. Bradley Ltd	2	-
1925	T. & I. Bradley Ltd	2	-
1926	T. & I. Bradley Ltd	2	-
1927	T. & I. Bradley Ltd	2	-
1928	T. & I. Bradley Ltd	2	-
1929	T. & I. Bradley Ltd	2	-
1930	T. & I. Bradley Ltd	2	-
1931	T. & I. Bradley Ltd	2	-
1932	T. & I. Bradley Ltd	2	-
1933	T. & I. Bradley Ltd	2	-
1934	Bradley & Foster Ltd	2	-
1935	Bradley & Foster Ltd	2	-
1936	Bradley & Foster Ltd	2	-
1937	Bradley & Foster Ltd	2	-

1805: output 4,600 tons. 1823–30: no output shown in either year. 1825: 100 tons a week, 4,500 tons p.a., comment (dated 20 March 1826): 'Blew out last week'. The B&W version of the list has the furnaces out of blast; the Staffs RO text has them both in blast. 1839: output 80 tons a week, 804 p.a. (actual); 'forge'; cold blast. 1841: 160 tons a week. 1843: 225 tons a week. 1849: Hunt lists 3 furnaces in blast. Truran: output 150 tons a week from each of 3 furnaces. In 1862–69 furnace-numbers for Capponfield are said to be combined with those for Chillington (qv), which in these years include all the works owned by the Chillington Co. In 1864–69, however, the entry for Goldshill (qv), the Bagnalls' other works, also states that the furnace-numbers include Capponfield. The latter attribution appears to be correct. Although the figure for 'Built' at Goldshill rises by only 2, whereas there were 3 furnaces at Capponfield in these years, the number of furnaces returned at Chillington (9) can be obtained by summing the figures for the works known to have been owned by the Chillington Co., without including Capponfield. There is no other evidence that Capponfield passed out of the Bagnalls' ownership in this period and their name has been inserted above accordingly. See also under Chillington. 1883, 1884: Production estimated. The Capponfield works, listed as Bilston from 1921, was dismantled in 1938. The owner's name as printed above between 1898 and 1933 cannot be found on the register and appears to be an error for T. & I. Bradley & Sons (incorporated as T. & I. Bradley & Sons Ltd in 1906); cf. Darlaston Green.

Castle: see Birchills (Old)

Chillington, Wolverhampton, Staffs. [SO 9298]

Year	Owner	Built	In Blast
1830	—	2	-
1839	Chillington Co.	4	4
1841	Chillington Co.	4	3

Year	Owner	Built	In Blast
1843	Jones, Barker & Foster	4	3
1847	Barker & Foster	4	3
1849	Chillington Co.	4	4
1852	Chillington Co.	4	4
1854	Chillington Co.	4	4
1855	Chillington Co.	4	4
1856	Chillington Co.	4	4
1857	Chillington Co.	4	4
1858	Chillington Co.	4	3
1859	Chillington Iron Co.	4	4
1860	Chillington Iron Co.	4	3
1861	Chillington Iron Co.	4	3
1862	Chillington Iron Co.	9	5
1863	Chillington Iron Co.	9	7
1864	Chillington Iron Co.	9	5
1865	Chillington Iron Co.	9	5
1866	Chillington Iron Co.	9	5
1867	Chillington Iron Co.	9	3
1868	Chillington Iron Co.	9	3
1869	Chillington Iron Co.	9	3
1870	Chillington Iron Co.	6	4
1871	Chillington Iron Co.	4	2
1872	Chillington Iron Co. Ltd	4	2
1873	Chillington Iron Co. Ltd	6	4
1874	Chillington Iron Co. Ltd	6	1
1875	Chillington Iron Co. Ltd	4	1
1876	Chillington Iron Co. Ltd	4	0
1877	Chillington Iron Co. Ltd	4	0
1878	Chillington Iron Co. Ltd	4	0
1879	Chillington Iron Co. Ltd	4	0
1880	Chillington Iron Co. Ltd	4	0
1881	Chillington Iron Co. Ltd	4	0
1882	Chillington Iron Co. Ltd	2	0
1883	Chillington Iron Co. Ltd	0	0

1823–30: nil return for 1823, note that 2 furnaces were built in 1829, making 6,240 tons p.a. in 1830. 1839: output 80 tons a week, 16,661 p.a. (actual); 'hard forge'; cold blast. 1841: output 240 tons a week. 1843: output 255 tons a week. Truran: output 110 tons a week from each of 4 furnaces; *Mineral Statistics* lists this site under Wolverhampton in 1855. The furnace-numbers for 1862–64 are said to include 3 at Capponfield, 3 at Moseley, 2 at Bentley and an undisclosed number at Leabrook (qqv), as well as the 4 at Chillington; for 1865–69 the Chillington entry brackets Leabrook, Bentley and Capponfield with Chillington; that for 1870 is said to include Chillington, Leabrook and Meadow, of which the latter is otherwise unrecorded in this period. The inclusion of Capponfield in 1862–69 appears to be an error, partly because the total of 9 furnaces listed under Chillington can be obtained by summing the figures for Moseley, Bentley and Chillington alone, but also because the entry for Goldshill in 1864–69 (owned, like Capponfield, by the Bagnalls) is similarly said to include Capponfield. Cf. further discussion under Capponfield. The number of furnaces 'Built' returned for Chillington in 1873–74 also suggests that other works are included, although this is not stated in *Mineral Statistics*. 1883: Dismantled.

Coneygre, Dudley Port, Staffs.　　[SO 9591]

Year	Owner	Built	In Blast
1847	Lord Ward	3	1
1849	Lord Ward	3	0
1852	Lord Ward	3	2
1854	Lord Ward	3	2
1855	Lord Ward	3	2
1856	Lord Ward	3	3
1857	Lord Ward	3	3
1858	Lord Ward	3	2
1859	Earl of Dudley	3	2
1860	Earl of Dudley	3	2
1861	Earl of Dudley	3	2
1862	Earl of Dudley	3	2
1863	Earl of Dudley	3	2
1864	Earl of Dudley	9	7
1865	Earl of Dudley	7	5
1866	Earl of Dudley	3	3
1867	Earl of Dudley	7	6
1868	Earl of Dudley	7	5
1869	Earl of Dudley	7	7
1870	Earl of Dudley	3	2
1871	Earl of Dudley	3	3
1872	Earl of Dudley	3	3
1873	Earl of Dudley	3	2
1874	Earl of Dudley	3	1
1875	Earl of Dudley	3	2
1876	Earl of Dudley	3	1
1877	Earl of Dudley	3	1
1878	Earl of Dudley	3	1
1879	Earl of Dudley	3	0
1880	Earl of Dudley	3	1
1881	Earl of Dudley	3	1
1882	Earl of Dudley	3	1
1883	Earl of Dudley	3	1
1884	Earl of Dudley	3	0
1885	Earl of Dudley	3	1
1886	Earl of Dudley	3	1
1887	Earl of Dudley	3	0
1888	Earl of Dudley	3	0
1889	Earl of Dudley	3	0
1890	Earl of Dudley	3	2
1891	Earl of Dudley	3	1
1892	Earl of Dudley	3	2
1893	Earl of Dudley	3	2
1894	Earl of Dudley	3	1
1895	Earl of Dudley	3	0

1849: Hunt lists 3 furnaces in blast. Truran: output 120 tons a week from each of 3 furnaces. 1864: furnace-numbers include Netherton and Level (New) (qqv). 1865, 1867–69: include Level (New).

Corbyn's Hall (Old), Staffs.　　[SO 9089]

Year	Owner	Built	In Blast
1825	Gibbons & Co.	3	3
1830	—	4	-
1839	Mathews & Dudley	2	2

Year	Owner	Built	In Blast
1841	Matthews & Dudley	4	3
1843	Matthews & Dudley	4	2
1847	Malins & Co.	4	2
1849	Galvanised Iron Co.	4	0
1852	William Mathews	4	3
1854	William Mathews & Co.	4	3
1855	William Mathews & Co.	4	3
1856	William Mathews & Co.	4	3
1857	William Mathews & Co.	4	3
1858	William Mathews & Co.	4	3
1859	William Mathews & Co.	4	0
1860	William Mathews & Co.	4	3
1861	William Mathews & Co.	4	2
1862	William Mathews & Co.	4	2
1863	William Mathews & Co.	4	3
1864	William Mathews & Co.	4	3
1865	William Mathews & Co.	4	3
1866	William Mathews & Co.	4	3
1867	William Mathews & Co.	4	2
1868	William Mathews & Co.	4	2
1869	William Mathews & Co.	2	2
1870	William Mathews & Co.	3	3
1871	Executors of late William Mathews	4	2
1872	Executors of late William Mathews	4	2
1873	Executors of late William Mathews	4	2
1874	Executors of late William Mathews	4	2
1875	Executors of late William Mathews	4	2
1876	William Mathews & Co. Ltd	3	2
1877	William Mathews & Co. Ltd	3	2
1878	William Mathews & Co. Ltd	3	1
1879	William Mathews & Co. Ltd	3	0
1880	William Mathews & Co. Ltd	3	1
1881	William Mathews & Co. Ltd	3	0
1882	William Mathews & Co. Ltd	3	0
1883	William Mathews & Co. Ltd	3	0
1884	William Mathews & Co. Ltd	3	0
1885	William Mathews & Co. Ltd	4	0
1886	William Mathews & Co. Ltd	3	0
1887	William Mathews & Co. Ltd	3	0
1888	William Mathews & Co. Ltd	3	0
1889	William Mathews & Co. Ltd	3	0
1890	William Mathews & Co. Ltd	3	0
1891	William Mathews & Co. Ltd	3	-

1823–30: nil return for 1823, notes that 3 furnaces were built in 1825 and 1 in 1829, which in 1830 had a total output of 7,350 tons p.a. 1825: weekly output 114 tons, 3,600 p.a., 'melting iron'. 1839: output 72 tons a week, 7,481 p.a. (actual); 'grey forge'; cold blast. 1841: output 250 tons a week. 1843: output 144 tons a week. In 1839 and 1847 two works are listed at Corbyn's Hall: the identification above is made on the basis of continuity of ownership at the newer works (qv). 1849: Hunt lists 6 furnaces in blast at Corbyn's Hall, which is probably a conflation of the two works. Truran: one of the three works listed under Corbyn's Hall is assigned an output of 120 tons a week from each of 3 furnaces which is presumably this site.

Corbyn's Hall (New) [I], Staffs. [SO 9089]

Year	Owner	Built	In Blast
1839	John Gibbons	2	2
1841	B. Gibbons	3	2
1843	B. Gibbons	2	2
1847	B. Gibbons	2	2
1849	Benjamin Gibbons	4	4
1852	B. Gibbons	3	3
1854	B. Gibbons	4	3
1855	B. Gibbons	4	4
1856	B. Gibbons	4	4
1857	B. Gibbons	4	3
1858	B. Gibbons	4	2
1859	Benjamin Gibbons	4	2
1860	Benjamin Gibbons	4	2
1861	Benjamin Gibbons	4	2
1862	Benjamin Gibbons	4	2
1863	Benjamin Gibbons	4	2
1864	Benjamin Gibbons Sen.	4	2
1865	Benjamin Gibbons Sen.	4	2
1866	Benjamin Gibbons Sen.	4	2
1867	Benjamin Gibbons Sen.	4	2
1868	Benjamin Gibbons Sen.	2	2
1869	Benjamin Gibbons Sen.	2	0
1870	Benjamin Gibbons Sen.	2	0
1871	Corbyn's Hall New Furnaces Co. Ltd	4	0
1872	Corbyn's Hall New Furnaces Co. Ltd	3	2
1873	Corbyn's Hall New Furnaces Co. Ltd	3	2
1874	Bromley Hall Coal & Iron Co. Ltd	4	1
1875	Bromley Hall Coal & Iron Co. Ltd	4	1
1876	Bromley Hall Coal & Iron Co. Ltd	4	1
1877	Bromley Hall Coal & Iron Co. Ltd	4	0
1878	Bromley Hall Coal & Iron Co. Ltd	4	0
1879	Bromley Hall Coal & Iron Co. Ltd	4	0
1880	Bromley Hall Coal & Iron Co. Ltd	4	0
1881	Bromley Hall Coal & Iron Co. Ltd	4	0
1882	Bromley Hall Coal & Iron Co. Ltd	4	0
1883	Bromley Hall Coal & Iron Co. Ltd	4	0
1884	J.S. Gibbons	4	0
1885	J.S. Gibbons	4	0

1839: output 86 tons a week, 8,976 p.a. (actual); 'cinder forge'; 1 hot blast, 1 cold blast. 1841: output 220 tons a week. 1843: an entry under Shut End appears to belong here. 1849: see previous entry. Truran: one of three works listed under Corbyn's Hall is assigned an output of 110 tons a week from each of 4 furnaces, which was presumably this site. 1874–75: two stray entries under Bromley Hall appear to be duplicates for those printed as above under Corbyn's Hall; in 1874 the furnaces were said to be under repair.

Corbyn's Hall (New) [II], Staffs. [SO 9089]

Year	Owner	Built	In Blast
1852	Hall, Holcroft & Pearson	1	1

Truran: one of the three works listed under Corbyn's Hall is assigned an output of 100 tons a week from a single furnace, presumably meaning this site. It may be identical with the works named Meadow (qv) listed in 1847.

Corngreaves, Staffs. [SO 9485]

Year	Owner	Built	In Blast
1847	British Iron Co.	2	2
1849	British Iron Co.	2	1
1852	New British Iron Co.	2	2
1854	New British Iron Co.	4	3
1855	New British Iron Co.	4	4

Year	Owner	Built	In Blast
1860	New British Iron Co.	6	4
1861	New British Iron Co.	6	4
1862	New British Iron Co.	6	3
1863	New British Iron Co.	6	4
1864	New British Iron Co.	6	4
1865	New British Iron Co.	6	3
1866	New British Iron Co.	6	5
1867	New British Iron Co.	6	4
1868	New British Iron Co.	6	4
1869	New British Iron Co.	6	4
1870	New British Iron Co.	6	4
1871	New British Iron Co.	6	4
1872	New British Iron Co.	6	4
1873	New British Iron Co.	6	3
1874	New British Iron Co.	6	2
1875	New British Iron Co.	6	3
1876	New British Iron Co.	6	3
1877	New British Iron Co.	6	1
1878	New British Iron Co.	6	2
1879	New British Iron Co.	6	1
1880	New British Iron Co.	6	2
1881	New British Iron Co.	6	1
1882	New British Iron Co.	6	3
1883	New British Iron Co. Ltd	6	3
1884	New British Iron Co. Ltd	6	3
1885	New British Iron Co. Ltd	5	3
1886	New British Iron Co. Ltd	5	2
1887	New British Iron Co. Ltd	5	2
1888	New British Iron Co. Ltd	5	3
1889	New British Iron Co. Ltd	5	3
1890	New British Iron Co. Ltd	5	3
1891	New British Iron Co. Ltd	5	2
1892	New British Iron Co. Ltd	5	3
1893	New British Iron Co. Ltd	5	2
1894	Corngreaves Furnace Co.	5	1
1895	Corngreaves Furnace Co.	3	1
1896	Corngreaves Furnace Co.	3	1
1897	Corngreaves Furnace Co.	3	2
1898	Corngreaves Furnace Co.	4	1
1899	W. Bassano & Co.	2	1
1900	Robert Fellows	2	1
1901	Robert Fellows	2	0
1902	Robert Fellows	2	0
1903	Robert Fellows	2	0
1904	Robert Fellows	2	0
1905	Robert Fellows	2	0
1906	Robert Fellows	2	0
1907	Robert Fellows	2	0
1908	Robert Fellows	2	0
1909	Robert Fellows	2	0
1910	Robert Fellows Ltd	4	0
1911	Robert Fellows Ltd	4	0
1912	Robert Fellows Ltd	4	0

1849: Hunt lists 2 furnaces in blast. Truran: output 100 tons a week from each of 2 furnaces.

Coseley, Staffs. [SO 9494]

Year	Owner	Built	In Blast
1823	—	2	-
1825	George Jones	3	3
1830	—	3	-
1839	George Jones	3	2
1841	George Jones	3	2
1843	George Jones	3	2
1847	G. Jones	2	2
1849	Turley Brothers	2	1
1852	J. & T. Turley	2	2
1854	J. & T. Turley	2	2
1855	J. & T. Turley	2	2
1856	J. & T. Turley	2	2
1857	J. & T. Turley	2	2
1858	Jos. & Thomas Turley	2	2
1859	Jos. & Thomas Turley	2	2
1860	Jos. & Thomas Turley	2	2
1861	Jos. & Thomas Turley	2	2
1862	Jos. & Thomas Turley	2	2
1863	Jos. & Thomas Turley	2	2
1864	W.E. Gibbons & Co.	2	2
1870	J. & T. Turley	2	2
1871	J. & T. Turley	2	2
1872	Joseph [&] Thomas Turley	2	2
1874	Thomas Turley & Sons	2	0
1875	Thomas Turley & Sons	2	1
1876	Thomas Turley & Sons	2	1
1877	Thomas Turley & Sons	2	0
1878	Thomas Turley & Sons	2	1
1879	Thomas Turley & Sons	2	1
1880	Thomas Turley & Sons	2	1
1881	Thomas Turley & Sons	2	1
1882	Thomas Turley & Sons	4	1
1883	Thomas Turley & Sons	2	1
1884	Thomas Turley & Sons	2	1
1885	Thomas Turley & Sons	2	1
1886	Thomas Turley & Sons	2	0
1887	Thomas Turley & Sons	2	0
1888	Thomas Turley & Sons	2	0
1889	Thomas Turley & Sons	2	0
1890	Wones (*sic; recte* Jones?) Brothers	2	0

1823–30: 2 furnaces in 1823; 1 built 1826; 3 furnaces with output of 10,140 tons p.a. in 1830. 1825: output 100 tons a week, 5,000 tons p.a., 'forge, very rough'; the B&W version of the list calls the works 'Coseley New', the Staffs RO version uses the name 'New Deepfield' (cf. Deepfields). 1839: output 75 tons a week, annual output for Coseley and Bilston (Old) (qv), 14,447 tons (actual); 'forge sale, in part'; cold blast. 1841: output 170 tons a week. 1843: 160 tons a week. 1849: Hunt lists 2 furnaces in blast. Truran: output 85 tons a week from each of 2 furnaces. In *Mineral Statistics* the works is called Coseley Hall in 1862–69 and Coseley Moor from 1874.

Coseley: see also Deepfields; Priorfield

Cotham, ?Staffs.

Year	Owner	Built	In Blast
1823	—	2	-
1825	Tristram	1	0
1830	—	2	-
1839	R. Mainwaring	1	1
1841	R. Manwarring	1	0
1849	John Mainwaring	0	0

1823–30: output nil in both years. 1825: called 'Cotam'; 'Not likely to work' (20 March 1826). 1839: an entry for 'Cotain' is assumed to belong here; output 40 tons a week, 2,080 p.a.

(estimated); 'foundry'; hot blast. 1841: output nil. 1849: works called 'Coltham'.

Crookhay, West Bromwich, Staffs. [SO 9993]

Year	Owner	Built	In Blast
1841	T. Davis	2	1
1843	T. Davis	2	1
1847	Dawes & Sons	3	3
1849	Thomas Davies	3	2
1852	T. Davies & Son	3	3
1854	T. Davies & Sons	4	3
1855	T. Davies & Sons	4	3
1856	T. Davies & Sons	4	0
1857	Geo. Thompson & Co.	4	1
1858	Geo. Thompson & Co.	4	2
1859	Geo. Thompson & Co.	4	0
1860	Geo. Thompson & Co.	4	2
1865	W. & G. Firmstone	4	2
1866	W. & G. Firmstone	4	2
1867	W. & G. Firmstone	4	3
1868	W. & G. Firmstone	4	3
1869	W. & G. Firmstone	4	2
1870	W. & G. Firmstone	4	2
1871	W. & G. Firmstone	3	2
1872	H.O. Firmstone	4	2
1873	W. & G. Firmstone	4	2
1874	W. & G. Firmstone	4	2
1875	W. & G. Firmstone	4	0
1876	W. & G. Firmstone	4	0
1877	H.O. Firmstone	4	0
1878	H.O. Firmstone	4	0
1879	H.O. Firmstone	4	0
1880	H.O. Firmstone	4	0
1881	H.O. Firmstone	4	0
1882	W. & G. Firmstone	2	0
1883	W. & G. Firmstone	4	0
1884	H.O. Firmstone	4	0
1885	H.O. Firmstone	4	0
1886	H.O. Firmstone	4	0
1887	H.O. Firmstone	4	0
1888	H.O. Firmstone	4	0

1841: output 90 tons a week. 1843: 90 tons a week. 1849: Hunt lists 3 furnaces in blast. Truran: output 110 tons a week from each of 3 furnaces.

Darlaston, Staffs. [SO 9797]

Year	Owner	Built	In Blast
1849	David Jones	1	1
1852	D. Jones	1	1

1849: called Darlaston Green by English, but placed here on the basis of the owner's name. Another works at Darlaston Green (qv) appears in 1852. Truran: output 110 tons a week from a single furnace. The works may be identical with that listed under Herberts Park, Bilston (qv) from 1854.

Darlaston (New): see Rough Hay

Darlaston Green, Staffs. [SO 9797]

Year	Owner	Built	In Blast
1847	Bills & Mills	1	1
1849	Mills & Co.	1	1
1852	S. Mills	3	3
1854	Samuel Mills	3	3
1855	Samuel Mills	3	3
1856	Samuel Mills	3	3
1857	Samuel Mills	3	3
1858	Samuel Mills	3	3
1859	Samuel Mills	3	3
1860	Samuel Mills	3	3
1861	Samuel Mills	3	3
1862	Samuel Mills	3	3
1863	Samuel Mills	3	3
1864	Darlaston Steel & Iron Co. Ltd	3	2
1865	Darlaston Steel & Iron Co. Ltd	3	3
1866	Darlaston Steel & Iron Co. Ltd	3	2
1867	Darlaston Steel & Iron Co. Ltd	3	2
1868	Darlaston Steel & Iron Co. Ltd	3	2
1869	Darlaston Steel & Iron Co. Ltd	3	3
1870	Darlaston Steel & Iron Co. Ltd	3	3
1871	Darlaston Steel & Iron Co. Ltd	3	2
1872	Darlaston Steel & Iron Co. Ltd	3	3
1873	Darlaston Steel & Iron Co. Ltd	3	2
1874	Darlaston Steel & Iron Co. Ltd	3	2
1875	Darlaston Steel & Iron Co. Ltd	3	2
1876	Darlaston Steel & Iron Co. Ltd	3	1
1877	Darlaston Steel & Iron Co. Ltd	3	0
1878	Darlaston Steel & Iron Co. Ltd	3	0
1879	Darlaston Steel & Iron Co. Ltd	1	0
1880	Darlaston Coal & Iron Co. Ltd	1	0
1881	Darlaston Coal & Iron Co. Ltd	1	0
1882	T. & I. Bradley	4	0
1883	T. & I. Bradley & Sons	2	1
1884	T. & I. Bradley & Sons	2	1
1885	T. & I. Bradley & Sons	2	1
1886	T. & I. Bradley & Sons	2	1
1887	T. & I. Bradley & Sons	2	1
1888	T. & I. Bradley & Sons	2	1
1889	T. & I. Bradley & Sons	2	2
1890	T. & I. Bradley & Sons	2	1
1891	T. & I. Bradley & Sons	2	2
1892	T. & I. Bradley & Sons	2	2
1893	T. & I. Bradley & Sons	2	2
1894	T. & I. Bradley & Sons	2	2
1895	T. & I. Bradley & Sons	2	1
1896	T. & I. Bradley & Sons	2	2
1897	T. & I. Bradley & Sons	2	2
1898	T. & I. Bradley & Sons	2	1
1899	T. & I. Bradley & Cons	2	1
1900	T. & I. Bradley & Sons	2	1
1901	T. & I. Bradley & Sons	2	1
1902	T. & I. Bradley & Sons	1	1
1903	T. & I. Bradley & Sons	1	1
1904	T. & I. Bradley & Sons	1	1
1905	T. & I. Bradley & Sons	1	1
1906	T. & I. Bradley & Sons	1	1
1907	T. & I. Bradley & Sons	1	1
1908	T. & I. Bradley & Sons	1	1
1909	T. & I. Bradley & Sons	1	1
1910	T. & I. Bradley & Sons	1	1
1911	T. & I. Bradley & Sons Ltd	1	1
1912	T. & I. Bradley & Sons Ltd	1	1
1913	T. & I. Bradley & Sons Ltd	1	1

Year	Owner	Built	In Blast
1921	Bradley & Foster Ltd	2	-
1922	Bradley & Foster Ltd	2	-
1923	Bradley & Foster Ltd	2	-
1924	Bradley & Foster Ltd	2	-
1925	Bradley & Foster Ltd	2	-
1926	Bradley & Foster Ltd	2	-
1927	Bradley & Foster Ltd	2	-
1928	Bradley & Foster Ltd	2	-
1929	Bradley & Foster Ltd	2	-
1930	Bradley & Foster Ltd	2	-
1931	Bradley & Foster Ltd	2	-
1932	Bradley & Foster Ltd	2	-
1933	Bradley & Foster Ltd	2	-
1934	Bradley & Foster Ltd	2	-

Truran: output 95 tons a week from each of 3 furnaces. 1883: at work 6 months. Furnaces dismantled during 1935.

Deepdale: see Dibdale

Deepfields (Old), Bilston, Staffs. [SO 9494]

Year	Owner	Built	In Blast
1794	Stokes, Pemberton & Co.	2	-
1796	—	2	2
1805	Stokes	2	2
1810	Stokes & Co.	2	2
1823	—	2	-
1825	Pemberton & Co.	2	2
1830	—	2	-
1839	Pemberton & Co.	3	2
1841	Pemberton & Co.	2	1
1843	Pemberton & Co.	3	1
1847	Pemberton & Co.	3	2
1849	Benton & Pemberton	3	2
1852	Benton & Pemberton	2	2
1854	Benton & Pemberton	2	2
1855	Benton & Pemberton	2	2
1856	Benton & Pemberton	2	2
1857	Benton & Pemberton	2	2
1858	Benton & Pemberton	3	1
1859	Thomas H. Pemberton	3	1
1860	Thomas H. Pemberton	3	0
1861	Samuel Pemberton	3	0
1862	Samuel Pemberton	3	0
1863	Samuel Pemberton	3	1
1864	Samuel Pemberton	3	1
1865	Deepfields Iron Co.	3	1
1866	Deepfields Iron Co.	3	2
1867	Deepfields Iron Co.	3	1
1868	Deepfields Iron Co.	3	1
1869	Deepfields Iron Co.	3	1
1870	Deepfields Iron Co.	3	2
1871	Gibbons & Elkington	3	2
1872	Gibbons & Elkington	3	2
1873	Samuel Pemberton	3	2
1874	Samuel Pemberton	3	1
1875	Deepfields Iron Co.	3	1
1876	Deepfields Iron Co.	3	1
1877	Deepfields Iron Co.	3	0
1878	Deepfields Iron Co.	3	0
1879	Deepfields Iron Co.	3	0
1880	Deepfields Iron Co.	3	0
1881	Deepfields Iron Co.	3	0
1882	Deepfields Iron Co.	2	0
1883	Deepfields Iron Co.	3	0
1884	Deepfields Iron Co.	3	0
1885	Deepfields Iron Co.	3	0
1886	Deepfields Iron Co.	3	0
1887	Unoccupied	3	0
1888	Unoccupied	3	0
1889	Unoccupied	3	0
1890	Unoccupied	3	0
1891	Unoccupied	3	0

The ground landlord in 1794, when the works was called 'Deepfield or Coasley', was Mr Penn & Co.; the furnaces were coke-fired, blown by engine and built in 1788. The only forge plant was 4 fineries. 1796: Excise and actual output 2,600 tons p.a. (i.e. 50 tons a week), Exact Return 2,526 tons. 1805: 3,660 tons. 1823–30: nil output both years. 1825: weekly output 90 tons, 4,500 p.a., 'No 3 melting' (B&W text); 'No 3 for sale' (Staffs RO). 1839: output 50 tons a week, 5,200 p.a. (estimated); 'forge, sale'; hot and cold blast. 1841: output 60 tons a week. 1843: output 65 tons a week. See also next entry. The two works at Deepfields in 1854 have been assigned to this entry and the next on the basis of continuity of ownership. Truran: output from one of the two works listed under Deepfield 100 tons a week from each of 2 furnaces, which is presumably this site. See also Coseley.

Deepfields (New), Bilston, Staffs. [SO 9494]

Year	Owner	Built	In Blast
1852	Groucutt & Co.	1	1
1854	S. Groucutt & Sons	1	1
1855	S. Groucutt & Sons	1	1
1856	S. Groucutt & Sons	1	1
1857	S. Groucutt & Sons	1	1
1859	S. Groucutt & Sons	-	-
1860	S. Groucutt & Sons	0	0
1861	S. Groucutt & Sons	-	-
1862	S. Groucutt & Sons	1	0
1863	S. Groucutt & Sons	1	0
1864	Samuel Groucutt & Sons	1	0

Cf. previous entry for the distinction between the two works listed at Deepfields in 1854. Truran: one of the two works listed at Deepfields had an output of 100 tons a week from a single furnace, which is presumably this site.

Dibdale Bank, Staffs. [SO 9291]

Year	Owner	Built	In Blast
1805	Dixon & Co.	1	1
1810	Dixon & Co.	1	1
1823	—	1	-
1825	Crockett	1	1
1830	—	1	-

1805: output 300 tons p.a. 1825: 35 tons a week, 2,100 tons p.a., comment dated 20 March 1826: 'Out last week' (B&W text); 'Blows out next week' (Staffs RO). 1823: a furnace named 'Deepdale' appears to belong here. Output 2,084 tons p.a. in 1823, 1,634 tons in 1830.

Dixon's Green, Dudley, Worcs. [SO 9589]

Year	Owner	Built	In Blast
1849	Joseph Haden	1	1
1852	J. Haden	2	1
1854	William Haden	1	1
1855	William Haden	1	1
1856	William Haden	1	1
1857	William Haden	1	1
1858	William Haden	1	1
1859	William Haden	1	0
1860	William Haden	1	1
1861	William Haden	1	0
1862	William Haden & Son	1	1
1863	William Haden & Son	1	1
1864	William Haden & Son	1	1
1865	William Haden & Son	1	1
1866	William Haden & Son	1	1
1867	Assignees of William Haden & Co.	1	0
1868	John Jones	1	0
1869	John Jones	1	0
1870	John Jones	1	0
1871	Walsall Iron Co.	1	1
1872	Walsall Iron Co.	2	2

Truran: output 110 tons a week from each of 2 furnaces.

Dudley Port (Old), Staffs. [SO 9691]

Year	Owner	Built	In Blast
1794	Mr Parkes	1	-
1796	—	1	1
1805	Parkers	1	1
1810	Parkes	1	1
1823	—	1	-
1825	Parkes	1	1
1830	—	1	-
1839	Earl of Dudley's Trustees	2	2
1841	Earl [of] Dudley's Trustees	2	1
1843	[Trustees of] Earl of Dudley	2	1
1847	J. Hopkins & Son	1	1
1849	— Hopkins	2	2
1852	Hopkins & Son	2	2
1854	Hopkins & Son	2	2
1855	Hopkins & Son	2	2
1856	Hopkins & Son	2	2
1857	Hopkins & Son	2	2
1858	Hopkins & Son	2	2
1859	Hopkins & Son	2	2
1860	Hopkins & Son	2	2
1861	Hopkins & Son	2	2
1862	Hopkins & Son	1	1

The 1794 list notes that the furnace was coke-fired and blown by engine but does not give a date of building or name the ground landlord. 1796: Excise and actual output 1,040 tons p.a. (i.e. 20 tons a week), Exact Return 869 tons. 1805: 1,196 tons p.a. 1823–30: 2,340 tons in both years. 1825: 40 tons a week, 2,000 tons p.a., 'used by themselves'. 1839: 45 tons a week, 4,250 p.a. (actual); 'forge, sale'; cold blast. 1841: 95 tons a week. 1843: 50 tons a week. The 1847 and 1852 lists, unlike those of the 1820s, 1839 and 1854, includes only one works at Dudley Port, which has been assumed to be the older site; the two entries from the 1854 list have then been assigned on the basis of continuity of ownership. Neither of the owners' names listed in 1839 fits those of adjacent lists for either works and the division is therefore arbitrary. 1849: Hunt lists one works at Dudley Port, with 3 furnaces in blast, which may be a conflation of this site and the next. Truran: one works listed under Dudley Port, output 110 tons a week from each of 2 furnaces; presumably this entry could refer either to this site or the next entry.

Dudley Port (New), Staffs. [SO 9691]

Year	Owner	Built	In Blast
1825	J.T. Fereday	2	2
1830	—	2	-
1839	D. & G. Horton	2	2
1843	T. Morris	1	1
1849	Thomas Morris	1	1
1854	Thomas Morris	2	2
1855	Thomas Morris & Son	2	2
1856	Thomas Morris & Son	2	2
1857	Thomas Morris & Son	2	2
1858	Thomas Morris & Son	2	2
1859	Thomas Morris & Son	2	2
1860	Thomas Morris & Son	0	0
1861	Thomas Morris & Son	-	-
1862	Thomas Morris & Son	2	0
1863	Thomas Morris & Son	2	0

1823–30: nil return for 1823, 2 furnaces built in 1824, output 4,060 tons p.a. in 1830. 1825: output 100 tons a week, 5,000 tons p.a.; 'Forge, consumed by themselves'. 1839: output 50 tons a week, 5,200 p.a. (estimated); 'foundry'; hot blast. 1843: output 60 tons a week. Cf. previous entry concerning the lists of 1839, 1847, 1849 and 1854 and Truran.

Dudley Port [III], Staffs. [SO 9691]

Year	Owner	Built	In Blast
1841	Joseph Gill	2	2
1843	J. Gill	2	1

1841: output 100 tons a week. 1843: output 50 tons a week.

Dudley Port [IV], Staffs. [SO 9691]

Year	Owner	Furnaces built	In Blast
1870	George Vernon	2	1
1871	George Vernon	3	0

Dudley Port [V], Staffs. [SO 9691]

Year	Owner	Built	In Blast
1870	J. & G. Onions	1	1
1871	J. & G. Onions	1	1
1872	J. & G. Onions	2	2
1873	J. & G. Onions	2	2
1874	J. & G. Onions	1	1
1875	J. & G. Onions	1	1

Dudley Port [VI], Staffs. [SO 9691]

Year	Owner	Built	In Blast
1892	Dudley Port Furnace Co.	1	0
1893	Dudley Port Furnace Co.	1	0
1894	Dudley Port Furnace Co.	1	0
1895	Dudley Port Furnace Co.	1	0
1896	Dudley Port Furnace Co.	1	0
1897	Dudley Port Furnace Co.	1	0
1898	Dudley Port Furnace Co.	1	0
1899	Dudley Port Furnace Co.	1	0
1900	Dudley Port Furnace Co.	1	0
1901	Dudley Port Furnace Co.	1	0
1902	Dudley Port Furnace Co.	1	0

The furnace-numbers for 1872–73 include those for Stour Valley Ironworks (qv). 1875: an isolated entry in *Mineral Statistics* for a works at Horseley Heath appears to belong here.

Dudley Wood, Worcs. [SO 9486]

Year	Owner	Built	In Blast
1823	—	4	-
1825	British Iron Co.	-	-
1830	—	4	-
1839	British Iron Co.	4	3
1841	British Iron Co.	4	2
1843	British Iron Co.	4	2
1847	British Iron Co.	6	2
1849	British Iron Co.	4	1
1852	New British Iron Co.	4	2
1854	New British Iron Co.	4	2
1855	New British Iron Co.	4	2
1856	New British Iron Co.	4	2
1857	New British Iron Co.	4	2
1858	New British Iron Co.	4	4
1859	New British Iron Co.	6	4
1863	N. Hingley & Co.	4	2
1864	N. Hingley & Co.	3	2
1865	N. Hingley & Sons	2	2
1866	N. Hingley & Sons	2	2
1867	N. Hingley & Sons	4	2
1868	N. Hingley & Sons	4	2
1869	N. Hingley & Sons	4	2
1870	N. Hingley & Sons	4	2

1823–30: output of 10,467 tons p.a. in 1823, 8,664 tons in 1830. 1825: see Netherton (Old) and Withymoor. 1839: output 70 tons a week, 10,920 p.a. (estimated); 'forge'; cold blast. 1841: output 160 tons a week. 1843: 164 tons a week. 1847 and 1859: furnace-numbers above include Dudley Wood and Netherton (Old). 1849: Hunt lists 2 furnaces in blast.

Duffield: see Bilston

Eagle Furnaces, ?Staffs.

Year	Owner	Built	In Blast
1823	—	2	-
1825	W. Aston	2	2
1830	—	2	-
1839	Eagle Furnace Co.	2	2
1841	Eagle Furnace Co.	2	0
1843	Eagle Furnace Co.	2	0

1823: output 4,900 tons p.a. 1830: 6,656 tons. 1825: output 105 tons a week, 5,500 tons p.a., comment (dated 20 March 1826): 'Out last week I believe'. The B&W text lists one furnace in blast, the Staffs RO version has two. 1839: output 60 tons a week, 6,009 p.a. (actual); 'forge and castings'; hot blast. 1841, 1843: output nil. Cf. also Toll End.

Ettingshall, Bilston, Staffs. [SO 9396]

Year	Owner	Built	In Blast
1839	T. Banks & Sons	2	2
1841	T. Banks & Sons	2	1
1843	T. Banks & Sons	2	2
1847	Banks & Son	2	1
1849	Thomas Banks & Son	2	1
1852	T. Banks & Son	2	1
1854	T. Banks & Son	2	1
1855	T. Banks & Son	2	1
1856	T. Banks & Son	2	1
1857	T. Banks & Son	2	1
1858	T. Banks & Son	2	1
1859	T. Banks & Son	3	3
1860	T. Banks & Son	0	0
1861	T. Banks & Son	-	-
1862	T. Banks & Son	3	0
1863	T. Banks & Son	3	0

1839: output 66 tons a week, 6,877 (actual) p.a.; 'forge'; cold blast. 1841: 80 tons a week. 1843: 140 tons a week. 1849: Hunt lists 2 furnaces in blast. Truran: 110 tons a week from each of 2 furnaces.

Ettingshall: see also Bilston

Fiery Holes, ?Staffs. [SO 9191?]

Year	Owner	Built	In Blast
1823	—	1	-
1825	Z. Parkes & Co.	1	1
1830	—	1	-

1823–30: nil output in 1823, 1,634 tons p.a. in 1830. 1825: works called 'Gornal or Fire Holes' in B&W text (cf. Gornalwood); 'Fiery Hole' in Staffs RO version; output 50 tons a week, 2,500 tons p.a. (thus B&W; 2,300 tons in Staffs RO), 'used by themselves'.

Glebefields, [?Tipton, Staffs.] [SO 9593?]

Year	Owner	Built	In Blast
1823	—	1	-
1825	Thomas Price	1	0
1830	—	1	-

Neither the 1823–30 list, which calls the works 'Glebe', nor that of 1825 lists records any output.

Goldenhill: see under North Staffordshire

Golds Green: see Goldshill

Goldshill, West Bromwich, Staffs. [SO 9893]

Year	Owner	Built	In Blast
1823	—	2	-
1830	—	3	-
1839	J. Bagnall & Sons	3	3
1841	J. Bagnall & Sons	3	2
1843	J. Bagnall & Son	3	2
1847	Bagnall & Sons	3	2
1849	Bagnall & Sons	3	3
1852	J. Bagnall & Sons	3	3
1854	John Bagnall & Sons	3	3
1855	John Bagnall & Sons	3	3
1856	John Bagnall & Sons	3	3
1857	John Bagnall & Sons	3	3
1858	John Bagnall & Sons	3	3
1859	John Bagnall & Sons	3	3
1860	John Bagnall & Sons	3	2
1861	John Bagnall & Sons	3	2
1862	John Bagnall & Sons	5	2
1863	John Bagnall & Sons	5	2
1864	John Bagnall & Sons	5	4
1865	John Bagnall & Sons	5	4
1866	John Bagnall & Sons	5	3
1867	John Bagnall & Sons	5	4
1868	John Bagnall & Sons	5	4
1869	John Bagnall & Sons	5	3
1870	John Bagnall & Sons	3	2
1871	John Bagnall & Sons	3	2
1872	John Bagnall & Sons	3	1
1873	John Bagnall & Sons	3	1
1874	John Bagnall & Sons	5	1
1875	John Bagnall & Sons Ltd	3	1
1876	John Bagnall & Sons Ltd	6	1
1877	John Bagnall & Sons Ltd	3	0
1878	John Bagnall & Sons Ltd	5	0
1879	John Bagnall & Sons Ltd	3	2
1880	John Bagnall & Sons Ltd	3	2
1881	John Bagnall & Sons Ltd	3	1
1882	John Bagnall & Sons Ltd	3	0

1823–30: notes building of third furnace in 1825; output in 1823 was 4,888 tons p.a., in 1830 9,412 tons. 1839: output 86 tons a week, 13,512 p.a. (actual); 'hard forge'; cold blast. 1841: output (at Goldsgreen) 170 tons a week. 1843: output (at Goldsgreen) 180 tons a week. The *Mineral Statistics* entry for 1854 is the first list to use the name 'Goldshill', rather than 'Golds Green'; the latter name, used in 1839 and 1847, reappears in 1859–67 and 1872–75, whereas the site is called Goldshill (or Gold(s) Hill) on other occasions: the two have been assumed to be identical on the basis of Bagnalls' ownership. Truran: output (at Goldshill) 110 tons from each of 3 furnaces. In 1864–69 the furnace-numbers at Goldshill also include Capponfield (qv); confusingly, the entry for Capponfield for 1862–69 is bracketed with Chillington (qv), apparently in error. In the table above, the figure in the 'Built' column for 1862–63 has been inflated by 2 on the assumption that Capponfield was in fact included with Goldshill, rather than with Chillington, in these years also.

Gornal: see Fiery Hole

Gornalwood, Staffs. [SO 9190]

Year	Owner	Built	In Blast
1796	—	1	0
1805	Banks	1	1
1810	Banks & Co.	1	1
1823	—	1	-
1825	J. Bradley & Co.	1	1
1830	—	1	-

1796: 1 furnace, out of blast. 1805: output 432 tons p.a. 1823–30: 1,671 tons in 1823, nil in 1830. 1825: 45 tons a week, 2,300 p.a., 'used by themselves'. The furnace is listed as out of blast in the B&W text, in blast in the Staffs RO version.

Gospel Oak, Staffs. [SO 9694]

Year	Owner	Built	In Blast
1794	Hawkes	1	-
1796	—	1	1
1805	Read	2	2
1810	J. Read	3	3
1823	—	2	-
1825	Samuel Walker & Co.	2	2
1830	—	4	-
1839	J. Bagnall & Sons	2	0

The ground landlord's name in 1794 appears to read 'Bank & Dernregin'; the furnace was coke-fired and blown by engine; the date of building is given as 1794 (the entry appears to be a late addition to the list). This may explain Gosepl Oak's omission from the early versions of the 1796 list, in which the only output figure is an Exact Return of 1,613 tons. 1805: output 4,667 tons p.a. 1823–30: output 5,312 tons p.a. in 1823, 2 furnaces built 1827, output 6,840 tons in 1830. 1825: 95 tons a week, 4,500 tons p.a.; 'Forge (own use)'. 1839: 'Now pulled down', but an output of 2,804 tons p.a. (actual) is listed.

Graveyard, Staffs. [SO 9190]

Year	Owner	Built	In Blast
1796	—	1	1
1805	Hawkes & Co.	2	1
1810	Hawkes & Co.	2	2
1823	—	1	-

Year	Owner	Built	In Blast
1825	Dudley Bagley	2	1
1830	—	1	-

1796: Excise output 1,260 tons p.a.; 1,000 tons actual, Exact Return 213 tons. 1805: 1,274 tons. 1823–30: output nil in both years. 1825: 25 tons a week, 1,250 tons p.a., 'melting iron'.

Green Lane, Walsall, Staffs. [SK 0000]

Year	Owner	Built	In Blast
1854	Highway Brothers	2	2
1855	T. & C. Highway	2	2
1856	T. & C. Highway	2	2
1857	T. & C. Highway	2	2
1858	T. & C. Highway	2	2
1859	T. & C. Highway	2	0
1860	T. & C. Highway	2	0
1861	T. & C. Highway	-	-
1862	T. & C. Highway	2	0
1863	T. & C. Highway	2	0
1864	T. & C. Highway	2	0
1865	T. & C. Highway	2	0
1866	T. & C. Highway	2	0
1867	John Jones	2	2
1868	John Jones	2	2
1869	John Jones	2	2
1870	Walsall Iron Co.	2	2
1871	John Jones & Son	2	2
1872	Walsall Iron Co.	2	2
1873	Walsall Iron Co.	2	1
1874	Walsall Iron Co.	2	1
1875	Walsall Iron Co.	2	1
1876	Walsall Iron Co.	2	1
1877	Walsall Iron Co.	2	1
1878	Walsall Iron Co.	2	2
1879	Walsall Iron Co.	2	1
1880	Walsall Iron Co.	2	1
1881	Walsall Iron Co.	2	1
1882	Walsall Iron Co., in liquidation	2	0
1883	Jones Brothers	2	0
1884	Jones Brothers	2	0
1885	Jones Brothers	2	1
1886	Jones Brothers	2	1
1887	Jones Brothers	2	1
1888	Jones Brothers	2	1
1889	Jones Brothers	2	1
1890	Jones Brothers	2	1

This site is called Bloxwich, Green Lane(s), in 1854–66; in 1867 the entry is for Green Lanes (but alphabetised as though it were Bloxwich); in 1868–69 the name Bloxwich is used again and in 1870 there are duplicate entries under both Bloxwich and Green Lane, with the owners named as John Jones and the Walsall Iron Co. respectively. From 1871 the heading Green Lanes is used, corrected to Green Lane from 1874. There are two isolated entries under Walsall in 1874–75 for a works owned by John Jones, with 2 furnaces, neither in blast in 1874 and 1 in 1875. These appear to be duplicates for Green Lane.

Groveland, Smethick, Staffs. [SO 9691]

Year	Owner	Built	In Blast
1854	H. Richards	1	1
1855	H. Richards	1	1
1856	H. Richards	2	1
1857	H. Rickards	2	1
1859	H. Rickards	-	-
1860	G.H. & A. Hickman	1	0
1863	Geo. H. Hickman	1	1
1864	Geo. H. Hickman	1	0
1865	Geo. H. Hickman	1	0
1866	Geo. H. Hickman	1	0
1867	Geo. H. Hickman	1	1
1868	Geo. H. Hickman	1	1
1869	Geo. H. Hickman	1	1
1870	Geo. H. Hickman	1	1
1871	Geo. H. Hickman	1	1
1872	Geo. H. Hickman	2	2
1873	Geo. H. Hickman	2	2
1874	Geo. H. Hickman	0	0
1875	Geo. H. Hickman	1	0
1876	Geo. H. Hickman	1	0
1877	Geo. H. Hickman	1	0
1878	Geo. H. Hickman	1	0
1879	Geo. H. Hickman	1	0
1880	Geo. H. Hickman	1	0
1881	Geo. H. Hickman	1	0
1882	G.H. Hickman	1	0
1883	G.H. Hickman	1	0
1884	Unoccupied	1	0
1885	Unoccupied	1	0
1886	Unoccupied	1	0
1887	Unoccupied	1	0
1888	Unoccupied	1	0

Hallfields, Staffs.

Year	Owner	Built	In Blast
1823	—	1	-
1825	Robert Cooper	1	1
1830	—	1	-
1849	B. Gibbons	1	1
1852	B. Gibbons jun.	1	1
1854	J.B. Gibbons jun.	1	1
1855	B. Gibbons jun.	1	1
1856	B. Gibbons jun.	1	1
1857	B. Gibbons jun.	1	1
1858	B. Gibbons jun.	1	1
1859	B. Gibbons jun.	1	1
1860	Moorcroft Colliery Co.	1	0
1861	Moorcroft Colliery Co.	-	-
1862	Moorcroft Colliery Co.	1	1
1863	Moorcroft Colliery Co.	1	0
1864	Moorcroft Colliery Co.	1	0
1865	Moorcroft Colliery Co.	1	0
1866	Moorcroft Colliery Co.	1	0
1867	Moorcroft Colliery	1	0
1868	Moorcroft Colliery	1	0
1869	Moorcroft Colliery	1	0
1870	Moorcroft Colliery	1	0

1823–30: output 2,454 tons p.a. in both years. 1825: 50 tons a week, 2,340 tons p.a., 'Forge, consumed by themselves in part'. Truran: output 100 tons a week from a single furnace.

Hange, Tividale, Staffs. [SO 9690]

Year	Owner	Built	In Blast
1867	Round Brothers	2	2
1868	Round Brothers	2	1
1869	Round Brothers	2	1
1870	Round Brothers	2	1
1871	Round Brothers	2	2
1872	Round Brothers	2	2
1873	Round Brothers	2	2
1874	Round Brothers	2	1
1875	Round Brothers	2	1
1876	Round Brothers	2	1
1877	Round Brothers	2	1
1878	Round Brothers	2	1
1879	Round Brothers	2	0
1880	Round Brothers	2	1
1881	Round Brothers	2	1
1882	Round Brothers	2	1
1883	Round Brothers	2	1
1884	Round Brothers	2	1
1885	Round Brothers	2	1
1886	Round Brothers	2	1
1887	Round Brothers	2	1
1888	Round Brothers	2	2
1889	Round Brothers	2	2
1890	Round Brothers	2	2
1891	Round Brothers	2	2
1892	Round Brothers	2	2
1893	Round Brothers	2	2
1894	Round Brothers	2	1
1895	Round Brothers	2	1
1896	Round Brothers	2	1
1897	Round Brothers	2	1
1898	Round Brothers	2	1
1899	Round Brothers	2	1
1900	Round Brothers	2	1

The works appears under Tividale in 1867, thereafter Hange or The Hange, Tividale.

Hatherton, Bloxwich, Staffs. [SJ 9902]

Year	Owner	Built	In Blast
1849	W. Fryer	1	1
1852	W. Fryer	2	1
1854	Highway Brothers	2	2
1855	Highway Brothers	2	0
1856	Highway Brothers	2	2
1857	Highway Brothers	2	2
1858	Highway Brothers	2	1
1859	G.B. Thorneycroft & Co.	2	2
1860	William F. Fryer	2	1
1861	William F. Fryer	2	1
1862	William F. Fryer	2	1
1863	William F. Fryer	2	1
1864	William F. Fryer	2	1
1865	William F. Fryer	2	1
1866	William F. Fryer	2	1
1867	William F. Fryer	2	1
1868	William F. Fryer	2	1
1869	William F. Fryer	2	1
1870	George & Richard Thomas	2	1
1871	George & Richard Thomas	2	2
1872	George & Richard Thomas	2	2
1873	George & Richard Thomas	2	2
1874	George & Richard Thomas	2	1
1875	George & Richard Thomas	2	1
1876	George & Richard Thomas	2	1
1877	George & Richard Thomas	2	2
1878	George & Richard Thomas	2	1
1879	George & Richard Thomas	2	1
1880	George & Richard Thomas	2	0
1881	George & Richard Thomas	2	2
1882	George & Richard Thomas	2	2
1883	George & Richard Thomas	2	1
1884	George & Richard Thomas	2	1
1885	George & Richard Thomas	2	1
1886	George & Richard Thomas	2	1
1887	George & Richard Thomas	2	2
1888	George & Richard Thomas	2	2
1889	George & Richard Thomas	2	2
1890	George & Richard Thomas	2	1
1891	George & Richard Thomas	2	1
1892	George & Richard Thomas	2	1
1893	George & Richard Thomas	2	1
1894	George & Richard Thomas	2	0
1895	George & Richard Thomas	2	0
1896	George & Richard Thomas	2	0
1897	George & Richard Thomas	2	1
1898	George & Richard Thomas	2	1
1899	George & Richard Thomas	2	1
1900	George & Richard Thomas	2	1
1901	George & Richard Thomas	2	1
1902	George & Richard Thomas	2	1
1903	George & Richard Thomas	2	1
1904	George & Richard Thomas	2	1
1905	George & Richard Thomas	2	1
1906	George & Richard Thomas	2	1
1907	George & Richard Thomas	2	1
1908	George & Richard Thomas	2	1
1909	George & Richard Thomas	2	1
1910	George & Richard Thomas	2	1
1911	George & Richard Thomas	2	1
1912	George & Richard Thomas	2	1
1913	George & Richard Thomas	2	1
1921	G. & R. Thomas	2	-
1922	G. & R. Thomas	2	-
1923	G. & R. Thomas	2	-
1924	G. & R. Thomas	2	-
1925	G. & R. Thomas	2	-
1926	G. & R. Thomas	2	-
1927	G. & R. Thomas	2	-
1928	G. & R. Thomas	2	-
1929	G. & R. Thomas	2	-
1930	G. & R. Thomas	2	-
1931	G. & R. Thomas	2	-
1932	G. & R. Thomas	2	-
1933	G. & R. Thomas Ltd	2	-
1934	G. & R. Thomas Ltd	2	-
1935	G. & R. Thomas Ltd	2	-
1936	G. & R. Thomas Ltd	2	-
1937	G. & R. Thomas Ltd	2	-
1938	G. & R. Thomas Ltd	2	-
1939	G. & R. Thomas Ltd	2	-
1940	G. & R. Thomas Ltd	2	-
1941	G. & R. Thomas Ltd	2	-
1942	G. & R. Thomas Ltd	2	-
1943	G. & R. Thomas Ltd	2	-
1944	G. & R. Thomas Ltd	2	-
1945	G. & R. Thomas Ltd	2	-
1946	G. & R. Thomas Ltd	2	-

| 1947 | G. & R. Thomas Ltd | 2 | - |

1849: listed by English (only) under Bloxwich. Truran: output 100 tons a week from each of 2 furnaces. 1883: Production estimated.

Herberts Park, Bilston, Staffs. [SO 9497]

Year	Owner	Built	In Blast
1854	David Jones	1	1
1855	David Jones	1	1
1856	David Jones	1	1
1857	David Jones	1	1
1858	David Jones	1	0
1859	David Jones	-	-
1860	David Jones	1	1
1861	David Jones	1	0
1862	David Jones	1	1
1863	David Jones	1	1
1864	David Jones	1	1
1865	David Jones	1	1
1866	David Jones	1	1
1867	David Jones	1	0
1868	David Jones	1	0
1869	David Jones	1	0
1870	David Jones	1	0
1871	David Jones & Sons	1	0
1872	David Jones & Sons	1	1
1873	David Jones & Sons	1	1
1874	David Jones & Sons	1	1
1875	David Jones & Sons	1	0
1876	David Jones & Sons	1	0
1877	David Jones & Sons	1	0
1878	David Jones & Sons	1	0
1879	David Jones & Sons	1	0
1880	David Jones & Sons	1	0
1881	David Jones & Sons	1	0
1882	David Jones & Sons	1	0
1883	David Jones & Sons	1	0
1884	David Jones & Sons	1	0
1885	David Jones & Sons	1	0

See Darlaston for what may be earlier references to this works.

Highfields, Staffs. [SO 9550]

Year	Owner	Built	In Blast
1823	—	2	-
1825	J. & W. Firmstone's Trustees	2	0
1830	—	2	-

1823–30 and 1825: nil output in all three years.

Horseley, Tipton, Staffs. [SO 9792]

Year	Owner	Built	In Blast
1823	—	2	-
1825	Oliver & Co.	2	2
1830	—	2	-
1839	Horseley Co.	2	1
1841	Horseley Co.	2	1
1843	Horseley Iron Co.	2	0
1847	J. Hartland	2	2
1849	Horseley Co.	2	2
1852	Colbourn & Co.	2	2
1854	Colbourn & Sons	2	2
1855	Colbourn & Sons	2	2
1856	Colbourn & Sons	2	2
1857	Colbourn & Sons	4	3
1858	Colbourn & Sons	4	3
1859	Colbourn & Sons	4	0
1860	Colbourn & Sons	4	3
1861	Colbourn & Sons	4	3
1862	John Colbourn & Sons	4	3
1863	John Colbourn & Sons	4	3
1864	John Colbourn & Sons	2	2
1865	John Colbourn & Sons	2	2
1866	John Colbourn & Sons	2	1
1867	John Colbourn & Sons	2	2
1868	John Colbourn & Sons	-	-
1869	John Colbourn & Sons	-	-
1870	John Colbourn & Sons	-	-
1871	John Colbourn & Sons	2	2
1872	John Colbourn & Sons	-	-
1873	John Colbourn & Sons	-	-
1874	John Colbourn & Sons	-	-
1875	John Colbourn & Sons	-	-
1876	John Colbourn & Sons	-	-
1877	John Colbourn & Sons	-	-
1878	John Colbourn & Sons	2	0
1879	John Colbourn & Sons	-	-
1880	John Colbourn & Sons	-	-
1881	John Colbourn & Sons	-	-
1882	John Colbourn, Sons & Co.	2	0
1883	John Colbourn, Sons & Co.	2	0
1884	John Colbourn, Sons & Co.	2	0
1885	John Colbourn, Sons & Co.	2	0
1886	John Colbourn, Sons & Co.	2	0
1887	John Colbourn, Sons & Co.	2	0
1888	John Colbourn, Sons & Co.	2	0

1823–30: output 4,368 tons p.a. in 1823, 4,680 tons in 1830. 1825: 90 tons a week, 4,940 tons p.a., 'casting trade'. 1839: output 60 tons a week, 3,064 p.a. (actual); 'castings'; cold blast. 1841: output 55 tons a week. 1843: output nil. In 1847 (only) there is a separate entry for a works at Horsley Hole (qv). 1849: owner's name printed as 'Horseley & Co.' by English; Hunt lists 3 furnaces in blast at Horseley, which may include this works and that listed here as Horsley Hole (qv). Truran: output 100 tons a week from each of 2 furnaces. In 1868–70, 1872–77 and 1879–81 furnace-numbers for Horseley are printed with those for Park Lane (qv).

Horseley Fields, Staffs.

A note prefacing the 1841 list for South Staffs. refers to one furnace then building by 'Mr Morris' at 'Horsley Field'. This is presumably Thomas Morris, who can be found at several other works in the district around this date, but not Osier Bed (qv), the name under which the later works at Horseley Fields is generally known.

Horseley Heath: see Dudley Port (V)

Horseley Hole, Staffs. [SO 9792]

Year	Owner	Built	In Blast
1847	Chillington & Co.	2	2

Cf. Horseley. The owner's name at Horseley Hole should possibly not include the ampersand.

Ketley's, Dudley, Worcs. [SO 9390?]

Year	Owner	Built	In Blast
1841	Blackwell, Jones & Co.	2	1
1843	Blackwell, Jones & Co.	2	1
1847	Jones & Oakes	3	0
1849	Jones & Oakes	3	0
1852	B. Gibbons	3	3
1854	B. Gibbons	3	2
1855	B. Gibbons	3	3
1856	B. Gibbons	3	3
1857	B. Gibbons	3	3
1858	B. Gibbons	3	3
1859	B. Gibbons	3	0
1860	B. Gibbons	3	0
1861	B. Gibbons	3	0
1862	B. Gibbons	3	0
1863	B. Gibbons	3	0
1864	B. Gibbons	3	0
1865	B. Gibbons	2	0

1841: output 90 tons a week. 1843: 75 tons a week. 1849: Hunt lists 3 furnaces in blast. Truran: output 95 tons a week from each of 3 furnaces.

Lane End: see under North Staffs.

Lays, Brockmoor, Staffs. [SO 9187]

Year	Owner	Built	In Blast
1830	—	2	-
1839	W. & G. Firmstone	3	3
1841	W. & G. Firmstone	3	2
1843	W. & G. Firmstone	3	3
1847	W. & G. Firmstone	3	2
1849	W. & G. Firmstone	4	3
1852	Firmstone & Co.	3	3
1854	W. & G. Firmstone	3	3
1855	W. & G. Firmstone	3	3
1856	W. & G. Firmstone	3	3
1857	W. & G. Firmstone	3	3
1858	W. & G. Firmstone	3	3
1859	W. & G. Firmstone	3	3
1860	W. & G. Firmstone	3	2
1861	W. & G. Firmstone	3	3
1862	W. & G. Firmstone	3	2
1863	W. & G. Firmstone	3	2
1864	W. & G. Firmstone	3	2
1867	W. & G. Firmstone	3	2
1868	W. & G. Firmstone	3	2
1869	W. & G. Firmstone	3	2
1870	W. & G. Firmstone	3	2
1871	W. & G. Firmstone	3	3
1872	W. & G. Firmstone	3	2
1873	W. & G. Firmstone	3	2
1874	W. & G. Firmstone	3	2
1875	W. & G. Firmstone	4	2
1876	W. & G. Firmstone	3	1
1877	W. & G. Firmstone	3	1
1878	W. & G. Firmstone	3	1
1879	W. & G. Firmstone	3	1
1880	W. & G. Firmstone	3	1
1881	W.H. & G. Firmstone	3	1
1882	W.H. & G. Firmstone	3	1
1883	W.H. & G. Firmstone	3	1
1884	W. & G. Firmstone	3	1
1885	W. & G. Firmstone	3	1
1886	W. & G. Firmstone	3	1
1887	W. & G. Firmstone	3	1
1888	W. & G. Firmstone	3	1
1889	W. & G. Firmstone	3	0
1890	W. & G. Firmstone	3	0
1891	W. & G. Firmstone	3	0

1823–30: nil return for 1823, note that 2 furnaces were built in 1828 and that output was 4,160 tons p.a. in 1830. Also a note that 1 furnace was built at Lays in 1831. 1839: output 72 tons a week, $11,226^{3}/_{4}$ p.a. (actual); 'foundry'; hot blast. 1841: output 150 tons a week. 1843: output 216 tons a week; the owner's name has been emended from W. & J. Firmstone, which is presumably an error. The name is spelt 'Leys' in 1823–30 and 'Lays' in 1839, 1843, 1847, 1852 and from 1854. Truran: output 110 tons a week from each of 3 furnaces.

Leabrook [I], ?Staffs. [SO 9794?]

Year	Owner	Built	In Blast
1810	Read & Co.	1	1
1823	—	1	-
1825	Bailey, Caddick & Co.	1	1
1830	—	1	-

1823–30: output nil in both years. 1825: 40 tons a week, 2,000 p.a., comment (dated 20 March 1826): 'will stand shortly' (B&W); 'If not at a stand, will be shortly' (Staffs RO). The owner's name is spelt Bayley in the B&W text, Bailey in the Staffs RO version.

Leabrook [II], ?Staffs. [SO 9794?]

Year	Owner	Built	In Blast
1862	Chillington Iron Co.	-	-
1863	Chillington Iron Co.	-	-
1864	Chillington Iron Co.	-	-
1865	Chillington Iron Co.	-	-
1866	Chillington Iron Co.	-	-
1867	Chillington Iron Co.	-	-
1868	Chillington Iron Co.	-	-
1869	Chillington Iron Co.	-	-
1870	Chillington Iron Co.	-	-

The furnace-numbers are printed under Chillington (qv).

Level (Old), Brierley Hill, Staffs. SO 9287

Year	Owner	Built	In Blast
1794	Gibbons & Co.	2	-
1796	—	1	1
1805	Gibbons	3	2
1810	Gibbons & Co.	3	3
1823	—	1	-
1825	Izons & Co	1	1
1830	—	1	-
1839	W. Izon	2	1
1841	William Izon	2	1
1843	William Izon	2	1
1847	W. Izons & Co.	2	1
1849	John Lyon	2	1
1852	Hall, Holcroft & Pearson	2	1
1854	Hall, Holcroft & Pearson	2	2
1855	Hall, Holcroft & Pearson	2	2
1856	Hall, Holcroft & Pearson	2	2
1857	Hall, Holcroft & Pearson	2	2
1858	Hall, Holcroft & Pearson	2	1
1859	Hall, Holcroft & Pearson	2	1
1860	Hall, Holcroft & Pearson	2	1
1861	Hall, Holcroft & Pearson	2	1
1862	Hall, Holcroft & Pearson	2	1
1863	Hall, Holcroft & Pearson	2	1
1864	Hall, Holcroft & Pearson	2	0
1865	Hall, Holcroft & Pearson	2	0
1866	Hall, Holcroft & Pearson	4	3
1867	Hall, Holcroft & Pearson	4	0
1868	Hall, Holcroft & Pearson	4	0
1869	Hall, Holcroft & Pearson	4	0
1870	Hall, Holcroft & Pearson	3	2
1871	Hall, Holcroft & Pearson	2	2
1872	James Holcroft	3	2
1873	J. & C. Holcroft	3	2
1874	J. & C. Holcroft	3	1
1875	James Holcroft	2	1
1876	James Holcroft	2	1
1877	James Holcroft	2	1
1878	James Holcroft	2	1
1879	James Holcroft	2	0
1880	James Holcroft	2	0
1881	James Holcroft	2	0
1882	James Holcroft	2	1
1883	James Holcroft	2	1
1884	James Holcroft	2	1
1885	James Holcroft	2	1
1886	James Holcroft	2	0
1887	James Holcroft	2	0
1888	James Holcroft	2	0
1889	James Holcroft	2	0
1890	James Holcroft	2	0
1891	James Holcroft	2	0
1892	James Holcroft	2	0
1893	James Holcroft	2	0
1894	—	2	0
1895	—	2	0
1896	—	2	0
1897	—	2	0
1898	Henry Hall & Co.	2	0

The ground landlord in 1794 was Lord Ward; the furnaces were coke-fired, blown by engine and built in 1786. The forge consisted of a chafery, 2 melting furnaces and 2 balling furnaces, built in 1787. 1796: output 1,560 tons p.a. (i.e. 30 tons a week), Excise and actual, Exact Return 1,391 tons. 1805: 3,351 tons. 1823–30: 2,072 tons p.a. in 1823; 1,028 tons in 1830. 1825: 36 tons a week, 1,750 p.a., 'used by themselves'; the furnace is shown as out of blast in the B&W text, in blast in the Staffs RO version. 1839: 50 tons a week, 2,600 p.a. (estimated); 'grey forge'; cold blast. 1841: 60 tons a week. 1843: 46 tons a week; the owner's name has been emended from 'William Iron' in the original. 1849: Hunt lists 2 furnaces in blast at 'Level Iron Works', which may include both this site and the next. Truran: two works listed under 'Level', one with an output of 100 tons a week from each of 2 furnaces, which is presumably this site. 1866–70: furnace-numbers include Brettells Lane (qv). From 1871 the site is called 'Old Level'. 1883: Production estimated.

Level (New), Brierley Hill, Staffs. SO 9287

Year	Owner	Built	In Blast
1823	—	4	-
1825	Gibbons & Co.	4	3
1830	—	4	-
1839	B. Gibbons	4	3
1841	B. Gibbons	4	2
1847	Lord Ward	3	1
1849	Lord Ward	3	0
1852	Lord Ward	3	2
1854	Lord Ward	3	3
1855	Lord Ward	3	3
1856	Lord Ward	3	3
1857	Lord Ward	3	3
1858	Lord Ward	3	3
1859	Earl of Dudley	3	3
1860	Earl of Dudley	3	2
1861	Earl of Dudley	3	3
1862	Earl of Dudley	3	3
1863	Earl of Dudley	4	3
1864	Earl of Dudley	-	-
1865	Earl of Dudley	-	-
1866	Earl of Dudley	4	3
1867	Earl of Dudley	-	-
1868	Earl of Dudley	-	-
1869	Earl of Dudley	-	-
1870	Earl of Dudley	4	3
1871	Earl of Dudley	4	3
1872	Earl of Dudley	4	3
1873	Earl of Dudley	2	2
1874	Earl of Dudley	5	2
1875	Earl of Dudley	5	2
1876	Earl of Dudley	5	2
1877	Earl of Dudley	5	3
1878	Earl of Dudley	5	2
1879	Earl of Dudley	5	2
1880	Earl of Dudley	5	3
1881	Earl of Dudley	5	2
1882	Earl of Dudley	5	2
1883	Earl of Dudley	5	2
1884	Earl of Dudley	5	2
1885	Earl of Dudley	5	2
1886	Earl of Dudley	5	2
1887	Earl of Dudley	5	2
1888	Earl of Dudley	5	2

Year	Owner	Built	In Blast
1889	Earl of Dudley	5	2
1890	Earl of Dudley	5	3
1891	Earl of Dudley	5	2
1892	Earl of Dudley	5	3
1893	Earl of Dudley	5	2
1894	Earl of Dudley	5	2
1895	Earl of Dudley	5	2
1896	Earl of Dudley	5	2
1897	Earl of Dudley	5	3
1898	Earl of Dudley	5	2
1899	Earl of Dudley	5	2
1900	Earl of Dudley	5	2
1901	Earl of Dudley	4	2
1902	Earl of Dudley	4	2
1903	Earl of Dudley	4	2
1904	Earl of Dudley	4	2
1905	Earl of Dudley	4	2
1906	Earl of Dudley	4	2
1907	Earl of Dudley	4	2
1908	Earl of Dudley	4	2
1909	Earl of Dudley	4	2
1910	Earl of Dudley	4	2
1911	Earl of Dudley	4	3
1912	Earl of Dudley	4	3
1913	Earl of Dudley	4	3
1921	Earl of Dudley	4	-
1922	Earl of Dudley	4	-
1923	Earl of Dudley	4	-
1924	Earl of Dudley	4	-
1925	Earl of Dudley	4	-
1926	Earl of Dudley	4	-
1927	Earl of Dudley	4	-
1928	Earl of Dudley	4	-
1929	Earl of Dudley	4	-
1930	Earl of Dudley	4	-
1931	Earl of Dudley	4	-
1932	Earl of Dudley	4	-
1933	Earl of Dudley	4	-
1934	Earl of Dudley	4	-
1935	Earl of Dudley's Round Oak Works Ltd	4	-
1936	Round Oak Steel Works Ltd	4	-
1937	Round Oak Steel Works Ltd	4	-
1938	Round Oak Steel Works Ltd	4	-
1939	Round Oak Steel Works Ltd	4	-
1940	Round Oak Steel Works Ltd	4	-
1941	Round Oak Steel Works Ltd	2	-
1942	Round Oak Steel Works Ltd	2	-
1943	Round Oak Steel Works Ltd	2	-
1944	Round Oak Steel Works Ltd	2	-
1945	Round Oak Steel Works Ltd	3	-
1946	Round Oak Steel Works Ltd	3	-
1947	Round Oak Steel Works Ltd	3	-
1948	Round Oak Steel Works Ltd	3	-
1949	Round Oak Steel Works Ltd	3	-
1950	Round Oak Steel Works Ltd	3	-
1951	Round Oak Steel Works Ltd	2	-
1952	Round Oak Steel Works Ltd	2	-
1953	Round Oak Steel Works Ltd	2	-
1954	Round Oak Steel Works Ltd	2	-
1955	Round Oak Steel Works Ltd	2	-
1956	Round Oak Steel Works Ltd	2	-

1823–30: output 6,464 tons p.a in 1823, nil in 1830. 1825: 120 tons a week, 5,550 tons p.a., 'melting iron'. The B&W text has 4 furnaces in blast, the Staffs RO version has 3. 1839: output 85 tons a week, 13,200 p.a. (actual); 'foundry and forge'; 2 furnaces hot blast, 1 cold. 1841: output 180 tons a week. 1849: see note to previous entry. Truran: two works listed at 'Level', one with an output of 120 tons a week from each of 3 furnaces, which is presumably this site. 1859: 1 furnace on cold blast for 8 months and hot blast for 4; the others hot blast all year. In 1864–65 and 1867–69 furnace-numbers were combined with Coneygre (qv). From 1871 the site is called 'New Level'. After 1921 the works is listed initially under the Earl of Dudley and from 1936 under Round Oak. From 1953 the location is given as Brierley Hill.

Leys: see Lays

Meadow, ?Staffs.

Year	Owner	Built	In Blast
1847	Hall, Holcroft & Co.	1	1
1870	Chillington Iron Co.	-	-

See under Corbyn's Hall (New) for what may be another reference to this works. 1870: furnace-numbers combined with Chillington (qv).

Millfield, Bilston, Staffs. [SO 9396]

Year	Owner	Built	In Blast
1805	Fereday	2	2
1810	Fereday	2	2
1823	—	4	-
1825	Mrs Walker	4	4
1830	—	4	-
1839	William Riley	3	3
1841	William Riley	3	2
1843	William Riley	3	3
1847	W. Riley	3	2
1849	W. Riley	3	3
1852	W. Riley	3	2
1854	William Riley & Son	3	3
1855	William Riley & Son	3	3
1856	William Riley & Son	2	1
1857	William Riley & Son	3	3
1858	B. Gibbons Jun. & Co.	3	3
1859	B. Gibbons Jun.	3	3
1860	B. Gibbons Jun. & Co.	4	4
1861	Benjamin Gibbons	4	4
1862	Benjamin Gibbons	4	4
1863	Benjamin Gibbons	4	3
1864	Mrs Emily Gibbons	4	3
1865	Mrs Emily Gibbons	4	3
1866	Mrs Emily Gibbons	4	3
1867	Mrs Emily Gibbons	4	0
1868	Mrs Emily Gibbons	4	0
1869	Mrs Emily Gibbons	4	0
1870	W. & J.T. Sparrow	4	0
1871	W. & J.T. Sparrow & Co.	3	0
1873	W. & J.T. Sparrow & Co.	3	1
1874	W. & J.T. Sparrow & Co.	3	1
1875	W. & J.T. Sparrow & Co.	3	2
1876	W. & J.S. Sparrow & Co.	3	2
1877	W. & J.S. Sparrow & Co.	3	2
1878	W. & J.S. Sparrow & Co.	3	3

Year	Owner	Built	In Blast
1879	W. & J.S. Sparrow & Co.	3	1
1880	W. & J.S. Sparrow & Co.	3	1
1881	W. & J.S. Sparrow & Co.	3	1
1882	W. & J.S. Sparrow & Co.	3	2
1883	W. & J.S. Sparrow & Co.	3	2
1884	W. & J.S. Sparrow & Co.	3	1
1885	W. & J.S. Sparrow & Co.	3	1
1886	W. & J.S. Sparrow & Co.	3	1
1887	W. & J.S. Sparrow & Co.	3	1
1888	W. & J.S. Sparrow & Co.	3	1
1889	W. & J.S. Sparrow & Co.	3	0
1890	W. & J.S. Sparrow & Co.	3	0
1891	Executors of late J.W. Sparrow	3	0
1892	Executors of late J.W. Sparrow	3	0
1893	Executors of late J.W. Sparrow	3	0
1894	Executors of late J.W. Sparrow	3	0
1895	Executors of late J.W. Sparrow	3	0
1896	Trustees of J.W. Sparrow	3	0
1897	Trustees of J.W. Sparrow	3	0
1898	W.H. Sparrow	3	0
1899	W.H. Sparrow	3	0

The 1805 list names the works as 'Mill Field or Birds Wharf' and gives the output as 5,065 tons p.a. 1823–30: output 6,708 tons p.a. in 1823, 8,112 tons in 1830. 1825: weekly output 160 tons, 1,800 p.a., 'forge iron, own use'. The B&W text has 3 furnaces in blast, the Staffs RO version has 4. 1839: output 58 tons a week, 8,944 p.a. (actual); 'forge sale'; cold blast. 1841: output 160 tons a week. 1843: output 210 tons a week. 1849: Hunt lists 2 furnaces in blast. Truran: output 120 tons a week from each of 3 furnaces. In 1879 and 1890 the site is entered under 'Bilston'.

Mitre: see Wednesbury Oak

Moorcroft, Staffs. [SO 9695?]

Year	Owner	Built	In Blast
1805	Addenbrooke	2	1
1810	J. Read	2	2
1823	—	2	-
1825	J. Addenbrooke	2	2
1830	—	2	-
1839	E.H. & J. Addenbrooke	2	2
1843	E.H. & J. Addenbrooke	2	0

1805: output 1,955 tons p.a.; 1823: 3,700 tons p.a. 1825: weekly output 90 tons, 4,500 p.a., 'melting and forge' (B&W); 'Consumed by themselves, the forge; make melting also' (Staffs RO). 1830: 4,791 tons p.a. 1839: output 50 tons a week, 5,013 p.a. (actual); 'forge'; hot and cold blast. 1843: output nil.

Moseley, Wolverhampton, Staffs. [SO 9398]

Year	Owner	Built	In Blast
1849	Chillington Iron Co.	3	2
1852	Chillington Co.	3	3
1854	Chillington Co.	3	2
1855	Chillington Co.	3	3
1856	Chillington Co.	3	3
1857	Chillington Co.	3	3
1858	Chillington Co.	3	3
1859	Chillington Co.	3	2
1860	Chillington Iron Co.	3	0
1861	Chillington Iron Co.	3	0
1862	Chillington Iron Co.	-	-
1863	Chillington Iron Co.	-	-

1849: Hunt lists 3 furnaces in blast. Truran: output 120 tons a week from each of 3 furnaces. In 1862–63 furnace-numbers were combined with Chillington (qv).

Moxley, Wednesbury, Staffs. [SO 9795]

Year	Owner	Built	In Blast
1870	David Rose	2	1
1871	David Rose	2	0
1872	David Rose	2	1
1873	David Rose	2	1
1874	David Rose	2	1
1875	David Rose	2	1
1876	David Rose	2	0
1877	David Rose	2	0
1878	David Rose	2	0
1879	David Rose	2	2
1880	David Rose	2	0
1881	David Rose	2	0
1882	David Rose	2	0
1883	David Rose & Sons	2	0
1884	David Rose & Sons	2	0
1885	David Rose & Sons	2	0
1886	David Rose & Sons	2	0
1887	David Rose & Sons	2	0
1888	David Rose & Sons	2	0
1889	David Rose & Sons	2	0
1890	Late David Rose & Sons	2	0
1891	Late David Rose & Sons	2	0

Netherton (Old), Dudley, Worcs. [SO 9388]

Year	Owner	Built	In Blast
1805	Attwood	2	1
1810	Attwood & Co.	2	1
1823	—	2	-
1825	British Iron Co.	4	4
1830	—	2	-
1839	British Iron Co.	2	2
1841	British Iron Co.	2	2
1843	British Iron Co.	2	2
1847	British Iron Co.	-	-
1849	British Iron Co.	2	1
1852	New British Iron Co.	2	2
1854	N. Hingley & Sons	3	2
1855	N. Hingley & Sons	3	2
1856	N. Hingley & Sons	2	2
1857	N. Hingley & Sons	2	2
1858	N. Hingley & Sons	2	2
1859	New British Iron Co.	-	-
1862	James & George Onions	-	-

Year	Owner	Built	In Blast
1863	Earl of Dudley	2	2
1864	Earl of Dudley	-	-
1865	James & George Onions	2	2
1868	Earl of Dudley	2	2
1869	Earl of Dudley	2	2
1870	N. Hingley & Sons	2	2
1871	N. Hingley & Sons	2	2
1872	N. Hingley & Sons	-	-
1874	N. Hingley & Sons	2	1
1875	N. Hingley & Sons	2	1
1876	N. Hingley & Sons	2	1
1877	N. Hingley & Sons	2	1
1878	Earl of Dudley	2	0
1879	Joseph H. Pearson	2	2
1880	Joseph H. Pearson	2	2
1881	Joseph H. Pearson	2	2
1882	Joseph H. Pearson	2	2
1883	Joseph H. Pearson	2	2
1884	Joseph H. Pearson	2	2
1885	Joseph H. Pearson	2	2
1886	Joseph H. Pearson	2	1
1887	Joseph H. Pearson	2	2
1888	Joseph H. Pearson	2	2
1889	Joseph H. Pearson	2	2
1890	Joseph H. Pearson	2	2
1891	Joseph H. Pearson	2	2
1892	Joseph H. Pearson	2	2
1893	Joseph H. Pearson	2	2
1894	Joseph H. Pearson	2	1
1895	Joseph H. Pearson	2	1
1896	Joseph H. Pearson	2	1
1897	Joseph H. Pearson	2	1
1898	Joseph H. Pearson	2	1
1899	Joseph H. Pearson	2	1
1900	Joseph H. Pearson	2	1
1901	Joseph H. Pearson	2	1
1902	Joseph H. Pearson	2	1
1903	Joseph H. Pearson	2	1
1904	Joseph H. Pearson	2	1
1905	Joseph H. Pearson	2	1
1906	Joseph H. Pearson	2	1
1907	Joseph H. Pearson	2	1
1908	Joseph H. Pearson	2	1
1909	Joseph H. Pearson	2	1
1910	Joseph H. Pearson	2	1
1911	Joseph H. Pearson	2	1
1912	Joseph H. Pearson	2	2
1913	Joseph H. Pearson	2	1
1921	Baldwin's Ltd	2	-
1922	Baldwin's Ltd	2	-
1923	Baldwin's Ltd	2	-
1924	Baldwin's Ltd	2	-
1925	Baldwin's Ltd	2	-
1926	Baldwin's Ltd	2	-
1927	Baldwin's Ltd	2	-

1805: no output. 1823: 1,406 tons p.a. 1830: 5,053 tons. 1825: Furnace-numbers appear to include Dudley Wood (qv), as presumably does the output of 200 tons weekly, 10,000 tons p.a., 'used by themselves'. 1839: output 60 tons a week, 7,280 p.a. (estimated); 'forge'; cold blast. 1841: output 150 tons a week. 1843: 164 tons a week. The 1847 list couples Netherton with Dudley Wood, as apparently does *Mineral Statistics* in 1859. Named as 'Bumble Hole, Netherton Works' in 1849, when Hunt lists 2 furnaces in blast, and as 'Bumble Hole' in 1852. Truran: output 100 tons a week from each of 2 furnaces. In 1862 furnace-numbers are combined with Brades Hall (qv); in 1864 with Coneygre (qv); and in 1872 with Old Hill (qv). In 1871 this site is called Netherton (New), although the pattern of ownership at both Netherton works makes it clear that this is an error. The connection between Pearson and Baldwin's over the gap of 1913–21 has been made partly on the basis of location (entries from 1921 use the name Netherton) and partly by elimination, since this is the only works listed in 1913 not in the ownership of the same company in 1921.

Netherton (New), Dudley, Worcs. [SO 9388]

Year	Owner	Built	In Blast
1839	M. & W. Grazebrook	2	2
1841	M. & W. Grazebrook	2	1
1843	M. & W. Grazebrook	2	1
1847	M. & W. Grazebrook	2	1
1849	M. & W. Grazebrook	2	1
1852	M. & W. Grazebrook	2	1
1854	M. & W. Grazebrook	2	1
1855	M. & W. Grazebrook	2	2
1856	M. & W. Grazebrook	2	2
1857	M. & W. Grazebrook	2	2
1858	M. & W. Grazebrook	2	2
1859	M. & W. Grazebrook	2	2
1860	M. & W. Grazebrook	2	2
1861	M. & W. Grazebrook	2	2
1862	M. & W. Grazebrook	2	2
1863	M. & W. Grazebrook	2	2
1864	M. & W. Grazebrook	2	2
1865	M. & W. Grazebrook	2	2
1866	M. & W. Grazebrook	2	2
1867	M. & W. Grazebrook	2	2
1868	M. & W. Grazebrook	2	2
1869	M. & W. Grazebrook	2	2
1870	M. & W. Grazebrook	2	2
1871	M. & W. Grazebrook	2	2
1872	M. & W. Grazebrook	2	2
1873	M. & W. Grazebrook	2	2
1874	M. & W. Grazebrook	2	1
1875	M. & W. Grazebrook	2	0
1876	M. & W. Grazebrook	2	1
1877	M. & W. Grazebrook	2	1
1878	M. & W. Grazebrook	2	1
1879	M. & W. Grazebrook	2	1
1880	M. & W. Grazebrook	2	1
1881	M. & W. Grazebrook	2	1
1882	M. & W. Grazebrook	2	1
1883	M. & W. Grazebrook	2	1
1884	M. & W. Grazebrook	2	1
1885	M. & W. Grazebrook	2	1
1886	M. & W. Grazebrook	2	1
1887	M. & W. Grazebrook	2	1
1888	M. & W. Grazebrook	2	1
1889	M. & W. Grazebrook	2	1
1890	M. & W. Grazebrook	2	1
1891	M. & W. Grazebrook	2	1
1892	M. & W. Grazebrook	2	1
1893	M. & W. Grazebrook	2	1
1894	M. & W. Grazebrook	2	1
1895	M. & W. Grazebrook	2	1
1896	M. & W. Grazebrook	2	1

Year	Owner	Built	In Blast
1897	M. & W. Grazebrook	2	1
1898	M. & W. Grazebrook	2	1
1899	M. & W. Grazebrook	2	1
1900	M. & W. Grazebrook	2	1
1901	M. & W. Grazebrook	2	1
1902	M. & W. Grazebrook	2	1
1903	M. & W. Grazebrook	2	1
1904	M. & W. Grazebrook	2	1
1905	M. & W. Grazebrook	2	1
1906	M. & W. Grazebrook	2	1
1907	M. & W. Grazebrook	2	1
1908	M. & W. Grazebrook	2	1
1909	M. & W. Grazebrook	2	1
1910	M. & W. Grazebrook	2	1
1911	M. & W. Grazebrook	2	1
1912	M. & W. Grazebrook	2	1
1913	M. & W. Grazebrook	2	2
1921	M. & W. Grazebrook	2	-
1922	M. & W. Grazebrook	2	-
1923	M. & W. Grazebrook	2	-
1924	M. & W. Grazebrook	2	-
1925	M. & W. Grazebrook	2	-
1926	M. & W. Grazebrook	2	-
1927	M. & W. Grazebrook	2	-
1928	M. & W. Grazebrook	2	-
1929	M. & W. Grazebrook	2	-
1930	M. & W. Grazebrook	2	-
1931	M. & W. Grazebrook	2	-
1932	M. & W. Grazebrook	2	-
1933	M. & W. Grazebrook Ltd	2	-
1934	M. & W. Grazebrook Ltd	2	-
1935	M. & W. Grazebrook Ltd	2	-
1936	M. & W. Grazebrook Ltd	2	-
1937	M. & W. Grazebrook Ltd	2	-
1938	M. & W. Grazebrook Ltd	2	-
1939	M. & W. Grazebrook Ltd	2	-
1940	M. & W. Grazberook Ltd	2	-
1941	M. & W. Grazebrook Ltd	2	-
1942	M. & W. Grazebrook Ltd	2	-
1943	M. & W. Grazebrook Ltd	2	-
1944	M. & W. Grazebrook Ltd	2	-
1945	M. & W. Grazebrook Ltd	2	-
1946	M. & W. Grazebrook Ltd	2	-
1947	Grazebrook Cold Blast Ltd	2	-

1839: output 60 tons a week, 6,420 p.a. (estimated); 'castings and forge'; cold blast. 1841: output 65 tons a week. 1843: 70 tons a week. 1849: Hunt lists 1 furnace in blast. Truran: output 110 tons a week from each of 2 furnaces. In 1856, 1858, 1861, 1863, 1866 and 1868 there are notes indicating that the furnaces were working entirely on cold blast.

New Birchills: see Birchills (New)

New Darlaston: see Rough Hay

New Duffield: see Bilston

New Furnaces: see Bilston (New)

New Level: see Level (New)

New Priestfield: see Priestfield (New)

Oak Farm, Dudley, Worcs. [SO 8990]

Year	Owner	Built	In Blast
1839	Oak Farm Co.	2	2
1841	Oak Farm Co.	2	2
1843	Oak Farm Iron Co.	2	2
1847	Oak Farm Co.	2	2
1849	Oak Farm Co.	2	0
1852	G. Bennet & Co.	2	2
1854	Geo. Bennet & Co.	2	2
1855	Geo. Bennett & Co.	2	2
1856	Geo. Bennett & Co.	2	2
1857	Oakfarm Furnace Co.	2	2
1858	Oakfarm Furnace Co.	2	2
1859	G. & W. Firmstone	2	2
1860	G. & W. Firmstone	2	0
1861	G. & W. Firmstone	2	2
1862	G. & W. Firmstone	2	2
1863	G. & W. Firmstone	2	2
1864	H. Sparrow	2	0
1865	H. Sparrow	2	0
1866	H. Sparrow	2	0
1867	Sir S. Glynn Bt	2	0
1868	Sir S. Glynn Bt	2	0

1839: output 70 tons a week, 7,000 p.a. (estimated); 'forge'; cold blast. 1841: output 140 tons a week at 'Oak Works'. 1843: 170 tons a week. The 1847 entry (in both Parliamentary Papers and Poole) lists 2 furnaces built, 2 in blast and 2 out of blast; the entry above seems the most reasonable correction. 1849: Hunt lists 1 furnace in blast. Truran: output 110 tons a week from each of 2 furnaces.

Oldbury, Salop [SO 9888]

Year	Owner	Built	In Blast
1805	Parker	1	1
1810	Parker	2	2
1823	—	2	-
1825	Parker & Co.	2	2
1830	—	2	-
1839	J. Dawes & Sons	2	2
1841	J. Dawes & Sons	2	2
1843	J. Davis & Son	2	2
1847	Dawes & Sons	2	0
1849	John Dawes & Sons	2	2
1852	W. Bennitt	3	2
1854	William Bennitt	4	3
1855	William Bennitt	4	3
1856	William Bennitt	4	4
1857	William Bennitt	4	3
1858	William Bennitt	4	4
1859	William Bennitt	4	4
1860	William Bennitt	4	4
1861	William Bennitt	4	4
1862	William Bennitt	4	2
1863	William Bennitt	4	2
1864	William Bennitt	4	2
1865	William Bennitt	4	3
1866	William Bennitt	4	2
1867	Assignees of William Bennitt	4	0
1868	Assignees of William Bennitt	4	0
1869	Assignees of William Bennitt	4	0
1870	Edward Onions & Co.	3	2
1871	J. & S. Onions	4	0

The 1805 list combines the output of this works with that at Tipton (qv) at 4,500 tons p.a. altogether. 1823–30: output for Oldbury alone of 2,600 tons p.a. in 1823, 5,720 in 1830. 1825: weekly output of 90 tons, 4,500 tons annual, 'use it themselves'. The works is listed under South Staffs. in the B&W text and under Shropshire in the Staffs RO version, with the note, 'Shropshire with Staffordshire'. 1839: output 65 tons a week, 6,760 p.a. (estimated); 'forge'. 1841: output 170 tons a week. 1843: output 180 tons a week. Truran: output 110 tons a week from each of 4 furnaces.

Old Dock, ?Staffs.

Year	Owner	Built	In Blast
1825	T. Morris	2	0

No output listed; 'Building'.

Old Hill, near Dudley, Staffs.   [SO 9586]

Year	Owner	Built	In Blast
1849	T. & J. Badger	1	1
1852	T. & J. Badger	1	1
1854	T. & J. Badger	2	1
1855	T. & J. Badger	2	1
1856	T. & J. Badger	2	1
1857	T. & J. Badger	2	1
1858	T. & J. Badger	2	1
1859	T. & J. Badger	2	1
1860	T. & J. Badger	2	1
1861	T. & J. Badger	2	0
1862	T. & J. Badger	2	0
1863	T. & J. Badger	2	0
1864	T. & J. Badger	2	0
1865	Suspended	2	0
1870	David Rose	2	1
1871	David Rose	2	1
1872	N. Hingley & Sons	2	1
1873	N. Hingley & Sons	2	1
1874	N. Hingley & Sons	2	1
1875	N. Hingley & Sons	2	1
1876	N. Hingley & Sons	2	1
1877	N. Hingley & Sons	2	0
1878	N. Hingley & Sons	2	1
1879	N. Hingley & Sons	2	1
1880	N. Hingley & Sons	2	1
1881	N. Hingley & Sons	2	1
1882	N. Hingley & Sons	2	1
1883	N. Hingley & Sons	2	1
1884	N. Hingley & Sons	2	1
1885	N. Hingley & Sons	2	1
1886	N. Hingley & Sons	2	1
1887	N. Hingley & Sons	2	1
1888	N. Hingley & Sons	2	1
1889	N. Hingley & Sons	2	1
1890	N. Hingley & Sons Ltd	2	1
1891	N. Hingley & Sons Ltd	2	1
1892	N. Hingley & Sons Ltd	2	1
1893	N. Hingley & Sons Ltd	2	1
1894	N. Hingley & Sons Ltd	2	1
1895	N. Hingley & Sons Ltd	2	1
1896	N. Hingley & Sons Ltd	2	1
1897	N. Hingley & Sons Ltd	2	1
1898	N. Hingley & Sons Ltd	2	1
1899	N. Hingley & Sons Ltd	2	1
1900	N. Hingley & Sons Ltd	2	1
1901	N. Hingley & Sons Ltd	2	1
1902	N. Hingley & Sons Ltd	2	1
1903	N. Hingley & Sons Ltd	2	1
1904	N. Hingley & Sons Ltd	2	1
1905	N. Hingley & Sons Ltd	2	1
1906	N. Hingley & Sons Ltd	2	1
1907	N. Hingley & Sons Ltd	2	1
1908	N. Hingley & Sons Ltd	2	1
1909	N. Hingley & Sons Ltd	2	1
1910	N. Hingley & Sons Ltd	2	1
1911	N. Hingley & Sons Ltd	2	1
1912	N. Hingley & Sons Ltd	2	1
1913	N. Hingley & Sons Ltd	2	1
1921	N. Hingley & Sons Ltd	2	-
1922	N. Hingley & Sons Ltd	2	-
1923	N. Hingley & Sons Ltd	2	-
1924	N. Hingley & Sons Ltd	2	-
1925	N. Hingley & Sons Ltd	2	-
1926	N. Hingley & Sons Ltd	2	-
1927	N. Hingley & Sons Ltd	2	-
1928	N. Hingley & Sons Ltd	2	-
1929	N. Hingley & Sons Ltd	2	-
1930	N. Hingley & Sons Ltd	2	-
1931	N. Hingley & Sons Ltd	2	-
1932	N. Hingley & Sons Ltd	2	-
1933	N. Hingley & Sons Ltd	2	-
1934	N. Hingley & Sons Ltd	2	-
1935	N. Hingley & Sons Ltd	2	-
1936	N. Hingley & Sons Ltd	2	-

Truran: output 100 tons a week from a single furnace. The furnace-numbers for 1872 include Netherton (Old) (qv). The Old Hill works was dismantled during 1937.

Old Park, Wednesbury, Staffs.   [SO 9895]

Year	Owner	Built	In Blast
1823	—	1	-
1825	Lloyds	1	1
1830	—	2	-
1839	Lloyds & Co.	2	2
1841	Lloyds, Fosters & Co.	2	2
1843	Lloyds & Co.	2	2
1847	Lloyds, Foster & Co.	2	1
1849	Lloyds, Foster & Co.	2	1
1852	Lloyds, Foster & Co.	2	2
1854	Lloyds, Foster & Co.	3	3
1855	Lloyds, Foster & Co.	3	3
1856	Lloyds, Foster & Co.	3	3
1857	Lloyds, Foster & Co.	3	2
1858	Lloyds, Foster & Co.	3	3
1859	Lloyds, Foster & Co.	3	3
1860	Lloyds, Foster & Co.	3	3
1861	Lloyds, Foster & Co.	3	3
1862	Lloyds, Foster & Co.	3	3
1863	Lloyds, Foster & Co.	3	2
1864	Lloyds, Foster & Co.	3	2
1865	Lloyds, Foster & Co.	3	3
1866	Lloyds, Foster & Co.	3	3

Year	Owner	Built	In Blast
1867	Patent Shaft & Axletree Co. Ltd (Lloyds, Foster & Co. Dept)	3	3
1868	Patent Shaft & Axletree Co. Ltd (Lloyds, Foster & Co. Dept)	3	2
1869	Patent Shaft & Axletree Co. Ltd (Lloyds, Foster & Co. Dept)	3	2
1870	Patent Shaft & Axletree Co. Ltd (Lloyds, Foster & Co. Dept)	3	2
1871	Patent Shaft & Axletree Co. Ltd	3	2
1872	Patent Shaft & Axletree Co. Ltd	3	2
1873	Patent Shaft & Axletree Co. Ltd	3	2
1874	Patent Shaft & Axletree Co. Ltd	3	2
1875	Patent Shaft & Axletree Co. Ltd	3	2
1876	Patent Shaft & Axletree Co. Ltd	3	2
1877	Patent Shaft & Axletree Co. Ltd	3	1
1878	Patent Shaft & Axletree Co. Ltd	3	1
1879	Patent Shaft & Axletree Co. Ltd	3	0
1880	Patent Shaft & Axletree Co. Ltd	3	0
1881	Patent Shaft & Axletree Co. Ltd	3	0
1882	Patent Shaft & Axletree Co. Ltd	3	0
1883	Patent Shaft & Axletree Co. Ltd	3	0
1884	Patent Shaft & Axletree Co. Ltd	3	0

1823–30: output 2,600 tons p.a. for 1823, note that a second furnace was built in 1828, output in 1830 5,200 tons. The entry in the 1825 list for 'Old Park Field' probably refers to Parkfield (qv), not Old Park, and the Lloyds works is that listed as Wednesbury, with an output of 40 tons a week, 2,000 tons p.a., 'Forge and melting'. The B&W furnace-numbers are given above; the Staffs RO text has 2 furnaces, with 1 in blast, which seems unlikely, given the statement in the 1823–30 list. 1839: output 80 tons a week, 8,005 p.a. (actual); 'foundry and forge'; hot blast. 1841: output (at 'Wednesbury Old Park') 160 tons a week. 1843: output (at 'Wednesbury') 180 tons a week. In 1847 the works was simply called Wednesbury. 1849: Hunt lists 2 furnaces in blast. In 1852 it was called 'Wednesbury Old Park' (cf. Wednesbury Oaks), as it was by Truran in 1855, who assigns an output of 110 tons a week from each of 3 furnaces.

Old Park, Wolverhampton: see Parkfield

Old Park Field: see Parkfield

Osier Bed, Horseley Fields, Staffs. [SO 9792?]

Year	Owner	Built	In Blast
1847	W. & J. Sparrow	3	2
1849	—	3	2
1852	Osier Bed Co.	3	3
1854	W.H. Sparrow & Co.	3	3
1855	W.H. Sparrow & Co.	3	3
1856	W.H. Sparrow & Co.	3	3
1857	W.H. Sparrow & Co.	3	3
1858	W.H. Sparrow & Co.	3	3
1860	Osier Bed Iron Co.	3	2
1861	Osier Bed Iron Co.	3	2
1862	Osier Bed Iron Co.	3	2
1863	Osier Bed Iron Co.	3	2
1864	Osier Bed Iron Co.	3	2
1865	Osier Bed Iron Co.	3	2
1866	Osier Bed Iron Co.	3	2
1867	Osier Bed Iron Co.	3	1
1868	Osier Bed Iron Co.	3	1
1869	Osier Bed Iron Co.	3	1
1870	Osier Bed Iron Co.	4	1
1871	Osier Bed Iron Co.	4	0
1872	Osier Bed Iron Co.	3	1
1873	Osier Bed Iron Co.	3	1
1874	Osier Bed Iron Co.	3	1
1875	Osier Bed Iron Co.	3	2
1876	Osier Bed Iron Co.	3	2
1877	Osier Bed Iron Co.	3	2
1878	Osier Bed Iron Co.	3	0
1879	Osier Bed Iron Co.	3	0
1880	Osier Bed Iron Co.	3	0
1881	Osier Bed Iron Co.	3	0
1882	Osier Bed Iron Co.	3	0
1883	Osier Bed Iron Co.	3	0
1884	Osier Bed Iron Co.	3	0
1885	Osier Bed Iron Co.	3	0

1849: The dash printed in place of an owner's name in English may have been intended as a ditto mark indicating that the owner was W. Sparrow, as at Stow Heath (qv), the preceding works on the list; Hunt lists 3 furnaces in blast. Truran: output 110 tons a week from each of 3 furnaces. The name of the works changes to Horseley Fields Iron & Tin Plate in 1872, later shortened to Horseley Fields. See also under Horseley Fields. 1882: Works partly dismantled.

Park, Old: see Parkfield

Park, Wednesbury: see Old Park, Wednesbury

Parkfield, Wolverhampton, Staffs. [SO 9296]

Year	Owner	Built	In Blast
1825	Bishton & Underhill	2	0
1830	—	4	-
1839	Parkfield Co.	4	3
1841	Parkfield Co.	4	3
1843	Parkfield Iron Co.	4	2
1847	Parkfield Co.	4	3
1849	Parkfield Co.	4	3
1852	Parkfield Co.	4	3
1854	Parkfield Iron Co.	4	4
1855	Parkfield Iron Co.	4	4
1856	Parkfield Iron Co.	4	4
1857	Parkfield Iron Co.	4	4
1858	Parkfield Iron Co.	5	4
1859	Parkfield Iron Co.	5	3
1860	Parkfield Iron Co.	5	4
1861	Parkfield Iron Co.	5	4
1862	Parkfield Iron Co.	5	4
1863	Henry John Marten	5	5
1864	Parkfield Iron Co.	5	5
1865	Parkfield Iron Co.	5	5
1866	Parkfield Iron Co.	5	5
1867	Parkfield Iron Co. Ltd	5	5
1868	Parkfield Iron Co. Ltd	5	4
1869	Parkfield Iron Co. Ltd	5	4
1870	Parkfield Iron Co. Ltd	5	5
1871	Parkfield Iron Co. Ltd	5	4
1872	Henry John Marten	5	4
1873	Parkfield Iron Co. Ltd	5	3
1874	Parkfield Iron Co. Ltd	5	3
1875	Parkfield Iron Co. Ltd	5	0

Year	Owner	Built	In Blast
1876	Wolverhampton & Staffordshire Banking Co.	5	1
1877	Wolverhampton & Staffordshire Banking Co.	5	1
1878	Wolverhampton & Staffordshire Banking Co.	5	1
1879	Wolverhampton & Staffordshire Banking Co.	3	0
1880	Wolverhampton & Staffordshire Banking Co.	3	0
1881	Lydney & Wigpool Iron Ore Co. Ltd	3	0
1882	Lydney & Wigpool Iron Ore Co. Ltd	5	0
1883	Unoccupied	5	0
1884	Unoccupied	5	0
1885	Unoccupied	5	0
1886	Unoccupied	5	0
1887	Unoccupied	5	0

1823–30: nil return for 1823; note that 2 furnaces were built in 1826, one in 1827 and one in 1828; output in 1830 9,500 tons p.a. 1825: called Old Park Field in both B&W and Staffs RO texts; no figure for output but the comment (dated 20 March 1826): 'building'. The B&W list has 3 furnaces built, 1 in blast; the Staffs RO has 2 furnace built, 2 in blast, which seems more likely on the evidence of the 1823–30 list. 1839: output 60 tons a week, 9,512 p.a. (actual); 'forge sale'; cold blast. 1841: output 210 tons a week. 1843: output 160 tons a week. Truran: output 100 tons a week from each of 4 furnaces. The site appears as 'Park Field, Wolverhampton' in 1876–81.

Parkhead, Dudley, Worcs. [SO 9389]

Year	Owner	Built	In Blast
1805	Parkes & Co.	1	1
1810	Parkes & Co.	1	1
1823	—	1	-
1825	Z. Parkes & Co.	1	1
1830	—	1	-
1839	Evers & Martin	2	1
1841	Evers & Martin	2	2
1843	Evers & Martin	2	2
1847	Evers & Martin	2	1
1849	Evers & Martin	2	1
1852	Evers & Martin	2	1
1854	Evers & Martin	2	2
1855	Evers & Martin	2	2
1856	Evers & Martin	2	2
1857	Evers & Martin	2	2
1858	Evers & Martin	2	2
1859	Evers & Martin	2	1
1860	Evers & Martin	2	1
1861	Evers & Martin	2	1
1862	Evers & Martin	2	1
1863	Evers & Martin	2	1
1864	Evers & Martin	2	1
1865	Evers & Martin	2	1
1866	Evers & Martin	2	1
1867	Evers & Martin	2	1
1868	Evers & Martin	2	1
1869	Evers & Martin	2	2
1870	Evers & Martin	2	2
1871	Evers & Martin	2	2
1872	Evers & Martin	2	2
1873	Evers & Martin	2	2
1874	Evers & Martin	0	0
1875	Phillips & McEwen	2	1
1876	Phillips & McEwen	2	2
1877	Phillips & McEwen	2	2
1878	Phillips & McEwen	2	1
1879	Phillips & McEwen	2	1
1880	Phillips & McEwen	2	1
1881	Phillips & McEwen	2	0
1882	Unoccupied	2	0
1883	Unoccupied	2	0
1884	Unoccupied	2	0
1885	Unoccupied	2	0
1886	Unoccupied	2	0
1887	Unoccupied	2	0
1888	Unoccupied	2	0

1805: output 1,404 tons. 1823–30: 2,289 tons in 1823, 2,468 in 1830. 1825: 48 tons a week, 1,924 p.a., 'used by themselves'. The furnace is shown out of blast in the B&W text, in blast in the Staffs RO version. 1839: output 50 tons a week, 2,600 p.a. (estimated); 'forge'; cold blast. 1841: output 120 tons a week. 1843: output 120 tons a week. Truran: output 100 tons a week from each of 2 furnaces.

Park Lane, Tipton, Staffs. [SO 9592]

Year	Owner	Built	In Blast
1847	T. Morris	1	1
1852	T. Morris & Son	2	1
1858	Thomas Morris	2	1
1859	Thomas Morris	2	1
1860	Thomas Morris	2	1
1861	Thomas Morris	2	1
1862	Thomas Morris	2	1
1863	Thomas Morris jun.	-	-
1864	John Colbourn & Sons	2	1
1865	John Colbourn & Sons	1	1
1866	John Colbourn & Sons	1	1
1867	John Colbourn & Sons	2	2
1868	John Colbourn & Sons	4	3
1869	John Colbourn & Sons	4	3
1870	John Colbourn & Sons	4	3
1871	John Colbourn & Sons	2	2
1872	John Colbourn & Sons	3	3
1873	John Colbourn & Sons	3	3
1874	John Colbourn & Sons	3	2
1875	John Colbourn & Sons	2	1
1876	John Colbourn & Sons	2	1
1877	John Colbourn & Sons	4	1
1878	John Colbourn & Sons	2	1
1879	John Colbourn & Sons	4	1
1880	John Colbourn & Sons	4	1
1881	John Colbourn & Sons	4	0
1882	John Colbourn, Sons & Co.	2	0
1883	John Colbourn, Sons & Co.	2	0

Truran: output 100 tons a week from each of 2 furnaces. In 1868–70, 1872–77 and 1879–81 furnace-numbers include Horseley (qv).

Park Lane, Smethwick, Staffs. [SP 0287]

Year	Owner	Built	In Blast
1875	W. & G. Onions	2	2
1876	W. & E. Onions	2	2
1877	W. & E. Onions	2	0
1878	W. & E. Onions	2	0
1879	W. & E. Onions	2	0
1880	W. & E. Onions	2	0

Pelsall, Walsall, Staffs. [SK 0203]

Year	Owner	Built	In Blast
1841	R. Fryer	2	1
1847	R. Fryer	2	1
1849	William Fryer	2	1
1852	W. Fryer	2	1
1854	Davies & Bloomer	2	2
1855	Davies & Bloomer	2	2
1856	Davies & Bloomer	2	2
1857	Davies & Bloomer	2	2
1858	Davies & Bloomer	2	2
1859	Davies & Bloomer	2	2
1860	Davies & Bloomer & Co.	2	2
1861	Davis & Bloomer & Son	2	2
1862	Davis & Bloomer & Son	2	2
1863	Davis & Bloomer & Son	2	2
1864	D. Bloomer & Son	2	1
1865	D. Bloomer & Son	2	2
1866	Boaz, Bloomer & Son	2	2
1867	Boaz Bloomer & Son	2	2
1868	Boaz Bloomer & Son	2	2
1869	Boaz Bloomer & Son	2	2
1870	Boaz Bloomer & Son	2	2
1871	Boaz Bloomer & Son	2	2
1872	Boaz Bloomer & Son	2	2
1873	Pelsall Coal & Iron Co. Ltd	2	2
1874	Pelsall Coal & Iron Co. Ltd	2	2
1875	Pelsall Coal & Iron Co. Ltd	2	2
1876	Pelsall Coal & Iron Co. Ltd	2	0
1877	Pelsall Coal & Iron Co. Ltd	2	0
1878	Pelsall Coal & Iron Co. Ltd	2	0
1879	Pelsall Coal & Iron Co. Ltd	2	0
1880	Pelsall Coal & Iron Co. Ltd	2	1
1881	Pelsall Coal & Iron Co. Ltd	2	1
1882	Pelsall Coal & Iron Co. Ltd	2	2
1883	Pelsall Coal & Iron Co. Ltd	2	2
1884	Pelsall Coal & Iron Co. Ltd	2	0
1885	Pelsall Coal & Iron Co. Ltd	2	0
1886	Pelsall Coal & Iron Co. Ltd	2	0
1887	Pelsall Coal & Iron Co. Ltd	2	1
1888	Pelsall Coal & Iron Co. Ltd	2	2
1889	Pelsall Coal & Iron Co. Ltd	2	2
1890	Pelsall Coal & Iron Co. Ltd	2	2
1891	Pelsall Coal & Iron Co. Ltd	2	0

1841: output 90 tons a week. 1849: Hunt lists 2 furnaces in blast. Truran: output 100 tons a week from each of 2 furnaces. Davies and Davis are presumably one and the same; it is not clear whether Boaz is a Christian name belonging with Bloomer or the surname of another partner.

Priestfield, Staffs. [SO 9397]

Year	Owner	Built	In Blast
1823	—	3	-
1825	W. Ward & Co.	3	2
1830	—	3	-
1839	W. Ward	3	3
1841	William Ward	3	2
1843	W. Ward	3	2
1847	W. Ward	3	2
1849	W. Ward	3	2
1852	Executors of W. Ward	3	2
1854	Henry Ward	3	3
1855	Ward & Sons	3	3
1856	Ward & Sons	3	3
1857	Ward & Sons	3	3
1858	W.M. Ward & Sons	3	3
1859	W.M. Ward & Sons	3	2
1860	W.M. Ward & Sons	3	2
1861	W.M. Ward & Sons	3	2
1862	W.M. Ward & Sons	5	3
1863	William Ward & Sons	5	3
1864	William Ward & Sons	5	3
1865	William Ward & Sons	5	2
1866	William Ward & Sons	5	2

1823–30: output 3,664 tons p.a. in 1823, 4,897 tons in 1830. 1825: called Priestfields; output 80 tons a week, 4,000 p.a., 'in the casting trade'. 1839: output 65 tons a week, 10,230 p.a. (actual); 'forge sale'; cold blast. 1841: output 160 tons a week. 1843: output 180 tons a week. The entry 'W. Ward Priestfield' as the owner's name in 1847 is presumably a misprint, rather than a change of name. Truran: output 100 tons a week from each of 3 furnaces. Furnace-numbers above include Priestfield (New) (qv) in 1862–66; in 1867 there is an entry under Priestfield which in fact probably refers to the newer works, since only 2 furnaces are listed and there is no entry that year under Priestfield (New). The older works disappears entirely in 1868–69 and reappears for the last time in 1870, bracketed with the newer site, with only 2 furnaces in all, presumably those at Priestfield (New).

Priestfield (New), Staffs. [SO 9397]

Year	Owner	Built	In Blast
1859	W.M. Ward & Sons	2	1
1860	W.M. Ward & Sons	-	-
1861	W.M. Ward & Sons	2	1
1862	W.M. Ward & Sons	-	-
1863	William Ward & Sons	-	-
1864	William Ward & Sons	-	-
1865	William Ward & Sons	-	-
1866	William Ward & Sons	-	-
1867	William Ward & Sons	2	1
1868	William Ward & Sons	2	1
1869	William Ward & Sons	2	1
1870	William Ward & Sons	2	2
1871	William Ward & Sons	2	2
1872	William Ward & Sons	2	1
1873	William Ward & Sons	2	1
1874	William Ward & Sons	2	1
1875	William Ward & Sons	2	1

Year	Owner	Built	In Blast
1876	William Ward & Sons	2	0
1877	William Ward & Sons	2	1
1878	William Ward & Sons	2	1
1879	William Ward & Sons	2	0
1880	William Ward & Sons	2	0
1881	William Ward & Sons	2	0
1882	William Ward & Sons	2	1
1883	William Ward & Sons	2	0
1884	William Ward & Sons	2	0
1885	William Ward & Sons	2	0
1886	William Ward & Sons	2	0
1887	William Ward & Sons	2	0
1888	William Ward & Sons	2	0
1889	William Ward & Sons	2	0
1890	William Ward & Sons	2	0
1891	William Ward & Sons	2	0
1892	William Ward & Sons	2	0
1893	William Ward & Sons	2	0
1894	William Ward & Sons	2	0
1895	William Ward & Sons	2	0
1896	William Ward & Sons	2	0
1897	William Ward & Sons	2	0
1898	William Ward & Sons	2	0
1899	William Ward & Sons	2	0
1900	Patent Shaft & Axletree Co. Ltd	2	1
1901	Patent Shaft & Axletree Co. Ltd	2	0

1862–66: furnace-numbers included with Priestfield (qv).
1883: furnace at work for 6 weeks.

Priorfield, Deepfields, Bilston, Staffs. [SO 9596?]

Year	Owner	Built	In Blast
1841	H.B. Whitehouse	3	2
1843	H.B. Whitehouse	3	2
1847	H.B. Whitehouse	3	2
1849	H.B. Whitehouse	3	2
1852	H.B. Whitehouse	3	3
1854	H.B. Whitehouse	3	2
1855	H.B. Whitehouse	3	2
1856	H.B. Whitehouse	3	2
1857	H.B. Whitehouse	3	2
1858	H.B. Whitehouse	3	3
1859	H.B. Whitehouse	3	3
1860	H.B. Whitehouse	3	2
1861	H.B. Whitehouse	3	2
1862	H.B. Whitehouse	3	1
1863	H.B. Whitehouse	3	1
1864	H.B. Whitehouse	3	3
1865	H.B. Whitehouse	3	2
1866	H.B. Whitehouse	3	3
1867	Hy Bickerton Whitehouse	3	3
1868	Hy Bickerton Whitehouse	3	3
1869	Hy Bickerton Whitehouse	3	3
1870	Hy B. Whitehouse & Son	3	3
1871	H.B. Whitehouse & Son	3	3
1872	H.B. Whitehouse & Son	3	3
1873	H.B. Whitehouse & Son	2	2
1874	H.B. Whitehouse & Son	3	3
1875	H.B. Whitehouse & Son	3	3
1876	H.B. Whitehouse & Son	3	2
1877	H.B. Whitehouse & Son	3	3
1878	H.B. Whitehouse & Son	3	3
1879	H.B. Whitehouse & Son	3	3
1880	H.B. Whitehouse & Son	3	3
1881	H.B. Whitehouse & Son	3	3
1882	H.B. Whitehouse & Son	3	3
1883	H.B. Whitehouse & Son	3	2
1884	H.B. Whitehouse & Son	3	2
1885	H.B. Whitehouse & Son	3	2
1886	Benjamin Whitehouse	3	2
1887	H.B. Whitehouse & Sons	3	2
1888	H.B. Whitehouse & Sons	3	2
1889	H.B. Whitehouse & Son	3	3
1890	H.B. Whitehouse & Son	3	2
1891	H.B. Whitehouse & Son	3	2
1892	H.B. Whitehouse & Son	3	2
1893	H.B. Whitehouse & Son	3	1
1894	H.B. Whitehouse & Son	3	1
1895	H.B. Whitehouse & Son	3	1
1896	H.B. Whitehouse & Son	3	1
1897	H.B. Whitehouse & Son	3	2
1898	H.B. Whitehouse & Son	3	2
1899	H.B. Whitehouse & Son	3	2
1900	H.B. Whitehouse & Son Ltd	3	2
1901	H.B. Whitehouse & Son Ltd	3	1
1902	H.B. Whitehouse & Son Ltd	3	2
1903	H.B. Whitehouse & Son Ltd	3	2
1904	H.B. Whitehouse & Son Ltd	3	1
1905	H.B. Whitehouse & Son Ltd	3	1
1906	H.B. Whitehouse & Son Ltd	3	2
1907	H.B. Whitehouse & Son Ltd	3	2
1908	H.B. Whitehouse & Son Ltd	3	1
1909	H.B. Whitehouse & Son Ltd	3	1
1910	H.B. Whitehouse & Son Ltd	3	1

1841: output 160 tons a week. 1843: output 180 tons a week. The works is called Coseley and the owner's name is given as 'H.P. Whitehouse', presumably in error. 1849: Hunt lists 3 furnaces in blast. Truran: output 100 tons a week from each of 3 furnaces.

Ridgeacre [I], ?Staffs.

Year	Owner	Furnaces	In Blast
1839	Fowler	1	1
1841	— Fowler	1	0
1843	Fowler	1	0
1849	— Fowler	0	0

1839: output 50 tons a week, 2,600 p.a. (estimated); 'forge, sale'; cold blast. 1841, 1843: output nil.

Ridgeacre [II], ?Staffs.

Year	Owner	Built	In Blast
1839	T. Davis	2	1

Output 60 tons a week, 3,120 p.a. (estimated).

Roggin Row: see Springwood, North Staffs.

Rough Hay, Wednesbury, Staffs. [SO 9797]

Year	Owner	Built	In Blast
1847	Addenbrooke & Co.	2	1
1849	Addenbrooke & Co.	2	2

Year	Owner	Built	In Blast
1852	Addenbrooke & Co.	2	2
1854	Addenbrooke & Co.	2	2
1855	Addenbrooke & Co.	2	2
1856	Addenbrooke & Co.	2	2
1857	Addenbrooke & Co.	2	2
1858	Addenbrooke, Smith & Pidcock	2	2
1859	Addenbrooke, Smith & Pidcock	3	2
1860	Addenbrooke, Smith & Pidcock	3	1
1861	Addenbrooke, Smith & Pidcock	3	2
1862	Addenbrooke, Smith & Pidcock	3	2
1863	Addenbrooke, Smith & Pidcock	3	2
1864	Addenbrooke, Smith & Pidcock	3	2
1865	Addenbrooke, Smith & Pidcock	3	2
1866	Addenbrooke, Smith & Pidcock	3	2
1867	Addenbrooke, Smith & Pidcock	3	2
1868	Addenbrooke, Smith & Pidcock	3	2
1869	Addenbrooke, Smith & Pidcock	3	2
1870	Addenbrooke, Smith & Pidcock	3	2
1871	Addenbrooke, Smith & Pidcock	3	2
1872	Addenbrooke, Smith & Pidcock	3	2
1873	Addenbrooke, Smith & Pidcock	3	2
1874	Addenbrooke, Smith & Pidcock	3	2
1875	Addenbrooke, Smith & Pidcock	3	1
1876	Addenbrooke, Smith & Pidcock	3	1
1877	Addenbrooke, Smith & Pidcock	3	0
1878	Addenbrooke, Smith & Pidcock	3	0
1879	Addenbrooke, Smith & Pidcock	3	0
1880	Addenbrooke, Smith & Pidcock	3	1
1881	Addenbrooke, Smith & Pidcock	3	0
1882	Addenbrooke, Smith & Pidcock	3	0
1883	Addenbrooke, Smith & Pidcock	3	0

Called 'New Darlaston' in 1852, and also by Truran, who assigns an output of 100 tons a week from each of 2 furnaces.

Rough Hills, Staffs. [SO 9296]

Year	Owner	Built	In Blast
1805	Fereday	2	2
1810	Fereday & Co.	2	2
1823	—	2	-
1825	W. Aston	3	3
1830	—	2	-

1805: output 3,193 tons p.a. 1823–30: output nil in both years. 1825: 105 tons a week, 5,200 p.a., but adds the comment (dated 20 March 1826): 'blew out last week'. The B&W text has all 3 furnaces out of blast, the Staffs RO version all 3 in blast.

Roughwood: see Birchills (Old)

Round Oak: see Level (New)

'Rush Hall': see Russell's Hall

Russell's Hall, Dudley, Worcs. [SO 9289]

Year	Owner	Built	In Blast
1830	—	2	-
1839	D. & G. Horton	2	1
1841	Blackwell & Co.	2	1
1843	Blackwell, Jones & Co.	2	1
1847	Blackwell & Co.	3	3
1849	Blackwell	3	2
1852	Blackwell & Co.	3	3
1854	S.H. Blackwell & Co.	4	4
1855	S.H. Blackwell & Co.	4	4
1856	S.H. Blackwell & Co.	4	4
1857	S.H. Blackwell & Co.	4	4
1858	S.H. Blackwell & Co.	5	5
1859	S.H. Blackwell & Co.	5	5
1860	S.H. Blackwell & Co.	5	3
1861	S.H. Blackwell & Co.	5	1
1862	S.H. Blackwell & Co.	5	2
1863	Blackwell & Co.	5	2
1864	Russell Hall Iron Co.	5	2
1865	Russell Hall Iron Co.	5	1
1866	Russell Hall Iron Co.	5	2
1867	Russell Hall Iron Co.	5	0
1868	Russell Hall Iron Co.	2	0
1869	Russell Hall Iron Co.	2	0

1823–30: nil return in 1823, note of building 2 furnaces in 1828, output 2,080 tons p.a. in 1830. 1839: output $46\frac{1}{4}$ tons a week, $4,811\frac{3}{4}$ p.a. (actual); 'foundry and forge'; hot blast. 1841: output 80 tons a week. 1843: 75 tons a week at 'Rush Hall'. 1849: Hunt lists 3 furnaces in blast. Truran: output 120 tons a week from each of 5 furnaces.

Shut End, Kingswinford, Staffs. [SO 9089]

Year	Owner	Built	In Blast
1839	James Foster	4	3
1841	James Foster	4	3
1843	James Foster	4	2
1847	J. Foster	4	3
1849	John Bradley & Co.	4	4
1852	J. Bradley & Co.	4	4
1854	John Bradley & Co.	4	3
1855	John Bradley & Co.	4	3
1856	John Bradley & Co.	4	3
1857	John Bradley & Co.	4	3
1858	John Bradley & Co.	4	3
1859	John Bradley & Co.	4	2
1860	John Bradley & Co.	4	3
1861	John Bradley & Co.	4	2
1862	John Bradley & Co.	4	2
1863	John Bradley & Co.	4	2
1864	John Bradley & Co.	4	2
1865	John Bradley & Co.	4	3
1866	John Bradley & Co.	4	3
1867	John Bradley & Co.	4	2
1868	John Bradley & Co.	4	2
1869	John Bradley & Co.	4	3
1870	John Bradley & Co.	4	3
1871	John Bradley & Co.	4	4
1872	John Bradley & Co.	4	2
1873	John Bradley & Co.	4	2
1874	John Bradley & Co.	4	2
1875	John Bradley & Co.	4	2
1876	John Bradley & Co.	4	2
1877	John Bradley & Co.	4	2
1878	John Bradley & Co.	4	1
1879	John Bradley & Co.	4	1
1880	John Bradley & Co.	4	1
1881	John Bradley & Co.	4	1
1882	John Bradley & Co.	4	1
1883	John Bradley & Co.	4	1

Year	Owner	Built	In Blast
1884	John Bradley & Co.	4	1
1885	John Bradley & Co.	4	1
1886	John Bradley & Co.	4	1
1887	John Bradley & Co.	4	1
1888	John Bradley & Co.	4	0
1889	John Bradley & Co.	4	0
1890	John Bradley & Co.	4	0
1891	John Bradley & Co.	4	0
1892	John Bradley & Co.	4	0
1893	John Bradley & Co.	4	0
1894	John Bradley & Co.	4	0
1895	John Bradley & Co.	4	0
1896	John Bradley & Co.	4	0
1897	John Bradley & Co.	2	0
1898	John Bradley & Co.	2	0

The 1823–30 list has a note that 2 furnaces were erected at Shut End in 1831. 1839: output $86\frac{1}{2}$ tons a week, $13,496\frac{3}{4}$ p.a. (actual); 'forge'; cold blast. 1841: output 250 tons a week. 1843: output 172 tons a week. Truran: output 120 tons a week from each of 4 furnaces.

Spring Vale, Bilston, Staffs.　　　　SO 9395

Year	Owner	Built	In Blast
1855	Jones & Murcott	3	3
1856	Jones & Murcott	3	3
1857	Jones & Murcott	3	3
1858	Jones & Murcott	3	2
1858	Jones & Murcott	3	2
1859	Jones & Murcott	3	2
1860	Jones & Murcott	3	2
1861	Jones & Murcott	3	2
1862	Jones & Murcott	3	3
1863	Jones & Murcott	3	0
1864	John Jones	3	0
1865	John Jones	3	3
1866	John Jones	3	2
1867	Alfred Hickman	3	1
1868	Alfred Hickman	3	2
1869	Alfred Hickman	3	2
1870	Alfred Hickman	3	3
1871	Alfred Hickman	3	3
1872	Alfred Hickman	3	3
1873	Alfred Hickman	3	2
1874	Alfred Hickman	3	2
1875	Alfred Hickman	4	3
1876	Alfred Hickman	4	3
1877	Alfred Hickman	4	4
1878	Alfred Hickman	4	4
1879	Alfred Hickman	4	2
1880	Alfred Hickman	4	3
1881	Alfred Hickman	4	4
1882	Alfred Hickman	4	4
1883	Alfred Hickman	4	4
1884	Alfred Hickman	5	4
1885	Alfred Hickman	6	4
1886	Alfred Hickman	6	5
1887	Alfred Hickman	6	5
1888	Alfred Hickman	6	5
1889	Alfred Hickman	6	5
1890	Alfred Hickman	6	4
1891	Sir Alfred Hickman	6	5
1892	Sir Alfred Hickman	6	5
1893	Sir Alfred Hickman	6	5
1894	Sir Alfred Hickman	6	5
1895	Sir Alfred Hickman	6	4
1896	Sir Alfred Hickman	6	4
1897	Sir Alfred Hickman	6	4
1898	Alfred Hickman Ltd	6	4
1899	Alfred Hickman Ltd	6	4
1900	Alfred Hickman Ltd	5	4
1901	Alfred Hickman Ltd	5	4
1902	Alfred Hickman Ltd	5	4
1903	Alfred Hickman Ltd	5	4
1904	Alfred Hickman Ltd	5	4
1905	Alfred Hickman Ltd	5	4
1906	Alfred Hickman Ltd	5	5
1907	Alfred Hickman Ltd	5	5
1908	Alfred Hickman Ltd	5	4
1909	Alfred Hickman Ltd	5	5
1910	Alfred Hickman Ltd	5	5
1911	Alfred Hickman Ltd	5	5
1912	Alfred Hickman Ltd	5	5
1913	Alfred Hickman Ltd	5	5
1921	Alfred Hickman Ltd	5	-
1922	Alfred Hickman Ltd	4	-
1923	Alfred Hickman Ltd	5	-
1924	Alfred Hickman Ltd	5	-
1925	Alfred Hickman Ltd	5	-
1926	Alfred Hickman Ltd	5	-
1927	Alfred Hickman Ltd	5	-
1928	Alfred Hickman Ltd	5	-
1929	Alfred Hickman Ltd	5	-
1930	Alfred Hickman Ltd	5	-
1931	Alfred Hickman Ltd	5	-
1932	Alfred Hickman Ltd	3	-
1933	Stewarts & Lloyds Ltd	3	-
1934	Stewarts & Lloyds Ltd	3	-
1935	Stewarts & Lloyds Ltd	3	-
1936	Stewarts & Lloyds Ltd	3	-
1937	Stewarts & Lloyds Ltd	3	-
1938	Stewarts & Lloyds Ltd	3	-
1939	Stewarts & Lloyds Ltd	3	-
1940	Stewarts & Lloyds Ltd	3	-
1941	Stewarts & Lloyds Ltd	3	-
1942	Stewarts & Lloyds Ltd	3	-
1943	Stewarts & Lloyds Ltd	3	-
1944	Stewarts & Lloyds Ltd	3	-
1945	Stewarts & Lloyds Ltd	3	-
1946	Stewarts & Lloyds Ltd	3	-
1947	Stewarts & Lloyds Ltd	3	-
1948	Stewarts & Lloyds Ltd	3	-
1949	Stewarts & Lloyds Ltd	3	-
1950	Stewarts & Lloyds Ltd	3	-
1951	Stewarts & Lloyds Ltd	3	-
1952	Stewarts & Lloyds Ltd	3	-
1953	Stewarts & Lloyds Ltd	3	-
1954	Stewarts & Lloyds Ltd	4	-
1955	Stewarts & Lloyds Ltd	4	-
1956	Stewarts & Lloyds Ltd	3	-
1957	Stewarts & Lloyds Ltd	3	-
1958	Stewarts & Lloyds Ltd	2	-
1959	Stewarts & Lloyds Ltd	2	-
1960	Stewarts & Lloyds Ltd	2	-
1961	Stewarts & Lloyds Ltd	2	-
1962	Stewarts & Lloyds Ltd	1	-
1963	Stewarts & Lloyds Ltd	1	-
1964	Stewarts & Lloyds Ltd	1	-
1965	Stewarts & Lloyds Ltd	1	-
1966	Stewarts & Lloyds Ltd	1	-
1967	Stewarts & Lloyds Ltd	1	-
1968	Stewarts & Lloyds Ltd	1	-

Year	Owner	Built	In Blast
1969	Stewarts & Lloyds Ltd	1	-
1970	British Steel Corporation	1	-
1971	British Steel Corporation	1	-
1972	British Steel Corporation	1	-
1973	British Steel Corporation	1	-
1974	British Steel Corporation	1	-
1975	British Steel Corporation	1	-
1976	British Steel Corporation	1	-
1977	British Steel Corporation	1	-
1978	British Steel Corporation	1	-

1862: Blown out 22 February [1863?]. In 1933–34 'Hickman Works' was printed after the owner's name; in subsequent years the location Bilston was given.

'Star Valley': see Stour Valley

Stonefield, Staffs. [SO 9496]

Year	Owner	Built	In Blast
1839	Woolley & Co.	1	1
1841	Woolley & Co.	1	1
1843	Woolley & Co.	2	2
1847	Woolley & Co.	1	1
1849	E. Woolley (now T.W. Vernon)	1	1
1852	T.W. Vernon	1	0
1854	G.H. & A. Hickman	1	1
1855	G.H. & A. Hickman	1	1
1856	G.H. & A. Hickman	1	1
1857	G.H. & A. Hickman	1	1
1858	G.H. & A. Hickman	1	1
1859	G.H. & A. Hickman	1	1
1860	G.H. & A. Hickman	1	0
1861	G.H. & A. Hickman (Late)	1	1
1862	G.H. & A. Hickman	1	0
1863	G.H. & A. Hickman	1	0
1864	Stonefield Co.	1	0
1865	Stonefield Co.	1	1
1866	Alfred Hickman	1	1
1867	Stonefield Iron Co.	1	0
1868	Stonefield Iron Co.	1	0
1869	Stonefield Iron Co.	1	0
1870	Stonefield Iron Co.	1	0
1871	G.H. Hickman	1	0
1872	Stonefield Iron Co.	1	1
1873	Stonefield Iron Co.	1	1
1874	Thomas Crew	1	0
1875	Thomas Crew	1	1
1876	Thomas Crew	1	0
1877	Thomas Crew	1	0
1878	Thomas Crew	1	0
1879	Thomas Crew	1	0
1880	Thomas Crew	1	0
1881	Thomas Crew	1	0
1882	Thomas Crew	1	0
1883	Unoccupied	1	0

The entries for 1839–47 all appear under Bilston in the original lists and have been linked with those for Stonfield in later lists through the change in ownership noted in 1849. 1839: output 40 tons a week, 2,080 p.a. (estimated); 'forge'; cold blast. 1841: output 70 tons a week. 1843: output 140 tons a week. Truran: output 110 tons a week from a single furnace. 1874–76: name printed as 'Stoneyfield'.

Stour Valley, ?Staffs.

Year	Owner	Built	In Blast
1857	B. Richards	2	1
1858	B. Richards	2	0
1859	B. Richards	3	0
1860a	W.J. Gibbons	1	1
1860b	Frederick Giles	1	1
1861	W.J. & G. Onions	2	2
1864	Onions & Co.	2	2
1870	J. & G. Onions	2	2
1871	J. & G. Onions	2	2
1872	J. & G. Onions	-	-
1873	J. & G. Onions	-	-
1874	Stour Valley Coal & Iron Co. Ltd	1	0
1875	Stour Valley Coal & Iron Co. Ltd	3	1
1876	Stour Valley Coal & Iron Co. Ltd	1	1
1877	Stour Valley Coal & Iron Co. Ltd	2	1
1878	Stour Valley Coal & Iron Co. Ltd	2	1

Truran lists an output of 100 tons a week from a single furnace for 1855, but the works is not listed in *Mineral Statistics* until 1857, when it appears as 'Star Valley'. In 1860 there are two entries under Stour Valley, each with a single furnace, which possibly suggests that the site was briefly in the hands of two different owners (unless there were two different works with the same name). In 1878 the entry for 'Union Valley' appears to belong here, since Union Ironworks (qv), also owned by the Stour Valley Co. from 1879, seems then to have been out of use and in any case had 3 furnaces, rather than 2.

Stow Heath, Bilston, Staffs. [SO 9397]

Year	Owner	Built	In Blast
1830	—	3	-
1839	W. & J.S. Sparrow & Co.	5	4
1841	W. & J.S. Sparrow & Co.	5	3
1843	W. & J.S. Sparrow	5	3
1847	W. & J. Sparrow	5	0
1849	W. Sparrow	5	3
1852	W. Sparrow & Co.	5	3
1854	W.H. Sparrow & Co.	5	3
1855	W.H. Sparrow & Co.	5	3
1856	W.H. Sparrow & Co.	5	3
1857	W.H. Sparrow & Co.	5	3
1858	W.H. Sparrow & Co.	5	4
1860	W.H. Sparrow & Co.	5	3
1861	W.H. Sparrow & Co.	4	3
1862	W.H. Sparrow & Co.	4	3
1863	W.H. Sparrow & Co.	4	3
1864	W. & J. Sparrow & Co.	4	2
1865	W. & J. Sparrow & Co.	4	2
1866	W. & J. Sparrow & Co.	4	2
1867	W.J. Sparrow & Co.	4	2
1868	W.J. Sparrow & Co.	4	2
1869	W.J. Sparrow & Co.	4	2
1870	W. & J.T. Sparrow & Co.	4	2
1871	W. & J.T. Sparrow & Co.	4	2
1872	W. & J.T. Sparrow & Co.	3	1

Year	Owner	Built	In Blast
1873	W. & J.T. Sparrow & Co.	3	0
1874	W. & J.T. Sparrow & Co.	3	0

1823–30: nil return for 1823; note of building 2 furnaces in 1825 and one in 1826; output 5,408 tons p.a. in 1830. 1839: output 65 tons a week, 12,756 p.a. (actual); 'hard forge'; cold blast. 1841: output 250 tons a week and note that 2 additional furnaces were building at Stow Heath (although these do not appear in later lists). 1843: output 255 tons a week. Truran: output 110 tons a week from each of 5 furnaces.

Talke o' th' Hill: see under North Staffs.

Tipton, Staffs. [SO 9592]

Year	Owner	Built	In Blast
1794	Messrs Parker	2	-
1796	—	2	2
1805	Parker	2	2
1810	Parker	2	2
1823	—	1	-
1825	G. Parkes & Co.	1	1
1830	—	1	-
1839	E. Cresswell & Sons	1	1
1841	E. Cresswell & Sons	1	1
1843	E. Cresswell & Sons	1	1
1847	E. Cresswell & Sons	2	1
1849	E. Cresswell & Sons	2	0
1852	E. Cresswell & Sons	2	1
1854	E. Cresswell & Sons	2	2
1855	E. Cresswell & Sons	2	2
1856	E. Cresswell & Sons	2	2
1857	E. Cresswell & Sons	2	2
1858	E. Cresswell & Sons	2	2
1859	E. Cresswell & Sons	2	1
1860	E. Cresswell & Sons	2	2
1861	E. Cresswell & Sons	2	2
1862	E. Cresswell & Sons	2	2
1863	E. Cresswell & Sons	2	2
1864	E. Cresswell & Sons	2	2
1865	E. Cresswell & Sons	2	2
1866	E. Cresswell & Sons?	2	1
1867	E. Cresswell & Sons?	2	0
1868	E. Cresswell & Sons?	2	0
1869	E. Cresswell & Sons?	2	0
1870	E. Cresswell & Sons?	2	0
1871	J. & T. Turley	2	0
1872	J. & T. Turley	2	0
1873	J. & T. Turley	2	0
1874	John Colbourn & Sons	2	1

The ground landlord in 1794 was Lord Dudley; the furnaces were coke-fired, blown by engine and built in 1783. There was also a slitting mill, built 1790. 1796: output 2,080 tons p.a. (i.e. 40 tons a week), Excise and actual, Exact Return 2,203 tons. 1805: output for Tipton and Oldbury (qv) together 4,500 tons p.a. 1823–30: 2,040 tons p.a. both years. 1825: weekly output 40 tons, 2,000 p.a., 'used by themselves'. 1839: $87^{1}/_{2}$ tons a week, $4,449^{1}/_{2}$ p.a. (actual); 'forge, sale'; hot blast. 1841 and 1843: 90 tons a week. 1849: Hunt lists 2 furnaces in blast. Truran lists two works under Tipton and a third under Tipton Green. One of the Tipton works is assigned an output 110 tons a week from each of 2 furnaces and is presumably this site. The question marks printed in 1867–70 are as in *Mineral Statistics*, which in 1870 prints 4 in the 'In Blast' column.

Tipton Green, Staffs. [SO 9592]

Year	Owner	Built	In Blast
1810	Fereday & Co.	3	3
1823	Tipton Co.	3	-
1825	Dixon & Co.	3	1
1830	Tipton Co.	3	-
1849	B. Gibbons jun.	2	1
1852	Gibbons & Roberts	2	2
1854	Gibbons & Roberts	4	3
1855	Gibbons & Roberts	4	3
1856	Gibbons & Roberts	4	3
1857	Gibbons & Roberts	4	3
1858	Gibbons & Roberts	4	4
1859	Gibbons & Roberts	4	2
1860	Roberts & Humfrey	-	-
1861	Roberts & Humfrey	4	3
1862	Roberts & Co.	4	3
1863	Roberts & Co.	4	4
1864	Roberts & Co.	4	2
1865	Roberts & Co.	4	4
1866	Roberts & Co.	4	4
1867	Roberts & Co.	4	4
1868	Roberts & Co.	4	4
1869	Roberts & Co.	4	4
1870	Roberts & Co.	4	4
1871	Roberts & Co.	4	4
1872	Roberts & Co.	4	4
1873	Roberts & Co.	4	4
1874	Roberts & Co.	4	4
1875	Roberts & Co.	4	3
1876	Roberts & Co.	4	3
1877	Roberts & Co.	4	4
1878	Roberts & Co.	4	4
1879	Roberts & Co.	4	3
1880	Roberts & Co.	4	3
1881	Roberts & Co.	4	4
1882	Roberts & Co.	4	4
1883	Roberts & Co.	4	4
1884	Roberts & Co.	4	3
1885	Roberts & Co.	4	4
1886	Roberts & Co.	4	3
1887	Roberts & Co.	4	4
1888	Roberts & Co.	4	3
1889	Roberts & Co.	4	4
1890	Roberts & Co.	4	2
1891	Roberts & Co.	4	3
1892	Roberts & Co.	4	3
1893	Roberts & Co.	4	2
1894	Roberts & Co.	4	2
1895	Roberts & Co.	3	2
1896	Roberts & Co.	4	2
1897	Roberts & Co.	4	2
1898	Roberts & Co.	4	2
1899	Roberts & Co.	4	2
1900	Wm Roberts (Tipton) Ltd	4	2
1901	Wm Roberts (Tipton) Ltd	3	2
1902	Wm Roberts (Tipton) Ltd	3	2
1903	Wm Roberts (Tipton) Ltd	3	2
1904	Wm Roberts (Tipton) Ltd	3	2
1905	Wm Roberts (Tipton) Ltd	3	2
1906	Wm Roberts (Tipton) Ltd	3	2
1907	Wm Roberts (Tipton) Ltd	3	2
1908	Wm Roberts (Tipton) Ltd	3	2
1909	Wm Roberts (Tipton) Ltd	3	2
1910	Wm Roberts (Tipton) Ltd	3	2
1911	Wm Roberts (Tipton) Ltd	3	2

Year	Owner	Built	In Blast
1912	Wm Roberts (Tipton) Ltd	3	2
1913	Wm Roberts (Tipton) Ltd	3	2
1921	Wm Roberts (Tipton) Ltd	3	-
1922	Wm Roberts (Tipton) Ltd	3	-
1923	Wm Roberts (Tipton) Ltd	3	-
1924	Wm Roberts (Tipton) Ltd	3	-
1925	Wm Roberts (Tipton) Ltd	3	-
1926	Wm Roberts (Tipton) Ltd	3	-
1927	Wm Roberts (Tipton) Ltd	3	-
1928	Wm Roberts (Tipton) Ltd	3	-
1929	Wm Roberts (Tipton) Ltd	3	-
1930	Wm Roberts (Tipton) Ltd	3	-
1931	Wm Roberts (Tipton) Ltd	3	-
1932	Wm Roberts (Tipton) Ltd	3	-
1933	Wm Roberts (Tipton) Ltd	3	-
1934	Wm Roberts (Tipton) Ltd	3	-
1935	Wm Roberts (Tipton) Ltd	3	-
1936	Wm Roberts (Tipton) Ltd	3	-

1823–30: output 5,640 tons p.a. in 1823, 3,515 tons in 1830. 1825: weekly output 45 tons, 2,300 tons p.a., 'casting trade'. The B&W text has 2 furnaces in blast, the Staffs RO version has 1. Truran lists a works at Tipton Green with an output of 110 tons a week from each of 2 furnaces; on the other hand, one of the two works in his list at Tipton (cf. previous entry) is assigned the same output from each of 4 furnaces, which according to *Mineral Statistics* for the 1850s was the number then standing at Tipton Green. If the latter works is not the one listed here, it cannot be matched with any other site in South Staffs. Although it appears to be impossible to resolve this question with certainty, it seems likely that Truran has listed the Tipton works with only two furnaces twice, called it Tipton Green on the second occasion, and listed what is called elsewhere Tipton Green works as Tipton. The Tipton Green works was finally dismantled in 1937.

Toll End, Tipton, Staffs. [SO 9793]

Year	Owner	Built	In Blast
1805	R. Hawkes	2	1
1810	J. Read	2	1
1823	—	3	-
1825	Baldwin, Aston & Co.	3	3
1830	—	3	-
1839	Toll End Co.	3	2
1841	Hartland & Co., Taylor & Co.	3	2
1843	Toll End Iron Co.	3	0
1849	Eagle Furnace Co.	0	0
1849	Birmingham Coal Co.	0	0
1852	Toll End Co.	1	1
1854	Toll End Co.	2	1
1855	Toll End Co.	2	2
1856	Toll End Co.	2	2
1857	Toll End Co.	2	1
1858	Toll End Co.	2	0
1859	Toll End Co.	2	0
1860	Motteram & Deeley	2	0

No output is given in 1805. 1823–30: 5,075 tons p.a. in 1823, 6,112 tons in 1830. 1825: 135 tons a week, 6,500 tons p.a., 'casting trade'. The B&W text has 2 furnaces in blast, the Staffs RO version has 3. 1839: output 54 tons a week, 5,555 p.a. (actual); 'forge'; cold blast. 1841: output 160 tons a week. 1843: output nil. 1849: two separate entries in English (none in Hunt), both apparently for works out of use, neither appears to relate to those for adjacent years; cf. also Eagle Furnaces. Truran: output 110 tons a week from a single furnace.

Union, West Bromwich, Staffs. [SO 9992]

Year	Owner	Built	In Blast
1830	—	2	-
1839	P. Williams & Co.	3	2
1841	P. Williams & Co.	3	2
1843	P. Williams & Co.	3	2
1847	P. Williams & Son	3	2
1849	P. Williams & Sons	3	2
1852	P. Williams & Son	3	3
1854	P. Williams & Son	3	2
1855	P. Williams & Son	3	0
1856	P. Williams & Co.	3	3
1857	P. Williams & Co.	3	3
1858	Philip Williams & Co.	3	3
1859	Philip Williams & Co.	3	2
1860	Philip Williams & Sons	3	3
1861	Philip Williams & Co.	3	2
1862	Philip Williams & Co.	3	2
1863	Philip Williams & Co.	6	4
1864	Philip Williams & Co.	3	2
1865	Philip Williams & Co.	6	5
1866	Philip Williams & Co.	3	2
1867	Philip Williams & Co.	3	2
1868	Philip Williams & Co.	3	2
1869	Philip Williams & Co.	5	5
1870	Philip Williams & Co.	-	-
1871	Philip Williams & Co.	3	2
1872	Philip Williams & Co.	3	2
1873	Philip Williams & Co.	3	1
1874	Stour Valley Coal & Iron Co. Ltd	0	0
1879	Stour Valley Coal & Iron Co. Ltd	3	1
1880	Stour Valley Coal & Iron Co. Ltd	3	0
1881	Stour Valley Coal & Iron Co. Ltd	3	0
1882	Stour Valley Coal & Iron Co. Ltd	3	0
1883	Stour Valley Coal & Iron Co. Ltd	3	1
1884	Stour Valley Coal & Iron Co. Ltd	3	1
1885	Stour Valley Coal & Iron Co. Ltd	3	0
1886	Philip Williams & Co.	3	0
1887	Philip Williams & Co.	3	0
1888	Philip Williams & Co.	2	0
1889	Philip Williams & Co.	3	0
1890	Philip Williams & Co.	3	0
1891	Philip Williams & Co.	3	0
1892	Philip Williams & Co.	2	0
1893	Philip Williams & Co.	3	0
1894	J.W. Williams	3	0

1823–30: nil return for 1823, note of building 2 furnaces in 1828, output 4,650 tons in 1830. 1839: output 78 tons a week, 8,100 p.a. (actual); 'forge, sale'; hot blast. 1841: output 160 tons a week. 1843: 170 tons a week. 1849: Hunt lists 3 furnaces in blast. Truran: output 110 tons a week from each of 3 furnaces. Furnace-numbers for 1863 and 1865–69 include Wednesbury Oak (qv); in 1870 there is no entry under Union but the furnace-numbers under Wednesbury Oak clearly include Union. There are no entries for Union in 1875–77 and in 1878 an entry for 'Union Valley' has been placed under Stour Valley (qv) since the furnace-numbers appear to fit better. 1884: Production estimated.

Wallbrook, Staffs. [SO 9493]

Year	Owner	Built	In Blast
1823	—	1	-
1825	Whitehouse & Co.	1	1
1830	—	2	-
1839	H.B. Whitehouse	2	2
1841	H.B. Whitehouse	2	0

1823–30: output 2,359 tons p.a. in 1823, second furnace built in 1825, output 2,886 tons in 1830. 1825: 40 tons a week, 1,750 tons p.a., 'melting iron'. 1839: output 55 tons a week, 5,532 p.a. (actual); 'foundry'; hot blast. 1841: output nil.

Wallbut, ?Staffs.

Year	Owner	Built	In Blast
1862	W. Baldwin & Co.	5	0
1863	W. Baldwin	5	0

Cf. Bovereux.

Walsall: see Green Lane

Waterloo: see Broadwaters

Wednesbury: see Old Park

Wednesbury Oak, Staffs. [SO 9594]

Year	Owner	Built	In Blast
1794	Messrs Hallens	1	-
1805	Attwood	1	0
1810	Attwood & Co.	2	2
1823	—	2	-
1825	P. Williams & Son	3	3
1830	—	3	-
1839	P. Williams & Son	3	3
1841	P. Williams & Sons	3	2
1843	P. Williams & Sons	3	0
1847	P. Williams & Son	3	3
1849	P. Williams & Sons	3	3
1852	P. Williams & Co.	3	3
1854	P. Williams & Son	3	3
1855	P. Williams & Co.	3	3
1856	P. Williams & Co.	3	3
1857	P. Williams & Co.	3	3
1858	Philip Williams & Co.	3	2
1859	Philip Williams & Co.	3	2
1860	Philip Williams & Co.	3	3
1861	Philip Williams & Co.	3	2
1862	Philip Williams & Co.	3	2
1863	Philip Williams & Co.	-	-
1864	Philip Williams & Co.	3	2
1865	Philip Williams & Co.	-	-
1866	Philip Williams & Co.	-	-
1867	Philip Williams & Co.	-	-
1868	Philip Williams & Co.	-	-
1869	Philip Williams & Co.	-	-
1870	Philip Williams & Sons	5	2
1871	Philip Williams & Sons	3	2
1872	Philip Williams & Sons	3	2
1873	Philip Williams & Sons	3	2
1874	Philip Williams & Sons	3	2
1875	Philip Williams & Sons	3	1
1876	Philip Williams & Sons	3	1
1877	Philip Williams & Sons	2	1
1878	Philip Williams & Sons	1	1
1879	Philip Williams & Sons	2	1
1880	Philip Williams & Sons	2	1
1881	Philip Williams & Sons	2	1
1882	Philip Williams & Sons	2	1
1883	Philip Williams & Sons	2	1
1884	Philip Williams & Sons	2	1
1885	Philip Williams & Sons	2	1
1886	Philip Williams & Sons	2	1
1887	Philip Williams & Sons	2	1
1888	Philip Williams & Sons	2	1
1889	Philip Williams & Sons	2	1
1890	Philip Williams & Sons	2	1
1891	Philip Williams & Sons	2	1
1892	Philip Williams & Sons	2	1
1893	Philip Williams & Sons	2	1
1894	Philip Williams & Sons	2	1
1895	Philip Williams & Sons	2	1
1896	Philip Williams & Sons	2	1
1897	Philip Williams & Sons	2	1
1898	Philip Williams & Sons	2	1
1899	Philip Williams & Sons	2	1
1900	Philip Williams & Sons	2	1
1901	Philip Williams & Sons	2	1
1902	Philip Williams & Sons	2	0
1903	Philip Williams & Sons	2	1
1904	Philip Williams & Sons	2	1
1905	Philip Williams & Sons	2	1
1906	Philip Williams & Sons	2	1
1907	Philip Williams & Sons	2	1
1908	Philip Williams & Sons	2	1
1909	Philip Williams & Sons	2	1
1910	Philip Williams & Sons	2	1
1911	Philip Williams & Sons	2	1
1912	Philip Williams & Sons	2	1
1913	Philip Williams & Sons	2	1
1921	P. Williams & Sons (Furnaces) Ltd	2	-

The ground landlord in 1794 was Mr S. Hallen; the furnace was coke-fired, blown by engine and built in 1785. The forge consisted of a chafery, two melting furnaces and a balling furnace, built in 1786. The name Wednesbury Oak does not appear in 1796 and in 1805 the works is assigned no output. 1823: 6,240 tons p.a. 1830: 7,684 tons; the third furnace was built in 1824. 1825: weekly output 160 tons, 7,500 p.a., 'forge (own use)' (B&W); 'Use it themselves, forge only' (Staffs RO). The owner's name is as above in the B&W text, Williams & Sons in the Staffs RO version. 1839: output 66 tons a week, 10,317 p.a. (actual); 'forge'; cold blast. 1841: output 160 tons a week. 1843: output nil. Truran: output 95 tons a week from each of 3 furnaces. In 1863 and 1865–69 furnace-numbers for this site were combined with Union under that heading (qv); in 1870 there is no entry for Union but the furnace-numbers for Wednesbury Oaks must include both works. In 1876 the furnace was working on cold blast and in 1878 one furnace was building. In 1899–1900 what is obviously the entry for Wednesbury Oaks appears under 'Mitre, Tipton'.

Wednesbury Park, Wednesbury Old Park: see Old Park

Willenhall, Staffs. [SO 9698]

Year	Owner	Built	In Blast
1857	Fletcher, Solly & Urwick	3	3
1858	Fletcher, Solly & Urwick	3	2
1859	Fletcher, Solly & Urwick	3	3
1860	Fletcher, Solly & Urwick	3	2
1861	Fletcher, Solly & Urwick	3	2
1862	Fletcher, Solly & Urwick	3	2
1863	Fletcher, Solly & Urwick	3	3
1864	Fletcher, Solly & Urwick	3	2
1865	Fletcher, Solly & Urwick	3	3
1866	Fletcher, Solly & Urwick	3	3
1867	Fletcher, Solly & Urwick	3	3
1868	Fletcher, Solly & Urwick	3	2
1869	Fletcher, Solly & Urwick	3	2
1870	Fletcher, Solly & Urwick	3	2
1871	Fletcher, Solly & Urwick	3	2
1872	Fletcher, Solly & Urwick	3	3
1873	Fletcher, Solly & Urwick	3	3
1874	Fletcher, Solly & Urwick	3	3
1875	Fletcher, Solly & Urwick	3	2
1876	Willenhall Furnaces Ltd	3	1
1877	Willenhall Furnaces Ltd	3	2
1878	Willenhall Furnaces Ltd	3	2
1879	Willenhall Furnaces Ltd	3	0
1880	Willenhall Furnaces Ltd	3	1
1881	Willenhall Furnaces Ltd	3	0
1882	Willenhall Furnaces Ltd	0	0

In 1879–82 the owner's name is given as 'Willenhall Furnaces Co. Ltd'; there was no such company on the register and the name is presumably an error for that printed in 1876–78, which can be identified. 1882: Furnaces and works partly dismantled.

Willingsworth, Wednesbury, Staffs. [SO 9794]

Year	Owner	Built	In Blast
1830	—	3	-
1839	Sir H. St Paul	3	3
1841	Sir H. St Paul	3	2
1843	Sir H. St Paul	3	2
1847	Sir Horace St Paul	3	1
1849	Haines & Co.	3	2
1852	Haines & Co.	3	2
1853	Haines & Co.	3	2
1854	Haines & Co.	3	2
1855	Haines & Co.	3	2
1856	Haines & Co.	3	2
1857	Haines & Co.	3	2
1858	Haines & Co.	3	3
1859	Haines & Co.	3	3
1860	Job & Henry Haines	-	-
1861	Job & Henry Haines	3	2
1862	Job & Henry Haines	3	2
1863	Job & Henry Haines	3	2
1864	Job & Henry Haines	3	2
1865	Job & Henry Haines	3	2
1866	Job & Henry Haines	3	2
1867	Job & Henry Haines	3	1
1868	Sir Horace St Paul	3	2
1869	Sir Horace St Paul	3	2
1870	Willingsworth Iron Co.	3	2
1871	David Kendrick & Richard Pearson	3	2
1872	David Kendrick & Richard Pearson	2	2
1873	David Kendrick & Richard Pearson	3	1
1874	Willingsworth Iron Co.	2	0
1875	Willingsworth Iron Co.	3	1
1876	Willingsworth Iron Co.	3	1
1877	David Kendrick	3	0
1878	Willingsworth Iron Co.	3	1
1879	Willingsworth Iron Co.	2	1
1880	Willingsworth Iron Co.	2	1
1881	Willingsworth Iron Co.	2	1
1882	D. Kendrick	2	1
1883	David Kendrick	2	1
1884	David Kendrick	2	1
1885	David Kendrick	2	1
1886	David Kendrick	2	1
1887	Willingsworth Iron Co.	2	1
1888	Willingsworth Iron Co.	2	1
1889	Willingsworth Iron Co.	2	1
1890	John W. Yates	2	1
1891	John W. Yates	2	1
1892	John W. Yates	2	1
1893	John W. Yates	2	1
1894	Willingsworth Iron Co.	2	1
1895	Willingsworth Iron Co.	2	1
1896	Willingsworth Iron Co.	2	1
1897	Willingsworth Iron Co.	2	1
1898	Willingsworth Iron Co.	2	1
1899	Willingsworth Iron Co.	2	1
1900	Willingsworth Iron Co.	2	1
1901	Willingsworth Iron Co.	2	1
1902	Willingsworth Iron Co.	2	1
1903	Willingsworth Iron Co.	2	1
1904	Willingsworth Iron Co.	2	1
1905	Willingsworth Iron Co.	2	1
1906	Willingsworth Iron Co.	2	1
1907	Willingsworth Iron Co.	2	2
1908	Willingsworth Iron Co.	2	2
1909	Willingsworth Iron Co.	2	2
1910	Willingsworth Iron Co.	2	1
1911	Willingsworth Iron Co. Ltd	2	2
1912	Willingsworth Iron Co. Ltd	2	2
1913	Willingsworth Iron Co. Ltd	2	2
1921	Willingsworth Iron Co. Ltd	2	-
1922	Willingsworth Iron Co. Ltd	2	-
1923	Willingsworth Iron Co. Ltd	2	-
1924	Willingsworth Iron Co. Ltd	2	-
1925	Willingsworth Iron Co. Ltd	2	-
1926	Willingsworth Iron Co. Ltd	2	-
1927	Willingsworth Iron Co. Ltd	2	-
1928	Willingsworth Iron Co. Ltd	2	-
1929	Willingsworth Iron Co. Ltd	2	-
1930	Willingsworth Iron Co. Ltd	2	-
1931	Willingsworth Iron Co. Ltd	2	-
1932	Willingsworth Iron Co. Ltd	2	-
1933	Willingsworth Iron Co. Ltd	2	-

Year	Owner	Built	In Blast
1934	Willingsworth Iron Co. Ltd	2	-
1935	Willingsworth Iron Co. Ltd	2	-
1936	Willingsworth Iron Co. Ltd	2	-
1937	Willingsworth Iron Co. Ltd	2	-
1938	Willingsworth Iron Co. Ltd	2	-
1939	Willingsworth Iron Co. Ltd	2	-
1940	Willingsworth Iron Co. Ltd	2	-
1941	Willingsworth Iron Co. Ltd	2	-
1942	Willingsworth Iron Co. Ltd	2	-
1943	Willingsworth Iron Co. Ltd	2	-

1823–30: two furnaces built in 1827 and a third in 1828; output in 1830 5,764 tons p.a. 1839: output 60 tons a week, 8,923 p.a.; 'forge'; cold blast. 1841: output 160 tons a week. 1843: output 160 tons a week. Truran: output 100 tons a week from each of 3 furnaces. Furnaces dismantled 1944.

Windmill End, Dudley, Worcs. [SO 9588]

Year	Owner	Built	In Blast
1810	Bancks & Co.	2	2
1825	Jones & Fereday	3	2
1830	—	2	-
1839	Sir H. St Paul	2	2
1841	Sir H. St Paul	2	1
1843	Sir H. St Paul	3	2
1847	Sir Horace St Paul	2	0
1849	W. Hadden	2	1
1852	W. Haden	2	1
1854	C.H. Plevins & Co.	2	2
1855	Woodall & Smith	3	3
1856	Woodall & Smith	3	3
1857	Woodall & Smith	3	2
1858	Woodall & Smith	3	2
1859	Woodall & Smith	3	2
1860	Samuel Griffiths	-	-
1861	Samuel Griffiths	3	2
1862	Samuel Griffiths	3	0
1863	Samuel Griffiths	3	0
1867	Hickman & Co.	1	1
1868	Hickman & Co.	1	1
1869	Hickman & Co.	1	1
1870	Joseph H. Pearson	1	1
1871	J.H. Pearson	2	1
1872	Sir Horace St Paul Bt	3	2
1873	J.H. Pearson	3	2
1874	J.H. Pearson	3	2
1875	J.H. Pearson	3	2
1876	J.H. Pearson	3	2
1877	J.H. Pearson	3	2
1878	Sir Horace St Paul Bt	3	2
1879	Sir Horace St Paul Bt	3	1
1880	Sir Horace St Paul Bt	3	2
1881	Sir Horace St Paul Bt	3	2
1882	Joseph H. Pearson	3	2
1883	Joseph H. Pearson	3	2
1884	Joseph H. Pearson	3	1
1885	Joseph H. Pearson	3	0
1886	Joseph H. Pearson	3	0
1887	Joseph H. Pearson	3	0
1888	Joseph H. Pearson	3	0
1889	Joseph H. Pearson	3	0
1890	Joseph H. Pearson	3	0
1891	Joseph H. Pearson	3	0

1823–30: two furnaces built in 1825, output 3,776 tons p.a. in 1830; this information can only be reconciled with that given in 1810 if two separate sites are involved or the works was completely rebuilt in 1825. The list of that year gives a weekly output figure of 90 tons, 5,750 tons p.a., 'melting trade' (B&W), 'melting iron' (Staffs RO). 1839: output 66 tons a week, 6,938 p.a. (actual); 'foundry and forge'; cold blast. 1841: output 80 tons a week. 1843: output 132 tons a week. Truran: output 100 tons a week from each of 2 furnaces.

Withygrove: see Withymoor

Withymoor, Staffs. [SO 9587]

Year	Owner	Built	In Blast
1825	British Iron Co.	2	2
1839	James Griffin	2	2
1841	Best & Barrs	2	1
1843	Best & Barrs	2	1
1847	Best & Bars	2	1
1849	Best & Bars	2	0
1852	Withymoor Co.	2	1
1854	W. Dawes	1	1
1855	W. Dawes	2	1
1856	W. Dawes	2	1
1857	W. Dawes	2	2
1858	W. Dawes	2	2
1859	W. Dawes	2	2
1860	John H. Dawes & Sons	2	1
1861	William Henry Dawes	2	2
1862	Executors of James Griffin	2	2
1863	William Henry Dawes	2	2
1864	John Dawes & Sons	2	2
1865	W.H. & John Dawes & Sons	2	2
1866	W. Henry Dawes	2	2
1867	John Dawes & Sons	2	2
1868	W.H. Dawes	2	2
1869	W.H. Dawes	2	2
1870	W.H. Dawes	2	2
1871	W.H. Dawes	2	2
1872	W.H. Dawes	2	2
1873	W.H. Dawes	2	2
1874	John Dawes	2	1
1875	John & George Dunn	2	1
1876	John & George Dunn	2	0
1877	John & George Dunn	2	0
1878	John & George Dunn	2	0

1825: weekly output 90 tons, 4,500 tons p.a., 'used by themselves'. The B&W text has 1 furnace, out of blast, the Staffs RO version has 2 furnaces, both in blast. 1839: output 50 tons a week, 1,400 p.a. (actual); 'forge'; cold blast. 1841: output 80 tons a week at 'Withemoor'. 1843: output 60 tons a week. The 1847 entry is for 'Withygrove', which presumably belongs here. 1849: Hunt lists 1 furnace in blast. Truran: output 100 tons a week from each of 2 furnaces. See also Dudley Wood and Netherton (Old). 1863–65: entries printed above appear under Bromford, W. Bromwich, in *Mineral Statistics* but evidently fill the gap that would otherwise occur there under Withygrove.

Wolverhampton, Staffs. [SO 9198]

Year	Owner	Furnaces	In Blast
1825	Tarratt, Timmins & Co.	1	0
1830	—	2	-
1839	Dixon, Mere & Co.	3	3
1841	Dixon, Neve & Co.	3	2
1843	Dixon, Neve & Hill	3	2
1847	Dixon, Nevi & Co.	3	2
1849	Dixon	3	2
1852	Whitehouse & Poole	3	2
1854	Whitehouse & Poole	3	2
1855	Edward Poole & Co.	3	2
1856	Edward Poole & Co.	3	2
1857	Edward Poole & Co.	3	2
1858	Edward Poole & Co.	3	2
1859	Edward Poole & Co.	3	1
1860	John Aston & Co.	3	0
1861	Isaiah Aston & Co.	3	2
1862	Isaiah Aston & Co.	3	1
1863	Isaiah Aston & Co.	3	1
1864	Isaiah Aston & Co.	3	2
1865	Isaiah Aston & Co.	2	2
1866	Isaiah Aston & Co.	2	2
1867	Assignees of Isaiah Aston & Co.	2	0
1868	Assignees of Isaiah Aston & Co.	2	0
1869	Assignees of Isaiah Aston & Co.	2	0
1870	Assignees of Isaiah Aston & Co.	2	0
1874	Thorneycroft & Co.	1	1

1823–30: one furnace built in 1825 and a second in 1827; output in 1830 3,200 tons p.a. 1825: weekly output 35 tons, 1,800 p.a. The B&W text has 1 furnace, out of blast, which corresponds with the evidence of the 1823–30 list; the Staffs RO version has 2 furnaces, 1 in blast. 1839: output 55 tons a week, 8,580 p.a. (actual); 'forge sale'; cold blast. The second partners in 1839–47 are probably one and the same, but it is not clear which name is correct. 1841: output 160 tons a week. 1843: output 140 tons a week. Truran: output 100 tons a week from each of 3 furnaces.

Wolverhampton: see also Chillington

Woodside, Dudley, Worcs. [SO 9288]

Year	Owner	Built	In Blast
1841	Bramah & Co.	2	1
1847	Cochrane & Co.	2	1
1849	Bramah & Cochrane	2	1
1852	Cochrane & Co.	2	2
1854	Cochrane & Co.	2	2
1855	Cochrane & Co.	2	2
1856	Cochrane & Co.	2	2
1857	Cochrane & Co.	2	2
1858	Cochrane & Co.	3	2
1859	Cochrane & Co.	3	2
1860	Cochrane & Co.	3	2
1861	Cochrane & Co.	3	2
1862	Cochrane & Co.	3	2
1863	Cochrane & Co.	3	2
1864	Cochrane & Co.	3	2
1865	Cochrane & Co.	3	2
1866	Cochrane & Co.	3	3
1867	Cochrane & Co.	3	2
1868	Cochrane & Co.	3	1
1869	Cochrane & Co.	3	2
1870	Cochrane & Co.	3	1
1871	Cochrane & Co.	3	3
1872	Cochrane & Co.	3	3
1873	Cochrane & Co.	3	3
1874	Cochrane & Co.	3	2
1875	Cochrane & Co.	3	2
1876	Cochrane & Co.	3	1
1877	Cochrane & Co.	3	2
1878	Cochrane & Co.	3	1
1879	Cochrane & Co.	3	2
1880	Cochrane & Co.	2	2
1881	Cochrane & Co.	3	2
1882	Cochrane & Co.	3	2
1883	Cochrane & Co.	3	2
1884	Cochrane & Co.	3	2
1885	Cochrane & Co.	3	2
1886	Cochrane & Co.	3	1
1887	Cochrane & Co.	2	1
1888	Cochrane & Co.	2	1
1889	Cochrane & Co.	2	1
1890	Cochrane & Co.	2	1
1891	Cochrane & Co.	2	1
1892	Cochrane & Co.	2	1
1893	Cochrane & Co.	2	1
1894	Cochrane & Co.	2	1
1895	Cochrane & Co.	2	1
1896	Cochrane & Co.	2	1
1897	Cochrane & Co.	2	1
1898	Cochrane & Co.	2	1
1899	Cochrane & Co.	2	1
1900	Cochrane & Co.	2	1
1901	Cochrane & Co.	2	1
1902	Cochrane & Co.	2	1
1903	Cochrane & Co.	2	1
1904	Cochrane & Co.	2	1
1905	Cochrane & Co.	2	1
1906	Cochrane & Co.	2	1
1907	Cochrane & Co.	2	1
1908	Cochrane & Co.	2	1
1909	Cochrane & Co.	2	1
1910	Cochrane & Co.	2	1
1911	Cochrane & Co. (Woodside) Ltd	2	1
1912	Cochrane & Co. (Woodside) Ltd	2	1
1913	Cochrane & Co. (Woodside) Ltd	2	1
1921	Cochrane & Co. Ltd	2	-
1922	Cochrane & Co. Ltd	2	-
1923	Cochrane & Co. Ltd	2	-
1924	Cochrane & Co. Ltd	2	-
1925	Cochrane & Co. Ltd	2	-
1926	Cochrane & Co. Ltd	2	-

1841: output 60 tons a week. 1849: Hunt lists 2 furnaces in blast. Truran: output 130 tons a week from each of 2 furnaces.

North Staffordshire

Apedale SJ 8248

Year	Owner	Built	In Blast
1794	Mr Parker	1	-
1796	—	1	1
1805	Parker	1	1
1810	Parker	1	1
1825	T. Firmstone	2	2
1839	Thomas Firmstone	3	2
1841	R.E. Heathcote	3	3
1843	R.C. Heathcote	3	2
1847	Heathcote	4	4
1849	—	-	3
1854	J.E. Heathcote	4	2
1855	J.E. Heathcote	4	2
1856	J.E. Heathcote	4	2
1857	J.E. Heathcote	4	2
1858	J.E. Heathcote	4	2
1859	J.E. Heathcote	4	-
1860	J.E. Heathcote	4	2
1861	J.E. Heathcote	4	3
1862	J.E. Heathcote	4	2
1863	J.E. Heathcote	4	2
1864	J.E. Heathcote	4	2
1865	J.E. Heathcote	4	3
1866	Apedale Coal & Iron Co.	4	3
1867	Apedale Coal & Iron Co.	4	0
1868	Stanier & Co.	4	1
1869	Stanier & Co.	4	3
1870	Stanier & Co.	4	3
1871	Stanier & Co.	4	3
1872	Stanier & Co.	8	6
1873	Stanier & Co.	8	5
1874	Stanier & Co.	10	6
1875	Stanier & Co.	10	6
1876	Stanier & Co.	8	4
1877	Stanier & Co.	6	4
1878	Stanier & Co.	6	2
1879	Stanier & Co.	8	4
1880	Stanier & Co.	6	2
1881	Stanier & Co.	6	3
1882	Stanier & Co.	6	3
1883	Stanier & Co.	6	3
1884	Stanier & Co.	6	3
1885	Stanier & Co.	6	3
1886	Stanier & Co.	6	3
1887	Francis Stanier	6	2
1888	Francis Stanier	6	2
1898	Francis Stanier	6	2
1890	Midland Coal, Coke & Iron Co. Ltd	6	1
1891	Midland Coal, Coke & Iron Co. Ltd	6	2
1892	Midland Coal, Coke & Iron Co. Ltd	6	2
1893	Midland Coal, Coke & Iron Co. Ltd	6	1
1894	Midland Coal, Coke & Iron Co. Ltd	6	0
1895	Midland Coal, Coke & Iron Co. Ltd	6	0
1896	Midland Coal, Coke & Iron Co. Ltd	6	0
1897	Midland Coal, Coke & Iron Co. Ltd	6	1
1898	Midland Coal, Coke & Iron Co. Ltd	6	1
1899	Midland Coal, Coke & Iron Co. Ltd	6	2
1900	Midland Coal, Coke & Iron Co. Ltd	6	2
1901	Midland Coal, Coke & Iron Co. Ltd	6	2
1902	Midland Coal, Coke & Iron Co. Ltd	6	2
1903	Midland Coal, Coke & Iron Co. Ltd	6	2
1904	Midland Coal, Coke & Iron Co. Ltd	6	1
1905	Midland Coal, Coke & Iron Co. Ltd	6	2
1906	Midland Coal, Coke & Iron Co. Ltd	6	2
1907	Midland Coal, Coke & Iron Co. Ltd	6	2
1908	Midland Coal, Coke & Iron Co. Ltd	6	2
1909	Midland Coal, Coke & Iron Co. Ltd	6	2
1910	Midland Coal, Coke & Iron Co. Ltd	6	3
1911	Midland Coal, Coke & Iron Co. Ltd	6	3
1912	Midland Coal, Coke & Iron Co. Ltd	6	3
1913	Midland Coal, Coke & Iron Co. Ltd	6	2
1921	Midland Coal, Coke & Iron Co. Ltd	5	-
1922	Midland Coal, Coke & Iron Co. Ltd	5	-
1923	Midland Coal, Coke & Iron Co. Ltd	5	-
1924	Midland Coal, Coke & Iron Co. Ltd	5	-
1925	Midland Coal, Coke & Iron Co. Ltd	5	-
1926	Midland Coal, Coke & Iron Co. Ltd	5	-
1927	Midland Coal, Coke & Iron Co. Ltd	5	-
1928	Midland Coal, Coke & Iron Co. Ltd	5	-
1929	Midland Coal, Coke & Iron Co. Ltd	5	-

The ground landlord in 1794 was Sir N. Gresley; the furnace was coke-fired and blown by engine; the date of building is given as 1784. 1796: output 2,100 tons p.a. Excise; 1,00 tons actual, 728 tons 10 cwt Exact Return. 1805: output 1,400 tons p.a. 1825: output 55 tons a week, 2,531 p.a., 'melting iron' (the Staffs RO version omits this phrase and notes instead: 'One will blow out next week', i.e. presumably at the end of March 1826). 1841: output 120 tons a week. 1843: output 100 tons a week. 1847: output 18,720 tons p.a., i.e. 360 tons a week, presumably meaning 90 tons from each of 4 furnaces. Truran: output 120 tons a week from each of 4 furnaces. In 1872–76 and 1879 the furnace-numbers given for Apedale also include those for Silverdale (qv). 1867: 4 furnaces being built.

Biddulph Valley [SJ 8857?]

Year	Owner	Built	In Blast
1860	F. Heath	2	2
1861	Robert Heath	3	3
1862	Robert Heath	4	3
1863	Robert Heath	4	4
1864	Robert Heath	4	4
1865	Robert Heath	6	4
1866	Robert Heath	6	4
1867	Robert Heath	6	6
1868	Robert Heath & Sons	7	7
1869	Robert Heath & Sons	8	4
1870	Robert Heath & Sons	8	8
1871	Robert Heath & Sons	8	8

Year	Owner	Built	In Blast
1872	Robert Heath & Sons	8	8
1873	Robert Heath & Sons	8	7
1874	Robert Heath & Sons	8	6
1875	Robert Heath & Sons	8	5
1876	Robert Heath & Sons	8	5
1877	Robert Heath & Sons	4	2
1878	Robert Heath & Sons	4	3
1879	Robert Heath & Sons	3	3
1880	Robert Heath & Sons	4	4
1881	Robert Heath & Sons	8	6
1882	Robert Heath & Sons	4	4
1883	Robert Heath & Sons	4	3
1884	Robert Heath & Sons	4	3
1885	Robert Heath & Sons	4	2
1886	Robert Heath & Sons	4	3
1887	Robert Heath & Sons	4	3
1888	Robert Heath & Sons	4	3
1889	Robert Heath & Sons	4	3
1890	Robert Heath & Sons	4	4
1891	Robert Heath & Sons	4	3
1892	Robert Heath & Sons	4	3
1893	Robert Heath & Sons	8	5
1894	Robert Heath & Sons Ltd	8	6
1895	Robert Heath & Sons Ltd	8	5
1896	Robert Heath & Sons Ltd	8	5
1897	Robert Heath & Sons Ltd	8	5
1898	Robert Heath & Sons Ltd	8	5
1899	Robert Heath & Sons Ltd	8	6
1900	Robert Heath & Sons Ltd	8	6
1901	Robert Heath & Sons Ltd	8	4
1902	Robert Heath & Sons Ltd	8	5
1903	Robert Heath & Sons Ltd	8	5
1904	Robert Heath & Sons Ltd	8	5
1905	Robert Heath & Sons Ltd	8	4
1906	Robert Heath & Sons Ltd	8	5
1907	Robert Heath & Sons Ltd	8	5
1908	Robert Heath & Sons Ltd	8	5
1909	Robert Heath & Sons Ltd	8	5
1910	Robert Heath & Sons Ltd	8	5
1911	Robert Heath & Sons Ltd	8	4
1912	Robert Heath & Sons Ltd	8	5
1913	Robert Heath & Sons Ltd	8	4
1921	Robert Heath & Low Moor Ltd	6	-
1922	Robert Heath & Low Moor Ltd	6	-
1923	Robert Heath & Low Moor Ltd	7	-
1924	Robert Heath & Low Moor Ltd	4	-
1925	Robert Heath & Low Moor Ltd	4	-
1926	Robert Heath & Low Moor Ltd	4	-
1927	Robert Heath & Low Moor Ltd	4	-
1928	Robert Heath & Low Moor Ltd	4	-

1866: 1 furnace building. In 1872–73 and 1881 furnace-numbers include Norton and in 1874–76 include Norton and Ravensdale (qqv), although there is no discontinuity apparent in the figures printed in *Mineral Statistics* at the first of these dates. 1879: 1 furnace building. From 1893 to 1913 there is a single entry for 'Biddulph Valley and Norton'. For Heath's Low Moor works see under Yorkshire, West Riding.

Chatterley [SJ 8451]

Year	Owner	Built	In Blast
1874	Chatterley Iron Co. Ltd	3	2
1875	Chatterley Iron Co. Ltd	3	2
1876	Chatterley Iron Co. Ltd	3	2
1877	Chatterley Iron Co. Ltd	3	1
1878	Chatterley Iron Co. Ltd	3	2
1879	Chatterley Iron Co. Ltd	3	2
1880	Chatterley Iron Co. Ltd	3	0
1881	Chatterley Iron Co. Ltd	3	2
1882	Chatterley Iron Co. Ltd	3	2
1883	Chatterley Iron Co. Ltd	3	2
1884	Chatterley Iron Co. Ltd	3	2
1885	Chatterley Iron Co. Ltd	3	2
1886	Chatterley Iron Co. Ltd	3	2
1887	Chatterley Iron Co. Ltd	3	2
1888	Chatterley Iron Co. Ltd	3	1
1889	Chatterley Iron Co. Ltd	3	2
1890	Chatterley-Whitfield Collieries Ltd	3	2
1891	Chatterley-Whitfield Collieries Ltd	3	2
1892	Chatterley-Whitfield Collieries Ltd	3	0
1893	Chatterley-Whitfield Collieries Ltd	3	1
1894	Chatterley-Whitfield Collieries Ltd	3	0
1895	Chatterley-Whitfield Collieries Ltd	3	0
1896	Chatterley-Whitfield Collieries Ltd	3	0
1897	Chatterley-Whitfield Collieries Ltd	3	0
1898	Chatterley-Whitfield Collieries Ltd	3	0
1899	Chatterley-Whitfield Collieries Ltd	3	1
1900	Chatterley-Whitfield Collieries Ltd	3	1
1901	Chatterley-Whitfield Collieries Ltd	2	0
1902	Chatterley-Whitfield Collieries Ltd	2	0
1903	Chatterley-Whitfield Collieries Ltd	2	0
1904	Chatterley-Whitfield Collieries Ltd	2	0
1905	Chatterley-Whitfield Collieries Ltd	2	0
1906	Chatterley-Whitfield Collieries Ltd	2	0
1907	Chatterley-Whitfield Collieries Ltd	2	0
1908	Chatterley-Whitfield Collieries Ltd	2	0
1909	Chatterley-Whitfield Collieries Ltd	2	0
1910	Chatterley-Whitfield Collieries Ltd	2	0
1911	Chatterley-Whitfield Collieries Ltd	2	0
1912	Chatterley-Whitfield Collieries Ltd	2	0
1913	Chatterley-Whitfield Collieries Ltd	2	0

Clough Hall: see Kidsgrove

Crewe: see Madeley

Etruria: see Shelton

Fenton: see Great Fenton

Fenton Park [SJ 8944?]

Year	Owner	Built	In Blast
1839	Thornborrow & Co.	2	2
1841	Thompson & Mussey	2	0
1843	Thompson & Co.	2	0
1856	Lawton & Co.	2	1
1857	Lawton & Co.	2	1
1858	Lawton & Co.	2	1
1859	Lawton & Co.	2	1
1860	Lawton & Co.	2	1

Year	Owner	Built	In Blast
1861	Lawton & Co.	2	2
1862	Lawton & Co.	2	1
1863	Lawton & Co.	2	1
1864	Lawton & Co.	2	1
1865	Lawton & Co.	2	1
1866	Lawton & Co.	2	1
1867	C. Leighton & G.P. Knocker	2	0
1868	C. Leighton & G.P. Knocker	2	0
1869	C. Leighton & G.P. Knocker	2	0
1870	C. Leighton & G.P. Knocker	2	0
1871	C. Leighton & G.P. Knocker	2	0

1841 and 1843: output nil in both years. 1867: Change of owners, Oct. 1867. 1871: works closed in 1870.

Foley: see Lane End

Goldendale [SJ 8651?]

Year	Owner	Built	In Blast
1847	Williamsons	2	2
1849	—	-	2
1854	Williamson Brothers	3	3
1855	Williamson Brothers	3	2
1856	Williamson Brothers	3	2
1857	Williamson Brothers	3	2
1858	Williamson Brothers	3	3
1859	Williamson Brothers	4	4
1860	Williamson Brothers	4	4
1861	Williamson Brothers	4	2
1862	Williamson Brothers	4	2
1863	Williamson Brothers	4	2
1864	Williamson Brothers	4	3
1865	Williamson Brothers	4	3
1866	Williamson Brothers	4	3
1867	Williamson Brothers	4	3
1868	Williamson Brothers	4	2
1869	Williamson Brothers	4	3
1870	Williamson Brothers	4	3
1871	Williamson Brothers	4	4
1872	Williamson Brothers	4	4
1873	Williamson Brothers	4	3
1874	Williamson Brothers	4	3
1875	Williamson Brothers	4	2
1876	Williamson Brothers	4	2
1877	Williamson Brothers	4	2
1878	Williamson Brothers	4	2
1879	Williamson Brothers	4	2
1880	Williamson Brothers	4	2
1881	Williamson Brothers	4	2
1882	Williamson Brothers	4	2
1883	Williamson Brothers	4	2
1884	Williamson Brothers	4	2
1885	Williamson Brothers	4	2
1885	Williamson Brothers	4	2
1886	Williamson Brothers	4	2
1887	Williamson Brothers	4	1
1888	Williamson Brothers	3	1
1889	Goldendale Iron Co.	3	1
1890	Goldendale Iron Co.	3	1
1891	Goldendale Iron Co.	3	2
1892	Goldendale Iron Co.	3	2
1893	Goldendale Iron Co.	3	1
1894	Goldendale Iron Co.	3	1
1895	Goldendale Iron Co.	3	1
1896	Goldendale Iron Co.	3	2
1897	Goldendale Iron Co.	3	2
1898	Goldendale Iron Co.	3	2
1899	Goldendale Iron Co.	3	2
1900	Goldendale Iron Co.	3	1
1901	Goldendale Iron Co.	3	1
1902	Goldendale Iron Co.	3	1
1903	Goldendale Iron Co.	3	1
1904	Goldendale Iron Co.	3	1
1905	Goldendale Iron Co.	3	1
1906	Goldendale Iron Co.	3	1
1907	Goldendale Iron Co.	3	1
1908	Goldendale Iron Co.	3	1
1909	Goldendale Iron Co.	3	1
1910	H.H. Williamson	3	1
1911	H.H. Williamson	3	1
1912	H.H. Williamson	3	1
1913	H.H. Williamson	3	1
1921	Goldendale Iron Co. Ltd	2	-
1922	Goldendale Iron Co. Ltd	2	-
1923	Goldendale Iron Co. Ltd	2	-
1924	Goldendale Iron Co. Ltd	2	-
1925	Goldendale Iron Co. Ltd	2	-
1926	Goldendale Iron Co. Ltd	2	-
1927	Goldendale Iron Co. Ltd	2	-
1928	Goldendale Iron Co. Ltd	2	-
1929	Goldendale Iron Co. Ltd	2	-
1930	Goldendale Iron Co. Ltd	2	-
1931	Goldendale Iron Co. Ltd	2	-
1932	Goldendale Iron Co. Ltd	2	-
1933	Goldendale Iron Co. Ltd	3	-
1934	Goldendale Iron Co. Ltd	3	-
1935	Goldendale Iron Co. Ltd	3	-
1936	Goldendale Iron Co. Ltd	3	-
1937	Goldendale Iron Co. Ltd	3	-
1938	Goldendale Iron Co. Ltd	3	-
1939	Goldendale Iron Co. Ltd	2	-
1940	Goldendale Iron Co. Ltd	2	-
1941	Goldendale Iron Co. Ltd	2	-
1942	Goldendale Iron Co. Ltd	2	-
1943	Goldendale Iron Co. Ltd	2	-
1944	Goldendale Iron Co. Ltd	2	-
1945	Goldendale Iron Co. Ltd	2	-
1946	Goldendale Iron Co. Ltd	2	-
1947	Goldendale Iron Co. Ltd	2	-
1948	Goldendale Iron Co. Ltd	2	-
1949	Goldendale Iron Co. Ltd	2	-
1950	Goldendale Iron Co. Ltd	2	-
1951	Goldendale Iron Co. Ltd	2	-
1952	Goldendale Iron Co. Ltd	2	-
1953	Goldendale Iron Co. Ltd	2	-
1954	Goldendale Iron Co. Ltd	2	-
1955	Goldendale Iron Co. Ltd	2	-
1956	Goldendale Iron Co. Ltd	2	-
1957	Goldendale Iron Co. Ltd	2	-
1958	Goldendale Iron Co. Ltd	2	-
1959	Goldendale Iron Co. Ltd	2	-
1960	Goldendale Iron Co. Ltd	2	-
1961	Goldendale Iron Co. Ltd	2	-
1962	Goldendale Iron Co. Ltd	2	-
1963	Goldendale Iron Co. Ltd	2	-
1964	Goldendale Iron Co. Ltd	2	-
1965	Goldendale Iron Co. Ltd	2	-
1966	Goldeedale Iron Co. Ltd	2	-
1967	Goldendale Iron Co. Ltd	2	-
1968	Goldendale Iron Co. Ltd	2	-
1969	Goldendale Iron Co. Ltd	2	-

| 1970 | Goldendale Iron Co. Ltd | 2 | - |

1847: called Tunstall; output 6,240 tons p.a., i.e. 60 tons a week from each of two furnaces. 1849: see also Latebrook. Truran: called Tunstall; output 95 tons a week from each of 2 furnaces. From 1953 the location is given as Stoke-on-Trent.

Goldenhill [SJ 9144?]

Year	Owner	Built	In Blast
1805	Barker	1	1
1810	Barker & Co.	2	2
1825	W. Banks	1	0

The 1805 list gives the output as 184 tons, returned by T. Barker, presumably the owner; that of 1825 gives nil as the output but adds the comment 'melting iron'. The Staffs RO version of the 1825 list adds the comments: 'This furnace has worked a month, will blow out in a few days' and (in the column headed March 1826) 'Not likely to work together at any time'.

Great Fenton [SJ 8944?]

Year	Owner	Built	In Blast
1884	Stafford Coal & Iron Co. Ltd	2	2
1885	Stafford Coal & Iron Co. Ltd	2	2
1886	Stafford Coal & Iron Co. Ltd	2	2
1887	Stafford Coal & Iron Co. Ltd	2	2
1888	Stafford Coal & Iron Co. Ltd	2	2
1889	Stafford Coal & Iron Co. Ltd	2	2
1890	Stafford Coal & Iron Co. Ltd	2	2
1891	Stafford Coal & Iron Co. Ltd	2	2
1892	Stafford Coal & Iron Co. Ltd	3	2
1893	Stafford Coal & Iron Co. Ltd	3	2
1894	Stafford Coal & Iron Co. Ltd	3	2
1895	Stafford Coal & Iron Co. Ltd	3	0
1896	Stafford Coal & Iron Co. Ltd	3	2
1897	Stafford Coal & Iron Co. Ltd	3	3
1898	Stafford Coal & Iron Co. Ltd	3	3
1899	Stafford Coal & Iron Co. Ltd	3	3
1900	Stafford Coal & Iron Co. Ltd	3	3
1901	Stafford Coal & Iron Co. Ltd	4	3
1902	Stafford Coal & Iron Co. Ltd	4	3
1903	Stafford Coal & Iron Co. Ltd	4	3
1904	Stafford Coal & Iron Co. Ltd	4	3
1905	Stafford Coal & Iron Co. Ltd	4	3
1906	Stafford Coal & Iron Co. Ltd	4	3
1907	Stafford Coal & Iron Co. Ltd	4	3
1908	Stafford Coal & Iron Co. Ltd	4	3
1909	Stafford Coal & Iron Co. Ltd	4	3
1910	Stafford Coal & Iron Co. Ltd	4	3
1911	Stafford Coal & Iron Co. Ltd	4	3
1912	Stafford Coal & Iron Co. Ltd	4	3
1913	Stafford Coal & Iron Co. Ltd	4	3
1921	Stafford Coal & Iron Co. Ltd	4	-
1922	Stafford Coal & Iron Co. Ltd	4	-
1923	Stafford Coal & Iron Co. Ltd	4	-
1924	Stafford Coal & Iron Co. Ltd	4	-
1925	Stafford Coal & Iron Co. Ltd	4	-
1926	Stafford Coal & Iron Co. Ltd	4	-
1927	Stafford Coal & Iron Co. Ltd	4	-
1928	Stafford Coal & Iron Co. Ltd	4	-
1929	Stafford Coal & Iron Co. Ltd	4	-
1930	Stafford Coal & Iron Co. Ltd	4	-
1931	Stafford Coal & Iron Co. Ltd	4	-
1932	Stafford Coal & Iron Co. Ltd	4	-
1933	Stafford Coal & Iron Co. Ltd	4	-

Kidsgrove [SJ 8454]

Year	Owner	Built	In Blast
1841	Thomas Kinnersley	3	3
1843	Thomas Kinnersley	3	3
1847	Kinnersley	3	3
1849	—	-	3
1854	Thomas Kinnersley	4	4
1855	Thomas Kinnersley	4	3
1856	Thomas Kinnersley	4	3
1857	Trustees of T. Kinnersley	4	4
1858	Trustees of T. Kinnersley	4	4
1859	Trustees of T. Kinnersley	4	4
1860	Trustees of T. Kinnersley	4	4
1861	Trustees of T. Kinnersley	4	2
1862	Kinnersley & Co.	4	3
1863	Miss & Mrs Kinnersley	4	4
1864	Miss G.M. Attwood & Mrs Kinnersley	4	4
1865	Mrs Kinnersley & Miss G.M. Attwood	4	3
1866	Mrs Kinnersley & Miss J.M. Attwood	4	4
1867	Kinnersley & Co.	4	3
1868	Kinnersley & Co.	4	4
1869	Kinnersley & Co.	4	4
1870	Kinnersley & Co.	4	4
1871	Kinnersley & Co.	4	4
1872	Kinnersley & Co.	4	4
1873	Kinnersley & Co.	4	4
1874	Kinnersley & Co.	4	4
1875	Kinnersley & Co.	4	4
1876	Kinnersley & Co.	4	4
1877	Kinnersley & Co.	4	3
1878	Kinnersley & Co.	4	3
1879	Kinnersley & Co.	4	3
1880	Kinnersley & Co.	4	4
1881	Kinnersley & Co.	4	4
1882	Kinnersley & Co.	4	4
1883	Kinnersley & Co.	4	4
1884	Kinnersley & Co.	4	3
1885	Kinnersley & Co.	4	4
1886	Kinnersley & Co.	4	2
1887	Kinnersley & Co.	4	0
1888	Kidsgrove Steel, Iron & Coal Co. Ltd	4	1
1889	Kidsgrove Steel, Iron & Coal Co. Ltd	4	0
1890	Kidsgrove Steel, Iron & Coal Co. Ltd	4	1
1891	Kidsgrove Steel, Iron & Coal Co. Ltd	4	0
1892	Kidsgrove Steel, Iron & Coal Co. Ltd	4	0
1893	Birchenwood Colliery Co. Ltd	4	0
1894	Birchenwood Colliery Co. Ltd	4	0

1841: output 150 tons a week. 1843: output 150 tons a week. The 1847 list gives an annual output of 13,520 tons, i.e. 260 tons a week. Truran: output 110 tons a week from each of 3 furnaces. The 1843 list uses the name Clough Hall, as does *Mineral Statistics* from 1857.

Lane End SJ 9043

Year	Owner	Built	In Blast
1839	W. Sparrow & Co.	2	2
1841	W.H. Sparrow	3	2
1843	Sparrow & Co.	3	1
1847	Sparrow	3	2
1849	—	-	2
1854	W.H. Sparrow	3	2
1855	W.H. Sparrow	3	2
1856	W.H. Sparrow	3	2
1857	W.H. Sparrow	3	3
1858	W.H. Sparrow & Son	3	3
1859	W.H. Sparrow & Son	3	3
1860	W.H. Sparrow & Son	3	2
1861	W.H. Sparrow & Son	3	3
1862	W.H. Sparrow & Son	3	2
1863	W.H. Sparrow & Son	3	3
1864	Duke of Sutherland	3	2
1865	W.H. Sparrow & Son	3	2
1866	W.H. Sparrow & Son	3	2
1867	W.H. Sparrow & Son	3	2
1868	T. Goddard & Son	3	2
1869	T. Goddard & Brothers	3	2
1870	John H. & William Goddard	3	2
1871	John H. & William Goddard	3	3
1872	Thomas Goddard & Sons	2	2
1873	Thomas Goddard & Sons	2	2
1874	Thomas Goddard & Sons	2	2
1875	Thomas Goddard & Sons	2	1
1876	Thomas Goddard & Sons	2	1
1877	Thomas Goddard & Sons	2	0
1878	Thomas Goddard & Sons	2	0
1879	Thomas Goddard & Sons	2	0
1880	Thomas Goddard & Sons	2	0
1881	Balfour & Co.	2	0
1882	Balfour & Co.	2	0
1883	Balfour & Co.	2	0
1884	Balfour & Co.	2	0
1885	Balfour & Co.	2	0
1886	Balfour & Co.	2	0
1887	Lane End Works Ltd	2	0
1888	Lane End Works Ltd	2	0
1889	Lane End Works Ltd	2	0

1841: output 150 tons a week. 1843: output 75 tons a week. 1847: output 8,320 tons p.a., i.e. 160 tons a week, presumably meaning 80 tons from each furnace. Truran: output 100 tons a week from each of 3 furnaces. In *Mineral Statistics* the works appears under Foley in 1854–56 and Longton Lane End in 1860, otherwise Lane End. There are duplicate entries for Lane End in the South Staffs. section of *Mineral Statistics* in 1859 and 1865.

Latebrook [SJ 8453?]

Year	Owner	Built	In Blast
1849	—	-	2

This is either the only reference to an otherwise unrecorded short-lived site or a duplicate entry for Goldendale (qv).

Lawton, Ches. [SJ 8056]

Year	Owner	Built	In Blast
1839	Thomas Kinnersley	1	1

The owner's name has been amended from 'Kennersley'; this site was evidently not identical with the family's main works at Kidsgrove (qv).

Longton Hall [SJ 9043]

Year	Owner	Built	In Blast
1877	James & Alfred Glover	2	2
1878	James & Alfred Glover	2	2
1879	James & Alfred Glover	2	2
1880	James & Alfred Glover	2	2
1881	James & Alfred Glover	2	2
1882	James & Alfred Glover	2	1
1883	James & Alfred Glover	3	2
1884	James & Alfred Glover	3	2
1885	James & Alfred Glover	3	1
1886	James & Alfred Glover	3	0
1887	James & Alfred Glover	3	0
1888	James & Alfred Glover	3	0
1889	Longton Hall Co. Ltd	2	0
1890	Longton Hall Co. Ltd	3	0
1891	Longton Hall Co. Ltd	3	0
1892	Longton Hall Co. Ltd	3	0
1893	Longton Hall Co. Ltd	3	0
1894	Longton Hall Co. Ltd	3	0
1895	Longton Hall Co. Ltd	3	0
1896	Longton Hall Co. Ltd	3	0
1897	Longton Hall Co. Ltd	3	0
1898	Longton Hall Co. Ltd	3	0
1899	Longton Hall Co. Ltd	3	0
1900	Longton Hall Co. Ltd	3	0
1901	Longton Hall Co. Ltd	3	0
1902	Longton Hall Co. Ltd	3	0
1903	—	3	0

Longton Lane End: see Lane End

Madeley [SJ 7744]

Year	Owner	Built	In Blast
1841	T. Firmstone	2	0
1843	J. Firmstone	1	1
1847	Firmstone	2	1
1849	—	-	1
1854	Thomas Firmstone	2	1

1841: works called Crewe; output nil. 1843: works not named; output 50 tons a week; the initial shown above may be a misprint for T. 1847: output 4,160 tons p.a., i.e. 80 tons a week from the single furnace then in blast. Truran: output 100 tons a week from each of 2 furnaces.

Norton [SJ 8951?]

Year	Owner	Built	In Blast
1870	Robert Heath	4	4
1872	Robert Heath & Sons	-	-
1873	Robert Heath & Sons	-	-
1874	Robert Heath & Sons	-	-
1875	Robert Heath & Sons	-	-
1876	Robert Heath & Sons	-	-
1877	Robert Heath & Sons	4	4
1878	Robert Heath & Sons	4	4
1879	Robert Heath & Sons	4	3
1880	Robert Heath & Sons	4	2
1881	Robert Heath & Sons	-	-
1882	Robert Heath & Sons	4	3
1883	Robert Heath & Sons	4	3
1884	Robert Heath & Sons	4	3
1885	Robert Heath & Sons	4	2
1886	Robert Heath & Sons	4	3
1887	Robert Heath & Sons	4	3
1888	Robert Heath & Sons	4	3
1889	Robert Heath & Sons	4	3
1890	Robert Heath & Sons	4	4
1891	Robert Heath & Sons	4	4
1892	Robert Heath & Sons	4	2

There is no entry for Norton in 1871; the furnace-numbers may be subsumed within those for Biddulph (qv), although this is not explicitly stated. In 1872–76, 1881 and from 1893 figures for Norton are definitely included with Biddulph. In 1877–80 the entries given above are said to be for Norton and Ravensdale (qv); the latter works is also included in the Biddulph entries for 1874–76.

Partridge Nest: see Springwood

Ravensdale SJ 8551

Year	Owner	Built	In Blast
1874	Robert Heath & Sons	-	-
1875	Robert Heath & Sons	-	-
1876	Robert Heath & Sons	-	-
1877	Robert Heath & Sons	-	-
1878	Robert Heath & Sons	-	-
1879	Robert Heath & Sons	-	-
1880	Robert Heath & Sons	-	-

Furnace-numbers are combined with Biddulph Valley in 1874–76 and with Norton in 1877–80 (qqv).

Roggin Row: see Springwood

Shelton SJ 8648

Year	Owner	Built	In Blast
1839	Earl Granville	0	0
1841	Earl Granville	3	2
1843	Earl Granville	3	0
1847	Earl Granville	3	2
1849	—	-	3
1854	Earl Granville	8	5
1855	Earl Granville	8	6
1856	Earl Granville	8	7
1857	Earl Granville	8	8
1858	Earl Granville	8	6
1859	Earl Granville	8	7
1860	Earl Granville	8	8
1861	Earl Granville	8	7
1862	Earl Granville	8	7
1863	Earl Granville	8	6
1864	Earl Granville	8	6
1865	Earl Granville	8	6
1866	Earl Granville	8	6
1867	Earl Granville	8	6
1868	Earl Granville	8	6
1869	Earl Granville	8	8
1870	Earl Granville	8	8
1871	Earl Granville	8	7
1872	Earl Granville and the Shelton Bar Iron Co.	8	7
1873	Earl Granvile	8	6
1874	Earl Granville	8	5
1875	Earl Granville	8	5
1876	Earl Granville	8	6
1877	Earl Granville	4	4
1878	Earl Granville	4	4
1879	Earl Granville	5	5
1880	Earl Granville	5	5
1881	Earl Granville	6	4
1882	Earl Granville	6	4
1883	Earl Granville	6	4
1884	Earl Granville	6	4
1885	Earl Granville	6	4
1886	Earl Granville	6	4
1887	Earl Granville	6	4
1888	Earl Granville	6	5
1889	Earl Granville	6	5
1890	Shelton Iron, Steel & Coal Co. Ltd	6	5
1891	Shelton Iron, Steel & Coal Co. Ltd	6	3
1892	Shelton Iron, Steel & Coal Co. Ltd	6	4
1893	Shelton Iron, Steel & Coal Co. Ltd	6	3
1894	Shelton Iron, Steel & Coal Co. Ltd	6	4
1895	Shelton Iron, Steel & Coal Co. Ltd	6	4
1896	Shelton Iron, Steel & Coal Co. Ltd	6	4
1897	Shelton Iron, Steel & Coal Co. Ltd	6	4
1898	Shelton Iron, Steel & Coal Co. Ltd	6	5
1899	Shelton Iron, Steel & Coal Co. Ltd	6	5
1900	Shelton Iron, Steel & Coal Co. Ltd	6	4
1901	Shelton Iron, Steel & Coal Co. Ltd	6	4
1902	Shelton Iron, Steel & Coal Co. Ltd	6	4
1903	Shelton Iron, Steel & Coal Co. Ltd	6	4
1904	Shelton Iron, Steel & Coal Co. Ltd	6	4
1905	Shelton Iron, Steel & Coal Co. Ltd	6	4
1906	Shelton Iron, Steel & Coal Co. Ltd	6	4
1907	Shelton Iron, Steel & Coal Co. Ltd	6	5
1908	Shelton Iron, Steel & Coal Co. Ltd	6	4
1909	Shelton Iron, Steel & Coal Co. Ltd	4	3
1910	Shelton Iron, Steel & Coal Co. Ltd	4	3
1911	Shelton Iron, Steel & Coal Co. Ltd	4	3
1912	Shelton Iron, Steel & Coal Co. Ltd	4	3
1913	Shelton Iron, Steel & Coal Co. Ltd	4	3
1921	Shelton Iron, Steel & Coal Co. Ltd	4	-
1922	Shelton Iron, Steel & Coal Co. Ltd	4	-
1923	Shelton Iron, Steel & Coal Co. Ltd	4	-

Year	Owner	Built	In Blast
1924	Shelton Iron, Steel & Coal Co. Ltd	4	-
1925	Shelton Iron, Steel & Coal Co. Ltd	4	-
1926	Shelton Iron, Steel & Coal Co. Ltd	4	-
1927	Shelton Iron, Steel & Coal Co. Ltd	4	-
1928	Shelton Iron, Steel & Coal Co. Ltd	4	-
1929	Shelton Iron, Steel & Coal Co. Ltd	4	-
1930	Shelton Iron, Steel & Coal Co. Ltd	4	-
1931	Shelton Iron, Steel & Coal Co. Ltd	4	-
1932	Shelton Iron, Steel & Coal Co. Ltd	3	-
1933	Shelton Iron, Steel & Coal Co. Ltd	3	-
1934	Shelton Iron, Steel & Coal Co. Ltd	3	-
1935	Shelton Iron, Steel & Coal Co. Ltd	3	-
1936	Shelton Iron, Steel & Coal Co. Ltd	3	-
1937	Shelton Iron, Steel & Coal Co. Ltd	3	-
1938	Shelton Iron, Steel & Coal Co. Ltd	3	-
1939	Shelton Iron, Steel & Coal Co. Ltd	3	-
1940	Shelton Iron, Steel & Coal Co. Ltd	3	-
1941	Shelton Iron, Steel & Coal Co. Ltd	3	-
1942	Shelton Iron, Steel & Coal Co. Ltd	3	-
1943	Shelton Iron, Steel & Coal Co. Ltd	3	-
1944	Shelton Iron, Steel & Coal Co. Ltd	3	-
1945	Shelton Iron, Steel & Coal Co. Ltd	3	-
1946	Shelton Iron, Steel & Coal Co. Ltd	3	-
1947	Shelton Iron, Steel & Coal Co. Ltd	3	-
1948	Shelton Iron, Steel & Coal Co. Ltd	3	-
1949	Shelton Iron, Steel & Coal Co. Ltd	3	-
1950	Shelton Iron, Steel & Coal Co. Ltd	3	-
1951	Shelton Iron, Steel & Coal Co. Ltd	3	-
1952	Shelton Iron, Steel & Coal Co. Ltd	3	-
1953	Shelton Iron, Steel & Coal Co. Ltd	3	-
1954	Shelton Iron, Steel & Coal Co. Ltd	3	-
1955	Shelton Iron, Steel & Coal Co. Ltd	3	-
1956	Shelton Iron & Steel Ltd	3	-
1957	Shelton Iron & Steel Ltd	3	-
1958	Shelton Iron & Steel Ltd	3	-
1959	Shelton Iron & Steel Ltd	3	-
1960	Shelton Iron & Steel Ltd	3	-
1961	Shelton Iron & Steel Ltd	3	-
1962	Shelton Iron & Steel Ltd	3	-
1963	Shelton Iron & Steel Ltd	3	-
1964	Shelton Iron & Steel Ltd	3	-
1965	Shelton Iron & Steel Ltd	3	-
1966	Shelton Iron & Steel Ltd	3	-
1967	Shelton Iron & Steel Ltd	3	-
1968	Shelton Iron & Steel Ltd	3	-
1969	Shelton Iron & Steel Ltd	3	-
1970	British Steel Corporation	3	-
1971	British Steel Corporation	3	-
1972	British Steel Corporation	3	-
1973	British Steel Corporation	3	-
1974	British Steel Corporation	3	-
1975	British Steel Corporation	3	-
1976	British Steel Corporation	3	-
1977	British Steel Corporation	3	-

1839: 3 furnaces building. 1841: output 100 tons a week. 1843: output nil. 1847: output 7,280 tons p.a., i.e. 70 tons a week from each furnace. Truran: output 100 tons a week from each of 3 furnaces. In 1841, 1847 and Truran the works is called Etruria. From 1953 the location is given as Stoke-on-Trent.

Silverdale

SJ 8147

Year	Owner	Built	In Blast
1796	—	1	1
1805	G. Sneyd & Co.	1	1
1810	Parker	1	1
1825	W. Sneyd	2	1
1839	W. Sneyd	2	0
1841	R. Sneyd	2	2
1843	Ralph Sneyd	3	1
1847	R. Sneyd	2	2
1849	—	-	3
1854	F. Stanier & Co.	4	4
1855	F. Stanier & Co.	4	3
1856	F. Stanier & Co.	4	3
1857	F. Stanier & Co.	3	3
1858	F. Stanier & Co.	3	3
1859	Silverdale Co.	4	3
1860	Silverdale Co.	4	2
1861	F. Stanier & Son	4	2
1862	F. Stanier & Son	4	2
1863	Mrs Stanier & F. Stanier Broade	4	3
1864	Silverdale Co.	4	3
1865	Silverdale Co.	4	3
1866	Silverdale Co.	4	3
1867	Silverdale Iron Co.	4	3
1868	Stanier & Co.	4	2
1869	Stanier & Co.	4	3
1870	Stanier & Co.	4	3
1871	Stanier & Co.	-	-
1872	Stanier & Co.	-	-
1873	Stanier & Co.	-	-
1874	Stanier & Co.	-	-
1875	Stanier & Co.	-	-
1876	Stanier & Co.	-	-
1877	Stanier & Co.	2	2
1878	Stanier & Co.	2	2
1879	Stanier & Co.	-	-
1880	Stanier & Co.	2	2
1881	Stanier & Co.	2	2
1882	Stanier & Co.	2	2
1883	Butterley Co.	2	2
1884	Butterley Co.	1	1
1885	Butterley Co.	2	2
1886	Butterley Co.	2	2
1887	Butterley Co.	2	2
1888	Butterley Co. Ltd	2	2
1889	Butterley Co. Ltd	2	2
1890	Butterley Co. Ltd	2	2
1891	Butterley Co. Ltd	2	2
1892	Butterley Co. Ltd	2	2
1893	Butterley Co. Ltd	2	1
1894	Butterley Co. Ltd	2	1
1895	Butterley Co. Ltd	2	2
1896	Butterley Co. Ltd	2	2
1897	Butterley Co. Ltd	2	2
1898	Butterley Co. Ltd	2	2
1899	Butterley Co. Ltd	2	2
1900	Butterley Co. Ltd	2	2
1901	Butterley Co. Ltd	2	0
1902	Butterley Co. Ltd	2	0

1796: output 2,600 tons p.a. Excise, 1,200 tons actual, Exact Return 1,230 tons. 1805: output 1,010 tons p.a. 1825: weekly figure of 30 tons, 1,500 tons p.a., 'melting iron' (the Staffs RO version of the list comments: 'One will blow out next week'). 1841: output 100 tons a week. 1843: output 60 tons a week. 1847: output 7,280 tons p.a., i.e. 70 tons a week from each of two furnaces. Truran: output 90 tons a week from each of 2 furnaces. In 1871–76 and 1879 furnace-numbers for Silverdale and Apedale were given together under the latter heading (qv).

Springwood SJ 8249

Year	Owner	Built	In Blast
1794	Kinnersley	1	-
1825	Kinnersley & Heathcote	1	0

The 1794 list contains a defective entry towards the end of the Staffordshire section which, by comparison with other evidence, must refer to the short-lived, unsuccessful coke-fired furnace at Springwood. In the original MS the scribe has written 'Cannock Wood' in error on the line above that on which Cannock Wood rolling mill is described; he has crossed it through but not inserted anything else in its place. The other details, however, match what is known about Springwood: the ground landlord was Sir T. Heathcote, the occupier's name was Kinnersley and there was one coke-fired furnace, blown by engine, built in 1790. The only other list in which Springwood may appear is that of 1825, which includes, under South Staffs., a furnace at 'Roggin Row', owned by Kinnersley & Heathcote, with no output and the comment 'can't work'. The owners' names belong in North Staffs., rather than the Black Country, and fit with the entry in the 1794 list for Springwood. The name 'Roggin Row' has not been located anywhere in Staffordshire.

Talke o' th' Hill [SJ 8253]

Year	Owner	Built	In Blast
1862	Company Ltd	2	0
1863	Company Ltd	2	0
1864	North Staffordshire Coal & Iron Co. Ltd	2	0
1870	North Staffordshire Coal & Iron Co. Ltd	2	2
1871	North Staffordshire Coal & Iron Co. Ltd	2	2
1872	New North Staffordshire Coal & Iron Co. Ltd	2	2
1873	New North Staffordshire Coal & Iron Co. Ltd	2	1

The entries for 1862–63 were printed in the South Staffs. section of *Mineral Statistics*; it is not clear what the owner's name in these years is intended to be, although the company listed in 1864 was registered as early as 1857.

Tunstall: see Goldendale

Northamptonshire

Corby			SP 8989
Year	Owner	Built	In Blast
1910	Lloyds Ironstone Co. Ltd	2	1
1911	Lloyds Ironstone Co. Ltd	2	2
1912	Lloyds Ironstone Co. Ltd	2	2
1913	Lloyds Ironstone Co. Ltd	2	2
1921	Lloyds Ironstone Co. Ltd	2	-
1922	Lloyds Ironstone Co. Ltd	3	-
1923	Lloyds Ironstone Co. Ltd	3	-
1924	Lloyds Ironstone Co. Ltd	3	-
1925	Lloyds Ironstone Co. Ltd	3	-
1926	Lloyds Ironstone Co. Ltd	3	-
1927	Lloyds Ironstone Co. Ltd	3	-
1928	Lloyds Ironstone Co. Ltd	3	-
1929	Lloyds Ironstone Co. Ltd	3	-
1930	Lloyds Ironstone Co. Ltd	3	-
1931	Lloyds Ironstone Co. Ltd	3	-
1932	Lloyds Ironstone Co. Ltd	3	-
1933	Stewarts & Lloyds Ltd	3	-
1934	Stewarts & Lloyds Ltd	3	-
1935	Stewarts & Lloyds Ltd	3	-
1936	Stewarts & Lloyds Ltd	3	-
1937	Stewarrs & Lloyds Ltd	4	-
1938	Stewarts & Lloyds Ltd	4	-
1939	Stewarts & Lloyds Ltd	4	-
1940	Stewarts & Lloyds Ltd	4	-
1941	Stewarts & Lloyds Ltd	4	-
1942	Stewarts & Lloyds Ltd	4	-
1943	Stewarts & Lloyds Ltd	4	-
1944	Stewarts & Lloyds Ltd	4	-
1945	Stewarts & Lloyds Ltd	4	-
1946	Stewarts & Lloyds Ltd	4	-
1947	Stewarts & Lloyds Ltd	4	-
1948	Stewarts & Lloyds Ltd	4	-
1949	Stewarts & Lloyds Ltd	4	-
1950	Stewarts & Lloyds Ltd	4	-
1951	Stewarts & Lloyds Ltd	4	-
1952	Stewarts & Lloyds Ltd	4	-
1953	Stewarts & Lloyds Ltd	4	-
1954	Stewarts & Lloyds Ltd	4	-
1955	Stewarts & Lloyds Ltd	4	-
1956	Stewarts & Lloyds Ltd	4	-
1957	Stewarts & Lloyds Ltd	4	-
1958	Stewarts & Lloyds Ltd	4	-
1959	Stewarts & Lloyds Ltd	4	-
1960	Stewarts & Lloyds Ltd	4	-
1961	Stewarts & Lloyds Ltd	4	-
1962	Stewarts & Lloyds Ltd	4	-
1963	Stewarts & Lloyds Ltd	4	-
1964	Stewarts & Lloyds Ltd	4	-
1965	Stewarts & Lloyds Ltd	4	-
1966	Stewarts & Lloyds Ltd	4	-
1967	Stewarts & Lloyds Ltd	4	-
1968	Stewarts & Lloyds Ltd	4	-
1969	Stewarts & Lloyds Ltd	4	-
1970	British Steel Corporation	4	-
1971	British Steel Corporation	4	-
1972	British Steel Corporation	4	-
1973	British Steel Corporation	4	-
1974	British Steel Corporation	4	-
1975	British Steel Corporation	4	-
1976	British Steel Corporation	4	-
1977	British Steel Corporation	4	-
1978	British Steel Corporation	4	-
1979	British Steel Corporation	4	-

Cransley, Kettering			SP 8477
Year	Owner	Built	In Blast
1875	Cransley Iron Co. Ltd	2	0
1876	Cransley Iron Co. Ltd	2	0
1877	Cransley Iron Co. Ltd	2	1
1878	Cransley Iron Co. Ltd	2	2
1879	Cransley Iron Co. Ltd	2	2
1880	Cransley Iron Co. Ltd	2	2
1881	Cransley Iron Co. Ltd	2	0
1882	Cransley Iron Co. Ltd	3	2
1883	Cransley Iron Co. Ltd	3	2
1884	Cransley Iron Co. Ltd	3	1
1885	Cransley Iron Co. Ltd	3	2
1886	Cransley Iron Co. Ltd	3	0
1887	Cransley Iron Co. Ltd	2	0
1888	Cransley Iron Co. Ltd	2	0
1890	New Cransley Iron & Steel Co. Ltd	2	1
1891	New Cransley Iron & Steel Co. Ltd	1	1
1892	New Cransley Iron & Steel Co. Ltd	2	1
1893	New Cransley Iron & Steel Co. Ltd	2	1
1894	New Cransley Iron & Steel Co. Ltd	2	1
1895	New Cransley Iron & Steel Co. Ltd	2	2
1896	New Cransley Iron & Steel Co. Ltd	2	2
1897	New Cransley Iron & Steel Co. Ltd	2	1
1898	New Cransley Iron & Steel Co. Ltd	2	2
1899	New Cransley Iron & Steel Co. Ltd	2	2
1900	New Cransley Iron & Steel Co. Ltd	2	1
1901	New Cransley Iron & Steel Co. Ltd	2	1
1902	New Cransley Iron & Steel Co. Ltd	2	1
1903	New Cransley Iron & Steel Co. Ltd	2	1
1904	New Cransley Iron & Steel Co. Ltd	2	1
1905	New Cransley Iron & Steel Co. Ltd	2	1
1906	New Cransley Iron & Steel Co. Ltd	2	2
1907	New Cransley Iron & Steel Co. Ltd	2	1
1908	New Cransley Iron & Steel Co. Ltd	2	1
1909	New Cransley Iron & Steel Co. Ltd	2	1
1910	New Cransley Iron & Steel Co. Ltd	2	1
1911	New Cransley Iron & Steel Co. Ltd	2	1
1912	New Cransley Iron & Steel Co. Ltd	2	1
1913	New Cransley Iron & Steel Co. Ltd	2	1
1921	New Cransley Iron & Steel Co. Ltd	2	-
1922	New Cransley Iron & Steel Co. Ltd	2	-
1923	New Cransley Iron & Steel Co. Ltd	2	-
1924	New Cransley Iron & Steel Co. Ltd	2	-
1925	New Cransley Iron & Steel Co. Ltd	2	-
1926	New Cransley Iron & Steel Co. Ltd	2	-

Year	Owner	Built	In Blast
1927	New Cransley Iron & Steel Co. Ltd	2	-
1928	New Cransley Iron & Steel Co. Ltd	1	-
1929	New Cransley Iron & Steel Co. Ltd	1	-
1930	New Cransley Iron & Steel Co. Ltd	1	-
1931	New Cransley Iron & Steel Co. Ltd	2	-
1921	New Cransley Iron & Steel Co. Ltd	2	-
1932	New Cransley Iron & Steel Co. Ltd	2	-
1933	New Cransley Iron & Steel Co. Ltd	2	-
1934	New Cransley Iron & Steel Co. Ltd	2	-
1935	New Cransley Iron & Steel Co. Ltd	2	-
1936	New Cransley Iron & Steel Co. Ltd	2	-
1937	New Cransley Iron & Steel Co. Ltd	2	-
1938	New Cransley Iron & Steel Co. Ltd	2	-
1939	New Cransley Iron & Steel Co. Ltd	2	-
1940	New Cransley Iron & Steel Co. Ltd	2	-
1941	New Cransley Iron & Steel Co. Ltd	2	-
1942	New Cransley Iron & Steel Co. Ltd	2	-
1943	New Cransley Iron & Steel Co. Ltd	2	-
1944	New Cransley Iron & Steel Co. Ltd	2	-
1945	New Cransley Iron & Steel Co. Ltd	2	-
1946	New Cransley Iron & Steel Co. Ltd	2	-
1947	New Cransley Iron & Steel Co. Ltd	2	-
1948	New Cransley Iron & Steel Co. Ltd	2	-
1949	New Cransley Iron & Steel Co. Ltd	2	-
1950	New Cransley Iron & Steel Co. Ltd	2	-
1951	New Cransley Iron & Steel Co. Ltd	2	-
1952	New Cransley Iron & Steel Co. Ltd	2	-
1953	New Cransley Iron & Steel Co. Ltd	2	-
1954	New Cransley Iron & Steel Co. Ltd	2	-
1955	New Cransley Iron & Steel Co. Ltd	2	-
1956	New Cransley Iron & Steel Co. Ltd	2	-

1875: Building. 1880: 1 furnace building. 1881: 1 furnace in blast for 2 months and another building. 1883: Production estimated.

East End Ironworks: see Wellingborough

Finedon SP 8972

Year	Owner	Built	In Blast
1866	Glendon Ore Co.	1	1
1867	Glendon Iron Ore Co.	1	1
1868	Glendon Iron Ore Co.	2	2
1869	Glendon Iron Ore Co.	3	3
1870	Glendon Iron Ore Co.	3	3
1871	Glendon Iron Ore Co.	3	3
1872	Checkland & Fisher	3	3
1873	Checkland & Fisher	3	3
1874	Checkland & Fisher	3	3
1875	Checkland & Fisher	3	3
1876	Checkland & Fisher	5	3
1877	Checkland & Fisher	5	4
1878	Checkland & Fisher	5	5
1879	Checkland & Fisher	5	5
1880	Checkland & Fisher	5	5
1881	Checkland & Fisher	5	5
1882	G.E. Checkland & E.K. Fisher	6	5
1883	Glendon Iron Co.	6	5
1884	Glendon Iron Co.	6	4
1885	Glendon Iron Co.	6	4
1886	Glendon Iron Co. Ltd	6	3
1887	Glendon Iron Co. Ltd	6	3
1888	Glendon Iron Co. Ltd	6	3
1889	Glendon Iron Co. Ltd	6	4
1890	Glendon Iron Co. Ltd	6	2
1891	Glendon Iron Co. Ltd	6	1
1892	Islip Iron Co.	6	0
1893	Islip Iron Co.	6	0
1894	Islip Iron Co.	6	0
1895	Islip Iron Co.	6	0
1896	Islip Iron Co.	6	0
1897	Islip Iron Co.	6	0
1898	Islip Iron Co.	6	0
1899	Islip Iron Co.	6	0
1900	Islip Iron Co.	3	0
1901	Islip Iron Co.	3	0
1902	Islip Iron Co.	2	0
1903	Islip Iron Co. Ltd	2	0
1904	Islip Iron Co. Ltd	2	0
1905	Islip Iron Co. Ltd	2	0
1906	Islip Iron Co. Ltd	2	0
1907	Islip Iron Co. Ltd	2	0
1908	Islip Iron Co. Ltd	2	0

1873: 1 new furnace building. 1875: 2 furnaces building. 1877: fifth furnace put in blast Jan. 1878. 1879: 1 new furnace building. 1880: same comment as 1879. In 1866 the name of both works and owner was given (in obvious error) as 'Glendow'. See under Islip for the various concerns known as the Islip Iron Co.

Heyford SP 6557

Year	Owner	Built	In Blast
1857	Pell & Co.	2	2
1858	Pell & Co.	2	2
1859	Pell & Co.	3	2
1860	Pell & Co.	3	2
1861	S. Griffiths	3	2
1862	George Pell	3	2
1863	George Pell	3	2
1864	George Pell	2	2
1865	Heyford Co. Ltd	3	2
1866	Heyford Co. Ltd	3	2
1867	George Pell	3	2
1868	George Pell	3	2
1869	George Pell	3	2
1870	C.H. Plevins	3	3
1871	George Pell	3	3
1872	Plevins & Co.	3	2
1873	Heyford Iron Co. Ltd	3	2
1874	Heyford Iron Co. Ltd	3	2
1875	Heyford Iron Co. Ltd	3	2
1876	Heyford Iron Co. Ltd	3	2
1877	Heyford Iron Co. Ltd	3	2
1878	Heyford Iron Co. Ltd	3	2
1879	Heyford Iron Co. Ltd	3	2
1880	Heyford Iron Co. Ltd	3	2
1881	Heyford Iron Co. Ltd	3	2
1882	Heyford Iron Co. Ltd	3	2
1883	Heyford Iron Co. Ltd	3	2
1884	Heyford Iron Co. Ltd	3	2
1885	Heyford Iron Co. Ltd	3	2
1886	Heyford Iron Co. Ltd	3	2
1887	Heyford Iron Co. Ltd	3	2
1888	Heyford Iron Co. Ltd	3	2
1889	Heyford Iron Co. Ltd	3	3
1890	Heyford Iron Co. Ltd	3	3
1891	Heyford Iron Co. Ltd	3	0
1892	Heyford Iron Co. Ltd	3	0

Year	Owner	Built	In Blast
1893	Heyford Iron Co. Ltd	3	0
1894	Heyford Iron Co. Ltd	3	0
1895	Heyford Iron Co. Ltd	3	0
1896	Heyford Iron Co. Ltd	3	0
1897	Heyford Iron Co. Ltd	3	0
1898	Heyford Iron Co. Ltd	3	0

1873: note that the furnaces were in blast for 5 months in 1873 and that the change in ownership (i.e. presumably that signified from 1873) took place in March 1874. In 1862 the owner's name is given as 'George Dell', presumably in error.

Hunsbury Hill   SP 7359

Year	Owner	Built	In Blast
1873	Northampton Coal, Iron & Wagon Co. Ltd	2	0
1874	Northampton Coal, Iron & Wagon Co. Ltd	2	0
1875	Northampton Coal, Iron & Wagon Co. Ltd	2	2
1876	Hunsbury Hill Coal & Iron Co. Ltd	2	1
1877	Hunsbury Hill Coal & Iron Co. Ltd	2	1
1878	Hunsbury Hill Coal & Iron Co. Ltd	2	0
1879	Hunsbury Hill Coal & Iron Co. Ltd	2	0
1880	Hunsbury Hill Coal & Iron Co. Ltd	2	2
1881	Hunsbury Hill Coal & Iron Co. Ltd	2	2
1882	Hunsbury Hill Coal & Iron Co. Ltd	2	2
1883	Hunsbury Hill Coal & Iron Co. Ltd	2	2
1884	Hunsbury Hill Coal & Iron Co. Ltd	2	2
1885	Hunsbury Hill Coal & Iron Co. Ltd	2	2
1886	Hunsbury Hill Coal & Iron Co. Ltd	2	1
1887	Hunsbury Hill Coal & Iron Co. Ltd	2	1
1888	Hunsbury Hill Coal & Iron Co. Ltd	2	0
1890	Hunsbury Hill Coal & Iron Co. Ltd	1	1
1891	Executors of P. Phipps	1	1
1892	Executors of P. Phipps	1	1
1893	Executors of P. Phipps	2	1
1894	Executors of P. Phipps	2	2
1895	Executors of P. Phipps	2	2
1896	Executors of P. Phipps	2	2
1897	Executors of P. Phipps	2	2
1898	Executors of P. Phipps	2	2
1899	Executors of P. Phipps	2	2
1900	Executors of P. Phipps	2	1
1901	Executors of P. Phipps	2	1
1902	Executors of P. Phipps	2	1
1903	Executors of P. Phipps	2	2
1904	Executors of P. Phipps	2	2
1905	Executors of P. Phipps	2	2
1906	Executors of P. Phipps	2	2
1907	Executors of P. Phipps	2	2
1908	Executors of P. Phipps	2	2
1909	Executors of P. Phipps	2	2
1910	Executors of P. Phipps	2	2
1911	Executors of P. Phipps	2	2
1912	Executors of P. Phipps	2	2
1913	Executors of P. Phipps	2	2
1921	Executors of P. Phipps	2	-
1922	Executors of P. Phipps	2	-
1923	Executors of P. Phipps	2	-
1924	Hunsbury Iron Co.	2	-
1925	Hunsbury Iron Co.	2	-
1926	Hunsbury Iron Co.	2	-
1927	Hunsbury Iron Co.	2	-
1928	Hunsbury Iron Co.	2	-
1929	Hunsbury Iron Co.	2	-
1930	Hunsbury Iron Co.	2	-
1931	Hunsbury Iron Co.	2	-
1932	Husnbury Iron Co.	2	-
1933	Hunsbury Iron Co.	2	-
1934	Hunsbury Iron Co.	2	-
1935	Hunsbury Iron Co.	2	-
1936	Richard Thomas & Co. Ltd	2	-

1873: Furnaces approaching completion. 1874: 1 furnace blown in on 23 Oct., 1 on 20 Nov. Furnaces dismantled during 1937. The owner in 1924–35 is called 'Ltd' in the original returns but the name cannot be found on the register.

Irthlingborough   SP 9067

Year	Owner	Built	In Blast
1866	Thomas Butlin & Co.	2	0
1867	Thomas Butlin & Co.	-	-
1868	Thomas Butlin & Co.	-	-
1869	Thomas Butlin & Co.	-	-
1870	Thomas Butlin & Co.	-	-
1871	Thomas Butlin & Co.	-	-
1872	Thomas Butlin & Co.	-	-
1873	Thomas Butlin & Co.	2	2
1874	Thomas Butlin & Co.	2	2
1875	Thomas Butlin & Co.	2	1
1876	Thomas Butlin & Co.	2	1
1877	Thomas Butlin & Co.	2	2
1878	Thomas Butlin & Co.	2	2
1879	Thomas Butlin & Co.	3	1
1880	Thomas Butlin & Co.	3	2
1881	Thomas Butlin & Co.	3	2
1882	Thomas Butlin & Co.	4	1
1883	Thomas Butlin & Co.	4	2
1884	Thomas Butlin & Co.	4	1
1885	Thomas Butlin & Co.	4	1
1886	Thomas Butlin & Co.	4	1
1887	Thomas Butlin & Co.	2	2
1888	Thomas Butlin & Co.	4	2
1889	Thomas Butlin & Co.	4	2
1890	Thomas Butlin & Co.	2	2
1891	Thomas Butlin & Co. Ltd	2	1
1892	Thomas Butlin & Co. Ltd	4	1
1893	Thomas Butlin & Co. Ltd	3	2
1894	Thomas Butlin & Co. Ltd	4	2
1895	Thomas Butlin & Co. Ltd	4	2
1896	Thomas Butlin & Co. Ltd	4	2
1897	Thomas Butlin & Co. Ltd	4	2
1898	Thomas Butlin & Co. Ltd	4	2
1899	Thomas Butlin & Co. Ltd	4	3
1900	Thomas Butlin & Co. Ltd	4	2
1901	Thomas Butlin & Co. Ltd	4	2
1902	Thomas Butlin & Co. Ltd	4	2
1903	Thomas Butlin & Co. Ltd	4	2
1904	Thomas Butlin & Co. Ltd	4	2
1905	Thomas Butlin & Co. Ltd	4	2
1906	Thomas Butlin & Co. Ltd	4	2
1907	Thomas Butlin & Co. Ltd	4	2
1908	Thomas Butlin & Co. Ltd	4	2
1909	Thomas Butlin & Co. Ltd	4	2
1910	Thomas Butlin & Co. Ltd	4	2

Year	Owner	Built	In Blast
1911	Thomas Butlin & Co. Ltd	4	2
1912	Thomas Butlin & Co. Ltd	4	2
1913	Thomas Butlin & Co. Ltd	4	2
1921	Thomas Butlin & Co. Ltd	4	-
1922	Thomas Butlin & Co. Ltd	4	-
1923	Thomas Butlin & Co. Ltd	4	-
1924	United Steel Companies Ltd	4	-
1925	United Steel Companies Ltd	4	-
1926	United Steel Companies Ltd	4	-
1927	United Steel Companies Ltd	4	-
1928	United Steel Companies Ltd	4	-
1929	United Steel Companies Ltd	4	-

1867–72: furnace-numbers combined with those for East End Ironworks (see under Wellingborough). 1881: 1 furnace building. In 1866 the owner's name is given, in obvious error, as 'Bullin'.

Islip   SP 9678

Year	Owner	Built	In Blast
1871	C.H. Plevins	2	0
1872	—	-	-
1873	Plevins & Co.	2	0
1874	Plevins & Co.	2	2
1875	Plevins & Co.	2	2
1876	Plevins & Co.	2	2
1877	Plevins & Co.	2	2
1878	Islip Iron Co.	2	2
1879	Islip Iron Co.	4	2
1880	Islip Iron Co.	4	2
1881	Islip Iron Co.	4	2
1882	Islip Iron Co.	4	2
1883	Islip Iron Co.	4	3
1884	Islip Iron Co.	4	3
1885	Islip Iron Co.	4	3
1885	Islip Iron Co.	4	3
1886	Islip Iron Co.	4	3
1887	Islip Iron Co.	4	3
1888	Islip Iron Co.	4	3
1889	Islip Iron Co.	4	3
1890	Islip Iron Co.	4	3
1891	Islip Iron Co.	4	3
1892	Islip Iron Co.	4	3
1893	Islip Iron Co.	4	2
1894	Islip Iron Co.	4	3
1895	Islip Iron Co.	4	3
1896	Islip Iron Co.	4	3
1897	Islip Iron Co.	4	3
1898	Islip Iron Co.	4	3
1899	Islip Iron Co.	4	3
1900	Islip Iron Co.	4	3
1901	Islip Iron Co.	4	2
1902	Islip Iron Co.	4	3
1903	Islip Iron Co. Ltd	4	3
1904	Islip Iron Co. Ltd	4	3
1905	Islip Iron Co. Ltd	4	3
1906	Islip Iron Co. Ltd	4	3
1907	Islip Iron Co. Ltd	4	3
1908	Islip Iron Co. Ltd	4	3
1909	Islip Iron Co. Ltd	4	3
1910	Islip Iron Co. Ltd	4	3
1911	Islip Iron Co. Ltd	4	3
1912	Islip Iron Co. Ltd	4	3
1913	Islip Iron Co. Ltd	4	3
1921	Islip Iron Co. Ltd	4	-
1922	Islip Iron Co. Ltd	4	-
1923	Islip Iron Co. Ltd	4	-
1924	Islip Iron Co. Ltd	4	-
1925	Islip Iron Co. Ltd	4	-
1926	Islip Iron Co. Ltd	4	-
1927	Islip Iron Co. Ltd	4	-
1928	Islip Iron Co. Ltd	4	-
1929	Islip Iron Co. Ltd	4	-
1930	Islip Iron Co. Ltd	4	-
1931	Islip Iron Co. Ltd	4	-
1932	Islip Iron Co. Ltd	4	-
1933	Stewarts & Lloyds Ltd	4	-
1934	Stewarts & Lloyds Ltd	4	-
1935	Stewarts & Lloyds Ltd	4	-
1936	Stewarts & Lloyds Ltd	4	-
1937	Stewarts & Lloyds Ltd	4	-
1938	Stewarts & Lloyds Ltd	3	-
1939	Stewarts & Lloyds Ltd	3	-
1940	Stewarts & Lloyds Ltd	3	-
1941	Stewarts & Lloyds Ltd	3	-
1942	Stewarts & Lloyds Ltd	3	-
1943	Stewarts & Lloyds Ltd	3	-
1944	Stewarts & Lloyds Ltd	3	-
1945	Stewarts & Lloyds Ltd	3	-

1871: 'Building'. 1878: 2 furnaces building. An Islip Iron Co. Ltd was registered on 24 December 1874, with the object of acquiring from Charles Henry Plevins of Woodford, Northants., the furnaces at Islip and other property. The company was voluntarily wound-up on 2 December 1875 and the ironworks taken over by an unincorporated partnership which traded as the Islip Iron Co. (see BT 31/2058/9061). A new Islip Iron Co. Ltd, which as Brierley Hill Investments Ltd is still on the register, was established in 1903 and both this concern and its predecessor also operated Finedon (qv).

Kettering: see Cransley; Warren Hills

Stowe   SP 6557

Year	Owner	Built	In Blast
1866	Stowe Iron Ore Co. Ltd	1	1
1867	Stowe Iron Ore Co. Ltd	1	0
1868	Stowe Iron Ore Co. Ltd	1	0
1873	William McClure	2	0
1874	William McClure	2	1
1875	William McClure	2	1
1876	William McClure	2	1
1877	William McClure	2	0
1878	William McClure	2	0
1879	William McClure	2	0
1880	William McClure	2	0
1881	William McClure	2	0
1882	William McClure	2	0
1883	William McClure	2	0
1884	William Lees McClure	2	0
1885	William Lees McClure	2	0
1886	William Lees McClure	2	0
1887	William Lees McClure	2	0
1888	William Lees McClure	2	0
1889	Steel & Iron Co. Ltd	2	0
1890	Steel & Iron Co. Ltd	1	0
1891	Steel & Iron Co. Ltd	1	1

Year	Owner	Built	In Blast
1892	Steel & Iron Co. Ltd	1	0
1893	Steel & Iron Co. Ltd	1	0
1894	Steel & Iron Co. Ltd	1	0

1873: 'In course of reconstruction'.

Towcester   SP 6950

Year	Owner	Built	In Blast
1875	Towcester Co. Ltd	2	0
1876	Towcester Co. Ltd	2	0
1877	Towcester Co. Ltd	2	0
1878	Towcester Co. Ltd	2	0
1879	Towcester Co. Ltd	2	0
1880	Towcester Co. Ltd	2	0
1881	Towcester Co. Ltd	2	0
1884	Easton Estate [&] Mining Co. [Ltd]	2	0
1885	Easton Estate & Mining Co. [Ltd]	3	0
1886	Easton Estate & Mining Co. [Ltd]	3	0
1887	Easton Estate & Mining Co. [Ltd]	3	0
1888	Easton Estate & Mining Co. [Ltd]	3	0

The 2 furnaces listed between 1875 and 1881 were described as Dr C.W. Siemens's patent rotatory furnaces for making wrought iron direct from the ore; they were not included in the district total for Northants. and it is not clear whether they were ever put into use. Those listed in 1884–88 were apparently conventional blast furnaces. The owner named in *Mineral Statistics* in these latter years is presumably the Easton Estate & Mining Co. Ltd, registered on 17 July 1878 to take over the existing mining activities of Samuel Lloyd and the Towcester Co. Ltd at Easton Neston and elsewhere, and to build blast furnaces etc, although this concern was voluntarily wound-up on 2 June 1883 (BT 31/2442/12393).

Warren Hills, Kettering   SP 8680

Year	Owner	Built	In Blast
1877	Kettering Iron & Coal Co. Ltd	2	0
1878	Kettering Iron & Coal Co. Ltd	2	2
1879	Kettering Iron & Coal Co. Ltd	2	0
1880	Kettering Iron & Coal Co. Ltd	2	2
1881	Kettering Iron & Coal Co. Ltd	2	2
1882	Kettering Iron & Coal Co. Ltd	2	1
1883	Kettering Iron & Coal Co. Ltd	2	2
1884	Kettering Iron & Coal Co. Ltd	2	2
1885	Kettering Iron & Coal Co. Ltd	2	1
1886	Kettering Iron & Coal Co. Ltd	2	2
1887	Kettering Iron & Coal Co. Ltd	2	2
1888	Kettering Iron & Coal Co. Ltd	2	2
1889	Kettering Iron & Coal Co. Ltd	3	3
1890	Kettering Iron & Coal Co. Ltd	3	2
1891	Kettering Iron & Coal Co. Ltd	3	2
1892	Kettering Iron & Coal Co. Ltd	3	2
1893	Kettering Iron & Coal Co. Ltd	3	2
1894	Kettering Iron & Coal Co. Ltd	3	3
1895	Kettering Iron & Coal Co. Ltd	3	3
1896	Kettering Iron & Coal Co. Ltd	3	3
1897	Kettering Iron & Coal Co. Ltd	3	3
1898	Kettering Iron & Coal Co. Ltd	3	2
1899	Kettering Iron & Coal Co. Ltd	3	3
1900	Kettering Iron & Coal Co. Ltd	3	3
1901	Kettering Iron & Coal Co. Ltd	3	2
1902	Kettering Iron & Coal Co. Ltd	3	2
1903	Kettering Iron & Coal Co. Ltd	3	2
1904	Kettering Iron & Coal Co. Ltd	3	2
1905	Kettering Iron & Coal Co. Ltd	3	2
1906	Kettering Iron & Coal Co. Ltd	3	2
1907	Kettering Iron & Coal Co. Ltd	3	2
1908	Kettering Iron & Coal Co. Ltd	3	2
1909	Kettering Iron & Coal Co. Ltd	3	2
1910	Kettering Iron & Coal Co. Ltd	3	2
1911	Kettering Iron & Coal Co. Ltd	3	2
1912	Kettering Iron & Coal Co. Ltd	3	2
1913	Kettering Iron & Coal Co. Ltd	3	2
1921	Kettering Iron & Coal Co. Ltd	3	-
1922	Kettering Iron & Coal Co. Ltd	3	-
1923	Kettering Iron & Coal Co. Ltd	3	-
1924	Kettering Iron & Coal Co. Ltd	3	-
1925	Kettering Iron & Coal Co. Ltd	3	-
1926	Kettering Iron & Coal Co. Ltd	3	-
1927	Kettering Iron & Coal Co. Ltd	3	-
1928	Kettering Iron & Coal Co. Ltd	2	-
1929	Kettering Iron & Coal Co. Ltd	3	-
1930	Kettering Iron & Coal Co. Ltd	3	-
1931	Kettering Iron & Coal Co. Ltd	3	-
1932	Kettering Iron & Coal Co. Ltd	3	-
1933	Kettering Iron & Coal Co. Ltd	2	-
1934	Kettering Iron & Coal Co. Ltd	2	-
1935	Kettering Iron & Coal Co. Ltd	2	-
1936	Kettering Iron & Coal Co. Ltd	2	-
1937	Kettering Iron & Coal Co. Ltd	2	-
1938	Kettering Iron & Coal Co. Ltd	2	-
1939	Kettering Iron & Coal Co. Ltd	2	-
1940	Kettering Iron & Coal Co. Ltd	2	-
1941	Kettering Iron & Coal Co. Ltd	2	-
1942	Kettering Iron & Coal Co. Ltd	2	-
1943	Kettering Iron & Coal Co. Ltd	2	-
1944	Kettering Iron & Coal Co. Ltd	2	-
1945	Kettering Iron & Coal Co. Ltd	2	-
1946	Kettering Iron & Coal Co. Ltd	2	-
1947	Kettering Iron & Coal Co. Ltd	2	-
1948	Kettering Iron & Coal Co. Ltd	2	-
1949	Kettering Iron & Coal Co. Ltd	2	-
1950	Kettering Iron & Coal Co. Ltd	2	-
1951	Kettering Iron & Coal Co. Ltd	2	-
1952	Kettering Iron & Coal Co. Ltd	2	-
1953	Kettering Iron & Coal Co. Ltd	2	-
1954	Kettering Iron & Coal Co. Ltd	2	-
1955	Kettering Iron & Coal Co. Ltd	2	-
1956	Kettering Iron & Coal Co. Ltd	2	-
1957	Kettering Iron & Coal Co. Ltd	2	-
1958	Kettering Iron & Coal Co. Ltd	2	-

1877: 'Building, not yet in blast'. 1883: Production estimated. Between 1939 and 1947 the owner's name is printed as 'Kettering Coal & Iron Co. Ltd', presumably in error.

Wellingborough   SP 9069

Year	Owner	Built	In Blast
1885	Rixon's Iron & Brick Co. Ltd	1	1
1886	Rixon's Iron & Brick Co. Ltd	2	1
1887	Rixon's Iron & Brick Co. Ltd	2	2
1888	Wellingboro' Iron Co. Ltd	2	2
1889	Wellingboro' Iron Co. Ltd	2	2
1890	Wellingboro' Iron Co. Ltd	2	2
1891	Wellingboro' Iron Co. Ltd	2	2

Year	Owner		
1892	Wellingboro' Iron Co. Ltd	2	2
1893	Wellingboro' Iron Co. Ltd	2	2
1894	Wellingboro' Iron Co. Ltd	2	2
1895	Wellingboro' Iron Co. Ltd	2	2
1896	Wellingboro' Iron Co. Ltd	2	2
1897	Wellingboro' Iron Co. Ltd	2	2
1898	Wellingboro' Iron Co. Ltd	3	2
1899	Wellingboro' Iron Co. Ltd	3	2
1900	Wellingboro' Iron Co. Ltd	3	2
1901	Wellingboro' Iron Co. Ltd	3	2
1902	Wellingboro' Iron Co. Ltd	3	2
1903	Wellingboro' Iron Co. Ltd	3	2
1904	Wellingboro' Iron Co. Ltd	3	2
1905	Wellingboro' Iron Co. Ltd	3	2
1906	Wellingboro' Iron Co. Ltd	3	2
1907	Wellingboro' Iron Co. Ltd	3	2
1908	Wellingboro' Iron Co. Ltd	3	2
1909	Wellingboro' Iron Co. Ltd	3	2
1910	Wellingboro' Iron Co. Ltd	3	2
1911	Wellingboro' Iron Co. Ltd	3	2
1912	Wellingboro' Iron Co. Ltd	3	2
1913	Wellingboro' Iron Co. Ltd	3	2
1921	Wellingboro' Iron Co. Ltd	3	-
1922	Wellingboro' Iron Co. Ltd	3	-
1923	Wellingboro' Iron Co. Ltd	3	-
1924	Wellingboro' Iron Co. Ltd	3	-
1925	Wellingboro' Iron Co. Ltd	3	-
1926	Wellingboro' Iron Co. Ltd	3	-
1927	Wellingboro' Iron Co. Ltd	3	-
1928	Wellingboro' Iron Co. Ltd	3	-
1929	Wellingboro' Iron Co. Ltd	3	-
1930	Wellingboro' Iron Co. Ltd	3	-
1931	Wellingboro' Iron Co. Ltd	3	-
1934	Wellingboro' Iron Co. Ltd	1	-
1935	Wellingboro' Iron Co. Ltd	1	-
1936	Wellingboro' Iron Co. Ltd	2	-
1937	Wellingboro' Iron Co. Ltd	2	-
1938	Wellingboro' Iron Co. Ltd	2	-
1939	Wellingboro' Iron Co. Ltd	2	-
1940	Wellingboro' Iron Co. Ltd	2	-
1941	Wellingboro' Iron Co. Ltd	2	-
1942	Wellingboro' Iron Co. Ltd	3	-
1943	Wellingboro' Iron Co. Ltd	3	-
1944	Wellingboro' Iron Co. Ltd	3	-
1945	Wellingboro' Iron Co. Ltd	3	-
1946	Wellingboro' Iron Co. Ltd	3	-
1947	Wellingboro' Iron Co. Ltd	3	-
1948	Wellingboro' Iron Co. Ltd	3	-
1949	Wellingboro' Iron Co. Ltd	3	-
1950	Wellingboro' Iron Co. Ltd	3	-
1951	Wellingboro' Iron Co. Ltd	3	-
1952	Wellingboro' Iron Co. Ltd	3	-
1953	Wellingboro' Iron Co. Ltd	3	-
1954	Wellingboro' Iron Co. Ltd	3	-
1955	Wellingboro' Iron Co. Ltd	3	-
1956	Wellingboro' Iron Co. Ltd	3	-
1957	Wellingboro' Iron Co. Ltd	3	-
1958	Wellingboro' Iron Co. Ltd	3	-
1959	Wellingboro' Iron Co. Ltd	3	-
1960	Wellingboro' Iron Co. Ltd	3	-
1961	Wellingboro' Iron Co. Ltd	3	-

Wellingborough: East End Ironworks SP 8968

Year	Owner	Built	In Blast
1857	Thomas Butlin & Co.	1	1
1858	Thomas Butlin & Co.	1	1
1859	Thomas Butlin & Co.	1	1
1860	Thomas Butlin & Co.	1	1
1861	Thomas Butlin & Co.	1	1
1862	Thomas Butlin & Co.	1	1
1863	Thomas Butlin & Co.	2	1
1864	Thomas Butlin & Co.	2	1
1865	Thomas Butlin & Co.	2	2
1866	Thomas Butlin & Co.	2	2
1867	Thomas Butlin & Co.	4	2
1868	Thomas Butlin & Co.	2	2
1869	Thomas Butlin & Co.	2	2
1870	Thomas Butlin & Co.	4	4
1871	Thomas Butlin & Co.	4	3
1872	Thomas Butlin & Co.	4	4
1873	Thomas Butlin & Co.	2	2
1874	Thomas Butlin & Co.	4	2
1875	Thomas Butlin & Co.	2	1
1876	Lyttle's Iron Agency Ltd	2	1

The owner's name in 1857–58 and 1860–61 is given as Thomas Butler & Co., and in 1866 as Thomas Bullin & Co., in both cases in error. Furnace-numbers for 1867–72 are for East End and Irthlingborough (qv) combined. In 1857–59 the furnaces at East End were said to be working on cold blast; in 1863 one furnace was said to be building and in 1865 two more building. 1873: 'Blown out March 1874'.

Lincolnshire

Appleby SE 9211

Year	Owner	Built	In Blast
1875	Appleby Iron Co. Ltd	2	0
1876	Appleby Iron Co. Ltd	2	0
1877	Appleby Iron Co. Ltd	2	2
1878	Appleby Iron Co. Ltd	2	2
1879	Appleby Iron Co. Ltd	2	2
1880	Appleby Iron Co. Ltd	2	2
1881	Appleby Iron Co. Ltd	2	2
1882	Appleby Iron Co. Ltd	2	2
1883	Appleby Iron Co. Ltd	2	2
1884	Appleby Iron Co. Ltd	3	2
1885	Appleby Iron Co. Ltd	3	3
1886	Appleby Iron Co. Ltd	3	3
1887	Appleby Iron Co. Ltd	3	3
1888	Appleby Iron Co. Ltd	3	3
1889	Appleby Iron Co. Ltd	3	3
1890	Appleby Iron Co. Ltd	3	3
1891	Appleby Iron Co. Ltd	3	3
1892	Appleby Iron Co. Ltd	3	3
1893	Appleby Iron Co. Ltd	3	3
1894	Appleby Iron Co. Ltd	3	3
1895	Appleby Iron Co. Ltd	3	3
1896	Appleby Iron Co. Ltd	3	3
1897	Appleby Iron Co. Ltd	3	3
1898	Appleby Iron Co. Ltd	4	3
1899	Appleby Iron Co. Ltd	4	4
1900	Appleby Iron Co. Ltd	4	4
1901	Appleby Iron Co. Ltd	4	4
1902	Appleby Iron Co. Ltd	4	4
1903	Appleby Iron Co. Ltd	4	4
1904	Appleby Iron Co. Ltd	4	4
1905	Appleby Iron Co. Ltd	4	4
1906	Appleby Iron Co. Ltd	4	4
1907	Appleby Iron Co. Ltd	4	4
1908	Appleby Iron Co. Ltd	4	4
1909	Appleby Iron Co. Ltd	4	4
1910	Appleby Iron Co. Ltd	4	4
1911	Appleby Iron Co. Ltd	4	4
1912	Appleby Iron Co. Ltd	4	3
1913	Appleby Iron Co. Ltd	4	3
1921	Appleby Iron Co. Ltd	4	-
1922	Appleby Iron Co. Ltd	4	-
1923	Appleby Iron Co. Ltd	4	-
1924	Appleby Iron Co. Ltd	4	-
1925	Appleby Iron Co. Ltd	4	-
1926	Appleby Iron Co. Ltd	5	-
1927	Appleby Iron Co. Ltd	5	-
1928	Appleby Iron Co. Ltd	6	-
1929	Appleby Iron Co. Ltd	6	-
1930	Appleby Iron Co. Ltd	4	-
1931	Appleby Iron Co. Ltd	4	-
1932	Appleby Iron Co. Ltd	4	-
1933	Appleby Iron Co. Ltd	4	-
1934	Appleby-Frodingham Steel Co. Ltd	8	-
1935	Appleby-Frodingham Steel Co. Ltd	8	-
1936	Appleby-Frodingham Steel Co. Ltd	8	-
1937	Appleby-Frodingham Steel Co. Ltd	8	-
1938	Appleby-Frodingham Steel Co. Ltd	8	-
1939	Appleby-Frodingham Steel Co. Ltd	10	-
1940	Appleby-Frodingham Steel Co. Ltd	10	-
1941	Appleby-Frodingham Steel Co. Ltd	10	-
1942	Appleby-Frodingham Steel Co. Ltd	10	-
1943	Appleby-Frodingham Steel Co. Ltd	10	-
1944	Appleby-Frodingham Steel Co. Ltd	10	-
1945	Appleby-Frodingham Steel Co. Ltd	10	-
1946	Appleby-Frodingham Steel Co.	10	-
1947	Appleby-Frodingham Steel Co.	10	-
1948	Appleby-Frodingham Steel Co.	9	-
1949	Appleby Frodingham Steel Co.	9	-
1950	Appleby Frodingham Steel Co.	8	-
1951	Appleby-Frodingham Steel Co.	8	-
1952	Appleby-Frodingham Steel Co.	7	-
1953	Appleby-Frodingham Steel Co.	6	-
1954	Appleby-Frodingham Steel Co.	6	-
1955	Appleby-Frodingham Steel Co.	4	-
1956	Appleby-Frodingham Steel Co.	4	-
1957	Appleby-Frodingham Steel Co.	4	-
1958	Appleby-Frodingham Steel Co.	4	-
1959	Appleby-Frodingham Steel Co.	4	-
1960	Appleby-Frodingham Steel Co.	4	-
1961	Appleby-Frodingham Steel Co.	4	-
1962	Appleby-Frodingham Steel Co.	4	-
1963	Appleby-Frodingham Steel Co.	4	-
1964	Appleby-Frodingham Steel Co.	4	-
1965	Appleby-Frodingham Steel Co.	4	-
1966	Appleby-Frodingham Steel Co.	4	-
1967	Appleby-Frodingham Steel Co.	4	-
1968	Appleby-Frodingham Steel Co.	4	-
1969	Appleby-Frodingham Steel Co.	4	-
1970	British Steel Corporation	4	-
1971	British Steel Corporation	4	-
1972	British Steel Corporation	4	-
1973	British Steel Corporation	4	-
1974	British Steel Corporation	4	-
1975	British Steel Corporation	4	-
1976	British Steel Corporation	7	-
1977	British Steel Corporation	7	-
1978	British Steel Corporation	7	-
1979	British Steel Corporation	4	-
1980	British Steel Corporation	4	-

1875: 'Will be ready for blast in July' (i.e. 1876?). 1876: 2 furnaces put in blast Dec. 1876. After the merger of the Appleby and Frodingham companies in 1934 a single entry appeared each year for the two sites, so that the figures above include Frodingham (qv) as well as Appleby. From 1946 the word 'Ltd' ceases to appear in the company's title. From 1953 the location of the works is given as Scunthorpe. The three additional furnaces listed in 1976–78 are presumably those at the adjoining Redbourn works (qv), which loses its separate entry in the returns in 1976. The Appleby-Frodingham site remains in use today.

Frodingham　　　　　　　　　　　　　　SE 9011

Year	Owner	Built	In Blast
1864	Cliff & Hurst	2	1
1865	Cliff & Hurst	1	1
1866	Cliff & Hurst	2	1
1867	Joseph Cliff	2	2
1868	Frodingham Iron Co.	2	2
1869	Frodingham Iron Co.	2	2
1870	Frodingham Iron Co.	2	2
1871	Frodingham Iron Co.	2	2
1872	Frodingham Iron Co.	4	4
1873	Frodingham Iron Co.	4	4
1874	Frodingham Iron Co.	4	4
1875	Frodingham Iron Co.	4	4
1876	Frodingham Iron Co.	4	2
1877	Frodingham Iron Co.	4	2
1878	Frodingham Iron Co.	4	2
1879	Frodingham Iron Co.	4	2
1880	Frodingham Iron Co.	4	3
1881	Frodingham Iron Co.	4	3
1882	Frodingham Iron Co.	4	4
1883	Frodingham Iron Co.	4	4
1884	Frodingham Iron Co.	4	4
1885	Frodingham Iron Co.	4	2
1886	Frodingham Iron Co.	4	2
1887	Frodingham Iron Co.	4	2
1888	Frodingham Iron Co.	4	2
1889	Frodingham Iron Co.	4	3
1890	Cliff Brothers	4	3
1891	Frodingham Iron & Steel Co.	4	2
1892	Frodingham Iron & Steel Co.	4	3
1893	Frodingham Iron & Steel Co.	4	2
1894	Frodingham Iron & Steel Co.	4	3
1895	Frodingham Iron & Steel Co.	4	3
1896	Frodingham Iron & Steel Co.	4	3
1897	Frodingham Iron & Steel Co.	4	3
1898	Frodingham Iron & Steel Co.	4	3
1899	Frodingham Iron & Steel Co.	4	3
1900	Frodingham Iron & Steel Co.	4	3
1901	Frodingham Iron & Steel Co.	4	3
1902	Frodingham Iron & Steel Co.	4	3
1903	Frodingham Iron & Steel Co.	4	3
1904	Frodingham Iron & Steel Co.	4	3
1905	Frodingham Iron & Steel Co.	4	4
1906	Frodingham Iron & Steel Co.	4	4
1907	Frodingham Iron & Steel Co.	4	4
1908	Frodingham Iron & Steel Co.	4	3
1909	Frodingham Iron & Steel Co.	3	3
1910	Frodingham Iron & Steel Co.	4	3
1911	Frodingham Iron & Steel Co. Ltd	4	3
1912	Frodingham Iron & Steel Co. Ltd	4	3
1913	Frodingham Iron & Steel Co. Ltd	4	4
1921	Frodingham Iron & Steel Co. Ltd	4	-
1922	Frodingham Iron & Steel Co. Ltd	4	-
1923	Frodingham Iron & Steel Co. Ltd	4	-
1924	Frodingham Iron & Steel Co. Ltd	4	-
1925	Frodingham Iron & Steel Co. Ltd	4	-
1926	Frodingham Iron & Steel Co. Ltd	4	-
1927	Frodingham Iron & Steel Co. Ltd	4	-
1928	Frodingham Iron & Steel Co. Ltd	4	-
1929	Frodingham Iron & Steel Co. Ltd	4	-
1930	Frodingham Iron & Steel Co. Ltd	4	-
1931	Frodingham Iron & Steel Co. Ltd	4	-
1932	Frodingham Iron & Steel Co. Ltd	4	-
1933	Frodingham Iron & Steel Co. Ltd	4	-

Mineral Statistics does not use the suffix Ltd until 1911, although the company's number (80861) gives it a date of registration of 1904. From 1934 a combined entry has been printed for the two works owned by the Appleby-Frodingham concern, for which see Appleby.

Holwell, Leics.　　　　　　　　　　　　　[SK 7323]

Year	Owner	Built	In Blast
1883	Holwell Iron Co. Ltd	2	2
1884	Holwell Iron Co. Ltd	2	2
1885	Holwell Iron Co. Ltd	2	2
1886	Holwell Iron Co. Ltd	3	2
1887	Holwell Iron Co. Ltd	3	2
1888	Holwell Iron Co. Ltd	3	3
1889	Holwell Iron Co. Ltd	3	3
1890	Holwell Iron Co. Ltd	3	3
1891	Holwell Iron Co. Ltd	4	3
1892	Holwell Iron Co. Ltd	4	3
1893	Holwell Iron Co. Ltd	4	3
1894	Holwell Iron Co. Ltd	4	3
1895	Holwell Iron Co. Ltd	4	3
1896	Holwell Iron Co. Ltd	4	3
1897	Holwell Iron Co. Ltd	4	3
1898	Holwell Iron Co. Ltd	4	3
1899	Holwell Iron Co. Ltd	4	4
1900	Holwell Iron Co. Ltd	4	3
1901	Holwell Iron Co. Ltd	4	3
1902	Holwell Iron Co. Ltd	4	3
1903	Holwell Iron Co. Ltd	4	2
1904	Holwell Iron Co. Ltd	4	2
1905	Holwell Iron Co. Ltd	4	3
1906	Holwell Iron Co. Ltd	4	3
1907	Holwell Iron Co. Ltd	4	3
1908	Holwell Iron Co. Ltd	3	3
1909	Holwell Iron Co. Ltd	4	3
1910	Holwell Iron Co. Ltd	4	3
1911	Holwell Iron Co. Ltd	4	3
1912	Holwell Iron Co. Ltd	4	3
1913	Holwell Iron Co. Ltd	4	3
1921	Holwell Iron Co. Ltd	3	-
1922	Holwell Iron Co. Ltd	3	-
1923	Holwell Iron Co. Ltd	5	-
1924	Holwell Iron Co. Ltd	5	-
1925	Holwell Iron Co. Ltd	5	-
1926	Holwell Iron Co. Ltd	5	-
1927	Holwell Iron Co. Ltd	5	-
1928	Holwell Iron Co. Ltd	5	-
1929	Holwell Iron Co. Ltd	5	-
1930	Holwell Iron Co. Ltd	5	-
1931	Holwell Iron Co. Ltd	5	-
1932	Holwell Iron Co. Ltd	5	-
1933	Holwell Iron Co. Ltd	5	-
1934	Stanton Ironworks Co. Ltd	5	-
1935	Stanton Ironworks Co. Ltd	5	-
1936	Stanton Ironworks Co. Ltd	5	-
1937	Stanton Ironworks Co. Ltd	5	-
1938	Stanton Ironworks Co. Ltd	5	-
1939	Stanton Ironworks Co. Ltd	5	-
1940	Stanton Ironworks Co. Ltd	5	-
1941	Stanton Ironworks Co. Ltd	5	-
1942	Stanton Ironworks Co. Ltd	5	-
1943	Stanton Ironworks Co. Ltd	5	-
1944	Stanton Ironworks Co. Ltd	5	-
1945	Stanton Ironworks Co. Ltd	5	-

Year	Owner	Built	In Blast
1946	Stanton Ironworks Co. Ltd	5	-
1947	Stanton Ironworks Co. Ltd	5	-
1948	Holwell Iron Co. Ltd	5	-
1949	Holwell Iron Co. Ltd	4	-
1950	Holwell Iron Co. Ltd	4	-
1951	Holwell Iron Co. Ltd	4	-
1952	Holwell Iron Co. Ltd	4	-
1953	Holwell Iron Co. Ltd	4	-
1954	Holwell Iron Co. Ltd	4	-
1955	Holwell Iron Co. Ltd	4	-
1956	Holwell Iron Co. Ltd	4	-
1957	Holwell Iron Co. Ltd	4	-
1958	Holwell Iron Co. Ltd	4	-
1959	Holwell Iron Co. Ltd	4	-
1960	Holwell Iron Co. Ltd	3	-
1961	Holwell Iron Co. Ltd	3	-

1884: 1 furnace building.

Lindsey   SE 9011

Year	Owner	Built	In Blast
1875	Lincolnshire Iron Smelting Co. Ltd	2	2
1876	Lincolnshire Iron Smelting Co. Ltd	2	2
1877	Lincolnshire Iron Smelting Co. Ltd	2	1
1878	Lincolnshire Iron Smelting Co. Ltd	2	2
1879	Lincolnshire Iron Smelting Co. Ltd	2	2
1880	Lincolnshire Iron Smelting Co. Ltd	2	2
1881	Lincolnshire Iron Smelting Co. Ltd	2	0
1882	Redbourn Hill Iron & Coal Co. Ltd	2	0
1883	Redbourn Hill Iron & Coal Co. Ltd	2	0
1884	Redbourn Hill Iron & Coal Co. Ltd	2	2
1885	Redbourn Hill Iron & Coal Co. Ltd	2	1
1886	Redbourn Hill Iron & Coal Co. Ltd	2	0
1887	Redbourn Hill Iron & Coal Co. Ltd	2	0
1888	Redbourn Hill Iron & Coal Co. Ltd	2	0
1889	Redbourn Hill Iron & Coal Co. Ltd	2	2
1890	Redbourn Hill Iron & Coal Co. Ltd	2	2
1891	Redbourn Hill Iron & Coal Co. Ltd	2	2
1892	Redbourn Hill Iron & Coal Co. Ltd	2	2
1893	Redbourn Hill Iron & Coal Co. Ltd	2	1
1894	Redbourn Hill Iron & Coal Co. Ltd	2	1
1895	Redbourn Hill Iron & Coal Co. Ltd	2	1
1896	Redbourn Hill Iron & Coal Co. Ltd	2	1
1897	Redbourn Hill Iron & Coal Co. Ltd	-	-
1898	Redbourn Hill Iron & Coal Co. Ltd	-	-
1899	Redbourn Hill Iron & Coal Co. Ltd	-	-
1900	Redbourn Hill Iron & Coal Co. Ltd	-	-
1901	Redbourn Hill Iron & Coal Co. Ltd	-	-
1902	Redbourn Hill Iron & Coal Co. Ltd	-	-

1883: 2 furnaces returned as being in blast but with a footnote saying that they were at work for 3 months only. From 1897 there is a combined entry for 'Redbourn Hill and Lindsey' (for which see Redbourn Hill), which changes to Redbourn Hill only in 1903, although the furnace-numbers suggest that the plant at Lindsey was included that year and in 1904.

Normanby Park   SE 8813

Year	Owner	Built	In Blast
1921	John Lysaght Ltd	5	-
1922	John Lysaght Ltd	5	-
1923	John Lysaght Ltd	5	-
1924	John Lysaght Ltd	5	-
1925	John Lysaght Ltd	5	-
1926	John Lysaght Ltd	5	-
1927	John Lysaght Ltd	5	-
1928	John Lysaght Ltd	5	-
1929	John Lysaght Ltd	5	-
1930	John Lysaght Ltd	5	-
1931	John Lysaght Ltd	5	-
1932	John Lysaght Ltd	5	-
1933	John Lysaght Ltd	5	-
1934	John Lysaght Ltd	5	-
1935	John Lysaght Ltd	5	-
1936	John Lysaght Ltd	5	-
1937	John Lysaght Ltd	5	-
1938	John Lysaght Ltd	5	-
1939	John Lysaght Ltd	5	-
1940	John Lysaght Ltd	5	-
1941	John Lysaght Ltd	5	-
1942	John Lysaght Ltd	5	-
1943	John Lysaght Ltd	5	-
1944	John Lysaght Ltd	5	-
1945	John Lysaght Ltd	5	-
1946	John Lysaght Ltd	3	-
1947	John Lysaght Ltd	4	-
1948	John Lysaght Ltd	4	-
1949	John Lysaght Ltd	4	-
1950	John Lysaght Ltd	4	-
1951	John Lysaght Ltd	5	-
1952	John Lysaght Ltd	5	-
1953	John Lysaght Ltd	4	-
1954	John Lysaght Ltd	3	-
1955	John Lysaght Ltd	4	-
1957	John Lysaght Ltd	4	-
1958	John Lysaght Ltd	3	-
1959	John Lysaght Ltd	3	-
1960	John Lysaght Ltd	4	-
1961	Lysaghts Scunthorpe Works	4	-
1962	Lysaghts Scunthorpe Works	4	-
1963	Lysaghts Scunthorpe Works	4	-
1964	Lysaghts Scunthorpe Works	4	-
1965	Lysaghts Scunthorpe Works	4	-
1966	Lysaghts Scunthorpe Works	4	-
1967	Lysaghts Scunthorpe Works	3	-
1968	Normanby Park Steel Works	3	-
1969	Normanby Park Steel Works	3	-
1970	British Steel Corporation	3	-
1971	British Steel Corporation	3	-
1972	British Steel Corporation	3	-
1973	British Steel Corporation	3	-
1974	British Steel Corporation	3	-
1975	British Steel Corporation	3	-
1976	British Steel Corporation	3	-
1977	British Steel Corporation	3	-
1978	British Steel Corporation	3	-
1979	British Steel Corporation	3	-
1980	British Steel Corporation	3	-

The owner's name was printed in the original returns as J. Lysaght & Co. Ltd in 1921–33 and J. Lysaght's Scunthorpe Works Ltd in 1947–60. Neither can be found on the register and both appear to be errors for that used in 1934–46, which has been inserted here throughout the period 1921–60. In 1961–65 the owner was described as a branch of GKN Steel Co. Ltd. 1980 was the last year in which an entry for Normanby Park appeared in the returns.

North Lincolnshire   SE 9110

Year	Owner	Built	In Blast
1864	Adamson & Co.	2	0
1865	North Lincolnshire Iron Works Co.	1	1
1866	North Lincolnshire Iron Works Co.	1	1
1867	North Lincolnshire Iron Works	1	1
1868	North Lincolnshire Iron Works	1	1
1869	North Lincolnshire Iron Works	1	1
1870	North Lincolnshire Iron Works	1	1
1871	North Lincolnshire Iron Works	2	1
1872	North Lincolnshire Iron Co. Ltd	2	1
1873	North Lincolnshire Iron Co. Ltd	2	2
1874	North Lincolnshire Iron Co. Ltd	4	2
1875	North Lincolnshire Iron Co. Ltd	4	2
1876	North Lincolnshire Iron Co. Ltd	4	2
1877	North Lincolnshire Iron Co. Ltd	4	2
1878	North Lincolnshire Iron Co. Ltd	4	2
1879	North Lincolnshire Iron Co. Ltd	4	2
1880	North Lincolnshire Iron Co. Ltd	4	3
1881	North Lincolnshire Iron Co. Ltd	4	4
1882	North Lincolnshire Iron Co. Ltd	4	4
1883	North Lincolnshire Iron Co. Ltd	4	4
1884	North Lincolnshire Iron Co. Ltd	4	3
1885	North Lincolnshire Iron Co. Ltd	4	2
1886	North Lincolnshire Iron Co. Ltd	4	2
1887	North Lincolnshire Iron Co. Ltd	4	3
1888	North Lincolnshire Iron Co. Ltd	4	3
1889	North Lincolnshire Iron Co. Ltd	4	4
1890	North Lincolnshire Iron Co. Ltd	4	3
1891	North Lincolnshire Iron Co. Ltd	4	3
1892	North Lincolnshire Iron Co. Ltd	4	3
1893	North Lincolnshire Iron Co. Ltd	4	2
1894	North Lincolnshire Iron Co. Ltd	4	3
1895	North Lincolnshire Iron Co. Ltd	4	3
1896	North Lincolnshire Iron Co. Ltd	4	4
1897	North Lincolnshire Iron Co. Ltd	4	4
1898	North Lincolnshire Iron Co. Ltd	4	4
1899	North Lincolnshire Iron Co. Ltd	4	4
1900	North Lincolnshire Iron Co. Ltd	4	3
1901	North Lincolnshire Iron Co. Ltd	3	2
1902	North Lincolnshire Iron Co. Ltd	3	3
1903	North Lincolnshire Iron Co. Ltd	3	3
1904	North Lincolnshire Iron Co. Ltd	3	2
1905	North Lincolnshire Iron Co. Ltd	3	3
1906	North Lincolnshire Iron Co. Ltd	3	3
1907	North Lincolnshire Iron Co. Ltd	3	2
1908	North Lincolnshire Iron Co. Ltd	3	2
1909	North Lincolnshire Iron Co. Ltd	3	2
1910	North Lincolnshire Iron Co. Ltd	2	2
1911	North Lincolnshire Iron Co. Ltd	3	2
1912	North Lincolnshire Iron Co. Ltd	3	2
1913	North Lincolnshire Iron Co. Ltd	3	2
1921	North Lincolnshire Iron Co. Ltd	3	-
1922	North Lincolnshire Iron Co. Ltd	3	-
1923	North Lincolnshire Iron Co. Ltd	3	-
1924	North Lincolnshire Iron Co. Ltd	3	-
1925	North Lincolnshire Iron Co. Ltd	3	-
1926	North Lincolnshire Iron Co. Ltd	3	-
1927	North Lincolnshire Iron Co. Ltd	3	-
1928	North Lincolnshire Iron Co. Ltd	3	-
1929	North Lincolnshire Iron Co. Ltd	3	-
1930	North Lincolnshire Iron Co. Ltd	3	-
1931	North Lincolnshire Iron Co. Ltd	3	-
1932	North Lincolnshire Iron Co. Ltd	3	-
1933	North Lincolnshire Iron Co. Ltd	3	-

1864: 'Building'.

Redbourn Hill   SE 9110

Year	Owner	Built	In Blast
1875	Redbourn Hill Iron & Coal Co. Ltd	2	2
1876	Redbourn Hill Iron & Coal Co. Ltd	2	2
1877	Redbourn Hill Iron & Coal Co. Ltd	2	0
1878	Redbourn Hill Iron & Coal Co. Ltd	2	0
1879	Redbourn Hill Iron & Coal Co. Ltd	2	0
1880	Redbourn Hill Iron & Coal Co. Ltd	2	2
1881	Redbourn Hill Iron & Coal Co. Ltd	2	2
1882	Redbourn Hill Iron & Coal Co. Ltd	2	2
1883	Redbourn Hill Iron & Coal Co. Ltd	2	2
1884	Redbourn Hill Iron & Coal Co. Ltd	2	2
1885	Redbourn Hill Iron & Coal Co. Ltd	2	2
1886	Redbourn Hill Iron & Coal Co. Ltd	2	2
1887	Redbourn Hill Iron & Coal Co. Ltd	2	2
1888	Redbourn Hill Iron & Coal Co. Ltd	2	2
1889	Redbourn Hill Iron & Coal Co. Ltd	2	2
1890	Redbourn Hill Iron & Coal Co. Ltd	2	1
1891	Redbourn Hill Iron & Coal Co. Ltd	2	0
1892	Redbourn Hill Iron & Coal Co. Ltd	2	0
1893	Redbourn Hill Iron & Coal Co. Ltd	2	1
1894	Redbourn Hill Iron & Coal Co. Ltd	2	2
1895	Redbourn Hill Iron & Coal Co. Ltd	2	2
1896	Redbourn Hill Iron & Coal Co. Ltd	2	2
1897	Redbourn Hill Iron & Coal Co. Ltd	4	3
1898	Redbourn Hill Iron & Coal Co. Ltd	4	2
1899	Redbourn Hill Iron & Coal Co. Ltd	4	3
1900	Redbourn Hill Iron & Coal Co. Ltd	4	2
1901	Redbourn Hill Iron & Coal Co. Ltd	4	2
1902	Redbourn Hill Iron & Coal Co. Ltd	4	2
1903	Redbourn Hill Iron & Coal Co. Ltd	4	2
1904	Redbourn Hill Iron & Coal Co. Ltd	4	2
1905	Redbourn Hill Iron & Coal Co. Ltd	2	2
1906	Redbourn Hill Iron & Coal Co. Ltd	2	2
1907	Redbourn Hill Iron & Coal Co. Ltd	2	2
1908	Redbourn Hill Iron & Coal Co. Ltd	2	2
1909	Redbourn Hill Iron & Coal Co. Ltd	2	2
1910	Redbourn Hill Iron & Coal Co. Ltd	3	2
1911	Redbourn Hill Iron & Coal Co. Ltd	3	2
1912	Redbourn Hill Iron & Coal Co. Ltd	3	2
1913	Redbourn Hill Iron & Coal Co. Ltd	3	2
1921	Redbourn Hill Iron & Coal Co. Ltd	4	-
1922	Redbourn Hill Iron & Coal Co. Ltd	4	-
1923	Redbourn Hill Iron & Coal Co. Ltd	4	-
1924	Redbourn Hill Iron & Coal Co. Ltd	4	-
1925	Redbourn Hill Iron & Coal Co. Ltd	4	-
1926	Redbourn Hill Iron & Coal Co. Ltd	4	-
1927	Richard Thomas & Co. Ltd	4	-
1928	Richard Thomas & Co. Ltd	4	-
1929	Richard Thomas & Co. Ltd	4	-
1930	Richard Thomas & Co. Ltd	4	-
1931	Richard Thomas & Co. Ltd	4	-
1932	Richard Thomas & Co. Ltd	4	-
1933	Richard Thomas & Co. Ltd	4	-
1934	Richard Thomas & Co. Ltd	4	-
1935	Richard Thomas & Co. Ltd	4	-
1936	Richard Thomas & Co. Ltd	4	-
1937	Richard Thomas & Co. Ltd	4	-
1938	Richard Thomas & Co. Ltd	4	-
1939	Richard Thomas & Baldwins Ltd	4	-

Year	Owner	Built	In Blast
1940	Richard Thomas & Baldwins Ltd	4	-
1941	Richard Thomas & Baldwins Ltd	4	-
1941	Richard Thomas & Baldwins Ltd	4	-
1942	Richard Thomas & Baldwins Ltd	4	-
1943	Richard Thomas & Baldwins Ltd	4	-
1944	Richard Thomas & Baldwins Ltd	4	-
1945	Richard Thomas & Baldwins Ltd	4	-
1946	Richard Thomas & Baldwins Ltd	4	-
1947	Richard Thomas & Baldwins Ltd	2	-
1948	Richard Thomas & Baldwins Ltd	2	-
1949	Richard Thomas & Baldwins Ltd	2	-
1950	Richard Thomas & Baldwins Ltd	2	-
1951	Richard Thomas & Baldwins Ltd	3	-
1952	Richard Thomas & Baldwins Ltd	3	-
1953	Richard Thomas & Baldwins Ltd	3	-
1954	Richard Thomas & Baldwins Ltd	3	-
1955	Richard Thomas & Baldwins Ltd	3	-
1956	Richard Thomas & Baldwins Ltd	3	-
1957	Richard Thomas & Baldwins Ltd	3	-
1958	Richard Thomas & Baldwins Ltd	3	-
1959	Richard Thomas & Baldwins Ltd	3	-
1960	Richard Thomas & Baldwins Ltd	3	-
1961	Richard Thomas & Baldwins Ltd	3	-
1962	Richard Thomas & Baldwins Ltd	3	-
1963	Richard Thomas & Baldwins Ltd	3	-
1964	Richard Thomas & Baldwins Ltd	3	-
1965	Richard Thomas & Baldwins Ltd	3	-
1966	Richard Thomas & Baldwins Ltd	3	-
1967	Richard Thomas & Baldwins Ltd	3	-
1968	Richard Thomas & Baldwins Ltd	3	-
1969	Richard Thomas & Baldwins Ltd	3	-
1970	British Steel Corporation	3	-
1971	British Steel Corporation	3	-
1972	British Steel Corporation	3	-
1973	British Steel Corporation	3	-
1974	British Steel Corporation	3	-
1975	British Steel Corporation	3	-

1879: In blast for a few months only. From 1897 there is a single entry for 'Redbourn Hill and Lindsey', which in 1903 changes to Redbourn Hill only, although the furnace-numbers above suggest that the plant at Lindsey (qv) was still included that year and in 1904. After the take-over by Richard Thomas, the site was initially called 'Redbourn Works'; from 1953 the location was given as Scunthorpe. In 1976–78, following the disappearance of an entry for Redbourn in the returns, the number of furnaces returned for Appleby-Frodingham increases by three, which must represent those at Redbourn.

Trent   SE 9011

Year	Owner	Built	In Blast
1863	W.H. Dawes & Co.	3	0
1864	W.H. & Geo. Dawes, Trent Iron Co.	3	2
1865	W.H. & Geo. Dawes	3	1
1866	W.H. & Geo. Dawes	3	1
1867	W.H. & Geo. Dawes	3	2
1868	W.H. & Geo. Dawes	3	2
1869	W.H. & Geo. Dawes	3	2
1870	W.H. & Geo. Dawes	3	1
1871	W.H. & Geo. Dawes	3	1
1872	W.H. & Geo. Dawes	3	2
1873	W.H. & Geo. Dawes	7	3
1874	W.H. & Geo. Dawes	7	2
1875	W.H. & Geo. Dawes	7	2
1876	W.H. & Geo. Dawes	7	3
1877	William Henry Dawes	7	3
1878	William Henry Dawes	7	3
1879	William Henry Dawes	7	3
1880	William Henry Dawes	7	3
1881	William Henry Dawes	7	3
1882	William Henry Dawes	7	5
1883	William Henry Dawes	6	4
1884	William Henry Dawes	6	4
1885	William Henry Dawes	6	4
1886	William Henry Dawes	6	4
1887	William Henry Dawes	6	4
1888	William Henry Dawes	6	4
1889	William Henry Dawes	6	4
1890	William Shakespeare	6	2
1891	William Shakespeare	6	2
1892	William Shakespeare	6	2
1893	William Shakespeare	6	1
1894	William Shakespeare	6	2
1895	William Shakespeare	6	2
1896	William Shakespeare	6	2
1897	William Shakespeare	6	2
1898	William Shakespeare	6	2
1899	William Shakespeare	6	2
1900	William Shakespeare	6	2
1901	William Shakespeare	6	1
1902	William Shakespeare	6	2
1903	William Shakespeare	6	2
1904	William Shakespeare	6	2
1905	William Shakespeare	6	2
1906	William Shakespeare	6	2
1907	William Shakespeare	2	2
1908	Trent Iron Co. Ltd	2	2
1909	Trent Iron Co. Ltd	2	2
1910	Trent Iron Co. Ltd	3	2
1911	Trent Iron Co. Ltd	3	2
1912	Trent Iron Co. Ltd	3	2
1913	Trent Iron Co. Ltd	3	2
1921	Trent Iron Co. Ltd	3	-
1922	Trent Iron Co. Ltd	3	-
1923	Trent Iron Co. Ltd	3	-
1924	Trent Iron Co. Ltd	3	-
1925	Trent Iron Co. Ltd	3	-
1926	Trent Iron Co. Ltd	3	-
1927	Trent Iron Co. Ltd	3	-
1928	Trent Iron Co. Ltd	3	-
1929	Trent Iron Co. Ltd	3	-
1930	Trent Iron Co. Ltd	3	-
1931	Trent Iron Co. Ltd	3	-
1932	Trent Iron Co. Ltd	3	-
1933	Trent Iron Co. Ltd	3	-
1934	John Lysaght Ltd	3	-
1935	John Lysaght Ltd	3	-

1863: 3 more furnaces building; entry headed Scunthorpe.
1875: 3 furnaces rebuilding. Furnaces dismantled during 1936.

Derbyshire

Adelphi: see Duckmanton

Alderwasley SK 3452

Year	Owner	Built	In Blast
1810	F. Hurt	2	2

See Morley Park, for which this appears to be a duplicate entry. In 1794 no furnace was listed at Alderwasley, although the date 1782 appears in the 'Built' column of the furnace section of the return, not the forge section, in which 3 fineries, 2 chaferies and a rolling and slitting mill are listed. The owner and occupier in 1794 was Mr Hurt.

Alfreton SK 4352

Year	Owner	Built	In Blast
1805	Saxleby, Edwards & Co.	1	1
1810	Edwards & Co.	1	1
1823	—	2	-
1825	Oakes & Co.	2	2
1830	—	2	-
1839	J. Oakes	2	2
1841	James Oakes & Co.	2	2
1843	James Oakes & Co.	2	2
1847	Oakes & Co.	3	3
1849	—	-	3
1854	Oakes & Co.	3	2
1854	Oakes & Co.	3	2
1855	Oakes & Co.	3	2
1856	Oakes & Co.	3	2
1857	Oakes & Co.	3	2
1858	James Oakes & Co.	3	2
1859	James Oakes & Co.	3	2
1860	James Oakes & Co.	3	2
1861	James Oakes & Co.	3	2
1862	James Oakes & Co.	3	2
1863	James Oakes & Co.	3	2
1864	James Oakes & Co.	3	3
1865	James Oakes & Co.	3	3
1866	James Oakes & Co.	3	2
1867	James Oakes & Co.	3	2
1868	James Oakes & Co.	3	2
1869	James Oakes & Co.	3	2
1870	James Oakes & Co.	3	2
1871	James Oakes & Co.	3	2
1872	James Oakes & Co.	3	2
1873	James Oakes & Co.	3	3
1874	James Oakes & Co.	3	3
1875	James Oakes & Co.	3	3
1876	James Oakes & Co.	3	2
1877	James Oakes & Co.	3	3
1878	James Oakes & Co.	3	3
1879	James Oakes & Co.	3	2
1880	James Oakes & Co.	3	3
1881	James Oakes & Co.	3	2
1882	James Oakes & Co.	3	3
1883	James Oakes & Co.	3	2
1884	James Oakes & Co.	3	3
1885	James Oakes & Co.	3	3
1886	James Oakes & Co.	3	3
1887	James Oakes & Co.	3	3
1888	James Oakes & Co.	3	2
1889	James Oakes & Co.	3	3
1890	James Oakes & Co.	3	3
1891	James Oakes & Co.	3	3
1892	James Oakes & Co.	3	3
1893	James Oakes & Co.	3	3
1894	James Oakes & Co.	3	2
1895	James Oakes & Co.	3	2
1896	James Oakes & Co.	3	2
1897	James Oakes & Co.	3	3
1898	James Oakes & Co.	3	3
1899	James Oakes & Co.	3	3
1900	James Oakes & Co.	3	3
1901	James Oakes & Co.	3	3
1902	James Oakes & Co.	3	2
1903	James Oakes & Co.	3	2
1904	James Oakes & Co.	3	2
1905	James Oakes & Co.	3	3
1906	James Oakes & Co.	3	3
1907	James Oakes & Co.	3	3
1908	James Oakes & Co.	3	2
1909	James Oakes & Co.	3	3
1910	James Oakes & Co.	3	2
1911	James Oakes & Co.	3	3
1912	James Oakes & Co.	3	3
1913	James Oakes & Co.	3	3
1921	James Oakes & Co.	3	-
1922	James Oakes & Co.	3	-
1923	James Oakes & Co.	3	-
1924	James Oakes & Co.	3	-
1925	James Oakes & Co.	3	-
1926	James Oakes & Co.	3	-
1927	James Oakes & Co.	3	-

1805: output 1,450 tons p.a. 1823–30: 2,690 tons in 1823, 2,950 tons in 1830. 1825: Works called 'Summercotes' (i.e. Somercotes); weekly output 70 tons, 3,000 tons p.a. 1839: 2 furnaces building. 1841: output 60 tons a week. 1843: output 65 tons a week. 1847: 6,240 tons p.a., i.e. 40 tons a week from each of the 3 furnaces. Truran: output 90 tons a week from each of 3 furnaces.

Ashby: see Moira

Awsworth: see Bennerley

Barlow: see Sheepbridge

Bennerley, Notts.   SK 4743

Year	Owner	Built	In Blast
1881	Awsworth Iron Co.	2	0
1882	Awsworth Iron Co.	3	3
1883	Awsworth Iron Co.	3	3
1884	Awsworth Iron Co.	3	3
1885	Awsworth Iron Co.	3	3
1886	Awsworth Iron Co.	3	1
1887	Awsworth Iron Co.	3	0
1888	E.P. Davis	3	1
1889	E.P. Davis	3	3
1890	E.P. Davis	3	2
1891	E.P. Davis	3	2
1892	E.P. Davis	3	2
1893	E.P. Davis	3	1
1894	E.P. Davis	3	2
1895	E.P. Davis	3	2
1896	E.P. Davis	3	2
1897	E.P. Davis	3	3
1898	E.P. Davis	3	2
1899	E.P. Davis	2	2
1900	E.P. Davis	3	2
1901	E.P. Davis	3	2
1902	E.P. Davis	3	2
1903	E.P. Davis	3	2
1904	E.P. Davis	3	2
1905	E.P. Davis	3	2
1906	E.P. Davis	3	2
1907	E.P. Davis	3	2
1908	E.P. Davis	3	2
1909	E.P. Davis	3	2
1910	E.P. Davis	3	2
1911	E.P. Davis	3	2
1912	E.P. Davis	3	2
1913	E.P. Davis	3	2
1921	E.P. Davis	3	-
1922	E.P. Davis	3	-
1923	E.P. Davis	3	-
1924	E.P. Davis	3	-
1925	E.P. Davis	3	-
1926	E.P. Davis	3	-
1927	E.P. Davis	3	-
1928	E.P. Davis	3	-
1929	Bennerley Iron Co. Ltd	3	-
1930	Bennerley Iron Co. Ltd	3	-
1931	Bennerley Iron Co. Ltd	3	-
1932	Bennerley Iron Co. Ltd	3	-
1933	Bennerley Iron Co. Ltd	3	-

The entries for 1881–87 are headed Awsworth in *Mineral Statistics* but clearly refer to the site listed as Bennerley from 1888 (with 'Awsworth' added in brackets from 1895). Five furnaces were returned for E.P. Davis in 1921–28, which evidently includes the two at the Erewash Valley Ironworks, Ilkeston. For 1929–33 only 3 furnaces were listed, with Bennerley Iron Co. as owner. The 1921–28 figures above have been adjusted and the 2 other furnaces entered under Erewash Valley (qv).

Bestwood, Notts.   SK 5547

Year	Owner	Built	In Blast
1881	Bestwood Coal & Iron Co. Ltd	2	2
1882	Bestwood Coal & Iron Co. Ltd	2	2
1883	Bestwood Coal & Iron Co. Ltd	2	2
1884	Bestwood Coal & Iron Co. Ltd	2	2
1885	Bestwood Coal & Iron Co. Ltd	2	2
1886	Bestwood Coal & Iron Co. Ltd	2	2
1887	Bestwood Coal & Iron Co. Ltd	3	2
1888	Bestwood Coal & Iron Co. Ltd	3	2
1889	Bestwood Coal & Iron Co. Ltd	3	3
1890	Bestwood Coal & Iron Co. Ltd	4	3
1891	Bestwood Coal & Iron Co. Ltd	4	3
1892	Bestwood Coal & Iron Co. Ltd	4	4
1893	Bestwood Coal & Iron Co. Ltd	4	3
1894	Bestwood Coal & Iron Co. Ltd	4	3
1895	Bestwood Coal & Iron Co. Ltd	4	3
1896	Bestwood Coal & Iron Co. Ltd	4	3
1897	Bestwood Coal & Iron Co. Ltd	4	3
1898	Bestwood Coal & Iron Co. Ltd	4	3
1899	Bestwood Coal & Iron Co. Ltd	4	3
1900	Bestwood Coal & Iron Co. Ltd	4	3
1901	Bestwood Coal & Iron Co. Ltd	4	3
1902	Bestwood Coal & Iron Co. Ltd	4	3
1903	Bestwood Coal & Iron Co. Ltd	4	3
1904	Bestwood Coal & Iron Co. Ltd	4	3
1905	Bestwood Coal & Iron Co. Ltd	4	3
1906	Bestwood Coal & Iron Co. Ltd	4	3
1907	Bestwood Coal & Iron Co. Ltd	4	3
1908	Bestwood Coal & Iron Co. Ltd	4	3
1909	Bestwood Coal & Iron Co. Ltd	4	3
1910	Bestwood Coal & Iron Co. Ltd	4	3
1911	Bestwood Coal & Iron Co. Ltd	4	3
1912	Bestwood Coal & Iron Co. Ltd	4	3
1913	Bestwood Coal & Iron Co. Ltd	4	3
1921	Bestwood Coal & Iron Co. Ltd	4	-
1922	Bestwood Coal & Iron Co. Ltd	4	-
1923	Bestwood Coal & Iron Co. Ltd	4	-
1924	Bestwood Coal & Iron Co. Ltd	4	-
1925	Bestwood Coal & Iron Co. Ltd	4	-
1926	Bestwood Coal & Iron Co. Ltd	4	-
1927	Bestwood Coal & Iron Co. Ltd	4	-
1928	Bestwood Coal & Iron Co. Ltd	4	-
1929	Bestwood Coal & Iron Co. Ltd	4	-
1930	Bestwood Coal & Iron Co. Ltd	4	-
1931	Bestwood Coal & Iron Co. Ltd	4	-
1932	Bestwood Coal & Iron Co. Ltd	4	-
1933	Bestwood Coal & Iron Co. Ltd	4	-
1934	Bestwood Coal & Iron Co. Ltd	4	-
1935	Bestwood Coal & Iron Co. Ltd	4	-

Furnaces demolished during first half of 1936.

Brampton: see Chesterfield

Brimington Moor   SK 4172

Year	Owner	Built	In Blast
1855	Knowles & Co.	1	1
1856	Knowles & Co.	1	1
1857	Knowles & Co.	1	1
1858	J. Knowles	1	1

1859	J. Knowles	1	0
1860	J. Knowles	1	0
1861	J. Knowles	1	0
1862	J. Knowles	1	0
1863	J. Knowles	1	0
1864	J. Knowles	1	0

Broad Oaks: see Wingerworth [II]

Butterley SK 4051

Year	*Owner*	*Built*	*In Blast*
1794	Outram, Jessop & Beresford	1	-
1796	—	1	1
1805	Outram & Co.	2	2
1810	Outram & Co.	3	3
1823	—	3	-
1825	Jessop & Co.	2	2
1830	—	3	-
1839	Jessop & Co.	3	2
1841	Butterley Co.	3	3
1843	Butterley Iron Co.	3	2
1847	Butterley Co.	3	3
1849	—	-	3
1854	Butterley Co.	3	3
1855	Butterley Co.	3	3
1856	Butterley Co.	3	3
1857	Butterley Co.	3	3
1858	Butterley Co.	3	3
1859	Butterley Co.	3	3
1860	Butterley Co.	3	2
1861	Butterley Co.	3	2
1862	Butterley Co.	3	3
1863	Butterley Co.	7	5
1864	Butterley Co.	7	6
1865	Butterley Co.	7	6
1866	F. Wright & W. Jessop	7	6
1867	Butterley Co.	7	6
1868	Butterley Co.	6	6
1869	Butterley Co.	6	5
1870	Butterley Co.	6	4
1871	Butterley Co.	7	4
1872	Butterley Co.	7	4
1873	Butterley Co.	7	3
1874	Butterley Co.	6	3
1875	Butterley Co.	6	3
1876	Butterley Co.	3	2
1877	Butterley Co.	3	2
1878	Butterley Co.	3	2
1879	Butterley Co.	3	1
1880	Butterley Co.	3	1
1881	Butterley Co.	5	2
1882	Butterley Co.	5	3
1883	Butterley Co.	5	2
1884	Butterley Co.	5	3
1885	Butterley Co.	5	2
1886	Butterley Co.	5	1
1887	Butterley Co.	5	1
1888	Butterley Co. Ltd	5	1
1889	Butterley Co. Ltd	2	2
1890	Butterley Co. Ltd	2	1
1891	Butterley Co. Ltd	2	2
1892	Butterley Co. Ltd	2	1
1893	Butterley Co. Ltd	2	1
1894	Butterley Co. Ltd	2	1
1895	Butterley Co. Ltd	2	1
1896	Butterley Co. Ltd	2	2
1897	Butterley Co. Ltd	2	2
1898	Butterley Co. Ltd	2	2
1899	Butterley Co. Ltd	2	2
1900	Butterley Co. Ltd	2	2
1901	Butterley Co. Ltd	2	2
1902	Butterley Co. Ltd	2	2
1903	Butterley Co. Ltd	2	2
1904	Butterley Co. Ltd	2	1
1905	Butterley Co. Ltd	2	1
1906	Butterley Co. Ltd	2	2
1907	Butterley Co. Ltd	2	2
1908	Butterley Co. Ltd	2	1
1909	Butterley Co. Ltd	2	0
1910	Butterley Co. Ltd	2	2
1911	Butterley Co. Ltd	2	2
1912	Butterley Co. Ltd	2	2
1913	Butterley Co. Ltd	2	2
1921	Butterley Co. Ltd	2	-
1922	Butterley Co. Ltd	2	-
1923	Butterley Co. Ltd	2	-

The ground landlord in 1794 was listed as 'Mr Otram' (i.e. Benjamin Outram); the furnace was coke-fired and said to have been built in 1792. 1796: output 936 tons (i.e. 18 tons a week), Excise, actual and Exact Return. 1805: output 1,766 tons p.a. 1823–30: 2,639 tons p.a. for 1823 and 3,981 tons for 1830. 1825: 70 tons a week, 3,000 tons p.a., 'castings &c'. 1841: output 148 tons a week. 1843: output 130 tons a week. 1847: 9,880 tons p.a., i.e. 190 tons a week from 3 furnaces. Truran: output 100 tons a week from each of 3 furnaces. 1876: 1 furnace rebuilding. 1877: 1 furnace building. In 1863–75 and 1881–88 furnace-numbers include Butterley and Codnor Park (qv).

Calow SK 4069

Year	*Owner*	*Built*	*In Blast*
1823	—	1	-
1825	Calow Iron Co.	1	1
1830	—	1	-

An output of nil was returned in 1823, 123 tons p.a. in 1830. The 1825 list gives a weekly figure of 23 tons, 1,040 p.a., 'castings &c'.

Chesterfield: Brampton SK 3770

Year	*Owner*	*Built*	*In Blast*
1794	Smith & Co.	2	-
1796	—	1	1
1805	Smith & Co.	3	2
1810	Smith & Co.	3	3
1823	—	2	-
1825	Ebenezer Smith & Co.	3	2
1830	—	2	-

This was the works about half a mile west of the centre of Chesterfield sometimes known as Griffin Foundry. The ground landlord in 1794 was James Shimels; the two coke-fired furnaces were blown by engine and said to have been built in 1777. The forge consisted of a finery and a chafery, plus a balling furnace, also built in 1777. 1796: output 1,800 tons p.a. (i.e. 36 tons a week), Excise and actual, 1,560 tons p.a. (i.e. 30 tons a week) Exact Return. In 1805 output was returned as 1,700 tons p.a.; in 1823–30 as 1,807 tons and 1,245 tons respectively. The 1825 list gives the weekly output as 46 (*sic*) tons and the annual figure as 2,080, 'castings &c'.

Chesterfield: Stonegravels [SK 3872?]

Year	Owner	Built	In Blast
1794	Barnes & Co.	2	-
1796	—	1	1
1805	Top & Co.	2	1
1810	Topps & Co.	2	1

This was the works about a mile north of the centre of Chesterfield near the terminus of the Chesterfield Canal. The 1794 list gives a date of building of 1780 for the two coke-fired furnaces, blown by engine; the forge consisted of a chafery, two melting furnaces and a balling furnace; no ground landlord is named. 1796: output 940 tons, Excise, actual and Exact Return, which (unusually) does not divide by either 50 or 52 into a whole number. The 1805 list returns the output as 700 tons p.a.

Chesterfield: Broad Oaks: see Wingerworth [II]

Clay Cross SK 3964

Year	Owner	Built	In Blast
1847	Stephenson & Co.	2	0
1849	—	-	2
1854	Clay Cross Co.	3	2
1855	Clay Cross Co.	3	2
1856	Clay Cross Co.	3	2
1857	Clay Cross Co.	3	2
1858	Clay Cross Co.	3	3
1859	Clay Cross Co.	3	3
1860	Clay Cross Co.	3	1
1861	Clay Cross Co.	3	1
1862	W. Jackson & Co.	3	1
1863	W. Jackson MP & Sir J. Walmsley	3	3
1864	W. Jackson MP & Sir J. Walmsley	3	3
1865	Clay Cross Co.	3	3
1866	Clay Cross Co.	3	3
1867	Clay Cross Iron Co.	3	2
1868	Clay Cross Iron Co.	3	2
1869	Clay Cross Iron Co.	3	2
1870	Clay Cross Iron Co.	3	2
1871	Clay Cross Iron Co.	3	3
1872	Clay Cross Co.	3	3
1873	Clay Cross Co.	3	3
1874	Clay Cross Co.	3	3
1875	Executors of Sir William Jackson Bt	3	3
1876	Executors of Sir William Jackson Bt	3	2
1877	Clay Cross Co.	3	3
1878	Clay Cross Co.	3	3
1879	Clay Cross Co.	3	2
1880	Clay Cross Co.	3	3
1881	Clay Cross Co.	3	3
1882	Clay Cross Co.	3	2
1883	Clay Cross Co.	3	3
1884	Clay Cross Co.	3	2
1885	Clay Cross Co.	3	2
1886	Clay Cross Co.	3	2
1887	Clay Cross Co.	3	2
1888	Clay Cross Co.	3	2
1889	Clay Cross Co.	3	2
1890	Clay Cross Co.	2	2
1891	Clay Cross Co.	3	2
1892	Clay Cross Co.	3	1
1893	Clay Cross Co.	3	1
1894	Clay Cross Co.	3	2
1895	Clay Cross Co.	3	2
1896	Clay Cross Co.	2	2
1897	Clay Cross Co.	3	2
1898	Clay Cross Co.	3	2
1899	Clay Cross Co.	3	2
1900	Clay Cross Co.	3	2
1901	Clay Cross Co.	3	2
1902	Clay Cross Co.	3	2
1903	Clay Cross Co.	3	2
1904	Clay Cross Co.	3	2
1905	Clay Cross Co.	3	2
1906	Clay Cross Co.	3	2
1907	Clay Cross Co.	3	3
1908	Clay Cross Co.	3	2
1909	Clay Cross Co.	3	2
1910	Clay Cross Co.	3	2
1911	Clay Cross Co.	3	2
1912	Clay Cross Co.	3	2
1913	Clay Cross Co. Ltd	3	2
1921	Clay Cross Co. Ltd	3	-
1922	Clay Cross Co. Ltd	3	-
1923	Clay Cross Co. Ltd	3	-
1924	Clay Cross Co. Ltd	3	-
1925	Clay Cross Co. Ltd	3	-
1926	Clay Cross Co. Ltd	3	-
1927	Clay Cross Co. Ltd	3	-
1928	Clay Cross Co. Ltd	3	-
1929	Clay Cross Co. Ltd	3	-
1930	Clay Cross Co. Ltd	3	-
1931	Clay Cross Co. Ltd	3	-
1932	Clay Cross Co. Ltd	3	-
1933	Clay Cross Co. Ltd	3	-
1934	Clay Cross Co. Ltd	3	-
1935	Clay Cross Co. Ltd	2	-
1936	Clay Cross Co. Ltd	1	-
1937	Clay Cross Co. Ltd	2	-
1938	Clay Cross Co. Ltd	2	-
1939	Clay Cross Co. Ltd	2	-
1940	Clay Cross Co. Ltd	2	-
1941	Clay Cross Co. Ltd	2	-
1942	Clay Cross Co. Ltd	2	-
1943	Clay Cross Co. Ltd	2	-
1944	Clay Cross Co. Ltd	2	-
1945	Clay Cross Co. Ltd	2	-
1946	Clay Cross Co. Ltd	1	-
1947	Clay Cross Co. Ltd	2	-
1948	Clay Cross Co. Ltd	2	-
1949	Clay Cross Co. Ltd	2	-
1950	Clay Cross Co. Ltd	2	-
1951	Clay Cross Co. Ltd	2	-
1952	Clay Cross Co. Ltd	2	-
1953	Clay Cross Co. Ltd	2	-

Year	Owner	Built	In Blast
1954	Clay Cross (Iron & Foundries) Ltd	2	-
1955	Clay Cross (Iron & Foundries) Ltd	2	-
1956	Clay Cross (Iron & Foundries) Ltd	2	-
1957	Clay Cross (Iron & Foundries) Ltd	1	-

The 1847 list gives an output figure of 8,320 tons p.a., i.e. 80 tons a week from each furnace, although both were then out of blast. Truran: output 100 tons a week from each of 2 furnaces. 1871: 1 furnace building. The company's name appears in the 1958 return but with no furnaces shown.

Codnor Park SK 4451

Year	Owner	Built	In Blast
1823	—	2	-
1825	Jessop & Co.	3	2
1830	—	3	-
1839	Jessop & Co.	3	3
1841	Butterley Co.	3	3
1843	Butterley Iron Co.	3	1
1847	Butterley Co.	3	3
1849	—	-	3
1854	Butterley Co.	4	4
1855	Butterley Co.	4	3
1856	Butterley Co.	4	4
1857	Butterley Co.	4	4
1858	Butterley Co.	4	4
1859	Butterley Co.	4	4
1860	Butterley Co.	4	3
1861	Butterley Co.	4	3
1862	Butterley Co.	4	2
1863	Butterley Co.	-	-
1864	Butterley Co.	-	-
1865	Butterley Co.	-	-
1866	F. Wright & W. Jessop	-	-
1867	Butterley Co.	-	-
1868	Butterley Co.	-	-
1869	Butterley Co.	-	-
1870	Butterley Co.	-	-
1871	Butterley Co.	-	-
1872	Butterley Co.	-	-
1873	Butterley Co.	-	-
1874	Butterley Co.	-	-
1875	Butterley Co.	-	-
1876	Butterley Co.	3	1
1877	Butterley Co.	2	2
1878	Butterley Co.	4	2
1879	Butterley Co.	3	1
1880	Butterley Co.	4	2
1881	Butterley Co.	-	-
1882	Butterley Co.	-	-
1883	Butterley Co.	-	-
1884	Butterley Co.	-	-
1885	Butterley Co.	-	-
1886	Butterley Co.	-	-
1887	Butterley Co.	-	-
1888	Butterley Co. Ltd	-	-
1889	Butterley Co. Ltd	3	1
1890	Butterley Co. Ltd	3	1
1891	Butterley Co. Ltd	3	1
1892	Butterley Co. Ltd	3	0
1893	Butterley Co. Ltd	3	0
1894	Butterley Co. Ltd	3	1
1895	Butterley Co. Ltd	3	0
1896	Butterley Co. Ltd	3	0
1897	Butterley Co. Ltd	3	0
1898	Butterley Co. Ltd	3	0
1899	Butterley Co. Ltd	3	0
1900	Butterley Co. Ltd	3	0
1901	Butterley Co. Ltd	3	0
1902	Butterley Co. Ltd	3	0

1823–30: output 2,096 tons p.a. in 1823 and 2,455 tons in 1830; the third furnace was built in 1828. 1825: output 70 tons a week, 3,000 p.a., 'castings &c'. 1841: output 140 tons a week. 1843: output 50 tons a week. 1847: 10,920 tons p.a., i.e. 70 tons a week from each of three furnaces. Truran: output 110 tons a week from each of 3 furnaces. 1863–75, 1881–88: furnace-numbers combined with Butterley (qv). 1877: 2 furnaces building. 1879: 1 building.

Dale Abbey SK 4738

Year	Owner	Built	In Blast
1794	Mr English	1	-
1796	—	1	1
1805	A. Raby	2	0
1810	A. Raby	2	0

The ground landlord in 1794 was Earl Stanhope; the furnace was coke-fired, blown by engine and said to have been built in 1790. 1796: output 474 tons, Excise and actual, 443 tons Exact Return. 1805: no output. See also Stanton.

Denby SK 3846

Year	Owner	Built	In Blast
1862	W.H. & G. Dawes	2	2
1863	W.H. & G. Dawes	4	2
1864	W.H. & G. Dawes	4	2
1865	W.H. & G. Dawes	4	2
1866	W.H. & G. Dawes	4	2
1867	W.H. & G. Dawes	4	2
1868	W.H. & G. Dawes	4	2
1869	W.H. & G. Dawes	4	2
1870	W.H. & G. Dawes	4	2
1871	W.H. & G. Dawes	4	3
1872	W.H. & G. Dawes	4	3
1873	W.H. & G. Dawes	4	3
1874	W.H. & G. Dawes	4	3
1875	W.H. & G. Dawes	4	3
1876	George Dawes	4	2
1877	George Dawes	4	2
1878	George Dawes	4	2
1879	George Dawes	4	2
1880	George Dawes	4	3
1881	George Dawes	4	3
1882	George Dawes	4	3
1883	George Dawes	4	3
1884	George Dawes	4	2
1885	George Dawes	4	1
1886	George Dawes	4	1
1887	George Dawes	4	0
1888	Executors of George Dawes	4	1
1889	Executors of George Dawes	4	0

Derbyshire

Year	Owner	Built	In Blast
1890	Denby Iron & Coal Co. Ltd	4	0
1891	Denby Iron & Coal Co. Ltd	4	1
1892	Denby Iron & Coal Co. Ltd	4	1
1893	Denby Iron & Coal Co. Ltd	4	1
1894	Denby Iron & Coal Co. Ltd	4	1
1895	Denby Iron & Coal Co. Ltd	4	2
1896	Denby Iron & Coal Co. Ltd	4	2
1897	Denby Iron & Coal Co. Ltd	4	2
1898	Denby Iron & Coal Co. Ltd	4	3
1899	Denby Iron & Coal Co. Ltd	4	3
1900	Denby Iron & Coal Co. Ltd	4	3
1901	Denby Iron & Coal Co. Ltd	4	2
1902	Denby Iron & Coal Co. Ltd	4	2
1903	Denby Iron & Coal Co. Ltd	4	3
1904	Denby Iron & Coal Co. Ltd	4	3
1905	Denby Iron & Coal Co. Ltd	4	3
1906	Denby Iron & Coal Co. Ltd	4	4
1907	Denby Iron & Coal Co. Ltd	4	4
1908	Denby Iron & Coal Co. Ltd	4	3
1909	Denby Iron & Coal Co. Ltd	4	4
1910	Denby Iron & Coal Co. Ltd	4	4
1911	Denby Iron & Coal Co. Ltd	4	3
1912	Denby Iron & Coal Co. Ltd	4	3
1913	Denby Iron & Coal Co. Ltd	4	4
1921	Denby Iron & Coal Co. Ltd	4	-
1922	Denby Iron & Coal Co. Ltd	4	-
1923	Denby Iron & Coal Co. Ltd	4	-
1924	Denby Iron & Coal Co. Ltd	4	-
1925	Denby Iron & Coal Co. Ltd	4	-
1926	Denby Iron & Coal Co. Ltd	4	-
1927	Denby Iron & Coal Co. Ltd	4	-
1928	Denby Iron & Coal Co. Ltd	4	-
1929	Denby Iron & Coal Co. Ltd	4	-

1863: 2 furnaces building.

Devonshire Works, Staveley   SK 4174

Year	Owner	Built	In Blast
1907	Staveley Coal & Iron Co. Ltd	2	1
1908	Staveley Coal & Iron Co. Ltd	3	3
1909	Staveley Coal & Iron Co. Ltd	3	3
1910	Staveley Coal & Iron Co. Ltd	3	3
1911	Staveley Coal & Iron Co. Ltd	3	3
1912	Staveley Coal & Iron Co. Ltd	3	3
1913	Staveley Coal & Iron Co. Ltd	3	3

These furnaces formed part of the Stavely Works complex and from 1921 a single figure was returned for both this site and the older furnaces (see under Staveley).

Duckmanton   SK 4271

Year	Owner	Built	In Blast
1805	Smith & Co.	2	1
1810	Smith & Co.	2	1
1823	—	1	-
1825	Smith Brothers	2	1
1830	—	1	-
1839	—	2	2
1841	Elsom & Smith	2	2
1843	Smith & Elsam	2	2
1847	Elsom & Co.	2	0
1849	—	-	2
1854	R. Arkwright	2	0
1855	R. Arkwright	0	0

1805: output 900 tons p.a. 1823–30: 1,091 tons p.a. in 1823, 1,446 tons in 1830. 1825: weekly output 25 tons, 1,144 p.a., 'castings &c'. 1841: output 71 tons a week. 1843: output 120 tons a week. In 1847, although the works had been abandoned, an output of 8,320 tons p.a. was returned, i.e. 80 tons a week from each furnace. The 1843 and 1847 lists use the name 'Adelphi' for the site. *Mineral Statistics* in 1855 noted that 'These old furnaces are pulled down'; Truran, nonetheless, lists 2 furnaces at 'Adelphi' with an output of 100 tons a week each, which is clearly wrong.

Dunston: see Sheepbridge

Erewash Valley, Ilkeston   SK 4740

Year	Owner	Built	In Blast
1874	Erewash Valley Iron Co. Ltd	1	1
1875	Erewash Valley Iron Co. Ltd	1	1
1876	Erewash Valley Iron Co. Ltd	4	1
1877	Erewash Valley Iron Co. Ltd	4	1
1878	Erewash Valley Iron Co. Ltd	4	1
1879	Erewash Valley Iron Co. Ltd	4	2
1880	Erewash Valley Iron Co. Ltd	4	3
1881	Erewash Valley Iron Co. Ltd	4	3
1882	Erewash Valley Iron Co. Ltd	4	2
1883	Erewash Valley Iron Co. Ltd	4	1
1884	Erewash Valley Iron Co. Ltd	4	1
1885	Erewash Valley Iron Co. Ltd	4	0
1886	Erewash Valley Iron Co. Ltd	4	0
1887	Erewash Valley Iron Co. Ltd	4	0
1888	Erewash Valley Iron Co. Ltd	4	0
1889	Erewash Valley Iron Co. Ltd	4	0
1890	E.P. Davis	4	1
1891	E.P. Davis	4	0
1892	E.P. Davis	4	0
1893	E.P. Davis	4	0
1894	E.P. Davis	4	0
1895	E.P. Davis	4	0
1896	E.P. Davis	4	0
1897	E.P. Davis	4	0
1898	E.P. Davis	3	1
1899	E.P. Davis	2	2
1900	E.P. Davis	2	2
1901	E.P. Davis	2	0
1902	E.P. Davis	2	0
1903	E.P. Davis	2	0
1904	E.P. Davis	2	0
1905	E.P. Davis	2	0
1906	E.P. Davis	2	1
1907	E.P. Davis	2	2
1908	E.P. Davis	2	1
1909	E.P. Davis	2	1
1910	E.P. Davis	2	1
1911	E.P. Davis	2	1
1912	E.P. Davis	2	1
1913	E.P. Davis	2	1
1921	E.P. Davis	2	-
1922	E.P. Davis	2	-
1923	E.P. Davis	2	-
1924	E.P. Davis	2	-

Year	Owner	Built	In Blast
1925	E.P. Davis	2	-
1926	E.P. Davis	2	-
1927	E.P. Davis	2	-
1928	E.P. Davis	2	-

1883: Production estimated. Five furnaces were returned for E.P. Davis in 1921–28, which must represent this site and Bennerley (qv); the figure has been divided by reference to the number of furnaces returned at the two works up to 1913.

Grassmoor: see Hasland

Hasland SK 4067

Year	Owner	Built	In Blast
1805	J. Brocksopp	1	1
1810	J. Brocksopp	2	2
1823	—	-	-
1825	Brocksopp	1	0
1830	—	-	-

The output returned in 1805 was 723 tons p.a. The 1823–30 list gives a nil return for this site, with the comment: 'Has not been in in Blast for many Years'; both in this list and that of 1825 (when again no output is shown) the works is called 'Grassmoor' and appears under Yorkshire. The Staffs RO version of the 1825 list names the owner as 'Brockshow' in undoubted error.

Ilkeston: see Erewash Valley

Moira, Leics.

Year	Owner	Built	In Blast
1805	Lord Moira	1	0
1810	Lord Moira	1	0
1825	Lord Moira	1	0

In all three lists this site is named as 'Ashby' (i.e. Ashby de la Zouch) but has long been known to historians as Moira. No output is given for either 1805 or 1825.

Morley Park SK 3849

Year	Owner	Built	In Blast
1794	Mr Hurt	1	-
1796	—	1	1
1805	F. Hurt	1	1
1810	F. Hurt	1	1
1823	—	1	-
1825	J. & C. Mold	2	1
1830	—	2	-
1839	Messrs Mold	2	2
1841	J. & C. Mold	2	2
1843	Mold & Co.	2	1
1847	Mold & Co.	2	2
1849	—	-	2
1854	—	2	2
1855	Mold & Co.	2	2
1856	Mold & Co.	2	2
1857	Mold & Co.	2	2
1858	W.H. Mold	2	2
1859	W.H. Mold	2	2
1860	W.H. Mold	2	0
1861	Charles C. Disney	2	1
1862	Charles C. Disney	2	2
1863	Charles C. Disney	2	2
1864	Charles C. Disney	2	2
1865	Charles C. Disney	2	2
1866	Charles C. Disney	2	2
1867	Charles C. Disney	2	1
1868	Charles C. Disney	2	2
1869	Charles C. Disney	2	2
1870	Henry Cathrow Disney	2	2
1871	Henry Cathrow Disney	2	2
1872	Henry Cathrow Disney	2	2
1873	Henry Cathrow Disney	2	2
1874	Henry Cathrow Disney	2	2
1875	Henry Cathrow Disney	2	2
1876	Henry Cathrow Disney	2	0
1877	Henry Cathrow Disney	2	0
1878	Henry Cathrow Disney	2	0
1879	Henry Cathrow Disney	2	0
1880	Henry Cathrow Disney	2	0
1881	Henry Cathrow Disney	2	0
1882	Henry Cathrow Disney	2	0

Hurt was both owner and occupier in 1794; the single furnace was coke-fired but no other details are given and the entry appears to be a late addition to the list. 1796: output 728 tons p.a. (i.e. 14 tons a week), Excise, actual and Exact Return. 1805: output 340 tons p.a. 1823–30: 544 tons in 1823; note that the second furnace was built in 1825; output 1,428 tons in 1830. 1825: weekly output 35 tons, 1,500 tons p.a., 'used by themselves'. 1841: output 45 tons a week. 1843: output 40 tons a week. 1847: output 4,680 tons, i.e. 90 tons a week from the two furnaces. 1858: 'The only cold-blast furnaces in Derbyshire'; the furnace in blast in 1861 was also working on cold blast. Truran: output 70 tons a week from each of 2 furnaces. In 1858–60 the works was called Alderwasley & Morley Park: the former (qv) was an associated forge, although there had been a blast furnace there briefly for a few years after 1764. The entry for Alderwasley in 1810, listing 2 furnaces, is probably a duplicate for Morley Park.

Newbold SK 3573

Year	Owner	Built	In Blast
1847	Scholefield & Co.	1	0
1849	—	-	1
1854	Samuel Beale & Co.	1	1
1855	Samuel Beale & Co.	1	1
1856	Samuel Beale & Co.	1	1
1857	Samuel Beale & Co.	1	1
1858	Samuel Beale & Co.	1	1
1859	Samuel Beale & Co.	1	1
1860	Samuel Beale & Co.	1	1
1861	Samuel Beale & Co.	1	1
1862	Samuel Beale & Co.	1	1
1863	Samuel Beale & Co.	1	1
1864	Samuel Beale & Co.	1	1
1865	Samuel Beale & Co.	1	1
1866	Samuel Beale & Co.	1	1
1867	Samuel Beale & Co.	1	1
1868	Samuel Beale & Co.	1	1

Year	Owner	Built	In Blast
1869	Samuel Beale & Co.	1	1
1870	C.H. Plevins	1	1
1871	C.H. Plevins	1	1
1872	Newbold Iron Co.	1	1
1873	Newbold Iron Co.	1	1
1874	Newbold Iron Co.	1	0
1875	Newbold Iron Co.	1	0
1876	Newbold Iron Co.	1	0
1877	C.H. Plevins	1	0
1878	C.H. Plevins	1	0
1879	C.H. Plevins	1	0
1880	Newbold Iron & Coal Co.	1	0
1881	Newbold Iron & Coal Co.	1	0
1882	Newbold Iron & Coal Co.	1	0
1883	Newbold Iron & Coal Co.	1	0
1884	Newbold Iron & Coal Co.	1	0
1885	Newbold Iron & Coal Co.	1	0

The 1847 list gives an output of 4,160 tons p.a., i.e. 80 tons a week, even though the furnace was out of blast. Truran: weekly output 100 tons from one furnace.

Oakerthorpe   SK 3954

Year	Owner	Built	In Blast
1857	Messrs Marshall	1	0
1858	Messrs Marshall	1	1
1859	Oakerthorpe Iron & Coal Co. Ltd	2	1
1860	Oakerthorpe Iron & Coal Co. Ltd	2	1
1861	Oakerthorpe Iron & Coal Co. Ltd	2	1
1862	Oakerthorpe Iron & Coal Co. Ltd	2	1
1863	Oakerthorpe Iron & Coal Co. Ltd	2	1
1864	Oakerthorpe Iron & Coal Co. Ltd	2	1
1865	Oakerthorpe Iron & Coal Co. Ltd	2	1
1866	Oakerthorpe Iron & Coal Co. Ltd	2	1
1867	Oakerthorpe Iron & Coal Co. Ltd	2	0
1868	J.B. Wilson	2	0
1869	J.B. Wilson	2	0
1870	J.B. Wilson	2	0
1871	James B. Wilson	2	0
1883	R. Strelley	2	0
1884	R.C. Strelley	2	0

The entries for 1857–58 appear under the heading 'Wingfield' (i.e. South Wingfield, in which Oakerthorpe lies); subsequent entries appear under the latter name but an entry for Wingfield, with one furnace, out of blast, continued to be printed in *Mineral Statistics* up to 1864. Cf. J. Armstrong and S. Jones, *Business Documents* (1987), pp. 39–41.

Renishaw   SK 4478

Year	Owner	Built	In Blast
1796	—	1	1
1805	Appleby & Co.	1	1
1810	Appleby	2	2
1823	—	2	-
1825	Appleby & Co.	2	2
1830	—	2	-
1839	—	2	2
1841	Appleby & Co.	1	1
1843	Appleby & Co.	2	1
1847	Appleby & Co.	2	1
1849	—	-	2
1854	Appleby & Co.	2	1
1855	Appleby & Co.	2	1
1856	Appleby & Co.	2	2
1857	Appleby & Co.	2	1
1858	Appleby & Co.	2	1
1859	Appleby & Co.	2	0
1860	Appleby & Co.	2	1
1861	F.R. & C.E. Appleby	2	1
1862	F.R. & C.E. Appleby	2	2
1863	F.R. & C.E. Appleby	2	2
1864	F.R. & C.E. Appleby	2	1
1865	F.R. & C.E. Appleby	2	2
1866	F.R. & C.E. Appleby	2	2
1867	F.R. & C.E. Appleby	2	2
1868	F.R. Appleby	2	2
1869	F.R. Appleby	2	2
1870	Appleby & Co.	2	1
1871	F.R. Appleby & Co.	2	2
1872	F.R. Appleby & Co.	4	2
1873	F.R. Appleby & Co.	4	3
1874	F.R. Appleby & Co.	4	3
1875	F.R. Appleby & Co.	4	3
1876	F.R. Appleby & Co.	4	2
1877	F.R. Appleby & Co.	4	2
1878	F.R. Appleby & Co.	4	4
1879	F.R. Appleby & Co.	3	2
1880	F.R. Appleby & Co.	3	3
1881	F.R. Appleby & Co.	3	3
1882	F.R. Appleby & Co.	3	3
1883	F.R. Appleby & Co.	3	2
1884	F.R. Appleby & Co.	2	2
1885	F.R. Appleby & Co.	2	2
1886	F.R. Appleby & Co.	2	2
1887	F.R. Appleby & Co.	2	2
1888	Appleby & Co.	2	2
1889	Appleby & Co.	2	2
1890	Appleby & Co.	2	2
1891	Appleby & Co.	3	2
1892	Appleby & Co.	3	2
1893	Renishaw Iron Co.	3	2
1894	Renishaw Iron Co.	3	2
1895	Renishaw Iron Co.	3	2
1896	Renishaw Iron Co.	3	3
1897	Renishaw Iron Co.	3	3
1898	Renishaw Iron Co.	3	3
1899	Renishaw Iron Co.	3	3
1900	Renishaw Iron Co.	3	3
1901	Renishaw Iron Co.	3	2
1902	Renishaw Iron Co. Ltd	3	3
1903	Renishaw Iron Co. Ltd	3	3
1904	Renishaw Iron Co. Ltd	3	3
1905	Renishaw Iron Co. Ltd	3	2
1906	Renishaw Iron Co. Ltd	3	3
1907	Renishaw Iron Co. Ltd	3	3
1908	Renishaw Iron Co. Ltd	3	2
1909	Renishaw Iron Co. Ltd	3	2
1910	Renishaw Iron Co. Ltd	3	3
1911	Renishaw Iron Co. Ltd	3	3
1912	Renishaw Iron Co. Ltd	3	3
1913	Renishaw Iron Co. Ltd	3	2
1921	Renishaw Iron Co. Ltd	3	-
1922	Renishaw Iron Co. Ltd	3	-
1923	Renishaw Iron Co. Ltd	2	-
1924	Renishaw Iron Co. Ltd	2	-
1925	Renishaw Iron Co. Ltd	2	-
1926	Renishaw Iron Co. Ltd	2	-

Year	Owner	Built	In Blast
1927	Renishaw Iron Co. Ltd	2	-
1928	Renishaw Iron Co. Ltd	2	-
1929	Renishaw Iron Co. Ltd	2	-
1930	Renishaw Iron Co. Ltd	2	-
1931	Renishaw Iron Co. Ltd	2	-
1932	Renishaw Iron Co. Ltd	2	-
1933	Renishaw Iron Co. Ltd	2	-
1934	Renishaw Iron Co. Ltd	2	-
1935	Renishaw Iron Co. Ltd	2	-
1936	Renishaw Iron Co. Ltd	2	-
1937	Renishaw Iron Co. Ltd	2	-
1938	Renishaw Iron Co. Ltd	2	-
1939	Renishaw Iron Co. Ltd	2	-
1940	Renishaw Iron Co. Ltd	2	-
1941	Renishaw Iron Co. Ltd	2	-
1942	Renishaw Iron Co. Ltd	2	-
1943	Renishaw Iron Co. Ltd	2	-
1944	Renishaw Iron Co. Ltd	2	-
1945	Renishaw Iron Co. Ltd	2	-
1946	Renishaw Iron Co. Ltd	2	-
1947	Renishaw Iron Co. Ltd	2	-
1948	Renishaw Iron Co. Ltd	2	-
1949	Renishaw Iron Co. Ltd	2	-
1950	Renishaw Iron Co. Ltd	2	-
1951	Renishaw Iron Co. Ltd	2	-
1952	Renishaw Iron Co. Ltd	2	-
1953	Renishaw Iron Co. Ltd	2	-
1954	Renishaw Iron Co. Ltd	2	-
1955	Renishaw Iron Co. Ltd	2	-
1956	Renishaw Iron Co. Ltd	2	-
1957	Renishaw Iron Co. Ltd	2	-
1958	Renishaw Iron Co. Ltd	2	-
1959	Renishaw Iron Co. Ltd	2	-
1960	Renishaw Iron Co. Ltd	2	-
1961	Renishaw Iron Co. Ltd	2	-
1962	Renishaw Iron Co. Ltd	2	-
1963	Renishaw Iron Co. Ltd	2	-
1964	Renishaw Iron Co. Ltd	2	-
1965	Renishaw Iron Co. Ltd	2	-
1966	Renishaw Iron Co. Ltd	2	-
1967	Renishaw Iron Co. Ltd	2	-

1796: Excise and actual output figures given for two furnaces; one was said to make 450 tons p.a. (i.e. 9 tons a week), the other 50 tons p.a., which suggests that it was a melting furnace rather than a blast furnace, especially as in 1805, when the output is given as 975 tons p.a., only one furnace is listed. The 1796 figures above have been amended on this assumption. The Exact Return in 1796 was 705 tons p.a. In both 1805 and 1810 Renishaw was listed under Yorkshire. 1823–30: output 2,120 tons p.a. in 1823, 2,810 tons in 1830. 1825: weekly output 60 tons, 2,600 p.a. 1841: output 62 tons a week. 1843: output 60 tons a week. 1847: 4,680 tons p.a., i.e. 90 tons a week from the two furnaces. Truran: output 110 tons a week from each of 2 furnaces.

Sheepbridge   SK 3774

Year	Owner	Built	In Blast
1857	Fowler & Co.	2	0
1858	John Chesterfield	3	0
1859	John Chesterfield	3	0
1860	William Fowler & Co.	3	2
1861	Dunston, Barlow & Co.	3	2
1862	Dunston, Barlow & Co.	4	3
1863	Fowlers & Hankey	4	4
1864	Sheepbridge Coal & Iron Co. Ltd	4	4
1865	Sheepbridge Coal & Iron Co. Ltd	4	4
1866	Sheepbridge Coal & Iron Co. Ltd	4	3
1867	Sheepbridge Coal & Iron Co. Ltd	4	2
1868	Sheepbridge Coal & Iron Co. Ltd	4	2
1869	Sheepbridge Coal & Iron Co. Ltd	4	4
1870	Sheepbridge Coal & Iron Co. Ltd	4	4
1871	Sheepbridge Coal & Iron Co. Ltd	5	5
1872	Sheepbridge Coal & Iron Co. Ltd	5	5
1873	Sheepbridge Coal & Iron Co. Ltd	5	5
1874	Sheepbridge Coal & Iron Co. Ltd	5	5
1875	Sheepbridge Coal & Iron Co. Ltd	6	4
1876	Sheepbridge Coal & Iron Co. Ltd	6	4
1877	Sheepbridge Coal & Iron Co. Ltd	6	5
1878	Sheepbridge Coal & Iron Co. Ltd	6	4
1879	Sheepbridge Coal & Iron Co. Ltd	6	3
1880	Sheepbridge Coal & Iron Co. Ltd	6	5
1881	Sheepbridge Coal & Iron Co. Ltd	7	5
1882	Sheepbridge Coal & Iron Co. Ltd	7	5
1883	Sheepbridge Coal & Iron Co. Ltd	7	5
1884	Sheepbridge Coal & Iron Co. Ltd	8	5
1885	Sheepbridge Coal & Iron Co. Ltd	8	4
1886	Sheepbridge Coal & Iron Co. Ltd	8	3
1887	Sheepbridge Coal & Iron Co. Ltd	8	3
1888	Sheepbridge Coal & Iron Co. Ltd	8	5
1889	Sheepbridge Coal & Iron Co. Ltd	8	5
1890	Sheepbridge Coal & Iron Co. Ltd	8	5
1891	Sheepbridge Coal & Iron Co. Ltd	8	5
1892	Sheepbridge Coal & Iron Co. Ltd	8	3
1893	Sheepbridge Coal & Iron Co. Ltd	8	3
1894	Sheepbridge Coal & Iron Co. Ltd	8	3
1895	Sheepbridge Coal & Iron Co. Ltd	8	3
1896	Sheepbridge Coal & Iron Co. Ltd	8	5
1897	Sheepbridge Coal & Iron Co. Ltd	8	5
1898	Sheepbridge Coal & Iron Co. Ltd	6	5
1899	Sheepbridge Coal & Iron Co. Ltd	6	5
1900	Sheepbridge Coal & Iron Co. Ltd	7	5
1901	Sheepbridge Coal & Iron Co. Ltd	7	4
1902	Sheepbridge Coal & Iron Co. Ltd	7	4
1903	Sheepbridge Coal & Iron Co. Ltd	7	3
1904	Sheepbridge Coal & Iron Co. Ltd	7	3
1905	Sheepbridge Coal & Iron Co. Ltd	7	3
1906	Sheepbridge Coal & Iron Co. Ltd	4	3
1907	Sheepbridge Coal & Iron Co. Ltd	4	3
1908	Sheepbridge Coal & Iron Co. Ltd	4	3
1909	Sheepbridge Coal & Iron Co. Ltd	4	3
1910	Sheepbridge Coal & Iron Co. Ltd	4	3
1911	Sheepbridge Coal & Iron Co. Ltd	4	2
1912	Sheepbridge Coal & Iron Co. Ltd	4	3
1913	Sheepbridge Coal & Iron Co. Ltd	4	3
1921	Sheepbridge Coal & Iron Co. Ltd	4	-
1922	Sheepbridge Coal & Iron Co. Ltd	4	-
1923	Sheepbridge Coal & Iron Co. Ltd	4	-
1924	Sheepbridge Coal & Iron Co. Ltd	4	-
1925	Sheepbridge Coal & Iron Co. Ltd	4	-
1926	Sheepbridge Coal & Iron Co. Ltd	4	-
1927	Sheepbridge Coal & Iron Co. Ltd	4	-
1928	Sheepbridge Coal & Iron Co. Ltd	4	-
1929	Sheepbridge Coal & Iron Co. Ltd	4	-
1930	Sheepbridge Coal & Iron Co. Ltd	2	-
1931	Sheepbridge Coal & Iron Co. Ltd	2	-
1932	Sheepbridge Coal & Iron Co. Ltd	2	-
1933	Sheepbridge Coal & Iron Co. Ltd	2	-
1934	Sheepbridge Coal & Iron Co. Ltd	2	-
1935	Sheepbridge Coal & Iron Co. Ltd	2	-
1936	Sheepbridge Coal & Iron Co. Ltd	2	-
1937	Sheepbridge Coal & Iron Co. Ltd	2	-

Year	Owner	Built	In Blast
1938	Sheepbridge Coal & Iron Co. Ltd	2	-
1939	Sheepbridge Coal & Iron Co. Ltd	2	-
1940	Sheepbridge Coal & Iron Co. Ltd	2	-
1941	Sheepbridge Coal & Iron Co. Ltd	2	-
1942	Sheepbridge Coal & Iron Co. Ltd	2	-
1943	Sheepbridge Coal & Iron Co. Ltd	2	-
1944	Sheepbridge Coal & Iron Co. Ltd	2	-
1945	Sheepbridge Coal & Iron Co. Ltd	2	-
1946	Sheepbridge Coal & Iron Co. Ltd	2	-
1947	Sheepbridge Coal & Iron Co. Ltd	2	-
1948	Sheepbridge Coal & Iron Co. Ltd	1	-
1949	Sheepbridge Coal & Iron Co. Ltd	1	-
1950	Sheepbridge Coal & Iron Co. Ltd	1	-
1951	Sheepbridge Co. Ltd	1	-
1952	Sheepbridge Co. Ltd	2	-
1953	Sheepbridge Co. Ltd	2	-
1954	Sheepbridge Co. Ltd	2	-
1955	Sheepbridge Co. Ltd	2	-
1956	Sheepbridge Co. Ltd	2	-
1957	Sheepbridge Co. Ltd	2	-
1958	Sheepbridge Co. Ltd	2	-
1959	Sheepbridge Co. Ltd	2	-
1960	Sheepbridge Co. Ltd	2	-
1961	Sheepbridge Co. Ltd	2	-

1857–59: works called Barlow & Dunston or Dunston & Barlow (both villages near Sheepbridge); the owner 'John Chesterfield' in 1858–59 is probably a confused combination of name and address (Sheepbridge is about two miles north of Chesterfield). 1863: 'A large proportion of the make is cold blast'. 1877–78: 2 furnaces building.

South Wingfield: see Oakerthorpe

Stanton SK 3847

Year	Owner	Built	In Blast
1847	Smith & Co.	3	3
1849	—	-	1
1854	Stanton Iron Co.	3	3
1855	Stanton Iron Co.	3	2
1856	Stanton Iron Co.	3	2
1857	Stanton Iron Co.	3	2
1858	Crompton & Co.	3	2
1859	Crompton & Co.	3	2
1859	Crompton & Co.	3	2
1860	Crompton & Co.	3	2
1861	Crompton & Co.	3	2
1862	Crompton & Co.	3	2
1863	Stanton Ironworks Co.	3	2
1864	Stanton Ironworks Co.	3	2
1865	Stanton Ironworks Co.	4	3
1866	Stanton Ironworks Co.	5	4
1867	Stanton Ironworks Co.	5	4
1868	Stanton Ironworks Co.	5	4
1869	Stanton Ironworks Co.	5	4
1870	Stanton Ironworks Co.	5	4
1871	Stanton Ironworks Co.	5	5
1872	Stanton Ironworks Co.	5	5
1873	Stanton Ironworks Co.	5	5
1874	Stanton Ironworks Co.	8	5
1875	Stanton Ironworks Co.	8	5
1876	Stanton Ironworks Co.	8	6
1877	Stanton Ironworks Co.	8	6
1878	Stanton Ironworks Co.	8	5
1879	Stanton Ironworks Co. Ltd	8	7
1880	Stanton Ironworks Co. Ltd	8	6
1881	Stanton Ironworks Co. Ltd	8	7
1882	Stanton Ironworks Co. Ltd	8	7
1883	Stanton Ironworks Co. Ltd	8	7
1884	Stanton Ironworks Co. Ltd	9	7
1885	Stanton Ironworks Co. Ltd	9	8
1886	Stanton Ironworks Co. Ltd	9	6
1887	Stanton Ironworks Co. Ltd	8	6
1888	Stanton Ironworks Co. Ltd	8	8
1889	Stanton Ironworks Co. Ltd	8	8
1890	Stanton Ironworks Co. Ltd	8	7
1891	Stanton Ironworks Co. Ltd	8	7
1892	Stanton Ironworks Co. Ltd	8	8
1893	Stanton Ironworks Co. Ltd	8	7
1894	Stanton Ironworks Co. Ltd	8	7
1895	Stanton Ironworks Co. Ltd	8	8
1896	Stanton Ironworks Co. Ltd	8	8
1897	Stanton Ironworks Co. Ltd	8	8
1898	Stanton Ironworks Co. Ltd	8	8
1899	Stanton Ironworks Co. Ltd	9	9
1900	Stanton Ironworks Co. Ltd	9	9
1901	Stanton Ironworks Co. Ltd	9	7
1902	Stanton Ironworks Co. Ltd	9	8
1903	Stanton Ironworks Co. Ltd	9	8
1904	Stanton Ironworks Co. Ltd	9	9
1905	Stanton Ironworks Co. Ltd	9	9
1906	Stanton Ironworks Co. Ltd	9	9
1907	Stanton Ironworks Co. Ltd	9	9
1908	Stanton Ironworks Co. Ltd	9	8
1909	Stanton Ironworks Co. Ltd	9	8
1910	Stanton Ironworks Co. Ltd	9	8
1911	Stanton Ironworks Co. Ltd	9	9
1912	Stanton Ironworks Co. Ltd	9	8
1913	Stanton Ironworks Co. Ltd	9	9
1921	Stanton Ironworks Co. Ltd	9	-
1922	Stanton Ironworks Co. Ltd	9	-
1923	Stanton Ironworks Co. Ltd	9	-
1924	Stanton Ironworks Co. Ltd	9	-
1925	Stanton Ironworks Co. Ltd	9	-
1926	Stanton Ironworks Co. Ltd	4	-
1927	Stanton Ironworks Co. Ltd	5	-
1928	Stanton Ironworks Co. Ltd	6	-
1929	Stanton Ironworks Co. Ltd	4	-
1930	Stanton Ironworks Co. Ltd	4	-
1931	Stanton Ironworks Co. Ltd	5	-
1932	Stanton Ironworks Co. Ltd	5	-
1933	Stanton Ironworks Co. Ltd	5	-
1934	Stanton Ironworks Co. Ltd	5	-
1935	Stanton Ironworks Co. Ltd	5	-
1936	Stanton Ironworks Co. Ltd	5	-
1937	Stanton Ironworks Co. Ltd	5	-
1938	Stanton Ironworks Co. Ltd	5	-
1939	Stanton Ironworks Co. Ltd	5	-
1940	Stanton Ironworks Co. Ltd	5	-
1941	Stanton Ironworks Co. Ltd	5	-
1942	Stanton Ironworks Co. Ltd	5	-
1943	Stanton Ironworks Co. Ltd	5	-
1944	Stanton Ironworks Co. Ltd	5	-
1945	Stanton Ironworks Co. Ltd	5	-
1946	Stanton Ironworks Co. Ltd	5	-
1947	Stanton Ironworks Co. Ltd	5	-
1948	Stanton Ironworks Co. Ltd	5	-
1949	Stanton Ironworks Co. Ltd	5	-
1950	Stanton Ironworks Co. Ltd	5	-
1951	Stanton Ironworks Co. Ltd	5	-
1952	Stanton Ironworks Co. Ltd	5	-

Year	Owner	Built	In Blast
1953	Stanton Ironworks Co. Ltd	5	-
1954	Stanton Ironworks Co. Ltd	5	-
1955	Stanton Ironworks Co. Ltd	5	-
1956	Stanton Ironworks Co. Ltd	5	-
1957	Stanton Ironworks Co. Ltd	5	-
1958	Stanton Ironworks Co. Ltd	5	-
1959	Stanton Ironworks Co. Ltd	5	-
1960	Stanton Ironworks Co. Ltd	5	-
1961	Stanton Ironworks Co. Ltd	5	-
1962	Stanton & Staveley Ltd	5	-
1963	Stanton & Staveley Ltd	5	-
1964	Stanton & Staveley Ltd	5	-
1965	Stanton & Staveley Ltd	5	-
1966	Stanton & Staveley Ltd	5	-
1967	Stanton & Staveley Ltd	5	-
1968	Stanton & Staveley Ltd	5	-
1969	Stanton & Staveley Ltd	4	-
1970	British Steel Corporation	4	-
1971	British Steel Corporation	3	-
1972	British Steel Corporation	3	-
1973	British Steel Corporation	3	-

See Dale Abbey for the earlier works on this site. The 1847 list gives an output of 10,400 tons p.a., i.e. 200 tons a week. Truran: output 120 tons a week from each of 3 furnaces. 1888: 1 furnace building.

Staveley

SK 4174

Year	Owner	Built	In Blast
1794	Mr Mather	1	-
1796	—	1	1
1805	Lowe & Ward	1	1
1810	Ward & Barrow	1	1
1823	—	1	-
1825	G.H. Barrow	2	1
1830	—	2	-
1839	—	2	1
1841	George Barrow	2	1
1843	Barrow	4	1
1847	Barrow	4	3
1849	—	-	4
1854	Richard Barrow	4	2
1855	Richard Barrow	4	2
1856	Richard Barrow	3	2
1857	Richard Barrow	2	2
1858	Richard Barrow	2	2
1859	Richard Barrow	2	2
1860	Richard Barrow	2	2
1861	Richard Barrow	2	2
1862	Richard Barrow	2	2
1863	Staveley Coal & Iron Co. Ltd	2	2
1864	Staveley Coal & Iron Co. Ltd	2	2
1865	Staveley Coal & Iron Co. Ltd	2	2
1866	Staveley Coal & Iron Co. Ltd	2	2
1867	Staveley Coal & Iron Co. Ltd	3	3
1868	Staveley Coal & Iron Co. Ltd	3	3
1869	Staveley Coal & Iron Co. Ltd	4	4
1870	Staveley Coal & Iron Co. Ltd	4	4
1871	Staveley Coal & Iron Co. Ltd	6	4
1872	Staveley Coal & Iron Co. Ltd	7	6
1873	Staveley Coal & Iron Co. Ltd	8	6
1874	Staveley Coal & Iron Co. Ltd	8	7
1875	Staveley Coal & Iron Co. Ltd	8	7
1876	Staveley Coal & Iron Co. Ltd	8	7
1877	Staveley Coal & Iron Co. Ltd	8	7
1878	Staveley Coal & Iron Co. Ltd	8	7
1879	Staveley Coal & Iron Co. Ltd	8	6
1880	Staveley Coal & Iron Co. Ltd	8	6
1881	Staveley Coal & Iron Co. Ltd	8	7
1882	Staveley Coal & Iron Co. Ltd	8	7
1883	Staveley Coal & Iron Co. Ltd	8	7
1884	Staveley Coal & Iron Co. Ltd	8	6
1885	Staveley Coal & Iron Co. Ltd	8	5
1886	Staveley Coal & Iron Co. Ltd	6	5
1887	Staveley Coal & Iron Co. Ltd	6	5
1888	Staveley Coal & Iron Co. Ltd	6	6
1889	Staveley Coal & Iron Co. Ltd	8	7
1890	Staveley Coal & Iron Co. Ltd	7	6
1891	Staveley Coal & Iron Co. Ltd	7	6
1892	Staveley Coal & Iron Co. Ltd	8	7
1893	Staveley Coal & Iron Co. Ltd	8	6
1894	Staveley Coal & Iron Co. Ltd	8	7
1895	Staveley Coal & Iron Co. Ltd	8	7
1896	Staveley Coal & Iron Co. Ltd	8	8
1897	Staveley Coal & Iron Co. Ltd	8	7
1898	Staveley Coal & Iron Co. Ltd	8	7
1899	Staveley Coal & Iron Co. Ltd	8	8
1900	Staveley Coal & Iron Co. Ltd	8	8
1901	Staveley Coal & Iron Co. Ltd	8	7
1902	Staveley Coal & Iron Co. Ltd	8	7
1903	Staveley Coal & Iron Co. Ltd	8	8
1904	Staveley Coal & Iron Co. Ltd	8	7
1905	Staveley Coal & Iron Co. Ltd	8	7
1906	Staveley Coal & Iron Co. Ltd	8	7
1907	Staveley Coal & Iron Co. Ltd	8	7
1908	Staveley Coal & Iron Co. Ltd	8	5
1909	Staveley Coal & Iron Co. Ltd	8	4
1910	Staveley Coal & Iron Co. Ltd	8	4
1911	Staveley Coal & Iron Co. Ltd	8	4
1912	Staveley Coal & Iron Co. Ltd	8	7
1913	Staveley Coal & Iron Co. Ltd	8	7
1921	Staveley Coal & Iron Co. Ltd	12	-
1922	Staveley Coal & Iron Co. Ltd	12	-
1923	Staveley Coal & Iron Co. Ltd	11	-
1924	Staveley Coal & Iron Co. Ltd	11	-
1925	Staveley Coal & Iron Co. Ltd	9	-
1926	Staveley Coal & Iron Co. Ltd	9	-
1927	Staveley Coal & Iron Co. Ltd	9	-
1928	Staveley Coal & Iron Co. Ltd	4	-
1929	Staveley Coal & Iron Co. Ltd	4	-
1930	Staveley Coal & Iron Co. Ltd	4	-
1931	Staveley Coal & Iron Co. Ltd	4	-
1932	Staveley Coal & Iron Co. Ltd	4	-
1933	Staveley Coal & Iron Co. Ltd	4	-
1934	Staveley Coal & Iron Co. Ltd	4	-
1935	Staveley Coal & Iron Co. Ltd	4	-
1936	Staveley Coal & Iron Co. Ltd	4	-
1937	Staveley Coal & Iron Co. Ltd	4	-
1938	Staveley Coal & Iron Co. Ltd	4	-
1939	Staveley Coal & Iron Co. Ltd	4	-
1940	Staveley Coal & Iron Co. Ltd	4	-
1941	Staveley Coal & Iron Co. Ltd	4	-
1942	Staveley Coal & Iron Co. Ltd	4	-
1943	Staveley Coal & Iron Co. Ltd	4	-
1944	Staveley Coal & Iron Co. Ltd	4	-
1945	Staveley Coal & Iron Co. Ltd	4	-
1946	Staveley Coal & Iron Co. Ltd	4	-
1947	Staveley Coal & Iron Co. Ltd	4	-
1948	Staveley Iron & Chemical Co. Ltd	4	-
1949	Staveley Iron & Chemical Co. Ltd	4	-
1950	Staveley Iron & Chemical Co. Ltd	4	-
1951	Staveley Iron & Chemical Co. Ltd	4	-

Year	Owner	Built	In Blast
1952	Staveley Iron & Chemical Co. Ltd	4	-
1953	Staveley Iron & Chemical Co. Ltd	4	-
1954	Staveley Iron & Chemical Co. Ltd	4	-
1955	Staveley Iron & Chemical Co. Ltd	4	-
1956	Staveley Iron & Chemical Co. Ltd	4	-
1957	Staveley Iron & Chemical Co. Ltd	4	-
1958	Staveley Iron & Chemical Co. Ltd	4	-
1959	Staveley Iron & Chemical Co. Ltd	4	-
1960	Staveley Iron & Chemical Co. Ltd	4	-
1961	Staveley Iron & Chemical Co. Ltd	4	-
1962	Staveley Iron & Chemical Co. Ltd	4	-
1963	Staveley Iron & Chemical Co. Ltd	4	-
1964	Stanton & Staveley Ltd	4	-
1965	Stanton & Staveley Ltd	4	-

The 1794 list names Mather as ground landlord also (wrongly; the site lay on the Duke of Devonshire's estate). The furnace was coke-fired but no other information is given; the forge consisted of two fineries and a chafery. 1796: output 1,000 tons p.a. (i.e. 20 tons a week), Excise and actual, Exact Return 761 tons. 1805: output 596 tons p.a. 1823–30: 1,051 tons for 1823 and 1,561 for 1830; the additional furnace was built in 1825. 1825: weekly output 37 tons, 1,820 p.a. 1841: output 50 tons a week. 1843: output 50 tons a week. 1847: 8,840 tons p.a., i.e. 170 tons a week. Truran: output 90 tons a week from each of 4 furnaces. 1855: 'Two of these furnaces are pulled down'. 1873: 1 furnace building. The figures returned for Staveley from 1921 must include both the older furnaces and those at Devonshire Works (qv), which formed part of the Staveley Works complex but had its own entry in *Mineral Statistics* from its construction in 1907 until 1913.

'Summercotes': see Alfreton

Unstone [SK 3677]

Year	Owner	Built	In Blast
1849	—	-	1
1854	Rangely & Co.	1	1
1855	Rangely & Co.	1	1
1856	Rangely & Co.	1	1
1857	Rangely & Co.	1	1
1858	Henry Rangely	1	1
1859	Henry Rangely	1	1
1860	Henry Rangely	1	1
1861	Henry Rangely	1	1
1862	Henry Rangely	1	1
1863	Henry Rangely	1	1
1863	Henry Rangely	1	1
1864	Henry Rangely	1	1
1865	Henry Rangely	1	1
1866	Henry Rangely	1	1
1867	Henry Rangely	1	1
1868	Henry Rangely	1	0
1869	Henry Rangely	1	0
1870	Henry Rangely	1	0

West Hallam [SK 4341]

Year	Owner	Built	In Blast
1847	Whitehouse	2	0
1854	Whitehouse & Co.	2	1
1855	Whitehouse & Co.	3	2
1856	Whitehouse & Co.	3	2
1857	Whitehouse & Co.	3	2
1858	H.B. Whitehouse	3	3
1859	H.B. Whitehouse	3	3
1860	H.B. Whitehouse & Sons	3	3
1861	H.B. Whitehouse & Sons	3	2
1862	H.B. Whitehouse & Sons	3	3
1863	H.B. Whitehouse & Sons	3	2
1864	H.B. Whitehouse & Sons	3	2
1865	H.B. Whitehouse & Co.	3	2
1866	H.B. Whitehouse jun.	3	2
1867	H.B. Whitehouse & Sons	3	2
1868	H.B. Whitehouse & Sons	3	1
1869	H.B. Whitehouse & Sons	3	1
1870	E.J. & A.G. Whitehouse	3	1
1871	E.J. & A.G. Whitehouse	3	2
1872	West Hallam Coal & Iron Co.	2	2
1873	West Hallam Coal & Iron Co.	2	1
1874	West Hallam Coal & Iron Co.	2	1
1875	West Hallam Coal & Iron Co.	2	1
1876	West Hallam Coal & Iron Co.	2	1
1877	West Hallam Coal & Iron Co.	2	1
1878	West Hallam Coal & Iron Co.	2	1
1879	West Hallam Coal & Iron Co.	2	1
1880	West Hallam Coal & Iron Co.	2	1
1881	West Hallam Coal & Iron Co.	2	1
1882	West Hallam Coal & Iron Co.	2	1
1883	West Hallam Coal & Iron Co.	2	0
1884	West Hallam Coal & Iron Co.	2	0
1885	West Hallam Coal & Iron Co.	1	0
1886	West Hallam Coal & Iron Co.	1	0

The 1847 list has an output figure of 8,320 tons p.a., i.e. 160 tons a week, although neither furnace was in blast. 1861: 1 furnace hot blast; the other hot blast for 37 weeks and cold blast for 15. Truran: output 100 tons a week from each of 2 furnaces. 1883: 1 furnace at work for 4 months.

Wingerworth [I] SK 3866

Year	Owner	Built	In Blast
1794	Mr Butler	2	-
1796	—	1	1
1805	J. Butler	2	1
1810	J. Butler	2	2

The ground landlord in 1794 was Sir H. Hunloke; the two furnaces were coke-fired, blown by engine and said to have been built in 1780. 1796: output 1,274 tons p.a., Excise, actual and Exact Return. 1805: output returned by Butler himself as 819 tons.

Wingerworth [II] SK 3869

Year	Owner	Built	In Blast
1847	Yates & Co.	3	2
1849	—	-	3
1854	Wingerworth Iron Co.	3	3
1855	Wingerworth Iron Co.	3	2
1856	Wingerworth Iron Co.	3	2
1857	Wingerworth Iron Co.	3	2
1858	Yates & Co.	2	2
1859	Wingerworth Iron Co.	3	2
1860	Wingerworth Iron Co.	3	2

1861	Wingerworth Iron Co.	3	2
1862	Wingerworth Iron Co.	3	2
1863	Wingerworth Iron Co.	3	2
1864	Wingerworth Iron Co.	3	2
1865	Wingerworth Iron Co.	3	2
1866	Wingerworth Iron Co.	3	2
1867	Wingerworth Iron Co.	3	2
1868	Wingerworth Iron Co.	3	1
1869	Wingerworth Iron Co.	3	2
1870	Wingerworth Iron Co.	3	2
1871	Wingerworth Iron Co.	3	3
1872	Wingerworth Iron Co.	3	3
1873	Wingerworth Iron Co.	3	3
1874	Wingerworth Iron Co.	3	2
1875	Wingerworth Iron Co.	3	3
1876	Wingerworth Iron Co.	3	3
1877	Wingerworth Iron Co.	3	3
1878	Wingerworth Iron Co.	3	3
1879	Wingerworth Iron Co.	3	3
1880	Wingerworth Iron Co.	3	3
1881	Wingerworth Iron Co.	3	3
1882	Wingerworth Iron Co.	3	3
1883	Wingerworth Iron Co.	3	1
1884	Wingerworth Iron Co.	3	2
1885	Wingerworth Iron Co.	3	3
1886	Wingerworth Iron Co.	3	3
1887	Wingerworth Iron Co.	3	0
1888	Wingerworth Iron Co.	3	0
1889	Wingerworth Iron Co.	3	3
1890	Wingerworth Iron Co.	3	2
1891	Wingerworth Iron Co.	3	3
1892	Wingerworth Iron Co.	3	3
1893	Wingerworth Iron Co.	3	1
1894	Wingerworth Iron Co.	3	0
1895	Wingerworth Iron Co.	3	0
1896	Wingerworth Iron Co.	3	0
1897	Staveley Coal & Iron Co. Ltd	3	2
1898	Staveley Coal & Iron Co. Ltd	3	3
1899	Staveley Coal & Iron Co. Ltd	3	3
1900	Staveley Coal & Iron Co. Ltd	3	3
1901	Staveley Coal & Iron Co. Ltd	3	2
1902	Staveley Coal & Iron Co. Ltd	3	2
1903	Staveley Coal & Iron Co. Ltd	3	2
1904	Staveley Coal & Iron Co. Ltd	3	2
1905	Staveley Coal & Iron Co. Ltd	3	2
1906	Staveley Coal & Iron Co. Ltd	3	3
1907	Staveley Coal & Iron Co. Ltd	3	3

1847: output 10,400 tons p.a., i.e. 200 tons a week. These furnaces were on a different site from that of Butler's works, about two miles away at Birdholme, on the outskirts of Chesterfield. Truran: output 120 tons a week from each of 3 furnaces. Although *Mineral Statistics* uses the style 'Wingerworth Iron Co. Ltd' from 1872 to 1883, no such company can be found on the register and local sources do not use the suffix. 1883: 2 furnaces rebuilding. From 1897 the works appears under the name Broad Oaks and its location is given as Chesterfield.

'Wingfield': see Oakerthorpe

Yorkshire, West Riding

Aireside, Leeds

Year	Owner	Built	In Blast
1874	Aireside Haematite Iron Co.	3	2
1875	Aireside Haematite Iron Co.	3	3
1876	Aireside Haematite Iron Co.	3	2
1877	Aireside Haematite Iron Co.	3	1
1878	Aireside Haematite Iron Co.	3	1
1879	Aireside Haematite Iron Co.	3	2
1880	Aireside Haematite Iron Co.	3	3
1881	Aireside Haematite Iron Co.	3	2
1882	Aireside Haematite Iron Co.	3	2
1883	Aireside Haematite Iron Co.	3	2
1884	Aireside Haematite Iron Co.	3	1
1885	Aireside Haematite Iron Co.	3	0
1886	Aireside Haematite Iron Co.	3	0
1887	Aireside Steel & Iron Co.	3	1

Ardsley: see West Yorkshire

Atlas, Sheffield

Year	Owner	Built	In Blast
1875	John Brown & Co. Ltd	3	3
1876	John Brown & Co. Ltd	3	3
1877	John Brown & Co. Ltd	3	2
1878	John Brown & Co. Ltd	3	2
1879	John Brown & Co. Ltd	3	3
1880	John Brown & Co. Ltd	3	3
1881	John Brown & Co. Ltd	3	1
1882	John Brown & Co. Ltd	3	2
1883	John Brown & Co. Ltd	3	2
1884	John Brown & Co. Ltd	3	2
1885	John Brown & Co. Ltd	3	2
1886	John Brown & Co. Ltd	3	1
1887	John Brown & Co. Ltd	3	1
1888	John Brown & Co. Ltd	3	2
1889	John Brown & Co. Ltd	3	2
1890	John Brown & Co. Ltd	3	3
1891	John Brown & Co. Ltd	3	2
1892	John Brown & Co. Ltd	3	2
1893	John Brown & Co. Ltd	3	1
1894	John Brown & Co. Ltd	3	1
1895	John Brown & Co. Ltd	3	1
1896	John Brown & Co. Ltd	3	2
1897	John Brown & Co. Ltd	3	2
1898	John Brown & Co. Ltd	3	2
1899	John Brown & Co. Ltd	3	2
1900	John Brown & Co. Ltd	3	2
1901	John Brown & Co. Ltd	3	1
1902	John Brown & Co. Ltd	3	1
1903	John Brown & Co. Ltd	3	1
1904	John Brown & Co. Ltd	3	1
1905	John Brown & Co. Ltd	3	1
1906	John Brown & Co. Ltd	3	2
1907	John Brown & Co. Ltd	3	2
1908	John Brown & Co. Ltd	3	1
1909	John Brown & Co. Ltd	3	1
1910	John Brown & Co. Ltd	3	2
1911	John Brown & Co. Ltd	2	1

Beeston Manor, Leeds [SE 2830?]

Year	Owner	Built	In Blast
1855	Harding & Co.	1	1
1856	Harding & Co.	1	1
1857	Harding & Co.	1	1
1858	Harding & Co.	1	1
1859	Harding & Co.	1	1
1860	Harding & Co.	1	1
1861	A. Harding & Co.	2	2
1862	A. Harding & Co.	2	1
1863	A. Harding & Co.	2	2
1864	A. Harding & Co.	2	2
1865	A. Harding & Co.	2	2
1866	A. Harding & Co.	2	2
1867	A. Harding & Co.	2	1
1868	A. Harding & Co.	2	1
1869	A. Harding & Co.	2	1
1870	A. Harding & Co.	2	1
1871	A. Harding & Co.	2	1
1872	A. Harding & Co.	2	1
1873	A. Harding & Co.	2	1
1874	A. Harding & Co.	2	1
1875	A. Harding & Co.	2	1
1876	A. Harding & Co.	2	1
1877	A. Harding & Co.	2	0
1878	A. Harding & Co.	2	0
1879	A. Harding & Co.	2	0
1880	—	-	-

1880: Works dismantled.

Bierley SE 1628

Year	Owner	Built	In Blast
1810	—	1	1
1823	—	1	-
1825	Marshall, Lea & Co.	2	2
1830	—	2	-
1839	—	3	3
1841	Leah, Clayton & Co.	4	4
1843	Leah, Clayton & Co.	4	3
1847	Clayton & Co.	4	3
1849	—	-	3
1854	Hird, Dawson & Hardy	4	3
1855	Hird, Dawson & Hardy	4	3
1856	Hird, Dawson & Hardy	4	3
1857	Hird, Dawson & Hardy	4	3
1858	Hird, Dawson & Hardy	4	3
1859	Hird, Dawson & Hardy	4	3
1860	Hird, Dawson & Hardy	4	3

YORKSHIRE, WEST RIDING

Year	Owner	Built	In Blast
1861	Hird, Dawson & Hardy	4	3
1862	Hird, Dawson & Hardy	-	-
1863	Hird, Dawson & Hardy	-	-
1864	Hird, Dawson & Hardy	-	-
1865	Hird, Dawson & Hardy	-	-
1866	Hird, Dawson & Hardy	-	-
1867	Hird, Dawson & Hardy	-	-
1868	Hird, Dawson & Hardy	-	-
1869	Hird, Dawson & Hardy	-	-
1870	Hird, Dawson & Hardy	-	-
1871	Hird, Dawson & Hardy	-	-
1872	Hird, Dawson & Hardy	-	-
1873	Hird, Dawson & Hardy	-	-
1874	Hird, Dawson & Hardy	-	-
1875	Hird, Dawson & Hardy	-	-
1876	Hird, Dawson & Hardy	-	-
1877	Hird, Dawson & Hardy	-	-
1878	Hird, Dawson & Hardy	-	-
1879	Hird, Dawson & Hardy	-	-
1880	Hird, Dawson & Hardy	-	-
1881	Hird, Dawson & Hardy	-	-

The entry in the 1810 list (unusually) lacks the name of the owner and looks as if it may have been a late addition. The 1823–30 list has an output of 2,450 tons in 1823; notes the building of a second furnace in 1824; and has an output of 4,590 tons in 1830. 1825: output 90 tons a week, 4,160 tons p.a., 'melting and forge'. 1841: output 169 tons a week. 1843: output 143 tons a week. 1847: output 8,320 tons p.a., i.e. 160 tons a week. Truran: output 80 tons a week from each of 4 furnaces. From 1862 furnace-numbers for Bierley and Low Moor are combined under the latter heading (qv).

Birkenshaw [SE 2028]

Year	Owner	Built	In Blast
1794	Mr Emmett	1	-
1796	—	1	1
1805	Emmett	1	1
1810	Emmett	1	1

In 1794 the ground landlord was Sir T. Gascoigne; the single coke-fired furnace was blown by engine and said to have been built in 1780. A note across the columns ruled for forge plant reads 'John Emanuel's Will'; the significance of this is not clear. 1796: output 780 tons p.a. (i.e. 15 tons a week), Excise and actual, Exact Return 846 tons. 1805: output 612 tons.

Bowling SE 1832

Year	Owner	Built	In Blast
1794	Sturges & Poley	2	-
1796	—	2	1
1805	Sturges & Co.	3	2
1810	Sturges	3	3
1823	—	3	-
1825	John Sturges & Co.	3	2
1830	—	3	-
1839	—	3	3
1841	Sturges & Co.	4	4
1843	Sturges & Co.	4	4
1847	Sturges & Co.	5	4
1849	—	-	3
1854	Sturges & Co.	5	4
1855	Sturges & Co.	5	4
1856	Sturges & Co.	5	4
1857	Sturges & Co.	5	4
1858	Sturges & Co.	5	4
1859	Sturges & Co.	6	5
1860	Sturges & Co.	6	5
1861	Sturges & Co.	6	5
1862	Sturges & Co.	6	5
1863	Sturges & Co.	6	5
1864	Sturges & Co.	6	5
1865	Sturges & Co.	6	5
1866	Bowling Iron Co.	6	5
1867	Bowling Iron Co.	6	4
1868	Bowling Iron Co.	6	3
1869	Bowling Iron Co.	6	4
1870	Bowling Iron Co. Ltd	6	4
1871	Bowling Iron Co. Ltd	6	4
1872	Bowling Iron Co. Ltd	6	5
1873	Bowling Iron Co. Ltd	6	4
1874	Bowling Iron Co. Ltd	6	4
1875	Bowling Iron Co. Ltd	6	4
1876	Bowling Iron Co. Ltd	6	3
1877	Bowling Iron Co. Ltd	5	3
1878	Bowling Iron Co. Ltd	5	2
1879	Bowling Iron Co. Ltd	6	2
1880	Bowling Iron Co. Ltd	6	2
1881	Bowling Iron Co. Ltd	6	2
1882	Bowling Iron Co. Ltd	6	2
1883	Bowling Iron Co. Ltd	6	2
1884	Bowling Iron Co. Ltd	6	2
1885	Bowling Iron Co. Ltd	6	1
1886	Bowling Iron Co. Ltd	6	2
1887	Bowling Iron Co. Ltd	6	2
1888	Bowling Iron Co. Ltd	3	1
1889	Bowling Iron Co. Ltd	6	1
1890	Bowling Iron Co. Ltd	6	1
1891	Bowling Iron Co. Ltd	6	1
1892	Bowling Iron Co. Ltd	6	2
1893	Bowling Iron Co. Ltd	6	1
1894	Bowling Iron Co. Ltd	6	1
1895	Bowling Iron Co. Ltd	6	0
1896	Bowling Iron Co. Ltd	6	0
1897	Bowling Iron Co. Ltd	6	0

Sturges & Poley were also named as ground landlords in 1794; the two coke-fired furnaces were blown by engine and said to have been built in 1791; other plant consisted of two fineries and a rolling mill. 1796: output 2,000 tons p.a. Excise, actual and Exact Return. 1805: output 2,473 tons p.a. 1823–30: 5,366 tons p.a. for 1823 and 5,117 tons for 1830. 1825: output 90 tons a week, 4,160 p.a., 'melting and forge'. 1841: 159 tons a week. 1843: 180 tons a week. 1847: 10,400 tons, i.e. 50 tons a week from each of the 4 furnaces in blast. Truran: 70 tons a week from each of 5 furnaces. The owner's name in *Mineral Statistics* for 1854–65 is 'Sturge & Co.', which has been corrected on the basis of earlier lists. In 1870 and 1871 the return notes that the works had 100 furnaces for making crucible (or cast) steel. In 1878 and 1880 one blast furnace was said to be building on each occasion. In 1894 the owner is named as 'Bowling Iron & Steel Co. Ltd', presumably in error, since no company of this name can be found on the register.

Bretton SE 2906

Year	Owner	Built	In Blast
1794	Cook & Cockshutt	1	-
1796	—	1	1
1805	Cooke & Co.	1	1
1810	—	1	1

In 1794 the ground landlord was Col. Britton; the furnace was charcoal-fired. 1796: output 250 tons p.a. Excise and Exact Return, 220 tons actual. In 1805 the furnace was said to be in blast but no output was listed. These entries appear to refer to the site now called Low Mill, where there are substantial remains of a small blast furnace with no known history.

Calder [SE 2219]

Year	Owner	Built	In Blast
1805	Emmett	1	1
1810	Crawshaw	1	1

Output 1,040 tons p.a. (i.e. 20 tons a week) in 1805.

Chapeltown [SK 3596]

Year	Owner	Built	In Blast
1794	Mr Swallow	2	-
1796	—	1	1
1805	Swallow	5	3
1810	—	1	1
1823	—	1	-
1825	J. Darwin & Co.	2	2
1830	—	1	-
1839	—	2	1
1841	Nesbitt & Marsden	2	1
1843	Nesbitt, Marsden & Co.	2	0
1847	Scholefield & Co.	2	2
1849	—	-	2
1854	Newton, Chambers & Co.	2	0
1855	Newton, Chambers & Co.	2	0
1856	Newton, Chambers & Co.	2	0
1857	Newton, Chambers & Co.	2	0
1858	Newton, Chambers & Co.	2	0
1859	Newton, Chambers & Co.	2	0
1860	Newton, Chambers & Co.	2	0
1861	Newton, Chambers & Co.	2	0
1862	Newton, Chambers & Co.	-	-
1863	Newton, Chambers & Co.	-	-
1864	Newton, Chambers & Co.	-	-
1865	Newton, Chambers & Co.	-	-
1866	Newton, Chambers & Co.	-	-
1868	Newton, Chambers & Co.	-	-
1869	Newton, Chambers & Co.	-	-
1870	Newton, Chambers & Co.	-	-
1871	Newton, Chambers & Co.	-	-

The ground landlord in 1794 was the Duke of Norfolk; the two coke-fired furnaces were blown by engine and the other plant consisted of a finery and a chafery. 1796: output 1,456 tons p.a. (i.e. 28 tons a week), Excise, actual and Exact Return. The 1805 list couples Chapeltown with Swallowhill (qv): the two sites together had 5 furnaces (3 in blast) and a total output of 3,737 tons. No owner's name appears in 1810. 1823–30: output 1,400 tons in 1823 and 1,631 tons in 1830. 1825: output 60 tons a week, 2,600 tons p.a., 'melting iron'. 1841: output 68 tons a week. 1843: output nil. 1847: output 5,200 tons p.a., i.e. 50 tons a week from each of the two furnaces. Truran: output 65 tons a week from each of 2 furnaces. In *Mineral Statistics* there are separate entries for Chapeltown and Thorncliffe (qv) for 1854–61, but Chapeltown appears to have been out of use. For 1862–71 the figures for Thorncliffe are said to include Chapeltown, except in 1867, when there is no reference to Chapeltown at all. The Thorncliffe entries from 1872 onwards similarly omit any reference to Chapeltown.

Charlton [SK 3790]

Year	Owner	Built	In Blast
1875	Charlton Iron Works Co. Ltd	2	2
1876	Charlton Iron Works Co. Ltd	2	1
1877	Charlton Iron Works Co. Ltd	2	1
1878	Charlton Iron Works Co. Ltd	2	0
1879	Charlton Iron Works Co. Ltd	2	0
1880	Charlton Iron Works Co. Ltd	2	0
1881	Charlton Iron Works Co. Ltd	2	0
1882	Company in liquidation	2	0
1883	Company in liquidation	2	0
1884	Company in liquidation	2	0
1885	Company in liquidation	2	0

The company, named merely as the 'Charlton Iron Co.', was also said to be in liquidation in *Mineral Statistics* in 1878. The Charlton Iron Works Co. Ltd was registered in 1872 to acquire the Charlton Ironworks at Grimesthorpe, near Sheffield (BT 31/1756/6547). A winding-up order was made against the company in December 1875 and a final order for dissolution in December 1890.

Elsecar

Year	Owner	Built	In Blast
1796	—	1	1
1805	Darwin & Co.	2	2
1810	Darwin & Co.	3	3
1823	—	3	-
1825	J. Darwin & Co.	3	1
1830	—	3	-
1839	—	3	1
1841	Earl FitzWilliam	3	1
1843	Earl FitzWilliam	3	1
1847	Lord FitzWilliam	2	1
1849	—	-	3
1854	Dawes & Co.	3	1
1855	Dawes & Co.	3	1
1856	Dawes & Co.	3	1
1857	Dawes & Co.	3	2
1858	Dawes & Co.	2	2
1859	W.H. John Dawes	3	2
1860	W.H. John Dawes	3	2
1861	W.H. & George Dawes	2	2
1862	W.H. & George Dawes	6	4
1863	Earl FitzWilliam	6	4

Year	Owner	Built	In Blast
1864	Dawes & Co.	6	4
1865	W.H. & Geo. Dawes	6	4
1866	W.H. & Geo. Dawes	6	4
1867	W.H. & Geo. Dawes	6	4
1868	W.H. & Geo. Dawes	6	4
1869	W.H. & Geo. Dawes	6	4
1870	W.H. & Geo. Dawes	6	4
1871	W.H. & Geo. Dawes	6	4
1872	W.H. & Geo. Dawes	6	4
1873	W.H. & Geo. Dawes	6	4
1874	W.H. & Geo. Dawes	6	4
1875	George Dawes	6	5
1876	George Dawes	6	4
1877	George Dawes	4	3
1878	George Dawes	4	3
1879	George Dawes	4	4
1880	George Dawes	6	6
1881	George Dawes	6	2
1882	George Dawes	6	2
1883	George Dawes	4	0
1884	George Dawes	4	0

1796: output 800 tons p.a. (i.e. 16 tons a week), Excise and actual, Exact Return 950 tons. 1805: output 2,495 tons p.a. 1823–30: output 1,400 tons p.a. in 1823, 1,460 in 1830. 1825: 30 tons a week, 1,560 p.a., 'melting iron'. 1841: output 27 tons a week. 1843: output 40 tons a week. 1847: output 2,340 tons, i.e. 45 tons a week. Truran: output 60 tons a week from each of 3 furnaces. In 1862–76 and 1880–82 furnace-numbers include Milton (qv). The figures for Elsecar in *Mineral Statistics* for 1857 (5 furnaces, 4 in blast) also appear to include both works, although separate figures are given for Milton for that year and those for Elsecar have been amended accordingly.

Emroyd: see Mirfield

Farnley [SE 2532]

Year	Owner	Built	In Blast
1847	Armitage	2	1
1849	—	-	1
1854	Armitage & Co.	-	-
1855	Armitage & Co.	2	2
1856	Armitage & Co.	4	2
1857	Armitage & Co.	4	2
1858	Armitage & Co.	4	3
1859	Armitage & Co.	4	3
1860	Armitage & Co.	4	3
1861	Armitage & Co.	4	4
1862	Armitage & Co.	4	3
1863	Farnley Iron Co.	4	2
1864	Farnley Iron Co.	4	2
1865	Farnley Iron Co.	4	3
1866	Farnley Iron Co.	4	3
1867	Farnley Iron Co.	4	2
1868	Farnley Iron Co.	4	2
1869	Farnley Iron Co.	4	1
1870	Farnley Iron Co.	4	2
1871	Farnley Iron Co. Ltd	4	2
1872	Farnley Iron Co. Ltd	4	2
1873	Farnley Iron Co. Ltd	4	2
1874	Farnley Iron Co. Ltd	4	2
1875	Farnley Iron Co. Ltd	3	2
1876	Farnley Iron Co. Ltd	2	2
1877	Farnley Iron Co. Ltd	2	2
1878	Farnley Iron Co. Ltd	2	2
1879	Farnley Iron Co. Ltd	2	1
1880	Farnley Iron Co. Ltd	2	2
1881	Farnley Iron Co. Ltd	2	2
1882	Farnley Iron Co. Ltd	2	2
1883	Farnley Iron Co. Ltd	2	2
1884	Farnley Iron Co. Ltd	2	1
1885	Farnley Iron Co. Ltd	2	1
1886	Farnley Iron Co. Ltd	2	1
1887	Farnley Iron Co. Ltd	2	1
1888	Farnley Iron Co. Ltd	2	1
1889	Farnley Iron Co. Ltd	2	1
1890	Farnley Iron Co. Ltd	2	1
1891	Farnley Iron Co. Ltd	2	1
1892	Farnley Iron Co. Ltd	2	2
1893	Farnley Iron Co. Ltd	2	1
1894	Farnley Iron Co. Ltd	2	1
1895	Farnley Iron Co. Ltd	2	1
1896	Farnley Iron Co. Ltd	2	1
1897	Farnley Iron Co. Ltd	2	1
1898	Farnley Iron Co. Ltd	2	1
1899	Farnley Iron Co. Ltd	2	1
1900	Farnley Iron Co. Ltd	2	1
1901	Farnley Iron Co. Ltd	2	1
1902	Farnley Iron Co. Ltd	2	1
1903	Farnley Iron Co. Ltd	2	1
1904	Farnley Iron Co. Ltd	2	1
1905	Farnley Iron Co. Ltd	2	1
1906	Farnley Iron Co. Ltd	2	1
1907	Farnley Iron Co. Ltd	2	1
1908	Farnley Iron Co. Ltd	2	1
1909	Farnley Iron Co. Ltd	2	1
1910	Farnley Iron Co. Ltd	2	1
1911	Farnley Iron Co. Ltd	2	0
1912	Farnley Iron Co. Ltd	2	0
1913	Farnley Iron Co. Ltd	2	0
1921	William Woodhead & Son Ltd	1	-
1922	William Woodhead & Son Ltd	1	-
1923	William Woodhead & Son Ltd	1	-
1924	William Woodhead & Son Ltd	1	-
1925	William Woodhead & Son Ltd	1	-

1847: output 2,600 tons p.a., i.e. 50 tons a week. 1854: furnace-numbers printed. Truran: output 60 tons a week from each of 2 furnaces. William Woodhead & Son Ltd appear for a few years in the Yorkshire (WR) and south Lancashire section of the post-1921 returns; the site cannot be matched for certain with any pre-1913 works but has been placed here since the company's registered office was Lawns House, Farnley (cf. BT 31/17872/90290).

Fieldhead [SE 3050]

Year	Owner	Built	In Blast
1805	Parker	1	1
1810	Parker	1	1
1823	—	-	-
1825	Parker	1	0
1830	—	-	-

No output is shown in the 1805 list, although the furnace was said to be in blast; the name appears in the 1823–30 list but with the comment: 'have not been worked for several years'. No output is given there or in the 1825 list.

'Glasshouse'

Hunt in 1849 and *Mineral Statistics* in 1854 list a works under this name, which Hunt's map places to the SE of Bradford. Two furnaces are said to be in blast in 1849; no furnace-numbers are given in 1854. The site has not been identified or linked to any other West Riding works.

Hepworth [SE 1606]

Year	Owner	Built	In Blast
1865	Hepworth Iron Co.	1	1
1866	Hepworth Iron Co.	2	1
1867	Hepworth Iron Co.	2	1
1868	Hepworth Iron Co.	2	0
1869	Hepworth Iron Co.	2	0
1870	Hepworth Iron Co.	2	0
1871	Hepworth Iron Co.	2	0
1884	Hepworth Iron Co.	2	0
1885	Hepworth Iron Co.	2	0

1865: Cold blast.

Holmes [SE 4192]

Year	Owner	Built	In Blast
1794	Messrs Walker	3	–
1796	—	3	3
1805	Walker	2	2
1810	Walkers & Co.	3	3
1823	—	3	–
1825	Samuel Walker & Co.	3	2
1830	—	3	–
1839	—	2	1
1841	Clarke	2	0
1843	Clarke	2	1
1849	—	–	2
1854	Samuel Beale & Co.	2	2
1855	Samuel Beale & Co.	2	2
1856	Samuel Beale & Co.	2	2
1857	Samuel Beale & Co.	2	2
1858	Samuel Beale & Co.	2	2
1859	Samuel Beale & Co.	2	2
1860	Samuel Beale & Co.	2	2
1861	Samuel Beale & Co.	2	2
1862	Samuel Beale & Co.	2	2
1863	Samuel Beale & Co.	4	3
1864	Park Gate Iron Co. Ltd	4	3
1865	Park Gate Iron Co. Ltd	4	3
1866	Park Gate Iron Co. Ltd	3	3
1867	Park Gate Iron Co. Ltd	3	3
1868	Park Gate Iron Co. Ltd	3	2
1869	Park Gate Iron Co. Ltd	3	3
1870	Park Gate Iron Co. Ltd	3	3
1871	Park Gate Iron Co. Ltd	3	2
1872	Park Gate Iron Co. Ltd	5	5
1873	Park Gate Iron Co. Ltd	5	5
1874	Park Gate Iron Co. Ltd	6	4
1875	Park Gate Iron Co. Ltd	6	3
1876	Park Gate Iron Co. Ltd	6	2
1877	Park Gate Iron Co. Ltd	3	0
1878	Park Gate Iron Co. Ltd	3	0

The ground landlord in 1794 was Lord Effingham; there were two coke-fired furnaces and one charcoal-fired; the date of building (of which is not made clear) is given as 1765. They were blown by engine. The forge consisted of three fineries, a chafery and a balling furnace; there was also a rolling and slitting mill. The works is named as Masbrough, the village on the outskirts of Rotherham where the Holmes is situated; in later lists the name Holmes is used (although in 1810 the name apears as 'Masper or Holmes'). 1796: output 6,000 tons from 3 coke furnaces (i.e. 40 tons a week from each furnace), Excise and actual, Exact Return 2,000 tons total. Only 1 furnace is listed in the original return, against which has been written 'should be 3', which is undoubtedly the case. In 1805 a single output (3,000 tons p.a.) was returned for Holmes and the Walkers' other works at Milton (qv), although separate furnace-numbers were given for the two sites. 1823–30: output 2,000 tons p.a. in 1823, 1,000 tons p.a. in 1830. 1825: 36 tons a week, 1,560 p.a. 1841: output nil. 1843: output 40 tons a week. Truran: output 60 tons a week from each of 2 furnaces. For 1863–76 the furnace-numbers above include Holmes and Park Gate; the two works have separate entries in 1877–78 and thereafter a single entry appears under Park Gate (qv).

Leather & Co.: see Thorpe Hall

Leeds Steel Works, Hunslet [SE 3031]

Year	Owner	Built	In Blast
1888	Leeds Steel Works Ltd	3	2
1889	Leeds Steel Works Ltd	3	2
1890	Leeds Steel Works Ltd	3	2
1891	Leeds Steel Works Ltd	3	2
1892	Leeds Steel Works Ltd	3	2
1893	Leeds Steel Works Ltd	3	2
1894	Leeds Steel Works Ltd	3	2
1895	Leeds Steel Works Ltd	3	3
1896	Leeds Steel Works Ltd	3	3
1897	Leeds Steel Works Ltd	3	3
1898	Leeds Steel Works Ltd	3	3
1899	Leeds Steel Works Ltd	3	3
1900	Walter Scott Ltd	3	3
1901	Walter Scott Ltd	3	2
1902	Walter Scott Ltd	3	2
1903	Walter Scott Ltd	3	3
1904	Walter Scott Ltd	3	3
1905	Walter Scott Ltd	3	3
1906	Walter Scott Ltd	3	3
1907	Walter Scott Ltd	3	3
1908	Walter Scott Ltd	4	3
1909	Walter Scott Ltd	4	3
1910	Walter Scott Ltd	4	3
1911	Walter Scott Ltd	4	3
1912	Walter Scott Ltd	4	3
1913	Walter Scott Ltd	4	3

Year	Owner	Built	In Blast
1921	Walter Scott Ltd	4	-
1922	Walter Scott Ltd	4	-
1923	Walter Scott Ltd	4	-
1924	Walter Scott Ltd	4	-
1925	Walter Scott Ltd	4	-
1926	Walter Scott Ltd	4	-
1927	Walter Scott Ltd	3	-
1928	Walter Scott Ltd	4	-
1929	Walter Scott Ltd	4	-
1930	Walter Scott Ltd	4	-
1931	Walter Scott Ltd	4	-
1932	Walter Scott Ltd	4	-
1933	Walter Scott Ltd	4	-
1934	Walter Scott Ltd	4	-

Furnaces dismantled 1935.

Low Mill: see Bretton

Low Moor SE 1528

Year	Owner	Built	In Blast
1794	Messrs Jarratt	2	-
1796	—	2	2
1805	Jarratt & Dawson	4	4
1810	Jarratt & Co.	4	4
1823	—	4	-
1825	Hird, Dawson & Co.	7	5
1830	—	4	-
1839	—	6	6
1841	Hird, Dawson & Hardy	6	6
1843	Hird, Dawson & Co.	6	4
1847	Hird, Dawson & Co.	6	5
1849	—	-	4
1854	Hird, Dawson & Hardy	5	5
1855	Hird, Dawson & Hardy	5	4
1856	Hird, Dawson & Hardy	5	4
1857	Hird, Dawson & Hardy	5	3
1858	Hird, Dawson & Hardy	5	3
1859	Hird, Dawson & Hardy	5	3
1860	Hird, Dawson & Hardy	5	3
1861	Hird, Dawson & Hardy	5	3
1862	Hird, Dawson & Hardy	9	7
1863	Hird, Dawson & Hardy	9	6
1864	Hird, Dawson & Hardy	9	6
1865	Hird, Dawson & Hardy	9	6
1866	Hird, Dawson & Hardy	8	6
1867	Hird, Dawson & Hardy	8	6
1868	Hird, Dawson & Hardy	8	5
1869	Hird, Dawson & Hardy	8	5
1870	Hird, Dawson & Hardy	8	5
1871	Hird, Dawson & Hardy	8	6
1872	Hird, Dawson & Hardy	8	6
1873	Hird, Dawson & Hardy	8	6
1874	Hird, Dawson & Hardy	8	6
1875	Hird, Dawson & Hardy	8	6
1876	Hird, Dawson & Hardy	8	7
1877	Hird, Dawson & Hardy	8	7
1878	Hird, Dawson & Hardy	8	6
1879	Hird, Dawson & Hardy	8	6
1880	Hird, Dawson & Hardy	8	5
1881	Hird, Dawson & Hardy	7	5
1882	Hird, Dawson & Hardy	8	5
1883	Hird, Dawson & Hardy	7	5
1884	Hird, Dawson & Hardy	8	4
1885	Hird, Dawson & Hardy	8	4
1886	Hird, Dawson & Hardy	8	4
1887	Hird, Dawson & Hardy	8	3
1888	Low Moor Co. Ltd	8	3
1889	Low Moor Co. Ltd	8	3
1890	Low Moor Co. Ltd	8	2
1891	Low Moor Co. Ltd	8	3
1892	Low Moor Co. Ltd	7	3
1893	Low Moor Co. Ltd	9	2
1894	Low Moor Co. Ltd	9	1
1895	Low Moor Co. Ltd	9	1
1896	Low Moor Co. Ltd	9	1
1897	Low Moor Co. Ltd	4	1
1898	Low Moor Co. Ltd	3	1
1899	Low Moor Co. Ltd	3	1
1900	Low Moor Co. Ltd	4	1
1901	Low Moor Co. Ltd	2	1
1902	Low Moor Co. Ltd	2	1
1903	Low Moor Co. Ltd	2	1
1904	Low Moor Co. Ltd	1	1
1905	Low Moor Co. Ltd	2	1
1906	Low Moor Co. Ltd	2	1
1907	Low Moor Co. Ltd	2	1
1908	Low Moor Co. Ltd	2	1
1909	Low Moor Co. Ltd	2	1
1910	Low Moor Co. Ltd	2	1
1911	Low Moor Co. Ltd	2	1
1912	Low Moor Co. Ltd	2	1
1913	Low Moor Co. Ltd	2	1
1921	Robert Heath & Low Moor Ltd	2	-
1922	Robert Heath & Low Moor Ltd	2	-
1923	Robert Heath & Low Moor Ltd	2	-
1924	Robert Heath & Low Moor Ltd	2	-
1925	Robert Heath & Low Moor Ltd	2	-
1926	Robert Heath & Low Moor Ltd	2	-
1927	Robert Heath & Low Moor Ltd	2	-
1928	Robert Heath & Low Moor Ltd	2	-
1929	Low Moor Iron Co. Ltd	2	-
1930	Low Moor Iron Co. Ltd	2	-
1931	Low Moor Iron Co. Ltd	2	-
1932	Low Moor Iron Co. Ltd	2	-
1933	Low Moor Iron Co. Ltd	2	-
1934	Low Moor Iron Co. Ltd	2	-
1935	Low Moor Iron Co. Ltd	2	-
1936	Low Moor Iron Co. Ltd	2	-
1937	Low Moor Iron Co. Ltd	2	-

The ground landlord in 1794 was — Leeds Esq.; the two coke-fired furnaces were blown by engine and said to have been built in 1791. The occupier's name is given as Messrs Jarard in obvious error. 1796: works called Wibsey Moor; output 2,000 tons (i.e. 40 tons a week), Excise and actual, Exact Return 2,500 tons. 1805: output 5,143 tons. 1823: 6,200 tons. 1830: nil. The 1825 list couples Low Moor with Shelf (qv); the combined output of the two works (7 furnaces, 5 in blast) was 210 tons a week, 10,400 tons p.a., 'melting and forge'. The furnace-numbers are also combined in 1839, 1841, 1843 and 1847. 1841: output 307 tons a week from both sites. 1843: output 180 tons a week from both sites. 1847: output (at Low Moor alone) 14,560 tons, i.e. 280 tons a week. Truran: output 70 tons a week from each of 6 furnaces. From 1862 the furnace-numbers above include Bierley (qv). Low Moor furnaces were dismantled during 1938.

Masbrough: see Holmes

Milton [SE 3700]

Year	Owner	Built	In Blast
1805	Walker	1	1
1810	Walkers & Co.	2	2
1823	—	2	-
1825	Henry Hartopp	2	2
1830	—	2	-
1839	—	2	2
1841	W. Graham & Co.	2	2
1843	Graham & Co.	2	2
1847	Graham	2	2
1849	—	-	2
1854	Dawes & Co.	2	2
1855	Dawes & Co.	2	2
1856	Dawes & Co.	2	2
1857	Dawes & Co.	2	2
1858	Dawes & Co.	2	2
1859	W.H. John Dawes	2	2
1860	W.H. John Dawes	2	2
1861	W.H. & George Dawes	2	2
1862	W.H. & George Dawes	-	-
1863	Earl FitzWilliam	-	-
1864	Dawes & Co.	-	-
1865	W.H. & Geo. Dawes	-	-
1866	W.H. & Geo. Dawes	-	-
1867	W.H. & Geo. Dawes	-	-
1868	W.H. & Geo. Dawes	-	-
1869	W.H. & Geo. Dawes	-	-
1870	W.H. & Geo. Dawes	-	-
1871	W.H. & Geo. Dawes	-	-
1872	W.H. & Geo. Dawes	-	-
1873	W.H. & Geo. Dawes	-	-
1874	W.H. & Geo. Dawes	-	-
1875	George Dawes	-	-
1876	George Dawes	-	-
1877	George Dawes	2	2
1878	George Dawes	2	2
1879	George Dawes	2	2
1880	George Dawes	-	-
1881	George Dawes	-	-
1882	George Dawes	-	-
1883	George Dawes	2	2
1884	George Dawes	2	-

The 1805 list couples Milton with Holmes (qv), with a total output of 3,000 tons p.a. for the three furnaces at the two works. 1823–30: output 2,187 tons p.a. for 1823, 1,715 tons for 1830. 1825: output 60 tons a week, 2,600 tons p.a. 1841: output 110 tons a week. 1843: 120 tons a week. 1847: output 6,240 tons p.a., i.e. 60 tons a week from each of two furnaces. Truran: output 80 tons a week from each of 2 furnaces. For 1862–76 and 1880–82 furnace-numbers for Milton include Elsecar (qv).

Mirfield [SE 2618?]

Year	Owner	Built	In Blast
1810	Day & Co.	1	1
1823	—	-	-
1825	Miln	1	0
1830	—	-	-

No output is shown for 1825, when the owner's name is given as Milns in the Staffs RO version of the list; the 1823–30 list comments: 'Have not been worked for several years'. What appears to be the same works is listed as 'Emroyd' in 1810.

New Park: see Park Gate

Park, Sheffield [SK 3489?]

Year	Owner	Built	In Blast
1794	Booth & Co.	2	-
1796	—	1	1
1805	Booth & Co.	1	1
1810	Booth & Co.	2	2
1823	—	2	-
1825	Booth & Co.	2	2
1830	—	2	-
1839	—	2	2
1841	Booth & Co.	2	2
1843	Booth & Co.	2	0

The ground landlord in 1794 was the Duke of Norfolk; the two coke-fired furnaces were blown by water and said to have been built in 1786. 1796: output 1,092 tons p.a. (i.e. 21 tons a week), Excise and actual, Exact Return 853 tons. 1805: output 1,905 tons p.a. 1823–30: 2,018 tons p.a. in 1823, 2,081 tons in 1830 (*sic*; a curious coincidence if not a misprint). 1825: 60 tons a week, 2,600 tons p.a., 'melting iron'. 1841: 50 tons a week. 1843: output nil. The works was also known as 'Sheffield Park' and lay about two miles from the town.

Park Gate [SK 4395]

Year	Owner	Built	In Blast
1839	—	1	1
1841	W. Scholefield	1	1
1843	Scholefield & Co.	1	1
1847	Scholefield & Co.	1	1
1849	—	-	1
1854	Samuel Beale & Co.	1	1
1855	Samuel Beale & Co.	1	1
1856	Samuel Beale & Co.	1	1
1857	Samuel Beale & Co.	1	1
1858	Samuel Beale & Co.	1	1
1859	Samuel Beale & Co.	1	1
1860	Samuel Beale & Co.	1	1
1861	Samuel Beale & Co.	2	2
1862	Samuel Beale & Co.	2	2
1863	Samuel Beale & Co.	-	-
1864	Park Gate Iron Co. Ltd	-	-
1865	Park Gate Iron Co. Ltd	-	-
1866	Park Gate Iron Co. Ltd	-	-
1867	Park Gate Iron Co. Ltd	-	-

Year	Owner	Built	In Blast
1868	Park Gate Iron Co. Ltd	-	-
1869	Park Gate Iron Co. Ltd	-	-
1870	Park Gate Iron Co. Ltd	-	-
1871	Park Gate Iron Co. Ltd	-	-
1872	Park Gate Iron Co. Ltd	-	-
1873	Park Gate Iron Co. Ltd	-	-
1874	Park Gate Iron Co. Ltd	-	-
1875	Park Gate Iron Co. Ltd	-	-
1876	Park Gate Iron Co. Ltd	-	-
1877	Park Gate Iron Co. Ltd	3	2
1878	Park Gate Iron Co. Ltd	3	3
1879	Park Gate Iron Co. Ltd	6	6
1880	Park Gate Iron Co. Ltd	6	6
1881	Park Gate Iron Co. Ltd	6	5
1882	Park Gate Iron Co. Ltd	6	6
1883	Park Gate Iron Co. Ltd	6	5
1884	Park Gate Iron Co. Ltd	5	5
1885	Park Gate Iron Co. Ltd	5	3
1886	Park Gate Iron Co. Ltd	5	2
1887	Park Gate Iron Co. Ltd	5	3
1888	Park Gate Iron & Steel Co. Ltd	5	4
1889	Park Gate Iron & Steel Co. Ltd	5	5
1890	Park Gate Iron & Steel Co. Ltd	5	4
1891	Park Gate Iron & Steel Co. Ltd	5	3
1892	Park Gate Iron & Steel Co. Ltd	5	5
1893	Park Gate Iron & Steel Co. Ltd	5	2
1894	Park Gate Iron & Steel Co. Ltd	5	3
1895	Park Gate Iron & Steel Co. Ltd	5	1
1896	Park Gate Iron & Steel Co. Ltd	5	5
1897	Park Gate Iron & Steel Co. Ltd	5	5
1898	Park Gate Iron & Steel Co. Ltd	5	5
1899	Park Gate Iron & Steel Co. Ltd	5	5
1900	Park Gate Iron & Steel Co. Ltd	5	5
1901	Park Gate Iron & Steel Co. Ltd	5	5
1902	Park Gate Iron & Steel Co. Ltd	5	5
1903	Park Gate Iron & Steel Co. Ltd	5	4
1904	Park Gate Iron & Steel Co. Ltd	4	3
1905	Park Gate Iron & Steel Co. Ltd	6	4
1906	Park Gate Iron & Steel Co. Ltd	6	4
1907	Park Gate Iron & Steel Co. Ltd	4	4
1908	Park Gate Iron & Steel Co. Ltd	5	3
1909	Park Gate Iron & Steel Co. Ltd	5	2
1910	Park Gate Iron & Steel Co. Ltd	5	2
1911	Park Gate Iron & Steel Co. Ltd	5	2
1912	Park Gate Iron & Steel Co. Ltd	5	3
1913	Park Gate Iron & Steel Co. Ltd	5	3
1921	Park Gate Iron & Steel Co. Ltd	3	-
1922	Park Gate Iron & Steel Co. Ltd	3	-
1923	Park Gate Iron & Steel Co. Ltd	3	-
1924	Park Gate Iron & Steel Co. Ltd	3	-
1925	Park Gate Iron & Steel Co. Ltd	3	-
1926	Park Gate Iron & Steel Co. Ltd	3	-
1927	Park Gate Iron & Steel Co. Ltd	3	-
1928	Park Gate Iron & Steel Co. Ltd	3	-
1929	Park Gate Iron & Steel Co. Ltd	3	-
1930	Park Gate Iron & Steel Co. Ltd	3	-
1931	Park Gate Iron & Steel Co. Ltd	3	-
1932	Park Gate Iron & Steel Co. Ltd	3	-
1933	Park Gate Iron & Steel Co. Ltd	3	-
1934	Park Gate Iron & Steel Co. Ltd	3	-
1935	Park Gate Iron & Steel Co. Ltd	3	-
1936	Park Gate Iron & Steel Co. Ltd	3	-
1937	Park Gate Iron & Steel Co. Ltd	3	-
1938	Park Gate Iron & Steel Co. Ltd	3	-
1939	Park Gate Iron & Steel Co. Ltd	3	-
1940	Park Gate Iron & Steel Co. Ltd	3	-
1941	Park Gate Iron & Steel Co. Ltd	3	-
1942	Park Gate Iron & Steel Co. Ltd	3	-
1943	Park Gate Iron & Steel Co. Ltd	2	-
1944	Park Gate Iron & Steel Co. Ltd	2	-
1945	Park Gate Iron & Steel Co. Ltd	2	-
1946	Park Gate Iron & Steel Co. Ltd	2	-
1947	Park Gate Iron & Steel Co. Ltd	2	-
1948	Park Gate Iron & Steel Co. Ltd	2	-
1949	Park Gate Iron & Steel Co. Ltd	2	-
1950	Park Gate Iron & Steel Co. Ltd	2	-
1951	Park Gate Iron & Steel Co. Ltd	2	-
1952	Park Gate Iron & Steel Co. Ltd	2	-
1953	Park Gate Iron & Steel Co. Ltd	2	-
1954	Park Gate Iron & Steel Co. Ltd	2	-
1955	Park Gate Iron & Steel Co. Ltd	2	-
1956	Park Gate Iron & Steel Co. Ltd	2	-
1957	Park Gate Iron & Steel Co. Ltd	2	-
1958	Park Gate Iron & Steel Co. Ltd	2	-
1959	Park Gate Iron & Steel Co. Ltd	2	-
1960	Park Gate Iron & Steel Co. Ltd	2	-
1961	Park Gate Iron & Steel Co. Ltd	2	-
1962	Park Gate Iron & Steel Co. Ltd	2	-
1963	Park Gate Iron & Steel Co. Ltd	2	-
1964	Park Gate Iron & Steel Co. Ltd	2	-
1965	Park Gate Iron & Steel Co. Ltd	2	-
1966	Park Gate Iron & Steel Co. Ltd	2	-
1967	Park Gate Iron & Steel Co. Ltd	2	-
1968	Park Gate Iron & Steel Co. Ltd	2	-
1969	Park Gate Iron & Steel Co. Ltd	2	-
1970	British Steel Corporation	2	-
1971	British Steel Corporation	2	-
1972	British Steel Corporation	2	-
1973	British Steel Corporation	2	-
1974	British Steel Corporation	2	-

1839: 'New Park' has been assumed to be identical with Park Gate in later lists. 1841: output 41 tons a week. 1843: output 50 tons a week. 1847: output 5,200 tons p.a., i.e. 100 tons a week. Truran: ouput 140 tons a week from a single furnace. In 1863–76 furnace-numbers for Park Gate are combined with those for Holmes (qv); the two works have separate entries in 1877–78 and thereafter a single entry was printed under Park Gate. From 1953 the location of the works was given as Rotherham.

Rotherham: see Holmes; Park Gate

Royds [SE 2721?]

Year	Owner	Built	In Blast
1810	Shaw & Co.	2	2

Seacroft [SE 3335]

Year	Owner	Built	In Blast
1794	—	-	-

Seacroft appears in the 1794 list without any owner or occupier's name, and the letter 'D' ('Down'?) in the column ruled for coke-fired furnaces, with the additional information that the furnace was blown by water and built in 1780.

Sheffield Park: see Park

Shelf [SE 1228]

Year	Owner	Built	In Blast
1794	Crawshay & Ellwell	1	-
1796	—	1	1
1805	Haydon & Co.	3	2
1810	Aydon & Co.	3	2
1823	—	3	-
1825	Hird, Dawson & Co.	-	-
1830	—	3	-
1841	Hird, Dawson & Hardy	-	-
1843	Hird, Dawson & Co.	-	-
1847	Hird, Dawson & Co.	-	-
1849	—	-	3
1854	—	-	-

Crawshay & Ellwell were also ground landlords in 1794; the furnace was coke-fired, blown by engine, and said to have been built in 1794. 1796: output 1,000 tons p.a. (i.e. 20 tons a week), Excise and actual, Exact Return 1,140 tons. 1805: output 2,716 tons. 1823–30: output nil in 1823, 7,480 tons p.a. in 1830. The 1825, 1841 and 1843 lists couple Shelf with Low Moor (qv), with furnace-numbers and output given for the two works together; judging by the furnace-numbers, the same is also true in 1847. In 1854 the name of the works appears but with no other information.

Swallowhill [SE 3209?]

Year	Owner	Built	In Blast
1805	Swallow	-	-
1810	Swallow	3	2
1823	—	-	-
1825	Swallow	3	0
1830	—	-	-

The 1805 list couples this site and Chapeltown (qv) together, with 5 furnaces (3 in blast) at the two works, producing 3,737 tons p.a. in all. The 1823–30 list uses the name 'Swallow Wood' and comments: 'Have not been worked for several years'; no output is given. The 1825 list calls the the site 'Swalwell'.

Thorncliffe [SK 3597?]

Year	Owner	Built	In Blast
1796	—	2	2
1805	Chambers & Co.	2	2
1810	Chambers & Co.	3	3
1823	—	3	-
1825	Newton, Scott, Chambers & Co.	3	3
1830	—	3	-
1839	—	3	2
1841	Newton, Chambers & Co.	3	2
1843	Chambers, Newton & Co.	3	1
1847	Chambers & Co.	2	2
1849	—	-	3
1854	Newton, Chambers & Co.	3	2
1855	Newton, Chambers & Co.	3	2
1856	Newton, Chambers & Co.	3	2
1857	Newton, Chambers & Co.	3	2
1858	Newton, Chambers & Co.	3	2
1859	Newton, Chambers & Co.	3	2
1860	Newton, Chambers & Co.	2	2
1861	Newton, Chambers & Co.	2	2
1862	Newton, Chambers & Co.	3	2
1863	Newton, Chambers & Co.	3	2
1864	Newton, Chambers & Co.	3	2
1865	Newton, Chambers & Co.	3	2
1866	Newton, Chambers & Co.	2	2
1867	Newton, Chambers & Co.	2	2
1868	Newton, Chambers & Co.	2	2
1869	Newton, Chambers & Co.	2	1
1870	Newton, Chambers & Co.	2	1
1871	Newton, Chambers & Co.	2	1
1872	Newton, Chambers & Co.	2	1
1873	Newton, Chambers & Co.	2	2
1874	Newton, Chambers & Co.	2	1
1875	Newton, Chambers & Co.	2	2
1876	Newton, Chambers & Co.	2	2
1877	Newton, Chambers & Co.	2	2
1878	Newton, Chambers & Co.	2	2
1879	Newton, Chambers & Co.	2	2
1880	Newton, Chambers & Co.	2	2
1881	Newton, Chambers & Co. Ltd	2	2
1882	Newton, Chambers & Co. Ltd	2	2
1883	Newton, Chambers & Co. Ltd	2	2
1884	Newton, Chambers & Co. Ltd	2	2
1885	Newton, Chambers & Co. Ltd	2	2
1886	Newton, Chambers & Co. Ltd	2	2
1887	Newton, Chambers & Co. Ltd	2	2
1888	Newton, Chambers & Co. Ltd	2	2
1889	Newton, Chambers & Co. Ltd	2	2
1890	Newton, Chambers & Co. Ltd	2	2
1891	Newton, Chambers & Co. Ltd	2	2
1892	Newton, Chambers & Co. Ltd	2	2
1893	Newton, Chambers & Co. Ltd	2	2
1894	Newton, Chambers & Co. Ltd	2	2
1895	Newton, Chambers & Co. Ltd	2	2
1896	Newton, Chambers & Co. Ltd	2	2
1897	Newton, Chambers & Co. Ltd	2	2
1898	Newton, Chambers & Co. Ltd	2	2
1899	Newton, Chambers & Co. Ltd	2	2
1900	Newton, Chambers & Co. Ltd	2	2
1901	Newton, Chambers & Co. Ltd	2	2
1902	Newton, Chambers & Co. Ltd	2	2
1903	Newton, Chambers & Co. Ltd	2	2
1904	Newton, Chambers & Co. Ltd	2	2
1905	Newton, Chambers & Co. Ltd	2	2
1906	Newton, Chambers & Co. Ltd	2	2
1907	Newton, Chambers & Co. Ltd	2	2
1908	Newton, Chambers & Co. Ltd	2	2
1909	Newton, Chambers & Co. Ltd	2	2
1910	Newton, Chambers & Co. Ltd	2	2
1911	Newton, Chambers & Co. Ltd	2	2
1912	Newton, Chambers & Co. Ltd	2	2
1913	Newton, Chambers & Co. Ltd	3	2
1921	Newton, Chambers & Co. Ltd	3	-
1922	Newton, Chambers & Co. Ltd	3	-
1923	Newton, Chambers & Co. Ltd	3	-
1924	Newton, Chambers & Co. Ltd	3	-
1925	Newton, Chambers & Co. Ltd	3	-
1926	Newton, Chambers & Co. Ltd	3	-

Year	Owner	Built	In Blast
1927	Newton, Chambers & Co. Ltd	2	-
1928	Newton, Chambers & Co. Ltd	2	-
1929	Newton, Chambers & Co. Ltd	2	-
1930	Newton, Chambers & Co. Ltd	2	-
1931	Newton, Chambers & Co. Ltd	2	-
1932	Newton, Chambers & Co. Ltd	2	-
1933	Newton, Chambers & Co. Ltd	2	-
1934	Newton, Chambers & Co. Ltd	2	-
1935	Newton, Chambers & Co. Ltd	2	-
1936	Newton, Chambers & Co. Ltd	1	-
1937	Newton, Chambers & Co. Ltd	1	-
1938	Newton, Chambers & Co. Ltd	1	-
1939	Newton, Chambers & Co. Ltd	1	-
1940	Newton, Chambers & Co. Ltd	1	-
1941	Newton, Chambers & Co. Ltd	1	-
1942	Newton, Chambers & Co. Ltd	1	-

1796: 2 furnaces, output of each 546 tons p.a., Excise and actual, 1,092 tons total; Exact Return 712 tons total. 1805: output 2,500 tons p.a. 1823–30: 2,909 tons in 1823, 2,188 tons in 1830. 1825: 90 tons a week, 4,368 p.a., 'melting iron'. 1841: 85 tons a week. 1843: 45 tons a week. 1847: 6,750 tons p.a., presumably meaning 135 tons a week. Truran: 80 tons a week from each of 2 furnaces. In 1862–66 furnace-numbers for Thorncliffe and Chapeltown (qv) are combined under the former heading; in 1867 Chapeltown is listed separately but with blanks in both columns; in 1868–71 the two works are once again combined. In 1872–73 Thorncliffe and Chapeltown are listed separately but no furnace-numbers are given for the latter; from 1874 Thorncliffe alone is listed. In the Thorncliffe entry for 1873 one furnace was said to be in course of construction. The last furnace was dismantled in 1943.

Thorpe Hall   SE 3331

Year	Owner	Built	In Blast
1839	—	1	1
1847	Fenton	1	1
1849	—	-	1
1854	Leather & Co.	-	-
1855	J. & H. Hains	1	1
1856	J. & H. Hains	1	1
1857	T. & H. Hains	1	1
1858	T. & H. Hains	1	1
1859	T. & H. Hains	1	1
1860	T. & H. Hains	1	1

1839–47: named Waterloo, from an adjacent colliery. 1847: output 2,340 tons p.a., i.e. 45 tons a week. 1849: listed as Leather & Co., with no works name: J.T. Leather of Leventhorpe Hall was the owner of Waterloo Colliery. His name also appears as the heading in *Mineral Statistics* in 1854, with no further information. Truran: output (at Waterloo) 70 tons a week from a single furnace.

Tinsley, Sheffield   [SK 4090]

Year	Owner	Built	In Blast
1875	William Cooke & Co. Ltd	2	2
1876	William Cooke & Co. Ltd	2	2
1877	William Cooke & Co. Ltd	2	2
1878	William Cooke & Co. Ltd	2	2
1879	William Cooke & Co. Ltd	2	0
1880	William Cooke & Co. Ltd	2	0
1881	William Cooke & Co. Ltd	2	0
1882	William Cooke & Co. Ltd	2	0
1883	William Cooke & Co. Ltd	2	1
1884	William Cooke & Co. Ltd	2	1
1885	William Cooke & Co. Ltd	2	1
1886	William Cooke & Co. Ltd	2	1
1887	William Cooke & Co. Ltd	2	1
1888	William Cooke & Co. Ltd	2	1
1889	William Cooke & Co. Ltd	2	1
1890	William Cooke & Co. Ltd	2	1
1891	William Cooke & Co. Ltd	2	1
1892	William Cooke & Co. Ltd	2	1
1893	William Cooke & Co. Ltd	2	1
1894	William Cooke & Co. Ltd	2	1
1895	William Cooke & Co. Ltd	2	1
1896	William Cooke & Co. Ltd	2	1
1897	William Cooke & Co. Ltd	2	1
1898	William Cooke & Co. Ltd	2	1
1899	William Cooke & Co. Ltd	2	1
1900	William Cooke & Co. Ltd	2	0

Waterloo: see Thorpe Hall

West Yorkshire, East Ardsley, Leeds   [SE 3025]

Year	Owner	Built	In Blast
1868	West Yorkshire Iron & Coal Co. Ltd	2	1
1869	West Yorkshire Iron & Coal Co. Ltd	2	2
1870	West Yorkshire Iron & Coal Co. Ltd	2	2
1871	West Yorkshire Iron & Coal Co. Ltd	3	3
1872	West Yorkshire Iron & Coal Co. Ltd	5	4
1873	West Yorkshire Iron & Coal Co. Ltd	5	4
1874	West Yorkshire Iron & Coal Co. Ltd	5	4
1875	West Yorkshire Iron & Coal Co. Ltd	5	4
1876	West Yorkshire Iron & Coal Co. Ltd	5	4
1877	West Yorkshire Iron & Coal Co. Ltd	5	2
1878	West Yorkshire Iron & Coal Co. Ltd	5	2
1879	West Yorkshire Iron & Coal Co. Ltd	5	1
1880	West Yorkshire Iron & Coal Co. Ltd	5	3
1881	West Yorkshire Iron & Coal Co. Ltd	5	3
1882	West Yorkshire Iron & Coal Co. Ltd	5	4
1883	West Yorkshire Iron & Coal Co. Ltd	5	4
1884	West Yorkshire Iron & Coal Co. Ltd	5	3
1885	West Yorkshire Iron & Coal Co. Ltd	5	2
1886	West Yorkshire Iron & Coal Co. Ltd	5	2
1887	West Yorkshire Iron & Coal Co. Ltd	5	2
1888	West Yorkshire Iron & Coal Co. Ltd	5	2
1889	West Yorkshire Iron & Coal Co. Ltd	5	3
1890	West Yorkshire Iron & Coal Co. Ltd	5	2
1891	West Yorkshire Iron & Coal Co. Ltd	5	2
1892	West Yorkshire Iron & Coal Co. Ltd	5	3
1893	West Yorkshire Iron & Coal Co. Ltd	5	2
1894	West Yorkshire Iron & Coal Co. Ltd	5	2
1895	West Yorkshire Iron & Coal Co. Ltd	5	2
1896	West Yorkshire Iron & Coal Co. Ltd	5	2
1897	West Yorkshire Iron & Coal Co. Ltd	5	2
1898	West Yorkshire Iron & Coal Co. Ltd	5	3
1899	West Yorkshire Iron & Coal Co. Ltd	5	3
1900	West Yorkshire Iron & Coal Co. Ltd	5	3
1901	West Yorkshire Iron & Coal Co. Ltd	5	2
1902	Yorkshire Iron & Coal Co. Ltd	5	3
1903	Yorkshire Iron & Coal Co. Ltd	5	3
1904	Yorkshire Iron & Coal Co. Ltd	5	3
1905	Yorkshire Iron & Coal Co. Ltd	5	3
1906	Yorkshire Iron & Coal Co. Ltd	5	3

Year	Owner	Built	In Blast
1907	Yorkshire Iron & Coal Co. Ltd	5	3
1908	Yorkshire Iron & Coal Co. Ltd	5	2
1909	Yorkshire Iron & Coal Co. Ltd	5	2
1910	Yorkshire Iron & Coal Co. Ltd	5	2
1911	Yorkshire Iron & Coal Co. Ltd	5	2
1912	Yorkshire Iron & Coal Co. Ltd	5	2
1913	Yorkshire Iron & Coal Co. Ltd	5	2
1921	Yorkshire Iron & Coal Co. Ltd	5	-
1922	Yorkshire Iron & Coal Co. Ltd	5	-
1923	Yorkshire Iron & Coal Co. Ltd	5	-
1924	Yorkshire Iron & Coal Co. Ltd	4	-
1925	Yorkshire Iron & Coal Co. Ltd	4	-
1926	Yorkshire Iron & Coal Co. Ltd	4	-
1927	Yorkshire Iron & Coal Co. Ltd	4	-
1928	Yorkshire Iron & Coal Co. Ltd	3	-

1871: 2 new furnaces nearly ready.

White Horse, York Road, Leeds   SE 3234

Year	Owner	Built	In Blast
1865	R. & W. Garside	2	2
1866	R. & W. Garside	2	2
1867	R. & W. Garside	2	2
1868	R. & W. Garside	2	2
1869	R. & W. Garside	2	1
1870	R. & W. Garside	2	0
1871	Trustees of R. & W. Garside	2	1
1872	York Road Iron & Coal Co.	2	2
1873	York Road Iron & Coal Co.	2	1
1874	York Road Iron & Coal Co.	2	1
1875	York Road Iron & Coal Co.	2	1
1876	York Road Iron & Coal Co.	2	1
1877	York Road Iron & Coal Co.	2	1
1878	York Road Iron & Coal Co.	2	1
1879	York Road Iron & Coal Co.	2	1
1880	York Road Iron & Coal Co.	2	1
1881	York Road Iron & Coal Co.	2	1
1882	York Road Iron & Coal Co.	2	1
1883	York Road Iron & Coal Co.	2	1
1884	York Road Iron & Coal Co.	2	1
1885	York Road Iron & Coal Co.	2	1
1886	York Road Iron & Coal Co.	2	1
1887	York Road Iron Co.	2	1
1888	York Road Iron Co.	2	1
1889	York Road Iron Co.	2	1
1890	York Road Iron Co.	2	1
1891	York Road Iron Co.	2	0
1892	York Road Iron Co.	2	0
1893	York Road Iron Co.	2	0
1894	York Road Iron Co.	2	0
1895	York Road Iron Co.	2	0
1896	York Road Iron Co.	2	0
1897	York Road Iron Co.	2	1
1898	York Road Iron Co.	2	1
1899	York Road Iron Co.	2	1
1900	York Road Iron Co.	2	1
1901	York Road Iron Co.	2	1
1902	York Road Iron Co.	2	1
1903	York Road Iron Co.	2	1
1904	York Road Iron Co.	2	0
1905	York Road Iron Co.	2	1
1906	York Road Iron Co.	2	1
1907	York Road Iron Co.	2	1
1908	York Road Iron Co.	2	0
1909	York Road Iron Co.	2	0
1910	York Road Iron Co.	2	0
1911	York Road Iron Co.	2	0
1912	York Road Iron Co.	2	0

The works is called White Horse in 1866, 1868–72 and from 1883, York Road in other years. 1869: 'Cold blast, part of year only'. In 1882–86 the owner's name is given the suffix 'Ltd', apparently in error, since no company of this name can be found on the register.

Wibsey Lowmoor: see Low Moor

Worsbrough   [SE 3503]

Year	Owner	Built	In Blast
1810	—	1	1
1823	—	1	-
1825	J. Darwin & Co.	1	1
1830	—	1	-
1839	—	1	1
1841	Field, Cooper & Co.	1	1
1843	Field, Cooper & Co.	1	1
1847	Field, Cooper & Co.	1	1
1849	—	-	1
1854	Field, Cooper & Co.	1	1
1855	Field, Cooper & Co.	1	0
1856	Field, Cooper & Co.	1	0
1857	Field, Cooper & Co.	1	0
1858	Field, Cooper & Co.	1	0
1859	Field, Cooper & Co.	1	0
1860	Field, Cooper & Co.	1	0
1861	Field, Cooper & Co.	1	0
1862	Worsborough Iron Co.	1	0
1863	Worsborough Iron Co.	1	0
1864	Worsborough Iron Co.	1	1
1865	Worsborough Iron Co.	1	1
1866	Worsborough Iron Co.	1	1
1867	Worsborough Iron Co.	1	0
1868	Worsborough Iron Co.	1	0
1869	Worsborough Iron Co.	1	0
1870	Worsborough Iron Co.	1	0
1871	Worsborough Iron Co.	1	0

1823–30: output 1,381 tons p.a. in 1823, 1,664 tons in 1830, with the comment 'This quantity is estimated' against 1830. The 1825 list (like that of 1847) calls the works Worsbrough Dale, and gives a weekly output of 26 tons, 1,300 tons p.a., 'melting iron'. 1841: output 43 tons a week. 1843: output 50 tons a week. 1847: output 2,600 tons p.a., i.e. 50 tons a week. Truran: output 70 tons a week from a single furnace. The works is called Worsbrough Dale in *Mineral Statistics* in 1854–61; in 1865 the furnace was said to be working on cold blast.

York Road: see White Horse

North West England

Askam, Lancs. SD 2177

Year	Owner	Built	In Blast
1865	Furness Iron & Steel Co. Ltd	2	0
1866	Furness Iron & Steel Co. Ltd	2	0
1867	Furness Iron & Steel Co. Ltd	2	0
1868	Furness Iron & Steel Co. Ltd	2	0
1869	Furness Iron & Steel Co. Ltd	2	0
1870	Furness Iron & Steel Co. Ltd	2	0
1871	Furness Iron & Steel Co. Ltd	2	2
1872	Furness Iron & Steel Co. Ltd	3	3
1873	Furness Iron & Steel Co. Ltd	4	4
1874	Furness Iron & Steel Co. Ltd	4	2
1875	Furness Iron & Steel Co. Ltd	4	4
1876	Furness Iron & Steel Co. Ltd	4	4
1877	Furness Iron & Steel Co. Ltd	4	4
1878	Furness Iron & Steel Co. Ltd	4	4
1879	Furness Iron & Steel Co. Ltd	4	4
1880	Furness Iron & Steel Co. Ltd	4	4
1881	Askam & Mouzell Iron Co. Ltd	4	1
1882	Askam & Mouzell Iron Co. Ltd	4	3
1883	Askam & Mouzell Iron Co. Ltd	4	3
1884	Askam & Mouzell Iron Co. Ltd	4	3
1885	Askam & Mouzell Iron Co. Ltd	4	3
1886	Askam & Mouzell Iron Co. Ltd	4	3
1887	Askam & Mouzell Iron Co. Ltd	4	3
1888	Askam & Mouzell Iron Co. Ltd	4	3
1889	Askam & Mouzell Iron Co. Ltd	4	2
1890	Millom & Askam Hematite Iron Co. Ltd	4	3
1891	Millom & Askam Hematite Iron Co. Ltd	4	3
1892	Millom & Askam Hematite Iron Co. Ltd	4	2
1893	Millom & Askam Hematite Iron Co. Ltd	4	2
1894	Millom & Askam Hematite Iron Co. Ltd	4	2
1895	Millom & Askam Hematite Iron Co. Ltd	4	2
1896	Millom & Askam Hematite Iron Co. Ltd	4	3
1897	Millom & Askam Hematite Iron Co. Ltd	4	2
1898	Millom & Askam Hematite Iron Co. Ltd	4	2
1899	Millom & Askam Hematite Iron Co. Ltd	3	2
1900	Millom & Askam Hematite Iron Co. Ltd	4	1
1901	Millom & Askam Hematite Iron Co. Ltd	4	0
1902	Millom & Askam Hematite Iron Co. Ltd	4	1
1903	Millom & Askam Hematite Iron Co. Ltd	4	1
1904	Millom & Askam Hematite Iron Co. Ltd	4	0
1905	Millom & Askam Hematite Iron Co. Ltd	4	0
1906	Millom & Askam Hematite Iron Co. Ltd	4	1
1907	Millom & Askam Hematite Iron Co. Ltd	4	0
1908	Millom & Askam Hematite Iron Co. Ltd	4	0
1909	Millom & Askam Hematite Iron Co. Ltd	4	0
1910	Millom & Askam Hematite Iron Co. Ltd	4	0
1911	Millom & Askam Hematite Iron Co. Ltd	4	0
1912	Millom & Askam Hematite Iron Co. Ltd	4	0
1913	Millom & Askam Hematite Iron Co. Ltd	4	0

A second entry in 1870 for 'Askam Haematite Iron Works' (1 furnace, not in blast) and another in 1871 under Furness Iron Co. (2 furnaces, neither in blast) appear to be duplicates for the entries printed above, which in 1872–76 are listed under Furness, rather than Askam.

Backbarrow, Lancs. SD 3584

Year	Owner	Built	In Blast
1794	B. Barrow & Co.	1	-
1796	—	1	1
1805	—	1	1
1810	Knott & Co.	1	1
1825	Harrison & Co.	1	-
1854	Harrison Ainslie & Co.	1	1
1855	Harrison Ainslie & Co.	1	1
1856	Harrison Ainslie & Co.	1	1
1857	Harrison Ainslie & Co.	1	1
1858	Harrison Ainslie & Co.	1	1
1859	Harrison Ainslie & Co.	1	1
1860	Harrison Ainslie & Co.	1	1
1861	Harrison Ainslie & Co.	1	1
1862	Harrison Ainslie & Co.	2	2
1863	Harrison Ainslie & Co.	2	1
1864	Harrison Ainslie & Co.	1	1
1865	Harrison Ainslie & Co.	1	1
1866	Harrison Ainslie & Co.	2	2
1867	Harrison Ainslie & Co.	2	2
1868	Harrison Ainslie & Co.	2	2
1869	Harrison Ainslie & Co.	2	2
1870	Harrison Ainslie & Co.	2	1
1871	Harrison Ainslie & Co.	2	2
1872	Harrison Ainslie & Co.	2	2
1873	Harrison Ainslie & Co.	2	2
1873	Harrison Ainslie & Co.	2	1
1874	Harrison Ainslie & Co.	2	2

Year	Owner	Built	In Blast
1875	Harrison Ainslie & Co.	2	1
1876	Harrison Ainslie & Co.	2	1
1877	Harrison Ainslie & Co.	2	2
1878	Harrison Ainslie & Co.	2	2
1879	Harrison Ainslie & Co.	2	2
1880	Harrison Ainslie & Co.	2	2
1881	Harrison Ainslie & Co.	2	2
1882	Harrison Ainslie & Co.	1	1
1883	Harrison Ainslie & Co.	1	1
1884	Harrison Ainslie & Co.	1	1
1885	Harrison Ainslie & Co.	1	1
1886	Harrison Ainslie & Co.	2	2
1887	Harrison Ainslie & Co.	1	1
1888	Harrison Ainslie & Co.	1	1
1889	Harrison Ainslie & Co.	1	1
1890	Harrison Ainslie & Co.	1	0
1891	Harrison Ainslie & Co.	1	0
1892	Harrison Ainslie & Co.	1	1
1893	Harrison Ainslie & Co. Ltd	1	1
1894	Harrison Ainslie & Co. Ltd	1	1
1895	Harrison Ainslie & Co. Ltd	1	0
1896	Harrison Ainslie & Co. Ltd	1	1
1897	Harrison Ainslie & Co. Ltd	1	0
1898	Harrison Ainslie & Co. Ltd	1	1
1899	Harrison Ainslie & Co. Ltd	1	1
1900	Harrison Ainslie & Co. Ltd	1	1
1901	Harrison Ainslie & Co. Ltd	1	1
1902	Harrison Ainslie & Co. Ltd	1	1
1903	Harrison Ainslie & Co. Ltd	1	1
1904	Harrison Ainslie & Co. Ltd	1	1
1905	Harrison Ainslie & Co. Ltd	1	1
1906	Harrison Ainslie & Co. Ltd	1	1
1907	Harrison Ainslie & Co. Ltd	1	1
1908	Harrison Ainslie & Co. Ltd	1	0
1909	Harrison Ainslie & Co. Ltd	1	1
1910	Harrison Ainslie & Co. Ltd	1	1
1911	Harrison Ainslie & Co. Ltd	1	0
1912	Harrison Ainslie & Co. Ltd	1	1
1913	Harrison Ainslie & Co. Ltd	1	1
1921	Charcoal Iron Co. Ltd	1	-
1922	Charcoal Iron Co. Ltd	1	-
1923	Charcoal Iron Co. Ltd	1	-
1924	Charcoal Iron Co. Ltd	1	-
1925	Charcoal Iron Co. Ltd	1	-
1926	Charcoal Iron Co. Ltd	1	-
1927	Charcoal Iron Co. Ltd	1	-
1928	Charcoal Iron Co. Ltd	1	-
1929	Charcoal Iron Co. Ltd	1	-
1930	Charcoal Iron Co. Ltd	1	-
1931	Charcoal Iron Co. Ltd	1	-
1932	Charcoal Iron Co. Ltd	1	-
1933	Charcoal Iron Co. Ltd	1	-
1934	Charcoal Iron Co. Ltd	1	-
1935	Charcoal Iron Co. Ltd	1	-
1936	Charcoal Iron Co. Ltd	1	-
1937	Charcoal Iron Co. Ltd	1	-
1938	Charcoal Iron Co. Ltd	1	-
1939	Charcoal Iron Co. Ltd	1	-
1940	Charcoal Iron Co. Ltd	1	-
1941	Charcoal Iron Co. Ltd	1	-
1942	Charcoal Iron Co. Ltd	1	-
1943	Charcoal Iron Co. Ltd	1	-
1944	Charcoal Iron Co. Ltd	1	-
1945	Charcoal Iron Co. Ltd	1	-
1946	Charcoal Iron Co. Ltd	1	-
1947	Charcoal Iron Co. Ltd	1	-
1948	Charcoal Iron Co. Ltd	1	-
1949	Charcoal Iron Co. Ltd	1	-
1950	Charcoal Iron Co. Ltd	1	-
1951	Charcoal Iron Co. Ltd	1	-
1952	Charcoal Iron Co. Ltd	1	-
1953	Charcoal Iron Co. Ltd	1	-
1954	Charcoal Iron Co. Ltd	1	-
1955	Charcoal Iron Co. Ltd	1	-
1956	Charcoal Iron Co. Ltd	1	-
1957	Charcoal Iron Co. Ltd	1	-
1958	Charcoal Iron Co. Ltd	1	-
1959	Charcoal Iron Co. Ltd	1	-
1960	Charcoal Iron Co. Ltd	1	-
1961	Charcoal Iron Co. Ltd	1	-
1962	Charcoal Iron Co. Ltd	1	-
1963	Charcoal Iron Co. Ltd	1	-
1964	Charcoal Iron Co. Ltd	1	-
1965	Charcoal Iron Co. Ltd	1	-
1966	Charcoal Iron Co. Ltd	1	-
1967	Charcoal Iron Co. Ltd	1	-
1968	Charcoal Iron Co. Ltd	1	-

In 1794 the ground landlord was John Machel; the single water-powered charcoal furnace was said to have been built in 1705. There was also a finery and a chafery. 1796: output 700 tons p.a., Excise and actual; Exact Return 769 tons. 1805: output 446 tons. In 1825 all the Harrison Ainslie furnaces are bracketed together with the comment: 'These are Charcoal Furnaces & of which I have no return'; no output figures are given. In 1854–56 *Mineral Statistics* describes in some detail the operation of Backbarrow, Newland and Duddon (qqv), the last charcoal-fired furnaces in England. Truran: 1 furnace, output 1,200 tons p.a. In 1862–63 and 1865–70 the furnace-numbers printed for Backbarrow and Newland also include Duddon and Lorn (Argyllshire, qv), which have their own returns, and the figures above have been adjusted accordingly. Backbarrow and Newland continue to be combined up to 1881 and the figures above include both sites. In 1882, when Newland has its own furnace-numbers, those for Backbarrow list 1 furnace built, $1^1/_2$ in blast. 1883: 1 furnace building at Backbarrow. The company was first registered in September 1893 under the name printed above (i.e. with no comma, a form also been used here for the earlier partnership). This concern was voluntarily wound-up and liquidated (by Alfred Fell, the historian of the Furness iron industry) in 1903–05, and succeeded by another company of the same name, registered in October 1904 and dissolved in November 1917 (BT 31/5662/39522; BT 31/17309/82203).

Barrow Hæmatite, Lancs.   SD 1870

Year	Owner	Built	In Blast
1859	Schneider & Hannay	3	3
1860	Schneider & Hannay	4	3
1861	Schneider & Hannay	6	5
1862	Schneider, Hannay & Co.	6	5
1863	Schneider, Hannay & Co.	8	6
1864	Schneider, Hannay & Co.	8	7
1865	Barrow Hæmatite Steel Co. Ltd	10	8
1866	Barrow Hæmatite Steel Co. Ltd	11	10
1867	Barrow Hæmatite Steel Co. Ltd	11	10
1868	Barrow Hæmatite Steel Co. Ltd	11	10
1869	Barrow Hæmatite Steel Co. Ltd	11	11
1870	Barrow Hæmatite Steel Co. Ltd	11	11
1871	Barrow Hæmatite Steel Co. Ltd	14	11
1872	Barrow Hæmatite Steel Co. Ltd	14	12

Year	Owner	Built	In Blast
1873	Barrow Hæmatite Steel Co. Ltd	16	13
1874	Barrow Hæmatite Steel Co. Ltd	16	13
1875	Barrow Hæmatite Steel Co. Ltd	16	12
1876	Barrow Hæmatite Steel Co. Ltd	16	12
1877	Barrow Hæmatite Steel Co. Ltd	16	12
1878	Barrow Hæmatite Steel Co. Ltd	16	11
1879	Barrow Hæmatite Steel Co. Ltd	14	12
1880	Barrow Hæmatite Steel Co. Ltd	14	13
1881	Barrow Hæmatite Steel Co. Ltd	14	13
1882	Barrow Hæmatite Steel Co. Ltd	14	13
1883	Barrow Hæmatite Steel Co. Ltd	14	12
1884	Barrow Hæmatite Steel Co. Ltd	14	11
1885	Barrow Hæmatite Steel Co. Ltd	14	9
1886	Barrow Hæmatite Steel Co. Ltd	14	10
1887	Barrow Hæmatite Steel Co. Ltd	14	12
1888	Barrow Hæmatite Steel Co. Ltd	14	13
1889	Barrow Hæmatite Steel Co. Ltd	14	13
1890	Barrow Hæmatite Steel Co. Ltd	14	12
1891	Barrow Hæmatite Steel Co. Ltd	14	12
1892	Barrow Hæmatite Steel Co. Ltd	14	10
1893	Barrow Hæmatite Steel Co. Ltd	14	9
1894	Barrow Hæmatite Steel Co. Ltd	14	9
1895	Barrow Hæmatite Steel Co. Ltd	14	8
1896	Barrow Hæmatite Steel Co. Ltd	14	10
1897	Barrow Hæmatite Steel Co. Ltd	14	10
1898	Barrow Hæmatite Steel Co. Ltd	14	10
1899	Barrow Hæmatite Steel Co. Ltd	12	10
1900	Barrow Hæmatite Steel Co. Ltd	12	10
1901	Barrow Hæmatite Steel Co. Ltd	12	9
1902	Barrow Hæmatite Steel Co. Ltd	12	8
1903	Barrow Hæmatite Steel Co. Ltd	12	7
1904	Barrow Hæmatite Steel Co. Ltd	12	5
1905	Barrow Hæmatite Steel Co. Ltd	12	5
1906	Barrow Hæmatite Steel Co. Ltd	12	6
1907	Barrow Hæmatite Steel Co. Ltd	10	6
1908	Barrow Hæmatite Steel Co. Ltd	10	3
1909	Barrow Hæmatite Steel Co. Ltd	10	4
1910	Barrow Hæmatite Steel Co. Ltd	10	6
1911	Barrow Hæmatite Steel Co. Ltd	10	5
1912	Barrow Hæmatite Steel Co. Ltd	10	5
1913	Barrow Hæmatite Steel Co. Ltd	10	6
1921	Barrow Hæmatite Steel Co. Ltd	8	-
1922	Barrow Hæmatite Steel Co. Ltd	8	-
1923	Barrow Hæmatite Steel Co. Ltd	8	-
1924	Barrow Hæmatite Steel Co. Ltd	7	-
1925	Barrow Hæmatite Steel Co. Ltd	7	-
1926	Barrow Hæmatite Steel Co. Ltd	7	-
1927	Barrow Hæmatite Steel Co. Ltd	7	-
1928	Barrow Hæmatite Steel Co. Ltd	7	-
1929	Barrow Hæmatite Steel Co. Ltd	7	-
1930	Barrow Hæmatite Steel Co. Ltd	6	-
1931	Barrow Hæmatite Steel Co. Ltd	7	-
1932	Barrow Hæmatite Steel Co. Ltd	7	-
1933	Barrow Hæmatite Steel Co. Ltd	7	-
1934	Barrow Hæmatite Steel Co. Ltd	7	-
1935	Barrow Hæmatite Steel Co. Ltd	7	-
1936	Barrow Hæmatite Steel Co. Ltd	4	-
1937	Barrow Hæmatite Steel Co. Ltd	4	-
1938	Barrow Hæmatite Steel Co. Ltd	4	-
1939	Barrow Hæmatite Steel Co. Ltd	4	-
1940	Barrow Hæmatite Steel Co. Ltd	4	-
1941	Barrow Hæmatite Steel Co. Ltd	4	-
1942	Barrow Hæmatite Steel Co. Ltd	4	-
1943	Barrow Hæmatite Steel Co. Ltd	4	-
1944	Barrow Hæmatite Steel Co. Ltd	4	-
1945	Barrow Hæmatite Steel Co. Ltd	4	-
1946	Barrow Hæmatite Steel Co. Ltd	4	-
1947	Barrow Hæmatite Steel Co. Ltd	4	-
1948	Barrow Ironworks Ltd	3	-
1949	Barrow Ironworks Ltd	3	-
1950	Barrow Ironworks Ltd	3	-
1951	Barrow Ironworks Ltd	3	-
1952	Barrow Ironworks Ltd	4	-
1953	Barrow Ironworks Ltd	4	-
1954	Barrow Ironworks Ltd	4	-
1955	Barrow Ironworks Ltd	4	-
1956	Barrow Ironworks Ltd	4	-
1957	Barrow Ironworks Ltd	4	-
1958	Barrow Ironworks Ltd	4	-
1959	Barrow Ironworks Ltd	4	-
1960	Barrow Ironworks Ltd	2	-
1961	Barrow Ironworks Ltd	3	-
1962	Barrow Ironworks Ltd	3	-

1861: Works called Ulverston Hæmatite. In 1865 the owner is named as Barrow Hæmatite Huel (*sic*) Co. Ltd, and in 1872–73 as Barrow Hæmatite Iron & Steel Co. Ltd; the latter is used as the heading in *Mineral Statistics* in 1874. 1879: 1 furnace building. The registered title of the company established in 1864 used the spelling 'Hæmatite'; the post-1921 returns use 'Hematite' in 1921–34 and 1939–47.

Bearpot: see Seaton

Carnforth, Lancs. SD 4970

Year	Owner	Built	In Blast
1865	Carnforth Hæmatite Iron Co. Ltd	3	0
1866	Carnforth Hæmatite Iron Co. Ltd	3	2
1867	Carnforth Hæmatite Iron Co. Ltd	3	3
1868	Carnforth Hæmatite Iron Co. Ltd	3	3
1869	Carnforth Hæmatite Iron Co. Ltd	4	4
1870	Carnforth Hæmatite Iron Co. Ltd	4	4
1871	Carnforth Hæmatite Iron Co. Ltd	5	5
1872	Carnforth Hæmatite Iron Co. Ltd	5	5
1873	Carnforth Hæmatite Iron Co. Ltd	6	5
1874	Carnforth Hæmatite Iron Co. Ltd	6	3
1875	Carnforth Hæmatite Iron Co. Ltd	6	3
1876	Carnforth Hæmatite Iron Co. Ltd	6	3
1877	Carnforth Hæmatite Iron Co. Ltd	6	3
1878	Carnforth Hæmatite Iron Co. Ltd	6	2
1879	Carnforth Hæmatite Iron Co. Ltd	6	4
1880	Carnforth Hæmatite Iron Co. Ltd	6	4
1881	Carnforth Hæmatite Iron Co. Ltd	6	4
1882	Carnforth Hæmatite Iron Co. Ltd	6	4
1883	Carnforth Hæmatite Iron Co. Ltd	6	3
1884	Carnforth Hæmatite Iron Co. Ltd	6	2
1885	Carnforth Hæmatite Iron Co. Ltd	6	3
1886	Carnforth Hæmatite Iron Co. Ltd	6	2
1887	Carnforth Hæmatite Iron Co. Ltd	6	3
1888	Carnforth Hæmatite Iron Co. Ltd	6	2
1889	Carnforth Hæmatite Iron Co. Ltd	6	3
1890	Carnforth Hæmatite Iron Co. Ltd	6	3
1891	Carnforth Hæmatite Iron Co. Ltd	6	2
1892	Carnforth Hæmatite Iron Co. Ltd	6	2
1893	Carnforth Hæmatite Iron Co. Ltd	6	2
1894	Carnforth Hæmatite Iron Co. Ltd	6	2
1895	Carnforth Hæmatite Iron Co. Ltd	6	2
1896	Carnforth Hæmatite Iron Co. Ltd	6	2
1897	Carnforth Hæmatite Iron Co. Ltd	6	2
1898	Carnforth Hematite Iron Co. Ltd	6	2
1899	Carnforth Hematite Iron Co. Ltd	6	3

Year	Owner	Built	In Blast
1900	Carnforth Hematite Iron Co. Ltd	4	3
1901	Carnforth Hematite Iron Co. Ltd	4	3
1902	Carnforth Hematite Iron Co. Ltd	4	2
1903	Carnforth Hematite Iron Co. Ltd	4	2
1904	Carnforth Hematite Iron Co. Ltd	3	1
1905	Carnforth Hematite Iron Co. Ltd	4	2
1906	Carnforth Hematite Iron Co. Ltd	4	2
1907	Carnforth Hematite Iron Co. Ltd	4	2
1908	Carnforth Hematite Iron Co. Ltd	4	2
1909	Carnforth Hematite Iron Co. Ltd	2	1
1910	Carnforth Hematite Iron Co. Ltd	3	1
1911	Carnforth Hematite Iron Co. Ltd	3	1
1912	Carnforth Hematite Iron Co. Ltd	3	1
1913	Carnforth Hematite Iron Co. Ltd	3	1
1921	Carnforth Hematite Iron Co. Ltd	3	-
1922	Carnforth Hematite Iron Co. Ltd	3	-
1923	Carnforth Hematite Iron Co. Ltd	3	-
1924	Carnforth Hematite Iron Co. Ltd	3	-
1925	Carnforth Hematite Iron Co. Ltd	3	-
1926	Carnforth Hematite Iron Co. Ltd	3	-
1927	Carnforth Hematite Iron Co. Ltd	3	-
1928	Carnforth Hematite Iron Co. Ltd	3	-
1929	Carnforth Hematite Iron Co. Ltd	3	-

No owner's name is given in 1865 but the company listed from 1866 was registered in 1864. The change in spelling in 1897–98 reflects the establishment of a new company; a third concern, Carnforth Hematite Iron Co. (1915) Ltd was later registered but this title was not used in the 1921–29 entries.

Cleator Moor, Cumb.   NY 0215

Year	Owner	Built	In Blast
1849	—	-	2
1854	Whitehaven Iron Co.	2	2
1855	Whitehaven Iron Co. (Thomas Ainsworth & Co.)	3	2
1856	Whitehaven Hematite Iron Co.	4	3
1857	Whitehaven Iron Co.	4	3
1858	Whitehaven Iron Co.	4	3
1859	Whitehaven Iron Co.	4	2
1860	Whitehaven Hematite Iron Co.	4	4
1861	Whitehaven Hematite Iron Co.	4	4
1862	Whitehaven Hematite Iron Co.	4	4
1863	Whitehaven Hematite Iron Co.	4	4
1864	Whitehaven Hematite Iron Co.	4	4
1865	Whitehaven Hematite Iron Co.	4	4
1866	Whitehaven Hematite Iron Co.	6	4
1867	Whitehaven Hematite Iron Co.	6	4
1868	Whitehaven Hematite Iron Co.	6	3
1869	Whitehaven Hematite Iron Co.	6	3
1870	Whitehaven Hematite Iron Co.	6	4
1871	Whitehaven Hematite Iron Co.	6	5
1872	Whitehaven Hematite Iron Co. Ltd	6	5
1873	Whitehaven Hematite Iron Co. Ltd	6	4
1874	Whitehaven Hematite Iron Co. Ltd	6	3
1875	Whitehaven Hematite Iron Co. Ltd	6	2
1876	Whitehaven Hematite Iron Co. Ltd	6	2
1877	Whitehaven Hematite Iron Co. Ltd	5	2
1878	Whitehaven Hematite Iron Co. Ltd	6	2
1879	Whitehaven Hematite Iron Co. Ltd	4	2
1880	Whitehaven Hematite Iron & Steel Co. Ltd	4	2
1881	Whitehaven Hematite Iron & Steel Co. Ltd	5	2
1882	Whitehaven Hematite Iron & Steel Co. Ltd	5	2
1883	Whitehaven Hematite Iron & Steel Co. Ltd	5	2
1884	Whitehaven Hematite Iron & Steel Co. Ltd	5	2
1885	Whitehaven Hematite Iron & Steel Co. Ltd	5	2
1886	Whitehaven Hematite Iron & Steel Co. Ltd	5	2
1887	Whitehaven Hematite Iron & Steel Co. Ltd	5	1
1888	Whitehaven Hematite Iron & Steel Co. Ltd	3	1
1889	Whitehaven Hematite Iron & Steel Co. Ltd	3	1
1890	Whitehaven Hematite Iron & Steel Co. Ltd	2	2
1891	Whitehaven Hematite Iron & Steel Co. Ltd	4	2
1892	Whitehaven Hematite Iron & Steel Co. Ltd	4	2
1893	Whitehaven Hematite Iron & Steel Co. Ltd	4	2
1894	Whitehaven Hematite Iron & Steel Co. Ltd	4	2
1895	Whitehaven Hematite Iron & Steel Co. Ltd	4	1
1896	Whitehaven Hematite Iron & Steel Co. Ltd	4	2
1897	Whitehaven Hematite Iron & Steel Co. Ltd	4	2
1898	Whitehaven Hematite Iron & Steel Co. Ltd	4	2
1899	Whitehaven Hematite Iron & Steel Co. Ltd	4	2
1900	Whitehaven Hematite Iron & Steel Co. Ltd	4	2
1901	Whitehaven Hematite Iron & Steel Co. Ltd	4	2
1902	Whitehaven Hematite Iron & Steel Co. Ltd	4	2
1903	Whitehaven Hematite Iron & Steel Co. Ltd	4	2
1904	Whitehaven Hematite Iron & Steel Co. Ltd	4	2
1905	Whitehaven Hematite Iron & Steel Co. Ltd	4	2
1906	Whitehaven Hematite Iron & Steel Co. Ltd	4	2
1907	Whitehaven Hematite Iron & Steel Co. Ltd	4	2
1908	Whitehaven Hematite Iron & Steel Co. Ltd	4	2
1909	Whitehaven Hematite Iron & Steel Co. Ltd	4	2
1910	Whitehaven Hematite Iron & Steel Co. Ltd	3	2
1911	Whitehaven Hematite Iron & Steel Co. Ltd	2	2
1912	Whitehaven Hematite Iron & Steel Co. Ltd	3	2
1913	Whitehaven Hematite Iron & Steel Co. Ltd	3	2
1921	Whitehaven Hematite Iron & Steel Co. Ltd	3	-

Year	Owner	Built	In Blast
1922	Whitehaven Hematite Iron & Steel Co. Ltd	3	-
1923	Whitehaven Hematite Iron & Steel Co. Ltd	3	-
1924	Whitehaven Hematite Iron & Steel Co. Ltd	3	-
1825	Whitehaven Hematite Iron & Steel Co. Ltd	3	-
1926	Whitehaven Hematite Iron & Steel Co. Ltd	3	-
1927	Whitehaven Hematite Iron & Steel Co. Ltd	3	-
1928	Whitehaven Hematite Iron & Steel Co. Ltd	3	-
1929	Whitehaven Hematite Iron & Steel Co. Ltd	3	-
1930	Whitehaven Hematite Iron & Steel Co. Ltd	3	-
1931	Whitehaven Hematite Iron & Steel Co. Ltd	3	-
1932	Whitehaven Hematite Iron & Steel Co. Ltd	3	-
1933	Whitehaven Hematite Iron & Steel Co. Ltd	3	-

1857: Nothing but hematite used. 1877 and 1880: 1 furnace building. 1883: Owner said to be in liquidation. In 1865–71 and from 1877 the entry in *Mineral Statistics* is headed 'Whitehaven', but the works was actually at Cleator Moor.

Darwen, Lancs. SD 6923

Year	Owner	Built	In Blast
1874	Darwen Iron Co. Ltd	2	2
1875	Darwen Iron Co. Ltd	2	2
1876	Darwen Iron Co. Ltd	2	2
1877	Darwen Iron Co. Ltd	2	2
1878	Darwen Iron Co. Ltd	2	2
1879	Darwen Iron Co. Ltd	2	2
1880	Darwen Iron Co. Ltd	2	2
1881	Darwen Iron Co. Ltd	2	2
1882	Darwen Iron Co. Ltd	2	2
1883	Darwen Iron Co. Ltd	2	2
1884	Darwen Iron Co. Ltd	2	2
1885	Darwen Iron Co. Ltd	2	2
1886	Darwen Iron Co. Ltd	2	2
1887	Darwen & Mostyn Iron Co. Ltd	3	2
1888	Darwen & Mostyn Iron Co. Ltd	3	2
1889	Darwen & Mostyn Iron Co. Ltd	3	2
1890	Darwen & Mostyn Iron Co. Ltd	3	2
1891	Darwen & Mostyn Iron Co. Ltd	2	1
1892	Darwen & Mostyn Iron Co. Ltd	2	1
1893	Darwen & Mostyn Iron Co. Ltd	2	1
1894	Darwen & Mostyn Iron Co. Ltd	2	1
1895	Darwen & Mostyn Iron Co. Ltd	2	1
1896	Darwen & Mostyn Iron Co. Ltd	2	1
1897	Darwen & Mostyn Iron Co. Ltd	2	1
1898	Darwen & Mostyn Iron Co. Ltd	2	1
1899	Darwen & Mostyn Iron Co. Ltd	2	1
1900	Darwen & Mostyn Iron Co. Ltd	2	2
1901	Darwen & Mostyn Iron Co. Ltd	2	1
1902	Darwen & Mostyn Iron Co. Ltd	2	1
1903	Darwen & Mostyn Iron Co. Ltd	2	2
1904	Darwen & Mostyn Iron Co. Ltd	2	1
1905	Darwen & Mostyn Iron Co. Ltd	2	1
1906	Darwen & Mostyn Iron Co. Ltd	2	1
1907	Darwen & Mostyn Iron Co. Ltd	2	1
1908	Darwen & Mostyn Iron Co. Ltd	2	1
1909	Darwen & Mostyn Iron Co. Ltd	2	1
1910	Darwen & Mostyn Iron Co. Ltd	2	1
1911	Darwen & Mostyn Iron Co. Ltd	2	1
1912	Darwen & Mostyn Iron Co. Ltd	2	1
1913	Darwen & Mostyn Iron Co. Ltd	2	2

Post-1921 entries for this company are printed under Mostyn (North Wales).

Derwent, Workington, Cumb. NX 9828

Year	Owner	Built	In Blast
1876	Derwent Hæmatite Iron Co.	2	2
1877	Derwent Hæmatite Iron Co.	3	2
1878	Derwent Hæmatite Iron Co.	3	2
1879	Derwent Hæmatite Iron Co.	3	2
1880	Derwent Hæmatite Iron Co.	3	3
1881	Derwent Hæmatite Iron Co.	3	2
1882	Derwent Hæmatite Iron Co.	3	3
1883	Charles Cammell & Co. Ltd	3	3
1884	Charles Cammell & Co. Ltd	3	3
1885	Charles Cammell & Co. Ltd	3	2
1886	Charles Cammell & Co. Ltd	3	2
1887	Charles Cammell & Co. Ltd	3	3
1888	Charles Cammell & Co. Ltd	3	3
1889	Charles Cammell & Co. Ltd	3	3
1890	Charles Cammell & Co. Ltd	4	4
1891	Charles Cammell & Co. Ltd	5	3
1892	Charles Cammell & Co. Ltd	5	4
1893	Charles Cammell & Co. Ltd	5	4
1894	Charles Cammell & Co. Ltd	5	3
1895	Charles Cammell & Co. Ltd	5	4
1896	Charles Cammell & Co. Ltd	5	5
1897	Charles Cammell & Co. Ltd	5	5
1898	Charles Cammell & Co. Ltd	5	4
1899	Charles Cammell & Co. Ltd	5	5
1900	Charles Cammell & Co. Ltd	5	5
1901	Charles Cammell & Co. Ltd	5	5
1902	Charles Cammell & Co. Ltd	5	4
1903	Cammell Laird & Co. Ltd	5	4
1904	Cammell Laird & Co. Ltd	5	3
1905	Cammell Laird & Co. Ltd	5	5
1906	Cammell Laird & Co. Ltd	5	4
1907	Cammell Laird & Co. Ltd	5	4
1908	Cammell Laird & Co. Ltd	5	3
1909	Workington Iron & Steel Co. Ltd	-	-
1910	Workington Iron & Steel Co. Ltd	-	-
1911	Workington Iron & Steel Co. Ltd	-	-
1912	Workington Iron & Steel Co. Ltd	-	-
1913	Workington Iron & Steel Co. Ltd	-	-

In 1876–81 (but not 1882) *Mineral Statistics* adds the suffix 'Ltd' to the owner's name, although no such company can be found on the register. 1883: Production estimated. From 1909 furnace-numbers were combined with those for other sites owned by the same company under Workington (qv).

Distington, Cumb. NY 0124

Year	Owner	Built	In Blast
1881	Distington Hematite Iron Co. Ltd	2	2

Year	Owner	Built	In Blast
1882	Distington Hematite Iron Co. Ltd	2	1
1883	Distington Hematite Iron Co. Ltd	2	1
1884	Distington Hematite Iron Co. Ltd	2	2
1885	Distington Hematite Iron Co. Ltd	2	1
1886	Distington Hematite Iron Co. Ltd	2	2
1887	Distington Hematite Iron Co. Ltd	3	2
1888	Distington Hematite Iron Co. Ltd	3	2
1889	Distington Hematite Iron Co. Ltd	3	2
1890	Distington Hematite Iron Co. Ltd	3	2
1891	Distington Hematite Iron Co. Ltd	3	2
1892	Distington Hematite Iron Co. Ltd	3	2
1893	Distington Hematite Iron Co. Ltd	3	2
1894	Distington Hematite Iron Co. Ltd	3	1
1895	Distington Hematite Iron Co. Ltd	3	1
1896	Distington Hematite Iron Co. Ltd	3	2
1897	Distington Hematite Iron Co. Ltd	3	2
1898	Distington Hematite Iron Co. Ltd	3	2
1899	Distington Hematite Iron Co. Ltd	3	2
1900	Distington Hematite Iron Co. Ltd	3	2
1901	Distington Hematite Iron Co. Ltd	3	2
1902	Distington Hematite Iron Co. Ltd	3	2
1903	Distington Hematite Iron Co. Ltd	3	2
1904	Distington Hematite Iron Co. Ltd	3	2
1905	Distington Hematite Iron Co. Ltd	3	2
1906	Distington Hematite Iron Co. Ltd	3	2
1907	Distington Hematite Iron Co. Ltd	3	2
1908	Distington Hematite Iron Co. Ltd	3	2
1909	Distington Hematite Iron Co. Ltd	3	2
1910	Distington Hematite Iron Co. Ltd	3	2
1911	Distington Hematite Iron Co. Ltd	3	2
1912	Distington Hematite Iron Co. Ltd	3	2
1913	Distington Hematite Iron Co. Ltd	3	2
1921	United Steel Companies Ltd	3	-
1922	United Steel Companies Ltd	3	-
1923	United Steel Companies Ltd	3	-
1924	United Steel Companies Ltd	3	-
1925	United Steel Companies Ltd	3	-
1926	United Steel Companies Ltd	3	-
1927	United Steel Companies Ltd	3	-
1928	United Steel Companies Ltd	3	-
1929	United Steel Companies Ltd	3	-

Ditton Brook, Lancs. [SJ 4685]

Year	Owner	Built	In Blast
1868	Ditton Brook Iron Co. Ltd	3	3
1869	Ditton Brook Iron Co. Ltd	4	3
1870	Ditton Brook Iron Co. Ltd	4	3
1871	Ditton Brook Iron Co. Ltd	6	4
1872	Ditton Brook Iron Co. Ltd	6	4
1873	Ditton Brook Iron Co. Ltd	6	4
1874	Ditton Brook Iron Co. Ltd	6	3
1875	Ditton Brook Iron Co. Ltd	6	3
1876	Ditton Brook Iron Co. Ltd	6	3
1877	Ditton Brook Iron Co. Ltd	6	2
1878	Ditton Brook Iron Co. Ltd	6	1
1879	Ditton Brook Iron Co. Ltd	6	1
1880	Ditton Brook Iron Co. Ltd	6	3
1881	Ditton Brook Iron Co. Ltd	6	2
1882	Ditton Brook Iron Co. Ltd	6	0
1883	John T. Brunner	6	0
1884	John T. Brunner	6	0
1885	John T. Brunner	6	0
1886	John T. Brunner	6	0
1887	John T. Brunner	6	0
1888	John T. Brunner	6	0
1889	John T. Brunner	6	0
1890	John T. Brunner	6	0
1891	John T. Brunner MP	6	0
1892	John T. Brunner MP	6	0
1893	John T. Brunner MP	6	0
1894	John T. Brunner MP	6	0

1882: Company in liquidation. John Tomlinson Brunner (whose name is given as John F. Brunner in *Mineral Statistics* in 1883, in obvious error) was Liberal MP for Northwich (Cheshire) in 1885–86 and between 1887 and 1910. He was created a baronet in 1895.

Duddon, Cumb. SD 1988

Year	Owner	Built	In Blast
1794	Mr Latham	1	-
1796	—	1	1
1805	Mitchell & Co., Barrow	1	1
1810	Mitchell & Co.	1	1
1825	Harrison & Co.	1	-
1854	Harrison Ainslie & Co.	1	1
1855	Harrison Ainslie & Co.	1	1
1856	Harrison Ainslie & Co.	1	0
1857	Harrison Ainslie & Co.	1	1
1858	Harrison Ainslie & Co.	1	0
1859	Harrison Ainslie & Co.	1	0
1860	Harrison Ainslie & Co.	1	0
1861	Harrison Ainslie & Co.	1	0
1862	Harrison Ainslie & Co.	1	0
1863	Harrison Ainslie & Co.	1	0
1864	Harrison Ainslie & Co.	1	0
1865	Harrison Ainslie & Co.	1	0
1866	Harrison Ainslie & Co.	1	0
1867	Harrison Ainslie & Co.	1	0
1868	Harrison Ainslie & Co.	1	0
1869	Harrison Ainslie & Co.	1	0
1870	Harrison Ainslie & Co.	1	0
1871	Harrison Ainslie & Co.	1	1
1872	Harrison Ainslie & Co.	1	0
1873	Harrison Ainslie & Co.	1	0
1874	Harrison Ainslie & Co.	1	0
1875	Harrison Ainslie & Co.	1	0
1876	Harrison Ainslie & Co.	1	0
1877	Harrison Ainslie & Co.	1	0
1878	Harrison Ainslie & Co.	1	0
1879	Harrison Ainslie & Co.	1	0
1880	Harrison Ainslie & Co.	1	0
1881	Harrison Ainslie & Co.	1	0
1882	Harrison Ainslie & Co.	1	0
1883	Harrison Ainslie & Co.	1	0
1884	Harrison Ainslie & Co.	1	0
1885	Harrison Ainslie & Co.	1	0

In 1794 the ground landlord was Mr Coupland. The furnace was charcoal-fired, blown by water and said to have been built in 174–. 1796: output 1,664 tons p.a. Excise, 400 tons p.a. actual, 325 tons Exact Return. 1805: output 175 tons. 1825: see under Backbarrow for a general comment about Harrison Ainslie's works. Truran: output 1,000 ton p.a. 1857: Ulverston haematite only used, smelted with charcoal. Cf. Backbarrow.

Dukinfield, Cheshire　　　　　　　　SJ 9496

Year	Owner	Built	In Blast
1794	T. Bateman	1	-
1825	J.D. Astley Esq. & Co.	1	0

In 1794 the ground landlord was — Astley Esq.; the furnace was coke-fired, blown by water and built in 1775. There appears to have been an attempted revival in 1825–26: the list gives no output figure but the B&W text adds the comment 'Building', while the Staffs RO version has 'Will blow in April'; both notes presumably date from March 1826. The owner's name in the B&W text is as above; the Staffs RO version lists the 'Executors of Astley Esq.'

Furness: see Askam

Haigh, Lancs.　　　　　　　　　　　[SD 6009]

Year	Owner	Built	In Blast
1794	Lindsay & Co.	2	-
1805	Lord Balcarres	4	1
1810	Lord Balcarres	4	1
1825	James Lindsay & Co.	2	0

The ground landlord in 1794 was Earl Balcarres; the furnaces were coke-fired, blown by engine and built in 1789. No output is shown in either 1805 or 1825.

Halton, Lancs　　　　　　　　　　　SD 4965

Year	Owner	Built	In Blast
1794	Halton & Co.	1	-

The ground landlord was Mr Bradshaw; the furnace was charcoal-fired, water-powered and built in 1756. The date 1754 has been written in the 'Mill' column but no plant is listed.

Harrington, Cumb.　　　　　　　　　NX 9825

Year	Owner	Built	In Blast
1856	C.H. Plevins	1	0
1857	C.H. Plevins	1	1
1858	C.H. Plevins	1	0
1859	C.H. Plevins	1	0
1860	C.H. Plevins	1	0
1861	C.H. Plevins	1	0
1862	C.H. Plevins	1	0
1870	Bain & Patterson	4	4
1871	Bain & Patterson	4	4
1872	Bain & Patterson	4	4
1873	Bain & Patterson	4	4
1874	Bain & Patterson	4	3
1875	James Bain & Co.	4	3
1876	James Bain & Co.	2	2
1877	James Bain & Co.	4	2
1878	James Bain & Co.	4	2
1879	James Bain & Co.	4	2
1880	James Bain & Co.	4	3
1881	James Bain & Co.	4	4
1882	James Bain & Co.	4	2
1883	James Bain & Co.	4	2
1884	James Bain & Co.	4	2
1885	James Bain & Co.	4	2
1886	James Bain & Co.	4	2
1887	James Bain & Co.	4	2
1888	James Bain & Co.	4	2
1889	James Bain & Co.	4	3
1890	James Bain & Co.	4	2
1891	James Bain & Co.	4	2
1892	James Bain & Co.	4	2
1893	James Bain & Co.	4	2
1894	James Bain & Co.	4	2
1895	James Bain & Co.	4	2
1896	James Bain & Co.	4	2
1897	James Bain & Co.	4	2
1898	James Bain & Co.	4	2
1899	James Bain & Co.	4	2
1900	James Bain & Co.	4	2
1901	James Bain & Co.	4	2
1902	James Bain & Co.	4	2
1903	James Bain & Co.	4	2
1904	James Bain & Co.	4	2
1905	James Bain & Co.	4	2
1906	James Bain & Co.	4	2
1907	Harrington Iron & Coal Co. Ltd	4	2
1908	Harrington Iron & Coal Co. Ltd	4	2
1909	Workington Iron & Steel Co. Ltd	-	-
1910	Workington Iron & Steel Co. Ltd	-	-
1911	Workington Iron & Steel Co. Ltd	-	-
1912	Workington Iron & Steel Co. Ltd	-	-
1913	Workington Iron & Steel Co. Ltd	-	-

1856: Works not completed. 1876: 1 furnace building. From 1909 furnace-numbers combined with those for other sites owned by the same company under Workington (qv).

Irlam: see Partington

Kirkless Hall, Wigan, Lancs.　　　　　SD 6006

Year	Owner	Built	In Blast
1858	Kirkless Hall Co.	2	2
1859	Kirkless Hall Co.	4	2
1860	Kirkless Hall Co.	4	3
1861	Kirkless Hall Co.	4	3
1862	Kirkless Hall Co.	4	3
1863	Kirkless Hall Co.	5	4
1864	Kirkless Hall Iron & Coal Co.	5	5
1865	Wigan Coal & Iron Co. Ltd	5	5
1866	Wigan Coal & Iron Co. Ltd	5	5
1867	Wigan Coal & Iron Co. Ltd	5	4
1868	Wigan Coal & Iron Co. Ltd	5	5
1869	Wigan Coal & Iron Co. Ltd	7	5
1870	Wigan Coal & Iron Co. Ltd	7	7
1871	Wigan Coal & Iron Co. Ltd	10	9
1872	Wigan Coal & Iron Co. Ltd	10	9
1873	Wigan Coal & Iron Co. Ltd	10	9
1874	Wigan Coal & Iron Co. Ltd	10	5
1875	Wigan Coal & Iron Co. Ltd	10	5
1876	Wigan Coal & Iron Co. Ltd	10	4
1877	Wigan Coal & Iron Co. Ltd	10	4
1878	Wigan Coal & Iron Co. Ltd	10	4

Year	Owner	Built	In Blast
1879	Wigan Coal & Iron Co. Ltd	10	7
1880	Wigan Coal & Iron Co. Ltd	10	6
1881	Wigan Coal & Iron Co. Ltd	10	6
1882	Wigan Coal & Iron Co. Ltd	10	7
1883	Wigan Coal & Iron Co. Ltd	10	6
1884	Wigan Coal & Iron Co. Ltd	10	5
1885	Wigan Coal & Iron Co. Ltd	10	5
1886	Wigan Coal & Iron Co. Ltd	10	5
1887	Wigan Coal & Iron Co. Ltd	10	5
1888	Wigan Coal & Iron Co. Ltd	10	4
1889	Wigan Coal & Iron Co. Ltd	10	5
1890	Wigan Coal & Iron Co. Ltd	10	5
1891	Wigan Coal & Iron Co. Ltd	10	5
1892	Wigan Coal & Iron Co. Ltd	10	5
1893	Wigan Coal & Iron Co. Ltd	10	4
1894	Wigan Coal & Iron Co. Ltd	10	10
1895	Wigan Coal & Iron Co. Ltd	10	3
1896	Wigan Coal & Iron Co. Ltd	10	3
1897	Wigan Coal & Iron Co. Ltd	10	3
1898	Wigan Coal & Iron Co. Ltd	10	4
1899	Wigan Coal & Iron Co. Ltd	10	4
1900	Wigan Coal & Iron Co. Ltd	10	4
1901	Wigan Coal & Iron Co. Ltd	10	4
1902	Wigan Coal & Iron Co. Ltd	10	4
1903	Wigan Coal & Iron Co. Ltd	10	4
1904	Wigan Coal & Iron Co. Ltd	10	3
1905	Wigan Coal & Iron Co. Ltd	10	3
1906	Wigan Coal & Iron Co. Ltd	10	4
1907	Wigan Coal & Iron Co. Ltd	10	4
1908	Wigan Coal & Iron Co. Ltd	9	3
1909	Wigan Coal & Iron Co. Ltd	9	3
1910	Wigan Coal & Iron Co. Ltd	7	3
1911	Wigan Coal & Iron Co. Ltd	5	3
1912	Wigan Coal & Iron Co. Ltd	5	3
1913	Wigan Coal & Iron Co. Ltd	7	3
1921	Wigan Coal & Iron Co. Ltd	7	-
1922	Wigan Coal & Iron Co. Ltd	5	-
1923	Wigan Coal & Iron Co. Ltd	5	-
1924	Wigan Coal & Iron Co. Ltd	5	-
1925	Wigan Coal & Iron Co. Ltd	5	-
1926	Wigan Coal & Iron Co. Ltd	5	-
1927	Wigan Coal & Iron Co. Ltd	5	-
1928	Wigan Coal & Iron Co. Ltd	5	-
1929	Wigan Coal & Iron Co. Ltd	5	-
1930	Lancashire Steel Corporation Ltd	4	-
1931	Lancashire Steel Corporation Ltd	4	-
1932	Lancashire Steel Corporation Ltd	4	-
1933	Lancashire Steel Corporation Ltd	4	-
1934	Lancashire Steel Corporation Ltd	4	-
1935	Lancashire Steel Corporation Ltd	4	-

1866: 2 furnaces in course of erection. The 4 furnaces were dismantled during the first half of 1936.

Lawton: see under North Staffs.

Leighton, Lancs.   SD 4877

Year	Owner	Built	In Blast
1794	Halton Co.	1	-
1796	—	1	1
1805	—	1	1
1810	—	1	1
1825	—	1	-

In 1794 the ground landlord was Lord Derby; the furnace was charcoal-fired, blown by water and built in 1715. 1796: output 780 tons p.a., Excise, actual and Exact Return. 1805: no output is given, nor any owner named. In 1825 the owner's name is actually given as Lord Moira in obvious error. The mistake arose from the juxtaposition of Leighton and Lord Moira's furnace at Moira (Leics.) (qv), in the 1805 list. The compiler of the 1825 list was obviously working from the earlier list and transposed the owner's name.

Lonsdale, Cumb.   NX 9718

Year	Owner	Built	In Blast
1874	Lonsdale Hematite Iron Co.	3	2
1875	Lonsdale Hematite Iron Co.	3	3
1876	Lonsdale Hematite Iron & Steel Co.	3	2
1877	Lonsdale Hematite Iron & Steel Co.	4	3
1878	Lonsdale Hematite Iron & Steel Co.	4	3
1879	Lonsdale Hematite Iron & Steel Co.	4	2
1880	Lonsdale Hematite Iron & Steel Co.	4	4
1881	Lonsdale Hematite Iron & Steel Co.	4	3
1882	Lonsdale Hematite Iron Co.	3	3
1883	Lonsdale Hematite Iron & Steel Co. Ltd	4	3
1884	Lonsdale Hematite Iron & Steel Co. Ltd	4	3
1885	Lonsdale Hematite Iron & Steel Co. Ltd	4	2
1886	Lonsdale Hematite Iron & Steel Co. Ltd	4	2
1887	Lonsdale Hematite Iron & Steel Co. Ltd	4	3
1888	Lonsdale Hematite Iron & Steel Co. Ltd	4	2
1889	Lonsdale Hematite Iron & Steel Co. Ltd	3	2
1890	Lonsdale Hematite Iron & Steel Co. Ltd	3	2
1891	Lonsdale Hematite Iron & Steel Co. Ltd	3	2
1892	Lonsdale Hematite Iron & Steel Co. Ltd	3	2
1893	Lonsdale Hematite Iron & Steel Co. Ltd	3	2
1894	Lonsdale Hematite Iron & Steel Co. Ltd	3	2
1895	Lonsdale Hematite Iron & Steel Co. Ltd	3	2
1896	Lonsdale Hematite Iron & Steel Co. Ltd	3	2
1897	Lonsdale Hematite Iron & Steel Co. Ltd	3	1
1898	Lonsdale Hematite Smelting Co. Ltd	3	2
1899	Lonsdale Hematite Smelting Co. Ltd	3	2
1900	Lonsdale Hematite Smelting Co. Ltd	3	2
1901	Lonsdale Hematite Smelting Co. Ltd	3	1
1902	Lonsdale Hematite Smelting Co. Ltd	3	2
1903	Lonsdale Hematite Smelting Co. Ltd	3	0
1904	Lonsdale Hematite Smelting Co. Ltd	3	0

1875: 1 furnace building. The owner's name appears in 1876 as North Lonsdale Hæmatite Iron & Steel Co. Ltd. This appears to be an error, since the entry is placed under Cumberland and the North Lonsdale works listed from 1877 (qv) was in Lancashire. The furnace-numbers would fit either site. In 1902–04 the owner was said to be in liquidation.

Lowther, Workington, Cumb. NX 9929

Year	Owner	Built	In Blast
1872	North of England Iron Co.	2	1
1873	North of England Iron Co.	2	1
1874	North of England Iron Co.	2	0
1875	Lowther Hematite Iron Co. Ltd	2	2
1876	Lowther Hematite Iron Co. Ltd	2	2
1877	Lowther Hematite Iron Co. Ltd	2	1
1878	Lowther Hematite Iron Co. Ltd	2	1
1879	Lowther Hematite Iron Co. Ltd	2	0
1880	Lowther Hematite Iron Co. Ltd	3	2
1881	Lowther Hematite Iron Co. Ltd	3	1
1882	Lowther Hematite Iron Co. Ltd	3	3
1883	Lowther Hematite Iron Co. Ltd	3	3
1884	Lowther Hematite Iron Co. Ltd	3	3
1885	Lowther Hematite Iron Co. Ltd	3	2
1886	Lowther Hematite Iron Co. Ltd	3	2
1887	Lowther Hematite Iron Co. Ltd	3	3
1888	Lowther Hematite Iron Co. Ltd	3	2
1889	Lowther Hematite Iron Co. Ltd	3	2
1890	Lowther Hematite Iron Co. Ltd	3	2
1891	Lowther Hematite Iron Co. Ltd	3	1
1892	Lowther Hematite Iron Co. Ltd	3	2
1893	Lowther Hematite Iron Co. Ltd	3	0
1894	Lowther Hematite Iron Co. Ltd	3	0
1895	Lowther Hematite Iron Co. Ltd	3	0
1896	The Proprietor of Lowther Ironworks	3	0
1897	Lowther Hematite Iron & Steel Co. Ltd	3	1
1898	Lowther Hematite Iron & Steel Co. Ltd	3	2
1899	Lowther Hematite Iron & Steel Co. Ltd	3	2
1900	Lowther Hematite Iron & Steel Co. Ltd	3	2
1901	Lowther Hematite Iron & Steel Co. Ltd	3	0
1902	Lowther Hematite Iron & Steel Co. Ltd	3	0
1903	Lowther Hematite Iron & Steel Co. Ltd	3	0
1904	Lowther Hematite Iron & Steel Co. Ltd	3	0
1905	Lowther Hematite Iron & Steel Co. Ltd	3	0
1906	Cammell Laird & Co. Ltd	3	2
1907	Cammell Laird & Co. Ltd	3	1
1908	Workington Iron Co. Ltd	3	1
1909	Workington Iron & Steel Co. Ltd	-	-
1910	Workington Iron & Steel Co. Ltd	-	-
1911	Workington Iron & Steel Co. Ltd	-	-
1912	Workington Iron & Steel Co. Ltd	-	-
1913	Workington Iron & Steel Co. Ltd	-	-

1878: furnaces restarted in Jan. 1880. In 1903–05 the company was said to be in liquidation. From 1909 furnace-numbers combined with others owned by the same company under Workington (qv).

Marron: see New Yard

Maryport, Cumb. NY 0336

Year	Owner	Built	In Blast
1870	Maryport Iron Co.	4	4
1871	Maryport Iron Co.	4	3
1872	Gilmour & Co.	6	6
1873	Gilmour & Co.	6	6
1874	Gilmour & Co.	6	4
1875	Maryport Hematite Iron Co.	6	4
1876	Maryport Hematite Iron Co.	6	3
1877	Maryport Hematite Iron Co.	6	3
1878	Maryport Hematite Iron Co.	6	6
1879	Maryport Hematite Iron Co.	6	6
1880	Maryport Hematite Iron Co.	6	6
1881	Maryport Hematite Iron Co.	6	6
1882	Maryport Hematite Iron Co.	6	5
1883	Maryport Hematite Iron & Steel Co. Ltd	6	3
1884	Maryport Hematite Iron & Steel Co. Ltd	6	3
1885	Maryport Hematite Iron & Steel Co. Ltd	6	3
1886	Maryport Hematite Iron & Steel Co. Ltd	6	3
1887	Maryport Hematite Iron & Steel Co. Ltd	6	4
1888	Maryport Hematite Iron & Steel Co. Ltd	6	3
1889	Maryport Hematite Iron & Steel Co. Ltd	6	3
1890	Maryport Hematite Iron & Steel Co. Ltd	4	3
1891	Maryport Hematite Iron & Steel Co. Ltd	4	1
1892	Maryport Hematite Iron & Steel Co. Ltd	4	0
1893	Maryport Hematite Iron & Steel Co. Ltd	4	0
1894	The Owners of the Maryport Ironworks	5	0
1895	The Owners of the Maryport Ironworks	5	0
1896	The Owners of the Maryport Ironworks	5	0

1895–96: The owners are identified as W.B. Peat & Co., 125 Ramsden Square, Barrow in Furness.

Maryport: see also Solway

Millom, Cumb. SD 1879

Year	Owner	Built	In Blast
1870	Cumberland Iron Mining & Smelting Co. Ltd	5	4
1871	Cumberland Iron Mining & Smelting Co. Ltd	6	5

Year	Company		
1872	Cumberland Iron Mining & Smelting Co. Ltd	6	5
1873	Cumberland Iron Mining & Smelting Co. Ltd	8	5
1874	Cumberland Iron Mining & Smelting Co. Ltd	8	5
1875	Cumberland Iron Mining & Smelting Co. Ltd	8	4
1876	Cumberland Iron Mining & Smelting Co. Ltd	8	2
1877	Cumberland Iron Mining & Smelting Co. Ltd	6	4
1878	Cumberland Iron Mining & Smelting Co. Ltd	6	3
1879	Cumberland Iron Mining & Smelting Co. Ltd	6	3
1880	Cumberland Iron Mining Smelting Co. Ltd	6	5
1881	Cumberland Iron Mining & Smelting Co. Ltd	6	6
1882	Cumberland Iron Mining & Smelting Co. Ltd	6	5
1883	Cumberland Iron Mining & Smelting Co. Ltd	6	4
1884	Cumberland Iron Mining & Smelting Co. Ltd	6	4
1885	Cumberland Iron Mining & Smelting Co. Ltd	6	3
1886	Cumberland Iron Mining & Smelting Co. Ltd	6	3
1887	Cumberland Iron Mining & Smelting Co. Ltd	6	4
1888	Cumberland Iron Mining & Smelting Co. Ltd	6	4
1889	Cumberland Iron Mining & Smelting Co. Ltd	6	3
1890	Millom & Askam Hematite Iron Co. Ltd	6	3
1891	Millom & Askam Hematite Iron Co. Ltd	6	2
1892	Millom & Askam Hematite Iron Co. Ltd	6	3
1893	Millom & Askam Hematite Iron Co. Ltd	6	4
1894	Millom & Askam Hematite Iron Co. Ltd	6	4
1895	Millom & Askam Hematite Iron Co. Ltd	6	4
1896	Millom & Askam Hematite Iron Co. Ltd	6	4
1897	Millom & Askam Hematite Iron Co. Ltd	6	4
1898	Millom & Askam Hematite Iron Co. Ltd	6	4
1899	Millom & Askam Hematite Iron Co. Ltd	6	4
1900	Millom & Askam Hematite Iron Co. Ltd	6	3
1901	Millom & Askam Hematite Iron Co. Ltd	6	3
1902	Millom & Askam Hematite Iron Co. Ltd	6	3
1903	Millom & Askam Hematite Iron Co. Ltd	6	3
1904	Millom & Askam Hematite Iron Co. Ltd	6	1
1905	Millom & Askam Hematite Iron Co. Ltd	6	3
1906	Millom & Askam Hematite Iron Co. Ltd	6	3
1907	Millom & Askam Hematite Iron Co. Ltd	6	3
1908	Millom & Askam Hematite Iron Co. Ltd	6	2
1909	Millom & Askam Hematite Iron Co. Ltd	6	2
1910	Millom & Askam Hematite Iron Co. Ltd	6	3
1911	Millom & Askam Hematite Iron Co. Ltd	6	2
1912	Millom & Askam Hematite Iron Co. Ltd	6	2
1913	Millom & Askam Hematite Iron Co. Ltd	6	3
1921	Millom & Askam Hematite Iron Co. Ltd	7	-
1922	Millom & Askam Hematite Iron Co. Ltd	7	-
1923	Millom & Askam Hematite Iron Co. Ltd	7	-
1924	Millom & Askam Hematite Iron Co. Ltd	7	-
1925	Millom & Askam Hematite Iron Co. Ltd	7	-
1926	Millom & Askam Hematite Iron Co. Ltd	6	-
1927	Millom & Askam Hematite Iron Co. Ltd	6	-
1928	Millom & Askam Hematite Iron Co. Ltd	5	-
1929	Millom & Askam Hematite Iron Co. Ltd	5	-
1930	Millom & Askam Hematite Iron Co. Ltd	5	-
1931	Millom & Askam Hematite Iron Co. Ltd	5	-
1932	Millom & Askam Hematite Iron Co. Ltd	4	-
1933	Millom & Askam Hematite Iron Co. Ltd	3	-
1934	Millom & Askam Hematite Iron Co. Ltd	3	-
1935	Millom & Askam Hematite Iron Co. Ltd	3	-
1936	Millom & Askam Hematite Iron Co. Ltd	3	-
1937	Millom & Askam Hematite Iron Co. Ltd	3	-
1938	Millom & Askam Hematite Iron Co. Ltd	3	-
1939	Millom & Askam Hematite Iron Co. Ltd	3	-
1940	Millom & Askam Hematite Iron Co. Ltd	3	-
1941	Millom & Askam Hematite Iron Co. Ltd	3	-
1942	Millom & Askam Hematite Iron Co. Ltd	3	-
1943	Millom & Askam Hematite Iron Co. Ltd	3	-
1944	Millom & Askam Hematite Iron Co. Ltd	3	-
1945	Millom & Askam Hematite Iron Co. Ltd	3	-

Year	Owner	Built	In Blast
1946	Millom & Askam Hematite Iron Co. Ltd	3	-
1947	Millom & Askam Hematite Iron Co. Ltd	3	-
1948	Millom & Askam Hematite Iron Co. Ltd	3	-
1949	Millom & Askam Hematite Iron Co. Ltd	3	-
1950	Millom & Askam Hematite Iron Co. Ltd	3	-
1951	Millom & Askam Hematite Iron Co. Ltd	3	-
1952	Millom & Askam Hematite Iron Co. Ltd	3	-
1953	Millom & Askam Hematite Iron Co. Ltd	3	-
1954	Millom & Askam Hematite Iron Co. Ltd	3	-
1955	Millom & Askam Hematite Iron Co. Ltd	2	-
1956	Millom & Askam Hematite Iron Co. Ltd	2	-
1957	Millom & Askam Hematite Iron Co. Ltd	2	-
1958	Millom Hematite Ore & Iron Co. Ltd	2	-
1959	Millom Hematite Ore & Iron Co. Ltd	3	-
1960	Millom Hematite Ore & Iron Co. Ltd	3	-
1961	Millom Hematite Ore & Iron Co. Ltd	3	-
1962	Millom Hematite Ore & Iron Co. Ltd	3	-
1963	Millom Hematite Ore & Iron Co. Ltd	3	-
1964	Millom Hematite Ore & Iron Co. Ltd	3	-
1965	Millom Hematite Ore & Iron Co. Ltd	3	-
1966	Millom Hematite Ore & Iron Co. Ltd	3	-
1967	Millom Hematite Ore & Iron Co. Ltd	3	-

Moss Bay, Workington, Cumb. NX 9827

Year	Owner	Built	In Blast
1872	Moss Bay Hematite Iron Co.	2	2
1873	Moss Bay Hematite Iron Co.	3	2
1874	Moss Bay Hematite Iron Co.	3	2
1875	Moss Bay Hematite Iron Co.	3	3
1876	Moss Bay Hematite Iron & Steel Co.	3	3
1877	Moss Bay Hematite Iron & Steel Co.	3	3
1878	Moss Bay Hematite Iron & Steel Co.	3	2
1879	Moss Bay Hematite Iron & Steel Co.	3	3
1880	Moss Bay Hematite Iron & Steel Co.	4	3
1881	Moss Bay Hematite Iron & Steel Co. Ltd	4	4
1882	Moss Bay Hematite Iron & Steel Co. Ltd	4	4
1883	Moss Bay Hematite Iron & Steel Co. Ltd	4	3
1884	Moss Bay Hematite Iron & Steel Co. Ltd	4	3
1885	Moss Bay Hematite Iron & Steel Co. Ltd	4	2
1886	Moss Bay Hematite Iron & Steel Co. Ltd	4	2
1887	Moss Bay Hematite Iron & Steel Co. Ltd	4	3
1888	Moss Bay Hematite Iron & Steel Co. Ltd	4	3
1889	Moss Bay Hematite Iron & Steel Co. Ltd	4	3
1890	Moss Bay Hematite Iron & Steel Co. Ltd	4	3
1891	Moss Bay Hematite Iron & Steel Co. Ltd	4	1
1892	Moss Bay Hematite Iron & Steel Co. Ltd	4	2
1893	Moss Bay Hematite Iron & Steel Co. Ltd	4	2
1894	Moss Bay Hematite Iron & Steel Co. Ltd	4	2
1895	Moss Bay Hematite Iron & Steel Co. Ltd	4	2
1896	Moss Bay Hematite Iron & Steel Co. Ltd	4	2
1897	Moss Bay Hematite Iron & Steel Co. Ltd	4	2
1898	Moss Bay Hematite Iron & Steel Co. Ltd	4	2
1899	Moss Bay Hematite Iron & Steel Co. Ltd	4	3
1900	Moss Bay Hematite Iron & Steel Co. Ltd	4	2
1901	Moss Bay Hematite Iron & Steel Co. Ltd	4	3
1902	Moss Bay Hematite Iron & Steel Co. Ltd	4	3
1903	Moss Bay Hematite Iron & Steel Co. Ltd	4	3
1904	Moss Bay Hematite Iron & Steel Co. Ltd	4	3
1905	Moss Bay Hematite Iron & Steel Co. Ltd	4	3
1906	Moss Bay Hematite Iron & Steel Co. Ltd	4	3
1907	Moss Bay Hematite Iron & Steel Co. Ltd	4	3
1908	Moss Bay Hematite Iron & Steel Co. Ltd	4	3
1909	Workington Iron & Steel Co. Ltd	-	-
1910	Workington Iron & Steel Co. Ltd	-	-
1911	Workington Iron & Steel Co. Ltd	-	-
1912	Workington Iron & Steel Co. Ltd	-	-
1913	Workington Iron & Steel Co. Ltd	-	-

From 1909 furnace-numbers are included with those for other sites owned by the same company under Workington (qv).

Newland, Lancs. SD 2979

Year	Owner	Built	In Blast
1794	Executors of G. Knott	1	-
1796	—	1	1
1805	Knott & Co.	1	1
1810	Knott & Co.	1	1
1825	Harrison & Co.	1	0
1854	Harrison Ainslie & Co.	1	1
1855	Harrison Ainslie & Co.	1	1
1856	Harrison Ainslie & Co.	1	1
1857	Harrison Ainslie & Co.	1	1
1858	Harrison Ainslie & Co.	1	0
1859	Harrison Ainslie & Co.	1	1
1860	Harrison Ainslie & Co.	1	1
1861	Harrison Ainslie & Co.	1	1
1862	Harrison Ainslie & Co.	-	-

Year	Owner	Built	In Blast
1863	Harrison Ainslie & Co.	-	-
1864	Harrison Ainslie & Co.	1	1
1865	Harrison Ainslie & Co.	1	1
1866	Harrison Ainslie & Co.	-	-
1867	Harrison Ainslie & Co.	-	-
1868	Harrison Ainslie & Co.	-	-
1869	Harrison Ainslie & Co.	-	-
1870	Harrison Ainslie & Co.	-	-
1871	Harrison Ainslie & Co.	-	-
1872	Harrison Ainslie & Co.	-	-
1873	Harrison Ainslie & Co.	-	-
1874	Harrison Ainslie & Co.	-	-
1875	Harrison Ainslie & Co.	-	-
1876	Harrison Ainslie & Co.	-	-
1877	Harrison Ainslie & Co.	-	-
1878	Harrison Ainslie & Co.	-	-
1879	Harrison Ainslie & Co.	-	-
1880	Harrison Ainslie & Co.	-	-
1881	Harrison Ainslie & Co.	-	-
1882	Harrison Ainslie & Co.	1	0
1883	Harrison Ainslie & Co.	1	1
1884	Harrison Ainslie & Co.	1	1
1885	Harrison Ainslie & Co.	1	0
1886	Harrison Ainslie & Co.	2	1
1887	Harrison Ainslie & Co.	1	1
1888	Harrison Ainslie & Co.	1	1
1889	Harrison Ainslie & Co.	1	0
1890	Harrison Ainslie & Co.	1	1
1891	Harrison Ainslie & Co.	1	0
1892	Harrison Ainslie & Co.	1	0
1893	Harrison Ainslie & Co. Ltd	1	0
1894	Harrison Ainslie & Co. Ltd	1	0
1895	Harrison Ainslie & Co. Ltd	1	0
1896	Harrison Ainslie & Co. Ltd	1	0
1897	Harrison Ainslie & Co. Ltd	1	0

In 1794 the executors of G. Knott were also ground landlords; the furnace was charcoal-fired, blown by water and built in 1750. There was also a finery and a chafery. 1796: output 700 tons p.a. Excise, actual and Exact Return. 1805: No output shown. 1825: see under Backbarrow for a general note about Harrison Ainslie's works. Truran: output 1,200 tons p.a. In 1862–63 and 1866–81 furnace-numbers for Newland are combined with those for Backbarrow; in 1882 *Mineral Statistics* lists the two furnaces at Newland and Backbarrow separately but gives the number in use at the latter as 1½.

New Yard, Workington, Cumb.   NX 9828

Year	Owner	Built	In Blast
1881	Kirk Brothers & Co.	1	1
1882	Kirk Brothers & Co.	1	1
1883	Kirk Brothers & Co.	1	1
1884	Kirk Brothers & Co.	1	1
1885	Kirk Brothers & Co.	1	1
1886	Kirk Brothers & Co.	1	0
1887	Kirk Brothers & Co.	1	1
1888	Kirk Brothers & Co.	1	0
1889	Kirk Brothers & Co.	1	1
1890	Kirk Brothers & Co.	1	1
1891	Kirk Brothers & Co.	1	1
1892	Kirk Brothers & Co.	1	1
1893	Kirk Brothers & Co.	1	0
1894	Kirk Brothers & Co.	1	1
1895	Kirk Brothers & Co.	1	1
1896	Kirk Brothers & Co.	1	1
1897	Kirk Brothers & Co.	1	1
1898	Kirk Brothers & Co.	1	1
1899	Kirk Brothers & Co. Ltd	1	1
1900	Kirk Brothers & Co. Ltd	1	1
1901	Kirk Brothers & Co. Ltd	1	0
1902	Kirk Brothers & Co. Ltd	1	1
1903	Kirk Brothers & Co. Ltd	1	1
1904	Kirk Brothers & Co. Ltd	1	1
1905	Kirk Brothers & Co. Ltd	1	1
1906	Kirk Brothers & Co. Ltd	1	1
1907	Kirk Brothers & Co. Ltd	1	1
1908	Kirk Brothers & Co. Ltd	1	0
1910	Workington Iron & Steel Co. Ltd	-	-
1911	Workington Iron & Steel Co. Ltd	-	-
1912	Workington Iron & Steel Co. Ltd	-	-
1913	Workington Iron & Steel Co. Ltd	-	-

In 1886–87 the site is listed under Marron. There is no entry for New Yard in 1909, the year in which furnace-numbers for the other Workington Iron & Steel Co. works are first combined, although from 1910 it is included (see Workington).

North Lancashire, Lancs.

Year	Owner	Built	In Blast
1875	North Lancashire Iron Co.	3	0

The 1875 entry includes a note that the furnaces were blown-in in May 1876 but there are no further returns under this heading, which is perhaps an error for North Lonsdale (qv).

North Lonsdale, Ulverston, Lancs.   SD 3077

Year	Owner	Built	In Blast
1877	North Lonsdale Iron & Steel Co. Ltd	3	3
1878	North Lonsdale Iron & Steel Co. Ltd	3	3
1879	North Lonsdale Iron & Steel Co. Ltd	4	3
1880	North Lonsdale Iron & Steel Co. Ltd	4	3
1881	North Lonsdale Iron & Steel Co. Ltd	4	4
1882	North Lonsdale Iron & Steel Co. Ltd	4	4
1883	North Lonsdale Iron & Steel Co. Ltd	4	4
1884	North Lonsdale Iron & Steel Co. Ltd	4	3
1885	North Lonsdale Iron & Steel Co. Ltd	4	3
1886	North Lonsdale Iron & Steel Co. Ltd	4	3
1887	North Lonsdale Iron & Steel Co. Ltd	4	3
1888	North Lonsdale Iron & Steel Co. Ltd	4	3
1889	North Lonsdale Iron & Steel Co. Ltd	4	3
1890	North Lonsdale Iron & Steel Co. Ltd	4	3
1891	North Lonsdale Iron & Steel Co. Ltd	4	3
1892	North Lonsdale Iron & Steel Co. Ltd	4	2
1893	North Lonsdale Iron & Steel Co. Ltd	4	3
1894	North Lonsdale Iron & Steel Co. Ltd	4	3
1895	North Lonsdale Iron & Steel Co. Ltd	4	2
1896	North Lonsdale Iron & Steel Co. Ltd	4	3
1897	North Lonsdale Iron & Steel Co. Ltd	4	3
1898	North Lonsdale Iron & Steel Co. Ltd	4	3
1899	North Lonsdale Iron & Steel Co. Ltd	4	3
1900	North Lonsdale Iron & Steel Co. Ltd	4	3
1901	North Lonsdale Iron & Steel Co. Ltd	4	3
1902	North Lonsdale Iron & Steel Co. Ltd	4	2

Year	Owner	Built	In Blast
1903	North Lonsdale Iron & Steel Co. Ltd	4	2
1904	North Lonsdale Iron & Steel Co. Ltd	4	2
1905	North Lonsdale Iron & Steel Co. Ltd	4	2
1906	North Lonsdale Iron & Steel Co. Ltd	4	2
1907	North Lonsdale Iron & Steel Co. Ltd	4	2
1908	North Lonsdale Iron & Steel Co. Ltd	4	2
1909	North Lonsdale Iron & Steel Co. Ltd	4	2
1910	North Lonsdale Iron & Steel Co. Ltd	4	2
1911	North Lonsdale Iron & Steel Co. Ltd	4	2
1912	North Lonsdale Iron & Steel Co. Ltd	4	2
1913	North Lonsdale Iron & Steel Co. Ltd	4	2
1921	North Lonsdale Iron & Steel Co. Ltd	4	-
1922	North Lonsdale Iron & Steel Co. Ltd	4	-
1923	North Lonsdale Iron & Steel Co. Ltd	4	-
1924	North Lonsdale Iron & Steel Co. Ltd	4	-
1925	North Lonsdale Iron & Steel Co. Ltd	4	-
1926	North Lonsdale Iron & Steel Co. Ltd	4	-
1927	North Lonsdale Iron & Steel Co. Ltd	4	-
1928	North Lonsdale Iron & Steel Co. Ltd	4	-
1929	North Lonsdale Iron & Steel Co. Ltd	4	-
1930	North Lonsdale Iron & Steel Co. Ltd	4	-
1931	North Lonsdale Iron & Steel Co. Ltd	4	-
1932	North Lonsdale Iron & Steel Co. Ltd	4	-
1933	North Lonsdale Iron & Steel Co. Ltd	4	-
1934	North Lonsdale Iron & Steel Co. Ltd	4	-
1935	Millom & Askam Hematite Iron Co. Ltd	4	-
1936	Millom & Askam Hematite Iron Co. Ltd	4	-
1937	Millom & Askam Hematite Iron Co. Ltd	4	-
1938	Millom & Askam Hematite Iron Co. Ltd	4	-
1939	North Lonsdale Iron & Steel Co. Ltd	4	-
1940	North Lonsdale Iron & Steel Co. Ltd	4	-
1941	North Lonsdale Iron & Steel Co. Ltd	4	-
1942	North Lonsdale Iron & Steel Co. Ltd	4	-
1943	North Lonsdale Iron & Steel Co. Ltd	4	-
1944	North Lonsdale Iron & Steel Co. Ltd	4	-
1945	North Lonsdale Iron & Steel Co. Ltd	4	-
1946	North Lonsdale Iron & Steel Co. Ltd	4	-

1883: 1 furnace at work 7 months. Cf. Lonsdale and North Lancashire for possible confusion with other sites.

North of England: see Lowther

North Western Hematite: see West Cumberland

Outwood, Radcliffe, Lancs. [SD 7706]

Year	Owner	Built	In Blast
1874	Outwood Iron Co. Ltd	1	1
1875	Outwood Iron Co. Ltd	1	1
1876	Outwood Iron Co. Ltd	1	1
1877	Outwood Iron Co. Ltd	1	1
1878	Outwood Iron Co. Ltd	1	1
1879	Outwood Iron Co. Ltd	1	1
1880	Outwood Iron Co. Ltd	1	1
1881	Outwood Iron Co. Ltd	1	1
1882	Outwood Iron Co. Ltd	1	1
1883	Outwood Iron Co. Ltd	1	1
1884	Outwood Iron Co. Ltd	1	1
1885	Outwood Iron Co. Ltd	1	0
1886	Outwood Iron Co. Ltd	1	1
1887	Outwood Iron Co. Ltd	1	0

1883: Production estimated. The address of the works is also given as Stoneclough.

Partington, Lancs. [SJ 7191]

Year	Owner	Built	In Blast
1913	Partington Steel & Iron Co. Ltd	3	2
1921	Partington Steel & Iron Co. Ltd	6	-
1922	Partington Steel & Iron Co. Ltd	6	-
1923	Partington Steel & Iron Co. Ltd	6	-
1924	Partington Steel & Iron Co. Ltd	6	-
1925	Partington Steel & Iron Co. Ltd	6	-
1926	Partington Steel & Iron Co. Ltd	6	-
1927	Partington Steel & Iron Co. Ltd	6	-
1928	Partington Steel & Iron Co. Ltd	6	-
1929	Partington Steel & Iron Co. Ltd	6	-
1930	Lancashire Steel Corporation Ltd	5	-
1931	Lancashire Steel Corporation Ltd	4	-
1932	Lancashire Steel Corporation Ltd	4	-
1933	Lancashire Steel Corporation Ltd	4	-
1934	Lancashire Steel Corporation Ltd	4	-
1935	Lancashire Steel Corporation Ltd	4	-
1936	Lancashire Steel Corporation Ltd	4	-
1937	Lancashire Steel Corporation Ltd	5	-
1938	Lancashire Steel Corporation Ltd	5	-
1939	Lancashire Steel Corporation Ltd	5	-
1940	Lancashire Steel Corporation Ltd	5	-
1941	Lancashire Steel Corporation Ltd	5	-
1942	Lancashire Steel Corporation Ltd	5	-
1943	Lancashire Steel Corporation Ltd	5	-
1944	Lancashire Steel Corporation Ltd	5	-
1945	Lancashire Steel Corporation Ltd	5	-
1946	Lancashire Steel Corporation Ltd	4	-
1947	Lancashire Steel Corporation Ltd	4	-
1948	Lancashire Steel Corporation Ltd	4	-
1949	Lancashire Steel Corporation Ltd	4	-
1950	Lancashire Steel Corporation Ltd	4	-
1951	Lancashire Steel Corporation Ltd	4	-
1952	Lancashire Steel Corporation Ltd	4	-
1953	Lancashire Steel Corporation Ltd	3	-
1954	Lancashire Steel Corporation Ltd	3	-
1955	Lancashire Steel Corporation Ltd	3	-
1956	Lancashire Steel Corporation Ltd	4	-
1957	Lancashire Steel Corporation Ltd	3	-
1958	Lancashire Steel Manufacturing Co. Ltd	3	-
1959	Lancashire Steel Manufacturing Co. Ltd	3	-
1960	Lancashire Steel Manufacturing Co. Ltd	4	
1961	Lancashire Steel Manufacturing Co. Ltd	4	-
1962	Lancashire Steel Manufacturing Co. Ltd	4	-
1963	Lancashire Steel Manufacturing Co. Ltd	4	-
1964	Lancashire Steel Manufacturing Co. Ltd	4	-
1965	Lancashire Steel Manufacturing Co. Ltd	4	-
1966	Lancashire Steel Manufacturing Co. Ltd	4	-

Year	Owner	Built	In Blast
1967	Lancashire Steel Manufacturing Co. Ltd	4	-
1968	Lancashire Steel Manufacturing Co. Ltd	4	-
1969	Lancashire Steel Manufacturing Co. Ltd	4	-
1970	British Steel Corporation	4	-

From 1953 the location of the works is given as Irlam.

Parton, Cumb. NX 9720

Year	Owner	Built	In Blast
1872	Blair & Co.	2	0
1873	Blair & Vance	2	0
1874	Parton Hæmatite Iron Co. Ltd	2	0
1875	Parton Hæmatite Iron Co. Ltd	2	2
1876	Parton Hæmatite Iron Co. Ltd	2	2
1877	Parton Hæmatite Iron Co. Ltd	2	0
1878	Parton Hæmatite Iron Co. Ltd	2	0
1879	Parton Hæmatite Iron Co. Ltd	2	0
1880	Parton Hæmatite Iron Co. Ltd	2	1
1881	Parton Hæmatite Iron Co. Ltd	2	1
1882	Parton Hæmatite Iron Co. Ltd	2	2
1883	Parton Hæmatite Iron Co. Ltd	2	2
1884	Parton Hæmatite Iron Co. Ltd	3	0
1885	Parton Hæmatite Iron Co. Ltd	2	0
1886	Parton Hæmatite Iron Co. Ltd	2	0
1887	Parton Hæmatite Iron Co. Ltd	2	0
1888	Parton Hæmatite Iron Co. Ltd	2	0
1889	Parton Hæmatite Iron Co. Ltd	2	0
1890	Parton Hæmatite Iron Co. Ltd	2	0
1891	Parton Hæmatite Iron Co. Ltd	2	0

1883: In liquidation; furnaces at work 4 months. 1889–91: In liquidation.

Radcliffe: see Outwood

Seaton, Cumb. NY 0129

Year	Owner	Built	In Blast
1794	Seaton Co.	1	-
1796	—	1	1
1805	Spedding & Co.	1	1
1810	Spedding & Co.	1	1
1825	—	1	-
1856	S.W. Smith & Co.	2	0
1857	S.W. Smith & Co.	1	1
1858	S.W. Smith & Co.	1	0
1859	S.W. Smith & Co.	1	0
1860	S.W. Smith & Co.	1	0
1861	S.W. Smith & Co.	1	0
1862	S.W. Smith & Co.	1	0

The ground landlord in 1794 was Mr Christian; the furnace was coke-fired, blown by water, built in 1760. There were 3 fineries, a chafery and a slitting mill. 1796: Excise return 2,080 tons p.a.; 'may make' 1,200 tons p.a. (i.e. 40 or 24 tons a week), Exact Return 240 tons. 1805: output 670 tons p.a. In 1796, 1805 and 1810 the works is called Bearpot. In 1825 Seaton is bracketed with Harrison Ainslie's works (see Backbarrow) and the owner's name is given (wrongly) as Harrison & Co. It is not clear whether the furnace was in blast or not, although no output is shown. 1856: Works not completed.

Solway, Maryport, Cumb. NY 0235

Year	Owner	Built	In Blast
1870	Solway Hematite Iron Co. Ltd	2	2
1871	Solway Hematite Iron Co. Ltd	2	2
1872	Solway Hematite Iron Co. Ltd	4	3
1873	Solway Hematite Iron Co. Ltd	4	4
1874	Solway Hematite Iron Co. Ltd	4	3
1875	Solway Hematite Iron Co. Ltd	4	3
1876	Solway Hematite Iron Co. Ltd	4	2
1877	Solway Hematite Iron Co. Ltd	4	3
1878	Solway Hematite Iron Co. Ltd	4	3
1879	Solway Hematite Iron Co. Ltd	4	2
1880	Solway Hematite Iron Co. Ltd	4	2
1881	Solway Hematite Iron Co. Ltd	4	4
1882	Solway Hematite Iron Co. Ltd	4	4
1883	Solway Hematite Iron Co. Ltd	4	3
1884	Solway Hematite Iron Co. Ltd	2	2
1885	Solway Hematite Iron Co. Ltd	2	2
1886	Solway Hematite Iron Co. Ltd	2	1
1887	Solway Hematite Iron Co. Ltd	2	2
1888	Solway Hematite Iron Co. Ltd	2	2
1889	Solway Hematite Iron Co. Ltd	2	2
1890	Solway Hematite Iron Co. Ltd	2	2
1891	Solway Hematite Iron Co. Ltd	2	1
1892	Solway Hematite Iron Co. Ltd	3	2
1893	Solway Hematite Iron Co. Ltd	3	2
1894	Solway Hematite Iron Co. Ltd	2	2
1895	Solway Hematite Iron Co. Ltd (W.B. Peat & Co.)	2	0
1896	Charles Cammell & Co. Ltd	3	1
1897	Charles Cammell & Co. Ltd	3	2
1898	Charles Cammell & Co. Ltd	3	2
1899	Charles Cammell & Co. Ltd	2	2
1900	Charles Cammell & Co. Ltd	3	2
1901	Charles Cammell & Co. Ltd	3	3
1902	Charles Cammell & Co. Ltd	3	3
1903	Cammell Laird & Co. Ltd	3	2
1904	Cammell Laird & Co. Ltd	3	2
1905	Cammell Laird & Co. Ltd	3	2
1906	Cammell Laird & Co. Ltd	3	2
1907	Cammell Laird & Co. Ltd	3	2
1908	Cammell Laird & Co. Ltd	3	0
1909	Workington Iron & Steel Co. Ltd	-	-
1910	Workington Iron & Steel Co. Ltd	-	-
1911	Workington Iron & Steel Co. Ltd	-	-
1912	Workington Iron & Steel Co. Ltd	-	-
1913	Workington Iron & Steel Co. Ltd	-	-

1870: 1 furnace building; entry headed Maryport. From 1909 furnace-numbers are combined with other sites owned by the same company under Workington (qv).

Ulverston: see Barrow Hæmatite; North Lonsdale

West Cumberland, Workington, Cumb. NX 9930

Year	Owner	Built	In Blast
1863	West Cumberland Hematite Iron Co. Ltd	4	2
1864	West Cumberland Hematite Iron Co. Ltd	5	3
1865	West Cumberland Hematite Iron Co. Ltd	5	3
1866	West Cumberland Hematite Iron Co. Ltd	5	4
1867	West Cumberland Hematite Iron Co. Ltd	5	3
1868	West Cumberland Hematite Iron Co. Ltd	5	4
1869	West Cumberland Hematite Iron Co. Ltd	5	3
1870	West Cumberland Hematite Iron Co. Ltd	5	4
1871	West Cumberland Hematite Iron Co. Ltd	5	5
1872	West Cumberland Iron & Steel Co. Ltd	6	4
1873	West Cumberland Iron & Steel Co. Ltd	6	4
1874	West Cumberland Iron & Steel Co. Ltd	6	4
1875	West Cumberland Iron & Steel Co. Ltd	6	4
1876	West Cumberland Iron & Steel Co. Ltd	6	3
1877	West Cumberland Iron & Steel Co. Ltd	6	3
1878	West Cumberland Iron & Steel Co. Ltd	6	3
1879	West Cumberland Iron & Steel Co. Ltd	6	3
1880	West Cumberland Iron & Steel Co. Ltd	6	5
1881	West Cumberland Iron & Steel Co. Ltd	6	5
1882	West Cumberland Iron & Steel Co. Ltd	6	5
1883	West Cumberland Iron & Steel Co. Ltd	6	4
1884	West Cumberland Iron & Steel Co. Ltd	6	5
1885	West Cumberland Iron & Steel Co. Ltd	6	4
1886	West Cumberland Iron & Steel Co. Ltd	6	3
1887	West Cumberland Iron & Steel Co. Ltd	6	4
1888	West Cumberland Iron & Steel Co. Ltd	6	4
1889	West Cumberland Iron & Steel Co. Ltd	6	4
1890	West Cumberland Iron & Steel Co. Ltd	6	3
1891	West Cumberland Iron & Steel Co. Ltd	6	1
1892	West Cumberland Iron & Steel Co. Ltd	6	0
1893	West Cumberland Iron & Steel Co. Ltd	6	0
1894	West Cumberland Iron & Steel Co. Ltd	6	0
1895	West Cumberland Iron & Steel Co. Ltd (W.B. Peat & Co.)	6	0
1896	West Cumberland Iron & Steel Co. Ltd (W.B. Peat & Co.)	6	0
1897	West Cumberland Iron & Steel Co. Ltd (W.B. Peat & Co.)	6	0
1898	North Western Hematite Steel Co. Ltd	6	0
1899	North Western Hematite Steel Co. Ltd	5	2
1900	North Western Hematite Steel Co. Ltd	5	1
1901	North Western Hematite Steel Co. Ltd	5	0
1902	North Western Hematite Steel Co. Ltd	5	0

Whitehaven: see Cleator Moor

Wigan: see Kirkless Hall

Workington, Cumb. NX 9929

Year	Owner	Built	In Blast
1857	Workington Iron Co.	2	0
1858	Workington Iron Co.	2	2
1859	Workington Iron Co.	6	2
1860	Workington Iron Co.	6	4
1861	Workington Iron Co.	6	4
1862	Workington Iron Co.	6	3
1863	Workington Iron Co.	6	3
1864	Workington Iron Co.	6	4
1865	Workington Iron Co.	6	2
1866	Workington Iron Co.	6	4
1867	Workington Iron Co.	6	2
1868	Workington Iron Co. Ltd	6	2
1869	Workington Iron Co. Ltd	6	2
1870	Workington Iron Co. Ltd	6	2
1871	Workington Iron Co. Ltd	6	4
1872	Workington Iron Co. Ltd	6	4
1873	Workington Iron Co. Ltd	6	4
1874	Workington Iron Co. Ltd	6	2
1875	Workington Iron Co. Ltd	6	2
1876	Workington Iron Co. Ltd	4	2
1877	Workington Iron Co. Ltd	4	0
1878	Workington Iron Co. Ltd	6	0
1879	Workington Iron Co. Ltd	6	0
1880	Workington Hematite Iron & Steel Co. Ltd	4	3
1881	Workington Hematite Iron & Steel Co. Ltd	4	2
1882	Workington Hematite Iron & Steel Co. Ltd	5	5
1883	Workington Hematite Iron & Steel Co. Ltd	5	1
1884	Workington Hematite Iron & Steel Co. Ltd	5	2
1885	Workington Hematite Iron & Steel Co. Ltd	5	1
1886	Workington Hematite Iron & Steel Co. Ltd	5	2
1887	Workington Hematite Iron & Steel Co. Ltd	5	2
1888	Workington Hematite Iron & Steel Co. Ltd	5	1

Year	Company		
1889	Workington Hematite Iron & Steel Co. Ltd	3	1
1890	Workington Hematite Iron & Steel Co. Ltd	3	2
1891	Workington Hematite Iron & Steel Co. Ltd	3	1
1892	Workington Hematite Iron & Steel Co. Ltd	3	1
1893	Workington Hematite Iron & Steel Co. Ltd	3	1
1894	Workington Hematite Iron & Steel Co. Ltd	3	1
1895	Workington Hematite Iron & Steel Co. Ltd	3	1
1896	Workington Hematite Iron & Steel Co. Ltd	3	2
1897	Workington Hematite Iron & Steel Co. Ltd	3	2
1898	Workington Hematite Iron & Steel Co. Ltd	3	2
1899	Workington Hematite Iron & Steel Co. Ltd	3	2
1900	Workington Hematite Iron & Steel Co. Ltd	3	2
1901	Workington Iron Co. Ltd	3	2
1902	Workington Iron Co. Ltd	3	1
1903	Workington Iron Co. Ltd	3	1
1904	Workington Iron Co. Ltd	3	1
1905	Workington Iron Co. Ltd	3	1
1906	Workington Iron Co. Ltd	3	2
1907	Workington Iron Co. Ltd	3	2
1908	Workington Iron Co. Ltd	3	2
1909	Workington Iron & Steel Co. Ltd	22	12
1910	Workington Iron & Steel Co. Ltd	23	12
1911	Workington Iron & Steel Co. Ltd	23	8
1912	Workington Iron & Steel Co. Ltd	23	6
1913	Workington Iron & Steel Co. Ltd	23	10
1921	United Steel Companies Ltd	18	-
1922	United Steel Companies Ltd	18	-
1923	United Steel Companies Ltd	18	-
1924	United Steel Companies Ltd	18	-
1925	United Steel Companies Ltd	17	-
1926	United Steel Companies Ltd	17	-
1927	United Steel Companies Ltd	17	-
1928	United Steel Companies Ltd	17	-
1929	United Steel Companies Ltd	17	-
1930	United Steel Companies Ltd	17	-
1931	United Steel Companies Ltd	17	-
1932	United Steel Companies Ltd	17	-
1933	United Steel Companies Ltd	9	-
1934	Workington Iron & Steel Co. Ltd	6	-
1935	Workington Iron & Steel Co. Ltd	6	-
1936	Workington Iron & Steel Co. Ltd	6	-
1937	Workington Iron & Steel Co. Ltd	6	-
1938	Workington Iron & Steel Co. Ltd	6	-
1939	Workington Iron & Steel Co. Ltd	6	-
1940	Workington Iron & Steel Co. Ltd	6	-
1941	Workington Iron & Steel Co. Ltd	6	-
1942	Workington Iron & Steel Co. Ltd	5	-
1943	Workington Iron & Steel Co. Ltd	5	-
1944	Workington Iron & Steel Co. Ltd	5	-
1945	Workington Iron & Steel Co. Ltd	3	-
1946	Workington Iron & Steel Co.	3	-
1947	Workington Iron & Steel Co.	3	-
1948	Workington Iron & Steel Co.	3	-
1949	Workington Iron & Steel Co.	3	-
1950	Workington Iron & Steel Co.	3	-
1951	Workington Iron & Steel Co.	3	-
1952	Workington Iron & Steel Co.	3	-
1953	Workington Iron & Steel Co.	3	-
1954	Workington Iron & Steel Co.	3	-
1955	Workington Iron & Steel Co.	3	-
1956	Workington Iron & Steel Co.	3	-
1957	Workington Iron & Steel Co.	3	-
1958	Workington Iron & Steel Co.	3	-
1959	Workington Iron & Steel Co.	3	-
1960	Workington Iron & Steel Co.	3	-
1961	Workington Iron & Steel Co.	3	-
1962	Workington Iron & Steel Co.	3	-
1963	Workington Iron & Steel Co.	3	-
1964	Workington Iron & Steel Co.	3	-
1965	Workington Iron & Steel Co.	3	-
1966	Workington Iron & Steel Co.	3	-
1967	Workington Iron & Steel Co.	3	-
1968	Workington Iron & Steel Co.	3	-
1969	Workington Iron & Steel Co.	3	-
1970	British Steel Corporation	3	-
1971	British Steel Corporation	3	-
1972	British Steel Corporation	3	-
1973	British Steel Corporation	3	-
1974	British Steel Corporation	3	-
1975	British Steel Corporation	3	-
1976	British Steel Corporation	3	-
1977	British Steel Corporation	3	-
1978	British Steel Corporation	3	-
1979	British Steel Corporation	3	-
1980	British Steel Corporation	3	-

1858: 2 furnaces building. The National Grid reference is for the original (Oldside) Workington Ironworks; from 1909 the furnace-numbers also include Derwent, Harrington, Lowther, Moss Bay (the heading under which *Mineral Statistics* printed the figures) and Solway (qqv), to which in 1910 was added New Yard (qv), thus completing the Workington Iron & Steel combine. The original Workington Iron Co. was registered in 1861, although the word 'Ltd' does not appear in *Mineral Statistics* until 1868. The word 'Ltd' ceased to be used in the entry for Workington Iron & Steel from 1946. 1980 was the last year in which Workington appeared in the annual returns.

North East England

Acklam, N. Riding [NZ 4821]

Year	Owner	Built	In Blast
1863	Stevenson, Wilson, Jaques & Co.	3	0
1864	Stevenson, Wilson, Jaques & Co.	3	0
1865	Stevenson, Jaques & Co.	3	1
1866	Stevenson, Jaques & Co.	3	3
1867	Stevenson, Jaques & Co.	3	3
1868	Stevenson, Jaques & Co.	3	3
1869	Stevenson, Jaques & Co.	4	4
1870	Stevenson, Jaques & Co.	4	4
1871	Stevenson, Jaques & Co.	4	4
1872	Stevenson, Jaques & Co.	4	4
1873	Stevenson, Jaques & Co.	4	4
1874	Stevenson, Jaques & Co.	4	4
1875	Stevenson, Jaques & Co.	4	4
1876	Stevenson, Jaques & Co.	4	4
1877	Stevenson, Jaques & Co.	4	3
1878	Stevenson, Jaques & Co.	4	3
1879	Stevenson, Jaques & Co.	4	3
1880	Stevenson, Jaques & Co.	4	4
1881	Stevenson, Jaques & Co.	4	4
1882	Stevenson, Jaques & Co.	4	4
1883	Stevenson, Jaques & Co.	4	3
1884	Stevenson, Jaques & Co.	4	3
1885	Stevenson, Jaques & Co.	4	3
1886	Stevenson, Jaques & Co.	4	3
1887	Stevenson, Jaques & Co.	4	4
1888	Acklam Iron Co. Ltd	4	3
1889	Acklam Iron Co. Ltd	4	3
1890	Acklam Iron Co. Ltd	4	3
1891	Acklam Iron Co. Ltd	4	1
1892	Acklam Iron Co. Ltd	4	3
1893	Acklam Iron Co. Ltd	4	3
1894	Acklam Iron Co. Ltd	4	3
1895	Acklam Iron Co. Ltd	4	3
1896	Acklam Iron Co. Ltd	4	3
1897	North Eastern Steel Co. Ltd	4	3
1898	North Eastern Steel Co. Ltd	3	3
1899	North Eastern Steel Co. Ltd	4	3
1900	North Eastern Steel Co. Ltd	4	3
1901	North Eastern Steel Co. Ltd	4	2
1902	North Eastern Steel Co. Ltd	4	2
1903	North Eastern Steel Co. Ltd	4	2
1904	North Eastern Steel Co. Ltd	4	3
1905	North Eastern Steel Co. Ltd	4	3
1906	North Eastern Steel Co. Ltd	4	3
1907	North Eastern Steel Co. Ltd	4	3
1908	North Eastern Steel Co. Ltd	4	3
1909	North Eastern Steel Co. Ltd	4	3
1910	North Eastern Steel Co. Ltd	4	3
1911	North Eastern Steel Co. Ltd	4	3
1912	North Eastern Steel Co. Ltd	4	3
1913	North Eastern Steel Co. Ltd	4	3
1953	Dorman Long & Co. Ltd	4	-
1954	Dorman Long (Steel) Ltd	4	-
1955	Dorman Long (Steel) Ltd	4	-
1956	Dorman Long (Steel) Ltd	4	-
1957	Dorman Long (Steel) Ltd	4	-
1958	Dorman Long (Steel) Ltd	4	-
1959	Dorman Long (Steel) Ltd	4	-
1960	Dorman Long (Steel) Ltd	4	-
1961	Dorman Long (Steel) Ltd	4	-
1962	Dorman Long (Steel) Ltd	4	-

1863: Building. By 1921 North Eastern Steel was part of Bolckow, Vaughan & Co., later Dorman Long, and Acklam has no separate furnace-numbers until 1953. See Middlesbrough and Redcar for the intervening years.

Auckland, Durham [NZ 2129?]

Year	Owner	Built	In Blast
1855	—	4	0

'Building'.

Ayresome, Middlesbrough, N. Riding [NZ 4821]

Year	Owner	Built	In Blast
1870	Gjers, Mills & Co.	2	2
1871	Gjers, Mills & Co.	4	2
1872	Gjers, Mills & Co.	4	4
1873	Gjers, Mills & Co.	4	4
1874	Gjers, Mills & Co.	4	4
1875	Gjers, Mills & Co.	4	4
1876	Gjers, Mills & Co.	4	4
1877	Gjers, Mills & Co.	4	4
1878	Gjers, Mills & Co.	4	4
1879	Gjers, Mills & Co.	4	4
1880	Gjers, Mills & Co.	4	4
1881	Gjers, Mills & Co.	4	4
1882	Gjers, Mills & Co.	4	4
1883	Gjers, Mills & Co.	4	4
1884	Gjers, Mills & Co.	4	3
1885	Gjers, Mills & Co.	4	3
1886	Gjers, Mills & Co.	4	4
1887	Gjers, Mills & Co.	4	4
1888	Gjers, Mills & Co.	4	3
1889	Gjers, Mills & Co.	4	4
1890	Gjers, Mills & Co.	4	3
1891	Gjers, Mills & Co.	4	3
1892	Gjers, Mills & Co.	4	3
1893	Gjers, Mills & Co.	4	3
1894	Gjers, Mills & Co.	4	4
1895	Gjers, Mills & Co.	4	4
1896	Gjers, Mills & Co.	4	4
1897	Gjers, Mills & Co.	4	4
1898	Gjers, Mills & Co.	4	4
1899	Gjers, Mills & Co.	4	4
1900	Gjers, Mills & Co.	4	3
1901	Gjers, Mills & Co. Ltd	4	3
1902	Gjers, Mills & Co. Ltd	4	4
1903	Gjers, Mills & Co. Ltd	4	4

Year	Owner	Built	In Blast
1904	Gjers, Mills & Co. Ltd	4	3
1905	Gjers, Mills & Co. Ltd	4	3
1906	Gjers, Mills & Co. Ltd	4	4
1907	Gjers, Mills & Co. Ltd	4	4
1908	Gjers, Mills & Co. Ltd	4	4
1909	Gjers, Mills & Co. Ltd	4	4
1910	Gjers, Mills & Co. Ltd	4	3
1911	Gjers, Mills & Co. Ltd	4	4
1912	Gjers, Mills & Co. Ltd	4	3
1913	Gjers, Mills & Co. Ltd	4	4
1921	Gjers, Mills & Co. Ltd	5	-
1922	Gjers, Mills & Co. Ltd	5	-
1923	Gjers, Mills & Co. Ltd	5	-
1924	Gjers, Mills & Co. Ltd	5	-
1925	Gjers, Mills & Co. Ltd	4	-
1926	Gjers, Mills & Co. Ltd	5	-
1927	Gjers, Mills & Co. Ltd	5	-
1928	Gjers, Mills & Co. Ltd	5	-
1929	Gjers, Mills & Co. Ltd	5	-
1930	Gjers, Mills & Co. Ltd	5	-
1931	Gjers, Mills & Co. Ltd	5	-
1932	Gjers, Mills & Co. Ltd	5	-
1933	Gjers, Mills & Co. Ltd	5	-
1934	Gjers, Mills & Co. Ltd	5	-
1935	Gjers, Mills & Co. Ltd	4	-
1936	Gjers, Mills & Co. Ltd	5	-
1937	Gjers, Mills & Co. Ltd	5	-
1938	Gjers, Mills & Co. Ltd	5	-
1939	Gjers, Mills & Co. Ltd	4	-
1940	Gjers, Mills & Co. Ltd	4	-
1941	Gjers, Mills & Co. Ltd	4	-
1942	Gjers, Mills & Co. Ltd	4	-
1943	Gjers, Mills & Co. Ltd	4	-
1944	Gjers, Mills & Co. Ltd	4	-
1945	Gjers, Mills & Co. Ltd	5	-
1946	Gjers, Mills & Co. Ltd	5	-
1947	Gjers, Mills & Co. Ltd	5	-
1948	Gjers, Mills & Co. Ltd	5	-
1949	Gjers, Mills & Co. Ltd	5	-
1950	Gjers, Mills & Co. Ltd	5	-
1951	Gjers, Mills & Co. Ltd	5	-
1952	Gjers, Mills & Co. Ltd	5	-
1953	Gjers, Mills & Co. Ltd	5	-
1954	Gjers, Mills & Co. Ltd	5	-
1955	Gjers, Mills & Co. Ltd	5	-
1956	Gjers, Mills & Co. Ltd	5	-
1957	Gjers, Mills & Co. Ltd	3	-
1958	Gjers, Mills & Co. Ltd	3	-
1959	Gjers, Mills & Co. Ltd	3	-
1960	Gjers, Mills & Co. Ltd	3	-
1961	Gjers, Mills & Co. Ltd	3	-
1962	Gjers, Mills & Co. Ltd	3	-
1963	Gjers, Mills & Co. Ltd	3	-
1964	Gjers, Mills & Co. Ltd	3	-

Beckhole, N. Riding [NZ 8202]

Year	Owner	Built	In Blast
1856	Whitby Iron Co.	2	0
1857	Whitby Iron Co.	2	0
1858	Whitby Iron Co.	2	0
1859	Whitby Iron Co.	2	0
1860	Whitby Iron Co.	2	1
1861	Whitby Iron Co.	2	0
1862	Whitby Iron Co.	2	0
1863	Whitby Iron Co. Ltd	1	1
1864	Whitby Iron Co. Ltd	2	1
1865	Whitby Iron Co. Ltd	2	0
1866	Whitby Iron Co. Ltd	2	0
1867	Whitby Iron Co. Ltd	2	0
1868	Whitby Iron Co. Ltd	2	0
1869	Whitby Iron Co. Ltd	2	0
1870	Whitby Iron Co. Ltd	2	0

1856: Not completed. 1860: Put in blast in 1860. 1864: Not working for some months.

Bedlington, Northumberland [NZ 2681]

Year	Owner	Built	In Blast
1849	—	-	1
1854	Bedlington Iron Co.	2	2
1855	Bedlington Iron Co.	2	0
1856	Bedlington Iron Co.	2	0
1857	Bedlington Iron Co.	2	0
1858	Bedlington Iron Co.	2	0
1859	Bedlington Iron Co.	2	0
1860	Bedlington Iron Co.	2	0
1861	Bedlington Iron Co.	2	0
1862	Bedlington Iron Co.	2	0
1863	Bedlington Iron Co.	2	0
1864	Bedlington Iron Co.	2	0
1865	Bedlington Iron Co. Ltd	2	0
1866	Bedlington Iron Co. Ltd	2	0
1867	Bedlington Iron Co. Ltd	2	0
1868	Bedlington Iron Co. Ltd	2	0
1869	Bedlington Iron Co. Ltd	2	0

1849: only included by Hunt, as above. Truran: output 120 tons a week from each of 2 furnaces.

Benwell, Northumberland [NZ 2164]

Year	Owner	Built	In Blast
1839	—	1	1
1843	Thompson & Co.	-	1

The entry in 1843 is for a works named 'Bywell', with an output of 35 tons a week, which appears to be identical with the works at Benwell listed in 1839.

Bessemer, Middlesbrough, N. Riding [NZ 5521]

Year	Owner	Built	In Blast
1953	Dorman Long & Co. Ltd	3	-
1954	Dorman Long (Steel) Ltd	3	-
1955	Dorman Long (Steel) Ltd	3	-
1956	Dorman Long (Steel) Ltd	3	-
1957	Dorman Long (Steel) Ltd	3	-
1958	Dorman Long (Steel) Ltd	3	-
1959	Dorman Long (Steel) Ltd	3	-
1960	Dorman Long (Steel) Ltd	3	-
1961	Dorman Long (Steel) Ltd	3	-
1962	Dorman Long (Steel) Ltd	3	-
1963	Dorman Long (Steel) Ltd	3	-
1964	Dorman Long (Steel) Ltd	3	-
1965	Dorman Long (Steel) Ltd	3	-

Year	Owner	Built	In Blast
1966	Dorman Long (Steel) Ltd	3	-
1967	Dorman Long (Steel) Ltd	3	-
1968	Dorman Long (Steel) Ltd	3	-
1969	Dorman Long (Steel) Ltd	2	-
1970	British Steel Corporation	2	-
1971	British Steel Corporation	2	-
1972	British Steel Corporation	2	-
1973	British Steel Corporation	2	-
1974	British Steel Corporation	5	-
1975	British Steel Corporation	5	-
1976	British Steel Corporation	5	-
1977	British Steel Corporation	5	-
1978	British Steel Corporation	5	-
1979	British Steel Corporation	2	-
1980	British Steel Corporation	2	-

Between 1921 and 1952 a single figure was returned for all the furnaces operated by Bolckow, Vaughan (from 1929 Dorman Long), for which see under Middlesbrough and Redcar. From 1953 separate figures were printed for each of the Dorman Long sites, includes those given above for Bessemer. From 1974 Bessemer and Clay Lane (qv) lose their separate entries and a single figure, printed above, was returned, initially under the name Cleveland, which was replaced by 'South Teesside' from 1977. The two furnaces listed in 1980 have recently been demolished.

Birtley, Durham [NZ 2756]

Year	Owner	Built	In Blast
1830	—	2	-
1839	—	2	2
1841	Birtley Co.	2	2
1843	Pyrkins	-	2
1847	Birtley Iron Co.	3	2
1849	Birtley Iron Co.	3	2
1854	Birtley Iron Co.	3	2
1855	Birtley Iron Co.	3	2
1856	Birtley Iron Co.	3	2
1857	Birtley Iron Co.	3	2
1858	Birtley Iron Co.	3	2
1859	Birtley Iron Co.	3	2
1860	Birtley Iron Co.	3	2
1861	Birtley Iron Co.	3	2
1862	Birtley Iron Co.	3	2
1863	Birtley Iron Co.	3	3
1864	Birtley Iron Co.	3	2
1865	Birtley Iron Co.	3	2
1866	Birtley Iron Co.	3	2
1867	Birtley Iron Co.	3	0
1868	Birtley Iron Co.	3	0
1869	Birtley Iron Co.	3	0
1870	Birtley Iron Co.	3	0
1871	Birtley Iron Co.	3	0

1823–30: 2 furnaces erected in 1829; output 3,080 tons p.a. in 1830. 1841: No output indicated. 1843: output 100 tons a week. 1847: 8,320 tons p.a., i.e. 80 tons a week from each furnace. 1849: Hunt lists 3 furnaces in blast. Truran: output 110 tons a week from each of 3 furnaces.

Bishop Auckland: see Auckland?

Bishopwearmouth, Durham [NZ 3856]

Year	Owner	Built	In Blast
1860	Derwent & Consett Iron Co. Ltd	18	7
1861	Derwent & Consett Iron Co. Ltd	18	4
1862	Derwent & Consett Iron Co. Ltd	18	4
1863	Derwent & Consett Iron Co. Ltd	18	5

The furnace-numbers include Bradley, Consett and Crookhall (qqv), as well as Bishopwearmouth, all of which were owned by the same company. From 1864 the same entry appears under Bradley.

Bradley, Durham [NZ 1152?]

Year	Owner	Built	In Blast
1854	J. Richardson & Co.	4	4
1855	John Richardson & Co.	4	4
1856	John Richardson & Co.	4	4
1857	Richardson & Co.	4	4
1858	Derwent Iron Co.	4	4
1859	Derwent Iron Co.	4	4
1860	Derwent & Consett Iron Co. Ltd	-	-
1861	Derwent & Consett Iron Co. Ltd	-	-
1862	Derwent & Consett Iron Co. Ltd	-	-
1863	Derwent & Consett Iron Co. Ltd	-	-
1864	Consett Iron Co. Ltd	17	7
1865	Consett Iron Co. Ltd	17	7
1866	Consett Iron Co. Ltd	17	6
1867	Consett Iron Co. Ltd	17	6
1868	Consett Iron Co. Ltd	17	5
1869	Consett Iron Co. Ltd	17	5
1870	Consett Iron Co. Ltd	-	-
1871	Consett Iron Co. Ltd	-	-

Truran lists a works at Bradley, at which 4 furnaces were said to produce 150 tons a week each; in *Mineral Statistics* the entry appears under Shotley Bridge in 1854, 'Shotley Bridge or Bradley' in 1855–56, and Bradley in 1857–69. In 1860–63 furnace-numbers for Bradley and three other works owned by the same company are grouped under Bishopwearmouth (qv); for 1864–69 the same furnace-numbers are given above. There are no further entries under Bradley after 1869 but the furnace-numbers printed for Consett (qv) in 1870–71 must include Bradley as well. See also Crookhall, the other works owned by the Consett Company.

Brinkburn, Northumberland NZ 1099

Year	Owner	Built	In Blast
1856	Brinkburn Iron Co.	2	0
1857	Brinkburn Iron Co.	2	0
1858	Brinkburn Iron Co.	2	0
1859	Brinkburn Iron Co.	2	0
1860	Brinkburn Iron Co.	2	0
1861	Brinkburn Iron Co.	2	0
1862	Brinkburn Iron Co.	2	0
1863	Brinkburn Iron Co.	2	0
1864	Brinkburn Iron Co.	2	0
1865	Brinkburn Iron Co.	2	0

Year	Owner	Built	In Blast
1866	Brinkburn Iron Co.	2	0
1867	Brinkburn Iron Co.	2	0
1868	Brinkburn Iron Co.	2	0
1869	Brinkburn Iron Co.	2	0

1856: Building.

'Bywell': see Benwell

Cargo Fleet, Middlesbrough, N. Riding [NZ 5120]

Year	Owner	Built	In Blast
1864	Swan, Straubenzie, Coates & Co.	2	0
1865	Swan, Coates & Co.	2	0
1866	Swan, Coates & Co.	2	2
1867	Swan, Coates & Co.	2	2
1868	Swan, Coates & Co.	2	2
1869	Swan, Coates & Co.	2	2
1870	Swan, Coates & Co.	3	3
1871	Swan, Coates & Co.	4	3
1872	Swan, Coates & Co.	4	4
1873	Swan, Coates & Co.	4	4
1874	Swan, Coates & Co.	5	4
1875	Swan, Coates & Co.	5	5
1876	Swan, Coates & Co.	5	4
1877	Swan, Coates & Co.	5	3
1878	Swan, Coates & Co.	5	3
1879	Cargo Fleet Iron Co.	5	3
1880	Cargo Fleet Iron Co.	5	4
1881	Cargo Fleet Iron Co.	5	4
1882	Cargo Fleet Iron Co.	5	4
1883	Cargo Fleet Iron Co. Ltd	5	5
1884	Cargo Fleet Iron Co. Ltd	5	4
1885	Cargo Fleet Iron Co. Ltd	5	4
1886	Cargo Fleet Iron Co. Ltd	5	4
1887	Cargo Fleet Iron Co. Ltd	5	3
1888	Cargo Fleet Iron Co. Ltd	5	4
1889	Cargo Fleet Iron Co. Ltd	5	4
1890	Cargo Fleet Iron Co. Ltd	5	4
1891	Cargo Fleet Iron Co. Ltd	5	4
1892	Cargo Fleet Iron Co. Ltd	5	4
1893	Cargo Fleet Iron Co. Ltd	5	4
1894	Cargo Fleet Iron Co. Ltd	5	4
1895	Cargo Fleet Iron Co. Ltd	5	4
1896	Cargo Fleet Iron Co. Ltd	5	4
1897	Cargo Fleet Iron Co. Ltd	5	4
1898	Cargo Fleet Iron Co. Ltd	5	4
1899	Cargo Fleet Iron Co. Ltd	5	4
1900	Cargo Fleet Iron Co. Ltd	5	4
1901	Cargo Fleet Iron Co. Ltd	5	2
1902	Cargo Fleet Iron Co. Ltd	2	0
1903	Cargo Fleet Iron Co. Ltd	2	0
1904	Cargo Fleet Iron Co. Ltd	2	0
1905	Cargo Fleet Iron Co. Ltd	2	2
1906	Cargo Fleet Iron Co. Ltd	2	2
1907	Cargo Fleet Iron Co. Ltd	2	2
1908	Cargo Fleet Iron Co. Ltd	2	1
1909	Cargo Fleet Iron Co. Ltd	2	2
1910	Cargo Fleet Iron Co. Ltd	2	2
1911	Cargo Fleet Iron Co. Ltd	2	2
1912	Cargo Fleet Iron Co. Ltd	2	2
1913	Cargo Fleet Iron Co. Ltd	2	2
1921	Cargo Fleet Iron Co. Ltd	3	-
1922	Cargo Fleet Iron Co. Ltd	3	-
1923	Cargo Fleet Iron Co. Ltd	3	-
1924	Cargo Fleet Iron Co. Ltd	3	-
1925	Cargo Fleet Iron Co. Ltd	3	-
1926	Cargo Fleet Iron Co. Ltd	3	-
1927	Cargo Fleet Iron Co. Ltd	3	-
1928	Cargo Fleet Iron Co. Ltd	3	-
1929	Cargo Fleet Iron Co. Ltd	3	-
1930	Cargo Fleet Iron Co. Ltd	3	-
1931	Cargo Fleet Iron Co. Ltd	3	-
1932	Cargo Fleet Iron Co. Ltd	3	-
1933	Cargo Fleet Iron Co. Ltd	3	-
1934	Cargo Fleet Iron Co. Ltd	3	-
1935	Cargo Fleet Iron Co. Ltd	3	-
1936	Cargo Fleet Iron Co. Ltd	3	-
1937	Cargo Fleet Iron Co. Ltd	3	-
1938	Cargo Fleet Iron Co. Ltd	3	-
1939	Cargo Fleet Iron Co. Ltd	3	-
1940	Cargo Fleet Iron Co. Ltd	3	-
1941	Cargo Fleet Iron Co. Ltd	3	-
1942	Cargo Fleet Iron Co. Ltd	3	-
1943	Cargo Fleet Iron Co. Ltd	3	-
1944	Cargo Fleet Iron Co. Ltd	3	-
1945	Cargo Fleet Iron Co. Ltd	3	-
1946	Cargo Fleet Iron Co. Ltd	2	-
1947	Cargo Fleet Iron Co. Ltd	3	-
1948	Cargo Fleet Iron Co. Ltd	2	-
1949	Cargo Fleet Iron Co. Ltd	2	-
1950	Cargo Fleet Iron Co. Ltd	2	-
1951	Cargo Fleet Iron Co. Ltd	2	-
1952	Cargo Fleet Iron Co. Ltd	3	-
1953	South Durham Steel & Iron Co. Ltd	2	-
1954	South Durham Steel & Iron Co. Ltd	2	-
1955	South Durham Steel & Iron Co. Ltd	2	-
1956	South Durham Steel & Iron Co. Ltd	2	-
1957	South Durham Steel & Iron Co. Ltd	3	-
1958	South Durham Steel & Iron Co. Ltd	3	-
1959	South Durham Steel & Iron Co. Ltd	3	-
1960	South Durham Steel & Iron Co. Ltd	3	-
1961	South Durham Steel & Iron Co. Ltd	3	-
1962	South Durham Steel & Iron Co. Ltd	3	-
1963	South Durham Steel & Iron Co. Ltd	3	-
1964	South Durham Steel & Iron Co. Ltd	3	-
1965	South Durham Steel & Iron Co. Ltd	3	-
1966	South Durham Steel & Iron Co. Ltd	3	-
1967	South Durham Steel & Iron Co. Ltd	3	-
1968	South Durham Steel & Iron Co. Ltd	3	-
1969	South Durham Steel & Iron Co. Ltd	2	-
1970	British Steel Corporation	2	-

1865: Ready to blow-in.

Carlton, Durham [NZ 3921]

Year	Owner	Built	In Blast
1866	Bastow and Co.	1	1
1867	Bastow and Co.	1	1
1868	S. Bastow & Co.	2	0
1869	S. Bastow & Co.	2	0
1870	North of England Industrial Iron & Coal Co. Ltd	2	2
1871	North of England Industrial Iron & Coal Co. Ltd	2	2
1872	North of England Industrial Iron & Coal Co. Ltd	3	2
1873	North of England Industrial Iron & Coal Co. Ltd	3	3

Year	Owner	Built	In Blast
1874	North of England Industrial Iron & Coal Co. Ltd	3	3
1875	North of England Industrial Iron & Coal Co. Ltd	3	3
1876	North of England Industrial Iron & Coal Co. Ltd	3	3
1877	Carlton Iron Co. Ltd	3	3
1878	Carlton Iron Co. Ltd	3	2
1879	Carlton Iron Co. Ltd	3	2
1880	Carlton Iron Co. Ltd	3	3
1881	Carlton Iron Co. Ltd	3	3
1882	Carlton Iron Co. Ltd	3	3
1883	Carlton Iron Co. Ltd	3	2
1884	Carlton Iron Co. Ltd	3	2
1885	Carlton Iron Co, Ltd	3	2
1886	Carlton Iron Co. Ltd	3	2
1887	Carlton Iron Co. Ltd	3	3
1888	Carlton Iron Co. Ltd	3	3
1889	Carlton Iron Co. Ltd	3	3
1890	Carlton Iron Co. Ltd	3	3
1891	Carlton Iron Co. Ltd	3	3
1892	Carlton Iron Co. Ltd	3	2
1893	Carlton Iron Co. Ltd	3	2
1894	Carlton Iron Co. Ltd	3	2
1895	Carlton Iron Co. Ltd	3	2
1896	Carlton Iron Co. Ltd	3	2
1897	Carlton Iron Co. Ltd	3	2
1898	Carlton Iron Co. Ltd	3	2
1899	Carlton Iron Co. Ltd	3	2
1900	Carlton Iron Co. Ltd	3	3
1901	Carlton Iron Co. Ltd	3	2
1902	Carlton Iron Co. Ltd	3	2
1903	Carlton Iron Co. Ltd	3	2
1904	Carlton Iron Co. Ltd	3	2
1905	Carlton Iron Co. Ltd	3	1
1906	Carlton Iron Co. Ltd	3	2
1907	Carlton Iron Co. Ltd	3	1
1908	Carlton Iron Co. Ltd	3	1
1909	Carlton Iron Co. Ltd	3	2
1910	Carlton Iron Co. Ltd	3	2
1911	Carlton Iron Co. Ltd	3	2
1912	Carlton Iron Co. Ltd	3	2
1913	Carlton Iron Co. Ltd	3	2
1921	Carlton Iron Co. Ltd	3	-
1922	Carlton Iron Co. Ltd	3	-

This entry appears as above under Co. Durham in 1866–70. In 1870 there is a second entry for Carlton under the N. Riding, which is printed above; under the Durham works the owner is listed as S. Bastow & Co., with 2 furnaces, both out of blast. In 1871–74 entries as printed above are listed under the N. Riding in *Mineral Statistics*, from 1875 under Durham. In 1871 1 furnace was said to be building.

Clarence, Durham [NZ 4921]

Year	Owner	Built	In Blast
1854	Bell Brothers	3	3
1855	Bell Brothers	3	3
1856	Bell Brothers	3	3
1857	Bell Brothers	3	3
1858	Bell Brothers	5	3
1859	Bell Brothers	5	5
1860	Bell Brothers	5	4
1861	Bell Brothers	6	5
1862	Bell Brothers	6	5
1863	Bell Brothers	6	5
1864	Bell Brothers	6	5
1865	Bell Brothers & Co.	6	6
1866	Bell Brothers & Co.	8	7
1867	Bell Brothers & Co.	8	7
1868	Bell Brothers & Co.	8	7
1869	Bell Brothers & Co.	8	8
1870	Bell Brothers & Co.	8	8
1871	Bell Brothers & Co.	8	8
1872	Bell Brothers	8	8
1873	Bell Brothers	8	8
1874	Bell Brothers Ltd	10	8
1875	Bell Brothers Ltd	12	10
1876	Bell Brothers Ltd	12	12
1877	Bell Brothers Ltd	12	10
1878	Bell Brothers Ltd	12	8
1879	Bell Brothers Ltd	12	8
1880	Bell Brothers Ltd	12	12
1881	Bell Brothers Ltd	12	12
1882	Bell Brothers Ltd	12	11
1883	Bell Brothers Ltd	12	11
1884	Bell Brothers Ltd	12	9
1885	Bell Brothers Ltd	12	9
1886	Bell Brothers Ltd	12	8
1887	Bell Brothers Ltd	12	7
1888	Bell Brothers Ltd	12	8
1889	Bell Brothers Ltd	12	10
1890	Bell Brothers Ltd	12	11
1891	Bell Brothers Ltd	12	11
1892	Bell Brothers Ltd	12	8
1893	Bell Brothers Ltd	12	10
1894	Bell Brothers Ltd	12	11
1895	Bell Brothers Ltd	12	11
1896	Bell Brothers Ltd	12	10
1897	Bell Brothers Ltd	12	10
1898	Bell Brothers Ltd	12	10
1899	Bell Brothers Ltd	12	10
1900	Bell Brothers Ltd	12	10
1901	Bell Brothers Ltd	12	10
1902	Bell Brothers Ltd	12	9
1903	Bell Brothers Ltd	12	9
1904	Bell Brothers Ltd	12	8
1905	Bell Brothers Ltd	12	8
1906	Bell Brothers Ltd	12	8
1907	Bell Brothers Ltd	12	8
1908	Bell Brothers Ltd	12	8
1909	Bell Brothers Ltd	12	8
1910	Bell Brothers Ltd	11	8
1911	Bell Brothers Ltd	11	7
1912	Bell Brothers Ltd	11	7
1913	Bell Brothers Ltd	11	8
1921	Bell Brothers Ltd	11	-
1922	Bell Brothers Ltd	11	-

Truran: output 140 tons a week from each of 3 furnaces. 1857: 3 more furnaces building. 1859: 1 furnace building. The works is listed under Clarence in 1854–61 and 1865–67, Port Clarence in 1862–64 and 1875–82, and Clarence from 1883.

Clay Lane [I], Middlesbrough, N. Riding [NZ 5420]

Year	Owner	Built	In Blast
1857	Elwon & Co.	2	0
1858	Elwon, Malcolm & Co.	2	0

Year	Owner	Built	In Blast
1859	Clay Lane Iron Co.	2	2
1860	Clay Lane Iron Co.	3	2
1861	Clay Lane Iron Co.	3	2
1862	Clay Lane Iron Co.	3	2
1863	Clay Lane Iron Co.	6	3
1864	Clay Lane Iron Co.	6	6
1865	Clay Lane Iron Co.	6	6
1866	Clay Lane Iron Co.	6	6
1867	Clay Lane Iron Co.	6	6
1868	Clay Lane Iron Co.	6	5
1869	Clay Lane Iron Co.	6	6
1870	Thomas Vaughan	6	6
1871	Thomas Vaughan	6	6
1872	Thomas Vaughan & Co.	6	6
1873	Thomas Vaughan & Co.	6	6
1874	Thomas Vaughan & Co.	6	6
1875	Thomas Vaughan & Co.	6	4
1876	Thomas Vaughan & Co.	6	6
1877	Thomas Vaughan & Co.	6	6
1878	Trustees of Thomas Vaughan & Co.	6	3
1879	Owners of Clay Lane Ironworks	6	3
1880	Owners of Clay Lane Ironworks	6	3
1881	Owners of Clay Lane Ironworks	6	3
1882	Owners of Clay Lane Ironworks	6	4
1883	Clay Lane Iron Co. Ltd	6	6
1884	Clay Lane Iron Co. Ltd	6	5
1885	Clay Lane Iron Co. Ltd	6	5
1886	Clay Lane Iron Co. Ltd	6	5
1887	Clay Lane Iron Co. Ltd	6	5
1888	Clay Lane Iron Co. Ltd	6	5
1889	Clay Lane Iron Co. Ltd	6	6
1890	Clay Lane Iron Co. Ltd	6	6
1891	Clay Lane Iron Co. Ltd	6	6
1892	Clay Lane Iron Co. Ltd	6	4
1893	Clay Lane Iron Co. Ltd	6	4
1894	Clay Lane Iron Co. Ltd	6	5
1895	Clay Lane Iron Co. Ltd	6	5
1896	Clay Lane Iron Co. Ltd	6	5
1897	Clay Lane Iron Co. Ltd	6	5
1898	Clay Lane Iron Co. Ltd	6	5
1899	Clay Lane Iron Co. Ltd	6	5
1900	Bolckow, Vaughan & Co. Ltd	6	5
1901	Bolckow, Vaughan & Co. Ltd	6	5
1902	Bolckow, Vaughan & Co. Ltd	6	5
1903	Bolckow, Vaughan & Co. Ltd	6	5
1904	Bolckow, Vaughan & Co. Ltd	6	5
1905	Bolckow, Vaughan & Co. Ltd	6	5
1906	Bolckow, Vaughan & Co. Ltd	6	4
1907	Bolckow, Vaughan & Co. Ltd	6	5
1908	Bolckow, Vaughan & Co. Ltd	6	5
1909	Bolckow, Vaughan & Co. Ltd	6	5
1910	Bolckow, Vaughan & Co. Ltd	6	5
1911	Bolckow, Vaughan & Co. Ltd	6	5
1912	Bolckow, Vaughan & Co. Ltd	6	4
1913	Bolckow, Vaughan & Co. Ltd	6	5

1858: In blast for a few months only. 1859: Commenced Feb. 1859. For post-1921 entries for the entire Bolckow, Vaughan (later Dorman Long) group see under Middlesbrough and Redcar.

Clay Lane [II], Middlesbrough, N. Riding [NZ 5420]

Year	Owner	Built	In Blast
1956	Dorman Long (Steel) Ltd	1	-
1957	Dorman Long (Steel) Ltd	2	-
1958	Dorman Long (Steel) Ltd	2	-
1959	Dorman Long (Steel) Ltd	2	-
1960	Dorman Long (Steel) Ltd	2	-
1961	Dorman Long (Steel) Ltd	2	-
1962	Dorman Long (Steel) Ltd	3	-
1963	Dorman Long (Steel) Ltd	3	-
1964	Dorman Long (Steel) Ltd	3	-
1965	Dorman Long (Steel) Ltd	3	-
1966	Dorman Long (Steel) Ltd	3	-
1967	Dorman Long (Steel) Ltd	3	-
1968	Dorman Long (Steel) Ltd	3	-
1969	Dorman Long (Steel) Ltd	3	-
1970	British Steel Corporation	3	-
1971	British Steel Corporation	3	-
1972	British Steel Corporation	3	-
1973	British Steel Corporation	3	-

These entries refer to a new plant which took the name of the old Clay Lane works. From 1974 the two surviving BSC works at Middlesbrough (Clay Lane and Bessemer) were combined in a single entry, initially called Cleveland, later South Teesside. See under Bessemer.

Cleveland, Middlesbrough, N. Riding [NZ 5321]

Year	Owner	Built	In Blast
1854	Elwon & Co.	2	2
1855	T.L. Elwon & Co.	3	2
1856	T.L. Elwon & Co.	3	3
1857	Bolckow & Vaughan	3	3
1858	Bolckow & Vaughan	4	3
1859	Bolckow & Vaughan	4	3
1860	Bolckow & Vaughan	4	4
1861	Bolckow & Vaughan	12	12
1862	Bolckow & Vaughan	12	10
1863	Bolckow & Vaughan	13	13
1864	Bolckow & Vaughan	13	13
1865	Bolckow, Vaughan & Co. Ltd	18	18
1866	Bolckow, Vaughan & Co. Ltd	18	16
1867	Bolckow, Vaughan & Co. Ltd	18	14
1868	Bolckow, Vaughan & Co. Ltd	18	12
1869	Bolckow, Vaughan & Co. Ltd	18	12
1870	Bolckow, Vaughan & Co. Ltd	18	12
1871	Bolckow, Vaughan & Co. Ltd	15	15
1872	Bolckow, Vaughan & Co. Ltd	-	-
1873	Bolckow, Vaughan & Co. Ltd	-	-
1874	Bolckow, Vaughan & Co. Ltd	-	-
1875	Bolckow, Vaughan & Co. Ltd	-	-
1876	Bolckow, Vaughan & Co. Ltd	8	8
1877	Bolckow, Vaughan & Co. Ltd	1	1
1878	Bolckow, Vaughan & Co. Ltd	-	-
1879	Bolckow, Vaughan & Co. Ltd	11	11
1880	Bolckow, Vaughan & Co. Ltd	11	11
1881	Bolckow, Vaughan & Co. Ltd	11	11
1882	Bolckow, Vaughan & Co. Ltd	11	11
1883	Bolckow, Vaughan & Co. Ltd	11	11
1884	Bolckow, Vaughan & Co. Ltd	8	8
1885	Bolckow, Vaughan & Co. Ltd	8	8
1886	Bolckow, Vaughan & Co. Ltd	8	7

Year	Owner	Built	In Blast
1887	Bolckow, Vaughan & Co. Ltd	8	7
1888	Bolckow, Vaughan & Co. Ltd	8	7
1889	Bolckow, Vaughan & Co. Ltd	8	6
1890	Bolckow, Vaughan & Co. Ltd	8	6
1891	Bolckow, Vaughan & Co. Ltd	8	6
1892	Bolckow, Vaughan & Co. Ltd	8	4
1893	Bolckow, Vaughan & Co. Ltd	8	5
1894	Bolckow, Vaughan & Co. Ltd	8	5
1895	Bolckow, Vaughan & Co. Ltd	8	4
1896	Bolckow, Vaughan & Co. Ltd	8	5
1897	Bolckow, Vaughan & Co. Ltd	8	5
1898	Bolckow, Vaughan & Co. Ltd	8	5
1899	Bolckow, Vaughan & Co. Ltd	8	5
1900	Bolckow, Vaughan & Co. Ltd	8	5
1901	Bolckow, Vaughan & Co. Ltd	8	4
1902	Bolckow, Vaughan & Co. Ltd	5	4
1903	Bolckow, Vaughan & Co. Ltd	5	5
1904	Bolckow, Vaughan & Co. Ltd	5	5
1905	Bolckow, Vaughan & Co. Ltd	5	5
1906	Bolckow, Vaughan & Co. Ltd	5	5
1907	Bolckow, Vaughan & Co. Ltd	5	5
1908	Bolckow, Vaughan & Co. Ltd	5	4
1909	Bolckow, Vaughan & Co. Ltd	5	4
1910	Bolckow, Vaughan & Co. Ltd	5	4
1911	Bolckow, Vaughan & Co. Ltd	5	4
1912	Bolckow, Vaughan & Co. Ltd	5	3
1913	Bolckow, Vaughan & Co. Ltd	5	4
1953	Dorman Long & Co. Ltd	4	-
1954	Dorman Long (Steel) Ltd	4	-
1955	Dorman Long (Steel) Ltd	4	-
1956	Dorman Long (Steel) Ltd	4	-

In 1854 *Mineral Statistics* listed three works under the name 'Eston', the details for one of which are given above and those for the other two printed here under South Bank and Middlesbrough (qqv). Truran also lists three works under Eston, one of which (with 6 furnaces) is clearly that later known as Middlesbrough. One of the other two had 3 furnaces, producing 130 tons a week, the other had 2 furnaces producing 110 tons a week. The first of these appears to be the works later known as Cleveland Iron & Steel (later simply Cleveland); the second appears to be South Bank. The furnace-numbers given above for 1861–63 include Middlesbrough (qv); in 1864–71 they include Middlesbrough and Witton Park (qv), even though the additional furnaces at the latter site seem only to be added in from 1865. In 1870–71 the works otherwise known as Cleveland is listed under Eston. In 1872–75 and 1878 furnace-numbers printed above once again include Middlesbrough. In 1876 3 furnaces were said to be building at the Cleveland works. From 1884 the entry for Cleveland in *Mineral Statistics* is divided, with 8 (later 5) furnaces listed under 'Cleveland' (rather than Cleveland Iron & Steel) and 3 others under 'Eston Steel, South Bank' in 1884–87, thereafter under Cleveland Steel. The first of these series is printed above, the second forms the next entry. For post-1921 entries for the Bolckow, Vaughan (later Dorman Long) group see under Middlesbrough and Redcar; separate entries for individual works were only resumed in 1953. From 1974 the name Cleveland (later South Teesside) was used for an entry for the two British Steel plants at Middlesbrough, Bessemer and Clay Lane, for which separate figures had previously been returned. See under Bessemer.

Cleveland Steel, South Bank, N. Riding [NZ 5321]

Year	Owner	Built	In Blast
1884	Bolckow, Vaughan & Co. Ltd	3	3
1885	Bolckow, Vaughan & Co. Ltd	3	3
1886	Bolckow, Vaughan & Co. Ltd	3	2
1887	Bolckow, Vaughan & Co. Ltd	3	2
1888	Bolckow, Vaughan & Co. Ltd	3	2
1889	Bolckow, Vaughan & Co. Ltd	3	2
1890	Bolckow, Vaughan & Co. Ltd	3	2
1891	Bolckow, Vaughan & Co. Ltd	3	2
1892	Bolckow, Vaughan & Co. Ltd	3	2
1893	Bolckow, Vaughan & Co. Ltd	3	3
1894	Bolckow, Vaughan & Co. Ltd	3	3
1895	Bolckow, Vaughan & Co. Ltd	3	3
1896	Bolckow, Vaughan & Co. Ltd	3	3
1897	Bolckow, Vaughan & Co. Ltd	3	3
1898	Bolckow, Vaughan & Co. Ltd	3	3
1899	Bolckow, Vaughan & Co. Ltd	3	3
1900	Bolckow, Vaughan & Co. Ltd	3	3
1901	Bolckow, Vaughan & Co. Ltd	3	2
1902	Bolckow, Vaughan & Co. Ltd	3	2
1903	Bolckow, Vaughan & Co. Ltd	2	1
1904	Bolckow, Vaughan & Co. Ltd	2	1
1905	Bolckow, Vaughan & Co. Ltd	2	1
1906	Bolckow, Vaughan & Co. Ltd	2	2
1907	Bolckow, Vaughan & Co. Ltd	2	2
1908	Bolckow, Vaughan & Co. Ltd	2	2
1909	Bolckow, Vaughan & Co. Ltd	2	1
1910	Bolckow, Vaughan & Co. Ltd	2	1
1911	Bolckow, Vaughan & Co. Ltd	2	0
1912	Bolckow, Vaughan & Co. Ltd	2	0
1913	Bolckow, Vaughan & Co. Ltd	2	1

See note to previous entry.

Coatham, N. Riding [NZ 5925]

Year	Owner	Built	In Blast
1872	Downey & Co.	2	0
1873	Downey & Co.	2	2
1874	Downey & Co.	2	2
1875	Downey & Co.	2	2
1876	Downey & Co.	2	2
1877	Downey & Co.	2	2
1878	Downey & Co.	2	2
1879	Downey & Co.	2	2
1880	Downey & Co.	2	2
1881	Downey & Co.	2	2
1882	Downey & Co.	2	2
1883	Downey & Co.	2	2
1884	Downey & Co.	2	2
1885	Downey & Co.	2	2
1886	Downey & Co.	2	2
1887	Downey & Co.	2	0
1888	Downey & Co.	2	0
1889	Downey & Co.	2	0
1890	Downey & Co.	2	0
1891	Downey & Co.	2	0
1892	Downey & Co.	2	0
1893	National Provincial Bank	2	0
1894	National Provincial Bank	2	0
1895	National Provincial Bank of England	2	0
1896	J.M. Lennard & William Whitwell	2	0
1897	J.M. Lennard & William Whitwell	2	0

Year	Owner	Built	In Blast
1898	J.M. Lennard & William Whitwell	2	0
1899	J.M. Lennard & William Whitwell	3	0
1900	Walker, Maynard & Co. Ltd	2	0
1901	Walker, Maynard & Co. Ltd	2	0
1902	Walker, Maynard & Co. Ltd	2	0
1903	Walker, Maynard & Co. Ltd	2	2
1904	Walker, Maynard & Co. Ltd	2	2
1905	Walker, Maynard & Co. Ltd	-	-
1906	Walker, Maynard & Co. Ltd	-	-
1907	Walker, Maynard & Co. Ltd	-	-
1908	Walker, Maynard & Co. Ltd	-	-
1909	Walker, Maynard & Co. Ltd	-	-
1910	Walker, Maynard & Co. Ltd	-	-
1911	Walker, Maynard & Co. Ltd	-	-
1912	Walker, Maynard & Co. Ltd	-	-
1913	Walker, Maynard & Co. Ltd	-	-

1872: Blown-in 9 June 1873. Between 1905 and 1913 a single figure was returned for Coatham and Walker, Maynard's other works at Redcar (qv), a practice continued after 1921.

Consett, Durham [NZ 0951]

Year	Owner	Built	In Blast
1843	—	-	2
1847	Derwent Iron Co.	14	7
1849	Mounsey & Co.	14	5
1854	Derwent Iron Co.	7	5
1855	Derwent Iron Co.	7	6
1856	Derwent Iron Co.	7	7
1857	Derwent Iron Co.	7	6
1858	Derwent Iron Co.	7	6
1859	Derwent Iron Co.	7	5
1860	Derwent & Consett Iron Co. Ltd	-	-
1861	Derwent & Consett Iron Co. Ltd	-	-
1862	Derwent & Consett Iron Co. Ltd	-	-
1863	Derwent & Consett Iron Co. Ltd	-	-
1864	Consett Iron Co. Ltd	-	-
1865	Consett Iron Co. Ltd	-	-
1866	Consett Iron Co. Ltd	-	-
1867	Consett Iron Co. Ltd	-	-
1868	Consett Iron Co. Ltd	-	-
1869	Consett Iron Co. Ltd	-	-
1870	Consett Iron Co. Ltd	17	5
1871	Consett Iron Co. Ltd	12	5
1872	Consett Iron Co. Ltd	5	5
1873	Consett Iron Co. Ltd	6	6
1874	Consett Iron Co. Ltd	6	6
1875	Consett Iron Co. Ltd	6	5
1876	Consett Iron Co. Ltd	6	4
1877	Consett Iron Co. Ltd	6	5
1878	Consett Iron Co. Ltd	6	4
1879	Consett Iron Co. Ltd	6	4
1880	Consett Iron Co. Ltd	7	6
1881	Consett Iron Co. Ltd	7	7
1882	Consett Iron Co. Ltd	7	6
1883	Consett Iron Co. Ltd	7	6
1884	Consett Iron Co. Ltd	7	5
1885	Consett Iron Co. Ltd	7	6
1886	Consett Iron Co. Ltd	7	6
1887	Consett Iron Co. Ltd	7	6
1888	Consett Iron Co. Ltd	7	6
1889	Consett Iron Co. Ltd	7	6
1890	Consett Iron Co. Ltd	7	6
1891	Consett Iron Co. Ltd	7	5
1892	Consett Iron Co. Ltd	7	5
1893	Consett Iron Co. Ltd	7	4
1894	Consett Iron Co. Ltd	7	6
1895	Consett Iron Co. Ltd	7	5
1896	Consett Iron Co. Ltd	7	6
1897	Consett Iron Co. Ltd	7	7
1898	Consett Iron Co. Ltd	7	7
1899	Consett Iron Co. Ltd	7	7
1900	Consett Iron Co. Ltd	7	7
1901	Consett Iron Co. Ltd	7	6
1902	Consett Iron Co. Ltd	7	6
1903	Consett Iron Co. Ltd	7	6
1904	Consett Iron Co. Ltd	7	6
1905	Consett Iron Co. Ltd	7	6
1906	Consett Iron Co. Ltd	7	6
1907	Consett Iron Co. Ltd	7	7
1908	Consett Iron Co. Ltd	8	5
1909	Consett Iron Co. Ltd	8	6
1910	Consett Iron Co. Ltd	8	6
1911	Consett Iron Co. Ltd	8	6
1912	Consett Iron Co. Ltd	8	6
1913	Consett Iron Co. Ltd	8	6
1921	Consett Iron Co. Ltd	8	-
1922	Consett Iron Co. Ltd	8	-
1923	Consett Iron Co. Ltd	8	-
1924	Consett Iron Co. Ltd	8	-
1925	Consett Iron Co. Ltd	8	-
1926	Consett Iron Co. Ltd	8	-
1927	Consett Iron Co. Ltd	8	-
1928	Consett Iron Co. Ltd	8	-
1929	Consett Iron Co. Ltd	8	-
1930	Consett Iron Co. Ltd	8	-
1931	Consett Iron Co. Ltd	8	-
1932	Consett Iron Co. Ltd	8	-
1933	Consett Iron Co. Ltd	8	-
1934	Consett Iron Co. Ltd	8	-
1935	Consett Iron Co. Ltd	8	-
1936	Consett Iron Co. Ltd	8	-
1937	Consett Iron Co. Ltd	7	-
1938	Consett Iron Co. Ltd	7	-
1939	Consett Iron Co. Ltd	7	-
1940	Consett Iron Co. Ltd	6	-
1941	Consett Iron Co. Ltd	6	-
1942	Consett Iron Co. Ltd	6	-
1943	Consett Iron Co. Ltd	6	-
1944	Consett Iron Co. Ltd	6	-
1945	Consett Iron Co. Ltd	2	-
1946	Consett Iron Co. Ltd	2	-
1947	Consett Iron Co. Ltd	2	-
1948	Consett Iron Co. Ltd	2	-
1949	Consett Iron Co. Ltd	2	-
1950	Consett Iron Co. Ltd	2	-
1951	Consett Iron Co. Ltd	3	-
1952	Consett Iron Co. Ltd	3	-
1953	Consett Iron Co. Ltd	3	-
1954	Consett Iron Co. Ltd	3	-
1955	Consett Iron Co. Ltd	3	-
1956	Consett Iron Co. Ltd	3	-
1957	Consett Iron Co. Ltd	3	-
1958	Consett Iron Co. Ltd	3	-
1959	Consett Iron Co. Ltd	3	-
1960	Consett Iron Co. Ltd	3	-

Year	Owner	Built	In Blast
1961	Consett Iron Co. Ltd	3	-
1962	Consett Iron Co. Ltd	3	-
1963	Consett Iron Co. Ltd	3	-
1964	Consett Iron Co. Ltd	3	-
1965	Consett Iron Co. Ltd	3	-
1966	Consett Iron Co. Ltd	3	-
1967	Consett Iron Co. Ltd	3	-
1968	Consett Iron Co. Ltd	3	-
1969	Consett Iron Co. Ltd	3	-
1970	British Steel Corporation	3	-
1971	British Steel Corporation	3	-
1972	British Steel Corporation	3	-
1973	British Steel Corporation	3	-
1974	British Steel Corporation	3	-
1975	British Steel Corporation	3	-
1976	British Steel Corporation	3	-
1977	British Steel Corporation	3	-
1978	British Steel Corporation	3	-
1979	British Steel Corporation	3	-

1843: A works named 'Conside', with no owner's name and a weekly output of 110 tons, presumably belongs here. 1847: furnace-numbers and output returned for Consett and Crookhall (qv) together; total output 29,120 tons p.a., i.e. 80 tons a week from each of 7 furnaces at the two sites. 1849: English calls the works Derwent and Shotley Bridge; Hunt lists Derwent and Crookhall separately, each with 7 furnaces in blast. Truran: output 130 tons a week from each of 7 furnaces at Consett alone. For 1860–63 furnace-numbers for Consett, Bradley, Crookhall and Bishopwearmouth are printed under the latter heading (qv); for 1864–69 the same figures are combined under Bradley (qv); and for 1870–71 the figures given above under Consett must include Bradley and Crookhall. In 1875 the Consett entry includes the comment 'Furnaces building'; in 1876 1 furnace was said to be building; the same comment reappears in 1879. Consett closed in 1980.

Crookhall, Durham [NZ 1150]

Year	Owner	Built	In Blast
1847	Derwent Iron Co.	-	-
1849	Mounsey & Co.	-	-
1854	Derwent Iron Co.	7	6
1855	Derwent Iron Co.	7	6
1856	Derwent Iron Co.	7	6
1857	Derwent Iron Co.	7	6
1858	Derwent Iron Co.	7	6
1859	Derwent Iron Co.	7	6
1860	Derwent & Consett Iron Co. Ltd	-	-
1861	Derwent & Consett Iron Co. Ltd	-	-
1862	Derwent & Consett Iron Co. Ltd	-	-
1863	Derwent & Consett Iron Co. Ltd	-	-
1864	Consett Iron Co. Ltd	-	-
1865	Consett Iron Co. Ltd	-	-
1866	Consett Iron Co. Ltd	-	-
1867	Consett Iron Co. Ltd	-	-
1868	Consett Iron Co. Ltd	-	-
1869	Consett Iron Co. Ltd	-	-
1870	Consett Iron Co. Ltd	-	-
1871	Consett Iron Co. Ltd	-	-

1847–49: see Consett. Truran: output 130 tons a week from each of 7 furnaces at Crookhall alone. In 1860–63 furnace-numbers for Crookhall are combined with those for other works owned by the same company under Bishopwearmouth (qv); in 1864–69 they are combined under Bradley (qv); and in 1870–71 the numbers printed under Consett (qv) must include Crookhall and Bradley.

Darlington: see South Durham

Derwent: see Consett

Elswick, Northumberland NZ 2363

Year	Owner	Built	In Blast
1865	Elswick Iron Co.	2	2
1866	Sir W.G. Armstrong & Co.	2	2
1867	Sir W.G. Armstrong & Co.	2	2
1868	Sir W.G. Armstrong & Co.	2	1
1869	Sir W.G. Armstrong & Co.	2	1
1870	Sir W.G. Armstrong & Co.	2	1
1871	Sir W.G. Armstrong & Co.	2	1
1872	Sir W.G. Armstrong & Co.	2	2
1873	Sir W.G. Armstrong & Co.	2	2
1874	Sir W.G. Armstrong & Co.	2	1
1875	Sir W.G. Armstrong & Co.	2	1
1876	Sir W.G. Armstrong & Co.	2	1
1877	Sir W.G. Armstrong & Co.	2	1
1878	Sir W.G. Armstrong & Co.	2	1
1879	Sir W.G. Armstrong & Co.	2	0
1880	Sir W.G. Armstrong & Co.	2	2
1881	Sir W.G. Armstrong & Co.	2	2
1882	Sir W.G. Armstrong, Mitchell & Co. Ltd	3	2
1883	Sir W.G. Armstrong, Mitchell & Co. Ltd	3	2
1884	Sir W.G. Armstrong, Mitchell & Co. Ltd	3	2
1885	Sir W.G. Armstrong, Mitchell & Co. Ltd	3	2
1886	Sir W.G. Armstrong, Mitchell & Co. Ltd	3	1
1887	Sir W.G. Armstrong, Mitchell & Co. Ltd	3	1
1888	Sir W.G. Armstrong, Mitchell & Co. Ltd	3	1
1889	Sir W.G. Armstrong, Mitchell & Co. Ltd	3	1
1890	Sir W.G. Armstrong, Mitchell & Co. Ltd	3	1
1891	Sir W.G. Armstrong, Mitchell & Co. Ltd	3	1
1892	Sir W.G. Armstrong, Mitchell & Co. Ltd	3	1
1893	Sir W.G. Armstrong, Mitchell & Co. Ltd	3	1
1894	Sir W.G. Armstrong, Mitchell & Co. Ltd	3	1
1895	Sir W.G. Armstrong, Mitchell & Co. Ltd	3	1
1896	Sir W.G. Armstrong, Mitchell & Co. Ltd	2	1
1897	Sir W.G. Armstrong, Mitchell & Co. Ltd	2	1
1898	Sir W.G. Armstrong, Whitworth & Co. Ltd	2	1
1899	Sir W.G. Armstrong, Whitworth & Co. Ltd	2	1

In 1879, 1880 and 1881 one furnace was said to be building.

Eston, Middlesbrough, N. Riding [NZ 5422]

Year	Owner	Built	In Blast
1854	Bolckow & Vaughan	6	6
1855	Bolckow & Vaughan	6	6
1856	Bolckow & Vaughan	6	6
1857	Bolckow & Vaughan	6	6
1858	Bolckow & Vaughan	5	5
1859	Bolckow & Vaughan	5	5
1860	Bolckow & Vaughan	5	5

Truran lists three works at Eston, one of which had 6 furnaces as above. One of the other two had 3 furnaces, each producing 130 tons a week, and the other had 2 furnaces each producing 110 tons a week. In *Mineral Statistics* for 1854 there are also three works under Eston, one of which appears under Cleveland and another under South Bank from 1855. Truran's works with 3 furnaces has been identified as the Cleveland site and the other placed under South Bank. The third works listed by *Mineral Statistics* continues to appear under Eston until 1860 but from 1861 is absorbed into the entry for Cleveland Iron & Steel (qv). In 1884 a new entry appears in *Mineral Statistics* for 'Eston Steel, South Bank', containing 3 of the 11 furnaces previously listed under Cleveland Iron & Steel. The heading changes to 'Cleveland Steel (Eston), South Bank' in 1888 and has been printed here under that name (qv).

Etherley: see Witton Park

Felling, Durham [NZ 2862]

Year	Owner	Built	In Blast
1854	H.L. Pattinson & Co.	2	2
1855	H.L. Pattinson & Co.	2	2
1856	H.L. Pattinson & Co.	2	2
1857	H.L. Pattinson & Co.	2	2
1858	H.L. Pattinson & Co.	2	2
1859	H.L. Pattinson & Co.	2	2
1860	H.L. Pattinson & Co.	2	0
1861	H.L. Pattinson & Co.	2	0
1862	H.L. Pattinson & Co.	2	0
1863	H.L. Pattinson & Co.	2	0
1864	H.L. Pattinson & Co.	2	2
1865	H.L. Pattinson & Co.	2	0
1866	H.L. Pattinson & Co.	2	0
1867	H.L. Pattinson & Co.	2	0
1868	H.L. Pattinson & Co.	2	0
1869	H.L. Pattinson & Co.	2	0
1870	H.L. Pattinson & Co.	2	0
1871	H.L. Pattinson & Co.	2	0

Truran: output 140 tons a week from each of 2 furnaces.

Ferry Hill, Durham [NZ 2932]

Year	Owner	Built	In Blast
1859	James Morrison	3	0
1860	James Morrison	3	2
1861	James Morrison	3	2
1862	James Morrison	3	2
1863	James Morrison	3	3
1864	Rosedale & Ferry Hill Iron Co. Ltd	3	2
1865	Rosedale & Ferry Hill Iron Co. Ltd	6	6
1866	Rosedale & Ferry Hill Iron Co. Ltd	6	6
1867	Rosedale & Ferry Hill Iron Co. Ltd	7	6
1868	Rosedale & Ferry Hill Iron Co. Ltd	8	7
1869	Rosedale & Ferry Hill Iron Co. Ltd	8	8
1870	Rosedale & Ferry Hill Iron Co. Ltd	8	8
1871	Rosedale & Ferry Hill Iron Co. Ltd	8	8
1872	Rosedale & Ferry Hill Iron Co. Ltd	8	8
1873	Rosedale & Ferry Hill Iron Co. Ltd	8	8
1874	Rosedale & Ferry Hill Iron Co. Ltd	8	7
1875	Rosedale & Ferry Hill Iron Co. Ltd	10	7
1876	Rosedale & Ferry Hill Iron Co. Ltd	9	6
1877	Rosedale & Ferry Hill Iron Co. Ltd	10	5
1878	Rosedale & Ferry Hill Iron Co. Ltd	10	5
1879	Rosedale & Ferry Hill Iron Co. Ltd	10	0
1880	Rosedale & Ferry Hill Iron Co. Ltd	10	0
1881	Rosedale & Ferry Hill Iron Co. Ltd	10	0
1882	Rosedale & Ferry Hill Iron Co. Ltd	8	0
1883	John Rogerson	8	0
1884	John Rogerson	8	0
1885	John Rogerson	8	0
1886	John Rogerson	8	0
1887	John Rogerson	8	0
1888	John Rogerson	8	0
1889	John Rogerson	8	0
1890	John Rogerson	8	0
1891	John Rogerson & Co. Ltd	8	0
1892	John Rogerson	4	0
1893	John E. Rogerson	4	0
1894	Executors of late John Rogerson	4	0
1895	John E. Rogerson	3	0

1879: Company in liquidation; 3 furnaces to 15 Feb., 2 to 31 March.

Glaisdale, N. Riding [NZ 7705]

Year	Owner	Built	In Blast
1866	Firth & Hodgson	3	2
1867	Lonsdale Vale Iron Co. Ltd	3	2
1868	Firth & Hodgson	3	0
1869	Firth & Hodgson	3	0
1870	George Wilson & Co.	3	3
1871	George Wilson & Co.	3	2
1872	South Cleveland Ironworks Ltd	3	3
1873	South Cleveland Ironworks Ltd	3	3
1874	South Cleveland Ironworks Ltd	3	2
1875	South Cleveland Ironworks Ltd	3	0
1876	South Cleveland Ironworks Ltd	3	0
1877	South Cleveland Ironworks Ltd	3	0
1878	South Cleveland Ironworks Ltd	3	0
1879	South Cleveland Ironworks Ltd	3	0
1880	South Cleveland Ironworks Ltd	3	0
1881	South Cleveland Ironworks Ltd	3	0
1882	South Cleveland Ironworks Ltd	3	0
1883	South Cleveland Ironworks Ltd	3	0
1884	South Cleveland Ironworks Ltd	3	0
1885	South Cleveland Ironworks Ltd	4	0
1886	South Cleveland Ironworks Ltd	4	0
1887	South Cleveland Ironworks Ltd	4	0
1888	South Cleveland Ironworks Ltd	3	0
1889	South Cleveland Ironworks Ltd	3	0

| 1890 | South Cleveland Ironworks Ltd | 3 | 0 |

Grangetown, Middlesbrough, N. Riding [NZ 5520]

Year	Owner	Built	In Blast
1905	Bolckow, Vaughan & Co. Ltd	2	1
1906	Bolckow, Vaughan & Co. Ltd	2	2
1907	Bolckow, Vaughan & Co. Ltd	2	2
1908	Bolckow, Vaughan & Co. Ltd	2	2
1909	Bolckow, Vaughan & Co. Ltd	2	2
1910	Bolckow, Vaughan & Co. Ltd	2	2
1911	Bolckow, Vaughan & Co. Ltd	2	2
1912	Bolckow, Vaughan & Co. Ltd.	2	1
1913	Bolckow, Vaughan & Co. Ltd.	2	2

From 1921 a single entry was printed for all the Bolckow, Vaughan works, for which see Middlesbrough.

Grosmont, N. Riding [NZ 8205]

Year	Owner	Built	In Blast
1864	Charles & Thomas Bagnall	2	2
1865	Charles & Thomas Bagnall	2	2
1866	Charles & Thomas Bagnall	2	2
1867	Charles & Thomas Bagnall Jun.	2	2
1868	Charles & Thomas Bagnall Jun.	2	1
1869	Charles & Thomas Bagnall Jun.	2	2
1870	Charles & Thomas Bagnall Jun.	2	2
1871	Charles & Thomas Bagnall Jun.	2	2
1872	Charles & Thomas Bagnall Jun.	2	2
1873	Charles & Thomas Bagnall Jun.	2	2
1874	Charles & Thomas Bagnall Jun.	2	2
1875	Charles & Thomas Bagnall Jun.	3	2
1876	Charles & Thomas Bagnall Jun.	3	2
1877	Charles & Thomas Bagnall Jun.	3	2
1878	Charles & Thomas Bagnall Jun.	3	2
1879	Charles & Thomas Bagnall Jun.	3	1
1880	Charles & Thomas Bagnall Jun.	3	2
1881	Charles & Thomas Bagnall Jun.	3	2
1882	Charles & Thomas Bagnall Jun.	3	2
1883	Charles & Thomas Bagnall Jun.	3	2
1884	Charles & Thomas Bagnall Jun.	3	2
1885	Charles & Thomas Bagnall	3	2
1886	Charles & Thomas Bagnall	3	1
1887	Charles & Thomas Bagnall	3	1
1888	Charles & Thomas Bagnall	3	2
1889	Charles & Thomas Bagnall	3	2
1890	Charles & Thomas Bagnall	3	2
1891	C. & T. Bagnall's Trustees	3	1

1864: In blast part of the year only.

Haltwhistle, Northumberland [NY 7064]

Year	Owner	Built	In Blast
1856	Joseph Beasley Jun.	1	0
1857	Joseph Beasley Jun.	1	0
1858	Joseph Beasley Jun.	1	0
1859	Joseph Beasley Jun.	1	0
1860	Joseph Beasley Jun.	1	0
1861	Joseph Beasley Jun.	1	0
1862	Joseph Beasley Jun.	1	0
1863	Joseph Beasley Jun.	1	0
1864	Joseph Beasley Jun.	1	0
1865	Joseph Beasley Jun.	1	0
1866	Joseph Beasley Jun.	1	0
1867	Joseph Beasley Jun.	1	0
1868	Joseph Beasley Jun.	1	0
1869	Joseph Beasley Jun.	1	0

Hareshaw, Northumberland NY 8483

Year	Owner	Built	In Blast
1841	—	1	1
1843	Campeon	-	1
1847	—	3	2
1849	Hareshaw Iron Co.	3	0
1854	Hareshaw Iron Co.	3	0
1855	Hareshaw Iron Co.	3	0
1856	Hareshaw Iron Co.	3	0
1857	Hareshaw Iron Co.	3	0
1858	Hareshaw Iron Co.	3	0
1859	Hareshaw Iron Co.	3	0
1860	Hareshaw Iron Co.	3	0
1861	Hareshaw Iron Co.	3	0
1862	Hareshaw Iron Co.	3	0
1863	Hareshaw Iron Co.	3	0
1864	Hareshaw Iron Co.	3	0
1865	Hareshaw Iron Co.	3	0
1866	Hareshaw Iron Co.	3	0
1867	Hareshaw Iron Co.	3	0
1868	Hareshaw Iron Co.	3	0
1869	Hareshaw Iron Co.	3	0
1870	Hareshaw Iron Co.	2	0
1871	Hareshaw Iron Co.	2	0
1872	Hareshaw Iron Co.	-	-
1873	Hareshaw Iron Co.	2	-
1874	Hareshaw Iron Co.	-	-

1841: A works named 'Hareshead' presumably belongs here; no output or owner's name is given. 1843: output 50 tons a week. 1847: 8,320 tons p.a., i.e. 80 tons a week from each furnace. 1849: Hunt lists 1 furnace in blast. Truran: output 120 tons a week from each of 3 furnaces.

Hartlepool: see Seaton Carew; West Hartlepool

Jarrow, Durham [NZ 3465]

Year	Owner	Built	In Blast
1856	Palmer & Co.	2	0
1857	Palmer & Co.	4	0
1858	Palmer & Co.	4	1
1859	Jarrow Iron Works	4	3
1860	Jarrow Iron Works	4	2
1861	Jarrow Iron Co.	2	2
1862	Jarrow Iron Co.	3	2
1863	Jarrow Iron Co.	6	6
1864	Jarrow Iron Co.	4	3
1865	Palmers Shipbuilding & Iron Co. Ltd	4	3
1866	Palmers Shipbuilding & Iron Co. Ltd	5	5
1867	Palmers Shipbuilding & Iron Co. Ltd	5	3
1868	Palmers Shipbuilding & Iron Co. Ltd	5	4
1869	Palmers Shipbuilding & Iron Co. Ltd	4	4
1870	Palmers Shipbuilding & Iron Co. Ltd	5	4

Year	Owner	Built	In Blast
1871	Palmers Shipbuilding & Iron Co. Ltd	4	4
1872	Palmers Shipbuilding & Iron Co. Ltd	4	4
1873	Palmers Shipbuilding & Iron Co. Ltd	4	4
1874	Palmers Shipbuilding & Iron Co. Ltd	4	4
1875	Palmers Shipbuilding & Iron Co. Ltd	4	3
1876	Palmers Shipbuilding & Iron Co. Ltd	3	3
1877	Palmers Shipbuilding & Iron Co. Ltd	3	2
1878	Palmers Shipbuilding & Iron Co. Ltd	3	2
1879	Palmers Shipbuilding & Iron Co. Ltd	3	2
1880	Palmers Shipbuilding & Iron Co. Ltd	3	3
1881	Palmers Shipbuilding & Iron Co. Ltd	3	3
1882	Palmers Shipbuilding & Iron Co. Ltd	3	3
1883	Palmers Shipbuilding & Iron Co. Ltd	3	3
1884	Palmers Shipbuilding & Iron Co. Ltd	4	3
1885	Palmers Shipbuilding & Iron Co. Ltd	4	3
1886	Palmers Shipbuilding & Iron Co. Ltd	4	4
1887	Palmers Shipbuilding & Iron Co. Ltd	4	4
1888	Palmers Shipbuilding & Iron Co. Ltd	4	4
1889	Palmers Shipbuilding & Iron Co. Ltd	4	4
1890	Palmers Shipbuilding & Iron Co. Ltd	4	4
1891	Palmers Shipbuilding & Iron Co. Ltd	5	4
1892	Palmers Shipbuilding & Iron Co. Ltd	5	2
1893	Palmers Shipbuilding & Iron Co. Ltd	5	3
1894	Palmers Shipbuilding & Iron Co. Ltd	5	4
1895	Palmers Shipbuilding & Iron Co. Ltd	5	2
1896	Palmers Shipbuilding & Iron Co. Ltd	5	3
1897	Palmers Shipbuilding & Iron Co. Ltd	5	4
1898	Palmers Shipbuilding & Iron Co. Ltd	5	5
1899	Palmers Shipbuilding & Iron Co. Ltd	5	4
1900	Palmers Shipbuilding & Iron Co. Ltd	5	4
1901	Palmers Shipbuilding & Iron Co. Ltd	5	4
1902	Palmers Shipbuilding & Iron Co. Ltd	5	4
1903	Palmers Shipbuilding & Iron Co. Ltd	5	4
1904	Palmers Shipbuilding & Iron Co. Ltd	5	4
1905	Palmers Shipbuilding & Iron Co. Ltd	5	4
1906	Palmers Shipbuilding & Iron Co. Ltd	4	4
1907	Palmers Shipbuilding & Iron Co. Ltd	5	4
1908	Palmers Shipbuilding & Iron Co. Ltd	5	2
1909	Palmers Shipbuilding & Iron Co. Ltd	5	3
1910	Palmers Shipbuilding & Iron Co. Ltd	5	3
1911	Palmers Shipbuilding & Iron Co. Ltd	5	3
1912	Palmers Shipbuilding & Iron Co. Ltd	5	3
1913	Palmers Shipbuilding & Iron Co. Ltd	5	3
1921	Palmers Shipbuilding & Iron Co. Ltd	5	-
1922	Palmers Shipbuilding & Iron Co. Ltd	5	-
1923	Palmers Shipbuilding & Iron Co. Ltd	5	-
1924	Palmers Shipbuilding & Iron Co. Ltd	5	-
1925	Palmers Shipbuilding & Iron Co. Ltd	5	-
1926	Palmers Shipbuilding & Iron Co. Ltd	5	-
1927	Palmers Shipbuilding & Iron Co. Ltd	5	-
1928	Palmers Shipbuilding & Iron Co. Ltd	5	-
1929	Palmers Shipbuilding & Iron Co. Ltd	5	-
1930	Palmers Shipbuilding & Iron Co. Ltd	4	-
1931	Palmers Shipbuilding & Iron Co. Ltd	4	-
1932	Palmers Shipbuilding & Iron Co. Ltd	4	-
1933	Palmers Shipbuilding & Iron Co. Ltd	4	-
1934	Palmers Shipbuilding & Iron Co. Ltd	5	-

1856 and 1857: Not completed. 1935: dismantled.

'Jennington': see Lemington

Lackenby, N. Riding [NZ 5619]

Year	Owner	Built	In Blast
1871	Lackenby Iron Co.	2	2
1872	Lackenby Iron Co.	3	2
1873	Lackenby Iron Co.	3	2
1874	Lackenby Iron Co.	3	3
1875	Lackenby Iron Co.	3	3
1876	Lackenby Iron Co.	3	3
1877	Lackenby Iron Co.	3	3
1878	Lackenby Iron Co.	3	3
1879	Downey & Co.	3	3
1880	Downey & Co.	3	2
1881	Downey & Co.	3	3
1882	Downey & Co.	3	3
1883	Downey & Co.	3	3
1884	Downey & Co.	3	2
1885	Downey & Co.	3	2
1886	Downey & Co.	3	2
1887	Downey & Co.	3	3
1888	Downey & Co.	3	3
1889	Downey & Co.	3	3
1890	Downey & Co.	3	3
1891	Downey & Co.	3	3
1892	Bolckow, Vaughan & Co. Ltd	3	2
1893	Bolckow, Vaughan & Co. Ltd	3	3
1894	Bolckow, Vaughan & Co. Ltd	3	2
1895	Bolckow, Vaughan & Co. Ltd	3	3
1896	Bolckow, Vaughan & Co. Ltd	3	3
1897	Bolckow, Vaughan & Co. Ltd	3	2
1898	Bolckow, Vaughan & Co. Ltd	3	2
1899	Bolckow, Vaughan & Co. Ltd	3	2
1900	Bolckow, Vaughan & Co. Ltd	3	2
1901	Bolckow, Vaughan & Co. Ltd	3	2
1902	Tees Furnace Co. Ltd	3	2
1903	Tees Furnace Co. Ltd	3	2
1904	Tees Furnace Co. Ltd	3	2
1905	Tees Furnace Co. Ltd	3	2
1906	Tees Furnace Co. Ltd	3	2
1907	Tees Furnace Co. Ltd	3	2
1908	Tees Furnace Co. Ltd	3	2
1909	Tees Furnace Co. Ltd	2	0
1910	Tees Furnace Co. Ltd	2	2
1911	Tees Furnace Co. Ltd	2	2
1912	Tees Furnace Co. Ltd	2	2
1913	Tees Furnace Co. Ltd	2	2
1921	Tees Furnace Co. Ltd	3	-
1922	Tees Furnace Co. Ltd	3	-
1923	Tees Furnace Co. Ltd	3	-
1924	Tees Furnace Co. Ltd	3	-
1925	Tees Furnace Co. Ltd	3	-
1926	Tees Furnace Co. Ltd	3	-
1927	Tees Furnace Co. Ltd	3	-
1928	Tees Furnace Co. Ltd	3	-
1929	Pease & Partners Ltd	3	-
1930	Pease & Partners Ltd	3	-
1931	Pease & Partners Ltd	3	-

1871: 1 furnace building.

'Leaham': see Vane & Seaham

Lemington, Northumberland [NZ 1764]

Year	Owner	Built	In Blast
1805	Bulmer & Co.	2	1
1810	Bulmer & Co.	2	2
1823	—	2	-
1825	Bulmer & Co.	2	-
1830	—	2	-
1839	—	2	2
1841	Tyne Iron Co.	2	1
1843	Bulmer & Co.	-	1
1847	Tyne Iron Co.	2	2
1849	Tyne Iron Co.	2	1
1854	Tyne Iron Co.	2	2
1855	Tyne Iron Co.	2	2
1856	Tyne Iron Co.	2	2
1857	Tyne Iron Co.	2	2
1858	Tyne Iron Co.	2	2
1859	Tyne Iron Co.	2	1
1860	Tyne Iron Co.	2	1
1861	Tyne Iron Co.	2	1
1862	Bulmer & Co.	2	1
1863	Bulmer & Co.	2	1
1864	Bulmer & Co.	2	1
1865	Bulmer & Co.	2	1
1866	Bulmer & Co.	2	1
1867	Bulmer & Co.	2	1
1868	Bulmer & Co.	2	0
1869	Bulmer & Co.	2	0
1870	Bulmer & Co.	2	0
1871	Bulmer & Co.	2	0
1872	Bulmer & Co.	-	-
1873	Bulmer & Co.	2	-
1874	Bulmer & Co.	-	-

1805: no output shown; the owner's name has been emended from 'Buliner' in the original text. 1823–30: output 2,379 tons p.a. in 1823, 2,247 tons in 1830. 1825: no indication of whether furnaces in blast or not, no output; 'No Return'. 1843: output 60 tons a week. 1847: 8,320 tons p.a., i.e. 80 tons a week from each of two furnaces. 1849: Hunt lists 2 furnaces in blast at Tyne Ironworks. Truran: output 100 tons a week from each of 2 furnaces at 'Jennington'. *Mineral Statistics* lists this works as Tyne Ironworks in 1854–59 and in 1860 has duplicate entries under both that heading and Lemington; from 1861 the name Lemington is used. The site listed by Truran as Tyne Main belongs under Wallsend (qv).

Linthorpe, N. Riding [NZ 4818]

Year	Owner	Built	In Blast
1865	Lloyd & Co.	4	4
1866	Lloyd & Co.	4	4
1867	Lloyd & Co.	4	4
1868	Lloyd & Co.	4	4
1869	Lloyd & Co.	4	4
1870	Lloyd & Co.	6	6
1871	Lloyd & Co.	6	6
1872	Lloyd & Co.	6	6
1873	Lloyd & Co.	6	6
1874	Lloyd & Co.	6	5
1875	Lloyd & Co.	6	6
1876	Lloyd & Co.	6	6
1877	Lloyd & Co.	6	6
1878	Lloyd & Co.	6	5
1879	Edward Williams	6	6
1880	Edward Williams	6	3
1881	Edward Williams	6	4
1882	Edward Williams	6	5
1883	Edward Williams	6	5
1884	Edward Williams	6	4
1885	Edward Williams	6	4
1886	Edward Williams	6	4
1887	Executors of late Edward Williams	6	4
1888	Executors of late Edward Williams	6	4
1889	Executors of late Edward Williams	6	5
1890	Executors of late Edward Williams	6	4
1891	Executors of late Edward Williams	6	3
1892	Edward Williams	6	3
1893	Edward Williams	6	4
1894	Edward Williams	6	4
1895	Edward Williams	6	4
1896	Edward Williams	6	4
1897	Edward Williams	6	3
1898	Edward Williams	6	4
1899	Edward Williams	6	4
1900	Edward Williams	6	4
1901	Edward Williams	6	3
1902	Edward Williams	6	2
1903	Linthorpe Dinsdale Smelting Co. Ltd	6	2
1904	Linthorpe Dinsdale Smelting Co. Ltd	6	3
1905	Linthorpe Dinsdale Smelting Co. Ltd	6	4
1906	Linthorpe Dinsdale Smelting Co. Ltd	6	4
1907	Linthorpe Dinsdale Smelting Co. Ltd	6	4
1908	Linthorpe Dinsdale Smelting Co. Ltd	6	3
1909	Linthorpe Dinsdale Smelting Co. Ltd	6	3
1910	Linthorpe Dinsdale Smelting Co. Ltd	6	4
1911	Linthorpe Dinsdale Smelting Co. Ltd	6	3
1912	Linthorpe Dinsdale Smelting Co. Ltd	6	3
1913	Linthorpe Dinsdale Smelting Co. Ltd	6	4
1921	Linthorpe-Dinsdale Smelting Co. Ltd	10	-
1922	Linthorpe-Dinsdale Smelting Co. Ltd	10	-
1923	Linthorpe-Dinsdale Smelting Co. Ltd	10	-
1924	Linthorpe-Dinsdale Smelting Co. Ltd	10	-
1925	Linthorpe-Dinsdale Smelting Co. Ltd	10	-
1926	Linthorpe-Dinsdale Smelting Co. Ltd	10	-
1927	Linthorpe-Dinsdale Smelting Co. Ltd	10	-
1928	Linthorpe-Dinsdale Smelting Co. Ltd	10	-
1929	Linthorpe-Dinsdale Smelting Co. Ltd	10	-
1930	Linthorpe-Dinsdale Smelting Co. Ltd	10	-
1931	Linthorpe-Dinsdale Smelting Co. Ltd	10	-
1932	Linthorpe-Dinsdale Smelting Co. Ltd	10	-
1933	Linthorpe-Dinsdale Smelting Co. Ltd	10	-
1934	Linthorpe-Dinsdale Smelting Co. Ltd	10	-
1935	Linthorpe-Dinsdale Smelting Co. Ltd	10	-
1936	Linthorpe-Dinsdale Smelting Co. Ltd	10	-
1937	Linthorpe-Dinsdale Smelting Co. Ltd	4	-
1938	Linthorpe-Dinsdale Smelting Co. Ltd	4	-
1939	Linthorpe-Dinsdale Smelting Co. Ltd	4	-
1940	Linthorpe-Dinsdale Smelting Co. Ltd	4	-
1941	Linthorpe-Dinsdale Smelting Co. Ltd	4	-
1942	Linthorpe-Dinsdale Smelting Co. Ltd	3	-
1943	Linthorpe-Dinsdale Smelting Co. Ltd	3	-
1944	Linthorpe-Dinsdale Smelting Co. Ltd	3	-
1945	Linthorpe-Dinsdale Smelting Co. Ltd	3	-

1865: In blast from 13 Aug.: commencement of works. A new company, with a hyphenated name, was registered in 1920. The 1921–36 returns must include at least two of the works operated by the old company in 1913 (i.e. Linthorpe, Newport (Middlesbrough) and Stockton North Shore, qqv) but the distribution of the total number of furnaces between the three sites has not been established.

Loftus: see Skinningrove

Middlesbrough, N. Riding [NZ 4921]

Year	Owner	Built	In Blast
1854	Bolckow, Vaughan & Co.	3	3
1855	Bolckow, Vaughan & Co.	3	3
1856	Bolckow & Vaughan	3	3
1857	Bolckow & Vaughan	3	3
1858	Bolckow & Vaughan	3	3
1859	Bolckow & Vaughan	3	3
1860	Bolckow & Vaughan	3	3
1861	Bolckow & Vaughan	-	-
1862	Bolckow & Vaughan	-	-
1863	Bolckow & Vaughan	-	-
1864	Bolckow & Vaughan	-	-
1865	Bolckow, Vaughan & Co. Ltd	-	-
1866	Bolckow, Vaughan & Co. Ltd	-	-
1867	Bolckow, Vaughan & Co. Ltd	-	-
1868	Bolckow, Vaughan & Co. Ltd	-	-
1869	Bolckow, Vaughan & Co. Ltd	-	-
1870	Bolckow, Vaughan & Co. Ltd	-	-
1871	Bolckow, Vaughan & Co. Ltd	-	-
1872	Bolckow, Vaughan & Co. Ltd	15	15
1873	Bolckow, Vaughan & Co. Ltd	15	15
1874	Bolckow, Vaughan & Co. Ltd	15	14
1875	Bolckow, Vaughan & Co. Ltd	11	9
1876	Bolckow, Vaughan & Co. Ltd	3	1
1877	Bolckow, Vaughan & Co. Ltd	3	3
1878	Bolckow, Vaughan & Co. Ltd	14	13
1879	Bolckow, Vaughan & Co. Ltd	11	11
1880	Bolckow, Vaughan & Co. Ltd	11	11
1881	Bolckow, Vaughan & Co. Ltd	3	3
1882	Bolckow, Vaughan & Co. Ltd	3	3
1883	Bolckow, Vaughan & Co. Ltd	2	2
1884	Bolckow, Vaughan & Co. Ltd	2	2
1885	Bolckow, Vaughan & Co. Ltd	2	2
1886	Bolckow, Vaughan & Co. Ltd	2	2
1887	Bolckow, Vaughan & Co. Ltd	2	2
1888	Bolckow, Vaughan & Co. Ltd	2	2
1889	Bolckow, Vaughan & Co. Ltd	2	2
1890	Bolckow, Vaughan & Co. Ltd	2	2
1891	Bolckow, Vaughan & Co. Ltd	2	2
1892	Bolckow, Vaughan & Co. Ltd	2	2
1893	Bolckow, Vaughan & Co. Ltd	2	2
1894	Bolckow, Vaughan & Co. Ltd	2	2
1895	Bolckow, Vaughan & Co. Ltd	2	2
1896	Bolckow, Vaughan & Co. Ltd	2	2
1897	Bolckow, Vaughan & Co. Ltd	2	2
1898	Bolckow, Vaughan & Co. Ltd	2	2
1899	Bolckow, Vaughan & Co. Ltd	2	2
1900	Bolckow, Vaughan & Co. Ltd	2	2
1901	Bolckow, Vaughan & Co. Ltd	2	1
1902	Bolckow, Vaughan & Co. Ltd	2	2
1903	Bolckow, Vaughan & Co. Ltd	2	2
1904	Bolckow, Vaughan & Co. Ltd	2	1
1905	Bolckow, Vaughan & Co. Ltd	2	2
1906	Bolckow, Vaughan & Co. Ltd	2	2
1907	Bolckow, Vaughan & Co. Ltd	2	1
1908	Bolckow, Vaughan & Co. Ltd	2	2
1909	Bolckow, Vaughan & Co. Ltd	2	2
1910	Bolckow, Vaughan & Co. Ltd	2	2
1911	Bolckow, Vaughan & Co. Ltd	2	1
1912	Bolckow, Vaughan & Co. Ltd	2	2
1913	Bolckow, Vaughan & Co. Ltd	2	1
1921	Bolckow, Vaughan & Co. Ltd	22	-
1922	Bolckow, Vaughan & Co. Ltd	22	-
1923	Bolckow, Vaughan & Co. Ltd	21	-
1924	Bolckow, Vaughan & Co. Ltd	19	-
1925	Bolckow, Vaughan & Co. Ltd	19	-
1926	Bolckow, Vaughan & Co. Ltd	13	-
1927	Bolckow, Vaughan & Co. Ltd	13	-
1928	Bolckow, Vaughan & Co. Ltd	13	-

Truran lists two works under Middlesbrough, one with 4 furnaces and the other with 3, to all of which he assigns an output per furnace of 140 tons a week. The second works is presumably this site; cf. also Tees. For furnace-numbers between 1861 and 1871 see Cleveland. The numbers printed above include Cleveland and Witton Park (qv) in 1872–74 and Cleveland only in 1875 and 1878. Those for 1879–80 above are said to be for Middlesbrough alone. Between 1921 and 1928 a single figure was returned (under Middlesbrough) for all the Bolckow, Vaughan sites, which is printed above; after 1929 this total is absorbed into a yet larger figure for Dorman Long (see Redcar).

Middlesbrough: see also Cleveland; Eston; Tees

Middleton, Durham [NZ 3413]

Year	Owner	Built	In Blast
1864	Middleton Iron Co. Ltd	2	0
1865	Middleton Iron Co. Ltd	2	1
1866	Middleton Iron Co. Ltd	2	2
1867	Middleton Iron Co. Ltd	2	0
1868	Middleton Iron Co. Ltd	2	0
1869	Middleton Iron Co. Ltd	2	0
1870	George Wythes & Co.	3	3
1871	George Wythes & Co.	3	3
1872	George Wythes & Co.	3	3
1873	George Wythes & Co.	3	3
1874	George Wythes & Co.	4	3
1875	George Wythes & Co.	4	4
1876	George Wythes & Co.	4	3
1877	George Wythes & Co.	4	0
1878	George Wythes & Co.	4	0
1879	George Wythes & Co.	4	0
1880	George Wythes & Co.	4	0
1881	George Wythes & Co.	4	2
1882	Executors of late George Wythes	4	2
1883	Executors of late George Wythes	4	4
1884	Executors of late George Wythes	4	0
1885	Executors of late George Wythes	4	0
1886	Executors of late George Wythes	4	0
1887	Executors of late George Wythes	4	0
1888	Executors of late George Wythes	4	0
1889	Executors of late George Wythes	4	0
1890	Executors of late George Wythes	4	0

Year	Owner	Built	In Blast
1891	Executors of late George Wythes	4	0
1892	Joseph Torbock	4	0
1893	Joseph Torbock	4	0
1894	Joseph Torbock	4	0
1895	Joseph Torbock	4	0
1896	Joseph Torbock	4	0
1897	Joseph Torbock	4	0
1898	Joseph Torbock	4	0
1899	Joseph Torbock	4	0
1900	Dinsdale Smelting Co. Ltd	4	0
1901	Dinsdale Smelting Co. Ltd	4	1
1902	Linthorpe Dinsdale Smelting Co. Ltd	4	1
1903	Linthorpe Dinsdale Smelting Co. Ltd	4	2
1904	Linthorpe Dinsdale Smelting Co. Ltd	4	2
1905	Linthorpe Dinsdale Smelting Co. Ltd	4	1
1906	Linthorpe Dinsdale Smelting Co. Ltd	4	3
1907	Linthorpe Dinsdale Smelting Co. Ltd	4	3
1908	Linthorpe Dinsdale Smelting Co. Ltd	4	2
1909	Linthorpe Dinsdale Smelting Co. Ltd	4	2
1910	Linthorpe Dinsdale Smelting Co. Ltd	4	3
1911	Linthorpe Dinsdale Smelting Co. Ltd	4	2
1912	Linthorpe Dinsdale Smelting Co. Ltd	4	2
1913	Linthorpe Dinsdale Smelting Co. Ltd	4	3

1883: at work 9 months. From 1921 a single figure was returned for the Linthorpe-Dinsdale works, for which see under Linthorpe.

Newport, Middlesbrough, N. Riding [NZ 4819]

Year	Owner	Built	In Blast
1864	B. Samuelson & Co.	3	3
1865	B. Samuelson & Co.	4	3
1866	B. Samuelson & Co.	4	4
1867	B. Samuelson & Co.	4	4
1868	B. Samuelson & Co.	5	5
1869	B. Samuelson & Co.	5	5
1870	B. Samuelson & Co.	7	7
1871	B. Samuelson & Co.	7	7
1872	B. Samuelson & Co.	8	8
1873	B. Samuelson & Co.	8	8
1874	B. Samuelson & Co.	8	5
1875	B. Samuelson & Co.	6	5
1876	B. Samuelson & Co.	6	3
1877	B. Samuelson & Co.	6	6
1878	B. Samuelson & Co.	7	5
1879	B. Samuelson & Co.	7	6
1880	B. Samuelson & Co.	8	7
1881	B. Samuelson & Co.	8	8
1882	B. Samuelson & Co.	8	7
1883	B. Samuelson & Co.	8	7
1884	B. Samuelson & Co.	8	6
1885	B. Samuelson & Co.	8	6
1886	B. Samuelson & Co.	8	7
1887	Sir B. Samuelson & Co. Ltd	8	8
1888	Sir B. Samuelson & Co. Ltd	8	7
1889	Sir B. Samuelson & Co. Ltd	8	6
1890	Sir B. Samuelson & Co. Ltd	8	8
1891	Sir B. Samuelson & Co. Ltd	8	7
1892	Sir B. Samuelson & Co. Ltd	8	5
1893	Sir B. Samuelson & Co. Ltd	8	5
1894	Sir B. Samuelson & Co. Ltd	8	5
1895	Sir B. Samuelson & Co. Ltd	8	6
1896	Sir B. Samuelson & Co. Ltd	8	6
1897	Sir B. Samuelson & Co. Ltd	8	6
1898	Sir B. Samuelson & Co. Ltd	8	6
1899	Sir B. Samuelson & Co. Ltd	8	7
1900	Sir B. Samuelson & Co. Ltd	8	7
1901	Sir B. Samuelson & Co. Ltd	8	4
1902	Sir B. Samuelson & Co. Ltd	8	5
1903	Sir B. Samuelson & Co. Ltd	8	5
1904	Sir B. Samuelson & Co. Ltd	8	5
1905	Sir B. Samuelson & Co. Ltd	8	5
1906	Sir B. Samuelson & Co. Ltd	8	5
1907	Sir B. Samuelson & Co. Ltd	8	5
1908	Sir B. Samuelson & Co. Ltd	8	5
1909	Sir B. Samuelson & Co. Ltd	8	4
1910	Sir B. Samuelson & Co. Ltd	8	5
1911	Sir B. Samuelson & Co. Ltd	8	5
1912	Sir B. Samuelson & Co. Ltd	8	5
1913	Sir B. Samuelson & Co. Ltd	8	6
1921	Sir B. Samuelson & Co. Ltd	8	-
1922	Sir B. Samuelson & Co. Ltd	8	-

1864: Blown-in in August. 1875 and 1876: 1 furnace building.

Normanby, N. Riding [NZ 5518]

Year	Owner	Built	In Blast
1860	Jones, Dunning & Co.	2	0
1861	Jones, Dunning & Co.	2	2
1862	Jones, Dunning & Co.	2	2
1863	Jones, Dunning & Co.	2	2
1864	Jones, Dunning & Co.	3	2
1865	Jones, Dunning & Co.	3	3
1866	Jones, Dunning & Co.	3	3
1867	Jones, Dunning & Co.	3	2
1868	Jones, Dunning & Co.	3	3
1869	Jones, Dunning & Co.	3	3
1870	Jones, Dunning & Co.	3	3
1871	Jones, Dunning & Co.	3	3
1872	Jones, Dunning & Co.	3	3
1873	Jones, Dunning & Co.	3	3
1874	Jones, Samuelson & Co.	3	3
1875	Jones, Dunning & Co.	3	3
1876	Jones, Dunning & Co.	3	3
1877	Jones, Dunning & Co.	3	0
1878	Jones, Dunning & Co.	3	3
1879	Jones, Dunning & Co.	3	3
1880	Jones, Dunning & Co.	3	3
1881	Jones, Dunning & Co.	3	3
1882	Jones, Dunning & Co.	3	3
1883	Jones, Dunning & Co.	3	3
1884	Jones, Dunning & Co.	3	3
1885	Jones, Dunning & Co.	3	3
1886	Jones, Dunning & Co.	3	3
1887	Jones, Dunning & Co.	3	2
1888	Jones, Pearce & Crewdson	3	2
1889	Jones, Dunning & Co.	3	2
1890	Normanby Iron Works Co.	3	2
1891	Normanby Iron Works Co.	3	2
1892	Normanby Iron Works Co.	3	1
1893	A.A.F. & H.P. Pease	3	2
1894	A.A.F. & H.P. Pease	3	2
1895	Arthur Pease	3	2
1896	Normanby Iron Works Co. Ltd	3	3
1897	Normanby Iron Works Co. Ltd	3	3
1898	Normanby Iron Works Co. Ltd	3	3
1899	Normanby Iron Works Co. Ltd	3	3
1900	Normanby Ironworks Co. Ltd	3	3
1901	Normanby Ironworks Co. Ltd	4	2

Year	Owner	Built	In Blast
1902	Normanby Ironworks Co. Ltd	4	3
1903	Normanby Ironworks Co. Ltd	4	2
1904	Normanby Ironworks Co. Ltd	4	2
1905	Normanby Ironworks Co. Ltd	4	3
1906	Normanby Ironworks Co. Ltd	4	3
1907	Normanby Ironworks Co. Ltd	4	2
1908	Normanby Ironworks Co. Ltd	4	2
1909	Normanby Ironworks Co. Ltd	4	2
1910	Normanby Ironworks Co. Ltd	4	3
1911	Pease & Partners Ltd	4	2
1912	Pease & Partners Ltd	4	2
1913	Pease & Partners Ltd	4	3
1921	Pease & Partners Ltd	3	-
1922	Pease & Partners Ltd	3	-
1923	Pease & Partners Ltd	3	-
1924	Pease & Partners Ltd	3	-
1925	Pease & Partners Ltd	3	-
1926	Pease & Partners Ltd	2	-
1927	Pease & Partners Ltd	2	-
1935	Pease & Partners Ltd	3	-
1936	Pease & Partners Ltd	3	-
1937	Pease & Partners Ltd	3	-
1938	Pease & Partners Ltd	3	-
1939	Pease & Partners Ltd	3	-
1940	Pease & Partners Ltd	3	-
1941	Pease & Partners Ltd	3	-
1942	Pease & Partners Ltd	3	-
1943	Pease & Partners Ltd	3	-
1944	Pease & Partners Ltd	3	-
1945	Pease & Partners Ltd	3	-
1946	Pease & Partners Ltd	3	-
1947	Normanby Iron Works Co. Ltd	3	-
1948	Normanby Iron Works Co. Ltd	3	-
1949	Normanby Iron Works Co. Ltd	3	-
1950	Normanby Iron Works Co. Ltd	3	-
1951	Normanby Iron Works Co. Ltd	3	-
1952	Normanby Iron Works Co. Ltd	3	-
1953	Normanby Iron Works Co. Ltd	3	-
1954	Normanby Iron Works Co. Ltd	3	-
1955	Normanby Iron Works Co. Ltd	3	-
1956	Normanby Iron Works Co. Ltd	3	-
1957	Normanby Iron Works Co. Ltd	3	-
1958	Normanby Iron Works Co. Ltd	3	-
1959	Normanby Iron Works Co. Ltd	3	-

The change in spelling in 1899–1900 reflects the establishment of a new company. Normanby disappears from the returns between 1928 and 1934. In 1947–52 the owner is named in the original returns as 'Pease & Partners, Normanby Iron Works, Ltd', which was not registered and must have been a variant devised by the new company, whose legal style was a revival of that used by the company of 1895–99.

North Shore: see Stockton

Norton, Durham [NZ 4422]

Year	Owner	Built	In Blast
1855	Warner, Lucas & Barrett	2	0
1856	Warner, Lucas & Barrett	2	2
1857	Warner, Lucas & Barrett	3	1
1858	Warner, Lucas & Barrett	3	2
1859	Warner, Lucas & Barrett	3	2
1860	Warner, Lucas & Barrett	3	2
1861	Warner, Lucas & Barrett	3	2
1862	Warner, Lucas & Barrett	3	3
1863	Warner, Lucas & Barrett	3	3
1864	Warner, Lucas & Barrett	3	3
1865	Norton Iron Co. Ltd	3	3
1866	Norton Iron Co. Ltd	4	3
1867	Norton Iron Co. Ltd	4	3
1868	Norton Iron Co. Ltd	4	1
1869	Norton Iron Co. Ltd	4	2
1870	Norton Iron Co. Ltd	4	2
1871	Norton Iron Co. Ltd	3	3
1872	Norton Iron Co. Ltd	6	3
1873	Norton Iron Co. Ltd	3	3
1874	Norton Iron Co. Ltd	3	3
1875	Norton Iron Co. Ltd	3	3
1876	Norton Iron Co. Ltd	3	3
1877	Norton Iron Co. Ltd	3	2
1878	Norton Iron Co. Ltd	6	0
1879	Norton Iron Co. Ltd	6	0
1880	Norton Iron Co. Ltd	6	0
1881	Norton Iron Co. Ltd	6	0
1882	Norton Iron Co. Ltd	6	0
1883	Norton Iron Co. Ltd	6	0
1884	Norton Iron Co. Ltd	3	0
1885	Norton Iron Co. Ltd	3	0
1886	Norton Iron Co. Ltd	3	0
1887	Norton Iron Co. Ltd	3	0
1888	Norton Iron Co. Ltd	3	0
1889	William Slater & Sons	3	0
1890	William Slater & Sons	3	0
1891	William Slater & Sons	3	0
1892	Norton Iron Co.	3	0
1893	Norton Iron Co.	3	0

1855: Building. The first partner's name is spelt 'Warners' in 1858–64.

Norwegian, N. Riding

Year	Owner	Built	In Blast
1870	Titanic Ore Co.	1	1
1871	Titanic Ore Co.	2	2
1872	Titanic Iron Co.	2	2
1873	Titanic Iron Co. Ltd	2	1
1874	Titanic Iron Co. Ltd	2	1
1875	Titanic Iron Co. Ltd	2	1
1876	Titanic Iron Co. Ltd	2	1
1877	Titanic Iron Co. Ltd	2	0

No company matching the owner's name printed in *Mineral Statistics* in 1873–77 can be found on the register; the works appears to have been operated by either the Titanic Steel & Iron Co. Ltd or the Titanium Ore Co. Ltd or both. The former concern was registered in 1862; its shareholders resolved in favour of voluntary winding-up in June 1871 and the last meeting was held in August 1874 (BT 31/679/2894). The other company was registered in June 1864, sought voluntary winding-up in September 1866, and was struck off in 1882, not having traded for many years (BT 31/962/1338C).

Ormesby, N. Riding [NZ 5317]

Year	Owner	Built	In Blast
1854	Cochrane & Co.	4	2
1855	Cochrane & Co.	4	3
1856	Cochrane & Co.	4	4
1857	Cochrane & Co.	4	4
1858	Cochrane & Co.	4	2
1859	Cochrane & Co.	4	2
1860	Cochrane & Co.	4	3
1861	Cochrane & Co.	4	3
1862	Cochrane & Co.	4	4
1863	Cochrane & Co.	4	4
1864	Cochrane & Co.	4	4
1865	Cochrane & Co.	4	4
1866	Cochrane & Co.	4	4
1867	Cochrane & Co.	2	2
1868	Cochrane & Co.	3	3
1869	Cochrane & Co.	3	2
1870	Cochrane & Co.	3	2
1871	Cochrane & Co.	3	3
1872	Cochrane & Co.	4	3
1873	Cochrane & Co.	4	2
1874	Cochrane & Co.	4	3
1875	Cochrane & Co.	4	3
1876	Cochrane & Co.	4	3
1877	Cochrane & Co.	4	3
1878	Cochrane & Co.	4	3
1879	Cochrane & Co.	4	3
1880	Cochrane & Co.	4	4
1881	Cochrane & Co.	4	4
1882	Cochrane & Co.	4	4
1883	Cochrane & Co.	5	4
1884	Cochrane & Co.	5	4
1885	Cochrane & Co.	5	4
1886	Cochrane & Co.	5	4
1887	Cochrane & Co.	5	3
1888	Cochrane & Co.	5	3
1889	Cochrane & Co.	5	3
1890	Cochrane & Co. Ltd	5	3
1891	Cochrane & Co. Ltd	5	3
1892	Cochrane & Co. Ltd	5	3
1893	Cochrane & Co. Ltd	5	3
1894	Cochrane & Co. Ltd	4	3
1895	Cochrane & Co. Ltd	4	3
1896	Cochrane & Co. Ltd	4	3
1897	Cochrane & Co. Ltd	4	3
1898	Cochrane & Co. Ltd	4	3
1899	Cochrane & Co. Ltd	4	3
1900	Cochrane & Co. Ltd	4	3
1901	Cochrane & Co. Ltd	4	3
1902	Cochrane & Co. Ltd	4	3
1903	Cochrane & Co. Ltd	4	3
1904	Cochrane & Co. Ltd	4	3
1905	Cochrane & Co. Ltd	4	3
1906	Cochrane & Co. Ltd	4	3
1907	Cochrane & Co. Ltd	4	3
1908	Cochrane & Co. Ltd	4	3
1909	Cochrane & Co. Ltd	4	3
1910	Cochrane & Co. Ltd	4	3
1911	Cochrane & Co. Ltd	4	3
1912	Cochrane & Co. Ltd	4	3
1913	Cochrane & Co. Ltd	4	3
1921	Cochrane & Co. Ltd	3	-
1922	Cochrane & Co. Ltd	3	-
1923	Cochrane & Co. Ltd	3	-
1924	Cochrane & Co. Ltd	3	-
1925	Cochrane & Co. Ltd	3	-
1926	Cochrane & Co. Ltd	3	-
1927	Cochrane & Co. Ltd	3	-
1928	Cochrane & Co. Ltd	3	-
1929	Cochrane & Co. Ltd	3	-
1930	Cochrane & Co. Ltd	3	-
1931	Cochrane & Co. Ltd	3	-
1932	Cochrane & Co. Ltd	3	-
1933	Cochrane & Co. Ltd	3	-

Truran: output 120 tons a week from each of 4 furnaces. 1871: 1 furnace building. 1882: 1 furnace building.

Port Clarence: see Clarence

Redcar, N. Riding [NZ 6124]

Year	Owner	Built	In Blast
1874	Robson, Maynard & Co.	2	2
1875	Robson, Maynard & Co.	4	2
1876	Robson, Maynard & Co.	4	4
1877	Robson, Maynard & Co.	4	4
1878	Robson, Maynard & Co.	4	4
1879	Robson, Maynard & Co.	4	4
1880	Robson, Maynard & Co.	4	4
1881	Robson, Maynard & Co.	4	4
1882	Walker, Maynard & Co.	4	4
1883	Walker, Maynard & Co.	4	4
1884	Walker, Maynard & Co.	4	3
1885	Walker, Maynard & Co.	4	3
1886	Walker, Maynard & Co.	4	3
1887	Walker, Maynard & Co.	4	3
1888	Walker, Maynard & Co.	4	4
1889	Walker, Maynard & Co.	4	4
1890	Walker, Maynard & Co.	4	4
1891	Walker, Maynard & Co.	4	3
1892	Walker, Maynard & Co.	4	2
1893	Walker, Maynard & Co.	4	2
1894	Walker, Maynard & Co.	4	4
1895	Walker, Maynard & Co.	4	4
1896	Walker, Maynard & Co.	4	4
1897	Walker, Maynard & Co.	4	4
1898	Walker, Maynard & Co.	4	4
1899	Walker, Maynard & Co.	4	4
1900	Walker, Maynard & Co.	4	4
1901	Walker, Maynard & Co. Ltd	4	4
1902	Walker, Maynard & Co. Ltd	4	4
1903	Walker, Maynard & Co. Ltd	4	4
1904	Walker, Maynard & Co. Ltd	4	2
1905	Walker, Maynard & Co. Ltd	6	5
1906	Walker, Maynard & Co. Ltd	6	5
1907	Walker, Maynard & Co. Ltd	6	6
1908	Walker, Maynard & Co. Ltd	6	4
1909	Walker, Maynard & Co. Ltd	6	5
1910	Walker, Maynard & Co. Ltd	6	4
1911	Walker, Maynard & Co. Ltd	6	5
1912	Walker, Maynard & Co. Ltd	6	5
1913	Walker, Maynard & Co. Ltd	6	4
1921	Dorman Long & Co. Ltd	10	-
1922	Dorman Long & Co. Ltd	10	-
1923	Dorman Long & Co. Ltd	30	-

Year	Owner	Built	In Blast
1924	Dorman Long & Co. Ltd	31	-
1925	Dorman Long & Co. Ltd	29	-
1926	Dorman Long & Co. Ltd	29	-
1927	Dorman Long & Co. Ltd	29	-
1928	Dorman Long & Co. Ltd	29	-
1929	Dorman Long & Co. Ltd	40	-
1930	Dorman Long & Co. Ltd	34	-
1931	Dorman Long & Co. Ltd	34	-
1932	Dorman Long & Co. Ltd	34	-
1933	Dorman Long & Co. Ltd	34	-
1934	Dorman Long & Co. Ltd	34	-
1935	Dorman Long & Co. Ltd	34	-
1936	Dorman Long & Co. Ltd	21	-
1937	Dorman Long & Co. Ltd	21	-
1938	Dorman Long & Co. Ltd	21	-
1939	Dorman Long & Co. Ltd	20	-
1940	Dorman Long & Co. Ltd	20	-
1941	Dorman Long & Co. Ltd	20	-
1942	Dorman Long & Co. Ltd	20	-
1943	Dorman Long & Co. Ltd	20	-
1944	Dorman Long & Co. Ltd	20	-
1945	Dorman Long & Co. Ltd	20	-
1946	Dorman Long & Co. Ltd	20	-
1947	Dorman Long & Co. Ltd	20	-
1948	Dorman Long & Co. Ltd	20	-
1949	Dorman Long & Co. Ltd	20	-
1950	Dorman Long & Co. Ltd	20	-
1951	Dorman Long & Co. Ltd	16	-
1952	Dorman Long & Co. Ltd	16	-
1953	Dorman Long & Co. Ltd	2	-
1954	Dorman Long (Steel) Ltd	2	-
1955	Dorman Long (Steel) Ltd	2	-
1956	Dorman Long (Steel) Ltd	2	-
1957	Dorman Long (Steel) Ltd	2	-
1958	Dorman Long (Steel) Ltd	2	-
1959	Dorman Long (Steel) Ltd	2	-
1960	Dorman Long (Steel) Ltd	2	-
1961	Dorman Long (Steel) Ltd	2	-
1962	Dorman Long (Steel) Ltd	2	-
1978	British Steel Corporation	-	-
1979	British Steel Corporation	1	-
1980	British Steel Corporation	1	-

1905–13: furnace-numbers include Coatham (qv), as do the figures from 1921. From 1929 the entry above includes the previously separate Bolckow, Vaughan works (see under Middlesbrough). From 1953 the Dorman Long total was distributed between five sites, besides Redcar: Acklam, Bessemer, Clay Lane, Cleveland and South Bank (qqv). The new furnace built at Redcar in 1978–79 remains in use today.

Ridsdale, Northumberland NZ 9084

Year	Owner	Built	In Blast
1841	Redesdale	3	0
1843	Redesdale Iron Co.	-	1
1847	Redesdale Iron Co.	3	2
1849	Redesdale Iron Co.	3	1

1843: output 60 tons a week. 1847: 8,320 tons p.a., i.e. 80 tons a week from each of two furnaces. 1849: Hunt lists 3 furnaces in blast. The spelling 'Ridsdale' (which is used for the company name in 1849 but not other years) has been adopted here in deference to current local usage.

Royal Greek: see Wallsend

Seaham: see Vane & Seaham

Seaton Carew, Durham [NZ 5229]

Year	Owner	Built	In Blast
1883	Seaton Carew Iron Co. Ltd	3	2
1884	Seaton Carew Iron Co. Ltd	3	2
1885	Seaton Carew Iron Co. Ltd	3	2
1886	Seaton Carew Iron Co. Ltd	3	2
1887	Seaton Carew Iron Co. Ltd	3	3
1888	Seaton Carew Iron Co. Ltd	3	3
1889	Seaton Carew Iron Co. Ltd	3	3
1890	Seaton Carew Iron Co. Ltd	3	3
1891	Seaton Carew Iron Co. Ltd	3	2
1892	Seaton Carew Iron Co. Ltd	3	2
1893	Seaton Carew Iron Co. Ltd	3	2
1894	Seaton Carew Iron Co. Ltd	3	2
1895	Seaton Carew Iron Co. Ltd	3	3
1896	Seaton Carew Iron Co. Ltd	3	3
1897	Seaton Carew Iron Co. Ltd	3	3
1898	Seaton Carew Iron Co. Ltd	3	3
1899	Seaton Carew Iron Co. Ltd	3	3
1900	Seaton Carew Iron Co. Ltd	3	3
1901	Seaton Carew Iron Co. Ltd	3	2
1902	Seaton Carew Iron Co. Ltd	3	2
1903	Seaton Carew Iron Co. Ltd	3	3
1904	Seaton Carew Iron Co. Ltd	3	2
1905	Seaton Carew Iron Co. Ltd	3	2
1906	Seaton Carew Iron Co. Ltd	3	3
1907	Seaton Carew Iron Co. Ltd	3	3
1908	Seaton Carew Iron Co. Ltd	3	2
1909	Seaton Carew Iron Co. Ltd	3	3
1910	Seaton Carew Iron Co. Ltd	3	3
1911	Seaton Carew Iron Co. Ltd	4	3
1912	Seaton Carew Iron Co. Ltd	4	3
1913	Seaton Carew Iron Co. Ltd	4	3
1921	Seaton Carew Iron Co. Ltd	4	-
1922	Seaton Carew Iron Co. Ltd	4	-
1923	Seaton Carew Iron Co. Ltd	4	-
1924	Seaton Carew Iron Co. Ltd	4	-
1925	Seaton Carew Iron Co. Ltd	4	-
1926	Seaton Carew Iron Co. Ltd	2	-
1927	Seaton Carew Iron Co. Ltd	2	-
1928	Seaton Carew Iron Co. Ltd	2	-
1929	Seaton Carew Iron Co. Ltd	2	-
1930	South Durham Steel & Iron Co. Ltd	3	-
1931	South Durham Steel & Iron Co. Ltd	3	-
1932	South Durham Steel & Iron Co. Ltd	3	-
1933	South Durham Steel & Iron Co. Ltd	2	-
1934	South Durham Steel & Iron Co. Ltd	2	-
1935	South Durham Steel & Iron Co. Ltd	2	-
1936	South Durham Steel & Iron Co. Ltd	2	-
1937	South Durham Steel & Iron Co. Ltd	2	-
1938	South Durham Steel & Iron Co. Ltd	2	-
1939	South Durham Steel & Iron Co. Ltd	2	-
1940	South Durham Steel & Iron Co. Ltd	2	-
1941	South Durham Steel & Iron Co. Ltd	2	-
1942	South Durham Steel & Iron Co. Ltd	2	-
1943	South Durham Steel & Iron Co. Ltd	2	-

Year	Owner	Built	In Blast
1944	South Durham Steel & Iron Co. Ltd	2	-
1945	South Durham Steel & Iron Co. Ltd	2	-
1946	South Durham Steel & Iron Co. Ltd	3	-
1947	South Durham Steel & Iron Co. Ltd	3	-
1948	South Durham Steel & Iron Co. Ltd	3	-
1949	South Durham Steel & Iron Co. Ltd	2	-
1950	South Durham Steel & Iron Co. Ltd	3	-
1951	South Durham Steel & Iron Co. Ltd	3	-
1952	South Durham Steel & Iron Co. Ltd	2	-
1953	South Durham Steel & Iron Co. Ltd	2	-
1954	South Durham Steel & Iron Co. Ltd	2	-
1955	South Durham Steel & Iron Co. Ltd	2	-
1956	South Durham Steel & Iron Co. Ltd	3	-
1957	South Durham Steel & Iron Co. Ltd	2	-
1958	South Durham Steel & Iron Co. Ltd	2	-
1959	South Durham Steel & Iron Co. Ltd	3	-
1960	South Durham Steel & Iron Co. Ltd	3	-
1961	South Durham Steel & Iron Co. Ltd	3	-
1962	South Durham Steel & Iron Co. Ltd	3	-
1963	South Durham Steel & Iron Co. Ltd	3	-
1964	South Durham Steel & Iron Co. Ltd	2	-
1965	South Durham Steel & Iron Co. Ltd	2	-
1966	South Durham Steel & Iron Co. Ltd	2	-
1967	South Durham Steel & Iron Co. Ltd	2	-
1968	South Durham Steel & Iron Co. Ltd	2	-
1969	South Durham Steel & Iron Co. Ltd	2	-
1970	British Steel Corporation	2	-
1971	British Steel Corporation	1	-
1972	British Steel Corporation	1	-
1973	British Steel Corporation	1	-
1974	British Steel Corporation	1	-
1975	British Steel Corporation	1	-
1976	British Steel Corporation	1	-

1883: 2 furnaces only partially at work. From 1953 the location of the works is given as West Hartlepool. From 1961 the original Seaton Carew works is known as the North Works, to distinguish it from a new South Works (see below). From 1970 the two sites become Hartlepool (North) and Hartlepool (South); in 1976 there is a single entry for Hartlepool (printed above).

Seaton Carew: South Works [NZ 5229]

Year	Owner	Built	In Blast
1961	South Durham Steel & Iron Co. Ltd	1	-
1962	South Durham Steel & Iron Co. Ltd	1	-
1963	South Durham Steel & Iron Co. Ltd	1	-
1964	South Durham Steel & Iron Co. Ltd	1	-
1965	South Durham Steel & Iron Co. Ltd	1	-
1966	South Durham Steel & Iron Co. Ltd	1	-
1967	South Durham Steel & Iron Co. Ltd	1	-
1968	South Durham Steel & Iron Co. Ltd	1	-
1969	South Durham Steel & Iron Co. Ltd	1	-
1970	British Steel Corporation	1	-
1971	British Steel Corporation	1	-
1972	British Steel Corporation	1	-
1973	British Steel Corporation	1	-
1974	British Steel Corporation	1	-
1975	British Steel Corporation	1	-

See note to previous entry.

Shotley Bridge: see Bradley; Consett

Skinningrove, N. Riding [NZ 7119]

Year	Owner	Built	In Blast
1874	Loftus Iron Co. Ltd	2	2
1875	Loftus Iron Co. Ltd	2	2
1876	Loftus Iron Co. Ltd	2	2
1877	Loftus Iron Co. Ltd	2	0
1878	Loftus Iron Co. Ltd	2	0
1879	Skinningrove Iron Co. Ltd	2	0
1880	Skinningrove Iron Co. Ltd	2	0
1881	Skinningrove Iron Co. Ltd	2	2
1882	Skinningrove Iron Co. Ltd	2	2
1883	Skinningrove Iron Co. Ltd	2	2
1884	Skinningrove Iron Co. Ltd	2	2
1885	Skinningrove Iron Co. Ltd	2	2
1886	Skinningrove Iron Co. Ltd	2	2
1887	Skinningrove Iron Co. Ltd	2	2
1888	Skinningrove Iron Co. Ltd	2	2
1889	Skinningrove Iron Co. Ltd	2	2
1890	Skinningrove Iron Co. Ltd	2	2
1891	Skinningrove Iron Co. Ltd	2	2
1892	Skinningrove Iron Co. Ltd	2	2
1893	Skinningrove Iron Co. Ltd	2	2
1894	Skinningrove Iron Co. Ltd	2	2
1895	Skinningrove Iron Co. Ltd	4	2
1896	Skinningrove Iron Co. Ltd	4	4
1897	Skinningrove Iron Co. Ltd	4	4
1898	Skinningrove Iron Co. Ltd	4	4
1899	Skinningrove Iron Co. Ltd	4	4
1900	Skinningrove Iron Co. Ltd	4	4
1901	Skinningrove Iron Co. Ltd	5	4
1902	Skinningrove Iron Co. Ltd	5	4
1903	Skinningrove Iron Co. Ltd	5	3
1904	Skinningrove Iron Co. Ltd	5	3
1905	Skinningrove Iron Co. Ltd	5	3
1906	Skinningrove Iron Co. Ltd	5	4
1907	Skinningrove Iron Co. Ltd	5	4
1908	Skinningrove Iron Co. Ltd	5	4
1908	Skinningrove Iron Co. Ltd	5	4
1910	Skinningrove Iron Co. Ltd	5	4
1911	Skinningrove Iron Co. Ltd	5	4
1912	Skinningrove Iron Co. Ltd	5	4
1913	Skinningrove Iron Co. Ltd	5	4
1921	Skinningrove Iron Co. Ltd	5	-
1922	Skinningrove Iron Co. Ltd	5	-
1923	Skinningrove Iron Co. Ltd	5	-
1924	Skinningrove Iron Co. Ltd	5	-
1925	Skinningrove Iron Co. Ltd	5	-
1926	Skinningrove Iron Co. Ltd	5	-
1927	Skinningrove Iron Co. Ltd	5	-
1928	Skinningrove Iron Co. Ltd	5	-
1929	Pease & Partners Ltd	5	-
1930	Pease & Partners Ltd	5	-
1931	Pease & Partners Ltd	5	-
1932	Skinningrove Iron Co. Ltd	5	-
1933	Skinningrove Iron Co. Ltd	5	-
1934	Skinningrove Iron Co. Ltd	5	-
1935	Skinningrove Iron Co. Ltd	5	-
1936	Skinningrove Iron Co. Ltd	4	-
1937	Skinningrove Iron Co. Ltd	4	-
1938	Skinningrove Iron Co. Ltd	4	-
1939	Skinningrove Iron Co. Ltd	5	-
1940	Skinningrove Iron Co. Ltd	5	-
1941	Skinningrove Iron Co. Ltd	5	-
1942	Skinningrove Iron Co. Ltd	5	-
1921	Skinningrove Iron Co. Ltd	5	-

Year	Owner	Built	In Blast
1943	Skinningrove Iron Co. Ltd	5	-
1944	Skinningrove Iron Co. Ltd	4	-
1945	Skinningrove Iron Co. Ltd	2	-
1946	Skinningrove Iron Co. Ltd	2	-
1947	Skinningrove Iron Co. Ltd	2	-
1948	Skinningrove Iron Co. Ltd	2	-
1949	Skinningrove Iron Co. Ltd	2	-
1950	Skinningrove Iron Co. Ltd	2	-
1951	Skinningrove Iron Co. Ltd	2	-
1952	Skinningrove Iron Co. Ltd	3	-
1953	Skinningrove Iron Co. Ltd	3	-
1954	Skinningrove Iron Co. Ltd	3	-
1955	Skinningrove Iron Co. Ltd	3	-
1956	Skinningrove Iron Co. Ltd	3	-
1957	Skinningrove Iron Co. Ltd	3	-
1958	Skinningrove Iron Co. Ltd	3	-
1959	Skinningrove Iron Co. Ltd	3	-
1960	Skinningrove Iron Co. Ltd	3	-
1961	Skinningrove Iron Co. Ltd	3	-
1962	Skinningrove Iron Co. Ltd	2	-
1963	Skinningrove Iron Co. Ltd	2	-
1964	Skinningrove Iron Co. Ltd	2	-
1965	Skinningrove Iron Co. Ltd	1	-
1966	Skinningrove Iron Co. Ltd	1	-
1967	Skinningrove Iron Co. Ltd	1	-
1968	Skinningrove Iron Co. Ltd	1	-
1969	Skinningrove Iron Co. Ltd	1	-
1970	British Steel Corporation	1	-
1971	British Steel Corporation	1	-

Until 1879 the works is listed under Loftus, from 1880 under Skinningrove. The works closed in March 1972.

South Bank, Middlesbrough, N. Riding [NZ 5320]

Year	Owner	Built	In Blast
1854	B. Samuelson	2	2
1855	B. Samuelson	2	2
1856	B. Samuelson & Co.	3	3
1857	B. Samuelson & Co.	3	3
1858	B. Samuelson & Co.	3	3
1859	B. Samuelson & Co.	3	3
1860	B. Samuelson & Co.	3	2
1861	B. Samuelson & Co.	3	2
1862	South Bank Iron Co.	3	3
1863	South Bank Iron Co.	9	3
1864	South Bank Iron Co.	9	3
1865	South Bank Iron Co.	9	6
1866	South Bank Iron Co.	9	7
1867	South Bank Iron Co.	9	7
1868	South Bank Iron Co.	9	9
1869	South Bank Iron Co.	9	9
1870	Thomas Vaughan	9	9
1871	Thomas Vaughan	9	9
1872	Thomas Vaughan & Co.	9	8
1873	Thomas Vaughan & Co.	6	6
1874	Thomas Vaughan & Co.	8	6
1875	Thomas Vaughan & Co.	8	2
1876	Thomas Vaughan & Co.	8	2
1877	Trustees of Thomas Vaughan & Co.	8	2
1878	Trustees of Thomas Vaughan & Co.	8	2
1879	Bolckow, Vaughan & Co. Ltd	8	8
1880	Bolckow, Vaughan & Co. Ltd	8	8
1881	Bolckow, Vaughan & Co. Ltd	8	8
1882	Bolckow, Vaughan & Co. Ltd	8	8
1883	Bolckow, Vaughan & Co. Ltd	8	6
1884	Bolckow, Vaughan & Co. Ltd	8	8
1885	Bolckow, Vaughan & Co. Ltd	8	6
1886	Bolckow, Vaughan & Co. Ltd	8	6
1887	Bolckow, Vaughan & Co. Ltd	8	6
1888	Bolckow, Vaughan & Co. Ltd	8	6
1889	Bolckow, Vaughan & Co. Ltd	8	6
1890	Bolckow, Vaughan & Co. Ltd	8	6
1891	Bolckow, Vaughan & Co. Ltd	8	6
1892	Bolckow, Vaughan & Co. Ltd	8	5
1893	Bolckow, Vaughan & Co. Ltd	8	6
1894	Bolckow, Vaughan & Co. Ltd	8	6
1895	Bolckow, Vaughan & Co. Ltd	8	7
1896	Bolckow, Vaughan & Co. Ltd	8	7
1897	Bolckow, Vaughan & Co. Ltd	8	7
1898	Bolckow, Vaughan & Co. Ltd	8	7
1899	Bolckow, Vaughan & Co. Ltd	8	7
1900	Bolckow, Vaughan & Co. Ltd	8	7
1901	Bolckow, Vaughan & Co. Ltd	8	5
1902	Bolckow, Vaughan & Co. Ltd	8	5
1903	Bolckow, Vaughan & Co. Ltd	8	5
1904	Bolckow, Vaughan & Co. Ltd	8	5
1905	Bolckow, Vaughan & Co. Ltd	8	5
1906	Bolckow, Vaughan & Co. Ltd	8	5
1907	Bolckow, Vaughan & Co. Ltd	8	5
1908	Bolckow, Vaughan & Co. Ltd	8	5
1909	Bolckow, Vaughan & Co. Ltd	8	4
1910	Bolckow, Vaughan & Co. Ltd	8	4
1911	Bolckow, Vaughan & Co. Ltd	8	4
1912	Bolckow, Vaughan & Co. Ltd	7	4
1913	Bolckow, Vaughan & Co. Ltd	7	5
1953	Dorman Long & Co. Ltd	3	-
1954	Dorman Long (Steel) Ltd	3	-
1955	Dorman Long (Steel) Ltd	3	-

In 1854 this is one of three works listed under Eston, the name also used by Truran the following year. One of these had 6 furnaces (see under Eston); one of the other two, later known as Cleveland (qv) had 3 furnaces, and the third, South Bank, had 2, each producing 110 tons a week. In 1856 Samuelson's works was called Eston South Bank and in 1888 Cleveland South Bank. 1863: 6 furnaces building. 1866: At work for 11 months, closed during a strike in July. Between 1921 and 1952 a single figures was returned for all the works owned by Bolckow, Vaughan (from 1929 Dorman Long), for which see under Middlesbrough and Redcar. From 1953 separate figures were given for each Dorman Long works.

South Durham, Darlington, Durham [NZ 2814]

Year	Owner	Built	In Blast
1854	South Durham Iron Co.	2	2
1855	H. Pease & Co.	2	2
1856	H. Pease & Co.	3	2
1857	South Durham Iron Co.	3	2
1858	South Durham Iron Co.	3	2
1859	South Durham Iron Co.	3	2
1860	South Durham Iron Co.	3	2
1861	South Durham Iron Co.	3	2
1862	South Durham Iron Co.	3	2
1863	South Durham Iron Co.	3	3
1864	South Durham Iron Co.	3	3
1865	South Durham Iron Co.	3	3
1866	South Durham Iron Co.	3	2
1867	South Durham Iron Co.	3	2
1868	South Durham Iron Co.	3	2

Year	Owner	Built	In Blast
1869	South Durham Iron Co.	3	2
1870	South Durham Iron Co.	3	2
1871	South Durham Iron Co.	3	3
1872	South Durham Iron Co.	3	3
1873	South Durham Iron Co.	3	3
1874	South Durham Iron Co.	3	3
1875	South Durham Iron Co. Ltd	3	3
1876	South Durham Iron Co. Ltd	3	3
1877	South Durham Iron Co. Ltd	3	3
1878	South Durham Iron Co. Ltd	3	0
1879	South Durham Iron Co. Ltd	3	0
1880	South Durham Iron Co. Ltd	3	0
1881	South Durham Iron Co. Ltd	3	0
1882	South Durham Iron Co. Ltd	3	0
1883	South Durham Iron Co. Ltd	3	0
1884	South Durham Iron Co. Ltd	3	0

Truran: output (at Darlington) 120 tons a week from each of 2 furnaces. 1867: in blast from 12 June; rebuilding up to then. 1879: Company in liquidation. 1883–84: In liquidation. In 1854–59 the works was listed under Darlington, thereafter South Durham.

South Teesside: see Bessemer; Clay Lane

Spennymoor: see Tudhoe

Stanhope, Durham [NZ 9939]

Year	Owner	Built	In Blast
1847	Weardale Iron Co.	1	1
1849	—	-	3
1854	Weardale Iron Co.	1	0
1855	Weardale Iron Co.	1	0
1856	Weardale Iron Co.	1	0
1857	Weardale Iron Co.	1	0
1858	Weardale Iron Co.	1	1
1859	Weardale Iron Co.	1	1
1860	Weardale Iron Co.	1	0
1861	Weardale Iron Co.	1	0
1862	Weardale Iron Co.	1	1
1863	Weardale Iron Co.	1	0
1864	Weardale Iron Co.	6	5
1865	Weardale Iron & Coal Co. Ltd	1	0
1866	Weardale Iron & Coal Co. Ltd	1	0
1867	Weardale Iron & Coal Co. Ltd	6	3

1847: output 4,160 tons p.a, i.e. 80 tons a week. 1849: English has an entry for 'Weardale & Towlaw' (see Tow Law); Hunt lists Stanhope as above, as well as Tow Law, although there appears to be some double-counting. Truran: output (at Stanhope) 120 tons a week from a single furnace. The furnace-numbers for 1864 and 1867 include Tow Law.

Stockton, North Shore, Durham [NZ 4320]

Year	Owner	Built	In Blast
1854	Stockton Iron Co.	3	0
1855	Holdsworth, Bennington, Byers & Co.	3	1
1856	Holdsworth, Bennington, Byers & Co.	3	3
1857	Holdsworth, Bennington, Byers & Co.	3	1
1858	Holdsworth, Bennington, Byers & Co.	3	2
1859	Holdsworth, Bennington, Byers & Co.	3	3
1860	Holdsworth, Bennington, Byers & Co.	3	2
1861	Holdsworth, Bennington, Byers & Co.	3	2
1862	Holdsworth, Bennington, Byers & Co.	3	2
1863	Holdsworth, Bennington, Byers & Co.	3	3
1864	Stockton Iron Furnace Co. Ltd	3	3
1865	Stockton Iron Furnace Co. Ltd	3	3
1866	Stockton Iron Furnace Co. Ltd	3	3
1867	Stockton Rail Mill Co. Ltd	3	3
1868	Stockton Rail Mill Co. Ltd	3	1
1869	Stockton Rail Mill Co. Ltd	3	1
1870	Stockton Rail Mill Co. Ltd	3	3
1874	Stockton Iron Furnace Co. Ltd	3	2
1875	Stockton Iron Furnace Co. Ltd	3	2
1876	Stockton Iron Furnace Co. Ltd	3	2
1877	Stockton Iron Furnace Co. Ltd	3	0
1878	Stockton Iron Furnace Co. Ltd	3	0
1879	Stockton Iron Furnace Co. Ltd	3	0
1880	Stockton Iron Furnace Co. Ltd	3	0
1881	Stockton Iron Furnace Co. Ltd	3	0
1882	Stockton Iron Furnace Co. Ltd	3	0
1883	Stockton Iron Furnace Co. Ltd	3	0
1884	Stockton Iron Furnace Co. Ltd, in liquidation	3	0
1885	Stockton Iron Furnace Co. Ltd, in liquidation	3	0
1886	Stockton Iron Furnace Co. Ltd, in liquidation	3	0
1887	Unoccupied	3	0
1888	Unoccupied	3	0
1892	Joseph Torbock	2	0
1893	Joseph Torbock	2	0
1894	Joseph Torbock	2	0
1895	Joseph Torbock	2	0
1896	Joseph Torbock	2	0
1897	Joseph Torbock	2	0
1898	Joseph Torbock	2	0
1899	Joseph Torbock	2	0

1854: Building. Truran: output 120 tons a week from each of 3 furnaces. 1874: entry above printed in *Mineral Statistics* under Stockton-on-Tees (the heading used since 1854); another entry under North Shore, with 3 furnaces, all in blast, appears to be a duplicate. 1875: single entry under Stockton as above; 1876–80: entry printed above listed under Stockton, North Shore; 1881: heading is simply North Shore. The owner's name in 1864–86 has been amended with reference to BT 31/1036/1749C and 1750C.

Tees, Middlesbrough, N. Riding [NZ 5020]

Year	Owner	Built	In Blast
1854	Gilkes, Wilson, Leatham & Co.	4	4

Year	Owner	Built	In Blast
1855	Gilkes, Wilson & Co.	4	4
1856	Gilkes, Wilson & Co.	4	4
1858	Gilkes, Wilson & Co.	5	3
1859	Gilkes, Wilson & Co.	5	3
1860	Gilkes, Wilson, Pease & Co.	5	3
1861	Gilkes, Wilson, Pease & Co.	5	2
1862	Gilkes, Wilson, Pease & Co.	5	2
1863	Gilkes, Wilson, Pease & Co.	5	4
1864	Gilkes, Wilson, Pease & Co.	7	5
1865	Gilkes, Wilson, Pease & Co.	7	4
1866	Gilkes, Wilson, Pease & Co.	8	4
1867	Gilkes, Wilson, Pease & Co.	8	3
1868	Gilkes, Wilson, Pease & Co.	8	3
1869	Gilkes, Wilson, Pease & Co.	8	3
1870	Gilkes, Wilson, Pease & Co.	5	3
1871	Gilkes, Wilson, Pease & Co.	5	4
1872	Gilkes, Wilson, Pease & Co.	5	5
1873	Gilkes, Wilson, Pease & Co.	5	5
1874	Gilkes, Wilson, Pease & Co.	5	5
1875	Gilkes, Wilson, Pease & Co.	5	5
1876	Gilkes, Wilson, Pease & Co.	4	4
1877	Gilkes, Wilson, Pease & Co.	5	5
1878	Gilkes, Wilson, Pease & Co.	5	4
1879	Gilkes, Wilson, Pease & Co.	5	4
1880	Wilsons, Pease & Co.	5	5
1881	Wilsons, Pease & Co.	5	5
1882	Wilsons, Pease & Co.	5	5
1883	Wilsons, Pease & Co.	5	5
1884	Wilsons, Pease & Co.	5	4
1885	Wilsons, Pease & Co.	5	4
1886	Wilsons, Pease & Co.	5	5
1887	Wilsons, Pease & Co.	5	4
1888	Wilsons, Pease & Co.	5	4
1889	Wilsons, Pease & Co.	5	5
1890	Wilsons, Pease & Co.	5	5
1891	Wilsons, Pease & Co.	5	4
1892	Wilsons, Pease & Co.	5	3
1893	Wilsons, Pease & Co.	5	5
1894	Wilsons, Pease & Co.	5	5
1895	Wilsons, Pease & Co.	5	5
1896	Wilsons, Pease & Co.	5	5
1897	Wilsons, Pease & Co.	4	4
1898	Wilsons, Pease & Co.	4	4
1899	Wilsons, Pease & Co.	4	4
1900	Wilsons, Pease & Co.	5	4
1901	Wilsons, Pease & Co.	3	2
1902	Wilsons, Pease & Co. Ltd	3	2
1903	Wilsons, Pease & Co. Ltd	3	3
1904	Wilsons, Pease & Co. Ltd	3	3
1905	Wilsons, Pease & Co. Ltd	3	3
1906	Wilsons, Pease & Co. Ltd	3	3
1907	Wilsons, Pease & Co. Ltd	3	3
1908	Wilsons, Pease & Co. Ltd	3	2
1909	Wilsons, Pease & Co. Ltd	3	2
1910	Wilsons, Pease & Co. Ltd	3	3
1911	Wilsons, Pease & Co. Ltd	3	3
1912	Wilsons, Pease & Co. Ltd	3	2
1913	Wilsons, Pease & Co. Ltd	3	2
1921	Pease & Partners Ltd	6	-
1922	Pease & Partners Ltd	6	-
1923	Pease & Partners Ltd	6	-
1924	Pease & Partners Ltd	6	-
1925	Pease & Partners Ltd	6	-
1926	Pease & Partners Ltd	6	-
1927	Pease & Partners Ltd	6	-
1928	Pease & Partners Ltd	6	-
1929	Pease & Partners Ltd	6	-
1930	Pease & Partners Ltd	6	-
1931	Pease & Partners Ltd	6	-
1932	Pease & Partners Ltd	6	-
1933	Pease & Partners Ltd	6	-
1934	Pease & Partners Ltd	6	-
1935	Pease & Partners Ltd	3	-

In 1854 three works were listed under Middlesbrough, two of which were owned by Bolckow & Vaughan (for which see Eston and Middlesbrough). The third appears from 1855 under Tees and the 1854 entry has been moved here accordingly. Truran lists two works under Middlesbrough, one of which had 4 furnaces, with an output of 140 tons a week from each; this presumably refers to the Tees works. 1876: 2 furnaces building.

Tees Bridge, Stockton-on-Tees, Durham [NZ 4418]

Year	Owner	Built	In Blast
1874	Tees-Bridge Iron Co. Ltd	2	2
1875	Tees-Bridge Iron Co. Ltd	3	2
1876	Tees-Bridge Iron Co. Ltd	3	3
1877	Tees-Bridge Iron Co. Ltd	3	3
1878	Tees-Bridge Iron Co. Ltd	3	3
1879	Tees-Bridge Iron Co. Ltd	3	3
1880	Tees-Bridge Iron Co. Ltd	3	3
1881	Tees-Bridge Iron Co. Ltd	3	3
1882	Tees-Bridge Iron Co. Ltd	3	3
1883	Tees-Bridge Iron Co. Ltd	3	3
1884	Tees-Bridge Iron Co. Ltd	3	3
1885	Tees-Bridge Iron Co. Ltd	3	2
1886	Tees-Bridge Iron Co. Ltd	3	2
1887	Tees-Bridge Iron Co. Ltd	3	2
1888	Tees-Bridge Iron Co. Ltd	3	3
1889	Tees-Bridge Iron Co. Ltd	3	3
1890	Tees-Bridge Iron Co. Ltd	3	2
1891	Tees-Bridge Iron Co. Ltd	3	2
1892	Tees-Bridge Iron Co. Ltd	3	1
1893	Tees-Bridge Iron Co. Ltd	3	2
1894	Tees-Bridge Iron Co. Ltd	3	2
1895	Tees-Bridge Iron Co. Ltd	3	2
1896	Tees-Bridge Iron Co. Ltd	3	2
1897	Tees-Bridge Iron Co. Ltd	3	2
1898	Tees-Bridge Iron Co. Ltd	3	2
1899	Tees-Bridge Iron Co. Ltd	3	2
1900	Tees-Bridge Iron Co. Ltd	3	2
1901	Tees-Bridge Iron Co. Ltd	3	2
1902	Tees-Bridge Iron Co. Ltd	3	2
1903	Tees-Bridge Iron Co. Ltd	3	2
1904	Tees-Bridge Iron Co. Ltd	3	2
1905	Tees-Bridge Iron Co. Ltd	3	2
1906	Tees-Bridge Iron Co. Ltd	3	2
1907	Tees-Bridge Iron Co. Ltd	3	2
1908	Tees-Bridge Iron Co. Ltd	3	2
1909	Tees-Bridge Iron Co. Ltd	3	2
1910	Tees-Bridge Iron Co. Ltd	3	2
1911	Tees-Bridge Iron Co. Ltd	3	2
1912	Tees-Bridge Iron Co. Ltd	3	2
1913	Tees-Bridge Iron Co. Ltd	3	2

The works appears to have gone out of use before the resumption of returns in 1921.

Tees Side, Middlesborough, N. Riding [NZ 4821]

Year	Owner	Built	In Blast
1856	Snowdon & Hopkins	2	0
1857	Snowdon & Hopkins	2	0
1858	Snowdon & Hopkins	2	0
1859	Snowdon & Hopkins	2	2
1860	Hopkins & Co.	2	2
1861	Hopkins & Co.	2	2
1862	Hopkins & Co.	2	2
1863	Hopkins & Co.	2	2
1864	Hopkins & Co.	2	2
1865	Hopkins, Gilkes & Co. Ltd	4	2
1866	Hopkins, Gilkes & Co. Ltd	2	2
1867	Hopkins, Gilkes & Co. Ltd	4	3
1868	Hopkins, Gilkes & Co. Ltd	4	4
1869	Hopkins, Gilkes & Co. Ltd	4	4
1870	Hopkins, Gilkes & Co. Ltd	4	4
1871	Hopkins, Gilkes & Co. Ltd	4	4
1872	Hopkins, Gilkes & Co. Ltd	4	4
1873	Hopkins, Gilkes & Co. Ltd	4	4
1874	Hopkins, Gilkes & Co. Ltd	4	4
1875	Hopkins, Gilkes & Co. Ltd	4	4
1876	Hopkins, Gilkes & Co. Ltd	5	5
1877	Hopkins, Gilkes & Co. Ltd	4	4
1878	Hopkins, Gilkes & Co. Ltd	4	2
1879	Hopkins, Gilkes & Co. Ltd	4	2
1880	Hopkins, Gilkes & Co. Ltd	4	4
1881	Hopkins, Gilkes & Co. Ltd	4	4
1882	Tees-side Iron & Engine Works Co. Ltd	4	4
1883	Tees-side Iron & Engine Works Co. Ltd	4	4
1884	Tees-side Iron & Engine Works Co. Ltd	4	3
1885	Tees-side Iron & Engine Works Co. Ltd	4	2
1886	Tees-side Iron & Engine Works Co. Ltd	4	2
1887	Tees-side Iron & Engine Works Co. Ltd	4	2
1888	Tees-side Iron & Engine Works Co. Ltd	4	1
1889	Tees Side Iron & Engine Works Co. Ltd	4	2
1890	Tees Side Iron & Engine Works Co. Ltd	4	2
1891	Tees Side Iron & Engine Works Co. Ltd	4	1
1892	Tees Side Iron & Engine Works Co. Ltd	4	2
1893	Tees Side Iron & Engine Works Co. Ltd	4	3
1894	Tees Side Iron & Engine Works Co. Ltd	4	2
1895	Tees Side Iron & Engine Works Co. Ltd	4	2
1896	Tees Furnace Co. Ltd	4	2

1856: Not completed. 1858: Only just completed. 1877: 2 furnaces building. The change in spelling in 1888–89 reflects the establishment of a new company.

Thornaby, N. Riding [NZ 4516]

Year	Owner	Built	In Blast
1859	Whitwell & Co.	2	0
1860	W. Whitwell & Co.	3	0
1861	W. Whitwell & Co.	3	0
1862	W. Whitwell & Co.	3	2
1863	W. Whitwell & Co.	3	3
1864	W. Whitwell & Co.	3	3
1865	William Whitwell & Co.	3	3
1866	William Whitwell & Co.	3	3
1867	William Whitwell & Co.	3	3
1868	William Whitwell & Co.	3	3
1869	William Whitwell & Co.	3	3
1870	William Whitwell & Co.	3	3
1871	William Whitwell & Co.	3	3
1872	William Whitwell & Co.	5	3
1873	William Whitwell & Co.	5	3
1874	William Whitwell & Co.	5	2
1875	William Whitwell & Co.	2	2
1876	William Whitwell & Co.	3	3
1877	William Whitwell & Co.	3	3
1878	William Whitwell & Co.	3	3
1879	William Whitwell & Co.	3	3
1880	William Whitwell & Co.	3	3
1881	William Whitwell & Co.	3	3
1882	William Whitwell & Co.	3	3
1883	William Whitwell & Co.	3	3
1884	William Whitwell & Co.	3	2
1885	William Whitwell & Co.	3	2
1886	William Whitwell & Co.	3	2
1887	William Whitwell & Co.	3	3
1888	William Whitwell & Co.	3	3
1889	William Whitwell & Co. Ltd	3	3
1890	William Whitwell & Co. Ltd	3	3
1891	William Whitwell & Co. Ltd	3	3
1892	William Whitwell & Co. Ltd	3	2
1893	William Whitwell & Co. Ltd	3	3
1894	William Whitwell & Co. Ltd	3	3
1895	William Whitwell & Co. Ltd	3	3
1896	William Whitwell & Co. Ltd	3	3
1897	William Whitwell & Co. Ltd	3	3
1898	William Whitwell & Co. Ltd	3	3
1899	William Whitwell & Co. Ltd	3	3
1900	William Whitwell & Co. Ltd	3	3
1901	William Whitwell & Co. Ltd	3	3
1902	William Whitwell & Co. Ltd	3	3
1903	William Whitwell & Co. Ltd	3	3
1904	William Whitwell & Co. Ltd	3	2
1905	William Whitwell & Co. Ltd	3	2
1906	William Whitwell & Co. Ltd	3	3
1907	William Whitwell & Co. Ltd	3	3
1908	William Whitwell & Co. Ltd	3	2
1909	William Whitwell & Co. Ltd	3	3
1910	William Whitwell & Co. Ltd	3	3
1911	William Whitwell & Co. Ltd	3	2
1912	William Whitwell & Co. Ltd	3	3
1913	William Whitwell & Co. Ltd	3	3
1921	William Whitwell & Co. Ltd	3	-
1922	William Whitwell & Co. Ltd	3	-
1923	William Whitwell & Co. Ltd	3	-
1924	William Whitwell & Co. Ltd	3	-
1925	William Whitwell & Co. Ltd	3	-
1926	William Whitwell & Co. Ltd	3	-
1927	William Whitwell & Co. Ltd	3	-
1928	William Whitwell & Co. Ltd	3	-

Year	Owner	Built	In Blast
1929	William Whitwell & Co. Ltd	3	-
1930	William Whitwell & Co. Ltd	3	-
1931	William Whitwell & Co. Ltd	3	-
1932	William Whitwell & Co. Ltd	3	-
1933	William Whitwell & Co. Ltd	3	-
1934	William Whitwell & Co. Ltd	3	-
1935	William Whitwell & Co. Ltd	3	-

In 1859 this works is listed under Witton, thereafter under Thornaby. The furnaces were dismantled during the first half of 1936.

Tow Law, Durham [NZ 1138]

Year	Owner	Built	In Blast
1847	Weardale Iron Co.	3	2
1849	Weardale Iron Co.	3	2
1854	Weardale Iron Co.	6	4
1855	Weardale Iron Co.	5	4
1856	Weardale Iron Co.	5	4
1857	Weardale Iron Co.	5	4
1858	Weardale Iron Co.	5	5
1859	Weardale Iron Co.	5	5
1860	Weardale Iron Co.	5	5
1861	Weardale Iron Co.	5	3
1862	Weardale Iron Co.	5	3
1863	Weardale Iron Co.	5	4
1864	Weardale Iron Co.	-	-
1865	Weardale Iron & Coal Co. Ltd	5	5
1866	Weardale Iron & Coal Co. Ltd	5	3
1867	Weardale Iron & Coal Co. Ltd	-	-
1868	Weardale Iron & Coal Co. Ltd	5	3
1869	Weardale Iron & Coal Co. Ltd	5	3
1870	Weardale Iron & Coal Co. Ltd	7	4
1871	Weardale Iron & Coal Co. Ltd	4	3
1872	Weardale Iron & Coal Co. Ltd	4	2
1873	Weardale Iron & Coal Co. Ltd	4	2
1874	Weardale Iron & Coal Co. Ltd	4	1
1875	Weardale Iron & Coal Co. Ltd	4	1
1876	Weardale Iron & Coal Co. Ltd	4	2
1877	Weardale Iron & Coal Co. Ltd	4	2
1878	Weardale Iron & Coal Co. Ltd	4	2
1879	Weardale Iron & Coal Co. Ltd	4	1
1880	Weardale Iron & Coal Co. Ltd	4	0
1881	Weardale Iron & Coal Co. Ltd	4	0
1882	Weardale Iron & Coal Co. Ltd	4	1
1883	Weardale Iron & Coal Co. Ltd	4	1
1884	Weardale Iron & Coal Co. Ltd	4	1
1885	Weardale Iron & Coal Co. Ltd	4	1
1886	Weardale Iron & Coal Co. Ltd	4	1
1887	Weardale Iron & Coal Co. Ltd	4	0
1888	Weardale Iron & Coal Co. Ltd	4	0
1889	Weardale Iron & Coal Co. Ltd	2	0
1890	Weardale Iron & Coal Co. Ltd	2	0
1891	Weardale Iron & Coal Co. Ltd	2	0
1892	Weardale Iron & Coal Co. Ltd	2	0
1893	Weardale Iron & Coal Co. Ltd	2	0
1894	Weardale Iron & Coal Co. Ltd	2	0
1895	Weardale Iron & Coal Co. Ltd	2	0

1847: output 8,320 tons p.a., i.e. 80 tons a week from each of 2 furnaces. 1849: called Weardale & Towlaw by English; cf. Stanhope. Truran: output 140 tons a week from each of 6 furnaces. 1864 and 1867: see Stanhope for combined furnace-numbers for the two sites. 1870: numbers above include Tudhoe (qv). In 1861 the owner at Tow Law is returned as W. Whitwell & Co., which is almost certainly an error arising from confusion with Thornaby (qv).

Tudhoe, Durham [NZ 2635]

Year	Owner	Built	In Blast
1870	Weardale Iron Co.	-	-
1872	Weardale Iron Co.	2	2
1873	Weardale Iron Co.	2	2
1874	Weardale Iron Co.	2	2
1875	Weardale Iron & Coal Co. Ltd	2	1
1876	Weardale Iron & Coal Co. Ltd	2	0
1877	Weardale Iron & Coal Co. Ltd	2	0
1878	Weardale Iron & Coal Co. Ltd	2	0
1879	Weardale Iron & Coal Co. Ltd	2	0
1880	Weardale Iron & Coal Co. Ltd	2	0
1881	Weardale Iron & Coal Co. Ltd	2	2
1882	Weardale Iron & Coal Co. Ltd	2	2
1883	Weardale Iron & Coal Co. Ltd	2	2
1884	Weardale Iron & Coal Co. Ltd	2	2
1885	Weardale Iron & Coal Co. Ltd	2	2
1886	Weardale Iron & Coal Co. Ltd	2	2
1887	Weardale Iron & Coal Co. Ltd	2	1
1888	Weardale Iron & Coal Co. Ltd	2	1
1889	Weardale Iron & Coal Co. Ltd	2	1
1890	Weardale Iron & Coal Co. Ltd	2	1
1891	Weardale Iron & Coal Co. Ltd	2	1
1892	Weardale Iron & Coal Co. Ltd	2	1
1893	Weardale Iron & Coal Co. Ltd	2	1
1894	Weardale Iron & Coal Co. Ltd	2	1
1895	Weardale Iron & Coal Co. Ltd	2	1
1896	Weardale Iron & Coal Co. Ltd	2	1
1897	Weardale Iron & Coal Co. Ltd	2	2
1898	Weardale Iron & Coal Co. Ltd	2	2
1899	Weardale Iron & Coal Co. Ltd	2	2
1900	Weardale Steel, Coal & Coke Co. Ltd	2	2
1901	Weardale Steel, Coal & Coke Co. Ltd	2	1
1902	Weardale Steel, Coal & Coke Co. Ltd	2	2
1903	Weardale Steel, Coal & Coke Co. Ltd	2	1
1904	Weardale Steel, Coal & Coke Co. Ltd	2	1
1905	Weardale Steel, Coal & Coke Co. Ltd	2	1
1906	Weardale Steel, Coal & Coke Co. Ltd	2	1
1907	Weardale Steel, Coal & Coke Co. Ltd	2	1
1908	Weardale Steel, Coal & Coke Co. Ltd	2	1
1909	Weardale Steel, Coal & Coke Co. Ltd	2	1
1910	Weardale Steel, Coal & Coke Co. Ltd	2	1
1911	Weardale Steel, Coal & Coke Co. Ltd	2	1

Year	Owner	Built	In Blast
1912	Weardale Steel, Coal & Coke Co. Ltd	2	1
1913	Weardale Steel, Coal & Coke Co. Ltd	2	1
1921	Weardale Steel, Coal & Coke Co. Ltd	2	-
1922	Weardale Steel, Coal & Coke Co. Ltd	2	-
1923	Weardale Steel, Coal & Coke Co. Ltd	2	-
1924	Weardale Steel, Coal & Coke Co. Ltd	2	-
1925	Weardale Steel, Coal & Coke Co. Ltd	2	-
1926	Weardale Steel, Coal & Coke Co. Ltd	2	-

1870: furnace-numbers combined with Tow Law (qv); there was no entry under Tudhoe the following year.

Tyne Ironworks: see Lemington

Tyne Main: see Wallsend

Vane & Seaham, Durham [NZ 4149]

Year	Owner	Built	In Blast
1859	Marchioness of Londonderry	4	0
1860	Marchioness of Londonderry	2	0
1861	Marchioness of Londonderry	2	0
1862	Marchioness of Londonderry	2	0
1863	Marchioness of Londonderry	2	2
1864	Earl Vane	2	2
1865	Earl Vane	2	2
1866	Earl Vane	2	0
1867	Earl Vane	2	0
1868	Earl Vane	2	0
1869	Earl Vane	2	0
1870	Earl Vane	2	0
1871	Watson, Kipling & Co.	1	0
1872	Watson, Kipling & Co.	1	1
1873	Watson, Kipling & Co.	1	1
1874	Watson, Kipling & Co.	1	1
1875	Watson, Kipling & Co.	2	1
1876	Watson, Kipling & Co.	2	0
1877	Watson, Kipling & Co. Ltd	2	0
1878	Watson, Kipling & Co. Ltd	2	0
1879	Watson, Kipling & Co. Ltd	2	0
1880	Watson, Kipling & Co. Ltd	2	0
1881	Watson, Kipling & Co. Ltd	2	0
1882	Watson, Kipling & Co. Ltd	2	0
1883	Watson, Kipling & Co. Ltd	2	0
1884	Watson, Kipling & Co. Ltd	2	0
1885	Watson, Kipling & Co. Ltd	2	0
1886	Watson, Kipling & Co. Ltd	2	0
1887	Watson, Kipling & Co. Ltd	2	0
1888	Watson, Kipling & Co. Ltd	2	0
1890	Watson, Kipling & Co. Ltd	2	0
1889	Watson, Kipling & Co. Ltd	2	0
1891	Watson, Kipling & Co. Ltd	2	0
1892	Watson, Kipling & Co. Ltd	2	0
1893	Marquess of Londonderry	2	0

1859: Works named as 'Leaham' in error for Seaham, which itself appears as the heading in 1871–73. In other years the works is called Vane & Seaham.

Walker, Northumberland [NZ 2964]

Year	Owner	Built	In Blast
1847	Losh, Wilson & Co.	2	2
1849	Losh, Wilson & Bell	2	2
1854	Losh, Wilson & Bell	5	4
1855	Losh, Wilson & Bell	5	4
1856	Losh, Wilson & Bell	5	3
1857	Losh, Wilson & Bell	5	3
1858	Losh, Wilson & Bell	5	3
1859	Losh, Wilson & Bell	5	3
1860	Losh, Wilson & Bell	5	3
1861	Losh, Wilson & Bell	5	3
1862	Losh, Wilson & Bell	5	2
1863	Losh, Wilson & Bell	5	3
1864	Losh, Wilson & Bell	4	3
1865	Losh, Wilson & Bell	3	2
1866	Losh, Wilson & Bell	3	2
1867	Losh, Wilson & Bell	3	0
1868	Losh, Wilson & Bell	3	0
1869	Losh, Wilson & Bell	3	0
1870	Losh, Wilson & Bell	3	2
1871	Losh, Wilson & Bell	3	2
1872	Losh, Wilson & Bell	2	2
1873	Bell Brothers	3	2
1874	Bell Brothers Ltd	2	1
1875	Bell Brothers Ltd	2	1
1876	Bell Brothers Ltd	2	0
1877	Bell Brothers Ltd	2	0
1878	Bell Brothers Ltd	2	0
1879	Bell Brothers Ltd	2	0
1880	Bell Brothers Ltd	2	0
1881	Bell Brothers Ltd	2	0
1882	Bell Brothers Ltd	2	2
1883	Bell Brothers Ltd	2	2
1884	Bell Brothers Ltd	2	0
1885	Bell Brothers Ltd	2	0
1886	Bell Brothers Ltd	2	0
1887	Bell Brothers Ltd	2	0
1888	Magnetic Iron Mountains Smelting Co. Ltd, late Bell Brothers Ltd	2	2
1889	Magnetic Iron Mountains Smelting Co. Ltd, late Bell Brothers Ltd	2	1
1890	Bell Brothers Ltd	2	1
1891	Bell Brothers Ltd	2	1
1892	Bell Brothers Ltd	2	0
1893	Bell Brothers Ltd	2	0
1894	Bell Brothers Ltd	2	0
1895	Bell Brothers Ltd	2	0
1896	Bell Brothers Ltd	2	0
1897	Bell Brothers Ltd	2	0

1847: output 8,320 tons p.a., i.e. 80 tons a week from each of two furnaces. Truran: output 150 tons a week from each of 5 furnaces.

Wallsend, Northumberland [NZ 2966]

Year	Owner	Built	In Blast
1854	J. Carr & Co.	2	2

Year	Owner	Built	In Blast
1855	J. Carr & Co.	2	2
1856	Palmer & Co.	2	2
1857	Palmer & Co.	2	2
1858	Palmer & Co.	2	0
1859	Jarrow Iron Co.	2	2
1860	Jarrow Iron Co.	2	2
1861	Jarrow Iron Co.	2	2
1862	Jarrow Iron Co.	3	2
1863	Jarrow Iron Co.	3	2
1864	Jarrow Iron Co.	2	2
1865	Palmers Shipbuilding & Iron Co. Ltd	2	0
1866	Palmers Shipbuilding & Iron Co. Ltd	2	0
1867	Palmers Shipbuilding & Iron Co. Ltd	2	0
1868	Palmers Shipbuilding & Iron Co. Ltd	2	0
1869	Palmers Shipbuilding & Iron Co. Ltd	2	0
1870	Palmers Shipbuilding & Iron Co. Ltd	2	0
1881	Royal Greek Iron Work Co.	2	0
1882	Crédit Général Ottoman, Constantinople	2	0
1883	Crédit Général Ottoman, Constantinople	2	0
1884	Crédit Général Ottoman, Constantinople	2	0
1885	Crédit Général Ottoman, Constantinople	2	0
1886	Crédit Général Ottoman, Constantinople	2	0
1887	Crédit Général Ottoman, Constantinople	2	0
1888	Crédit Général Ottoman, Constantinople	2	0
1889	Crédit Général Ottoman, Constantinople	2	0
1890	—	2	0

In 1855–58 the works is called 'Wallsend or Tyne Main'; in Truran the latter name only appears, where 2 furnaces were each said to make 120 tons a week. Cf. Tyne Ironworks.

Washington, Durham [NZ 3157]

Year	Owner	Built	In Blast
1858	Washington Iron Co.	1	0
1859	Washington Iron Co.	1	0
1860	Washington Iron Co.	1	0
1861	Washington Iron Co.	1	0
1862	Washington Iron Co.	1	0
1863	Washington Iron Co.	1	0
1864	Washington Iron Co.	1	1
1865	Washington Iron Co.	1	0
1866	Washington Iron Co.	1	0
1867	Washington Iron Co.	1	0
1868	Washington Iron Co.	1	0
1869	Washington Iron Co.	1	0
1870	Washington Iron Co.	1	0

1858: in blast 4 months. 1859: in blast $5^1/_2$ months.

Wear, Washington, Durham [NZ 3157]

Year	Owner	Built	In Blast
1856	Bell, Hawks & Co.	1	0
1857	Bell, Hawks & Co.	1	0
1858	Bell, Hawks & Co.	1	0
1859	Bell, Hawks & Co.	1	1
1860	Bell, Hawks & Co.	1	1
1861	Bell, Hawks & Co.	1	1
1862	Bell, Hawks & Co.	1	1
1863	Bell, Hawks & Co.	1	1
1864	Bell, Hawks & Co.	1	1
1865	Bell, Hawks & Co.	1	1
1866	Bell, Hawks & Co.	1	1
1867	Bell, Hawks & Co.	1	0
1868	Bell Brothers	1	0
1869	Bell Brothers	1	0
1870	Bell Brothers	1	1
1871	Bell Brothers	1	1
1872	Bell Brothers	1	1
1873	Bell Brothers	1	1
1874	Bell Brothers Ltd	1	1
1875	Bell Brothers Ltd	1	1
1876	Bell Brothers Ltd	1	0
1877	Bell Brothers Ltd	1	0
1878	Bell Brothers Ltd	1	0
1879	Bell Brothers Ltd	1	0
1880	Bell Brothers Ltd	1	0
1881	Bell Brothers Ltd	1	0
1882	Bell Brothers Ltd	1	0

1856: Building. 1858: 'Only blown-in at the end of the year'. In 1856 and 1858–67 the first partner's name is spelt 'Bells'; in 1857–60 the second name is 'Hawkes'.

Weardale: see Towlaw

West Hartlepool, Durham [NZ 5032]

Year	Owner	Built	In blast
1874	West Hartlepool Iron Co. Ltd	3	3
1875	West Hartlepool Iron Co. Ltd	3	0
1876	West Hartlepool Iron Co. Ltd	3	0
1877	West Hartlepool Iron Co. Ltd	3	0
1878	West Hartlepool Iron Co. Ltd	3	0
1879	West Hartlepool Iron Co. Ltd	3	0
1880	West Hartlepool Iron Co. Ltd	3	0
1881	West Hartlepool Iron Co. Ltd	3	0
1882	West Hartlepool Iron Co. Ltd	3	0

In 1876, 1878, 1879 and 1880 *Mineral Statistics* adds the comment 'In liquidation'.

West Hartlepool: see also Seaton Carew

Witton: see Thornaby

Witton Park, Durham [NZ 1730]

Year	Owner	Built	In Blast
1847	Witton Park Co.	4	3
1849	Bolckow & Vaughan	4	3
1854	Bolckow & Vaughan	4	0
1855	Bolckow & Vaughan	4	4
1856	Bolckow & Vaughan	4	4
1857	Bolckow & Vaughan	4	4
1858	Bolckow & Vaughan	4	4

Year	Owner	Built	In Blast
1859	Bolckow & Vaughan	4	4
1860	Bolckow & Vaughan	4	4
1861	Bolckow & Vaughan	4	4
1862	Bolckow & Vaughan	4	4
1863	Bolckow & Vaughan	4	4
1864	Bolckow & Vaughan	-	-
1865	Bolckow, Vaughan & Co. Ltd	-	-
1866	Bolckow, Vaughan & Co. Ltd	-	-
1867	Bolckow, Vaughan & Co. Ltd	-	-
1868	Bolckow, Vaughan & Co. Ltd	-	-
1869	Bolckow, Vaughan & Co. Ltd	-	-
1870	Bolckow, Vaughan & Co. Ltd	-	-
1871	Bolckow, Vaughan & Co. Ltd	-	-
1872	Bolckow, Vaughan & Co. Ltd	-	-
1873	Bolckow, Vaughan & Co. Ltd	-	-
1874	Bolckow, Vaughan & Co. Ltd	-	-
1875	Bolckow, Vaughan & Co. Ltd	5	2
1876	Bolckow, Vaughan & Co. Ltd	6	3
1877	Bolckow, Vaughan & Co. Ltd	6	4
1878	Bolckow, Vaughan & Co. Ltd	6	4
1879	Bolckow, Vaughan & Co. Ltd	6	4
1880	Bolckow, Vaughan & Co. Ltd	6	3
1881	Bolckow, Vaughan & Co. Ltd	6	2
1882	Bolckow, Vaughan & Co. Ltd	6	3
1883	Bolckow, Vaughan & Co. Ltd	2	2
1884	Bolckow, Vaughan & Co. Ltd	2	1
1885	Bolckow, Vaughan & Co. Ltd	2	0
1886	Bolckow, Vaughan & Co. Ltd	2	0
1887	Bolckow, Vaughan & Co. Ltd	2	0
1888	Bolckow, Vaughan & Co. Ltd	2	0
1889	Bolckow, Vaughan & Co. Ltd	2	0
1890	Bolckow, Vaughan & Co. Ltd	2	0
1891	Bolckow, Vaughan & Co. Ltd	2	0
1892	Bolckow, Vaughan & Co. Ltd	2	0
1893	Bolckow, Vaughan & Co. Ltd	2	0
1894	Bolckow, Vaughan & Co. Ltd	2	0
1895	Bolckow, Vaughan & Co. Ltd	2	0
1896	Bolckow, Vaughan & Co. Ltd	2	0

1847: output 12,480 tons p.a., i.e. 80 tons a week from each of 3 furnaces. 1849: Hunt lists 4 furnaces in blast. Truran: output 140 tons a week from each of 4 furnaces. In 1855–60 the works is called 'Witton Park & Etherley'. Furnace-numbers for several Bolckow, Vaughan works are combined under Cleveland (qv) for 1864–71 and Middlesbrough (qv) for 1872–74.

Wreck Hill, N. Riding [NZ 8016]

Year	Owner	Built	In Blast
1856	Victoria Iron Works Co.	2	0
1857	Victoria Iron Works Co.	2	0

1856: Not completed. 1857: Works destroyed.

Wylam, Northumberland NZ 1164

Year	Owner	Built	In Blast
1841	Wylam Co.	1	0
1847	Bell Brothers	1	1
1849	Bell Brothers	1	1
1854	Bell Brothers	1	1
1855	Bell Brothers	1	1
1856	Bell Brothers	1	1
1857	Bell Brothers	1	1
1858	Bell Brothers	1	1
1859	Bell Brothers	1	0
1860	Bell Brothers	1	1
1861	Bell Brothers	1	1
1862	Bell Brothers	1	1
1863	Bell Brothers	1	1
1864	Bell Brothers	1	1
1865	—	1	0
1866	Bell Brothers	1	0
1867	Bell Brothers	1	0
1868	Bell Brothers	1	0
1869	Bell Brothers	1	0
1870	Bell Brothers	1	0
1871	Bell Brothers	1	0
1872	Bell Brothers	-	-
1873	Bell Brothers	1	-
1874	Bell Brothers	1	-

1847: output 4,160 tons p.a., i.e. 80 tons a week. Truran: output 140 tons a week from a single furnace. No owner is listed in 1865.

Scotland

Airdrie: see Chapelhall; Monkland

Almond, Stirlingshire   NS 9676

Year	Owner	Built	In Blast
1854	James Russel & Son	1	0
1855	James Russel & Son	2	2
1856	James Russel & Son	2	2
1857	James Russel & Son	2	2
1858	James Russel & Son	3	2
1859	James Russel & Son	3	1
1860	James Russel & Son	3	1
1861	James Russel & Son	3	2
1862	Trustees of late James Russel	3	2
1863	James Russel & Son	3	2
1864	James Russel & Son	3	2
1865	James Russel & Son	3	2
1866	James Russel & Son	3	2
1867	James Russel & Son	3	2
1868	James Russel & Son	3	2
1869	James Russel & Son	3	2
1870	James Russel & Son	3	2
1871	James Russel & Son	3	2
1872	James Russel & Sons	3	2
1873	James Russel & Sons	3	2
1874	James Russel & Sons	3	2
1875	James Russel & Sons	3	2
1876	James Russel & Sons	3	1
1877	James Russel & Sons	3	1
1878	James Russel & Sons	3	1
1879	James Russel & Sons	3	1
1880	James Russel & Sons	3	1
1881	James Russel & Sons	3	1
1882	James Russel & Son	3	0
1883	James Russel & Son	3	0
1884	James Russel & Son	3	0
1885	James Russel & Son	3	0
1886	James Russel & Son	3	0
1887	James Russel & Son	3	0
1888	James Russel & Son	3	0

The works is called Cawseyend in 1854 and Almond Bank in 1855–60; from 1878 Cawseyend reappears as an address following the name Almond. The works was in Stirlingshire, although from 1874 *Mineral Statistics* uses the suffix Linlithgow, which is the nearest town. The owner's name is spelt Russel between 1857 and 1872, Russell in 1854–56 and from 1873; local sources use the former spelling throughout the period. In 1880 *Mineral Statistics* appends the comment, 'Works closed permanently March 1881'.

Ardeer, Ayrshire   [NS 2742]

Year	Owner	Built	In Blast
1854	Merry & Cunninghame	4	2
1855	Merry & Cunninghame	4	3
1856	Merry & Cunninghame	4	4
1857	Merry & Cunninghame	4	4
1858	Merry & Cunninghame	4	4
1859	Merry & Cunninghame	4	4
1860	Merry & Cunninghame	4	4
1861	Merry & Cunninghame	4	4
1862	Merry & Cunninghame	4	4
1863	Merry & Cunninghame	4	4
1864	Merry & Cunninghame	4	4
1865	Merry & Cunninghame	4	4
1866	Merry & Cunninghame	4	3
1867	Merry & Cunninghame	4	4
1868	Merry & Cunninghame	4	4
1869	Merry & Cunninghame	4	4
1870	Merry & Cunninghame	5	4
1871	Merry & Cunninghame	5	4
1872	Merry & Cunninghame Ltd	5	4
1873	Merry & Cunninghame Ltd	5	4
1874	Merry & Cunninghame Ltd	5	4
1875	Merry & Cunninghame Ltd	5	4
1876	Merry & Cunninghame Ltd	5	4
1877	Merry & Cunninghame Ltd	4	4
1878	Merry & Cunninghame Ltd	5	2
1879	Merry & Cunninghame Ltd	14	7
1880	Merry & Cunninghame Ltd	5	3
1881	Merry & Cunninghame Ltd	5	5
1882	Merry & Cunninghame Ltd	5	5
1883	Merry & Cunninghame Ltd	5	5
1884	Merry & Cunninghame Ltd	5	3
1885	Merry & Cunninghame Ltd	5	2
1886	Merry & Cunninghame Ltd	5	1
1887	Merry & Cunninghame Ltd	5	0
1888	Merry & Cunninghame Ltd	5	1
1889	Merry & Cunninghame Ltd	5	3
1890	Merry & Cunninghame Ltd	5	3
1891	Merry & Cunninghame Ltd	5	1
1892	Glengarnock Iron & Steel Co. Ltd	5	2
1893	Glengarnock Iron & Steel Co. Ltd	5	2
1894	Glengarnock Iron & Steel Co. Ltd	5	2
1895	Glengarnock Iron & Steel Co. Ltd	5	3
1896	Glengarnock Iron & Steel Co. Ltd	5	3
1897	Glengarnock Iron & Steel Co. Ltd	5	3
1898	Glengarnock Iron & Steel Co. Ltd	5	3
1899	Glengarnock Iron & Steel Co. Ltd	5	3
1900	Glengarnock Iron & Steel Co. Ltd	5	3
1901	Glengarnock Iron & Steel Co. Ltd	5	3
1902	Glengarnock Iron & Steel Co. Ltd	5	2
1903	Glengarnock Iron & Steel Co. Ltd	5	3
1904	Glengarnock Iron & Steel Co. Ltd	5	3
1905	Glengarnock Iron & Steel Co. Ltd	5	3
1906	Glengarnock Iron & Steel Co. Ltd	5	4
1907	Glengarnock Iron & Steel Co. Ltd	5	5
1908	Glengarnock Iron & Steel Co. Ltd	5	4
1909	Glengarnock Iron & Steel Co. Ltd	5	4
1910	Glengarnock Iron & Steel Co. Ltd	5	4
1911	Glengarnock Iron & Steel Co. Ltd	5	4
1912	Glengarnock Iron & Steel Co. Ltd	5	4
1913	Glengarnock Iron & Steel Co. Ltd	5	4

Year	Owner	Built	In Blast
1921	Merry & Cunninghame Ltd	5	-
1922	Merry & Cunninghame Ltd	5	-
1923	Merry & Cunninghame Ltd	5	-
1924	Merry & Cunninghame Ltd	5	-
1925	Merry & Cunninghame Ltd	5	-
1926	Merry & Cunninghame Ltd	5	-
1927	Merry & Cunninghame Ltd	5	-
1928	Merry & Cunninghame Ltd	5	-
1929	Merry & Cunninghame Ltd	5	-
1930	Merry & Cunninghame Ltd	5	-

1877: 1 furnace building. 1879: furnace-numbers include Glengarnock (qv).

Argyll: see Craleckan

Ayrshire: see Portland

Blair, Ayrshire [NS 2948]

Year	Owner	Built	In Blast
1847	Ayrshire Iron Co.	5	0
1849	Ayrshire Iron Co.	5	0
1854	Eglinton Iron Co.	5	2
1855	Eglinton Iron Co.	5	2
1856	Eglinton Iron Co.	5	3
1857	William Baird & Co.	5	4
1858	William Baird & Co.	5	4
1859	William Baird & Co.	5	4
1860	William Baird & Co.	5	4
1861	William Baird & Co.	5	4
1862	William Baird & Co.	5	2
1863	William Baird & Co.	5	4
1864	William Baird & Co.	5	4
1865	William Baird & Co.	5	4
1866	William Baird & Co.	5	3
1867	William Baird & Co.	5	3
1868	William Baird & Co.	5	3
1869	William Baird & Co.	5	3
1870	William Baird & Co.	5	2

1849: Hunt lists 6 furnaces in blast. Truran: output 140 tons a week from each of 5 furnaces.

Bonawe: see Lorn

Bridgeness, Linlithgowshire [NT 0181]

Year	Owner	Built	In Blast
1871	—	2	1
1872	Henry Cadell	2	1
1873	Henry Cadell	2	1
1874	Henry Cadell	2	0
1875	Henry Cadell	2	0
1876	Henry Cadell	2	0
1877	Henry Cadell	2	0
1878	Henry Cadell	2	0
1879	Henry Cadell	2	0
1880	Henry Cadell	2	0
1881	Henry Cadell	2	0
1882	Henry Cadell	2	0
1883	Henry Cadell	2	0
1884	Henry Cadell	2	0
1885	Henry Cadell	2	0
1886	Henry Cadell	2	0
1887	Henry Cadell	2	0
1888	Henry Cadell	2	0

1876 and 1877: Works given up and not likely to be resumed. 1881: Not likely to be blown-in again. 1883: Partly dismantled.

Calder, Lanarkshire [NS 7263]

Year	Owner	Built	In Blast
1805	Dixon & Co.	2	1
1810	Dalrymple & Co.	3	2
1823	—	3	-
1825	John & William Dixon	4	2
1830	—	4	-
1839	—	6	6
1841	W. Dixon & Co.	8	7
1843	W. Dixon & Co.	8	5
1847	William Dixon	8	3
1849	William Dixon	8	5
1854	William Dixon	6	4
1855	William Dixon	7	4
1856	William Dixon	8	5
1857	William Dixon	8	5
1858	William Dixon	8	5
1859	William Dixon	8	5
1860	William Dixon	8	6
1861	William Dixon	8	6
1862	William Dixon	8	6
1863	William Dixon	8	6
1864	William Dixon	8	7
1865	William Dixon	8	6
1866	William Dixon	8	6
1867	William Dixon	8	7
1868	William Dixon	8	7
1869	William Dixon	8	6
1870	William Dixon	8	6
1871	William Dixon	8	6
1872	William Dixon Ltd	8	6
1873	William Dixon Ltd	8	6
1874	William Dixon Ltd	8	6
1875	William Dixon Ltd	8	3
1876	William Dixon Ltd	7	5
1877	William Dixon Ltd	6	5
1878	William Dixon Ltd	6	3
1879	William Dixon Ltd	6	4
1880	William Dixon Ltd	6	4
1881	William Dixon Ltd	5	4
1882	William Dixon Ltd	5	4
1883	William Dixon Ltd	5	5
1884	William Dixon Ltd	5	5
1885	William Dixon Ltd	5	3
1886	William Dixon Ltd	5	4
1887	William Dixon Ltd	5	5
1888	William Dixon Ltd	5	4
1889	William Dixon Ltd	5	3
1890	William Dixon Ltd	5	2
1891	William Dixon Ltd	5	3
1892	William Dixon Ltd	6	4
1893	William Dixon Ltd	6	5
1894	William Dixon Ltd	5	2
1895	William Dixon Ltd	5	5
1896	William Dixon Ltd	5	5

Year	Owner	Built	In Blast
1897	William Dixon Ltd	5	4
1898	William Dixon Ltd	6	5
1899	William Dixon Ltd	6	6
1900	William Dixon Ltd	7	6
1901	William Dixon Ltd	6	5
1902	William Dixon Ltd	7	5
1903	William Dixon Ltd	7	5
1904	William Dixon Ltd	7	5
1905	William Dixon Ltd	7	5
1906	William Dixon Ltd	7	6
1907	William Dixon Ltd	7	6
1908	William Dixon Ltd	7	5
1909	William Dixon Ltd	7	5
1910	William Dixon Ltd	7	6
1911	William Dixon Ltd	7	5
1912	William Dixon Ltd	7	5
1913	William Dixon Ltd	7	5
1921	William Dixon Ltd	13	-
1922	William Dixon Ltd	13	-
1923	William Dixon Ltd	12	-
1924	William Dixon Ltd	12	-
1925	William Dixon Ltd	12	-
1926	William Dixon Ltd	12	-
1927	William Dixon Ltd	12	-
1928	William Dixon Ltd	12	-
1929	William Dixon Ltd	12	-
1930	William Dixon Ltd	12	-
1931	William Dixon Ltd	12	-
1932	William Dixon Ltd	12	-
1933	William Dixon Ltd	12	-
1934	William Dixon Ltd	12	-
1935	William Dixon Ltd	12	-
1936	William Dixon Ltd	12	-
1937	William Dixon Ltd	12	-
1938	William Dixon Ltd	12	-
1939	William Dixon Ltd	6	-
1940	William Dixon Ltd	6	-
1941	William Dixon Ltd	6	-
1942	William Dixon Ltd	6	-
1943	William Dixon Ltd	6	-
1944	William Dixon Ltd	6	-
1945	William Dixon Ltd	6	-
1946	William Dixon Ltd	6	-
1947	Dixons' Ironworks Ltd	6	-
1948	Dixons' Ironworks Ltd	6	-
1949	Dixons' Ironworks Ltd	6	-
1950	Dixons' Ironworks Ltd	6	-
1951	Dixons' Ironworks Ltd	6	-
1952	Dixons' Ironworks Ltd	6	-
1953	Dixons' Ironworks Ltd	6	-
1954	Dixons' Ironworks Ltd	6	-
1955	Dixons' Ironworks Ltd	6	-
1956	Dixons' Ironworks Ltd	6	-
1957	Dixons' Ironworks Ltd	6	-
1958	Dixons' Ironworks Ltd	6	-

1805: output 1,077 tons p.a. 1823–30: output in 1823 4,000 tons p.a.; 1830: 9,000 tons p.a.; additional furnace built in 1824. 1825: output 80 tons a week, 4,00 tons p.a. 1839: 1 furnace contemplated. 1841: output 595 tons a week. 1843: output 425 tons a week. 1849: Hunt lists 7 furnaces in blast. Truran: output 140 tons a week from each of 8 furnaces. In 1868 *Mineral Statistics* lists 3 furnaces built, 7 in blast; it seems more likely that the first figure is a misprint for 8 than that the 3 and 7 have been transposed. After 1921 a single figure was returned for Dixons' two works at Calder and Govan (qv).

Calderbank, Lanarkshire [NS 7662]

Year	Owner	Built	In Blast
1839	—	2	2

1839: Two further furnaces contemplated. Monkland (qv) was called Calderbank from 1878 but has its own entry in 1839; the above entry is therefore apparently for another works.

Carnbroe, Lanarkshire [NS 7463]

Year	Owner	Built	In Blast
1839	—	2	2
1841	Alison & Co.	5	5
1843	Aleson & Co.	6	5
1847	Merry & Cunninghame	6	3
1849	Merry & Cunninghame	6	3
1854	Merry & Cunninghame	6	4
1855	Merry & Cunninghame	6	4
1856	Merry & Cunninghame	6	4
1857	Merry & Cunninghame	6	4
1858	Merry & Cunninghame	6	4
1859	Merry & Cunninghame	6	4
1860	Merry & Cunninghame	6	4
1861	Merry & Cunninghame	6	4
1862	Merry & Cunninghame	6	4
1863	Merry & Cunninghame	6	4
1864	Merry & Cunninghame	6	4
1865	Merry & Cunninghame	6	5
1866	Merry & Cunninghame	6	4
1867	Merry & Cunninghame	6	4
1868	Merry & Cunninghame	6	5
1869	Merry & Cunninghame	6	6
1870	Merry & Cunninghame	6	6
1871	Merry & Cunninghame	6	6
1872	Merry & Cunninghame Ltd	6	6
1873	Merry & Cunninghame Ltd	6	6
1874	Merry & Cunninghame Ltd	6	4
1875	Merry & Cunninghame Ltd	6	5
1876	Merry & Cunninghame Ltd	6	5
1877	Merry & Cunninghame Ltd	6	5
1878	Merry & Cunninghame Ltd	6	3
1879	Merry & Cunninghame Ltd	6	4
1880	Merry & Cunninghame Ltd	6	3
1881	Merry & Cunninghame Ltd	6	4
1882	Merry & Cunninghame Ltd	6	4
1883	Merry & Cunninghame Ltd	6	4
1884	Merry & Cunninghame Ltd	5	4
1885	Merry & Cunninghame Ltd	5	4
1886	Merry & Cunninghame Ltd	5	3
1887	Merry & Cunninghame Ltd	5	4
1888	Merry & Cunninghame Ltd	4	4
1889	Merry & Cunninghame Ltd	4	4
1890	Merry & Cunninghame Ltd	4	2
1891	Merry & Cunninghame Ltd	4	2
1892	Merry & Cunninghame Ltd	5	4
1893	Merry & Cunninghame Ltd	5	3
1894	Merry & Cunninghame Ltd	5	3
1895	Merry & Cunninghame Ltd	5	4
1896	Merry & Cunninghame Ltd	5	4
1897	Merry & Cunninghame Ltd	5	4
1898	Merry & Cunninghame Ltd	5	4
1899	Merry & Cunninghame Ltd	5	4
1900	Merry & Cunninghame Ltd	5	4
1901	Merry & Cunninghame Ltd	5	4

Year	Owner	Built	In Blast
1902	Merry & Cunninghame Ltd	5	4
1903	Merry & Cunninghame Ltd	5	3
1904	Merry & Cunninghame Ltd	5	4
1905	Merry & Cunninghame Ltd	5	4
1906	Merry & Cunninghame Ltd	5	4
1907	Merry & Cunninghame Ltd	5	4
1908	Merry & Cunninghame Ltd	5	4
1909	Merry & Cunninghame Ltd	5	4
1910	Merry & Cunninghame Ltd	5	4
1911	Merry & Cunninghame Ltd	5	4
1912	Merry & Cunninghame Ltd	5	3
1913	Merry & Cunninghame Ltd	5	4
1921	Merry & Cunninghame Ltd	5	-
1922	Merry & Cunninghame Ltd	5	-
1923	Merry & Cunninghame Ltd	5	-
1924	Merry & Cunninghame Ltd	5	-
1925	Merry & Cunninghame Ltd	5	-
1926	Merry & Cunninghame Ltd	5	-
1927	Merry & Cunninghame Ltd	5	-
1928	Merry & Cunninghame Ltd	5	-
1929	Merry & Cunninghame Ltd	5	-

1841: output 425 tons a week. 1843: 450 tons a week. 1849: Hunt lists 6 furnaces in blast. Truran: output 140 tons a week from each of 6 furnaces.

Carron, Stirlingshire NS 8882

Year	Owner	Built	In Blast
1794	Carron Co.	5	-
1796	—	4	4
1805	Carron Co.	5	5
1810	Carron Co.	5	5
1823	—	5	-
1825	Carron Co.	5	4
1830	—	5	-
1839	—	4	4
1841	Carron Co.	5	3
1843	Carron Co.	4	3
1847	Carron Co.	4	3
1849	Carron Co.	5	2
1854	Carron Co.	4	2
1855	Carron Co.	4	3
1856	Carron Co.	4	3
1857	Carron Co.	4	3
1858	Carron Co.	4	3
1859	Carron Co.	4	4
1860	Carron Co.	4	4
1861	Carron Co.	4	4
1862	Carron Co.	4	4
1863	Carron Co.	4	4
1864	Carron Co.	4	4
1865	Carron Co.	4	4
1866	Carron Co.	4	3
1867	Carron Co.	4	3
1868	Carron Co.	4	3
1869	Carron Co.	4	3
1870	Carron Co.	3	1
1871	Carron Co.	4	3
1872	Carron Co.	4	3
1873	Carron Co.	4	3
1874	Carron Co.	6	5
1875	Carron Co.	6	5
1876	Carron Co.	6	4
1877	Carron Co.	5	4
1878	Carron Co.	4	3
1879	Carron Co.	4	2
1880	Carron Co.	4	2
1881	Carron Co.	4	2
1882	Carron Co.	4	4
1883	Carron Co.	4	4
1884	Carron Co.	4	2
1885	Carron Co.	4	2
1886	Carron Co.	4	2
1887	Carron Co.	4	2
1888	Carron Co.	4	2
1889	Carron Co.	4	2
1890	Carron Co.	4	3
1891	Carron Co.	4	3
1892	Carron Co.	4	3
1893	Carron Co.	4	2
1894	Carron Co.	4	1
1895	Carron Co.	4	2
1896	Carron Co.	4	3
1897	Carron Co.	4	4
1898	Carron Co.	4	4
1899	Carron Co.	4	3
1900	Carron Co.	4	4
1901	Carron Co.	4	4
1902	Carron Co.	4	4
1903	Carron Co.	4	4
1904	Carron Co.	4	3
1905	Carron Co.	4	3
1906	Carron Co.	4	4
1907	Carron Co.	4	3
1908	Carron Co.	4	3
1909	Carron Co.	4	3
1910	Carron Co.	4	3
1911	Carron Co.	4	3
1912	Carron Co.	4	3
1913	Carron Co.	4	3
1921	Carron Co.	4	-
1922	Carron Co.	4	-
1923	Carron Co.	4	-
1924	Carron Co.	4	-
1925	Carron Co.	4	-
1926	Carron Co.	4	-
1927	Carron Co.	4	-
1928	Carron Co.	4	-
1929	Carron Co.	4	-
1930	Carron Co.	4	-
1931	Carron Co.	4	-
1932	Carron Co.	4	-
1933	Carron Co.	4	-
1934	Carron Co.	4	-
1935	Carron Co.	4	-
1936	Carron Co.	4	-
1937	Carron Co.	4	-
1938	Carron Co.	4	-
1939	Carron Co.	4	-
1940	Carron Co.	4	-
1941	Carron Co.	4	-
1942	Carron Co.	4	-
1943	Carron Co.	4	-
1944	Carron Co.	4	-
1945	Carron Co.	4	-
1946	Carron Co.	4	-
1947	Carron Co.	4	-
1948	Carron Co.	4	-
1949	Carron Co.	4	-
1950	Carron Co.	4	-
1951	Carron Co.	4	-

Year	Owner	Built	In Blast
1952	Carron Co.	4	-
1953	Carron Co.	4	-
1954	Carron Co.	4	-
1955	Carron Co.	4	-
1956	Carron Co.	4	-
1957	Carron Co.	4	-
1958	Carron Co.	4	-
1959	Carron Co.	2	-
1960	Carron Co.	2	-
1961	Carron Co.	2	-
1962	Carron Co.	2	-
1963	Carron Co.	2	-
1964	Carron Co.	2	-
1965	Carron Co.	2	-

The ground landlord in 1794 was Bruce of Kinnard; the furnaces were coke-fired, blown by water, built in 1760. The forge consisted of three fineries, a chafery and a balling furnace; no date of construction is given for the forge, although 1769 appears in the mill section of the table. 1796: output 5,200 tons p.a., i.e. 25 tons a week from each of four furnaces (not, according to the original return, 20 tons a week from each of five). 1805: output 7,380 tons p.a. 1823-30: output 7,000 tons p.a. in both years. 1825: output 120 tons a week, 5,000 tons p.a.; although there were said to be 5 furnaces built and 4 in blast the figure in the 'Out of blast' column is 0. 1841: output 255 tons a week. 1843: 180 tons a week. 1849: Hunt lists 3 furnaces in blast. Truran: output 120 tons a week from each of 5 furnaces. In 1869 *Mineral Statistics* listed 3 furnaces built, 4 in blast, which has been treated above as a simple transposition error, although only 3 furnaces were listed at Carron the following year.

Castlehill, Lanarkshire [NS 8451]

Year	Owner	Built	In Blast
1839	—	2	2
1841	Shotts Iron Co.	4	3
1843	Shotts Iron Co.	2	0
1847	Shotts Iron Co.	3	3
1849	Shotts Iron Co.	3	2
1854	Shotts Iron Co.	3	3
1855	Shotts Iron Co.	3	3
1856	Shotts Iron Co.	3	3
1857	Shotts Iron Co.	3	2
1858	Shotts Iron Co.	3	2
1859	Shotts Iron Co.	3	0
1860	Shotts Iron Co.	3	0
1861	Shotts Iron Co.	3	0
1862	Shotts Iron Co.	3	0
1863	Shotts Iron Co.	8	4
1864	Shotts Iron Co.	3	0
1865	Shotts Iron Co.	3	0
1866	Shotts Iron Co.	3	0
1867	Shotts Iron Co.	3	0
1868	Shotts Iron Co.	3	2
1869	Shotts Iron Co.	7	6
1870	Shotts Iron Co.	4	3
1871	Shotts Iron Co.	3	2
1872	Shotts Iron Co.	3	3
1873	Shotts Iron Co.	4	3
1874	Shotts Iron Co.	3	1
1875	Shotts Iron Co.	3	2
1876	Shotts Iron Co.	3	2
1877	Shotts Iron Co.	3	2
1878	Shotts Iron Co.	3	2
1879	Shotts Iron Co.	3	2
1880	Shotts Iron Co.	3	3
1881	Shotts Iron Co.	3	3
1882	Shotts Iron Co.	3	3
1883	Shotts Iron Co.	3	3
1884	Shotts Iron Co.	3	2
1885	Shotts Iron Co.	3	0
1886	Shotts Iron Co.	3	0
1887	Shotts Iron Co.	3	0
1888	Shotts Iron Co.	3	0

1841: Furnace-numbers are for Castlehill and Shotts (qv) combined; output of 3 furnaces 255 tons a week. 1843: output (at Castlehill) nil. Truran: output 140 tons a week from each of 3 furnaces. In 1863 and 1869 the furnace-numbers include Shotts as well as Castlehill.

Cawseyend: see Almond

Cessnock, Ayrshire [NS 5135?]

Year	Owner	Furnaces	In Blast
1841	—	2	0
1843	M'Cullum & Co.	2	0

The works appears as 'Cepnock' in 1841 and 'Gessnock' in 1843. The output was nil in both years.

Chapelhall, Lanarkshire [NS 7862]

Year	Owner	Built	In Blast
1879	Monkland Iron & Coal Co. Ltd	3	3
1880	Monkland Iron & Coal Co. Ltd	3	3
1881	Monkland Iron & Coal Co. Ltd	-	-
1882	Monkland Iron Co. Ltd	3	2
1883	Monkland Iron Co. Ltd	3	2
1884	Monkland Iron Co. Ltd	3	2
1885	Monkland Iron Co. Ltd	3	2
1886	Monkland Iron Co. Ltd	3	2
1887	Monkland Iron Co. Ltd	3	0
1888	Monkland Iron Co. Ltd	3	0
1889	Owners of Chapelhall	3	0
1890	Monkland Iron Co. Ltd	3	0
1891	Monkland Iron Co. Ltd	3	0

For earlier entries for this works see under Monkland, the name usually used in nationally compiled lists. Separate furnace-numbers were given for Chapelhall in 1879–80 and again in 1882–90; they were combined for the last time in 1881.

Cleland: see Omoa

Clyde Ironworks, Lanarkshire   NS 6362

Year	Owner	Built	In Blast
1794	Edington & Co.	2	-
1796	—	3	3
1805	Cadell & Co.	3	2
1810	Cadell & Co.	3	3
1823	—	3	-
1825	Colin Dunlop & Co.	3	2
1830	—	4	-
1839	—	4	4
1841	J. Dunlop	6	4
1843	C. Dunlop & Co.	7	4
1847	Colin Dunlop & Co.	7	5
1849	C. Dunlop & Co.	7	6
1854	Colin Dunlop & Co.	7	5
1855	Colin Dunlop & Co.	7	5
1856	Colin Dunlop & Co.	9	5
1857	Colin Dunlop & Co.	9	6
1858	Colin Dunlop & Co.	9	7
1859	Colin Dunlop & Co.	9	7
1860	Colin Dunlop & Co.	8	7
1861	Colin Dunlop & Co.	8	7
1862	Colin Dunlop & Co.	9	7
1863	Colin Dunlop & Co.	9	7
1864	Colin Dunlop & Co.	9	7
1865	Colin Dunlop & Co.	7	5
1866	Colin Dunlop & Co.	6	3
1867	Colin Dunlop & Co.	6	4
1868	Colin Dunlop & Co.	6	4
1869	James Dunlop & Co.	6	4
1870	James Dunlop & Co.	6	5
1871	James Dunlop & Co.	6	5
1872	Colin Dunlop & Co.	6	5
1873	James Dunlop & Co.	6	5
1874	James Dunlop & Co.	6	6
1875	James Dunlop & Co.	6	5
1876	James Dunlop & Co.	6	5
1877	James Dunlop & Co.	5	3
1878	James Dunlop & Co.	6	4
1879	James Dunlop & Co.	6	4
1880	James Dunlop & Co.	5	5
1881	James Dunlop & Co.	5	4
1882	James Dunlop & Co.	5	4
1883	James Dunlop & Co.	5	4
1884	James Dunlop & Co.	4	4
1885	James Dunlop & Co.	4	4
1886	James Dunlop & Co.	4	3
1887	James Dunlop & Co.	4	3
1888	James Dunlop & Co. Ltd	4	3
1889	James Dunlop & Co. Ltd	4	4
1890	James Dunlop & Co. Ltd	4	3
1891	James Dunlop & Co. Ltd	4	3
1892	James Dunlop & Co. Ltd	4	4
1893	James Dunlop & Co. Ltd	4	4
1894	James Dunlop & Co. Ltd	4	3
1895	James Dunlop & Co. Ltd	4	4
1896	James Dunlop & Co. Ltd	4	4
1897	James Dunlop & Co. Ltd	5	4
1898	James Dunlop & Co. Ltd	4	4
1899	James Dunlop & Co. Ltd	5	4
1900	James Dunlop & Co. (1900) Ltd	5	4
1901	James Dunlop & Co. (1900) Ltd	5	4
1902	James Dunlop & Co. (1900) Ltd	5	4
1903	James Dunlop & Co. Ltd	5	4
1904	James Dunlop & Co. Ltd	5	4
1905	James Dunlop & Co. Ltd	5	4
1906	James Dunlop & Co. Ltd	5	4
1907	James Dunlop & Co. Ltd	5	4
1908	James Dunlop & Co. Ltd	5	4
1909	James Dunlop & Co. Ltd	5	4
1910	James Dunlop & Co. Ltd	5	4
1911	James Dunlop & Co. Ltd	5	4
1912	James Dunlop & Co. Ltd	5	4
1913	James Dunlop & Co. Ltd	5	4
1921	James Dunlop & Co. Ltd	5	-
1922	James Dunlop & Co. Ltd	5	-
1923	James Dunlop & Co. Ltd	5	-
1924	James Dunlop & Co. Ltd	5	-
1925	James Dunlop & Co. Ltd	5	-
1926	James Dunlop & Co. Ltd	5	-
1927	James Dunlop & Co. Ltd	5	-
1928	James Dunlop & Co. Ltd	5	-
1929	James Dunlop & Co. Ltd	5	-
1930	Colvilles Ltd	12	-
1931	Colvilles Ltd	12	-
1932	Colvilles Ltd	12	-
1933	Colvilles Ltd	12	-
1934	Colvilles Ltd	12	-
1935	Colvilles Ltd	12	-
1936	Colvilles Ltd	3	-
1937	Colvilles Ltd	3	-
1938	Colvilles Ltd	3	-
1939	Colvilles Ltd	3	-
1940	Colvilles Ltd	3	-
1941	Colvilles Ltd	3	-
1942	Colvilles Ltd	3	-
1943	Colvilles Ltd	3	-
1944	Colvilles Ltd	3	-
1945	Colvilles Ltd	2	-
1946	Colvilles Ltd	2	-
1947	Colvilles Ltd	3	-
1948	Colvilles Ltd	3	-
1949	Colvilles Ltd	3	-
1950	Colvilles Ltd	3	-
1951	Colvilles Ltd	3	-
1952	Colvilles Ltd	3	-
1953	Colvilles Ltd	3	-
1954	Colvilles Ltd	3	-
1955	Colvilles Ltd	3	-
1956	Colvilles Ltd	3	-
1957	Colvilles Ltd	3	-
1958	Colvilles Ltd	3	-
1959	Colvilles Ltd	3	-
1960	Colvilles Ltd	3	-
1961	Colvilles Ltd	3	-
1962	Colvilles Ltd	3	-
1963	Colvilles Ltd	3	-
1964	Colvilles Ltd	3	-
1965	Colvilles Ltd	3	-
1966	Colvilles Ltd	3	-
1967	Colvilles Ltd	3	-
1968	Colvilles Ltd	3	-
1969	Colvilles Ltd	3	-
1970	British Steel Corporation	3	-
1971	British Steel Corporation	3	-
1972	British Steel Corporation	3	-
1973	British Steel Corporation	3	-
1974	British Steel Corporation	3	-
1975	British Steel Corporation	3	-
1976	British Steel Corporation	3	-

The ground landlord in 1794 was Ed. Dunlop; the furnaces were coke-fired, blown by engine and built in 1787. In 1796 the works appears as 'Edington', output 3,640 tons p.a., i.e. 70 tons a week from the three furnaces together. 1805: output 2,687 tons p.a. 1823–30: output in 1823 2,500 tons p.a.; in 1830 8,000 tons p.a.; additional furnace built 1828. 1825: output 90 tons a week, 4,500 tons p.a. 1841: output 340 tons a week. 1843: 320 tons a week. 1849: Hunt lists 7 furnaces in blast. Truran: output 130 tons a week from each of 7 furnaces. 1856–65: furnace-numbers include Quarter (qv). In 1854–56 the owner's Christian name appears as 'Colm', presumably in error. The reappearance of 'Colin' in 1872 may also be an error. In 1930 James Dunlop was acquired by Colvilles and from that year a single figure was returned for furnaces at Clyde and Glengarnock. Three-quarters of Colvilles' furnaces were dismantled in 1936, including all those at Glengarnock, so that from that year the figures above relate solely to Clyde. See also Ravenscraig.

Coltness, Lanarkshire [NS 8056]

Year	Owner	Built	In Blast
1839	—	2	2
1841	Holdsworth	4	3
1843	Houldsworth	4	3
1847	Coltness Iron Co.	6	4
1849	Coltness Iron Co.	6	6
1854	Coltness Iron Co.	6	6
1855	Coltness Iron Co.	6	6
1856	Coltness Iron Co.	8	8
1857	Coltness Iron Co.	9	9
1858	Coltness Iron Co.	9	9
1859	Coltness Iron Co.	9	8
1860	Coltness Iron Co.	9	9
1861	Coltness Iron Co.	9	9
1862	Houldsworth & Hunter	10	10
1863	Houldsworth & Hunter	12	10
1864	Coltness Iron Co.	12	12
1865	Coltness Iron Co.	12	10
1866	Coltness Iron Co.	12	8
1867	Coltness Iron Co.	12	9
1868	Coltness Iron Co.	12	12
1869	Coltness Iron Co.	12	12
1870	Coltness Iron Co.	12	12
1871	Coltness Iron Co.	12	12
1872	Coltness Iron Co.	12	12
1873	Coltness Iron Co.	12	12
1874	Coltness Iron Co.	12	12
1875	Coltness Iron Co.	12	12
1876	Coltness Iron Co.	12	12
1877	Coltness Iron Co.	12	12
1878	Coltness Iron Co.	12	10
1879	Coltness Iron Co.	12	8
1880	Coltness Iron Co.	12	10
1881	Coltness Iron Co.	12	10
1882	Coltness Iron Co.	12	11
1883	Coltness Iron Co. Ltd	12	12
1884	Coltness Iron Co. Ltd	12	11
1885	Coltness Iron Co. Ltd	12	11
1886	Coltness Iron Co. Ltd	12	9
1887	Coltness Iron Co. Ltd	12	9
1888	Coltness Iron Co. Ltd	12	9
1889	Coltness Iron Co. Ltd	12	10
1890	Coltness Iron Co. Ltd	11	8
1891	Coltness Iron Co. Ltd	11	6
1892	Coltness Iron Co. Ltd	11	8
1893	Coltness Iron Co. Ltd	11	7
1894	Coltness Iron Co. Ltd	11	7
1895	Coltness Iron Co. Ltd	11	9
1896	Coltness Iron Co. Ltd	11	9
1897	Coltness Iron Co. Ltd	9	8
1898	Coltness Iron Co. Ltd	9	9
1899	Coltness Iron Co. Ltd	9	9
1900	Coltness Iron Co. Ltd	9	9
1901	Coltness Iron Co. Ltd	9	7
1902	Coltness Iron Co. Ltd	9	7
1903	Coltness Iron Co. Ltd	9	8
1904	Coltness Iron Co. Ltd	9	9
1905	Coltness Iron Co. Ltd	9	8
1906	Coltness Iron Co. Ltd	9	9
1907	Coltness Iron Co. Ltd	9	9
1908	Coltness Iron Co. Ltd	9	7
1909	Coltness Iron Co. Ltd	9	7
1910	Coltness Iron Co. Ltd	9	7
1911	Coltness Iron Co. Ltd	9	7
1912	Coltness Iron Co. Ltd	9	6
1913	Coltness Iron Co. Ltd	9	8
1921	Coltness Iron Co. Ltd	9	-
1922	Coltness Iron Co. Ltd	9	-
1923	Coltness Iron Co. Ltd	9	-
1924	Coltness Iron Co. Ltd	9	-
1925	Coltness Iron Co. Ltd	6	-
1926	Coltness Iron Co. Ltd	6	-
1927	Coltness Iron Co. Ltd	6	-
1928	Coltness Iron Co. Ltd	6	-
1929	Coltness Iron Co. Ltd	6	-
1930	Coltness Iron Co. Ltd	6	-
1931	Coltness Iron Co. Ltd	6	-
1932	Coltness Iron Co. Ltd	6	-
1933	Coltness Iron Co. Ltd	6	-
1934	Coltness Iron Co. Ltd	6	-
1935	Coltness Iron Co. Ltd	6	-
1936	Coltness Iron Co. Ltd	6	-

1841: output 255 tons a week. 1843: output 180 tons a week. Truran: output 150 tons a week from each of 6 furnaces. In 1870 there were said to be 13 furnaces in blast, which is presumably a simple misprint. Furnaces dismantled during 1937.

Craleckan, Argyllshire NM 0200

Year	Owner	Built	In Blast
1794	L.G. Knott	1	-
1796	—	1	1
1805	—	1	0
1810	—	2	0

In 1794 the Duke of Argyll was the ground landlord at what is called Argyll furnace, which was charcoal-fired, water-powered and built in 1755. The 1796 list combines Craleckan (or Argyll) furnace with Lorn (i.e. Bonawe) (qv), with 2 furnaces, both apparently in blast, with the total output given as 1,600 tons p.a. The number of furnaces given in 1810 must be an error, since Bonawe has its own entry that year.

Cramond, West Lothian [NT 1876]

The 1794 list includes an entry for Cramond, near Edinburgh, owned and occupied by Cadell & Edington, in which a figure

1 appears in the charcoal blast furnace column but with no other information; there was also a slitting mill, built in 1760. There is no other evidence that there was ever a blast furnace at Cramond and the entry in 1794 appears to be an error.

Cumnock: see New Cumnock

Dalmellington, Ayrshire NS 4408

Year	Owner	Built	In Blast
1849	Dalmellington Iron Co.	3	3
1854	Dalmellington Iron Co.	4	3
1855	Dalmellington Iron Co.	4	4
1856	Dalmellington Iron Co.	4	4
1857	Dalmellington Iron Co.	4	4
1858	Dalmellington Iron Co.	5	4
1859	Dalmellington Iron Co.	5	4
1860	Dalmellington Iron Co.	5	4
1861	Dalmellington Iron Co.	5	4
1862	Dalmellington Iron Co.	5	4
1863	Dalmellington Iron Co.	5	4
1864	Dalmellington Iron Co.	5	5
1865	Dalmellington Iron Co.	7	6
1866	Dalmellington Iron Co.	7	5
1867	Dalmellington Iron Co.	7	6
1868	Dalmellington Iron Co.	7	7
1869	Dalmellington Iron Co.	8	8
1870	Dalmellington Iron Co.	8	7
1871	Dalmellington Iron Co.	8	7
1872	Dalmellington Iron Co.	8	7
1873	Dalmellington Iron Co.	8	6
1874	Dalmellington Iron Co.	8	6
1875	Dalmellington Iron Co.	8	6
1876	Dalmellington Iron Co.	7	6
1877	Dalmellington Iron Co.	8	5
1878	Dalmellington Iron Co.	8	5
1879	Dalmellington Iron Co.	8	5
1880	Dalmellington Iron Co.	8	7
1881	Dalmellington Iron Co.	8	6
1882	Dalmellington Iron Co.	8	6
1883	Dalmellington Iron Co.	8	5
1884	Dalmellington Iron Co.	8	4
1885	Dalmellington Iron Co. Ltd	8	5
1886	Dalmellington Iron Co. Ltd	7	5
1887	Dalmellington Iron Co. Ltd	7	5
1888	Dalmellington Iron Co. Ltd	6	5
1889	Dalmellington Iron Co. Ltd	6	5
1890	Dalmellington Iron Co. Ltd	6	4
1891	Dalmellington Iron Co. Ltd	6	4
1892	Dalmellington Iron Co. Ltd	6	4
1893	Dalmellington Iron Co. Ltd	6	5
1894	Dalmellington Iron Co. Ltd	6	3
1895	Dalmellington Iron Co. Ltd	6	5
1896	Dalmellington Iron Co. Ltd	6	6
1897	Dalmellington Iron Co. Ltd	6	6
1898	Dalmellington Iron Co. Ltd	6	5
1899	Dalmellington Iron Co. Ltd	6	6
1900	Dalmellington Iron Co. Ltd	6	6
1901	Dalmellington Iron Co. Ltd	6	5
1902	Dalmellington Iron Co. Ltd	6	5
1903	Dalmellington Iron Co. Ltd	6	5
1904	Dalmellington Iron Co. Ltd	6	4
1905	Dalmellington Iron Co. Ltd	5	4
1906	Dalmellington Iron Co. Ltd	5	4
1907	Dalmellington Iron Co. Ltd	5	4
1908	Dalmellington Iron Co. Ltd	5	4
1909	Dalmellington Iron Co. Ltd	5	4
1910	Dalmellington Iron Co. Ltd	5	4
1911	Dalmellington Iron Co. Ltd	5	4
1912	Dalmellington Iron Co. Ltd	5	4
1913	Dalmellington Iron Co. Ltd	5	4
1921	Dalmellington Iron Co. Ltd	5	-
1922	Dalmellington Iron Co. Ltd	5	-
1923	Dalmellington Iron Co. Ltd	5	-
1924	Dalmellington Iron Co. Ltd	5	-
1925	Dalmellington Iron Co. Ltd	5	-
1926	Dalmellington Iron Co. Ltd	5	-

Truran: output 140 tons a week from each of 3 furnaces. 1876: 1 furnace building.

Dalry, Ayrshire [NS 2949]

Year	Owner	Furnaces	In Blast
1841	—	3	0
1843	—	3	0

The output was nil in both years.

Darngaber: see Quarter

Devon, Clackmannanshire [NS 7788?]

Year	Owner	Built	In Blast
1794	Roebuck & Co.	1	-
1796	Addison	2	2
1805	Gordon & Co.	2	2
1810	Edington & Co.	2	2
1823	—	3	-
1825	Devon Iron Co.	3	2
1830	—	3	-
1839	—	3	3
1841	Devon Iron Co.	3	2
1843	Devon Iron Co.	3	2
1847	Devon Iron Co.	1	1
1849	Wilson & Christie	5	4
1854	Andrew Christie	3	2
1855	Andrew Christie	3	1
1856	Andrew Christie	3	1
1857	Andrew Christie	3	1
1858	J. Miller	3	0
1859	J. Miller	3	0
1860	J. Miller	3	0
1861	J. Miller	3	0
1862	J. Miller	3	0
1863	Executors of late J. Miller	3	0
1864	Executors of late J. Miller	1	0
1865	Executors of late J. Miller	1	0

The works appears as Sauchie, near Alloa, in 1794, when the ground landlord was Lord Cathcart; the furnace was coke-fired, blown by engine and built in 1793. In 1796 the furnace called 'Addison' can only, by a process of elimination, be Devon, and the name is presumably that of the owner. Output combined with that of Omoa (qv). 1805: output 2,596 tons p.a. 1823–30: output 3,000 tons p.a. in 1823, 3,500 tons in 1830. 1825: output 75 tons a week, 3,700 tons p.a. 1841: 170 tons a week. 1843: 100 tons a week. 1849: Hunt lists 1 furnace in blast. Truran: output 120 tons a week from each of 2 furnaces.

Dundyvan, Lanarkshire [NS 7265?]

Year	Owner	Built	In Blast
1839	—	5	5
1841	Dunlop & Co.	9	8
1843	J. Wilson	9	9
1847	John Wilson	9	8
1849	John Wilson	9	8
1854	Trustees of the late John Wilson	9	6
1855	Trustees of the late John Wilson	9	6
1856	Trustees of the late John Wilson	8	6
1857	Trustees of the late John Wilson	8	5
1858	Trustees of the late John Wilson	8	5
1859	Trustees of the late John Wilson	8	4
1860	Trustees of the late John Wilson	8	4
1861	Trustees of the late John Wilson	8	3
1862	Trustees of the late John Wilson	8	3
1863	Trustees of the late John Wilson	4	3
1864	Trustees of the late John Wilson	8	2
1865	Trustees of the late John Wilson	8	2
1866	Trustees of the late John Wilson	3	1
1867	Trustees of the late John Wilson	3	1
1868	Trustees of the late John Wilson	1	1
1869	Trustees of the late John Wilson	0	0
1870	Trustees of the late John Wilson	-	-

1839: 3 further furnaces contemplated. 1841: output 680 tons a week. 1843: output 780 tons a week. 1849: Hunt lists 9 furnaces in blast. Truran: output 150 tons a week from each of 9 furnaces. The owner's name is given in various forms between 1854 and 1870, of which that used above is the fullest.

Eglinton, Ayrshire [NS 3242]

Year	Owner	Built	In Blast
1847	William Baird & Co.	3	0
1849	William Baird & Co.	4	3
1854	Eglinton Iron Co.	5	5
1855	Eglinton Iron Co.	5	5
1856	Eglinton Iron Co.	5	5
1857	William Baird & Co.	5	5
1858	William Baird & Co.	11	5
1859	William Baird & Co.	7	7
1860	William Baird & Co.	8	8
1861	William Baird & Co.	8	8
1862	William Baird & Co.	8	8
1863	William Baird & Co.	8	8
1864	William Baird & Co.	8	8
1865	William Baird & Co.	8	8
1866	William Baird & Co.	8	5
1867	William Baird & Co.	8	6
1868	William Baird & Co.	8	6
1869	William Baird & Co.	8	7
1870	William Baird & Co.	8	7
1871	William Baird & Co.	8	7
1872	Eglinton Iron Co.	7	7
1873	Eglinton Iron Co.	7	7
1874	Eglinton Iron Co.	8	6
1875	Eglinton Iron Co.	8	6
1876	Eglinton Iron Co.	8	6
1877	Eglinton Iron Co.	7	4
1878	Eglinton Iron Co.	7	4
1879	Eglinton Iron Co.	7	6
1880	Eglinton Iron Co.	7	6
1881	Eglinton Iron Co.	7	5
1882	Eglinton Iron Co.	7	5
1883	Eglinton Iron Co.	7	6
1884	Eglinton Iron Co.	7	3
1885	Eglinton Iron Co.	7	3
1886	Eglinton Iron Co.	7	3
1887	Eglinton Iron Co.	7	4
1888	Eglinton Iron Co.	7	5
1889	Eglinton Iron Co.	7	3
1890	Eglinton Iron Co.	7	2
1891	Eglinton Iron Co.	7	3
1892	William Baird & Co. Ltd	7	4
1893	William Baird & Co. Ltd	7	2
1894	William Baird & Co. Ltd	3	2
1895	William Baird & Co. Ltd	3	2
1896	William Baird & Co. Ltd	6	2
1897	William Baird & Co. Ltd	6	3
1898	William Baird & Co. Ltd	6	4
1899	William Baird & Co. Ltd	6	4
1900	William Baird & Co. Ltd	6	5
1901	William Baird & Co. Ltd	6	5
1902	William Baird & Co. Ltd	6	6
1903	William Baird & Co. Ltd	6	6
1904	William Baird & Co. Ltd	6	6
1905	William Baird & Co. Ltd	6	5
1906	William Baird & Co. Ltd	6	6
1907	William Baird & Co. Ltd	6	6
1908	William Baird & Co. Ltd	6	6
1909	William Baird & Co. Ltd	6	5
1910	William Baird & Co. Ltd	6	5
1911	William Baird & Co. Ltd	6	6
1912	William Baird & Co. Ltd	6	5
1913	William Baird & Co. Ltd	6	6
1921	William Baird & Co. Ltd	6	-
1922	William Baird & Co. Ltd	6	-
1923	William Baird & Co. Ltd	6	-
1924	William Baird & Co. Ltd	6	-
1925	William Baird & Co. Ltd	6	-
1926	William Baird & Co. Ltd	6	-
1927	William Baird & Co. Ltd	6	-
1928	William Baird & Co. Ltd	6	-
1929	William Baird & Co. Ltd	6	-
1930	William Baird & Co. Ltd	6	-
1931	William Baird & Co. Ltd	6	-
1932	William Baird & Co. Ltd	6	-
1933	William Baird & Co. Ltd	6	-
1934	William Baird & Co. Ltd	6	-
1935	Bairds & Dalmellington Ltd	6	-
1936	Bairds & Dalmellington Ltd	6	-

1849: Hunt lists 3 furnaces in blast at Kilwinning. Truran: output 140 tons a week from each of 4 furnaces. 1858: the furnace-numbers apparently include those for one of William Baird's others works, presumably either Blair (which then had 5 furnaces), Lugar (which had 4) or Muirkirk (with 3) (qqv), since Gartsherrie (qv) had 16 furnaces alone at this date. The other three smaller Baird works all have returns of their own for 1858 and it is impossible to establish what exactly is included in the totals given for Eglinton. In addition, 3 furnaces were said to be building at Eglinton in 1858. Furnaces dismantled 1937.

Forth, Fifeshire [NT 0388?]

Year	Owner	Built	In Blast
1847	Forth Iron Co.	6	4
1849	Forth Iron Co.	5	4
1854	Forth Iron Co.	6	6
1855	Forth Iron Co.	6	6
1856	Forth Iron Co.	6	6
1857	Forth Iron Co.	6	4
1858	Forth Iron Co.	7	6
1859	Forth Iron Co.	7	5
1860	Forth Iron Co.	7	5
1861	Forth Iron Co.	7	3
1862	Forth Iron Co.	7	1
1863	Forth Iron Co.	7	4
1864	Forth Iron Co.	7	3
1865	Forth Iron Co.	7	3
1866	Forth Iron Co.	7	3
1867	Forth Iron Co.	7	1
1868	Forth Iron Co.	7	1
1869	Forth Iron Co.	7	1

1849: English notes 1 further furnace building; Hunt lists 5 furnaces in blast. Truran: output 150 tons a week from each of 6 furnaces.

Garscube, Dunbartonshire [NS 7854?]

Year	Owner	Built	In Blast
1841	—	2	1
1843	—	2	0
1847	John Watson	2	0
1849	John Watson	2	0
1854	Montgomrie & Fleming	2	1
1855	Montgomrie & Fleming	2	0
1856	Montgomrie & Fleming	2	0
1857	Montgomrie & Fleming	2	0
1858	Montgomrie & Fleming	2	0
1859	Montgomrie & Fleming	2	0
1860	Montgomrie & Fleming	2	0

1841: output 85 tons a week. 1843: output nil. 1849: Hunt lists 1 furnace in blast. Truran: output 150 tons a week from each of 2 furnaces.

Gartsherrie, Lanarkshire [NS 7166]

Year	Owner	Built	In Blast
1830	—	1	-
1839	—	8	8
1841	W. Baird & Co.	15	12
1853	W. Baird & Co.	16	11
1847	William Baird & Co.	16	16
1849	William Baird & Co.	16	16
1854	William Baird & Co.	16	16
1855	William Baird & Co.	16	15
1856	William Baird & Co.	16	15
1857	William Baird & Co.	16	15
1858	William Baird & Co.	16	14
1859	William Baird & Co.	16	13
1860	William Baird & Co.	16	14
1861	William Baird & Co.	16	13
1862	William Baird & Co.	16	14
1863	William Baird & Co.	16	13
1864	William Baird & Co.	16	13
1865	William Baird & Co.	16	14
1866	William Baird & Co.	16	10
1867	William Baird & Co.	16	13
1868	William Baird & Co.	16	13
1869	William Baird & Co.	16	14
1870	William Baird & Co.	16	13
1871	William Baird & Co.	16	12
1872	William Baird & Co.	16	12
1873	William Baird & Co.	16	12
1874	William Baird & Co.	16	10
1875	William Baird & Co.	16	13
1876	William Baird & Co.	16	13
1877	William Baird & Co.	16	11
1878	William Baird & Co.	16	10
1879	William Baird & Co.	14	10
1880	William Baird & Co.	14	12
1881	William Baird & Co.	14	13
1882	William Baird & Co.	14	13
1883	William Baird & Co.	14	12
1884	William Baird & Co.	14	11
1885	William Baird & Co.	14	10
1886	William Baird & Co.	14	11
1887	William Baird & Co.	14	12
1888	William Baird & Co.	14	13
1889	William Baird & Co.	14	13
1890	William Baird & Co.	14	8
1891	William Baird & Co.	14	8
1892	William Baird & Co.	14	12
1893	William Baird & Co. Ltd	14	10
1894	William Baird & Co. Ltd	12	9
1895	William Baird & Co. Ltd	12	10
1896	William Baird & Co. Ltd	12	12
1897	William Baird & Co. Ltd	12	12
1898	William Baird & Co. Ltd	12	10
1899	William Baird & Co. Ltd	12	12
1900	William Baird & Co. Ltd	12	12
1901	William Baird & Co. Ltd	12	12
1902	William Baird & Co. Ltd	12	12
1903	William Baird & Co. Ltd	12	11
1904	William Baird & Co. Ltd	12	12
1905	William Baird & Co. Ltd	12	12
1906	William Baird & Co. Ltd	12	12
1907	William Baird & Co. Ltd	12	12
1908	William Baird & Co. Ltd	12	11
1909	William Baird & Co. Ltd	12	11
1910	William Baird & Co. Ltd	12	12
1911	William Baird & Co. Ltd	12	12
1912	William Baird & Co. Ltd	12	10
1913	William Baird & Co. Ltd	12	12
1921	William Baird & Co. Ltd	12	-
1922	William Baird & Co. Ltd	12	-
1923	William Baird & Co. Ltd	12	-
1924	William Baird & Co. Ltd	12	-
1925	William Baird & Co. Ltd	12	-
1926	William Baird & Co. Ltd	12	-
1927	William Baird & Co. Ltd	9	-
1928	William Baird & Co. Ltd	9	-
1929	William Baird & Co. Ltd	9	-
1930	William Baird & Co. Ltd	7	-
1931	William Baird & Co. Ltd	7	-
1932	William Baird & Co. Ltd	7	-
1933	William Baird & Co. Ltd	7	-
1934	William Baird & Co. Ltd	7	-
1935	William Baird & Co. Ltd	5	-
1936	William Baird & Co. Ltd	5	-

Year	Owner	Built	In Blast
1937	William Baird & Co. Ltd	5	-
1938	William Baird & Co. Ltd	5	-
1939	Bairds & Scottish Steel Ltd	5	-
1940	Bairds & Scottish Steel Ltd	5	-
1941	Bairds & Scottish Steel Ltd	5	-
1942	Bairds & Scottish Steel Ltd	5	-
1943	Bairds & Scottish Steel Ltd	5	-
1944	Bairds & Scottish Steel Ltd	5	-
1945	Bairds & Scottish Steel Ltd	5	-
1946	Bairds & Scottish Steel Ltd	5	-
1947	Bairds & Scottish Steel Ltd	5	-
1948	Bairds & Scottish Steel Ltd	5	-
1949	Bairds & Scottish Steel Ltd	5	-
1950	Bairds & Scottish Steel Ltd	5	-
1951	Bairds & Scottish Steel Ltd	5	-
1952	Bairds & Scottish Steel Ltd	5	-
1953	Bairds & Scottish Steel Ltd	5	-
1954	Bairds & Scottish Steel Ltd	5	-
1955	Bairds & Scottish Steel Ltd	5	-
1956	Bairds & Scottish Steel Ltd	5	-
1957	Bairds & Scottish Steel Ltd	4	-
1958	Bairds & Scottish Steel Ltd	3	-
1959	Bairds & Scottish Steel Ltd	3	-
1960	Bairds & Scottish Steel Ltd	4	-
1961	Bairds & Scottish Steel Ltd	4	-
1962	Bairds & Scottish Steel Ltd	3	-
1963	Bairds & Scottish Steel Ltd	3	-
1964	Bairds & Scottish Steel Ltd	1	-
1965	Bairds & Scottish Steel Ltd	1	-
1966	Bairds & Scottish Steel Ltd	1	-

1823–30: 1 furnace built 1829; no output shown in 1830. 1839: 12 further furnaces contemplated. 1841: output 1,020 tons a week. 1843: output 950 tons a week. Truran: output 150 tons a week from each of 16 furnaces. The 1963 return notes that 2 of the 3 furnaces listed were being dismantled in March 1964.

'Gessnock': see Cessnock

Gladsmuir or Westbank, East Lothian

Year	Owner	Built	In Blast
1854	Charles Christie	1	0
1855	Charles Christie	1	1
1856	Charles Christie	1	1
1857	Charles Christie	1	1
1858	C. & A. Christie	1	1
1859	C. & A. Christie	1	1
1860	C. & A. Christie	1	1
1861	C. & A. Christie	1	0
1862	C. & A. Christie	1	0
1863	C. & A. Christie	1	0
1864	C. & A. Christie	1	1
1865	C. & A. Christie	1	1
1866	C. & A. Christie	1	0
1867	C. & A. Christie	1	1
1868	C. & A. Christie	1	1
1869	C. & A. Christie	1	1
1870	C. & A. Christie	1	1
1871	C. & A. Christie	1	1

Glenbuck, Ayrshire [NS 7529]

Year	Owner	Built	In Blast
1805	Dixon & Co.	1	1
1810	Dalrymple	2	2

1805: output 790 tons p.a.

Glengarnock, Ayrshire NS 3253

Year	Owner	Built	In Blast
1843	—	2	0
1847	Merry & Cunninghame	7	6
1849	Merry & Cunninghame	9	9
1854	Merry & Cunninghame	9	9
1855	Merry & Cunninghame	9	7
1856	Merry & Cunninghame	9	7
1857	Merry & Cunninghame	9	8
1858	Merry & Cunninghame	9	8
1859	Merry & Cunninghame	9	9
1860	Merry & Cunninghame	9	9
1861	Merry & Cunninghame	9	8
1862	Merry & Cunninghame	9	8
1863	Merry & Cunninghame	9	9
1864	Merry & Cunninghame	9	9
1865	Glengarnock Iron Co.	9	9
1866	Glengarnock Iron Co.	9	5
1867	Glengarnock Iron Co.	9	7
1868	Glengarnock Iron Co.	10	5
1869	Merry & Cunninghame	10	6
1870	Merry & Cunninghame	9	6
1871	Glengarnock Iron Co.	9	7
1872	Merry & Cunninghame Ltd	9	8
1873	Merry & Cunninghame Ltd	9	7
1874	Merry & Cunninghame Ltd	9	7
1875	Merry & Cunninghame Ltd	9	7
1876	Merry & Cunninghame Ltd	9	7
1877	Merry & Cunninghame Ltd	9	6
1878	Merry & Cunninghame Ltd	9	6
1879	Merry & Cunninghame Ltd	-	-
1880	Merry & Cunninghame Ltd	9	6
1881	Merry & Cunninghame Ltd	9	6
1882	Merry & Cunninghame Ltd	9	6
1883	Merry & Cunninghame Ltd	9	5
1884	Merry & Cunninghame Ltd	7	3
1885	Merry & Cunninghame Ltd	7	4
1886	Merry & Cunninghame Ltd	7	5
1887	Merry & Cunninghame Ltd	7	5
1888	Merry & Cunninghame Ltd	7	5
1889	Merry & Cunninghame Ltd	8	5
1890	Merry & Cunninghame Ltd	8	5
1891	Glengarnock Iron & Steel Co. Ltd	7	4
1892	Glengarnock Iron & Steel Co. Ltd	7	4
1893	Glengarnock Iron & Steel Co. Ltd	7	2
1894	Glengarnock Iron & Steel Co. Ltd	6	3
1895	Glengarnock Iron & Steel Co. Ltd	6	6
1896	Glengarnock Iron & Steel Co. Ltd	6	6
1897	Glengarnock Iron & Steel Co. Ltd	6	6
1898	Glengarnock Iron & Steel Co. Ltd	5	3
1899	Glengarnock Iron & Steel Co. Ltd	6	6
1900	Glengarnock Iron & Steel Co. Ltd	6	6
1901	Glengarnock Iron & Steel Co. Ltd	7	4
1902	Glengarnock Iron & Steel Co. Ltd	7	6

Year	Owner	Built	In Blast
1903	Glengarnock Iron & Steel Co. Ltd	6	6
1904	Glengarnock Iron & Steel Co. Ltd	6	6
1905	Glengarnock Iron & Steel Co. Ltd	7	6
1906	Glengarnock Iron & Steel Co. Ltd	6	6
1907	Glengarnock Iron & Steel Co. Ltd	7	6
1908	Glengarnock Iron & Steel Co. Ltd	7	0
1909	Glengarnock Iron & Steel Co. Ltd	7	5
1910	Glengarnock Iron & Steel Co. Ltd	7	6
1911	Glengarnock Iron & Steel Co. Ltd	7	6
1912	Glengarnock Iron & Steel Co. Ltd	7	6
1913	Glengarnock Iron & Steel Co. Ltd	7	6
1921	David Colville & Sons Ltd	7	-
1922	David Colville & Sons Ltd	7	-
1923	David Colville & Sons Ltd	7	-
1924	David Colville & Sons Ltd	7	-
1925	David Colville & Sons Ltd	7	-
1926	David Colville & Sons Ltd	7	-
1927	David Colville & Sons Ltd	7	-
1928	David Colville & Sons Ltd	7	-
1929	David Colville & Sons Ltd	7	-

1843: output nil. 1849: Hunt lists 9 furnaces in blast at Kilbirnie. Truran: output 150 tons a week from each of 9 furnaces. In 1868 the number of furnaces built at Glengarnock was returned as 14, which clearly includes those at Merry & Cunninghame's other works at Ardeer (qv), which has its own return for that year. The figure above has been adjusted to 10 to eliminate double-counting. In 1874 both furnace-numbers for Glengarnock in *Mineral Statistics* include those for Ardeer and have once again been adjusted. In 1879 furnace-numbers for the two works were combined under Ardeer. In 1874 the return for Glengarnock notes that 6 furnaces were out of blast during a strike. In 1930 Colvilles took over the Clyde Ironworks of James Dunlop & Co. and a single figure was returned thereafter for Clyde and Glengarnock, for which see under Clyde. The company dismantled 6 furnaces in 1936, including all those at Glengarnock, and completely rebuilt Clyde the following year.

Govan, Lanarkshire [NS 5464]

Year	Owner	Built	In Blast
1839	—	2	2
1841	W. Dixon	5	4
1843	W. Dixon	5	5
1847	William Dixon	6	4
1849	William Dixon	6	4
1854	William Dixon	6	4
1855	William Dixon	6	4
1856	William Dixon	6	4
1857	William Dixon	6	4
1858	William Dixon	6	4
1859	William Dixon	6	3
1860	William Dixon	6	3
1861	William Dixon	5	3
1862	William Dixon	5	3
1863	William Dixon	5	4
1864	William Dixon	5	4
1865	William Dixon	5	4
1866	William Dixon	5	1
1867	William Dixon	5	2
1868	William Dixon	5	0
1869	William Dixon	5	3
1870	William Dixon	5	2
1871	William Dixon	5	5
1872	William Dixon Ltd	5	5
1873	William Dixon Ltd	5	4
1874	William Dixon Ltd	5	4
1875	William Dixon Ltd	5	4
1876	William Dixon Ltd	5	4
1877	William Dixon Ltd	5	3
1878	William Dixon Ltd	5	5
1879	William Dixon Ltd	5	5
1880	William Dixon Ltd	5	5
1881	William Dixon Ltd	6	6
1882	William Dixon Ltd	6	5
1883	William Dixon Ltd	6	1
1884	William Dixon Ltd	6	6
1885	William Dixon Ltd	6	5
1886	William Dixon Ltd	6	6
1887	William Dixon Ltd	6	6
1888	William Dixon Ltd	6	6
1889	William Dixon Ltd	6	6
1890	William Dixon Ltd	6	4
1891	William Dixon Ltd	6	6
1892	William Dixon Ltd	6	6
1893	William Dixon Ltd	6	6
1894	William Dixon Ltd	6	3
1895	William Dixon Ltd	6	6
1896	William Dixon Ltd	6	5
1897	William Dixon Ltd	6	5
1898	William Dixon Ltd	6	5
1899	William Dixon Ltd	6	6
1900	William Dixon Ltd	6	6
1901	William Dixon Ltd	6	5
1902	William Dixon Ltd	6	5
1903	William Dixon Ltd	6	6
1904	William Dixon Ltd	6	5
1905	William Dixon Ltd	6	5
1906	William Dixon Ltd	6	6
1907	William Dixon Ltd	6	6
1908	William Dixon Ltd	6	5
1909	William Dixon Ltd	6	6
1910	William Dixon Ltd	6	5
1911	William Dixon Ltd	6	5
1912	William Dixon Ltd	6	4
1913	William Dixon Ltd	6	5

1839: 2 further furnaces building. 1841: output 340 tons a week. 1843: 350 tons a week. 1849: Hunt lists 5 furnaces in blast. Truran: output 150 tons a week from each of 6 furnaces. From 1921 a single figure was returned for Dixons' two works, for which see under Calder.

Househill, Renfrewshire [NS 4762?]

Year	Owner	Built	In Blast
1841	Shotts Iron Co.	2	0
1843	Gallaway & Co.	2	0

Output nil in both years.

Kilbirnie: see Glengarnock

Kilwinning: see Eglinton

SCOTLAND

Kinneil, Linlithgowshire [NS 9880]

Year	Owner	Built	In Blast
1847	John Wilson	4	4
1849	John Wilson	4	4
1854	Trustees of the late John Wilson	4	2
1855	Trustees of the late John Wilson	4	3
1856	Trustees of the late John Wilson	4	4
1857	William Wilson & Co.	4	3
1858	William Wilson & Co.	4	4
1859	William Wilson & Co.	4	3
1860	William Wilson & Co.	4	4
1861	William Wilson & Co.	4	4
1862	William Wilson & Co.	4	4
1863	William Wilson & Co.	4	4
1864	George Wilson & Co.	4	3
1865	George Wilson & Co.	4	3
1866	George Wilson & Co.	4	3
1867	George Wilson & Co.	4	2
1868	George Wilson & Co.	4	2
1869	George Wilson & Co.	4	2
1870	George Wilson & Co.	4	3
1871	George Wilson & Co.	4	3
1872	George Wilson & Co.	4	4
1873	George Wilson & Co.	4	3
1874	George Wilson & Co.	4	3
1875	George Wilson & Co.	4	3
1876	George Wilson & Co.	4	3
1877	George Wilson & Co.	4	2
1878	George Wilson & Co.	4	0
1879	George Wilson & Co.	4	0
1880	George Wilson & Co.	2	1
1881	George Wilson & Co.	4	2
1882	Kinneil Iron & Coal Co. Ltd	4	2
1883	Kinneil Iron & Coal Co. Ltd	4	2
1884	Kinneil Iron & Coal Co. Ltd	4	2
1885	Kinneil Iron & Coal Co. Ltd	4	0
1886	Kinneil Iron & Coal Co. Ltd	4	0
1887	Kinneil Iron & Coal Co. Ltd	4	0
1888	Kinneil Iron & Coal Co. Ltd	4	0
1889	Kinneil Iron & Coal Co. Ltd	4	0
1890	Kinneil Iron & Coal Co. Ltd	4	0
1891	Kinneil Iron & Coal Co. Ltd	4	0
1892	Kinneil Iron & Coal Co. Ltd	4	0
1893	Kinneil Iron & Coal Co. Ltd	4	0
1894	Kinneil Iron & Coal Co. Ltd	4	0

Truran: output 140 tons a week from each of 4 furnaces.

Langloan, Lanarkshire [NS 7264]

Year	Owner	Built	In Blast
1841	—	3	2
1843	—	3	2
1847	Addie, Miller & Rankine	6	5
1849	Addie, Miller & Rankine	6	6
1854	Addie, Miller & Rankine	6	5
1855	Addie, Miller & Rankine	6	5
1856	Addie, Miller & Rankine	6	5
1857	Addie & Rankine	6	5
1858	Addie & Rankine	6	6
1859	Addie & Rankine	6	6
1860	Addie & Rankine	6	6
1861	Addie & Rankine	6	6
1862	Addie & Rankine	6	6
1863	Robert Addie	6	6
1864	Robert Addie	6	6
1865	Robert Addie	6	5
1866	Robert Addie	6	4
1867	Robert Addie	6	5
1868	Robert Addie	8	6
1869	Robert Addie	8	6
1870	Robert Addie	8	7
1871	Robert Addie	8	7
1872	Robert Addie & Sons	8	7
1873	Robert Addie & Sons	8	6
1874	Robert Addie & Sons	8	7
1875	Robert Addie & Sons	8	6
1876	Robert Addie & Sons	8	6
1877	Robert Addie & Sons	7	6
1878	Robert Addie & Sons	8	7
1879	Robert Addie & Sons	7	6
1880	Robert Addie & Sons	7	7
1881	Robert Addie & Sons	7	6
1882	Robert Addie & Sons	7	6
1883	Robert Addie & Sons	7	6
1884	Robert Addie & Sons	7	5
1885	Robert Addie & Sons	7	5
1886	Robert Addie & Sons	6	4
1887	Robert Addie & Sons	6	4
1888	Robert Addie & Sons	6	6
1889	Robert Addie & Sons	6	5
1890	Robert Addie & Sons	6	4
1891	Robert Addie & Sons	5	2
1892	Robert Addie & Sons	5	3
1893	Robert Addie & Sons	5	0
1894	Robert Addie & Sons	5	0
1895	Robert Addie & Sons	5	0
1896	Robert Addie & Sons	5	0
1897	Robert Addie & Sons	5	0
1898	Robert Addie & Sons	5	0
1899	Robert Addie & Sons	6	0
1900	Langloan Iron & Chemical Co. Ltd	4	0
1901	Langloan Iron & Chemical Co. Ltd	4	3
1902	Langloan Iron & Chemical Co. Ltd	4	4
1903	Langloan Iron & Chemical Co. Ltd	5	3
1904	Langloan Iron & Chemical Co. Ltd	5	4
1905	Langloan Iron & Chemical Co. Ltd	5	4
1906	Langloan Iron & Chemical Co. Ltd	5	4
1907	Langloan Iron & Chemical Co. Ltd	5	4
1908	Langloan Iron & Chemical Co. Ltd	5	3
1909	Langloan Iron & Chemical Co. Ltd	5	4
1910	Langloan Iron & Chemical Co. Ltd	5	4
1911	Langloan Iron & Chemical Co. Ltd	5	4
1912	Langloan Iron & Chemical Co. Ltd	5	3
1913	Langloan Iron & Chemical Co. Ltd	5	4
1921	Langloan Iron & Chemical Co. Ltd	5	-
1922	Langloan Iron & Chemical Co. Ltd	5	-
1923	Langloan Iron & Chemical Co. Ltd	5	-
1924	Langloan Iron & Chemical Co. Ltd	5	-
1925	Langloan Iron & Chemical Co. Ltd	5	-
1926	Langloan Iron & Chemical Co. Ltd	5	-
1927	Langloan Iron & Chemical Co. Ltd	5	-
1928	Langloan Iron & Chemical Co. Ltd	5	-
1929	Langloan Iron & Chemical Co. Ltd	5	-
1930	Langloan Iron & Chemical Co. Ltd	5	-
1931	Langloan Iron & Chemical Co. Ltd	5	-
1932	Langloan Iron & Chemical Co. Ltd	5	-
1933	Langloan Iron & Chemical Co. Ltd	5	-
1934	Langloan Iron & Chemical Co. Ltd	5	-
1935	Langloan Iron & Chemical Co. Ltd	5	-
1936	Langloan Iron & Chemical Co. Ltd	5	-

Year	Owner	Built	In Blast
1937	Langloan Iron & Chemical Co. Ltd	5	-

1841: output 170 tons a week. 1843: output 100 tons a week. Truran: output 150 tons a week from each of 6 furnaces. In 1858–62 the second partner's name is spelt Rankin. The furnaces were dismantled during 1938.

Leven, Fifeshire [NO 3800]

Year	Owner	Built	In Blast
1805	Losh & Co.	2	0
1810	Edington & Co.	2	0

In 1805 the works was listed as 'Markinch or Leven'.

Lochgelly, Fifeshire NT 1894

Year	Owner	Built	In Blast
1849	Lochgelly Iron Co.	2	1
1854	Lochgelly Iron Co.	2	2
1855	Lochgelly Iron Co.	2	2
1856	Lochgelly Iron Co.	3	3
1857	Lochgelly Iron Co.	4	1
1858	Lochgelly Iron Co.	4	1
1859	Lochgelly Iron Co.	4	0
1860	Lochgelly Iron Co.	4	1
1861	Lochgelly Iron Co.	4	0
1862	Lochgelly Iron Co.	4	0
1863	Lochgelly Iron Co.	4	2
1864	Lochgelly Iron Co.	4	2
1865	Lochgelly Iron Co.	4	2
1866	Lochgelly Iron Co.	4	1
1867	Lochgelly Iron Co.	4	1
1868	Lochgelly Iron Co.	4	1
1869	Lochgelly Iron Co.	4	2
1870	Lochgelly Iron Co.	4	2
1871	Lochgelly Iron Co.	4	2
1872	Lochgelly Iron & Coal Co. Ltd	4	2
1873	Lochgelly Iron & Coal Co. Ltd	4	2
1874	Lochgelly Iron & Coal Co. Ltd	4	2
1875	Lochgelly Iron & Coal Co. Ltd	4	2
1876	Lochgelly Iron & Coal Co. Ltd	4	0
1877	Lochgelly Iron & Coal Co. Ltd	4	0
1878	Lochgelly Iron & Coal Co. Ltd	4	0
1879	Lochgelly Iron & Coal Co. Ltd	4	0
1880	Lochgelly Iron & Coal Co. Ltd	4	0
1881	Lochgelly Iron & Coal Co. Ltd	4	0
1882	Lochgelly Iron & Coal Co. Ltd	4	0
1883	Lochgelly Iron & Coal Co. Ltd	4	0
1884	Lochgelly Iron & Coal Co. Ltd	4	0
1885	Lochgelly Iron & Coal Co. Ltd	4	0
1886	Lochgelly Iron & Coal Co. Ltd	2	0
1887	Lochgelly Iron & Coal Co. Ltd	2	0
1888	Lochgelly Iron & Coal Co. Ltd	4	0
1889	Lochgelly Iron & Coal Co. Ltd	4	0
1890	Lochgelly Iron & Coal Co. Ltd	2	0
1891	Lochgelly Iron & Coal Co. Ltd	2	0
1892	Lochgelly Iron & Coal Co. Ltd	4	0
1893	Lochgelly Iron & Coal Co. Ltd	2	0
1894	Lochgelly Iron & Coal Co. Ltd	2	0
1895	Lochgelly Iron & Coal Co. Ltd	2	0
1896	Lochgelly Iron & Coal Co. Ltd	2	0

1849: Hunt lists 2 furnaces in blast. Truran: output 120 tons a week from each of 2 furnaces.

Lorn, Argyllshire NN 0031

Year	Owner	Built	In Blast
1794	L.G. Knott	1	-
1796	—	1	1
1805	—	1	1
1810	—	1	1
1839	—	1	1
1855	Harrison Ainslie & Co.	1	1
1856	Harrison Ainslie & Co.	1	1
1857	Harrison Ainslie & Co.	1	1
1858	Harrison Ainslie & Co.	1	1
1859	Harrison Ainslie & Co.	1	0
1860	Harrison Ainslie & Co.	1	0
1861	Harrison Ainslie & Co.	1	0
1862	Harrison Ainslie & Co.	1	0
1863	Harrison Ainslie & Co.	1	1
1864	Harrison Ainslie & Co.	1	0
1865	Harrison Ainslie & Co.	1	0
1866	Harrison Ainslie & Co.	1	0
1867	Harrison Ainslie & Co.	1	0
1868	Harrison Ainslie & Co.	1	1
1869	Harrison Ainslie & Co.	1	1
1870	Harrison Ainslie & Co.	1	1
1871	Harrison Ainslie & Co.	1	0
1872	Harrison Ainslie & Co.	1	0
1873	Harrison Ainslie & Co.	1	1
1874	Harrison Ainslie & Co.	1	1
1875	Harrison Ainslie & Co.	1	1
1876	Harrison Ainslie & Co.	1	1
1877	Harrison Ainslie & Co.	1	0
1878	Harrison Ainslie & Co.	1	0
1879	Harrison Ainslie & Co.	1	0
1880	Harrison Ainslie & Co.	1	0
1881	Harrison Ainslie & Co.	1	0

In 1794 the Duke of Argyll was ground landlord of what was called Bonawe furnace, which was described as charcoal-fired and built in 174–. In 1796 'Argyll and Bower' (i.e. Craleckan (qv) and Bonawe) were coupled together as 2 charcoal furnaces with a combined output of 1,600 tons p.a. Similarly, in 1805 the two sites were combined, although no output is given. 1839: output (charcoal-fired) 400 tons p.a. Truran: output 800 tons p.a. from a single furnace (entered under the heading 'Lancashire Charcoal'). *Mineral Statistics* also notes that this was a charcoal furnace, using haematite from Cumberland. The site is usually known as Bonawe today.

Lugar, Ayrshire NS 5921

Year	Owner	Built	In Blast
1847	Lugar Iron Co.	4	0
1849	John Wilson	4	4
1854	Trustees of late John Wilson	4	0
1855	Trustees of late John Wilson	4	3
1856	Trustees of late John Wilson	4	2
1857	William Baird & Co.	4	0
1858	William Baird & Co.	4	0
1859	William Baird & Co.	4	0
1860	William Baird & Co.	4	0
1861	William Baird & Co.	4	0

Year	Owner	Built	In Blast
1862	William Baird & Co.	4	0
1863	William Baird & Co.	4	0
1864	William Baird & Co.	4	0
1865	William Baird & Co.	3	2
1866	William Baird & Co.	3	1
1867	William Baird & Co.	3	2
1868	William Baird & Co.	3	3
1869	William Baird & Co.	4	4
1870	William Baird & Co.	4	4
1871	William Baird & Co.	4	4
1872	Eglinton Iron Co.	4	4
1873	Eglinton Iron Co.	4	4
1874	Eglinton Iron Co.	4	4
1875	Eglinton Iron Co.	4	4
1876	Eglinton Iron Co.	4	4
1877	Eglinton Iron Co.	4	4
1878	Eglinton Iron Co.	4	3
1879	Eglinton Iron Co.	4	4
1880	Eglinton Iron Co.	5	4
1881	Eglinton Iron Co.	5	5
1882	Eglinton Iron Co.	5	4
1883	Eglinton Iron Co.	5	5
1884	Eglinton Iron Co.	5	5
1885	Eglinton Iron Co.	5	5
1886	Eglinton Iron Co.	5	5
1887	Eglinton Iron Co.	5	5
1888	Eglinton Iron Co.	5	5
1889	Eglinton Iron Co.	5	5
1890	Eglinton Iron Co.	5	4
1891	Eglinton Iron Co.	5	5
1892	William Baird & Co. Ltd	5	4
1893	William Baird & Co. Ltd	5	5
1894	William Baird & Co. Ltd	5	4
1895	William Baird & Co. Ltd	5	5
1896	William Baird & Co. Ltd	5	5
1897	William Baird & Co. Ltd	5	5
1898	William Baird & Co. Ltd	5	5
1899	William Baird & Co. Ltd	5	5
1900	William Baird & Co. Ltd	5	5
1901	William Baird & Co. Ltd	5	5
1902	William Baird & Co. Ltd	5	5
1903	William Baird & Co. Ltd	5	5
1904	William Baird & Co. Ltd	5	5
1905	William Baird & Co. Ltd	5	5
1906	William Baird & Co. Ltd	5	5
1907	William Baird & Co. Ltd	5	5
1908	William Baird & Co. Ltd	5	5
1909	William Baird & Co. Ltd	5	5
1910	William Baird & Co. Ltd	5	5
1911	William Baird & Co. Ltd	5	5
1912	William Baird & Co. Ltd	5	5
1913	William Baird & Co. Ltd	5	5
1921	William Baird & Co. Ltd	5	-
1922	William Baird & Co. Ltd	5	-
1923	William Baird & Co. Ltd	5	-
1924	William Baird & Co. Ltd	5	-
1925	William Baird & Co. Ltd	5	-
1926	William Baird & Co. Ltd	5	-
1927	William Baird & Co. Ltd	5	-
1928	William Baird & Co. Ltd	5	-
1929	William Baird & Co. Ltd	5	-
1930	William Baird & Co. Ltd	5	-
1931	William Baird & Co. Ltd	5	-
1932	William Baird & Co. Ltd	5	-
1933	William Baird & Co. Ltd	5	-
1934	William Baird & Co. Ltd	5	-
1935	Bairds & Dalmellington Ltd	5	-
1936	Bairds & Dalmellington Ltd	5	

Truran: output 140 tons a week from each of 4 furnaces. Furnaces dismantled during 1937.

Lumphinnans, Fifeshire [NT 1792]

Year	Owner	Built	In Blast
1854	Lumphinnans Iron Co.	1	1
1855	Lumphinnans Iron Co.	1	1
1856	Lumphinnans Iron Co.	1	1
1857	Lumphinnans Iron Co.	1	1
1858	A. Christie & Co.	1	1
1859	A. Christie & Co.	1	1
1860	A. Christie & Co.	1	1
1861	Alex. Christie & Co.	1	0
1862	Alex. Christie & Co.	1	1
1863	Lumphinnans Iron Co.	1	1
1864	Lumphinnans Iron Co.	1	1
1865	Lumphinnans Iron Co.	2	1
1866	Lumphinnans Iron Co.	1	0
1867	Lumphinnans Iron Co.	2	1
1868	Lumphinnans Iron Co.	2	1
1869	Lumphinnans Iron Co.	2	1
1870	Lumphinnans Iron Co.	2	1
1871	Lumphinnans Iron Co.	2	1
1872	Lumphinnans Iron Co.	2	1
1873	A. Christie & Co.	2	1
1874	A. Christie & Co.	2	1
1875	A. Christie & Co.	2	0
1876	A. Christie & Co.	2	0
1877	A. Christie & Co.	2	0
1878	A. Christie & Co.	2	0
1879	A. Christie & Co.	2	0
1880	A. Christie & Co.	2	0
1881	Lumphinnans Iron Co.	2	0
1882	Lumphinnans Iron Co.	2	0
1883	Lumphinnans Iron Co.	2	1
1884	Lumphinnans Iron Co.	2	1
1885	Lumphinnans Iron Co.	2	0
1886	Cowdenbeath Coal Co.	2	0
1887	Cowdenbeath Coal Co.	2	0
1888	Cowdenbeath Coal Co.	2	0
1889	Cowdenbeath Coal Co.	2	0
1890	Cowdenbeath Coal Co.	2	0
1891	Cowdenbeath Coal Co.	2	0
1892	Cowdenbeath Coal Co. Ltd	2	0
1893	Cowdenbeath Coal Co. Ltd	2	0
1894	Cowdenbeath Coal Co. Ltd	2	0
1895	Cowdenbeath Coal Co. Ltd	2	0
1896	Fife Coal Co. Ltd	2	0
1897	Fife Coal Co. Ltd	2	0
1898	Fife Coal Co. Ltd	2	0
1899	Fife Coal Co. Ltd	2	0
1900	Fife Coal Co. Ltd	2	0
1901	Fife Coal Co. Ltd	2	0
1902	Fife Coal Co. Ltd	2	0
1903	Fife Coal Co. Ltd	2	0

Markinch: see Leven

Monkland, Lanarkshire [NS 7663]

Year	Owner	Built	In Blast
1825	Monkland Steel Co.	1	0
1830	—	2	-
1839	—	3	3
1841	Monkland Iron Co.	5	4
1843	Monkland Iron & Steel Co.	5	5
1847	Monkland Iron & Steel Co.	9	9
1849	Monkland Iron & Steel Co.	9	9
1854	Monkland Iron & Steel Co.	9	7
1855	Monkland Iron & Steel Co.	9	8
1856	Monkland Iron & Steel Co.	9	8
1857	Monkland Iron & Steel Co.	9	9
1858	Monkland Iron & Steel Co.	9	9
1859	Monkland Iron & Steel Co.	9	9
1860	Monkland Iron & Steel Co.	9	9
1861	Monkland Iron & Steel Co.	9	8
1862	Monkland Iron & Steel Co.	9	9
1863	Monkland Iron & Steel Co.	9	9
1864	Monkland Iron & Steel Co.	9	8
1865	Monkland Iron & Steel Co.	9	9
1866	Monkland Iron & Steel Co.	9	6
1867	Monkland Iron & Steel Co.	9	7
1868	Monkland Iron & Steel Co.	9	9
1869	Monkland Iron & Steel Co.	9	9
1870	Monkland Iron & Steel Co.	9	9
1871	Monkland Iron & Steel Co.	9	8
1872	Monkland Iron & Coal Co. Ltd	9	8
1873	Monkland Iron & Coal Co. Ltd	9	8
1874	Monkland Iron & Coal Co. Ltd	9	6
1875	Monkland Iron & Coal Co. Ltd	9	9
1876	Monkland Iron & Coal Co. Ltd	9	9
1877	Monkland Iron & Coal Co. Ltd	9	9
1878	Monkland Iron & Coal Co. Ltd	9	8
1879	Monkland Iron & Coal Co. Ltd	6	5
1880	Monkland Iron & Coal Co. Ltd	6	5
1881	Monkland Iron & Coal Co. Ltd	9	7
1882	Monkland Iron Co. Ltd	6	5
1883	Monkland Iron Co. Ltd	6	4
1884	Monkland Iron Co. Ltd	6	4
1885	Monkland Iron Co. Ltd	5	4
1886	Monkland Iron Co. Ltd	5	3
1887	Monkland Iron Co. Ltd	5	2
1888	Monkland Iron Co. Ltd	5	0
1889	Monkland Iron Co. Ltd	5	0

1823–30: 1 furnace built 1826 and another in 1829; output in 1830 2,000 tons p.a. 1825: no output shown. 1841: output 340 tons a week. 1843: 400 tons a week. 1849: Hunt lists 3 furnaces in blast at Monkland and 3 at 'Chapel' (i.e. Chapelhall). Truran: output 150 tons a week from each of 9 furnaces. This works usually appears in nationally compiled lists as Monkland, although it was more commonly known locally as Chapelhall. In 1879–80 furnace-numbers were given separately for two works, called Monkland and Chapelhall (qv); in previous years, and in 1881, 3 of the 9 furnaces listed under Monkland were presumably those at Chapelhall. In 1875–77 the Monkland works is called 'Monkland, Calderbank'; from 1878 it is listed as 'Calderbank, Monkland'.

Muirkirk, Ayrshire NS 6926

Year	Owner	Built	In Blast
1794	Mr Greave & Co.	3	-
1796	—	2	2
1805	Robinson & Co.	3	2
1810	Robinson & Co.	3	2
1823	—	3	-
1825	Muirkirk Iron Co.	3	3
1830	—	3	-
1839	—	2	2
1841	Muirkirk Iron Co.	3	2
1843	Muirkirk Iron Co.	4	2
1847	Muirkirk Iron Co.	4	0
1849	Dunlop, Wilson & Co.	3	1
1854	Trustees of late J. Wilson	3	3
1855	Trustees of late J. Wilson	3	3
1856	Trustees of late J. Wilson	3	1
1857	William Baird & Co.	3	1
1858	William Baird & Co.	3	2
1859	William Baird & Co.	3	2
1860	William Baird & Co.	3	3
1861	William Baird & Co.	3	3
1862	William Baird & Co.	3	3
1863	William Baird & Co.	3	3
1864	William Baird & Co.	3	3
1865	William Baird & Co.	3	3
1866	William Baird & Co.	3	3
1867	William Baird & Co.	3	3
1868	William Baird & Co.	3	3
1869	William Baird & Co.	3	3
1870	William Baird & Co.	3	2
1871	William Baird & Co.	3	3
1872	Eglinton Iron Co.	3	3
1873	Eglinton Iron Co.	3	3
1874	Eglinton Iron Co.	3	3
1875	Eglinton Iron Co.	3	3
1876	Eglinton Iron Co.	3	3
1877	Eglinton Iron Co.	3	3
1878	Eglinton Iron Co.	3	3
1879	Eglinton Iron Co.	3	3
1880	Eglinton Iron Co.	3	3
1881	Eglinton Iron Co.	3	3
1882	Eglinton Iron Co.	3	2
1883	Eglinton Iron Co.	3	2
1884	Eglinton Iron Co.	3	3
1885	Eglinton Iron Co.	3	3
1886	Eglinton Iron Co.	3	3
1887	Eglinton Iron Co.	3	3
1888	Eglinton Iron Co.	3	3
1889	Eglinton Iron Co.	3	3
1890	Eglinton Iron Co.	3	2
1891	Eglinton Iron Co.	3	3
1892	William Baird & Co. Ltd	3	3
1893	William Baird & Co. Ltd	3	3
1894	William Baird & Co. Ltd	3	2
1895	William Baird & Co. Ltd	3	3
1896	William Baird & Co. Ltd	3	3
1897	William Baird & Co. Ltd	3	3
1898	William Baird & Co. Ltd	3	3
1899	William Baird & Co. Ltd	3	3
1900	William Baird & Co. Ltd	3	3
1901	William Baird & Co. Ltd	3	2
1902	William Baird & Co. Ltd	3	3
1903	William Baird & Co. Ltd	3	3
1904	William Baird & Co. Ltd	3	3
1905	William Baird & Co. Ltd	3	3

Year	Owner	Built	In Blast
1906	William Baird & Co. Ltd	3	3
1907	William Baird & Co. Ltd	3	3
1908	William Baird & Co. Ltd	3	3
1909	William Baird & Co. Ltd	3	3
1910	William Baird & Co. Ltd	3	3
1911	William Baird & Co. Ltd	3	3
1912	William Baird & Co. Ltd	3	3
1913	William Baird & Co. Ltd	3	3
1921	William Baird & Co. Ltd	3	-
1922	William Baird & Co. Ltd	3	-
1923	William Baird & Co. Ltd	3	-
1924	William Baird & Co. Ltd	3	-
1925	William Baird & Co. Ltd	3	-
1926	William Baird & Co. Ltd	3	-
1927	William Baird & Co. Ltd	3	-
1928	William Baird & Co. Ltd	3	-
1929	William Baird & Co. Ltd	3	-
1930	William Baird & Co. Ltd	3	-
1931	William Baird & Co. Ltd	3	-
1932	William Baird & Co. Ltd	3	-
1933	William Baird & Co. Ltd	3	-
1934	William Baird & Co. Ltd	3	-
1935	Bairds & Dalmellington Ltd	3	-
1936	Bairds & Dalmellington Ltd	3	-

The ground landlord in 1794 was Mr Strong; the furnaces were coke-fired, blown by engine and built in 1788. The forge consisted of a finery, 3 melting furnaces and a balling furnace; the date 1788 appears in the column ruled for the year of construction of mill-plant but no plant is listed. 1796: output 3,120 tons p.a., i.e. 30 tons a week from each of 2 furnaces. 1805: output 3,043 tons p.a. 1823–30: output 3,500 tons p.a. in 1823, 4,000 tons in 1830. 1825: output 120 tons a week, 5,000 p.a. 1841: 170 tons a week. 1843: 100 tons a week. 1849: Hunt lists 3 furnaces in blast. Truran: output 140 tons a week from each of 4 furnaces. Furnaces dismantled during 1937.

New Cumnock, Ayrshire [NS 6113]

Year	Owner	Built	In Blast
1854	New Cumnock Iron Co.	3	2
1855	New Cumnock Iron Co.	3	0
1856	New Cumnock Iron Co.	-	-
1857	New Cumnock Iron Co.	3	0
1858	New Cumnock Iron Co.	3	0
1859	New Cumnock Iron Co.	3	0
1860	New Cumnock Iron Co.	3	0

Newmains: see Coltness

Nithsdale, Ayrshire

Year	Owner	Built	In Blast
1849	Nithsdale Iron Co.	-	-
1855	—	3	0
1856	—	3	0

1849: English lists 3 furnaces building; Hunt lists 3 in blast. Truran: output 120 tons a week from each of 3 furnaces.

Omoa, Lanarkshire [NS 7959]

Year	Owner	Built	In Blast
1794	Col. Dalrymple	2	-
1796	Dalrymple	2	2
1805	Dalrymple	3	2
1810	Edington & Co.	3	3
1823	—	2	-
1825	Wm Young	2	1
1830	—	2	-
1839	—	1	1
1841	W. Young	1	1
1843	R. Stuart	1	0
1847	R. Stewart	4	4
1849	Robert Stewart	4	4
1854	Robert Stewart	4	3
1855	Robert Stewart	4	3
1856	Robert Stewart	4	3
1857	Robert Stewart	4	3
1858	J. Robert Stewart	4	3
1859	J. Robert Stewart	4	3
1860	Robert Stewart	4	3
1861	Robert Stewart	4	3
1862	Robert Stewart	4	2
1863	Robert Stewart	4	3
1864	Robert Stewart	4	3
1865	Robert Stewart	4	3
1866	Robert Stewart	4	2
1867	Robert Stewart	4	2
1868	Robert Stewart's Trustees	4	2
1869	Robert Stewart's Trustees	0	0
1870	Robert Stewart's Trustees	-	-

In 1794 the works appears as Cleland; the ground landlord was also Col. Dalrymple; the furnaces were coke-fired, blown by engine, and built in 1788. No forge or mill plant is listed but the date 1788 also appears in the column for the date of building in the mill section. In the 1796 list the works appears as 'Dalrymple', with two furnaces, coupled with 'Addison', with two more. The four together were said to produce 3,000 tons p.a., i.e. 15 tons a week from each. It is possible, by a process of elimination, to infer that the two latter furnaces can only be those at Devon (qv), which otherwise does not appear in the 1796 list. In 1805 output at Omoa was 1,852 tons p.a. 1823–30: output in 1823 2,500 tons p.a.; no figure returned in 1830. 1825: 40 tons a week, 1,500 p.a. 1841: output 85 tons a week. 1843: output nil. Truran: output 150 tons a week from each of 4 furnaces.

Portland, Kilmarnock, Ayrshire [NS 4237]

Year	Owner	Built	In Blast
1847	—	0	0
1849	Portland Iron Co.	2	2
1854	Portland Iron Co.	4	3
1855	Portland Iron Co.	4	4
1856	Portland Iron Co.	4	4
1857	Freeland & Lancaster	4	4
1858	Freeland & Lancaster	5	5
1859	Freeland & Lancaster	5	4
1860	Freeland & Lancaster	5	4
1861	Freeland & Lancaster	5	4
1862	Freeland & Lancaster	5	4
1863	Freeland & Lancaster	5	4
1864	William Baird & Co.	5	1

Year	Owner	Built	In Blast
1865	William Baird & Co.	6	5
1866	William Baird & Co.	6	3
1867	William Baird & Co.	6	3
1868	William Baird & Co.	6	3
1869	William Baird & Co.	6	3
1870	William Baird & Co.	4	2
1871	William Baird & Co.	6	3
1872	Eglinton Iron Co.	6	4
1873	Eglinton Iron Co.	6	3
1874	Eglinton Iron Co.	6	3
1875	Eglinton Iron Co.	6	3
1876	Eglinton Iron Co.	6	3
1877	Eglinton Iron Co.	6	3
1878	Eglinton Iron Co.	4	0
1879	Eglinton Iron Co.	6	0
1880	Eglinton Iron Co.	6	4
1881	Eglinton Iron Co.	6	4
1882	Eglinton Iron Co.	6	2
1883	Eglinton Iron Co.	4	2
1884	Eglinton Iron Co.	4	3
1885	Eglinton Iron Co.	6	3
1886	Eglinton Iron Co.	6	3
1887	Eglinton Iron Co.	6	3
1888	Eglinton Iron Co.	6	2
1889	Eglinton Iron Co.	6	2
1890	Eglinton Iron Co.	6	1
1891	Eglinton Iron Co.	4	0
1892	William Baird & Co. Ltd	6	0
1893	William Baird & Co. Ltd	6	0
1894	William Baird & Co. Ltd	6	0

1839: called 'Ayrshire'; 2 furnaces building. 1849: Hunt lists 4 furnaces in blast. Truran: output 140 tons a week from each of 2 furnaces.

Quarter, Lanarkshire [NS 7351]

Year	Owner	Built	In Blast
1856	Colin Dunlop & Co.	-	-
1857	Colin Dunlop & Co.	-	-
1858	Colin Dunlop & Co.	-	-
1859	Colin Dunlop & Co.	-	-
1860	Colin Dunlop & Co.	-	-
1861	Colin Dunlop & Co.	-	-
1862	Colin Dunlop & Co.	-	-
1863	Colin Dunlop & Co.	-	-
1864	Colin Dunlop & Co.	-	-
1865	Colin Dunlop & Co.	2	2
1866	Colin Dunlop & Co.	2	2
1867	Colin Dunlop & Co.	3	2
1868	Colin Dunlop & Co.	3	3
1869	Colin Dunlop & Co.	4	3
1870	Colin Dunlop & Co.	4	4
1871	Colin Dunlop & Co.	4	4
1872	Colin Dunlop & Co.	4	4
1873	Colin Dunlop & Co.	5	4
1874	Colin Dunlop & Co.	5	4
1875	Colin Dunlop & Co.	5	4
1876	Colin Dunlop & Co.	4	4
1877	Colin Dunlop & Co.	5	5
1878	Colin Dunlop & Co.	5	3
1879	Colin Dunlop & Co.	5	5
1880	Colin Dunlop & Co.	5	5
1881	Colin Dunlop & Co.	5	4
1882	Colin Dunlop & Co.	5	5
1883	Colin Dunlop & Co.	5	5
1884	Colin Dunlop & Co.	5	5
1885	Colin Dunlop & Co.	5	5
1886	Colin Dunlop & Co.	5	3
1887	Colin Dunlop & Co.	5	1
1888	Colin Dunlop & Co.	5	0
1889	Colin Dunlop & Co.	5	0
1890	Colin Dunlop & Co.	5	0
1891	Colin Dunlop & Co.	5	0
1892	Colin Dunlop & Co.	5	0
1893	Colin Dunlop & Co.	5	0
1894	Colin Dunlop & Co.	5	0
1895	Colin Dunlop & Co.	5	0
1896	Colin Dunlop & Co.	5	0
1897	Colin Dunlop & Co.	5	0
1898	Colin Dunlop & Co.	5	0
1899	Colin Dunlop & Co.	5	0
1900	Colin Dunlop & Co.	5	0

1856–64: furnace-numbers for Quarter and Clyde given together under the latter heading (qv). 1876: 1 furnace at Quarter building.

Ravenscraig, Lanarkshire NS 7756

Year	Owner	Built	In Blast
1957	Colvilles Ltd	1	-
1958	Colvilles Ltd	1	-
1959	Colvilles Ltd	1	-
1960	Colvilles Ltd	1	-
1961	Colvilles Ltd	2	-
1962	Colvilles Ltd	2	-
1963	Colivlles Ltd	3	-
1964	Colvilles Ltd	3	-
1965	Colvilles Ltd	3	-
1966	Colvilles Ltd	3	-
1967	Colvilles Ltd	3	-
1968	Colvilles Ltd	3	-
1969	Colvilles Ltd	3	-
1970	British Steel Corporation	3	-
1971	British Steel Corporation	3	-
1972	British Steel Corporation	3	-
1973	British Steel Corporation	3	-
1974	British Steel Corporation	3	-
1975	British Steel Corporation	3	-
1976	British Steel Corporation	3	-
1977	British Steel Corporation	3	-
1978	British Steel Corporation	3	-
1979	British Steel Corporation	3	-
1980	British Steel Corporation	3	-

The works, Scotland's last blast furnace plant, closed in 1992.

Sauchie: see Devon

Shotts, Lanarkshire NS 8759

Year	Owner	Built	In Blast
1805	Logan & Co.	2	1
1810	Logan	2	2
1823	—	1	-
1825	Shotts Iron Co.	2	1
1830	—	1	-

Year	Owner	Built	In Blast
1839	Shotts Co.	3	3
1841	Shotts Iron Co.	-	-
1843	Shotts Iron Co.	3	2
1847	Shotts Iron Co.	4	3
1849	Shotts Iron Co.	4	4
1854	Shotts Iron Co.	4	3
1855	Shotts Iron Co.	4	3
1856	Shotts Iron Co.	4	3
1857	Shotts Iron Co.	4	3
1858	Shotts Iron Co.	5	5
1859	Shotts Iron Co.	5	4
1860	Shotts Iron Co.	5	3
1861	Shotts Iron Co.	5	3
1862	Shotts Iron Co.	5	4
1863	Shotts Iron Co.	-	-
1864	Shotts Iron Co.	4	4
1865	Shotts Iron Co.	4	4
1866	Shotts Iron Co.	4	3
1867	Shotts Iron Co.	4	3
1868	Shotts Iron Co.	4	4
1869	Shotts Iron Co.	-	-
1870	Shotts Iron Co.	3	2
1871	Shotts Iron Co.	4	3
1872	Shotts Iron Co.	4	4
1873	Shotts Iron Co.	4	4
1874	Shotts Iron Co.	4	4
1875	Shotts Iron Co.	5	3
1876	Shotts Iron Co.	5	5
1877	Shotts Iron Co.	5	5
1878	Shotts Iron Co.	5	4
1879	Shotts Iron Co.	5	4
1880	Shotts Iron Co.	5	5
1881	Shotts Iron Co.	5	3
1882	Shotts Iron Co.	5	5
1883	Shotts Iron Co.	5	5
1884	Shotts Iron Co.	5	5
1885	Shotts Iron Co.	5	5
1886	Shotts Iron Co.	5	5
1887	Shotts Iron Co.	5	4
1888	Shotts Iron Co.	5	5
1889	Shotts Iron Co.	5	5
1890	Shotts Iron Co.	5	2
1891	Shotts Iron Co.	6	4
1892	Shotts Iron Co.	6	4
1893	Shotts Iron Co.	6	3
1894	Shotts Iron Co.	6	3
1895	Shotts Iron Co.	6	4
1896	Shotts Iron Co.	6	4
1897	Shotts Iron Co.	6	4
1898	Shotts Iron Co.	6	4
1899	Shotts Iron Co.	5	5
1900	Shotts Iron Co. Ltd	5	4
1901	Shotts Iron Co. Ltd	5	4
1902	Shotts Iron Co. Ltd	5	5
1903	Shotts Iron Co. Ltd	5	5
1904	Shotts Iron Co. Ltd	5	4
1905	Shotts Iron Co. Ltd	5	4
1906	Shotts Iron Co. Ltd	5	5
1907	Shotts Iron Co. Ltd	5	4
1908	Shotts Iron Co. Ltd	5	4
1909	Shotts Iron Co. Ltd	5	4
1910	Shotts Iron Co. Ltd	5	4
1911	Shotts Iron Co. Ltd	5	4
1912	Shotts Iron Co. Ltd	5	4
1913	Shotts Iron Co. Ltd	5	4
1921	Shotts Iron Co. Ltd	5	-
1922	Shotts Iron Co. Ltd	5	-
1923	Shotts Iron Co. Ltd	5	-
1924	Shotts Iron Co. Ltd	5	-
1925	Shotts Iron Co. Ltd	5	-
1926	Shotts Iron Co. Ltd	5	-
1927	Shotts Iron Co. Ltd	5	-
1928	Shotts Iron Co. Ltd	4	-
1929	Shotts Iron Co. Ltd	4	-
1930	Shotts Iron Co. Ltd	5	-
1931	Shotts Iron Co. Ltd	4	-
1932	Shotts Iron Co. Ltd	4	-
1933	Shotts Iron Co. Ltd	5	-
1934	Shotts Iron Co. Ltd	5	-
1935	Shotts Iron Co. Ltd	5	-
1936	Shotts Iron Co. Ltd	5	-
1937	Shotts Iron Co. Ltd	4	-
1938	Shotts Iron Co. Ltd	4	-
1939	Shotts Iron Co. Ltd	4	-
1940	Shotts Iron Co. Ltd	4	-
1941	Shotts Iron Co. Ltd	4	-
1942	Shotts Iron Co. Ltd	4	-
1943	Shotts Iron Co. Ltd	4	-
1944	Shotts Iron Co. Ltd	4	-
1945	Shotts Iron Co. Ltd	4	-
1946	Shotts Iron Co. Ltd	4	-

1805: output 2,034 tons p.a. 1823–30: output 2,000 tons p.a. in both years. 1825: 40 tons a week, 2,000 p.a. 1839: 2 further furnaces building. 1841: Furnace-numbers (4 furnaces, 3 in blast) and output (255 tons a week) for the two Shotts Iron Co. sites at Shotts and Castlehill are apparently combined under Shotts and have been printed here under Castlehill. A second entry for the Shotts Co., for a works called Househill (2 furnaces, none in blast, output nil), appears to refer to a third site and is not an error for Castlehill. 1843: output (at Shotts) 120 tons a week. 1849: Hunt lists 4 furnaces in blast under Shotts. Truran: output (at Shotts) 150 tons a week from each of 4 furnaces. In 1863 and 1869 furnace-numbers were combined with those for Castlehill under the latter heading (qv).

Summerlee, Lanarkshire [NS 7559?]

Year	Owner	Built	In Blast
1839	—	4	4
1841	Wilson & Co.	6	4
1843	Wilson & Co.	6	4
1847	Wilson & Co.	6	5
1849	Wilson & Co.	6	6
1854	Wilson & Co.	6	6
1855	Wilson & Co.	6	6
1856	Wilson & Co.	6	6
1857	Wilson & Co.	8	7
1858	Wilson & Co.	8	8
1859	Wilson & Co.	8	8
1860	Wilson & Co.	8	8
1861	Wilson & Co.	8	8
1862	Wilson & Co.	8	8
1863	Wilson & Co.	8	8
1864	Wilson & Co.	8	8
1865	Wilson & Co.	8	8

Year	Owner	Built	In Blast
1866	Wilson & Co.	8	5
1867	Wilson & Co.	8	6
1868	Wilson & Co.	8	6
1869	Wilson & Co.	8	3
1870	Wilson & Co.	8	7
1871	Wilson & Co.	8	7
1872	Wilson & Co.	8	7
1873	Summerlee Iron Co.	8	7
1874	Summerlee Iron Co.	8	6
1875	Summerlee Iron Co.	8	6
1876	Summerlee Iron Co.	8	6
1877	Summerlee Iron Co.	8	5
1878	Summerlee Iron Co.	8	5
1879	Summerlee Iron Co.	8	4
1880	Summerlee Iron Co.	8	6
1881	Summerlee Iron Co.	8	7
1882	Summerlee Iron Co.	7	6
1883	Summerlee Iron Co.	7	6
1884	Summerlee Iron Co.	8	6
1885	Summerlee Iron Co.	7	6
1886	Summerlee Iron Co.	8	6
1887	Summerlee Iron Co.	8	6
1888	Summerlee Iron Co.	8	6
1889	Summerlee & Mossend Iron & Steel Co. Ltd	8	4
1890	Summerlee & Mossend Iron & Steel Co. Ltd	8	5
1891	Summerlee & Mossend Iron & Steel Co. Ltd	7	5
1892	Summerlee & Mossend Iron & Steel Co. Ltd	7	6
1893	Summerlee & Mossend Iron & Steel Co. Ltd	7	5
1894	Summerlee & Mossend Iron & Steel Co. Ltd	7	5
1895	Summerlee & Mossend Iron & Steel Co. Ltd	7	6
1896	Summerlee & Mossend Iron & Steel Co. Ltd	7	6
1897	Summerlee & Mossend Iron & Steel Co. Ltd	7	6
1898	Summerlee & Mossend Iron & Steel Co. Ltd	7	6
1899	Summerlee & Mossend Iron & Steel Co. Ltd	7	6
1900	Summerlee & Mossend Iron & Steel Co. Ltd	7	6
1901	Summerlee & Mossend Iron & Steel Co. Ltd	7	6
1902	Summerlee & Mossend Iron & Steel Co. Ltd	7	6
1903	Summerlee & Mossend Iron & Steel Co. Ltd	7	6
1904	Summerlee & Mossend Iron & Steel Co. Ltd	7	6
1905	Summerlee & Mossend Iron & Steel Co. Ltd	7	6
1906	Summerlee & Mossend Iron & Steel Co. Ltd	7	6
1907	Summerlee & Mossend Iron & Steel Co. Ltd	7	6
1908	Summerlee & Mossend Iron & Steel Co. Ltd	7	5
1909	Summerlee & Mossend Iron & Steel Co. Ltd	7	5
1910	Summerlee & Mossend Iron & Steel Co. Ltd	7	6
1911	Summerlee & Mossend Iron & Steel Co. Ltd	7	6
1912	Summerlee & Mossend Iron & Steel Co. Ltd	7	4
1913	Summerlee & Mossend Iron & Steel Co. Ltd	7	6
1921	Summerlee Iron Co. Ltd	7	-
1922	Summerlee Iron Co. Ltd	7	-
1923	Summerlee Iron Co. Ltd	7	-
1924	Summerlee Iron Co. Ltd	7	-
1925	Summerlee Iron Co. Ltd	7	-
1926	Summerlee Iron Co. Ltd	7	-
1927	Summerlee Iron Co. Ltd	7	-
1928	Summerlee Iron Co. Ltd	7	-
1929	Summerlee Iron Co. Ltd	7	-
1930	Summerlee Iron Co. Ltd	7	-
1931	Summerlee Iron Co. Ltd	7	-
1932	Summerlee Iron Co. Ltd	7	-
1933	Summerlee Iron Co. Ltd	7	-
1934	Summerlee Iron Co. Ltd	7	-
1935	Summerlee Iron Co. Ltd	7	-
1936	Summerlee Iron Co. Ltd	7	-

1841: output: 340 tons a week. 1843: output 320 tons a week. Truran: output 150 tons a week from each of 6 furnaces. Furnaces dismantled during 1937.

Westbank: see Gladsmuir

Wilsontown, Lanarkshire NS 9554

Year	Owner	Built	In Blast
1794	Messrs Wilson	2	-
1796	—	2	2
1805	Wilson	2	1
1810	Wilson & Co.	2	2
1823	—	2	-
1825	John & William Dixon	2	2
1830	—	2	-
1839	—	1	1
1843	W. Dixon & Co.	1	0

In 1794 the ground landlord was Mr Wilson; the furnaces were coke-fired, blown by engine and were said to have been built in 1782. In 1796 the output was 2,080 tons p.a., i.e. 20 tons a week from each furnace. 1805: output 1,381 tons p.a. 1823–30: no output shown in 1823, 2,000 tons p.a. in 1830. 1825: 80 tons a week, 3,500 p.a. 1843: output nil.

Wishaw, Lanarkshire [NS 8055]

Year	Owner	Built	In Blast
1859	—	3	2
1860	Robert Bell	3	2
1861	Robert Bell	3	1
1862	Robert Bell	3	0
1863	Robert Bell	3	2
1864	Wishaw Iron Co.	3	3
1865	Wishaw Iron Co.	3	3
1866	Wishaw Iron Co.	3	3
1867	Wishaw Iron Co.	3	2
1868	Wishaw Iron Co.	3	3

Year	Owner	Built	In Blast
1869	Wishaw Iron Co.	3	3
1870	Wishaw Iron Co.	3	1
1871	Wishaw Iron Co.	3	2
1872	Glasgow Iron Co.	3	2
1873	Wishaw Iron Co.	3	2
1874	Wishaw Iron Co.	3	2
1875	Wishaw Iron Co.	3	2
1876	Glasgow Iron Co.	3	2
1877	Glasgow Iron Co.	3	2
1878	Glasgow Iron Co.	3	2
1879	Glasgow Iron Co.	3	2
1880	Glasgow Iron Co.	3	3
1881	Glasgow Iron Co.	3	3
1882	Glasgow Iron Co.	3	2
1883	Glasgow Iron Co.	3	2
1884	Glasgow Iron Co.	3	2
1885	Glasgow Iron Co.	3	1
1886	Glasgow Iron Co.	3	3
1887	Glasgow Iron Co.	3	3
1888	Glasgow Iron & Steel Co. Ltd	3	3
1889	Glasgow Iron & Steel Co. Ltd	3	3
1890	Glasgow Iron & Steel Co. Ltd	3	3
1891	Glasgow Iron & Steel Co. Ltd	3	3
1892	Glasgow Iron & Steel Co. Ltd	3	3
1893	Glasgow Iron & Steel Co. Ltd	3	2
1894	Glasgow Iron & Steel Co. Ltd	4	2
1895	Glasgow Iron & Steel Co. Ltd	4	4
1896	Glasgow Iron & Steel Co. Ltd	4	4
1897	Glasgow Iron & Steel Co. Ltd	4	4
1898	Glasgow Iron & Steel Co. Ltd	4	4
1899	Glasgow Iron & Steel Co. Ltd	4	4
1900	Glasgow Iron & Steel Co. Ltd	4	4
1901	Glasgow Iron & Steel Co. Ltd	4	4
1902	Glasgow Iron & Steel Co. Ltd	5	4
1903	Glasgow Iron & Steel Co. Ltd	5	4
1904	Glasgow Iron & Steel Co. Ltd	5	4
1905	Glasgow Iron & Steel Co. Ltd	5	5
1906	Glasgow Iron & Steel Co. Ltd	5	4
1907	Glasgow Iron & Steel Co. Ltd	6	5
1908	Glasgow Iron & Steel Co. Ltd	6	4
1909	Glasgow Iron & Steel Co. Ltd	6	4
1910	Glasgow Iron & Steel Co. Ltd	6	5
1911	Glasgow Iron & Steel Co. Ltd	6	4
1912	Glasgow Iron & Steel Co. Ltd	6	5
1913	Glasgow Iron & Steel Co. Ltd	6	6
1921	Glasgow Iron & Steel Co. Ltd	6	-
1922	Glasgow Iron & Steel Co. Ltd	6	-
1923	Glasgow Iron & Steel Co. Ltd	6	-
1924	Glasgow Iron & Steel Co. Ltd	6	-
1925	Glasgow Iron & Steel Co. Ltd	6	-
1926	Glasgow Iron & Steel Co. Ltd	6	-
1927	Glasgow Iron & Steel Co. Ltd	6	-
1928	Glasgow Iron & Steel Co. Ltd	6	-
1929	Glasgow Iron & Steel Co. Ltd	6	-
1930	Glasgow Iron & Steel Co. Ltd	6	-
1931	Glasgow Iron & Steel Co. Ltd	6	-
1932	Glasgow Iron & Steel Co. Ltd	6	-
1933	Glasgow Iron & Steel Co. Ltd	6	-
1934	Glasgow Iron & Steel Co. Ltd	6	-
1935	Glasgow Iron & Steel Co. Ltd	6	-
1936	Glasgow Iron & Steel Co. Ltd	6	-

Furnaces dismantled during 1937.

'New Works', Fifeshire

Year	Owner	Built	In Blast
1854	—	3	-

There is no name for either the works or its owner in *Mineral Statistics* for 1854; the following year there is no corresponding entry at all but merely the three other Fifeshire works at Forth, Lochgelly and Lumphinnans (qqv).

Index of Ironworks

Abbey Tintern: see Tintern
Abdon: see Bouldon
Aberaman, Glam. 1
'Abercarne': see Abercraf
Abercraf, Brecs. 1
Aberdare, Glam. 1–2
Aberderfyn, Denbighs. 49
'Aberdovey': see Dyfi
Abernant, Glam. 2
Abernant (Glyn-neath), Glam. 2
Abersychan, Mon. 2–3
Acklam, Yorks. 152
Acrefair, Denbighs. 49
Adelphi: see Duckmanton
Airdrie: see Chapelhall; Monkland
Aireside, Yorks. 125
Alderwasley, Derbys. 112
Alfreton, Derbys. 112
Almond, Stirlingshire 179
Amman, 'Amwain': see Brynamman; Cwmavon; Oakwood
Apedale, Staffs. 93
Appleby, Lincs. 107
Ardeer, Ayrshire 179–80
Ardsley: see West Yorkshire
Argyll: see Cralecken
Ashburnham, Sussex 37
Ashby: see Moira
Ashton Vale, Somerset 35
Askam, Lancs. 136
Atlas, Sheffield, Yorks. 125
Auckland, Durham 152
Awsworth: see Bennerley
Ayresome, Middlesbrough, Yorks. 152–3
Ayrshire: see Portland

Backbarrow, Lancs. 136–7
Bankfield: see Broadwaters
Banwen, Glam. 3
Barbor's Hill Field, Bilston, Staffs. 55
Barlow: see Sheepbridge
Barnetts Leasow, Broseley, Salop 38
Barrow Hæmatite, Lancs. 137–8
Batterfield, ?Staffs. 55
Bearpot: see Seaton
Beaufort, Brecs. 3–4
Beckhole, Yorks. 153
Bedlam: see Madeley Wood
Bedlington, Northumberland 153
Beeston Manor, Leeds, Yorks. 125
Bennerley, Notts. 113
Benthall, Salop 38
Bentley, Walsall, Staffs. 55–6
Benwell, Northumberland 153
Bessemer, Middlesbrough, Yorks. 153–4
Bestwood, Notts. 113
Biddulph Valley, Staffs. 93–4
Bierley, Yorks. 125–6
Billingsley, Salop 38
Bilston, Staffs. 56
 see also Ettingshall; Millfield; Spring Vale; Stonefield
Bilston Brook, Staffs. 56
Birchfield, ?Staffs. 56–7
Birchills, Walsall, Staffs. 57
Birds Wharf: see Millfields
Birkenshaw, Yorks. 126
Birtley, Durham 154
Bishop Auckland: see Auckland?
Bishopswood, Glos. 32
Bishopwearmouth, Durham 154
Blaenavon, Mon. 4–5
Blaendare, Mon. 5
Blaengwrach: see Venallt
Blain: see Cwmavon

Blaina, Mon. 5–6
Blair, Ayrshire 180
Blists Hill, Salop 38–9
Blowers Green, Dudley, Worcs. 58
Bloxwich: see Green Lane; Hatherton
Bonawe: see Lorn
Bouldon, Salop 39
Bovereux, Bilston, Staffs. 58
Bowling, Yorks. 126
Brades Hall, Tipton, Staffs. 58
Bradley, Durham 154
Bradley, Staffs. 58–9
Brampton: see Chesterfield
Brettell Lane, Staffs. 59
Bretton, Yorks. 127
Bridge, Bilston, Staffs. 59
Bridgeness, Linlithgowshire 180
Brierley, Staffs. 59
Brierley Hill, Staffs. 59
Brimington Moor, Derbys. 113–14
'Brin': see Onllwyn
Bringewood, Herefs. (formerly Salop) 39
Brinkburn, Northumberland 154–5
British: see Abersychan; Acrefair
Briton Ferry, Glam. 6
Broad Oaks: see Wingerworth
Broadwaters, Wednesbury, Staffs. 59–60
Bromford: see Withymoor
Bromley Hall: see Corbyn's Hall
Bromley Hill: see Oakwood
Brook: see Bilston Brook
Broseley, Salop 39
Brymbo, Denbighs. 49–50
Bryn: see Onllwyn
Bryn-du, Glam. 7
Brynamman, Glam. 6–7
Buffery, Dudley, Worcs. 60
Bull Field, ?Staffs. 60
Bumble Hole: see Netherton
Bute, Mon. 7
 see also Rhymney & Bute
Butterley, Derbys. 114
'Bywell': see Benwell

Caerphilly, Glam. 7
Calcutts, Salop 39
Calder, Lanarkshire 180–1
Calder, Yorks. 127
Calderbank, Lanarkshire 181
Calow, Derbys. 114
Cambrian: see Llynvi
Cape, Smethwick, Staffs. 60
Capponfield, Bilston, Staffs. 61
Cardiff Iron & Steel, Glam. 8
Cargo Fleet, Middlesborough, Yorks. 155
Carlton, Durham 155–6
Carmarthen, Carms. 8–9
Carnbroe, Lanarkshire 181–2
Carnforth, Lancs. 138–9
Carron, Stirlingshire 182–3
Castle: see Birchills (Old), Staffs.; Dawley Castle, Salop
Castlehill, Lanarkshire 183
Cawseyend: see Almond
Cefn Cribwr, Glam. 9
Cefn Cwsc, Glam. 9
Cefn, Denbighs. 50
Cessnock, Ayrshire 183
Chapeltown, Yorks. 127
Chappelhall, Lanarkshire 183
Charlton, Yorks. 127
Chatterley, Staffs. 94
Chesterfield, Derbys. 114–15
 see also Wingerworth
Chillington, Wolverhampton, Staffs. 61–2

Cinderford, Glos. 32
Clarence, Durham 156
Clay Cross, Derbys. 115–16
Clay Lane, Middlesbrough, Yorks. 156–7
Cleator Moor, Cumb. 139–40
Clee Hill, Salop 39
Cleland: see Omoa
Cleveland, Middlesbrough, Yorks. 157–8
Cleveland Steel, South Bank, Middlesbrough, Yorks. 158
Clough Hall: see Kidsgrove
Clydach, Brecs. 9
Clyde Ironworks, Lanarkshire 184–5
Coalbrookdale, Salop 39–40
Coalbrookvale, Mon. 10
'Coalford': see Bouldon
Coatham, Yorks. 158–9
Codnor Park, Derbys. 116
Coed Talon, Flints. 50–1
'Coelbrook': see Gwendraeth
Coltness, Lanarkshire 185
Coneybury: see Broseley
Coneygre, Dudley Port, Staffs. 62
Consett, Durham 159–60
Corby, Northants. 101
Corbyn's Hall, Staffs. 62–3
Cornbrook, Salop 40
Corngreaves, Dudley, Worcs. 63–4
Coseley, Tipton, Staffs. 64
 see also Deepfields; Priorfield
Cotham, ?Staffs. 64–5
Cralecken, Argyllshire 185
Cramond, West Lothian 185–6
Cransley, Northants. 101–2
Crewe: see Madeley
Crookhall, Durham 160
Crookhay, West Bromwich, Staffs. 65
Cumnock: see New Cumnock
Cwm Bychan: see Cwmavon
Cwm Neath: see Venallt
Cwm-celyn, Mon. 12
Cwmavon, Glam. 10–11
Cwmbran, Mon. 11–12
Cyfarthfa, Glam. 12–13

Dagenham, Essex 37
Dale Abbey, Derbys. 116
Dalmellington, Ayrshire 186
Dalry, Ayrshire 186
Dark Lane, Salop 40
Darkhill, Glos. 32
Darlaston, Staffs. 65
 see also Rough Hay
Darlaston Green, Staffs. 65–6
Darlington: see South Durham
Darngaber: see Quarter
Darwen, Lancs. 140
Dawley Castle, Salop 40–1
Deepdale: see Dibdale
Deepfields, Bilston, Staffs. 66
 see also Coseley
Denby, Derbys. 116–17
Derwent, Workington, Cumb. 140
 see also Consett
Devon, Clackmannanshire 186–7
Devonshire Works, Staveley, Derbys. 117
Dibdale Bank, Staffs. 66
Distington, Cumb. 140–1
Ditton Brook, Lancs. 141
Dixon's Green, Dudley, Worcs. 67
Dolydd, Denbighs. 51
Donnington Wood, Salop 41
Dowlais, Glam. 13–14
Duckmanton, Derbys. 117
Duddon, Cumb. 141

INDEX OF IRONWORKS

Dudley Port, Staffs. 67–8
Dudley Wood, Worcs. 68
Duffield: *see* Bilston
Duffryn, Glam. 14
Dukinfield, Ches. 142
Dundyvan, Lanarkshire 187
Dunston: *see* Sheepbridge
Dyfi, Cards. 51

Eagle Furnaces, ?Staffs. 68
East End Ironworks: *see* Wellingborough
East Moors: *see* Cardiff Iron & Steel
Ebbw Vale, Mon. 14–16
Eglinton, Ayrshire 187
Elsecar, Yorks. 127–8
Elswick, Northumberland 160–1
Emroyd: *see* Mirfield
Erewash Valley, Ilkeston, Derbys. 117–18
Eston, Middlesbrough, Yorks. 161
Etherley: *see* Witton Park
Etruria: *see* Shelton
Ettingshall, Bilston, Staffs. 68
  see also Bilston

Farnley, Yorks. 128
Felling, Durham 161
Fenton: *see* Great Fenton
Fenton Park, Staffs. 94
Ferry Hill, Durham 161
Ffrwd, Denbighs. 51
Fieldhead, Yorks. 128–9
Fiery Holes, ?Staffs. 68
Finedon, Northants. 102
Flaxley, Glos. 33
Foley: *see* Lane End
Forest of Dean: *see* Cinderford
Forest Iron & Steel: *see* Pontypridd
Forth, Fifeshire 188
Frodingham, Lincs. 108
Furnace Isaf: *see* Plymouth
Furness: *see* Askam

Gadlys, Glam. 16
Garscube, Dunbartonshire 188
Garth, Glam. 16
Gartsherrie, Lanarkshire 188–9
'Gessnock': *see* Cessnock
Gladsmuir or Westbank, East Lothian 189
Glaisdale, Yorks. 161–2
Glamorgan Coal & Iron Co.: *see* Tondu
'Glasshouse', Yorks. 129
Glebefields, ?Tipton, Staffs. 69
Glenbuck, Ayrshire 189
Glengarnock, Ayrshire 189–90
Glyn-neath: *see* Abernant (Glyn-neath)
Goldendale, Staffs. 95–6
Goldenhill, Staffs. 96
Golds Green: *see* Goldshill
Goldshill, West Bromwich, Staffs. 69
Golynos, Mon. 16–17
Gornal: *see* Fiery Hole
Gornalwood, Staffs. 69
Gospel Oak, Wednesbury, Staffs. 69
Govan, Lanarkshire 190
Grangetown, Middlesbrough, Yorks. 162
Grassmoor: *see* Hasland
Graveyard, Staffs. 69–70
Great Fenton, Staffs. 96
Great Western: *see* Soudley
Green Lane, Walsall, Staffs. 70
Grosmont, Yorks. 162
Groveland, Smethwick, Staffs. 70
Gwendraeth, Carms. 17

Hadley, Salop 41
Haigh, Lancs. 142
Hallfields, Staffs. 70
Halton, Lancs. 142
Haltwhistle, Northumberland 162
Hange, Tividale, Staffs. 71
Hareshaw, Northumberland 162
Harrington, Cumb. 142

Hartlepool: *see* Seaton Carew; West Hartlepool
Hasland, Derbys. 118
Hatherton, Bloxwich, Staffs. 71–2
Heathfield, Sussex 37
Hepworth, Yorks. 129
Herberts Park, Bilston, Staffs. 72
Heyford, Northants. 102–3
Highfields, Staffs. 72
Hinkshay, Salop 41
Hirwaun, Brecs. 17
Hollinswood, Salop 41
Holmes, Yorks. 129
Holwell, Leics. 108–9
Horsehay, Salop 42
Horseley, Tipton, Staffs. 72
Horseley Fields, Staffs. 72
Horseley Heath: *see* Dudley Port
Horseley Hole, Staffs. 73
Househill, Renfrewshire 190
Hunsbury Hill, Northants. 103

Ifor: *see* Dowlais
Ilkeston: *see* Erewash Valley
Irlam: *see* Partington
Irthlingborough, Northants 103–4
Islip, Northants. 104

Jackfield: *see* Calcutts
Jarrow, Durham 162–3
'Jennington': *see* Lemington
Jerry, The: *see* Hinkshay

Ketley, Salop 42
Ketley's, Dudley, Worcs. 73
Kettering: *see* Cransley; Warren Hills
Kidsgrove, Staffs. 96–7
Kilbirnie: *see* Glengarnock
Kilgetty, Pembs. 17–18
Kilwinning: *see* Eglinton
Kinneil, Linlithgowshire 191
Kirkless Hall, Wigan, Lancs. 142–3

Lackenby, Yorks. 163
Landore, Glam. 18
  see also Millbrook
Lane End, Staffs. 97
Langley, Salop 42–3
Langloan, Lanarkshire 191–2
Latebrook, Staffs. 97
Lawley, Salop 43
Lawton, Ches. 97
Lays, Brockmoor, Staffs. 73
Leabrook, ?Staffs 73
'Leaham': *see* Vane & Seaham
Leeds Steel Works, Hunslet, Yorks. 129–30
Leeswood, Flints. 51–2
Leighton, Lancs. 143
Lemington, Northumberland 164
Level, Brierley Hill, Staffs. 74–5
Leven, Fifeshire 192
Leys: *see* Lays
Lightmoor, Salop 43
Lilleshall: *see* Lodge Wood
Lindsey, Lincs. 109
Linthorpe, Yorks. 164–5
Llanelli, Carms. 18
Llanelly, Brecs. 18
Llanwern, Mon. 18
Llvynvi Vale, Glam. 19
Llwydcoed: *see* Aberdare
Llwyneinion, Denbighs. 52
Lochgelly, Fifeshire 192
Lodge Wood, Salop 44
Loftus: *see* Skinningrove
Longton Hall, Staffs. 97
Longton Lane End: *see* Lane End
Lonsdale, Cumb. 143–4
Lorn, Argyllshire 192
Low Mill: *see* Bretton
Low Moor, Yorks. 130–1
Lowther, Workington, Cumb. 144

Lugar, Ayrshire 192–3
Lumphinnans, Fifeshire 193
Lydney, Glos. 33

Machen: *see* Rudry
Madeley, Staffs. 97
Madeley Court, Salop 44–5
Madeley Wood, Salop 45
Maesteg, Glam. 19
Malinslee: *see* Old Park
Margam: *see* Port Talbot
Markinch: *see* Leven
Marron: *see* New Yard
Maryport, Cumb. 144
  see also Solway
Masbrough: *see* Holmes
Meadow, ?Staffs. 75
Melincourt, Glam. 19
Melingriffith: *see* Pentyrch
Middlesbrough, Yorks. 165
  see also Cleveland; Eston; Tees
Middleton, Durham 165–6
Millbrook and Landore, Glam. 20
Millfield, Bilston, Staffs. 75–6
Millom, Cumb. 144–6
Milton, Yorks. 131
Mirfield, Yorks. 131
Mitre: *see* Wednesbury Oak
Moira, Leics. 118
Monkland, Lanarkshire 194
Moorcroft, Staffs. 76
Morley Park, Derbys. 118
Morriston: *see* Millbrook
Moseley, Wolverhampton, Staffs. 76
Moss Bay, Workington, Cumb. 146
Mostyn, Flints. 52–3
Moxley, Wednesbury, Staffs. 76
Muirkirk, Ayrshire 194–5

Nantyglo, Mon. 20
Neath Abbey, Glam. 20–1
Neath Valley: *see* Abernant (Glyn-neath); Venallt
Netherton, Dudley, Worcs. 76–8
New Birchills: *see* Birchills (New)
New Broseley: *see* Broseley
New Cumnock, Ayrshire 195
New Darlaston: *see* Rough Hay
New Duffield: *see* Bilston
New Furnaces: *see* Bilston (New)
New Hadley: *see* Hadley
New Level: *see* Level (New)
New Park: *see* Park Gate
New Priestfield: *see* Priestfield (New)
New Yard, Workington, Cumb. 147
Newbold, Derbys. 118–19
Newbridge, Denbighs. 53
Newland, Lancs. 146–7
Newmains: *see* Coltness
Newnham: *see* Cinderford
Newport, Mon.: *see* Llanwern
Newport, Middlesbrough, Yorks. 166
Nithsdale, Ayrshire 195
Normanby, Yorks. 166–7
Normanby Park, Lincs. 109
North of England: *see* Lowther
North Lancashire, Lancs. 147
North Lincolnshire, Lincs. 110
North Lonsdale, Ulverston, Lancs. 147–8
North Shore: *see* Stockton
North Western Hematite: *see* West Cumberland
Norton, Durham 167
Norton, Staffs. 98
Norwegian, Yorks. 167

Oak Farm, Dudley, Worcs. 78
Oakengates: *see* Priorslee
Oakerthorpe, Derbys. 119
Oakwood, Glam. 21
Oakwood, Glos. 33
Old Dock, ?Staffs. 79

Old Hill, near Dudley, Staffs. 79
Old Lodge: *see* Lodge Wood
Old Park, Salop 45–6
Old Park, Wednesbury, Staffs. 79–80
Old Park, Wolverhampton: *see* Parkfield
Old Park Field: *see* Parkfield
Old Ruabon: *see* Acrefair; Ruabon
Oldbury, Salop 78–9
Omoa, Lanarkshire 195
Onllwyn, Glam. 21
Ormesby, Yorks. 167–8
Osier Bed, Horsley Fields, Staffs. 80
Outwood, Radcliffe, Lancs. 148

Paine's Lane Works: *see* Madeley Court
Pant, Denbighs. 53
Park: *see* Old Park
Park, Old: *see* Parkfield
Park, Sheffield, Yorks. 131
Park, Wednesbury: *see* Old Park, Wednesbury
Park Gate, Yorks. 131–2
Park Lane, Smethwick, Staffs. 82
Park Lane, Tipton, Staffs. 81
Parkend, Glos. 33
Parkfield, Wolverhampton, Staffs. 80–1
Parkhead, Dudley, Worcs. 81
Partington, Lancs. 148–9
Parton, Cumb. 149
Partridge Nest: *see* Springwood
Pelsall, Walsall, Staffs. 82
Pembrey, Carms. 21
Penallt: *see* Venallt
Pennywell Road, Somerset 35
Penrhiwtyn, Glam. 21
Pentwyn, Mon. 21–2
Pentyrch, Glam. 22
Penycae: *see* Ebbw Vale
Penydarren, Glam. 22–3
Plas Issa, Denbighs. 53
Plas Main: *see* Ffrwd
Plaskynaston, Denbighs. 53
Plymouth, Glam. 23
Ponciau, Denbighs. 53
Pontrhydyfen, Glam. 23
Pontrhydyryn: *see* Pontrhydyfen
Pontypool, Mon. 23–4
Pontypridd, Glam. 24–5
Port Clarence: *see* Clarence
Port Talbot, Glam. 25
Porthcawl: *see* Cefn Cwsc
Portland, Kilmarnock, Ayrshire 195–6
Priestfield, Staffs. 82–3
Priorfield, Deepfield, Bilston, Staffs. 83
Priorslee, Salop 46
Pyle: *see* Bryn-du; Cefn Cwsc

Quarter, Lanarkshire 196
Queenswood, Salop 47

Race: *see* Pontypool
Radcliffe: *see* Outwood
Ravenscraig, Lanarkshire 196
Ravensdale, Staffs. 98
Redbourn Hill, Lincs. 110–11
Redbrook, Glos. 33–4
Redcar, Yorks. 168–9
Redesdale: *see* Ridsdale
Renishaw, Derbys. 119–20
Rhymney & Bute, Mon. 25–6
Ridgeacre, ?Staffs 83
Ridsdale, Northumberland 169
Roggin Row: *see* Springwood
Rotherham: *see* Holmes; Park Gate
Rough Hay, Wednesbury, Staffs. 83–4
Rough Hills, Staffs. 84
Roughwood: *see* Birchills (Old)
Round Oak: *see* Level (New)
Royal Greek: *see* Wallsend
Royds, Yorks. 132
Ruabon, Denbighs. 53
  see also Acrefair; Pant

Rudry, Glam. 26
'Rush Hall': *see* Russell's Hall
Russell's Hall, Dudley, Worcs. 84

Sauchie: *see* Devon
Saundersfoot: *see* Kilgetty
Seacroft, Yorks. 132
Seaham: *see* Vane & Seaham
Seaton, Cumb. 149
Seaton Carew, Durham 169–70
Seend, Wilts. 35
Shakemantle, Glos. 34
Sheepbridge, Derbys. 120–1
Sheffield Park: *see* Park
Shelf, Yorks. 133
Shelton, Staffs. 98–9
Shotley Bridge: *see* Bradley; Consett
Shotton, Flints. 54
Shotts, Lanarkshire 196–7
Shut End, Kingswinford, Staffs. 84–5
Silverdale, Staffs. 99–100
Sirhowy, Mon. 26–7
Skinningrove, Yorks. 170–1
Snedshill, Salop 47
Solway, Maryport, Cumb. 149
Soudley, Glos. 34
South Bank, Middlesbrough, Yorks. 171
South Durham, Darlington, Durham 171–2
South Teesside: *see* Bessemer; Clay Lane
South Wingfield: *see* Oakerthorpe
Southsea, Denbighs. 54
Spennymoor: *see* Tudhoe
Spring Vale, Bilston, Staffs. 85–6
Springwood, Staffs. 100
Stanhope, Durham 172
Stanton, Derbys. 121–2
'Star Valley': *see* Stour Valley
Staveley, Derbys. 122–3
  see also Devonshire Works
Stirchley, Salop 47
Stirchley Old Park: *see* Old Park
Stockton, North Shore, Durham 172
Stonefield, Staffs. 86
Stonegravels: *see* Chesterfield
Stour Valley, ?Staffs. 86
Stow Heath, Bilston, Staffs. 86–7
Stowe, Northants. 104–5
'Summercotes': *see* Alfreton
Summerlee, Lanarkshire 197–8
Swallowhill, Yorks. 133

Taffvale: *see* Abernant
Talke o' th' Hill, Staffs. 100
Tees, Middlesbrough, Yorks. 172–3
Tees Bridge, Stockton-on-Tees, Durham 173
Tees Side, Middlesbrough, Yorks. 174
Thornaby, Yorks. 174–5
Thorncliffe, Yorks. 133–4
Thorpe Hall, Yorks. 134
Tinsley, Sheffield, Yorks. 134
Tintern, Mon. 34
Tipton, Staffs. 87
Tipton Green, Staffs. 87–8
Toll End, Tipton, Staffs. 88
Tondu, Glam. 27–8
Tow Law, Durham 175
Towcester, Northants. 105
Tredegar, Mon. 28
Treforest: *see* Pontypridd
Trent, Lincs. 111
Trimsaran, Carms. 28
Trosnant: *see* Pontypool
Tudhoe, Durham 175–6
Tunstall: *see* Goldendale
Tyne Ironworks: *see* Lemington
Tyne Main: *see* Wallsend
Typwca: *see* Cwmbran

Ulverston: *see* Barrow Hæmatite; North Lonsdale
Union, Mon.: *see* Rhymney

Union, West Bromwich, Staffs. 88
Unstone, Derbys. 123
'Urmbridge': *see* Wombridge

Vane & Seaham, Durham 176
Varteg, Mon. 29
Venallt, Glam. 29
Victoria, Mon. 29–30

Walker, Northumberland 176
Wallbrook, Staffs. 89
Wallbut, ?Staffs. 89
Wallsend, Northumberland 176–7
Walsall: *see* Green Lane
Warren Hills, Northants. 105
Warsash, Hants. 37
Washington, Durham 177
Waterloo: *see* Broadwaters
Waterloo, Yorks.: *see* Thorpe Hall
Wear, Washington, Durham 177
Weardale: *see* Tow Law
Wednesbury: *see* Old Park
Wednesbury Oak, Staffs. 89–90
Wednesbury Park, Wednesbury Old Park: *see* Old Park
Wellingborough, Northants. 105–6
Wellington: *see* Old Park
West Cumberland, Workington, Cumb. 150
West Hallam, Derbys. 123
West Hartlepool, Durham 177
  see also Seaton Carew
West Yorkshire, East Ardsley, Leeds, Yorks. 134–5
Westbank: *see* Gladsmuir
Westbury, Wilts. 35–6
White Horse, York Road, Leeds, Yorks. 135
Whitehaven: *see* Cleator Moor
Wibsey Lowmoor: *see* Low Moor
Wigan: *see* Kirkless Hall
Willenhall, Staffs. 90
Willey, Salop 47
Willingsworth, Wednesbury, Staffs. 90–1
Wilsontown, Lanarkshire 198
Windmill End, Dudley, Worcs. 91
Wingerworth, Derbys. 123–4
'Wingfield': *see* Oakerthorpe
Wishaw, Lanarkshire 198–9
Withygrove: *see* Withymoor
Withymoor, Staffs. 91
Witton: *see* Thornaby
Witton Park, Durham 177–8
Wolverhampton, Staffs. 92
  see also Chillington
Wombridge, Salop 47
Woodside, Dudley, Worcs. 92
Workington, Cumb. 150–1
Worsbrough, Yorks. 135
Wreck Hill, Yorks. 178
Wrockwardine, Salop 47–8
Wylam, Northumberland 178

Ynyscedwyn, Brecs. 30–1
Ynysfach, Glam. 31
York Road: *see* White Horse
Ystalyfera, Glam. 31

Index of Owners

The number and date in brackets following the names of companies are the registered number and year of registration; the prefix SC indicates that the company was registered in Scotland, not England. Registered companies have been indexed in precise alphabetical order (e.g. William Baird & Co. Ltd, not Baird, William, & Co. Ltd).

Abbots: see Knight, Abbots & Co.
Aberdare & Plymouth Co. Ltd (10077 : 1875) 1, 2, 22–3, 23
Aberdare Iron Co. 1, 2, 22, 29
Aberdare Works & Collieries Co. 1, 2
Abernant Iron Co. 2
Acklam Iron Co. Ltd (27281 : 1888) 152
Adamson & Co. 110
Addenbrooke, — 76
    E.H. & J. 76
    J. 76
Addenbrooke, Smith & Pidcock 84
Addenbrooke & Co. 43, 65, 83–4
Addenbrooke & Pidcock 43
Addie, Miller & Rankine 191
Addie, Robert 191
    Robert & Sons 191
Addie & Rankine 191
Addison, — 186
Ainslie: see Harrison Ainslie & Co.; Harrison Ainslie & Co. Ltd
Ainsworth, Thomas & Co. 139
Aireside Haematite Iron Co. 125
Aireside Steel & Iron Co. 125
Aleson & Co. 181
Alfred Hickman Ltd (17246 : 1882) 85
Alison & Co. 181
Allies: see Cruttwell, Allies & Co.
Alloway & Crawshay 32
Amman Iron & Tinplate Co. 7
Amman Iron Co. 7
Anson, Louisa Barbara Catherine (née Phillips), Countess of Lichfield 55
    trustees of 55
    Thomas William, Earl of Lichfield 55
Anstice, Messrs 39
    John 39
    W. & Co. 45
    William & Co. 39
Anthracite Iron & Steel Co. Ltd (24838 : 1887) 28
Apedale Coal & Iron Co. 93
Appleby, — 119
    F.R. 119
    F.R. & C.E. 119
    F.R. & Co. 119
Appleby & Co. 119
Appleby Iron Co. Ltd (8897 : 1874) 107
Appleby-Frodingham Steel Co. 107
Appleby-Frodingham Steel Co. Ltd (292747 : 1934) 107
Arkwright, R. 117
Armitage, — 128
Armitage & Co. 128
Armstrong, Sir W.G. & Co. 160
    see also Sir W.G. Armstrong, Mitchell & Co. Ltd
Arthur & Co. 29
Ashburnham, John, Earl of Ashburnham 37
Ashton Furnace Co. 35
Ashton Vale Iron Co. Ltd (1359C : 1864) 35
Askam & Mouzell Iron Co. Ltd (14936 : 1881) 136
    see also Millom & Askam Hematite Iron Co. Ltd
Astley, J.D., Esq. & Co. 142
Aston: see Baldwin, Aston & Co.
Aston, Isaiah & Co. 92
    assignees of 92

John & Co. 92
W. 61, 68, 84
Atkinson, Mr 26
Attwood, — 76, 89
    Miss G.M.: see Mrs Kinnersley & Miss G.M. Attwood
    Miss G.M. & Mrs Kinnersley 96
    Miss J.M.: see Mrs Kinnersley & Miss J.M. Attwood
Attwood & Co. 76, 89
Awsworth Iron Co. 113
Aydon & Co. 133
Ayrshire Iron Co. 180

Badger, T. & J. 79
Bagley, Dudley 70
Bagnall, C. & T., trustees of 162
    Charles & Thomas 162
    Charles & Thomas jun. 162
    J. & Son 69
    J. & Sons 61, 69
    John & Sons 61, 69
    see also John Bagnall & Sons Ltd
Bagnall & Sons 69
Bailey, Messrs 3, 20
    C. 1
    Crawshay 1
    Crawshay & Morgan, William 16, 29
    J. & C. 3, 20
    J. & J. 3, 20
    Jos. 20
    Sir Jos. & C. 3, 20
    Jos. & Crawshay 20
    Sir Jos. H. 20
    Joseph & C. 20
    Joseph & Co. 3
Bailey Bros. 3, 20
Bailey, Caddick & Co. 73
Bain, James & Co. 142
Bain & Patterson 142
Baird, W. & Co. 188
    William & Co. 180, 187, 188, 192–3, 194, 195–6
    see also William Baird & Co. Ltd
Bairds & Dalmellington Ltd (SC 16594 : 1931) 187, 193, 195
Bairds & Scottish Steel Ltd, formerly Scottish Iron & Steel Co. Ltd (SC 8313 : 1912) 189
Balcarres, Lord: see Lindsay, Alexander
Baldwin, W. 56, 89
    W. & Co. 56, 89
    William, reps. of late 58
    William & Co. 58
Baldwin & Co. 56, 58
Baldwin, Aston & Co. 88
Baldwin's Ltd (73336 : 1902) 11, 17–18, 25, 77
    see also British (Guest, Keen, Baldwins) Iron & Steel Co. Ltd; Richard Thomas & Co. Ltd
Balfour & Co. 97
Ball: see Horton, Simms & Ball
Bancks & Co. 91
    see also Banks
Banhest, Messrs 38, 39
Bank & Onions 59
Banks, — 69
    T. & Son 55, 68
    T. & Sons 68

Thomas 55
Thomas & Son 68
W. 96
see also Bancks
Banks & Co. 39, 69
Banks & Son 68
Banwen Co. 3
Barbor's Field Co. 55
Barker, — 96
    see also Jones, Barker & Foster
Barker & Co. 96
Barker & Foster 62
Barlow: see Dunston, Barlow & Co.
Barnaby, — 5
Barnes & Co. 115
Barrett: see Warner, Lucas & Barrett
Barrow, — 122
    B. & Co. 136
    George 122
    G.H. 122
    Richard 122
    see also Ward & Barrow
Barrow Hæmatite Steel Co. Ltd (1126C : 1864) 137–8
Barrow Ironworks Ltd (457441 : 1948) 138
Bassano, W. & Co. 64
Bastow, S. & Co. 155
Bastow & Co. 155
Bateman, T. 142
    see also Fothergill, Hankey & Bateman
Beale, Samuel & Co. 118–19, 129, 131
Beasley, Joseph jun. 162
Bedlington Iron Co. Ltd (2557C : 1865) 153
Bell, Hawks & Co. 177
Bell, Robert 198
    see also Losh, Wilson & Bell
Bell Brothers 156, 176, 177, 178
Bell Brothers & Co. 156
Bell Brothers Ltd (7855 : 1873; 44839 : 1895; 60411 : 1899) 156, 176, 177
Benet, G. & Co. 78
Bennerley Iron Co. Ltd (199244 : 1924) 113
Bennet, Geo. & Co. 78
Bennett, Geo. & Co. 78
Bennington: see Holdsworth, Bennington, Byers & Co.
Bennitt, W. 78
    William 78
    assignees of 78
Benton, George 34
    executors of late 34
Benton & Pemberton 66
Beresford: see Outram, Jessop & Beresford
Berridge, Richard 35
    executors of late 35
Best & Barrs 91
Best & Bars 91
Bestwood Coal & Iron Co. Ltd (6506 : 1872) 113
Bevan, — 20
Bickley & Gibbons 56
Bills & Mills 65
Bilston Brook Furnace Co. 56
Birchenwood Colliery Co. Ltd (37179 : 1892) 96
Birchills Furnaces Ltd (93205 : 1908) 57
Birmingham Coal Co. 88
Birtley Co. 154

Birtley Iron Co. 154
Bishton, — 41, 47
Bishton & Co. 41, 47
Bishton & Underhill 80
Bishton & Wright 42
Blackwell, — 84
Blackwell, Jones & Co. 60, 73, 84
Blackwell, S.H. & Co. 56, 84
Blackwell & Co. 56, 84
Blaenavon Co. Ltd (1312C : 1864; 13698 : 1880) 4
Blaenavon Iron & Steel Co. Ltd (4934 : 1870) 4
Blaenavon Iron Co. 4
Blaina Furnaces Co. Ltd (13676 : 1880) 5
    see also Cwmcelyn & Blaina Co.; Nant-y-Glo & Blaina Iron Works Co. Ltd; Pyle & Blaina Works Ltd
Blair & Co. 149
Blair & Vance 149
Blakemore, — 22
    R. 22
Blakemore & Co. 22
Blewitt, R.J. 11
Bloomer, D. & Son 82
Bloomer, Boaz & Son 82
    see also Boaz, Bloomer & Son; Davies & Bloomer; Davies & Bloomer & Co.; Davis, & Bloomer & Son
Blount, Sir W. 39
Boaz, Bloomer & Son 82
Bolckow, Vaughan & Co. 165
Bolckow, Vaughan & Co. Ltd (1705C : 1864) 157, 157–8, 158, 162, 163, 165, 171, 178
Bolckow & Vaughan 157, 161, 165, 177–8
Booker, T.W. 22
    T.W. & Co. 22
    Thomas W.: see Thomas W. Booker & Co. Ltd
    Thomas William & Co. 22
Booth & Co. 131
Botfield, — 40, 45, 47
    B. 40, 41, 42, 45
    Beriah 40, 41, 42
        reps. of late 40, 41
    Mrs Isabella 40, 41
    J.N. & B. 40, 45, 47
    T.W. & B. 45, 47
    W. & B. 40, 45, 47
    see also Brown, H. & Botfield
Botfield & Co. 39, 40, 45
Botfields & Co. 40, 45, 47
Bouzer & Co. 17
Bowling Iron Co. 126
Bowling Iron Co. Ltd (4917 : 1870) 126
Bradley, J. & Co. 38, 59, 69, 84
    John & Co. 44, 84–5
    T. & I. 61, 65
    T. & I. & Sons 65
    see also T. &. I. Bradley & Sons Ltd
Bradley & Foster Ltd: see T. & I. Bradley & Sons Ltd
Bramah & Co. 92
Brahah & Cochrane 92
    see also Cochrane & Co.
Brancker, Sir T. & Co. 31
Brancker & Co. 31
Brayford, — 57
    J. 57
    John 57
Brewer & Co. 10
Brinkburn Iron Co. 154–5
British (Guest, Keen, Baldwins) Iron & Steel Co. Ltd, later Guest Keen Baldwins Iron & Steel Co. Ltd, afterwards Guest Keen Iron & Steel Co. Ltd, subsequently GKN Steel Co. Ltd (246754 : 1930) 6, 8, 25, 50, 109
British Iron Co. 2, 49, 53, 63, 68, 76, 91
British Steel Corporation, formerly Dorman Long & Co. Ltd (30048 : 1889) (qv), now British Steel PLC (2280000 : 1988) 8, 15, 18, 25, 50, 54, 86, 99, 101, 107, 109, 111, 122, 132, 149, 151, 154, 157, 160, 169, 170, 171, 184, 196
Briton Ferry Iron Co. 6
Briton Ferry Works Reconstruction Co. Ltd, later Briton Ferry Works Ltd (30050 : 1889) 6
Broade: see Stanier, Mrs & Broade, F. Stanier
Brocksopp, — 118
    J. 118
Brodie, Mr 39
Brodie & Co. 39
Brogden, John & Sons 27
    Messrs 27
Brogden & Sons 27
Bromley Hall Coal & Iron Co. Ltd (8697 : 1874) 63
Brook Furnace Co. 56
Brook Furnaces Iron Co. 56
Brown, H. & Botfield 456
    see also Darby, Brown & Co.; Fothergill, Brown & Co.; John Brown & Co. Ltd; Russell & Brown
Brunner, John T., MP 141
Brymbo Co. 49
Brymbo Iron Co. 49–50
Brymbo Steel Co. Ltd (19895 : 1884) 50
Brymbo Steel (Successors) Co. Ltd (280284 : 1933) 50
Brymbo Steel Works 50
Brymbo Steel Works Ltd (48605 : 1896) 50
Buckley, Newton & Co. 53
Bulmer & Co. 164
Burton: see Kyrke & Burton
Bute, Marquess of: see Crichton-Stuart, John Patrick
Butler, J. 123
    Mr 123
    see also Wright Butler & Co. Ltd
Butlin, Thomas & Co. 103, 106
    see also Thomas Butlin & Co. Ltd
Butterley Co. 99, 114, 116
Butterley Co. Ltd (26306 : 1888) 99, 114, 116
Butterley Iron Co. 114, 116
Byers: see Holdsworth, Bennington, Byers & Co.

Caddick: see Bailey, Caddick & Co.
Cadell, Henry 180
Cadell & Co. 184
Cadell & Edington 185
Calow Iron Co. 114
Cambrian Co. 19
Cambrian Iron Co. 19
Cammell Laird & Co. 144
    see also Charles Cammell & Co. Ltd
Campeon, — 162
Cape Iron Co. 60
Cardiff Iron & Tin Plate Co. Ltd (19190 : 1883) 22
Cargo Fleet Iron Co. 155
Cargo Fleet Iron Co. Ltd (17822 : 1883) 155
Carlton Iron Co. Ltd: see North of England Industrial Iron & Coal Co. Ltd
Carnforth Hæmatite Iron Co. Ltd (1501C : 1864) 138
Carnforth Hematite Iron Co. (1915) Ltd (141131 : 1915) 139
Carnforth Hematite Iron Co. Ltd (57536 : 1898) 138–9
Carr, J. & Co. 176–7
Carron Co. (RC 93 : 1760) 182–3
Castle Coal & Iron Co. Ltd (7955 : 1874) 57
Cefn Iron Works Ltd (60601 : 1899) 9
Chambers & Co. 133
    see also Newton, Chambers & Co.; Newton, Chambers & Co. Ltd; Newton, Scott, Chambers & Co.
Chapelhall, owners of 183
Charcoal Iron Co. Ltd (146666 : 1917) 137
Charles Cammell & Co. Ltd, later Cammell Laird & Co. Ltd (1166C : 1864; 55513 : 1898) 140, 149
Charlton Iron Works Co. Ltd (6547 : 1872) 127
Chatterley Iron Co. Ltd (1898C : 1865) 94
Chatterley-Whitfield Collieries Ltd (33178 : 1891) 94
Checkland, G.E. & Fisher, E.K. 102
Checkland & Fisher 102
Cheney, Edward 45
Chesterfield, John 120
Chick, George 35
    see also Keeling & Chick
Chillington & Co. 55, 73
Chillington Co. 62, 76
Chillington Iron Co. 55, 61–2, 73, 75, 76
Chillington Iron Co. Ltd (6178 : 1872) 55, 62
Christie, A. & Co. 193
    Alex. & Co. 193
    Andrew 186
    C. & A. 189
    Charles 189
    see also Wilson & Christie
Cinderford Iron Co. 32
Clarke, — 129
    H. 55
Clarke & Jerome 55
Clay Cross Co. 115
Clay Cross Co. Ltd (126827 : 1913) 115
Clay Cross (Iron & Foundries) Ltd (541366 : 1954) 116
Clay Cross Iron Co. 115
Clay Lane Iron Co. 157
Clay Lane Iron Co. Ltd (16285 : 1882) 157
Clay Lane Ironworks, owners of 157
Clayton & Co. 125
    see also Leah, Clayton & Co.
Cliff, Joseph 108
Cliff & Hurst 108
Cliff Brothers 108
Clydach Iron Co. 9
Coalbrookdale Co. 39, 40, 42, 43
Coalbrookdale Co. Ltd (15648 : 1881) 40, 43
Coalbrookdale Iron Co. 40, 42, 43
Coates: see Swan, Coates & Co.; Swan, Straubenzie, Coates & Co.
Cochrane & Co. 92, 168
    see also Bramah & Cochrane
Cochrane & Co. Ltd (30503 : 1889) 92, 168
Cochrane & Co. (Woodside) Ltd (91167 : 1906) 92
Cockshutt: see Cook & Cockshutt
Cohen, J.C. 58
Colbourn, Groucutt & Co. 60
Colbourn, John, Sons & Co. 72, 81
    John & Sons 72, 81, 87
Colbourn & Co. 72
Colbourn & Sons 72
Collins: see Jukes, Collins & Co.
Coltness Iron Co. 185
Coltness Iron Co. Ltd (SC 1046 : 1881; SC 4315 : 1899) 185
Colvilles Ltd (SC 16249 : 1930) 184, 196
    see also David Colville & Sons Ltd
Consett Iron Co. Ltd (1140C : 1864) 154, 159–60, 160
    see also Derwent & Consett Iron Co. Ltd
Cook & Cockshutt 127
Cooke & Co. 127
Cooke & Frere 9
    see also Frere, Cooke & Co.; William Cooke & Co. Ltd
Cooley: see Downing & Cooley
Cooper, Robert 70

see also Field, Cooper & Co.
Copper Miners of England 10
Copper Mining Co. 10, 20
Corbyn's Hall New Furnaces Co. Ltd (5581 : 1871) 63
Corngreaves Furnace Co. 64
Cosham: see Hinde & Cosham
Cowdenbeath Coal Co. 193
Cowdenbeath Coal Co. Ltd (SC 2355 : 1892) 193
Crane, George 30
Crane & Co. 30
Crane Iron, Steel & Coal Co. Ltd (20350 : 1884) 30
Cransley Iron Co. Ltd (8994 : 1874) 101
Crawley, — 33
  T.B. 33
Crawley & Co. 33
Crawshaw, — 127
Crawshay, — 12, 17, 25, 31
  Francis 17, 24
  Henry 32
  Henry & Co. 32
  Henry & Sons 33
    see also Henry Crawshay & Co. Ltd
  R. 12
  Robert 12, 31
  W. 12, 17, 31
  W. & Sons 12, 31
  William 12, 31
  William & Sons 31
  see also Alloway & Crawshay
Crawshay & Co. 12, 17, 31, 32
Crawshay & Ellwell 133
Crawshay Brothers 12, 31
Crawshay Brothers, Cyfarthfa, Ltd (32142 : 1890) 12–13
Crédit Général Ottoman, Constantinople 177
Cresswell, E. & Sons 87
Crew, Thomas 86
Crewdson: see Jones, Pearce & Crewson
Crichton-Stuart, John Patrick, Marquess of Bute 17
Crockett, — 66
Crompton & Co. 121
Cruttwell, Messrs 5, 12
Cruttwell, Allies & Co. 5, 12
Cruttwell, Levick & Co. 5, 10, 12
Cruttwell & Levick 5, 10, 12
Cumberland Iron Mining & Smelting Co. Ltd (2266C : 1865) 144–5
Cunninghame: see Merry & Cunninghame; Merry & Cunninghame Ltd
Cure, A.C. 45
Cwm Avon Estate & Works Co. Ltd (15621 : 1881) 11
Cwm Avon Estate, receiver of 11
Cwm Avon Works, proprietors of 11
Cwm Celyn Co. 12
Cwmbran Iron Co. 11
Cwmcelyn & Blaina Co. 5, 12

Dale & Co. 40, 42
Dale Co. 39, 42, 45
Dalmellington Iron Co. 186
Dalmellington Iron Co. Ltd (SC 1464 : 1885) 186
  see also Bairds & Dalmellington Ltd
Dalrymple, — 188, 195
  Col. 195
Dalrymple & Co. 180
Dalton, Messrs 52
Darby, A. & Co. 40
Darby, Brown & Co. 2–3
Darby & Co. 14, 26, 29, 49
Darlaston Coal & Iron Co. Ltd (11712 : 1877) 65
Darlaston Steel & Iron Co. Ltd (1639C : 1864) 65
Darwen & Mostyn Iron Co. Ltd (24351 : 1887) 52, 140
Darwen Iron Co. 140

Darwen Iron Co. Ltd (8641 : 1874; 12378 : 1878) 140
Darwin, J. & Co. 127, 135
Darwin & Co. 127
Davey, George Henry 6
  see also Willett & Davey
David Colville & Sons Ltd (SC 2965 : 1895) 190
Davies, T. & Son 65
  T. & Sons 65
  Thomas 65
Davies & Bloomer 82
Davies & Bloomer & Co. 82
Davies & Co. 33
Davis, E.P. 113, 117–18
  J. & Son 78
  R. 65
  T. 83
Davis, Williams & Phillips 22
Davis & Bloomer & Son 82
Dawes, George 116, 128, 131
  executors of 116
  J. & Sons 78
  John 91
  John & Sons 91
  John H. & Sons 91
  W. 91
  W. Henry 91
  W.H. 91
  W.H. & Co. 111
  W.H. & G. 116
  W.H. & Geo. 111, 128, 131
  W.H. & George 127, 131
  W.H. & John & Sons 91
  W.H. John 127, 131
  William Henry 91, 111
Dawes & Co. 127–8, 130–1
Dawes & Sons 65, 78
Dawson: see Hird, Dawson & Co.; Hird, Dawson & Hardy; Jarratt & Dawson
Day & Co. 128
Deeley: see Motteram & Deeley
Deepfields Iron Co. 66
Denby Iron & Coal Co. Ltd (31201 : 1890) 117
Derwent & Consett Iron Co. Ltd (1275 : 1858) 154, 159, 160
Derwent Haematite Iron Co. 140
Derwent Iron Co. 154, 159, 160
Devon Iron Co. 186
Dickenson, B. & Co. 39, 40, 42
Dickin, John 53
Dinsdale Smelting Co. Ltd (66720 : 1900) 166
  see also Linthorpe Dinsdale Smelting Co. Ltd; Linthorpe-Dinsdale Smelting Co. Ltd
Disney, Charles C. 118
  Henry Cathrow 118
Distington Hematite Iron Co. Ltd (16146 : 1881) 140–1
Ditton Brook Iron Co. Ltd (2824 : 1862) 141
Dixon, John & William 180, 198
  W. 190
  W. & Co. 180, 198
  William 180, 190
  see also William Dixon Ltd
Dixon, Mere & Co. 92
Dixon, Neve & Co. 92
Dixon, Neve & Hill 92
Dixon, Nevi & Co. 92
Dixon & Co. 66, 87, 180, 188
Dixons' Ironworks Ltd (SC 25725 : 1947) 181
Dorman Long & Co. Ltd (30048 : 1889) 152, 153, 158, 168–9, 171
  see also British Steel Corporation
Dorman Long (Steel) Ltd (538416 : 1954) 152, 153–4, 157, 158, 169, 171
Dowlais Co. 13
Dowlais Iron Co. 8, 13

Downey & Co. 158, 163
Downing & Cooley 39
Ducal Iron & Coal Co. 35
Dudley, 1st Earl of: see Ward, John William
  1st Earl of (2nd creation): see Ward, William
  2nd Earl of: see Ward, William Humble
  3rd Earl of: see Ward, William Humble Eric
  see also Earl of Dudley's Round Oak Steelworks Ltd; Matthews & Dudley
Dudley Port Furnace Co. 68
Dudley, Bagley 70
Dunlop, C. & Co. 184
  Colin & Co. 184, 196
  J. 184
  James & Co. 184
    see also James Dunlop & Co. (1900) Ltd; James Dunlop & Co. Ltd
Dunlop & Co. 187
Dunlop, Wilson & Co. 194
Dunn, J. & G. 60
  John & George 91
Dunning, J. 60
  see also Jones, Dunning & Co.; Jones, Dunning & Co. Ltd
Dunston, Barlow & Co. 120

Eagle Furnace Co. 68, 88
Earl of Dudley's Round Oak Steel Works Ltd (133796 : 1891) 75
  see also Round Oak Steel Works Ltd
East Moors Works 8
Easton Estate & Mining Co. Ltd (12393 : 1878) 105
Ebbw Vale Co. 2–3, 14, 221, 26, 29, 33
Ebbw Vale Co. Ltd (1386C : 1864) 3, 14, 22, 24, 26, 29, 33
Ebbw Vale Iron & Coal Co. 26
Ebbw Vale Iron & Steel Co. 14
Ebbw Vale Iron Co. 3, 14, 22, 26, 29
Ebbw Vale Steel Iron & Coal Co. Ltd (3956 : 1868) 3, 14–15, 24, 27, 29–30, 33
Edington & Co. 184, 192, 195
Edington Iron Co. 186
  see also Cadell & Edington
Edwards & Co. 112
  see also Saxleby, Edwards & Co.
Eglinton Iron Co. 180, 187, 193, 194, 196
Elkington: see Gibbons & Elkington
Ellwell: see Crawshay & Ellwell
Elsam: see Smith & Elsam
Elsom & Co. 117
Elsom & Smith 117
Elswick Iron Co. 160
Elwon, Malcolm & Co. 156
  T.L. & Co. 157
Elwon & Co. 156, 157
Emmett, — 126, 127
English, Mr 116
Erewash Valley Iron Co. Ltd (5981 : 1872) 117
Evers & Martin 81

Farnley Iron Co. 128
Farnley Iron Co. Ltd (5316 : 1871) 128
Fellows, Robert 64
  see also Robert Fellows Ltd
Fenton, — 134
Fereday, — 58, 75, 84
  J.T. 58, 67
  see also Jones & Fereday
Fereday & Co. 41, 84, 87
Ferry Hill: see Rosedale & Ferry Hill Iron Co. Ltd
Field, Cooper & Co. 135
Fife Coal Co. Ltd (SC 449 : 1872; SC 2826 : 1895) 193
Firmstone, — 97
  G. & W. 78

H.O. 65
J. 97
J. & W., trustees of 72
T. 93, 97
Thomas 93, 97
W. & G. 65, 73
W.H. & G. 73
Firmstone & Co. 73
Firth & Hodgson 161
Fisher: see Checkland & Fisher; Checkland, G.E. & Fisher, E.K.
FitzWilliam, 3rd Earl: see Wentworth-FitzWilliam, C.W.
4th Earl: see Wentworth-FitzWilliam, W.T.S.
Fleming: see Montgomerie & Fleming
Fletcher, Solly & Urwick 90
Ford Motor Co. Ltd (235446 : 1928) 37
Forest of Dean Iron Co. 33
Forest of Dean Iron Co. Ltd (10442 : 1876) 33
Forest Iron & Steel Co. Ltd (6614 : 1872) 24–5
Forman, W.H. & Fothergill, R. 28
  William 22
  William Henry 22
Forman & Co. 7, 22, 25
Forman & Fothergill 28
Forth Iron Co. 188
Foster, J. 44, 84
  James 44, 47, 84
  William H. 45
  W.O. 44
  William Orme 44–5
  see also Barker & Foster; Bradley & Foster Ltd; Jones, Barker & Foster; Lloyds, Foster & Co.
Fosters: see Lloyds, Fosters & Co.
Fothergill, — 26, 27
  R.: see Forman, W.H. & Fothergill, R.
  R. & Hankey, T.A. 1, 2, 22, 23
  R. & Lewis, T.A. 14
  see also Forman & Fothergill; Scales, Fothergill & Co.
Fothergill, Brown & Co. 29
Fothergill, Hankey & Bateman 14, 23
Fothergill, Hankey & Lewis 1, 2, 14, 23
Fothergill & Co. 1, 2, 26
Fothergill & Hankey 1, 2, 14, 23
Fowler, — 83
  W.H. 55
  William & Co. 120
  see also Shale & Fowler
Fowler & Co. 120
Fowlers & Hankey 120
Fox & Co. 20
Foxes & Co. 20
Freeland & Lancaster 195
Frere, Cooke & Co. 9
Frere & Co. 9
  see also Cooke & Frere
Frodingham Iron & Steel Co. 108
Frodingham Iron & Steel Co. Ltd (80861 : 1904) 108
Frodingham Iron Co. 108
Frood Iron Co. 51
Fryer, R. 82
  W. 71, 82
  William 82
  William F. 71
Fuller, J. 37
Furness Iron & Steel Co. Ltd (2964 : 1866) 136

G. & R. Thomas Ltd (189630 : 1923) 71–2
GKN Rolled & Bright Steel Ltd (185151) 50
GKN Steel Co. Ltd: see British (Guest, Keen, Baldwins) Iron & Steel Co. Ltd; see also under Guest Keen
Gadlys Coal & Iron Co. Ltd (6736 : 1872) 16

Gadlys Iron Co. 16
Gallaway & Co. 190
Galvanised Iron Co. 63
Gandy, Messrs 52
Garside, R. & W. 135
  trustees of 135
George: see Leigh & George
George & Co. 39
Gibbons — 74
  B. 56, 73, 74
  B. jun. 34, 71, 75, 87
  B. jun. & Co. 75
  Benjamin 34, 56, 63, 75
  Benjamin sen. 63
  Emily 56, 75
  John 63
  J.S. 63
  W.E. & Co. 64
  W.J. 86
  see also Bickley & Gibbons
Gibbons & Co. 62, 74
Gibbons & Elkington 66
Gibbons & Roberts 87
Giles, Frederick 86
Gilkes, Wilson, Leatham & Co. 172
Gilkes, Wilson, Pease & Co. 173
  see also Wilsons, Pease & Co.; Wilsons, Pease & Co. Ltd
Gilkes, Wilson & Co. 173
  see also Hopkins, Gilkes & Co. Ltd
Gill, J. 67
  Joseph 67
Giller, Samuel 53
Gilmour & Co. 144
Gjers, Mills & Co. 152
Gjers, Mills & Co. Ltd (72017 : 1901) 152–3
Glasgow Iron & Steel Co. Ltd (SC 1722 : 1888) 199
Glasgow Iron Co. 199
Glendon Iron Co. 102
Glendon Iron Co. Ltd (22814 : 1886) 102
Glendon Iron Ore Co. 102
Glendon Ore Co. 102
Glengarnock Iron & Steel Co. Ltd (SC 2333 : 1892) 179, 189–90
Glengarnock Iron Co. 189
Glover, James & Alfred 97
  Mr 17
Glynn, Sir S., Bt 78
Goddard, John H. & William 97
  T. & Brothers 97
  T. & Son 97
  Thomas & Sons 97
Goldendale Iron Co. 95
Goldendale Iron Co. Ltd (143567 : 1916) 95–6
Golynos Co. 16
Golynos Iron Co. 16–17, 29
Goold Brothers 34
Gordon & Co. 186
Governor & Co. of Copper Miners in England 10–11, 21
Governor & Co. of Copper Mines 10, 21
Graham, — 131
  W. & Co. 131
Graham & Co. 131
Granville, 1st Earl: see Leveson-Gower, Granville
  2nd Earl: see Leveson-Gower, Granville George
Grazebrook, — 58
  M. & W. 77–8
  see also M. & W. Grazebrook Ltd
Grazebrook & Co. 58
Grazebrook & Sons 58
Grazebrook Cold Blast Ltd (436803 : 1947) 78
Great Western Iron Co. Ltd (9952 : 1875) 34, 51
Greave, Mr & Co. 194
Green & Price 9

Greenham: see James & Greenham
Greenhow, R.T. & R. 53
Greenhowe, — 53
Greenwell & Co. 35
Grenfell: see Leighton & Grenfell
Griffin, James 91
  executors of 91
Griffiths, S. 102
  Samuel 56, 91
Groucutt, S. & Sons 66
  Samuel & Sons 60, 66
Groucutt & Co. 66
  see also Colbourn, Groucutt & Co.
Guest, Sir J.J., & Co. 13
  Sir J.J., Bt, trustees of 13
Guest, Lewis & Co. 13
Guest & Co. 13
Guest Keen & Co. Ltd, later Guest Keen & Nettlefolds Ltd (66549 : 1900) 8, 11, 13
Guest Keen Iron & Steel Co. Ltd: see British (Guest, Keen, Baldwins) Iron & Steel Co. Ltd
Guest Keen Iron & Steel Works 8
  see also GKN Rolled & Bright Steel Ltd

H.B. Whitehouse & Son Ltd (63981 : 1899) 83
Haden, J. 60, 67
  Joseph 60, 67
  W. 91
  William 67
  William & Co., assignees of 67
  William & Son 67
Haines, Job & Henry 90
Haines & Co. 90
Hains, J. & H. 134
  T. & H. 134
Hall, B. 25
  Henry & Co. 74
Hall, Holcroft & Co. 75
Hall, Holcroft & Pearson 59, 63, 74
Hallens, Messrs 89
Halton & Co. 142
Halton Co. 143
Hankey, T.A.: see Fothergill, R. & Hankey, T.A.
  see also Fothergill, Hankey & Bateman; Fothergill, Hankey & Lewis; Fothergill & Hankey; Fowlers & Hankey
Hannay: see Schneider, Hannay & Co.; Schneider & Hannay
Harding, A. & Co. 125
Harding & Co. 125
Hardy: see Hird, Dawson & Hardy
Hareshaw Iron Co. 162
Harford, Daniel 33
Harford & Co. 7, 14, 26
Harford & Partridge 7
Harfords & Co. 14, 26
Harries, — 38
  F.B. 38
Harries & Co. 38
Harrington Iron & Coal Co. Ltd (97583 : 1908) 142
Harrison, Frederick 28
Harrison & Co. 136, 141, 146
Harrison Ainslie & Co. 37, 136–7, 141, 146–7, 192
Harrison Ainslie & Co. Ltd (39522 : 1893; 82203 : 1904) 137, 147
Hartland, J. 72
Hartland & Co. 88
Hartopp, Henry 131
Hawkes, — 69
  R. 88
Hawkes & Co. 69
Hawks: see Bell, Hawks & Co.
Haybridge Iron Co. Ltd (4759 : 1870) 40, 41, 45, 47
Haydon & Co. 133
Hazledine, W. 39

Heath, F. 93
   Robert 93, 98
   Robert & Sons 93–4, 98
     see also Low Moor Co. Ltd; Robert Heath & Sons Ltd
Heathcote, — 93
   J.E. 93
   R.C. 93
   R.E. 93
   see also Kinnersley & Heathcote
Henry Crawshay & Co. Ltd (29552 : 1889) 32
Hepworth Iron Co. 129
Heyford Co. Ltd (2394C : 1865) 102
Heyford Iron Co. Ltd (9510 : 1875; 32878 : 1890) 102–3
Hickman, Alfred (later Sir Alfred) 85, 86
   see also Alfred Hickman Ltd
   G.H. 70, 86
   G.H. & A. 56, 70, 86
   Geo. H. 70
Hickman & Co. 91
Hickman & Sons 56
Highway, T. & C. 70
Highway Brothers 70, 71
Hill, — 23
   A. 14, 23
   A. & Co. 23
   Anthony 13, 23
     trustees of late 14, 23
   Anthony & Co. 14, 23
   R. & A. 14, 23
   R. & Son 23
   see also Dixon, Neve & Hill
Hill & Co. 4, 20
Hill & Hopkins 4
Hill & Struttle 23
Hinde, Thomas & Co. 42
Hinde & Cosham 17
Hingley, N. & Co. 68
   N. & Sons 68, 76–7, 79
   see also N. Hingley & Sons Ltd
Hird, Dawson & Co. 130, 133
Hird, Dawson & Hardy 125–6, 130, 133
Hirwain Coal & Iron Co. Ltd (2088C : 1865) 17
Hodgson: see Firth & Hodgson
Holcroft, J. & C. 74
   James 74
   James & Thomas 58
   Thomas 58
   see also Hall, Holcroft & Co.; Hall, Holcroft & Pearson
Holdsworth, — 185
Holdsworth, Bennington, Byers & Co. 172
Holroyd, T. & Co. 48
Holwell Iron Co. Ltd (10083 : 1875; 68691 : 1900) 108–9
Homfray, — 22, 43
   J. & Watt 14
   S. & Co. 22, 28
Homfray & Co. 28
Hopkins, — 67
   J. & Son 67
Hopkins, Gilkes & Co. Ltd (1922C : 1865) 174
Hopkins & Co. 174
Hopkins & Son 67
   see also Hill & Hopkins; Snowdon & Hopkins
Horseley Co. 72
Horseley Iron Co. 72
Horton, D. & G. 67, 84
Horton, Simms & Ball 44
Houldsworth, — 185
Houldsworth & Hunter 185
Humfrey: see Roberts & Humfrey
Hunsbury Hill Coal & Iron Co. Ltd (10961 : 1876) 103
Hunsbury Iron Co. 103
Hunt, — 21
Hunter: see Houldsworth & Hunter

Hurst: see Cliff & Hurst
Hurt, — 118
   F. 112, 118

Islip Iron Co. 102, 104
Islip Iron Co. Ltd (9061 : 1874; 78271 : 1903) 102, 104
Iwons & Co. 29
Izon, W. 74
   William 74
Izons, William & Co. 74
Izons & Co. 59, 74

Jackson, Sir William, Bt, executors of 115
   W., MP & Walmsley, Sir J. 115
   W. & Co. 115
James & Greenham 33
James & Montague 33
James Dunlop & Co. (1900) Ltd, later James Dunlop & Co. Ltd (SC 4545 : 1900) 184
James Dunlop & Co. Ltd (SC 1515 : 1886) 184
Jaques: see Stevenson, Jaques & Co.; Stevenson, Wilson, Jaques & Co.
Jarratt, Messrs 130
Jarratt & Co. 130
Jarratt & Dawson 130
Jarrow Iron Co. 162, 177
Jarrow Iron Works 162
Jarvis, — 29
Jayne, John 9
Jerome: see Clarke & Jerome
Jesson, — 38
Jessop, W.: see F. Wright and W. Jessop
   see also Outram, Jessop & Beresford
Jessop & Co. 114, 116
Jevons & Co. 29
Jevons, Wood & Co. 29
John Bagnall & Sons Ltd (7101 : 1873) 61, 69
John Brown & Co. Ltd (1125C : 1864) 125
John Lysaght Ltd (71994 : 1901) 109, 111
John Rogerson & Co. Ltd (24409 : 1887) 161
John Russell & Co. Ltd (10744 : 1876; 140981 : 1915) 57
John Summers & Sons Ltd (56433 : 1897) 54
Jones, — 49
   D. 65
   David 59, 65, 72
   David & Sons 72
   G. 5, 56, 57, 64
   Geo. 56, 57
   George 56, 57, 64
   J. 60
   John 57, 67, 70, 85
   John & Co. 60
   John & Son 70
Jones, Barker & Foster 62
Jones, Dunning & Co. 166
Jones, Pearce & Crewdson 166
Jones & Fereday 91
Jones & Murcott 85
Jones & Oakes 60, 73
Jones & Rowland 53
Jones Brothers 64?, 70
Jones Brothers, Walsall, Ltd (27398 : 1888) 57
   see also Blackwell, Jones & Co.; Wainwright, Jones & Co.
Jukes, J. & Co. 53
   Joseph 53
Jukes, Collins & Co. 47
   see also Moss & Jukes

Keeling & Chick 35
Keen: see British (Guest, Keen, Baldwins) Iron & Steel Co. Ltd; GKN Rolled & Bright Steel Ltd; Guest Keen Iron & Steel Works

Kendall, — 3, 51
Kendall & Co. 3
Kendrick, D. 90
   David 90
   David & Pearson, Richard 90
Kenrick & Co. 29
Ketley Co. 42, 43
Ketley Iron Co. 42
Kettering Iron & Coal Co. Ltd (10528 : 1876) 105
Kidsgrove Steel, Iron & Coal Co. Ltd (26074 : 1888) 96
Kinneil Iron & Coal Co. Ltd (SC 923 : 1879) 191
Kinnersley, — 96, 99
   Miss and Mrs 96
   Mrs & Miss G.M. Attwood 96
   Mrs & Miss J.M. Attwood 96
   see also Attwood, Miss G.M. & Kinnersley, Mrs
   T., trustees of 96
   Thomas 96, 97
Kinnersley & Co. 96
Kinnersley & Heathcote 100
Kipling: see Watson, Kipling & Co.; Watson, Kipling & Co. Ltd
Kirk & Co. 53
Kirk Brothers & Co. 147
Kirk Brothers & Co. Ltd (57734 : 1898) 147
Kirkless Hall Co. 142
Kirkless Hall Iron & Coal Co. 142
Knight, Abbots & Co. 35
Knight, Edwin & Co. 35
Knight & Co. 29
Knocker: see Leighton, C. & Knocker, G.P.
Knott, G., executors of 146
   L.G. 185, 192
Knott & Co. 136, 146
Knowles, J. 113–14
Knowles & Co. 113
Kyrke & Burton 53

Lackenby Iron Co. 163
Laird: see Cammell Laird & Co. Ltd
Lancashire Steel Corporation Ltd (246417 : 1930) 143, 148
Lancashire Steel Manufacturing Co. Ltd (601555 : 1958) 148–9
Lancaster: see Freeland & Lancaster
Lane End Works Ltd (25676 : 1888) 97
Langford & Co. 35
Langley Co. 42
   mortgagees of 42
Langley Iron Co. 42
Langloan Iron & Chemical Co. Ltd (SC 3251 : 1896) 191–2
Lankaster, John & Co. 52
Latham, Mr 141
Lawley Co. 43
Lawley Iron Co. 43
Lawrence, J. 11
Lawton & Co. 94–5
Lea: see Marshall, Lea & Co.
Leah, Clayton & Co. 125
Leatham: see Gilkes, Wilson, Leatham & Co.
Leather & Co. 134
Leeds Steel Works Ltd (17615 : 1888) 129
Leeswood Iron Co. Ltd (2916 : 1862) 52
Leigh, — 23
   C.H. 24
Leigh & George 24
Leighton, C. & Knocker, G.P. 95
Leighton & Grenfell 40, 41
Lennard, J.M. & Whitwell, William 158–9
Lettsom, Dr, for Myers' Executors 19
Leveson-Gower, Granville, 1st Earl Granville 98
   Granville George, 2nd Earl Granville 98
   see also Sutherland-Leveson-Gower
Levick, Fred. 5, 10, 12

Fred. & Simpson, R. 5, 10, 12
Levick & Simpson 5, 10, 12
  see also Cruttwell, Levick & Co.; Cruttwell & Levick
Lewis, Mr 22
  T.A.: see Fothergill, R. & Lewis, T.A.
  see also Fothergill, Hankey & Lewis; Guest, Lewis & Co.
Lichfield, Countess of: see Anson, Louisa Barbara Catherine
  Earl of: see Anson, Thomas William
Lilleshall Co. 41, 44, 46, 48
Lilleshall Co. Ltd (14802 : 1880) 44, 46
Lilleshall Iron & Steel Co. Ltd (447281: 1947) 46
Lilleshall Iron Co. 41, 44, 47
Lincolnshire Iron Smelting Co. Ltd (6314 : 1872) 109
Lindsay, Alexander, Earl of Balcarres 142
  James & Co. 142
Lindsay & Co. 142
Linthorpe Dinsdale Smelting Co. Ltd (76930 : 1903) 164, 166
Linthorpe-Dinsdale Smelting Co. Ltd (165706 : 1920) 164
Llewellyn, L. 7, 21
  W. 21
  W. & Son 21
Llewellyn & Co. 6
Llewelyn & Co. 3
Lloyd & Co. 164
Lloyds 79
Lloyds, Foster & Co. 79–80
Lloyds, Fosters & Co. 79
Lloyds & Co. 79
Lloyds Ironstone Co. Ltd (94482 : 1907) 101
  see also Stewarts & Lloyds; Stewarts & Lloyds Ltd
Llynvi, Tondu & Ogmore Coal & Iron Co. Ltd (6258 : 1872) 19, 27
Llynvi & Tondû Co. Ltd (13783 : 1880) 19, 27
Llynvi Iron Co. 19
Llynvi Vale Iron Co. (518 : 1856) 19
Llynvi Vale Iron Co. Ltd (3415 : 1867) 19
Lochgelly Iron & Coal Co. Ltd (SC 400 : 1872; SC 3204 : 1896) 192
Lochgelly Iron Co. 192
Loftus Iron Co. Ltd (6354 : 1872) 170
Logan, — 196
Logan & Co. 196
Londonderry, Marchioness of: see Stewart, Elizabeth Frances Charlotte
  Marquess of: see Vane-Tempest, G.H.R.C.W.
Longton Hall Co. Ltd (29703 : 1889) 97
Lonsdale Hematite Iron & Steel Co. 143
Lonsdale Hematite Iron & Steel Co. Ltd (18567 : 1883; 48512 : 1896) 143
Lonsdale Hematite Iron Co. 143
Lonsdale Hematite Smelting Co. Ltd (53180 : 1897) 143
Lonsdale Vale Iron Co. Ltd (2166C : 1865) 161
Losh, Wilson & Bell 176
Losh, Wilson & Co. 176
Losh & Co. 192
Low Moor Co. Ltd, *later* Robert Heath & Low Moor Ltd (26367 : 1888) 94, 130
Low Moor Iron Co. Ltd (239705 : 1929) 130
Lowe & Ward 122
Lowther Hematite Iron & Steel Co. Ltd (51762 : 1897) 144
Lowther Hematite Iron Co. Ltd (9971 : 1875) 144
Lowther Ironworks, proprietor of 144
Lucas: see Warner, Lucas & Barrett
Lugar Iron Co. 192
Lumphinnans Iron Co. 193

Lydney & Wigpool Iron Ore Co. Ltd (5917 : 1871) 81
Lyon, John 74
Lysaghts Scunthorpe Works 109
  see also John Lysaght Ltd
Lyttle's Iron Agency Ltd (9137 : 1875) 106

M. & W. Grazebrook Ltd (137711 : 1914) 78
McClure, William 104
  William Lees 104
M'Cullum & Co. 183
McEwen: see Phillips & McEwen
Madeley Wood Co. 38, 39, 45
Madeley Wood Iron Co. 38
Madeley Wood Iron Co. Ltd (149617 : 1918) 39
Maesteg Iron Co. 19
Magnetic Iron Mountains Smelting Co. Ltd (25990 : 1888) 176
Mainwaring, John 64
  R. 64
Malcolm, W. & S.S. & Co. 35
  see also Elwon, Malcolm & Co.
Malcolm & Co. 35
Maling [&] Co. 9, 16
Malins & Co. 63
Marsden: see Nesbitt, Marsden & Co.; Nesbitt & Marsden
Marshall, Messrs 119
Marshall, Lea & Co. 125
Marten, Henry John 80
Martin & Co. 6
  see also Evers & Martin
Martole & Co. 28
Maryport Hematite Iron & Steel Co. Ltd (18539 : 1883) 144
Maryport Hematite Iron Co. 144
Maryport Iron Co. 144
Maryport Ironworks, owners of 144
Mather, Mr 122
Mathews, William 63
  executors of late 63
  William & Co. 63
  see also William Mathews & Co. Ltd
Mathews & Dudley 62–3
Matthews & Co. 59
Maynard: see Robson, Maynard & Co.; Walker, Maynard & Co.; Walker, Maynard & Co. Ltd
Melin, — 9
Mellins & Co. 9
Mere: see Dixon, Mere & Co.
Merry & Cunninghame 179, 181, 189
Merry & Cunninghame Ltd (SC 2114 : 1891) 179, 180, 181–2, 189
Middleton Iron Co. Ltd (1195C : 1864) 165
Midland Coal, Coke & Iron Co. Ltd (30551 : 1890; 40034 : 1893) 93
Millbrook Iron Co. 20
Millens & Co. 9
Miller, J. 186
  executors of late 186
  see also Addie, Miller & Rankine
Millom & Askam Hematite Iron Co. Ltd (32438 : 1890; 157429 : 1919) 136, 145–6, 148
Millom Hematite Ore & Iron Co. Ltd (572325 : 1956) 146
Mills, S. 65
  Samuel 65
  see also Bills & Mills; Gjers, Mills & Co.; Gjers, Mills & Co. Ltd
Milnes, — 131
Miners' Co. 10
Mitchell: see Sir W.G. Armstrong, Mitchell & Co. Ltd
Mitchell & Co., Barrow 141
Moira, Earl of: see Rawdon-Hastings, Francis
Mold, Messrs 118
  J. & C. 118

W.H. 118
Mold & Co. 118
Monkland Iron & Coal Co. Ltd (SC 429 : 1872) 183, 194
Monkland Iron & Steel Co. 193
Monkland Iron Co. 194
Monkland Iron Co. Ltd (SC 1052 : 1881) 183, 194
Monkland Steel Co. 194
Montague: see James & Montague
Montgomerie & Fleming 188
Moorcroft Colliery 70
Moorcroft Colliery Co. 70
Morgan, — 8
  William: see Bailey, Crawshay, & Morgan, William
Morris, Sir G.B. 20
  Sir J. 20
  Sir John, Bt 20
  T. 67, 79, 81
  T. & Son 81
  Thomas 67, 81
  Thomas & Son 67
  Thomas jun. 81
Morrison, James 161
Moss & Jukes 53
Moss Bay Hematite Iron & Steel Co. 146
Moss Bay Hematite Iron & Steel Co. Ltd (15042 : 1881; 33663 : 1891) 146
Moss Bay Iron Co. 146
Mossend: see Summerlee & Mossend Iron & Steel Co. Ltd
Mostyn Coal & Iron Co. Ltd (8502 : 1874) 52
  see also Darwen & Mostyn Iron Co. Ltd
Motteram & Deeley 88
Mounsey & Co. 159, 160
Mouzell: see Askam & Mouzell Iron Co. Ltd 136
Muirkirk Iron Co. 194
Murcott: see Jones & Murcott
Mushet, — 32
Mussey: see Thompson & Mussey
Myers, — 19
Myers & Co. 19
Myers' Executors: see Lettsom, Dr, for Myers' Executors

N. Hingley & Sons Ltd (32532 : 1890) 79
Nant-y-Glo & Blaina Iron Works Co. Ltd (5580 : 1871) 3–4, 5, 10, 20
Nartoh & Co. 28
Nartole & Co. 28
National Provincial Bank 158
National Provincial Bank of England 158
Neath Abbey Co. 2, 29
Neath Abbey Iron Co. 20
Nesbitt, Marsden & Co. 127
Nesbitt & Marsden 127
Nettlefolds: see Guest Keen & Co. Ltd
Neve: see Dixon, Neve & Co.; Dixon, Neve & Hill
Nevi: see Dixon, Nevi & Co.
New British Iron Co. 2, 49, 63–4, 68, 76
New British Iron Co. Ltd (19092 : 1883) 49, 64
New Clydach Sheet & Bar Iron Co. Ltd (1151C : 1864) 9
New Cransley Iron & Steel Co. Ltd (30330 : 1889; 149318 : 1918) 101–2
New Cumnock Iron Co. 195
New North Staffordshire Coal & Iron Co. Ltd (6456 : 1872) 100
New Westbury Iron Co. Ltd (77615 : 1903) 36
Newbold Iron & Coal Co. 119
Newbold Iron Co. 119
Newton, Chambers & Co. 127, 133
Newton, Chambers & Co. Ltd (15997 : 1881) 133-4
Newton, Scott, Chambers & Co. 133
  see also Buckley, Newton & Co.

Nithsdale Iron Co. 195
Normanby Iron Works Co. 166
Normanby Iron Works Co. Ltd (45380 : 1895; 438949 : 1947) 166, 167
Normanby Ironworks Co. Ltd (66673 : 1900) 166–7
Normanby Park Steel Works 109
North British Banking Co. 9
North Eastern Steel Co. Ltd (15639 : 1881) 152
North of England Industrial Iron & Coal Co. Ltd, *later* Carlton Iron Co. Ltd (4891 : 1870; 136855 : 1914) 155–6
North of England Iron Co. 144
North Lancashire Iron Co. 147
North Lincolnshire Iron Co. Ltd (6674 : 1872) 110
North Lincolnshire Iron Works 110
North Lincolnshire Iron Works Co. 110
North Lonsdale Iron & Steel Co. Ltd (7730 : 1873) 147–8, 148
North Staffordshire Coal & Iron Co. Ltd (865 : 1857) 100
North Western Hematite Steel Co. Ltd (57735 : 1898) 150
Northampton Coal, Iron & Wagon Co. Ltd (6611 : 1872) 103
North's Navigation Collieries (1889) Ltd (28099 : 1889) 27–8
North's Navigation Collieries Syndicate Ltd (27108 : 1888) 19, 27
Norton Iron Co. 167
Norton Iron Co. Ltd (2382C : 1865) 167

Oak Farm Co. 78
Oak Farm Iron Co. 78
Oakerthorpe Iron & Coal Co. Ltd (1677 : 1859) 119
Oakes, J. 112
   James & Co. 112
Oakes & Co. 112
   see also Jones & Oakes
Oakfarm Furnace Co. 78
Oakley, — 51, 52
   E. 51, 52
   Edward 51, 52
Oakley & Co. 51, 52
Oakwood Co. 21
Ogmore: *see* Llynvi, Tondu & Ogmore Coal & Iron Co. Ltd
Old Park Iron Co. Ltd (33 : 1856) 45
Oliver & Co. 72
O'Neil & Co. 7
Onions, — 59
   Edward & Co. 79
   J. & G. 67, 86
   J. & S. 78
   James & George 58, 76
   John 39
   W. & E. 58, 82
   W. & G. 58, 82
   W.J. & G. 86
   see also Bank & Onions
Onions & Co. 59, 86
Onllwyn Iron & Coal Co. Ltd (1367C : 1864) 21
Osier Bed Co. 80
Osier Bed Iron Co. 80
Outram, Jessop & Beresford 114
Outram & Co. 114
Outwood Iron Co. Ltd (6428 : 1872) 148

P. Williams & Sons (Furnaces) Ltd (138468 : 1914) 89
Palmer & Co. 162, 177
Palmers Shipbuilding & Iron Co. Ltd (2298C : 1865) 162–3, 177
Park Gate Iron Co. 129
Park Gate Iron Co. Ltd, *later* Park Gate Iron & Steel Co. Ltd (1179C : 1864) 129, 131–2
Parker, — 78, 87, 93, 99, 128

Parker & Co. 78
Parkers, — 67
Parkes, — 67
   G. & Co. 87
   Z. & Co. 68, 81
Parkes & Co. 81
Parkfield Co. 80
Parkfield Iron Co. 80
Parkfield Iron Co. Ltd (3741 : 1867) 80–1
Parson, J. 56
Parsons, — 30
   J. 56
   John 56
   W. 21
   William 21
Parsons & Co. 30
Partington Steel & Iron Co. Ltd (111330 : 1910) 148
Parton Hematite Iron Co. Ltd (7983 : 1874) 149
Partridge, — 32
   H. 33
   William 32
   see also Harford & Partridge
Partridge & Sons 16, 29
Patent Nut & Bolt Co. Ltd (1311C : 1862; 70989 : 1901) 11
Patent Shaft & Axletree Co. Ltd (964C : 1864; 29477 : 1889; 75857 : 1902) 80, 83
Patterson: *see* Bain & Patterson
Pattinson, H.L. & Co. 161
Pearce: *see* Jones, Pearce & Crewdson
Pearson, J.H. 91
   Joseph H. 77, 91
   see also Hall, Holcroft & Pearson; Kendrick, David & Pearson, Richard
Pease, A.A.F. & H.P. 166
   Arthur 166
   H. & Co. 171
   see also Gilkes, Wilson, Pease & Co.; Pease & Partners Ltd; Wilsons, Pease & Co.; Wilsons, Pease & Co. Ltd
Pease & Partners Ltd (17217 : 1882; 59106 : 1898) 163, 173, 167, 170
Peat, W.B. & Co. 144, 149, 150
Peel, C.E. & H.M., Swansea 28
Pell, George 102
Pell & Co. 102
Pelsall Coal & Iron Co. Ltd (7152 : 1873) 82
Pemberton, Samuel 66
   Thomas H. 66
   see also Benton & Pemberton; Stokes, Pemberton & Co.
Pemberton & Co. 66
Pembroke Iron & Coal Co. 17–18
Pembrokeshire Iron & Coal Co. Ltd (2301 : 1861) 18
Pentwyn Co. 21
Penydarren Iron Co. 22
Perkins: *see* Pyrkins
Perry, F.C. 57
Phillips & McEwen 81
Phillips & Wilson 20
   see also Davis, Williams & Phillips
Phipps, P., executors of 103
Pickering, Messrs 50
Pidcock: *see* Addenbrooke & Pidcock; Addenbrooke, Smith & Pidcock
Plevins, C.H. 102, 104, 119, 142
   C.H. & Co. 91
Plevins & Co. 102, 104
Plymouth: *see* Aberdare & Plymouth Co. Ltd
Plymouth Iron Co. 14, 23
Plymouth Works, mortgagees of 23
Poley: *see* Sturges & Poley
Ponkey Iron Co. Ltd (1381 : 1858) 53
Pontypool Iron Co. 24
Poole, Edward & Co. 92

   see also Sparrow, James & Poole; Sparrow & Poole; Whitehouse & Poole
Pope, Christopher 26
Portland Iron Co. 195
Powell & Co. 9
Price, — 20
   J. 20
   Sir R. 27
   Sir Robert 27
   Sir Robert & Co. 27
   T.B., executors of 56
   Thomas 56, 69
   see also Green & Price
Price & Co. 20
Prices & Co. 56
Protheroe, — 32
Pyle & Blaina Works Ltd (29580 : 1889) 5, 9
Pyle Works Ltd (14565 : 1880) 5, 9
Pyrkins, — 154

Raby, — 18, 21
   A. 18, 21, 116
Rangely & Co. 123
Rangley, Henry 123
Rankine: *see* Addie, Miller & Rankine; Addie & Rankine
Rawdon-Hastings, Francis, Earl of Moira etc 118
Read, — 69
   J. 69, 76, 88
   see also Smith, Read & Co.
Read & Co. 73
Redbourn Hill Iron & Coal Co. Ltd (6405 : 1872) 109, 110
Redesdale 169
Redesdale Iron Co. 169
Renishaw Iron Co. 119
Renishaw Iron Co. Ltd (73235, 75203 : 1902) 119–20
Reynolds, — 30
   R. & Co. 42
   William & Co. 41
Reynolds & Co. 23, 42, 45, 47
Rhymney Co. 7, 25
Rhymney Iron Co. 7, 25–6
Rhymney Iron Co. Ltd (5346 : 1871) 26
Richard, Benjamin 60
Richard Thomas & Co. Ltd, *later* Richard Thomas & Baldwins Ltd (20255 : 1884) 15, 18, 103, 110–11
Richards, B. 86
   H. 70
Richardson, J. & Co. 154
   John & Co. 154
Richardson & Co. 154
Riley, W. 75
   William 75
   William & Son 75
Riley & Co. 55
Rixon's Iron & Brick Co. Ltd (18470 : 1883) 105
Robert Fellows Ltd (95964 : 1907) 64
Robert Heath & Sons Ltd (42576 : 1894) 94
   see also Low Moor Co. Ltd
Roberts, J. & S. 58
   T. & S. 58
   see also Gibbons & Roberts; Wm Roberts (Tipton) Ltd
Roberts, Rogers & Co. 53
Roberts & Co. 87
Roberts & Humfrey 87
Robinson & Co. 194
Robson, Maynard & Co. 168
Roebuck & Co. 186
Rogers: *see* Roberts, Rogers & Co.
Rogerson, John 161
   executors of late 161
   John E. 161
   see also John Rogerson & Co. Ltd
Roper, R.S. & Co. 11

Rose, David 76, 79
    David & Sons 76
Rosedale & Ferry Hill Iron Co. Ltd (1347C : 1864) 161
Round Brothers 71
Round Oak Steel Works Ltd (156070 : 1919) 75
    see also Earl of Dudley's Round Oak Steel Works Ltd
Rowland, — 53
    E. & Co. 53
    see also Jones & Rowland
Royal Greek Iron Works Co. 177
Ruabon Coal Co. Ltd (2 : 1856) 53
Russel, James, trustees of late 179
    James & Son 179
    James & Sons 179
Russell & Brown 5
Russell Hall Iron Co. 84

St Paul, Sir H., Bt 59, 90, 91
St Paul, Sir H., Thorneycroft & Co. 59
St Paul, Sir Horace 59
Salisbury & Co. 60
Samuelson, B. 171
    B. & Co. 166, 171
    see also Sir B. Samuelson & Co. Ltd
Sarl & Sons 35
Saxleby, Edwards & Co. 112
Scale, Messrs 9
    H. 9
Scales & Co. 1
Scales, Fothergill & Co. 1, 2
Schneider, Hannay & Co. 137
Schneider & Hannay 137
Scholefield, W. 131
Scholefield & Co. 118, 127, 131
Scott: see Newton, Scott, Chambers & Co.; Walter Scott Ltd
Scottish Iron & Steel Co. Ltd: see Bairds & Scottish Steel Ltd
Seaton Carew Iron Co. Ltd (16711 : 1882) 169
Seaton Co. 149
Shakespeare, William 111
Shale & Fowler 55
Share: see Small, Share & Co.
Sharp & Co. 52
Shaw & Co. 132
Sheepbridge Coal & Iron Co. Ltd, later Sheepbridge Co. Ltd (1594C : 1864) 120–1
Shelton, Iron, Steel & Coal Co. Ltd, later Shelton Iron & Steel Ltd (30347 : 1889) 98–9
Shelton Bar Iron Co. 98
Shotts Co. 196
Shotts Iron Co. 183, 190, 196–7
Shotts Iron Co. Ltd (SC 3597 : 1897; SC 3633 : 1897) 197
Silverdale Co. 99
Silverdale Iron Co. 99
Simms: see Horton, Simms & Ball
Simpson, R.: see Levick & Simpson; Levick, Fred. & Simpson, R.
Sir B. Samuelson & Co. Ltd (25072 : 1887) 166
Sir W.G. Armstrong, Mitchell & Co. Ltd (17532 : 1882) 160
Sir W.G. Armstrong, Whitworth & Co. Ltd (46687 : 1896) 160
Skinningrove Iron Co. Ltd (14171 : 1880) 170–1
Slater, William & Sons 167
Small, Share & Co. 2
Smith, Ebenezer & Co. 114
    Henry 57
    Read & Co. 61
    S.W. & Co. 149
    see also Addenbrooke, Smith & Pidcock; Elsom & Smith; Vigors & Smith; Woodall & Smith

Smith & Co. 19, 114, 117, 121
Smith & Elsam 117
Smith Brothers 117
Sneyd, G. & Co. 99
    R. 99
    Ralph 99
    W. 99
Snowdon & Hopkins 174
Solly: see Fletcher, Solly & Urwick
Solway Hematite Co. Ltd (4730 : 1870) 149
South Bank Iron Co. 171
South Cleveland Ironworks Ltd (6003 : 1872) 161–2
South Durham Iron Co. 171–2
South Durham Iron Co. Ltd (6616 : 1872) 172
South Durham Steel & Iron Co. Ltd (60098 : 1898) 155, 169–70, 170
Sparrow, — 97
    H. 78
    James 51
    James & Poole 51
    James & Son 51
    J.W., executors/trustees of late 76
    W. 80, 86
    W. & Co. 51, 56, 86, 97
    W. & J. 80, 86
    W. & J. & Co. 86
    W. & J.S. 86
    W. & J.S. & Co. 75–6, 86
    W. & J.T. 75
    W. & J.T. & Co. 75, 86–7
    W.H. 76, 97
    W.H. & Co. 80, 86
    W.H. & Son 97
    W.J. & Co. 86
Sparrow & Co. 51, 97
Sparrow & Poole 51
Spedding & Co. 149
Stafford Coal & Iron Co. Ltd (7638 : 1873) 96
Stanier, F. & Co. 99
    F. & Son 99
    Francis 93
    Mrs & Broade, F. Stanier 99
Stanier & Co. 93, 99
Stanton & Staveley Ltd: see Stanton Ironworks Co. Ltd
Stanton Iron Co. 121
Stanton Ironworks Co. 121
Stanton Ironworks Co. Ltd, later Stanton & Staveley Ltd (11928 : 1877; 66522 : 1900) 108–9, 121–2, 123
Staveley Coal & Iron Co. Ltd (866C : 1863) 117, 122, 124
Staveley Iron & Chemical Co. Ltd (459090 : 1948) 122–3
    see also Stanton Ironworks Co. Ltd
Steel & Iron Co. Ltd (30115 : 1889) 104–5
Steel Company of Wales Ltd (434353 : 1947) 25
Stephenson & Co. 115
Stevenson, Jaques & Co. 152
Stevenson, Wilson, Jaques & Co. 152
Stewart, Elizabeth Frances Charlotte (formerly Wingfield, née Jocelyn), Marchioness of Londonderry 176
    J. Robert 195
    R. 195
    Robert 195
    trustees of 195
Stewarts & Lloyds Ltd (56764 : 1898) 85–6, 101, 104
Stockton Iron Co. 172
Stockton Iron Furnace Co. Ltd (1750C : 1864) 172
Stockton Rail Mill Co. Ltd (1749C : 1864) 172
Stokes, — 38, 66
Stokes, Pemberton & Co. 66
Stokes & Co. 66
Stonefield Co. 86

Stonefield Iron Co. 86
Stour Valley Coal & Iron Co. Ltd (7757 : 1873) 86, 88
Stowe Iron Ore Co. Ltd (2240 : 1861) 104
Straubenzie: see Swan, Straubenzie, Coates & Co.
Strelley, R. 119
    R.C. 119
Strick, Henry & Co. 7
Strickley, Frances 7
Struttle: see Hill & Struttle
Stuart, R. 195
    see also Crichton-Stuart; Stewart
Stuart Iron, Steel & Tin Plate Co. Ltd (13824 : 1880) 17
Sturges, — 126
    John & Co. 126
Sturges & Co. 126
Sturges & Poley 126
Summerlee & Mossend Iron & Steel Co. Ltd, later Summerlee Iron Co. Ltd (SC 3221 : 1896) 198
Summerlee Iron Co. 197
Summerlee Iron Co. Ltd: see Summerlee & Mossend Iron & Steel Co. Ltd
Summers: see John Summers & Sons Ltd
Sutherland, Duke of: see Sutherland-Leveson-Gower, G.G.W.
Sutherland-Leveson-Gower, George Granville William, 3rd Duke of Sutherland etc 97
    see also Leveson-Gower
Swallow, — 127, 133
Swan, Coates & Co. 155
Swan, Straubenzie, Coates & Co. 155
Swansea Blast Furnace Co. Ltd (13551 : 1879) 18
Swansea Hematite Iron Co. Ltd (28540 : 1889) 18

T. & I. Bradley & Sons Ltd, later Bradley & Foster Ltd (90670 : 1906) 61?, 65–6
'T. & I. Bradley Ltd' 61
Tait & Co. 13
Tame Iron Co. 58
Tanner, D. 5, 18, 23, 34
Tappenden, — 2
Tappenden & Co. 2
Tarratt, Timmins & Co. 92
Taylor & Co. 88
Teague & Co. 32
Tees Furnace Co. Ltd (48714 : 1896) 163, 174
Tees Side Iron & Engine Works Co. Ltd (29728 : 1889) 174
Tees-Bridge Iron Co. Ltd (5585 : 1871) 173
Tees-side Iron & Engine Works Co. Ltd (1922C : 1865) 174
Thomas, E.H. 28
    G. & R. 71
    George & Richard 71
    see also G. & R. Thomas Ltd
    Richard: see Richard Thomas & Co. Ltd
Thomas Butlin & Co. Ltd (29239 : 1889) 103–4
Thomas W. Booker & Co. Ltd (6803 : 1872) 22
Thompson, — 34, 51
    Geo. & Co. 65
    John 49, 51, 53
Thompson & Co. 1, 2, 22, 28, 34, 94, 153
Thompson & Mussey 94
Thornborrow & Co. 94
Thorneycroft, G.B. & Co. 59, 71
Thorneycroft & Co. 92
    see also St Paul, Sir H. & Thorneycroft & Co.
Timmins: see Tarratt, Timmins & Co.
Tipton Co. 87
Titanic Iron Co. 167
'Titanic Iron Co. Ltd' 167

Titanic Ore Co. 167
Titanic Steel & Iron Co. Ltd (2894 : 1862) 167
Titanium Ore Co. Ltd (1338C : 1864) 167
Toll End Co. 88
Toll End Iron Co. 88
Tondu: see Llynvi, Tondu & Ogmore Coal & Iron Co. Ltd; Llynvi & Tondû Co. Ltd
Top & Co. 115
Topps & Co. 115
Torbock, Joseph 166, 172
Towcester Co. Ltd (8270 : 1874) 105
Townshend, Wood & Co. 6
Tredegar Iron & Coal Co. Ltd (7116 : 1873) 28
Tredegar Iron Co. 28
Trent Iron Co. 111
Trent Iron Co. Ltd (94261 : 1907) 111
Tristram, — 64
Turley, J. & T. 64, 87
   Jos. & Thomas 64
   Joseph & Thomas 64
   Thomas & Sons 64
Turley Brothers 64
Tyler, E. 57
Tyne Iron Co. 164

Underhill: see Bishton & Underhill
United Steel Companies Ltd (250327: 1930) 104, 141, 151
Urwick: see Fletcher, Solly & Urwick

Vance: see Blair & Vance
Vane, Earl: see Vane-Tempest, G.H.R.C.W.
Vane-Tempest (formerly Vane), George Henry Robert Charles William, 5th Marquess of Londonderry, Earl Vane etc 176
Varteg Co. 29
Vaughan, N. 29
   Thomas 157, 171
   trustees of 171
   Thomas & Co. 157, 171
   trustees of 157
   see also Bolckow, Vaughan & Co.; Bolckow, Vaughan & Co. Ltd; Bolckow & Vaughan
Vernon, George 67
   T.W. 86
Vickerman & Co. 187
Victoria 29
Victoria Coal & Iron Co. 29
Victoria Iron Works Co. 178
Vigors & Co. 10
Vigors & Smith 10

Wainwright, Jones & Co. 60
Walker, — 129, 131
   Mrs 57, 75
   Samuel & Co. 69, 129
Walker, Maynard & Co. 168
Walker, Maynard & Co. Ltd (67934, 68092 : 1900) 159, 168
Walkers & Co. 129, 131
Walmsley, Sir J.: see Jackson, W., MP & Walmsley, Sir J.
Walsall Iron Co. 67, 70
Walter Scott Ltd (36095 : 1892; 68066 : 1900) 129–30
Walters, T. 1
Ward, E., executors of 82
   Henry 82
   John William, 1st Earl of Dudley, trustees of 67
   T.E. 53
   W. 82
   W. & Co. 82
   W.M. & Sons 82
   William 82
   William & Sons 82, 82–3

William, Baron Ward of Birmingham, later 1st Earl of Dudley (2nd creation) etc 62, 74-5, 77
William Humble, 2nd Earl of Dudley 62, 75
William Humble Eric, 3rd Earl of Dudley 75
Ward & Barrow 122
Ward & Sons 82
   see also Lowe & Ward
Ward, Lord: see Ward, William
Warner, Lucas & Barrett 167
Washington Iron Co. 177
Watney, Daniel 17
   T. 17
   T. & Co. 17
Watney & Co. 17
Watson, John 188
Watson, Kipling & Co. 176
Watson, Kipling & Co. Ltd (11552 : 1877) 176
Watt: see Homfray, J. & Watt
Wayne & Co. 16
Wayne's Merthyr Steam Coal & Iron Works Ltd (8046 : 1874) 16
Weardale Iron & Coal Co. Ltd (559C : 1863) 172, 175
Weardale Iron Co. 172, 175
Weardale Steel, Coal & Coke Co. Ltd (63715 : 1899) 175–6
Wellingboro' Iron Co. Ltd (27457 : 1888; 166083 : 1920) 105–6
Wellington Iron & Coal Co. Ltd (7482 : 1873) 456
Welsh Iron & Coal Co. 50, 52
Welsh Iron Co. 49
Wentworth-FitzWilliam, Charles William, 3rd Earl FitzWilliam 127
   William Thomas Spencer, 4th Earl Fitz-William 127, 131
West Cumberland Hematite Iron Co. Ltd (2027 : 1860) 150
West Cumberland Iron & Steel Co. Ltd (6618 : 1872) 150
West Hallam Coal & Iron Co. 123
West Hartlepool Iron Co. Ltd (8431 : 1874) 177
West Yorkshire Iron & Coal Co. Ltd (3140 : 1866) 134
Westbury Iron, Mining & Smelting Co. 36
Westbury Iron Co. 35, 35–6
Westbury Iron Co. Ltd (948 : 1857) 35
Wheeley, — 59
   J. & Co. 59
   J. & W. 59
   John & Co. 59
Wheely, W. & J. 59
Whitby Iron Co. (148C : 1862) 153
Whitby Iron Co. Ltd (815 : 1863) 153
Whitehaven Hematite Iron & Steel Co. Ltd (14257 : 1880; 26174 : 1888) 139–40
Whitehaven Hematite Iron Co. 139
Whitehaven Hematite Iron Co. Ltd (5383 : 1871) 139
Whitehaven Iron Co. 139
Whitehouse, — 123
   Benjamin 83
   E.J. & A.G. 123
   H.B. 83, 89, 123
   H.B. & Co. 123
   H.B. & Son 83
   H.B. & Sons 83, 123
   H.B. jun. 123
   Hy B. & Son 83
   Hy Bickerton 83
   see also H.B. Whitehouse & Son Ltd
Whitehouse & Co. 32, 89, 123
Whitehouse & Poole 92
Whitwell, W. & Co. 174
   William: see Lennard, J.M. & Whitwell, William
   William & Co. 174

   see also William Whitwell & Co. Ltd
Whitwell & Co. 174
Whitworth: see Sir W.G. Armstrong, Whitworth & Co. Ltd
Wigan Coal & Iron Co. Ltd (2650C : 1866) 142–3
Wilkinson, — 41, 47, 49, 58
   J. 41, 47, 49, 58
   trustees of 58
   J. & Co. 58
   J. & Son 58
Wilkinson's Executors 39, 40, 41
Willenhall Furnaces Ltd (10850 : 1876) 90
Willett & Davey 6
William Baird & Co. Ltd (7320 : 1873; SC 2440 : 1893; 59358 : 1898) 187, 188–9, 193, 194–5, 196
William Cooke & Co. Ltd (7320 : 1873; 59358 : 1898) 134
William Dixon Ltd (SC 491 : 1893; SC 6175 : 1906) 180–1, 190
William Mathews & Co. Ltd (10629 : 1876) 63
William Roberts (Tipton) Ltd: see Wm Roberts (Tipton) Ltd
William Whitwell & Co. Ltd (28225 : 1889) 174–5
William Woodhead & Son Ltd (90290 : 1906) 128
Williams, Edward 164
   executors of late 164
   J. 21
   J. & Co. 42
   John 21
   J.W. 88
   P. & Co. 88, 89
   P. & Son 88, 89
   P. & Sons 57, 89
   Philip & Co. 88, 89
   Philip & Sons 88, 89
   see also Davis, Williams & Phillips; P. Williams & Sons (Furnaces) Ltd
Williams & Co. 16, 21, 29, 42, 43
Williams Brothers 57
Williamson Brothers 95
Williamson, H.H. 95
Williamsons 95
Williamson's Executors 40
Willingsworth Iron Co. 90
Willingsworth Iron Co. Ltd (88089 : 1906; 100070 : 1908) 90–1
Wilson, — 198
   George & Co. 161, 191
   J. 187
   trustees of late 194
   James B. 119
   J.B. 119
   John 187, 191, 1920
   trustees of late 187, 191, 192
   William & Co. 191
   see also Dunlop, Wilson & Co.; Gilkes, Wilson, Leatham & Co.; Gilkes, Wilson, Pease & Co.; Gilkes, Wilson & Co.; Losh, Wilson & Bell; Losh, Wilson & Co.; Phillips & Wilson; Stevenson, Wilson, Jaques & Co.
Wilson & Christie 186
Wilson & Co. 197–8, 198
Wilsons, Pease & Co. 173
Wilsons, Pease & Co. Ltd (70712 : 1901) 173
Wingerworth Iron Co. 123–4
Wishaw Iron Co. 198–9
Withymoor Co. 91
Witton Park Co. 177
Wm Roberts (Tipton) Ltd (60930 : 1899) 87–8
Wolverhampton & Staffordshire Banking Co. 81
Wombridge & Co. 42
'Wones Brothers' 64

Wood: *see* Jevons, Wood & Co.; Townshend, Wood & Co.
Woodall & Smith 91
Woodhead: *see* William Woodhead & Son Ltd
Woolley, E. 86
Woolley & Co. 86
Workington Hematite Iron & Steel Co. Ltd (13604 : 1879) 150–1
Workington Iron & Steel Co. 151
Workington Iron & Steel Co. Ltd (104491 : 1909) 140, 142, 144, 146, 149, 151
Workington Iron Co. 150
Workington Iron Co. Ltd (2532 : 1861; 67821 : 1900) 144, 150, 151
Worsborough Iron Co. 135
Wright, F. & Jessop, W. 114, 116
Wright Butler & Co. Ltd (25588 : 1887) 11, 18
   see also Bishton & Wright
Wylam Co. 178
Wythes, George, executors of late 165–6
   George & Co. 165

Yates, John W. 90
Yates & Co. 123
Ynyscedwyn Iron, Steel & Coal Co. Ltd (4962 : 1870) 30–1
Ynyscedwyn Iron Co. 30
Ynyscedwyn Iron Co. Ltd (1148C : 1864) 30
York Road Iron & Coal Co. 135
York Road Iron Co. 135
Yorkshire Iron & Coal Co. Ltd (69629 : 1902) 134-5
Young, W. 195
   Wm 195
Ystalyfera Iron & Tin Plate Co. Ltd (23057 : 1886) 31
Ystalyfera Iron Co. 31